P9-CBH-808

UPHEAVALS
OF THOUGHT

The Intelligence of Emotions

MARTHA C. NUSSBAUM
The University of Chicago

CAMBRIDGE
UNIVERSITY PRESS

PUBLISHED BY THE PRESS SYNDICATE OF THE UNIVERSITY OF CAMBRIDGE
The Pitt Building, Trumpington Street, Cambridge, United Kingdom

CAMBRIDGE UNIVERSITY PRESS
The Edinburgh Building, Cambridge CB2 2RU, UK
40 West 20th Street, New York, NY 10011-4211, USA
10 Stamford Road, Oakleigh, VIC 3166, Australia
Ruiz de Alarcón 13, 28014 Madrid, Spain
Dock House, The Waterfront, Cape Town 8001, South Africa
http://www.cambridge.org

First published 2001

Printed in the United States of America

Typeface Sabon 10.25/13.5 pt.   *System* DeskTopPro$_{/UX}$ [BV]

A catalog record for this book is available from the British Library.

Library of Congress Cataloging in Publication data
Nussbaum, Martha Craven, 1947–
Upheavals of thought : the intelligence of emotions / Martha C. Nussbaum.
p. cm.
Includes bibliographical references and index.
ISBN 0-521-46202-9
1. Emotions and cognition. 2. Emotions – Moral and ethical aspects. 3.
Emotions – Sociological aspects. I. Title.
BF531.N87 2001
152.4 – dc21   2001018087

ISBN 0 521 46202 9 hardback

For Cass

It is almost impossible to understand the extent to which this upheaval agitated, and by that very fact had temporarily enriched, the mind of M. de Charlus. Love in this way produces real geological upheavals of thought. In the mind of M. de Charlus, which only several days before resembled a plane so flat that even from a good vantage point one could not have discerned an idea sticking up above the ground, a mountain range had abruptly thrust itself into view, hard as rock – but mountains sculpted as if an artist, instead of taking the marble away, had worked it on the spot, and where there twisted about one another, in giant and swollen groupings, Rage, Jealousy, Curiosity, Envy, Hate, Suffering, Pride, Astonishment, and Love.

Marcel Proust, *Remembrance of Things Past*

Thus, by being born we have made the step from an absolutely self-sufficient narcissism to the perception of a changing external world and the beginnings of the discovery of objects. And with this is associated the fact that we cannot endure the new state of things for long, that we periodically revert from it, in our sleep, to our former condition of absence of stimulation and avoidance of objects.

Sigmund Freud, *Group Psychology and the Analysis of the Ego*

CONTENTS

INTRODUCTION

Emotions shape the landscape of our mental and social lives. Like the "geological upheavals" a traveler might discover in a landscape where recently only a flat plane could be seen, they mark our lives as uneven, uncertain, and prone to reversal. Why and how? Is it because emotions are animal energies or impulses that have no connection with our thoughts, imaginings, and appraisals? Proust denies this, calling the emotions "geological upheavals of thought." In other words, what changes the Baron's mind from a flat plane into a mountain range is not some subterranean jolt, but the thoughts he has about Charlie Morel, a person who has suddenly become central to his well-being, and whom he sees as inscrutable, undependable, and utterly beyond his control. It is these thoughts about value and importance that make his mind project outward like a mountain range, rather than sitting inert in self-satisfied ease.

A lot is at stake in the decision to view emotions in this way, as intelligent responses to the perception of value. If emotions are suffused with intelligence and discernment, and if they contain in themselves an awareness of value or importance, they cannot, for example, easily be sidelined in accounts of ethical judgment, as so often they have been in the history of philosophy. Instead of viewing morality as a system of principles to be grasped by the detached intellect, and emotions as motivations that either support or subvert our choice to act according to principle, we will have to consider emotions as part and parcel of the system of ethical reasoning. We cannot plausibly omit them, once we acknowledge that emotions include in their content judgments that can be true or false, and good or bad guides to ethical choice. We will have to grapple with the messy material of grief and love, anger and fear, and the role these tumultuous experiences play in thought about the good and the just.

To say that emotions should form a prominent part of the subject matter of moral philosophy is not to say that moral philosophy should give emotions a privileged place of trust, or regard them as immune from rational criticism: for they may be no more reliable than any other set of entrenched beliefs. There may even be special reasons for regarding them with suspicion, given their specific content and the nature of their history. It does mean, however, that we cannot ignore them, as so often moral philosophy has done. It means that a central part of developing an adequate ethical theory will be to develop an adequate theory of the emotions, including their cultural sources, their history in infancy and childhood, and their sometimes unpredictable and disoderly operation in the daily life of human beings who are attached to things outside themselves.

Proust's account of the Baron's mind issues a challenge to conventional ethical thought in yet another way. It tells us something about what texts we need to turn to if we are to arrive at an adequate account of the emotions. If emotions involve judgments about the salience for our well-being of uncontrolled external objects, judgments in which the mind of the judge is projected unstably outward into a world of objects, we will need to be able to imagine those attachments, their delight and their terror, their intense and even obsessive focusing on their object, if we are ever to talk well about love, or fear, or anger. But then it seems that we will have reason to turn to texts such as Proust's novel, which encourage us in such imaginings, deepening and refining our grasp of upheavals of thought in our own lives. If Proust is right, we will not understand ourselves well enough to talk good sense in ethics unless we do subject ourselves to the painful self-examination a text such as his can produce.

Furthermore, if emotions are as Proust describes them, they have a complicated cognitive structure that is in part narrative in form, involving a story of our relation to cherished objects that extends over time. Ultimately, we cannot understand the Baron's love, for example, without knowing a great deal about the history of patterns of attachment that extend back into his childhood. Past loves shadow present attachments, and take up residence within them. This, in turn, suggests that in order to talk well about them we will need to turn to texts that contain a narrative dimension, thus deepening and refining our grasp of ourselves as beings with a complicated temporal history. It is for this reason that Proust's narrator comes to believe that certain truths about the human being can be told only in literary form. If we accept his view of what emotions are, we should agree, to the extent of making a place for literature (and other works of art) within moral philosophy, alongside more conventional philosophical texts. Once again: an account of human reasoning based only upon abstract texts such as are conventional in moral philosophy is likely to prove too simple to offer us the type of self-understanding we need.

Some of these claims might be maintained even by people who think of emotions as totally noncognitive: even such people might think that we need to understand human psychology better than we often do in order to write well about ethics. But if a cognitive/evaluative theory of emotions is correct, these claims have a particular salience: for what they mean is that not just a psychological adjunct to emotional thought, but a part of ethical thought itself will be omitted with the omission of emotions. Emotions are not just the fuel that powers the psychological mechanism of a reasoning creature, they are parts, highly complex and messy parts, of this creature's reasoning itself.

Thus a theoretical account of emotions is not only that: it has large consequences for the theory of practical reason, for normative ethics, and for the relationship between ethics and aesthetics. Such an account has consequences for political thought as well: for understanding the relationship between emotions and various conceptions of the human good will inform our deliberations as we ask how politics might support human flourishing. If we think of emotions as essential elements of human intelligence, rather than just as supports or props for intelligence, this gives us especially strong reasons to promote the conditions of emotional well-being in a political culture: for this view entails that without emotional development, a part of our reasoning capacity as political creatures will be missing.

In the first part of the book I shall develop a conception of the emotions that fleshes out the insight expressed in Proust's description, suggesting that diverse phenomena of our emotional life are well explained by a view that has its antecedents in the ideas of the ancient Greek Stoics.

This view holds that emotions are appraisals or value judgments, which ascribe to things and persons outside the person's own control great importance for that person's own flourishing.[1] It thus contains three salient ideas: the idea of a *cognitive appraisal* or *evaluation*; the idea of *one's own flourishing* or *one's important goals and projects*; and the idea of the *salience of external objects as elements in one's own scheme of goals.* Emotions typically combine these ideas with information about events in the world; they are our ways of registering how things are with respect to the external (i.e., uncontrolled)[2] items that we view as salient for our well-being. Focusing on a complex example of grief involving the death of a parent (an example chosen because of its ubiquity, as an apt device for encouraging readers to mine their own experiences of grief), I shall show how this particular type of cognitive account does justice to our experiences of emotion.

My strategy is to state the view initially in a relatively simple form, providing it with a preliminary defense (Chapter 1). Once we have seen its general structure, we can then consider several modifications that it needs to undergo in order to become more adequate. These modifications were not made by the Stoics themselves (so far as we know from the fragments of their work on this topic that survive). The view undergoes refinement and reshaping in four distinct stages. By the time we are finished with it, a general core will remain, but it will be a lot more subtle than the view first announced. The view that emerges may justly be called neo-Stoic, and I shall often use this term. But it has an independent character, emphasizing, as it does, the commonality between humans and other animals, the role of social norms, and the complexities of an individual human history.

To modify the view, we need, first, simply to elaborate it further, taking up issues the Stoics are not known to have addressed. We need to consider the role of imagination in emotions of various types. We need to make distinctions between general and particular emotions,

1 This analysis of emotion in no way entails the Stoics' controversial normative view that the evaluations involved in emotions are all false. It is this view that explains their recommendation that we extirpate all emotions, seeking an undisturbed life. For exegesis of both the analysis and the normative view, see Nussbaum (1994); for the normative view, and my critique of it, see Chapter 7.
2 Externality is a metaphorical way of referring to the fact that these elements are not securely controlled by the person's own will; in that sense many things inside the person's own body (health and disease, for example) are "external."

and between "background" and "situational" emotions. We need to ask how the diminution of grief over time can be explained within a cognitive/evaluative theory. We need to ask carefully whether all the evaluations involved in emotion do indeed relate to uncontrolled "external goods," and whether the object of emotion is always valued for some relation it bears to one's own flourishing. And, finally, we need to devote a good deal of attention to the thorny question of whether there are elements other than cognitive attitudes that are involved in emotion: feelings, bodily movements, dense perceptions that are not exhausted by the emotion's propositional content. In the latter half of the first chapter, I begin the refinement of the Stoic view – or, we might also say, the construction of a contemporary neo-Stoic view – by mapping out these further distinctions and confronting these further questions.

Second, any contemporary cognitive/evaluative view needs to advance a plausible account of the relationship between human emotions and the emotions of other animals. The original Stoics had an implausible account: they simply denied that nonhuman animals had emotions. This denial has led some thinkers to reject their view. But we need not take this course, since we may, instead, reject their low estimate of the intelligence of animals. At this point we need to turn to modern work in ethology and cognitive psychology, asking what forms of cognitive appraisal it is plausible to ascribe to animals of various types. I argue in Chapter 2 that we can give an adequate account of animal emotion in the general spirit of the Stoic view; but we need to broaden the Stoic account of evaluative cognition, focusing less on language and the acceptance of linguistically formulable propositions and more on the general ability to see X as Y, where Y involves a notion of salience or importance for the creature's own well-being. At this point I also focus on some general issues of emotional content, addressing the connection between animal emotions and the perception of helplessness, arguing that emotional health requires the belief that one's own voluntary actions will make a significant difference to one's most important goals and projects.

At this point in the argument, we are also in a position to discuss three important distinctions that help us to map further the geography of the emotional life: distinctions between emotions and appetites, between emotions and moods, and between emotions and motives for action. Showing that the view can provide an adequate account of these distinctions helps to strengthen our claim that the view provides a good account of emotional experience. These discussions conclude Chapter 2.

But a contemporary cognitive/evaluative account also needs an adequate account of the role of diverse social norms in constructing a society's emotional repertory. The original Stoics gave an important place to social norms in their accounts of emotion, but they said nothing about how variations in norms entail variations in emotion. The third major modification we must make in the simple view first advanced is, then, to pursue this issue, offering a sensible account of the role of "social construction" in the emotional life. Anthropological studies of emotion have yielded rich material on emotional variety, which I draw on in the third chapter in order to pursue these issues. The simple view is transformed yet again: and yet its main features (its emphasis on appraisal and on the role of important goals and projects) remain constant.

The Greek and Roman Stoics had no apparent interest in childhood, nor did they ever ask how early experiences shape the mature emotional life. Indeed, they appear to have had the implausible view that children, like animals, do not have emotions. We can see that this was an error – that the "geological upheavals of thought" that constitute the adult experience of emotion involve foundations laid down much earlier in life, experiences of attachment, need, delight, and anger. Early memories shadow later perceptions of objects, adult attachment relations bear the traces of infantile love and hate. Although this narrative dimension is a ubiquitous part of adult emotional experience, and in that sense should be a part of the analysis from the beginning, it could not be adequately described before we had elaborated the second chapter's flexible account of cognition and the third chapter's account of social variation. At this point, however, we can ask how the human infant's combination of extreme neediness and cognitive maturity, of intense attachment and nascent separateness, shapes, for better or for worse, the geography of the emotional life. On these questions, rarely treated by philosophers and almost never treated well, a philosopher needs to turn to psychology and to literature for help. Recently there has been an unprecedented degree of convergence and even cooperation between cognitive psychologists and psychoanalysts, especially those in the object-relations tradition, where some of these issues are concerned. I draw on this material – but also, and centrally, on Proust, in some ways the most profound object-relations psychoanalyst of all. The simple view thus undergoes yet one more stage of modification – this one being perhaps the most dramatic.

My account of childhood emotions focuses on the role of the imagination in promoting a good outcome to early emotional crises. My later accounts of compassion and love develop this insight, focusing on the role of the arts in cultivating these emotions. The Interlude and Chapter 5 therefore turn to experiences of emotion we have in connection with works of art. The Interlude develops a general framework for thinking about emotions directed toward works of art. Chapter 5 then focuses on music, since this case is much more difficult to treat than the case of literature, and yet crucial if we are to satisfy ourselves that the account we are developing is on the right track. Music is an especially rich source of emotional experiences and has frequently been taken to offer us insight into the nature of the emotional life. Many cognitive/evaluative views of emotion have difficulty explaining these phenomena; I argue that mine does not, because of its flexible nonlinguistic account of cognition. Indeed, it enables us to cut through a dilemma that has vexed analysts of musical experience. Mahler's music, and his remarkably perceptive statements about his music, are my guides here, and I offer interpretations of two songs from the *Kindertotelieder* to show what the view can make of a complex case of the musical expression of grief, love, guilt, and helplessness.

Thus Part I ends: with a far more complicated version of the view first mapped out in Chapter 1 – incorporating nonlinguistic cognitions, social norms, and individual history – and with an example of the way that such a view can go to work explaining a harrowing and yet subtle experience.

It will be evident that Part I focuses on some emotions more than others. Grief plays an especially prominent role in all of the chapters, as do the closely related emotions of fear and hope. (The focus broadens in Chapter 4, when shame, disgust, envy, and anger all become prominent.) And yet, despite this focus on certain cases, it is also clear that my project is to construct an analytical framework for thinking about emotions in general. This procedure requires comment, because some would claim that there is no interesting common ground among such a wide range of phenomena.[3] One can only defeat that kind of skepticism by forging ahead and proposing an account that is illuminating, and yet does not neglect significant differences among the emotions.[4] Differences are repeatedly confronted by the fact that the account does draw on an increasingly wide range of cases as it goes along. Starting with a detailed mapping of a single type of emotion,[5] it eventually includes analyses of many others. Parts II and III expand the range still further. I agree with the skeptical critic to the extent that I think any adequate account of emotions needs to go into complex details about the specific content of particular emotions; little of interest can be said without that. Nonetheless, when we do get into the analysis of particular emotions, we find that there are close relationships among them, both conceptual and causal, that we need to trace if we are to have a good understanding even of the specific varieties.

We will find, too, that the common ground within the class of emotions is actually greater than we might suppose if we simply looked at our casual and frequently loose use of words such as "feeling," "emotion," and "passion." Although, as I shall describe shortly, I do rely on people's ability to classify pretty reliably experiences of a particular type of emotion, even here my methodology makes room for error that will ultimately be corrected in dialogue with a theoretical account. Where large generic categories are concerned, ordinary use seems to me far less precise and thus less reliable than it is with the particular categories; so I will not take it for granted, for example, that every use of a term such as "feeling" designates a single phenomenon. There are multiple ambiguities in use, and a theory ought to be prepared to point this out.[6] Such a critical theory can nonetheless arrive at an interesting

3 See Griffiths (1997).
4 See also Ben-Ze'ev (2000), Solomon (1999).
5 Of course, each single type has tremendous internal variety, as my account stresses. I argue in Chapters 3 and 4 that social norms and personal history are sources of great diversity in the experience of grief.
6 It is particularly odd that Griffiths, who is a stern critic of the reliance on ordinary use and ordinary conceptions, should rely on them himself in a quite uncritical way when arguing that the category "emotion" contains such great heterogeneity that no interesting single account is possible. He uses the word quite loosely in order to establish that the things falling under it are multiple and not unified; and yet it is he who holds that our loose use is to be distrusted.

unified account of a core group of phenomena that do have significant commonalities. The reader must judge whether the theory has sufficient flexibility to explore differences among the different emotions, and among different experiences of a given emotion, while retaining enough definiteness to illuminate the diverse phenomena.[7]

What, then, is the starting point of the investigation? It is plain that it must be experience. Moreover, even when, as here, the results of scientific investigations are prominently consulted, the terrain of the *explanandum* has to be identified in some way that is, at least initially, independent of the explanatory theories scientists bring forward. Thus scientists who investigate the emotions typically rely on their subjects' (and their readers') ability to identify experientially instances of a given emotion, and to name them pretty reliably. The whole enterprise is one of establishing correlations – between a neural phenomenon, say, and the emotion of grief. So instances of grief have to be identified in some other way, usually by self-report. It is difficult to see how even the most parsimonious scientist could proceed otherwise: without experiential classification and the subsequent correlation, we would have simply a description of neural activity, and it would not hook onto any question that scientists typically ask. In a similar way, my own account assumes the general ability of readers to identify and classify instances of emotions such as grief, fear, and envy; intuitive judgments about these cases are consulted throughout, along with the results of philosophical and scientific investigations.

Two qualifications, however, must be firmly entered at this point. First, relying on people's ability to classify instances of emotion does not mean relying on people's theories about what emotions are.[8] Consider field linguists: they rely on the ability of their subjects to identify more or less correctly instances of proper and improper use. They do not rely on their ability to construct a correct theory of the language in

7 Admittedly, it is not always easy to draw a line between emotions and other closely related experiences, such as moods and appetites. The distinctions are slippery, and some cases may be genuinely indeterminate. This situation obtains, however, with many complex phenomena of human experience that philosophers try to investigate. Concepts such as belief and consciousness, virtue and justice, look far more difficult to specify in any interestingly unified way. And yet this has not stopped philosophers from investigating commonalities and saying things that are genuinely illuminating as a result.

8 Surprisingly, Griffiths (1997) does not seem to notice this distinction; his attack on "folk psychology" would appear to cover intuitions of both types.

question, and of course it would be ludicrous to rely on that. Most people have no idea how to write the grammar of their language, although it is to their competence that any grammar must be accountable. Consider, again, the career of Socrates. His procedure, as Plato records it, relied on the ability of his interlocutors to identify, more or less correctly, instances of a given virtue. Candidate definitions of courage, or justice, are standardly attacked by discovering what both Socrates and the interlocutor consider to be a genuine case of the virtue, not covered by the definition – or else by finding that the definition covers phenomena that neither Socrates nor the interlocutor is prepared to count as a genuine case of the virtue. What his procedure reveals is that people are more reliable when they are grouping instances than when they are trying to give them a theoretical explanation. That is not surprising, because the identification of instances is a ubiquitous part of their lives, part of being a competent speaker of that language and participant in that culture – whereas theory construction is usually something to which they have devoted no sustained thought at all. My procedure, then, is Socratic: it relies on the ability of readers to identify the instances that constitute the range of the *explanandum,* but it does not rely on them to produce good explanations. Indeed, my own explanation seems quite counterintuitive to start with, just as do many Socratic definitions. My hope is that it will ultimately seem convincing as a valuable explanatory theory.

Second, relying on people's ability to be generally correct in classifying phenomena does not mean assuming that they are always correct.[9] If I am searching for a scientific definition of water, I will have to begin somewhere: presumably, with instances of water identified by competent speakers of the language. But once I get the definition, in terms of a chemical analysis of water, the phenomena will need to be regrouped: if the speakers didn't know that ice was an instance of the same chemical compound, their classifications will have to be corrected. A core range of phenomena will have to remain, or else we will wonder whether the explanation is really explaining the thing that we began to investigate.[10] But it is only natural – given that people, as I've

9 Again, the possibility of an account of emotion that is both responsive to experience and critical seems to be ignored by Griffiths, in his contemptuous dismissal of most philosophical work on the topic.

10 That is the problem that has often been found in Plato's *Republic*: some interpreters hold that Socrates' definition of justice in terms of the order of the soul has moved so

said, are often less than thoughtful about their classifications – that they will not draw all the boundaries in the right places, and that this error will be revealed by a correct account.

In this way, I will start from instances of emotion as people identify them in daily life, but I will ultimately argue that we should admit other instances that are not always correctly identified: an ongoing fear of death, for example, that persists unnoticed in the fabric of one's life, explaining many actions and reactions; a submerged anger at a loved one, which is not acknowledged as such, but emerges in the form of depression – a depression that seems like an objectless mood, but that turns out, on inspection, to be the legacy of a childhood loss. In such cases, I do believe that we need to return, at the end, to people and their judgments: we need to be able to show people that positing a fear of death is a good way of unifying diverse experiences in the given case, and explaining actions that otherwise would not be so well explained. If we do not come back to the phenomena with a sense of new illumination, then our own explanatory account is in trouble. Nonetheless, we should insist that philosophy may, indeed should, be responsive to human experience and yet critical of the defective thinking it sometimes contains.

Part I says little about normative questions. Establishing that the emotions have rich cognitive/intentional content helps dispel one objection to them as elements in deliberation, namely the objection that they are blind forces that have no selectivity or intelligence about them. But this is hardly the only objection that one might make. Seeing the emotions as forms of evaluative thought shows us that the question about their role in a good human life is part and parcel of a general inquiry into the good human life. One cannot, then, say what role emotions should play in morality (or in the nonmoral aspects of a good life) without defending an overall normative view. To defend such an overall view is beyond the scope of this project. It also goes against its spirit, which is to show what emotions may offer to views of a number of different types.

Nonetheless, it still seems right to ask whether there is anything

far away from the range of cases that the interlocutors initially used to locate justice that he has really defined a different concept. I think this charge can be answered – but not here!

about emotions as such that makes them subversive of morality (or, in other ways, of human flourishing). If lack of discrimination or intelligence is not a fair complaint, are there other general complaints against emotions that should trouble us? In answering this question I make some assumptions about what an adequate normative view should be like. In particular, I assume that an adequate view should make room for mutual respect and reciprocity; that it should treat people as ends rather than as means, and as agents rather than simply as passive recipients of benefit; that it should include an adequate measure of concern for the needs of others, including those who live at a distance; and that it should make room for attachments to particular people, and for seeing them as qualitatively distinct from one another. These characteristics are left deliberately vague and general, in order to show that they can be exemplified by a number of different normative theories, and also (a separate point) that they can be further specified in many different ways.

To someone with these concerns (which a philosopher could associate either with a liberal brand of Aristotelianism or with a flexible virtue-oriented type of Kantianism), the emotions as I characterize them in Part I pose three problems. First, insofar as they involve acknowledgment of neediness and lack of self-sufficiency, emotions reveal us as vulnerable to events that we do not control; and one might hold that including a large measure of uncontrol in one's conception of a good life compromises too deeply the dignity of one's own agency. This is the reason why the original Stoics linked their extremely shrewd analysis of the emotions, which I follow here, to a radical normative thesis, that it is best to extirpate the emotions completely from human life. I do not accept that normative thesis here. I proceed on the assumption that at least some things and persons outside one's own control have real worth. But the Stoic challenge, drawing as it does on an attractive picture of agency and its integrity, raises questions that must be answered, in connection with any normative thesis that one does defend.

Second, emotions focus on our own goals, and they represent the world from the point of view of those goals and projects, rather than from a strictly impartial viewpoint. Moreover, they develop in connection with extremely close and intimate attachments, and my historical account suggests that these early, very particular attachments shadow later object relations. So the emotions seem to be too partial or unbalanced, and one might suppose that we could do better with the guidance of more detached forms of reasoning. Again, this issue will be handled differently by different normative theories; but it is one that any theory meeting my thin constraints needs to worry about, since we do want to provide a basis for respect for the dignity of agency and for concern about human need.

Third, emotions seem to be characterized by ambivalence toward their objects. In the very nature of our early object relations, I argue in Chapter 4, there lurks a morally subversive combination of love and resentment, which springs directly from the thought that we need others to survive and flourish, but do not at all control their movements. If love is in this way always, or even commonly, mixed up with hatred, then, once again, this might offer us some reasons not to trust to the emotions at all in the moral life, but rather to the more impersonal guidance of rules of duty. Chapter 4 also offers some preliminary reflections about how these problems might be overcome, developing a tentative account of psychological health that involves a willingness to live in interdependence with others. But this norm remains fragile and elusive; and to that extent the role of emotions in the good ethical life remains unclear.

Part II and Part III investigate these three objections, but they do not do so in a linear way. Instead, using the account of emotions in Part I as a basis, they focus on two emotions that seem particularly pertinent in crafting a reply: compassion and love. There would be indefinitely many ways of investigating connections between emotions and morality; and a general discussion of this question could easily come to lack the kind of specificity and detail that would make such an account valuable. So my choice has been to narrow my scope, both by focusing on these two emotions (although others, such as shame and disgust, also play an important role in my account), and by talking about them in a way that is sometimes indirect and unsystematic, focusing on the analysis of historical debates and the interpretation of texts.

Compassion is an emotion that has often been relied on to hook our imaginations to the good of others and to make them the object of our intense care. In Chapter 6 I investigate the structure of that emotion, asking what prospects and problems it contains for morality. In Chapter 7 I turn to historical texts, tracing the ways in which all of my three objections have been raised in debates about the social role of compassion. I discuss arguments favorable and unfavorable to that emotion made by thinkers including Plato, Aristotle, the Stoics, Adam Smith, Rousseau, Kant, Schopenhauer, and Nietzsche. I then assess the historical debate, examining each of the three objections in turn and concluding with a complex and highly qualified defense of that emotions' social role. Despite its potential for unevenness and partiality, I argue, compassion can be an invaluable way of extending our ethical awareness and of understanding the human meaning of events and policies. In Chapter 8 I propose some roles that compassion, in partnership with an adequate ethical theory, can play in the political life.

But defending compassion from the moral point of view is a relatively straightforward task. Far harder is the defense of the more intense and ambivalent emotions of the personal life, which are more thoroughly shaped by early object relations, with their intense delight and terror, their jealousy and frustration. Personal love has typically been thought too wonderful to remove from human life; but it has also been seen (not only by philosophers) as a source of great moral danger because of its partiality and the extreme form of vulnerability it involves, which make a connection with jealousy and anger virtually inevitable. There are indefinitely many ways in which a philosophical project might investigate this issue. I have chosen to focus on accounts of the "ascent" or "ladder" of love within highly restricted portions of the Western philosophical/literary traditions, asking which reforms in the structure of love seem to promise solutions to these problems, and whether, in solving the problems, they still leave in place the elements of life that I have said an adequate account must include. These attempts can be divided into three families: Platonic, Christian, and Romantic. Each family makes proposals of real merit, and yet all of them, in some ways, climb so high above real life that there are real doubts about whether they actually include, as they claim to do, everything that has genuine worth. Moreover, as we shall see, some of their proposals actually reinforce elements in the history of childhood emotion that (as I argue earlier) are especially dangerous to morality: in particular, shame at the limitations of the body and envy of others who control what we wish to control but don't. In that sense they make things worse rather than better. In the last two chapters, I therefore turn to two attempts to surmount shame and envy, and to propose, in the process, an inversion of the canonical "ladder," restoring our love and attention to the phenomena of daily life.

In Part III, I develop this argument through a focus on particular texts, some of them philosophical/religious (Plato, Augustine, Dante, Spinoza) but others literary (Proust, Emily Brontë, Whitman, Joyce) or even musical (Mahler) – although my way of addressing the literary and musical texts is to focus on the conversation they have (in both form and content) with the philosophical/religious tradition. Running through the concrete textual investigations, however, and connecting them, are my own questions about the role of emotions in the good life, as generated by the account in Part I. In that sense, Part III is less an exhaustive account of the texts than a philosophical meditation on them, with my own normative questions in mind. The turn to literature and music is significant in the light of the role played by the imagination in the account of childhood development and the account of compassion: any program for the ascent of love that is likely to prove valuable will involve cultivating this faculty, as well as the capacity for argument.

All the normative material in Parts II and III presupposes the analysis of Part I, and assumes, for purposes of the normative debate, that some such story about emotions and their development is true. The idea is to show that understanding the emotions (their relation to judgment, their evaluative dimensions, their childhood history) in this way raises a definite group of normative questions and problems, and also offers a set of resources for their solution. A different analysis of the emotions might leave some of the normative arguments of Parts II and III unchanged, but most of them would have to be heavily revised. (If we thought of the emotions as innate bodily processes, for example, proposals to modify them by altering our perceptions of objects would not seem feasible.) In that sense, the analysis of emotions does moral work: we see clearly what problems we do and don't have on our hands, we adopt plausible rather than implausible pictures of ethical change, and we understand (in connection with our normative arguments) what it might mean for a political community to extend to its citizens the social bases of imaginative and emotional health.

It is sometimes supposed that cognitive views of emotion are "Apollinian," leaving out what is messy and ungovernable in the life of the passions.[11] I hope to show that this criticism is misguided – or at least that it would not be correct to aim it at my view. As the passage from Proust indicates, thinking of emotions as thoughts hardly leaves out what is sometimes unsettling, indeed excruciating, about them. Indeed, I suspect that the criticism should be aimed the other way around. If we really were to think of emotions as like bodily tugs or stabs or flashes, then we would precisely leave out what is most disturbing about them. How simple life would be, if grief were only a pain in the leg, or jealousy but a very bad backache. Jealousy and grief torment us mentally; it is the thoughts we have about objects that are the source of agony – and, in other cases, delight. Even the grief and love of animals, as I shall argue, is a function of their capacity for thoughts about objects that they see as important to their well-being. But the peculiar depth and the potentially terrifying character of the human emotions derives from the especially complicated thoughts that humans are likely to form about their own need for objects, and about their imperfect control over them.

As Freud writes, in my second epigraph, the story of human birth is the story of the emergence of a sentient being from the womb of secure narcissism to the sharp perception that it is cast adrift in a world of objects, a world that it has not made and does not control. In that world, the infant is aware of being an unusually weak and helpless being. Bodily pain is nothing by contrast to the terrifying awareness of helplessness, close to unendurable without the shelter of a womblike sleep. When we wake up, we have to figure out how to live in that world of objects. Without the intelligence of the emotions, we have little hope of confronting that problem well.

11 This term is used by Blackburn (1998), p. 89; but the sentiment is more broadly shared.

PART I

NEED AND RECOGNITION

EMOTIONS AS
JUDGMENTS OF VALUE

Emotions, I shall argue, involve judgments about important things, judgments in which, appraising an external object as salient for our own well-being, we acknowledge our own neediness and incompleteness before parts of the world that we do not fully control. I therefore begin with a story of such evaluations, a story involving fear, and hope, and grief, and anger, and love.

I. NEED AND RECOGNITION

In April 1992 I was lecturing at Trinity College, Dublin.[1] Because my mother was in the hospital convalescing after a serious but routine operation, I phoned at regular intervals to get reports on her progress. One of these phone calls brought the news that she had had a serious complication during the night, a rupture of the surgical incision between her esophagus and her stomach. She had developed a massive internal infection and a fever, and, though she was receiving the best care in a fine hospital, her life was in jeopardy. This news felt like a nail suddenly driven into my stomach. With the help of my hosts I arranged to return on the next flight, which was not until the next day. That evening I delivered my scheduled lecture, on the subject of the emotions – a blueprint for the series of lectures on which this book is based. I was not the exuberant self-sufficient philosopher delivering a lecture – or rather, not only that – but at the same time a person invaded by the world, barely containing tears. That night I had a dream

---

1 Nussbaum (1998) recasts this material in the form of a philosophical dialogue; ultimately the dialogue will be revised for a book that I am writing on the topic of the dialogue form.

in which my mother appeared in my room in Trinity College, in her hospital bed, very emaciated and curled into a fetal position. I looked at her with a surge of tremendous love and said, "Beautiful Mommy." Suddenly she stood up, looking young and beautiful as in old photographs from the time when I was two or three. She smiled at me with her characteristically embracing wit, and said that others might call her wonderful, but she very much preferred to be called beautiful. I woke up and wept, knowing that things were not so.

During the transatlantic flight the next day, I saw, with hope, that image of health before me. But I also saw, more frequently, the image of her death, and my body wanted to interpose itself before that image, to negate it. With shaking hands I typed out paragraphs of a lecture on mercy, and the narrative understanding of criminal offenders. And I felt, all the while, a vague and powerful anger – at the doctors, for allowing this crisis to occur, at the flight attendants, for smiling as if everything were normal, above all at myself, for not having been able to stop this event from happening, or for not having been there with her when it did.

Arriving in Philadelphia I called the hospital's intensive care unit and was told by the nurse that my mother had died twenty minutes earlier. My sister, who lived there, had been with her and had told her that I was on my way. The nurse invited me to come over and see her laid out. I ran through the littered downtown streets as if something could be done. At the end of a maze of corridors, beyond the cafeteria where hospital workers were laughing and talking, I found the surgical intensive care unit. There, ushered in by a nurse, I saw, behind a curtain, my mother in bed, lying on her back, as so often I had seen her lying asleep at home. She was dressed in her best robe, the one with the lace collar. Her makeup was impeccable. (The nurses, who were very fond of her, told me that they knew how important it had been to her always to have her lipstick on straight.) A barely visible tube went into her nose, but it was not hooked up to anything. I wept incontrollably, while the nurses brought me glasses of water. An hour later I was on my way to my hotel in a hospital van, carrying her red overnight bag, with her clothes and the books I had given her to read in the hospital – strange relics that seemed to me not to belong in the world any more, as if they should have vanished with her life.

In the weeks that followed, I had periods of agonized weeping;

whole days of crushing fatigue; nightmares in which I felt altogether unprotected and alone, and seemed to feel a strange animal walking across my bed. I felt, again, anger – at the nurses for not prolonging her life until I arrived, although I knew that they were following her written instructions not to take "extraordinary measures"; at the doctors for letting a routine operation lead to catastrophe, although I had no reason to suspect malpractice; at people who phoned on business as if everything were normal, even though I knew they had no way of knowing otherwise. For it seemed appropriate to be angry, and not possible to be angry at mortality itself. Above all, I felt anger at myself for not being with her on account of my busy career and my unswerving determination to work, which had always caused me to see her less frequently than my sister had. And though I told myself that I had in fact seen her often in recent months and had checked her condition carefully with the doctors before going to Ireland, I blamed myself still, for all the inattentiveness and the anger and all the deficiencies in love that I could find in my history with her, and some that I may possibly have invented. As I completed my lecture about mercy and forgiveness, I blamed myself most acutely.

I did, however, complete my lecture, and delivered it shortly after traveling with my daughter to the funeral. And I noticed this: that the ongoing structure of daily life with my daughter, with my work, with friends and colleagues and people I love, the relatively unaltered structure of my expectations as to what would happen in that daily life the next day and the next, made the grief less chaotic for me than it was for my sister, who had lived close to my mother and seen her almost every day. Although I believe we loved her equally, there was an asymmetry in the way life dealt with that love, and this brought about an apparent asymmetry in emotional duration. On the other hand, although my present life was less disrupted I had the odd sensation of having been robbed of a history, of being no longer a person who had a family history. For this reason the sight of my ex-husband, arriving at the funeral, filled me with joy, because I could recognize in him twenty years of life with my mother, and knew that he could recognize it in me, and prove that it had existed. At the funeral the speeches of many whose lives she had helped also gave me joy, since they proved the continuity of her influence in the world. And the exertion of something like my usual professional activity, as I gave a speech on behalf of the family, made me feel less helpless, although I viewed this very fact with suspicion, as a possible sign of deficiency in love.

In this story we see several features of the emotions that it will be the business of my argument to try to explain: their urgency and heat; their tendency to take over the personality and to move it to action with overwhelming force; their connection with important attachments, in terms of which a person defines her life; the person's sense of passivity before them; their apparently adversarial relation to "rationality" in the sense of cool calculation or cost-benefit analysis; their close connections with one another, as hope alternates uneasily with fear, as a single event transforms hope into grief, as grief, looking about for a cause, expresses itself as anger, as all of these can be the vehicles of an underlying love.

In the light of all these features, it might seem very strange to suggest that emotions are forms of judgment. And yet it is something close to this thesis that I shall defend. I shall argue that all of these features not only are compatible with, but actually are best explained by, a modified version of the ancient Greek Stoic view, according to which emotions are forms of evaluative judgment that ascribe to certain things and persons outside a person's own control great importance for the person's own flourishing. Emotions are thus, in effect, acknowledgments of neediness and lack of self-sufficiency. My aim in Part I is to examine this view and the arguments that support it, adding some further distinctions and arguments to the original view.[2]

2 Some elements of a related philosophical position are in Lyons (1980), Gordon (1987), and de Sousa (1987). None of these, however, stresses the evaluative nature of the emotions' cognitive content. That aspect of emotions was already stressed in Pitcher (1965), one of the earliest and most forceful critiques of the dominant Humean view, and still one of the most interesting accounts of the emotions' intentionality; see also Kenny (1963), Thalberg (1964). Another pioneering work that stresses the connection of emotions to values is Solomon (1976, 2nd ed. 1993). Solomon also stresses the intentionality characteristic of emotions (pp. 111–19) and criticizes dominant "hydraulic" and "feeling" models (pp. 77–88, 96–102). But his approach is in other respects very different from the one taken here. Heavily influenced by existentialism, he thinks of emotions as involving value-positings that are willed and altogether subjective, and therefore speaks of emotions as "the source of our values" and things that "create our interests and our purposes," or even "constitute our world" (all p. 15). My approach does not take a stand one way or another on the nature of value, but tries to present the valuational nature of our appraisals from the internal viewpoint of the person having

As I shall argue in Chapter 2, we need to substitute a broader and more capacious account of cognition for the original Stoic emphasis on the grasp of linguistically formulable propositions. This modification is necessary in order to give an adequate account of animal emotions, of the emotions of human infants, and also of many emotions of adult human beings. Other modifications will involve investigating the role of social norms in emotions (Chapter 3), and providing an account of the development of emotions in infancy and early childhood (Chapter 4). Nonetheless, I shall argue that emotions always involve thought of an object combined with thought of the object's salience or importance; in that sense, they always involve appraisal or evaluation. I shall therefore refer to my view as a type of "cognitive-evaluative" view, and sometimes, more briefly, as a type of "cognitive" view. But by "cognitive" I mean nothing more than "concerned with receiving and processing information." I do not mean to imply the presence of elaborate calculation, of computation, or even of reflexive self-awareness.

My focus will be on developing an adequate philosophical account. But since any adequate account in this area must respond, I believe, not only to the data of one's own experience and to stories of the experience of others, but also to the best work done to systematize and account for emotional experience in the disciplines of psychology and anthropology, I shall turn, as well, to those disciplines, where it happens that views related to mine have recently been gaining the ascendancy – in cognitive psychology, in work on helplessness and control, and on emotion as "appraisal" of that which pertains to a creature's "thriving"; in anthropology, in work on emotion as an evaluative "social construction"; and in psychoanalysis, in work on early object relations and their evaluative dimensions.

Throughout, the *explananda* will be the genus of which some species

the emotional experience. More recently, Ben-Ze'ev (2000), in an excellent and wide-ranging book, has given appraisal a prominent role in his account, and has defended appraisal views against opponents. (See, in particular, his effective response on pp. 541–2, n, 49, to the objections against such views made by Griffiths [1997], with all points of which I am in strong agreement.) Although his account is more open-textured than the one to be presented here, and although he denies that the evaluative element is primary in distinguishing emotions from nonemotions (p. 70), he also grants, referring to the present book, that if the account of the appraisal or evaluation is sufficiently complex, his objections do not hold (p. 70 and p. 540, n. 44). Another significant recent account is Green (1992).

are grief, fear, love, joy, hope, anger, gratitude, hatred, envy, jealousy, pity, guilt. The members of this family are, I shall argue in Chapter 2, importantly distinct both from bodily appetites such as hunger and thirst and from objectless moods such as irritation and endogenous depression. There are numerous internal distinctions among members of the family; but they have enough in common to be analyzed together; and a long tradition in Western philosophy, beginning with Aristotle, has so grouped them. Nor is this grouping a peculiarity of the Western tradition: similar, though not identical, classifications also occur in other traditions of thought.[3] We also find this grouping in everyday experience, where we do treat emotions differently than we do moods, appetites, and desires, although we may not have a good theoretical account of why we do so. Therefore, we have at least a roughly demarcated category of phenomena before us that can be scrutinized to see what their common features might be, although we should be prepared, as well, to find that the boundaries of the class are not clear and that there are noncentral cases that share only some of the features of the central cases.[4] It is not to be expected that any explanatory theory will preserve all the phenomena intact; but my assumption will be that a criterion of correctness for a theory on this topic is that it should preserve the truth of the "greatest number and the most basic" of these experiences,[5] and that it should be able to provide a convincing explanation for any errors in classification that it eventually ascribes to experience.

II. THE ADVERSARY: INTENTIONALITY, BELIEF, EVALUATION

The Stoic view of emotion has an adversary. It is the view that emotions are "non-reasoning movements," unthinking energies that simply push the person around, without being hooked up to the ways in which

---

3 See Marks and Ames (1995) for Asian traditions. For conversations on this point about Chinese traditions I am indebted to Lothar von Falkenhausen, about Ghanaian traditions to Kwasi Wiredu, and about Balinese emotions to Unni Wikan (on whose work see further in Chapter 3). One salient feature of the Ghanaian tradition is that emotions are treated from the first as a sub-category of thought; this is apparently also the case in Bali.

4 See Pitcher (1965) for an excellent discussion of this issue.

5 See Aristotle, *Nicomachean Ethics* 1147a.

she perceives or thinks about the world. Like gusts of wind or the currents of the sea, they move, and move the person, but obtusely, without vision of an object or beliefs about it. In this sense they are "pushes" rather than "pulls." Sometimes this view is connected with the idea that emotions derive from an "animal" part of our nature, rather than from a specifically human part – usually by thinkers who do not have a high regard for animal intelligence. (I shall be arguing that animals are capable of a great deal of thought and discrimination, and that we have to invoke these capacities to explain their emotions.) Sometimes, too, the adversary's view is connected with the idea that emotions are "bodily" rather than "mental," as if this were sufficient to make them unintelligent rather than intelligent. Although I believe that emotions are, like other mental processes, bodily, I also believe, and shall argue, that seeing them as in every case taking place in a living body does not give us reason to reduce their intentional/cognitive components to nonintentional bodily movements.[6] We probably do not have reason even to include in the definition of a given emotion-type reference to any definite bodily state – though this is a much more contentious point that will require further argument. Certainly we are not left with a choice between regarding emotions as ghostly spiritual energies and taking them to be obtuse nonseeing bodily movements, such as a leap of the heart, or the boiling of the blood. Living bodies are capable of intelligence and intentionality.

The adversary's view is grossly inadequate, as we shall see. In that sense, it might seem to be a waste of time to consider it. The fact that it has until recently been very influential, both in empiricist-derived philosophy and in cognitive psychology[7] – and through both of these

6 For my general position on mind/body reduction, see Nussbaum and Putnam (1992).

7 For a good account of why it assumed preeminence, see Deigh (1994), who argues that removing intentionality came to seem characteristic of modern scientific approaches, by contrast with their medieval predecessors. See the illuminating criticisms of both philosophical and psychological versions of the approach in Kenny (1963), who realizes that there is a close kinship between Humean philosophy and behaviorist psychology. See also the account of the "Traditional View" in Pitcher (1965); of the "hydraulic" and "feeling" models in Solomon (1976), pp. 77–88, 96–102; of feeling and behaviorist views in Lyons (1980), Chapter 1; and cf. also Green (1992). Hume's own view is complex: see Davidson (1976) and Baier (1978). Kenny is certainly correct about some central passages, and these aspects of the view have had enormous influence; but Hume complicates his own account at crucial points, making it more plausible than some official statements suggest. A highly influential source of the adversary's view, which I

in fields such as law and public policy[8] – gives us somewhat more reason to spend time on it. An even stronger reason is given by the fact that the view, though inadequate, does capture some important aspects of emotional experience, aspects that need to figure in any adequate account. If we understand why the view has the power that it undeniably does, and then begin to see why and how further reflection moves us away from it, we will also understand what we must not ignore or efface in so moving away.

Turning back, now, to my account of my mother's death, we find that the "unthinking movements" view does appear to capture at least some of what went on: my feeling of terrible tumultuousness, of being at the mercy of currents that swept over me without my consent or complete understanding; the feeling of being buffeted between hope and fear, as if between two warring winds; the feeling that very powerful forces were pulling the self apart, or tearing it limb from limb; in short – the terrible power or urgency of the emotions, their problematic relationship to one's sense of self, the sense one has that one is passive or powerless before them. It comes as no surprise that even philosophers who argue for a cognitive view of emotion should speak of them this way: the Stoic philosopher Seneca, for example, is fond of comparisons of emotions to fire, to the currents of the sea, to fierce gales, to intruding forces that hurl the self about, cause it to explode, cut it up, tear it limb from limb.[9] Such images, furthermore, are found in many cultural traditions, and thus cannot be explained away as idiosyncrasies of the Western tradition.[10] It seems easy for the adversary's view to explain these phenomena: for if emotions are just unthinking forces

---

shall discuss further in Chapter 2, is Lange and James (1922). Psychoanalysis is another source of hydraulic and mechanist views of emotion: see Solomon (1976); Lyons (1980), Chapter 1; Kahan and Nussbaum (1996). In Chapter 4 I discuss psychoanalytic views that are not reductionistic in this way. For a very different nonreductionistic psychoanalytic view, see Wollheim (1999).

8 We see such views, for example, in the behaviorist psychology of Posner (1990), and to some extent in Posner (1992). For the role of such views in the criminal law, with many examples, see Kahan and Nussbaum (1996). The adversary's view is not the traditional common law view, but a recent incursion, under the influence of Humean and behaviorist psychology.

9 See Nussbaum (1994), Chapter 12, for discussion of these metaphors.

10 Lutz (1988) suggests that only the Western tradition treats emotions as forces of nature; but such metaphors are ubiquitous in poetry from India and China, in the African novel, and elsewhere.

that have no connection with our thoughts, evaluations, or plans, then they really are just like the invading currents of some ocean. And they really are, in a sense, nonself; and we really are passive before them. It seems easy, furthermore, for the adversary to explain their urgency: for once we imagine them as unthinking forces we can without difficulty imagine these forces as extremely strong.

By contrast, my neo-Stoic view appears to be in trouble on all of these points. For if emotions are a kind of judgment or thought, it seems difficult to account for their urgency and heat; thoughts are usually imagined as detached and calm. It seems difficult, too, to find in them the passivity that we undoubtedly experience: for judgments seem to be things that we actively make or do, not things that we suffer. And their ability to dismember the self also seems to be omitted: for thoughts are paradigmatic, it would seem, of what we control, and of the most securely managed parts of our identity. Let us now see what would cause us to move away from the adversary's view. Later on we shall see how a neo-Stoic view responds to our worries.

What, then, makes the emotions in my example unlike the thought-less natural energies I have described? First of all, they are *about* something: they have an object. My fear, my hope, my ultimate grief, all are about my mother and directed at her and her life. A wind may hit against something, a current in the blood may pound against something: but they are not in the same way *about* the things they strike in their way. My fear's very identity as fear depends on its having some such object: take that away and it becomes a mere trembling or heart-leaping. The identity of the wind as wind does not in the same way depend on any particular object against which it may pound.[11]

Second, the object is an *intentional* object: that is, it figures in the emotion as it is seen or interpreted by the person whose emotion it is. Emotions are not *about* their objects merely in the sense of being pointed at them and let go, the way an arrow is released toward its target. Their aboutness is more internal, and embodies a way of seeing. My fear perceived my mother both as tremendously important and as threatened; my grief saw her as valuable and as irrevocably cut off from me. (Both, we might add – beginning to approach the adversary's point about the self – contained a corresponding perception of myself

---

11 See Pitcher (1965) for an excellent formulation of this point.

and my life – as threatened in the one case, as bereft in the other.) This aboutness comes from my active ways of seeing and interpreting: it is not like being given a snapshot of the object, but requires looking at the object, so to speak, through one's own window.[12] This perception might contain an accurate view of the object, or it might not. (And indeed it might take as its target a real and present object, or it might also be directed at an object that is no longer in existence, or that has never existed at all. In this way, too, intentionality is distinct from a more mechanical sort of directedness.)[13] Once again, we should insist that aboutness is part of the emotions' identity. What distinguishes fear from hope, fear from grief, love from hate – is not so much the identity of the object, which might not change, but the way in which the object is seen. In fear, one sees oneself or what one loves as seriously threatened. In hope, one sees oneself or what one loves as in some uncertainty but with a good chance for a good outcome.[14] In grief, one sees an important object or person as lost; in love, as invested with a special sort of radiance. Again, the adversary's view proves unable to account either for the ways in which we actually identify and individuate emotions, or for a prominent feature of our experience of them.

Third, these emotions embody not simply ways of seeing an object, but beliefs – often very complex – about the object. (It is not always easy, or even desirable, to distinguish an instance of *seeing X as Y*, such as I have described here, from having a belief that X is Y. I shall deal with this issue in the next chapter; for now I continue to use the language of belief.) In order to have fear – as Aristotle already saw[15] – I must believe that bad events are impending; that they are not trivially, but seriously bad; and that I am not entirely in control of warding them off.[16] In order to have anger, I must have an even more complex

---

12 See Solomon (1976), Pitcher (1965), and Lyons (1980), Chapter 9. Ben-Ze'ev (2000) has valuable discussions of this aspect of emotions throughout his book: see, for example, pp. 49–51, 106–9.

13 On the role of this independence of an actual object in the concept of intentionality, see Caston (1992).

14 Fear and hope can often involve the same set of facts, but differ in their focus – on the danger in the former case, on the possible good outcome in the latter. As Seneca said, "You will cease to fear if you cease to hope. Both belong to a mind that is in suspense . . ." (*Moral Epistle* 5.7–8, on which see Nussbaum [1994], p. 389).

15 *Rhetoric* II.5.

16 Aristotle adds that one has fear only when one believes there is some chance for escape (*Rhet.* II.5, 1383a5–6). One might argue with this one, thinking of the way in which

set of beliefs: that some damage has occurred to me or to something or someone close to me;[17] that the damage is not trivial but significant; that it was done by someone; probably, that it was done willingly.[18] It seems plausible to suppose that every member of this family of beliefs is necessary in order for anger to be present. If I should discover that not A but B had done the damage, or that it was not done willingly, or that it was not serious, we could expect my anger to modify itself accordingly, or go away.[19] My anger at the flight attendants who smiled was quickly dissipated by the thought that they had done so without any thought of disturbing me or giving me offense.[20] Similarly, my fear would have turned to relief – as it so often has – had the medical news changed, or proved to be mistaken. Again, these beliefs are essential to the identity of the emotion: the feeling of agitation all by itself will not reveal to me whether what I am feeling is fear or grief or pity. Only an inspection of the thoughts discriminates. Nor is the thought purely a

one fears death even when one does know not just that it will occur but when. There is much to be said here: does even the man on death row ever know for sure that he will not get a reprieve? Does anyone ever know for sure what death consists in? And of course one never knows what death is like, or what may be beyond it. In that sense, there is always an element of uncertainty, since even the most determined atheist may hope for an afterlife. And yet Aristotle's assertion still seems too dogmatic: we fear bad things even when we know that they will happen. More precisely, we *dread* these things; if we should deny that dread is a species of fear, we might preserve Aristotle's claim. But I think we do think of dread as a type of fear.

17 Aristotle insists that the damage must take the form of a "slight," suggesting that what is wrong with wrongdoing is always that it shows a lack of respect (*Rhet.* II.2, 1378a31–3). This is a valuable and, I think, ultimately very plausible position for many cases, but I am not going to defend it here.

18 *Rhetoric* II.2–3. Aristotle adds that anger involves the thought that it would be good for the agent of the damage to be punished, and even that this is a pleasing thought (1378b1–2). The Stoics, similarly, categorize anger as an emotion involving thought about a future good event. This is plausible for some cases, but probably not for all. There may be genuine cultural difference between the *orgê* described by Aristotle and the anger described in my story; but in the anger I describe, the reactive side seems to be primary.

19 In my case, however, one can see that the very magnitude of an accidental grief sometimes prompts a search for someone to blame, even in the absence of any compelling evidence that there is a responsible agent involved. It seems better that there should be someone to blame than that the universe should be a place of accident in which one's loved ones are helpless. Blame is a valuable antidote to helplessness (see Chapter 2). One reason for our society's focus on anger associated with medical malpractice may be that there is often no way of proving that medical malpractice did not occur – so it becomes a useful target for those unwilling to blame hostile deities or evil spirits.

20 Anger at oneself is a more intractable phenomenon, since it is rarely about only the events at hand (see Chapter 4).

heuristic device that reveals what I am feeling, where feeling is understood as something without thought. For it seems necessary to put the thought into the definition of the emotion itself. Otherwise, we seem to have no good way of making the requisite discriminations among emotion types. Here again, then, the adversary's view is too simple: severing emotion from belief, it severs emotion from what is not only a necessary condition of itself, but also a part of its very identity.

Finally, we notice something marked in the intentional perceptions and the beliefs characteristic of the emotions: they are concerned with *value*, they see their object as invested with value or importance. Suppose that I did not love my mother or consider her a person of great importance; suppose I considered her about as important as a branch on a tree next to my house. Then (unless I had invested the tree-branch itself with an unusual degree of value) I would not fear her death, or hope so passionately for her recovery. My experience records this in many ways – not least in my dream, in which I saw her as beautiful and wonderful and, seeing her that way, wished her restored to health and wit. And of course in the grief itself there was the same perception – of enormous significance, permanently removed. This indeed is why the sight of the dead body of someone one loves is so intolerable: because the same sight that is a reminder of value is also an evidence of irrevocable loss.[21]

The value perceived in the object appears to be of a particular sort. It appears to make reference to the person's own flourishing. The object

---

21 One might wonder how value is being defined here, and whether it will not need to be defined with reference to emotion, thus creating a troublesome (though not necessarily vicious) circle. (For one version of this objection, see Gibbard [1990], pp. 130–1.) But this need not be so. Emotion judgments are a subclass of value judgments, on my view. They pertain to objects that figure in the person's own scheme of goals and projects – and, in central cases, to objects that are seen as not fully controlled by the person. There will therefore be other value judgments that won't involve emotion, and even other judgments involving the notion of the human good. For example, I might think that intellectual activity is a human good; for myself, however, I specify this good by doing philosophy; my attitude toward mathematics will be that it is very valuable, but I have no emotions about it one way or another, given that it isn't an important part of my life. Again, I might, as a musician, think that Indian classical music is very valuable – and yet have no emotions about it or its pursuit; I just don't know very much about it, I am not engaged in it. How to define value is yet another matter, not exactly the easiest definitional question in philosophy. We might mention notions of what's worth pursuing, what is a good use of someone's time, what it seems good to do or attend to.

of the emotion is seen as *important for* some role it plays in the person's own life.[22] I do not go about fearing any and every catastrophe any-where in the world, nor (so it seems) do I fear any and every catastro-phe that I know to be bad in important ways. What inspires fear is the thought of damages impending that cut to the heart of my own cher-ished relationships and projects. What inspires grief is the death of someone beloved, someone who has been an important part of one's own life. This does not mean that the emotions view these objects simply as tools or instruments of the agent's own satisfaction: they may be invested with intrinsic worth or value, as indeed my mother surely was. They may be loved for their own sake, and their good sought for its own sake. But what makes the emotion center around this particular mother, among all the many wonderful people and mothers in the world, is that she is *my* mother, a part of my life. The emotions are in this sense localized: they take their stand in my own life, and focus on the transition between light and darkness there, rather than on the general distribution of light and darkness in the universe as a whole. Even when they are concerned with events that take place at a distance, or events in the past, that is, I think, because the person has managed to invest those events with a certain importance in her own scheme of ends and goals. The notion of *loss* that is central to grief itself has this double aspect: it alludes to the value of the person who has left or died, but it alludes as well to that person's relation to the perspective of the mourner.

Another way of putting this point – to which I shall often return – is that the emotions appear to be *eudaimonistic*,[23] that is, concerned with the person's flourishing. And thinking for a moment about ancient Greek eudaimonistic ethical theories will help us to start thinking about the geography of the emotional life. In a eudaimonistic ethical theory,

22 On this aspect, see Lazarus (1991), to be further discussed in Chapter 2. Solomon (1976) holds that the goal of emotions is always to "maximize" "personal dignity and self-esteem" (see pp. 160, 181). This, I think, makes them far too egoistic, and my own account should be sharply distinguished from this one. Even compassion, as I argue in Chapter 6, is always eudaimonistic; but it can include the well-being of distant others as an element of value in my scheme of ends and purposes.

23 I retain this spelling, rather than using the English word "eudaemonistic," because I want to refer directly to the ancient Greek concept of *eudaimonia*, which is compatible with as many distinct conceptions of what that good is as one cares to propose; the English word has acquired associations with one specific type of view, namely, the view that the supreme good is happiness or pleasure.

the central question asked by a person is, "How should a human being live?" The answer to that question is the person's conception of *eudaimonia*, or human flourishing, a complete human life. A conception of *eudaimonia* is taken to be inclusive of all to which the agent ascribes intrinsic value: if one can show someone that she has omitted something without which she would not think her life complete, then that is a sufficient argument for the addition of the item in question.[24] Now the important point is this: in a eudaimonistic theory, the actions, relations, and persons that are included in the conception are not all valued simply on account of some instrumental relation they bear to the agent's satisfaction. This is a mistake commonly made about such theories, under the influence of Utilitarianism and the misleading use of "happiness" as a translation for *eudaimonia*.[25] Not only virtuous actions but also mutual relations of civic or personal love and friendship, in which the object is loved and benefited for his or her own sake, can qualify as constituent parts of a person's *eudaimonia*.[26] On the other hand, they are valued as constituents of a life that is my life and not someone else's, as my actions, as people who are in some relation with me.[27] For example, an Aristotelian really pursues social justice as a good in its own right: that is why she has put it into her conception of *eudaimonia*. She doesn't want just any old conception, she wants the one that values things aright, in the way that a human being ought to. Once she puts it into her conception, however, she both seeks the intrinsic good of justice and seeks to be a person who performs just actions for their own sake. It is not irrelevant to her that *she* get to perform those actions; if she is in prison and unable to act, she will view her life as incomplete. Her own presence in the action is ethically salient, although she does not view the action as simply a means to her own states of satisfaction. This, it seems, is what emotions are like.

---

24 On this see Aristotle, *Nicomachean Ethics*, I; and for a particular case, IX.9, on the value of *philia*. For an excellent discussion of this aspect of Aristotle's view, see Williams (1962).

25 For the misreading, and a brilliant correction, see Prichard (1935) and Austin (1970). "Happiness" is misleading if it is taken to suggest that the end or goal is a state of pleasure or contentment. As Austin shows, the English word once had a wider range, inclusive of fine actions that brought no pleasure in their train.

26 For a good account of this, where *philia* is concerned, see Cooper (1980).

27 The contrast between such eudaimonistic and more impartialist views is brought out, and distinguished from the contrast between egoism and altruism, in Williams (1973).

They insist on the real importance of their object, but they also embody the person's own commitment to the object as a part of her scheme of ends. This is why, in the negative cases, they are felt as tearing the self apart: because they have to do with me and my own, my plans and goals, what is important in my own conception (or more inchoate sense) of what it is for me to live well.[28]

There is much more to be said about types and levels of eudaimonism, and about the relationship between the self-referential element (the "my" in "my plans and goals") and the element of general evaluation (that the object is important, or valuable) in emotions of many types; we shall return to these issues in section V. For now, I simply insist that emotions look at the world from the subject's own viewpoint, mapping events onto the subject's own sense of personal importance or value.

III. NECESSITY AND CONSTITUENT PARTHOOD

We have now gone a long way toward answering the adversary. For I have argued that his view, while picking out certain features of emotional life that are real and important, has omitted others of equal and greater importance, central to the identity of an emotion and to discriminations between one emotion and another: their aboutness, their intentionality, their basis in beliefs, their connection with evaluation. All this makes them look very much like thoughts, after all; and we have even begun to see how a cognitive/evaluative view might itself explain some of the phenomena that the adversary has invoked on his side – the intimate relationship to selfhood, the urgency. But we are far from being all the way to a neo-Stoic view, according to which the emotions are defined in terms of evaluative judgment alone. For the considerations we have brought forward might be satisfied, it seems, by a weaker or more hybrid view, according to which beliefs and perceptions play a large role in emotions, but are not identical with them.

28 As we shall see, "have to do with" should not be construed as implying that the emotions simply take a conception of *eudaimonia* as their *object*, saying "X is part of my scheme of ends." If that were so, they would be in error only if they were wrong about what conception of value I actually hold. On the neo-Stoic view they are about the *world,* in both its evaluative and its circumstantial aspects.

We can begin to map the possibilities by posing three questions:

(1) Are the relevant beliefs[29] *constituent parts* of the emotion in question?

(2) Is having such beliefs a *necessary condition* for having the emotion in question?

(3) Is having such beliefs a *sufficient condition* for having the emotion in question?

The answers to these questions are logically independent. One may hold that the beliefs are necessary with or without holding them to be sufficient, and vice versa. A claim of necessity is compatible with, but does not entail, a claim of constituent parthood, since the beliefs might be necessary as external causes of something that in its own nature does not contain belief. So much is also true of a claim of sufficiency. Beliefs might be a constituent part with or without being a *necessary* constituent of the emotion's identity. And they might be a part that does not guarantee the presence of the whole or, on the other hand, a part that by itself suffices for the presence of the whole (whether causally or because it is the only part there is).

We have gone far enough, I think, to rule out the external-cause form of necessity and of sufficiency: for I have argued that the cognitive elements are an essential part of the emotion's identity, and of what differentiates one emotion from other emotions. Examination of philosophical attempts to define the emotions over the ages confirms this hypothesis: for again and again, whether the view announces itself as a cognitive view or not, the cognitive content is brought into the definition. Aristotle, Chrysippus, Cicero, Seneca, Spinoza, Smith, even Descartes and Hume (for whom this creates some tension within their general theories of mind) – all of these figures define emotions in terms of belief. Nor, as we shall see in Chapter 2, have attempts in psychology to jettison the cognitive elements of the definition met with success. Neither a characteristic feeling nor a characteristic mode of behavior would appear sufficient to define emotions such as envy, hope, grief, pity, and jealousy, or to differentiate one of these from the others. In some cases (for example, anger and fear) there are at least prima facie candidates for such a defining feeling, although I have argued that the

---

29 As I have noted, I shall ultimately include forms of seeing X as Y that may or may not count as belief, depending on how one defines the notion of belief.

full-fledged emotion requires more than this feeling (and shall later argue that this feeling isn't always present). In others, such as hope and envy, we can't even begin to specify such a defining feeling.[30] We seem to be left, then, at the least with constituent parthood, with, that is, the thesis that the cognitive elements are part of what the emotion *is* – whether in a form in which the belief part suffices for the presence of the other parts, or in a form in which it is merely necessary.

What might those other parts be? The adversary is ready with an answer: nonthinking movements of some sort, or perhaps (shifting over to the point of view of experience) objectless feelings of pain and/or pleasure. A number of questions immediately come to mind about these feelings: What are they like if they are not *about* anything? What is the pleasure *in*, or the pain *at*? How are they connected with the beliefs, if they do not themselves contain any thought or cognition? And so forth. I shall address those questions in section VI, arguing that no such feelings are absolutely necessary definitional elements in any of the emotion types.

A problem remains, however, for the claim of necessity, and we should investigate it before we proceed further. It appears that people sometimes change their minds about the beliefs that underlie their emotions, but continue to have the emotions nonetheless. Sandra, who was terrified by a dog during childhood, may learn that dogs are no danger to her well-being; but she still fears dogs. Jack may decide that he was wrong to accept his parents' belief that African-Americans are ruining the country; but he still has intense anger against them. Does this mean, after all, that one may remove the evaluative beliefs without removing the emotions?[31]

The examples do not support such a conclusion, for the simple reason that we may often hold contradictory beliefs, especially in cases involving long habituation. In childhood I came to think that the U.S. Supreme Court is in California. (I thought this because I often heard the words "Earl Warren" and "California," of which he had been the governor, coupled together, and also the words "Earl Warren" and "Supreme Court.") I put it on the map of my mind in that place, somewhere around Sacramento. To this day, whenever I hear the words

30 See Pitcher (1965), p. 338.
31 See Greenspan (1988).

"Supreme Court" I see that dot on the map. I have known for about forty-five years that this is a false belief, and yet I still retain the belief in some form. I find myself using it to make inferences about how far colleagues will be traveling when they go there, and what sort of weather they are likely to encounter. I sometimes get to the point of making embarrassing blunders in speech. I make similar errors in other matters involving spatial beliefs that have become deeply habitual. Having lived for forty-eight years on the East Coast, I formed the habit of thinking that when I am away from home and set out to drive home, I will be driving east. I have the greatest difficulty to the present time not thinking that Chicago is east of South Bend and even of Ann Arbor. I get on the highway going the wrong way sometimes, and even when I don't, I have the strong bodily feeling that I am driving east when I am on my way home. (When the sun is facing the wrong way, it strikes a dissonant note in my mental landscape, and I think that something is wrong with the sun.)

If this can be so with respect to matters on which nothing depends, it is likely to be far more true concerning the evaluative beliefs that we lay down in childhood, frequently in connection with attachment relations of deep intensity. Changing these, as Seneca knew, requires a lifetime of patient self-examination, and even that is not always successful. Sandra still sees dogs as dangerous to her well-being in particular cases, although she also holds a general belief that contradicts this. (And maybe it doesn't, notice: it would be irrational to believe that dogs never cause harm, so what she probably believes is that many dogs don't cause harm.) Jack may be teaching himself some moral truths, but his deep-seated habits wipe those off the slate at times, and he is again in the grip of his past. In the same way, Seneca believes that honor isn't very important, but: when someone seats him at a place at table that he thinks insulting, he is in the grip of his habits.[32] Here Seneca has no temptation to say that the emotion is nonjudgmental: the whole problem is that he *does* judge that he has been significantly insulted, even while he knows that the matter is not significant. So the case against necessity is unconvincing; to rebut it we need only point to the fact that the mind has a complex archaeology, and false beliefs, especially about matters of value, are difficult to shake.

32 See Seneca, *On Anger*, III.36.

IV. JUDGING AND ACKNOWLEDGING,
AND SUFFICIENT CONDITIONS

In order to prepare for a fuller elaboration and defense of the neo-Stoic view, we must now, however, say more about judgment. To understand the case for the view that emotions are judgments, we need to understand exactly what a Stoic means when she says that; I think we will find the picture intuitively appealing, and a valuable basis for a critique of a familiar Humean belief – desire framework for the explanation of action (see Chapter 2) – although the Stoic view will turn out to be overly focused on linguistically formulable propositional content, and will therefore need a good deal of modification. According to the Stoics, then, a judgment is an assent to an appearance. In other words, it is a process that has two stages. First, it occurs to me or strikes me that such and such is the case. It looks to me that way, I see things that way – but so far I haven't really accepted it. Note that this view does not require any metaphysics of internal representations that allegedly mirror the world: the Stoics are just talking about the way things look to people, and this way may or may not be conveyed to the mind through internal representational mechanisms.[33]

At this point there are three possibilities. I can accept or embrace the way things look, take it into me as the way things *are:* in this case the appearance has become my judgment, and that act of acceptance is what judging is. I can repudiate the appearance as not being the way things are: in that case I am judging the contradictory. Or I can let the appearance hang there without committing myself one way or another. In that case I have no belief or judgment about the matter one way or the other.[34] Consider a simple perceptual case introduced

33 See Frede (1986). On getting representationalism out of translations and interpretations of Aristotle, see Nussbaum (1978), essay 5.
34 Aristotle points out that such an unaccepted "appearance" may still have some motivating power, but only in a limited way: as when a sudden sight causes one to be startled (but not yet really afraid) – see *De Anima* III.9, *De Motu Animalium*, ch. 11. Seneca makes a similar point concerning the so-called pre-emotions or *propatheiai:* see *De Ira* II.3; it is remarkable that Richard Lazarus reinvents, apparently independently, the very same term, "pre-emotions," to describe the same phenomenon in the animals he observes – see Lazarus (1991), to be discussed in Chapter 2. The Greek skeptics suggest that one might live an entire life being motivated by appearances alone, without any beliefs – pointing to the alleged fact that animals are so moved. But their case is

by Aristotle.[35] The sun strikes me as being about a foot wide. (That's the way it looks to me, that is what I see it *as*.) Now I might embrace this appearance and talk and act accordingly; most children do so. If I am confused about astronomy, I may refuse to make any cognitive commitment on the matter. But if I have a confident belief that the sun is in fact tremendously large, and that the way it looks is deceptive, I will repudiate the appearance and embrace a contradictory appearance. There seems nothing odd here about saying both that the appearance presents itself to my cognitive faculties and that its acceptance or rejection is the activity of those faculties. Assenting to or embracing a way of seeing something in the world, acknowledging it as true, seems to be a job that *requires* the discriminating power of cognition. Cognition need not be imagined as inert, as it is in the Humean tradition. In this case, it is reason itself that reaches out and takes that appearance to itself, saying, so to speak, "Yes, that's the one I'll have. That's the way things really are." We might even say that this is a good way of thinking about what reasoning is: an ability in virtue of which we commit ourselves to a view of the way things really are.

Stoics thought that assent was always a voluntary act, and that we always had it in our power to assent or refuse to assent to any appearance. (Or at least adults had this power: for the voluntarist view was part of their argument for denying emotions to children and nonhuman animals.) Thus they developed an extreme voluntarist view of personality, coupled with an exigent doctrine of self-monitoring that Epictetus summarizes in the maxim, "Watch over yourself like an enemy lying in wait." We do not need to accept these aspects of Stoic psychology in order to accept their general picture of judgment. Indeed, we may remind Stoics that in other texts they spoke of appearances that "dragged us by the hair to assent" (although they did not include emotion-related appearances in that category). Even so, habit, attachment, and the sheer weight of events may frequently extract assent from us; it is not to be imagined as an act that we always deliberately perform.

When we understand assent in this broader way, we understand, too, how the view, so broadened, will ultimately be able to ascribe

dubious, since, for one thing, it seems to misdescribe the cognitive equipment of animals – see Chapter 2.

35 *De Anima* III.3.

emotions to young children and nonhuman animals, who, to a greater or lesser extent, lack the capacity to withhold assent from the appearances with which life confronts them. Whenever they accept a way the world seems as the way it is, they can be said to have judgment in my sense. We should notice, however, that the Stoic picture of animals and children is actually quite implausible: for very often, as soon as they gather experience, they are able to form thoughts of the sort, "This person is smiling, but he isn't really a friend," or "This looks good to eat, but it's really not."[36]

Let us now return to my central example. My mother has died. It strikes me, it appears to me, that a person of enormous value, who was central in my life, is there no longer. It seemed to me as if a nail from the world had entered my insides; it also felt as if life had suddenly a large rip or tear in it, a gaping hole. I saw, as well, her wonderful face – both as tremendously loved and as forever cut off from me. The appearance, in however many ways we picture it, has propositional content or at least combination: it combines the thought of importance with the thought of loss, its content is that this importance is lost. And, as I have said, it is evaluative and eudaimonistic: it does not just assert, "Betty Craven is dead." Central to the propositional content is my mother's enormous importance, both in herself and as an element in my life.

So far we are still at the stage of appearing – and notice that I was in this stage throughout the night before her death, throughout the long transatlantic plane ride, haunted by that value-laden picture but powerless to accept or reject it; for it was sitting in the hands of the world. (There are not always two stages in this way: for often the look of the world and the inexorability of the truth of that look bear in on one simultaneously.) I might have had reason to reject the appearance – if, for example, I had awakened and found that the whole experience of getting the bad news and planning my return trip had been a nightmare. Or in a different way I might have rejected it if the outcome had turned out to be good and she had in fact no longer been threatened. I did accept that she was endangered – so I did have fear. But whether or not she was or would be *lost* – that I could not say. But now I am

---

36 For a detailed discussion of these aspects of the Stoic view of judgment, see Deigh (2000) and my reply in Nussbaum (2000b).

in the hospital room with her body before me. I embrace the appearance as the way things are. Can I assent to the idea that someone tremendously beloved is forever lost to me, and yet preserve emotional equanimity?

The neo-Stoic claims that I cannot. Not if what I am accepting is that very set of propositions, with all of their evaluative elements. Suppose I had said to the nurses, "Yes, I see that a person I love deeply is dead and that I'll never see her again. But I am fine: I am not disturbed at all." If we put to one side considerations about reticence before strangers and take the utterance to be nondeceptive, we should say, I think, that one among three things is very likely to be the case. First, this person may really not attach much importance to the person who died. For social reasons, she may be claiming to do so, but she may have long ceased to love the dead person. We could figure this out, if we had enough evidence about her other statements and actions.

Second, and a more common possibility: the person may in fact be grieving already, but may not be ready to acknowledge this fact to herself, because it is scary to be helpless. This case, like the other cases of nonconscious emotion that I shall consider in section VIII, must be introduced with great caution, since it would compromise the entire argumentative strategy if we were to recognize too many such cases, granted that we are commending our view for its superior power to explain experience. But, as I shall later argue, we may admit some such cases under specific conditions: if the person's pattern of behavior seems best explained by the hypothesis of an unconsious fear, or anger, or grief. We have an even more powerful case if the person can be brought under certain circumstances to acknowledge this fact about the pattern of her conduct.

So: John's mother has recently died. He knows that she is dead, but he says he is fine and sincerely denies having grief. Still, he acts strangely. He is unjustifiably angry with people and things around him. He shows an unusual determination not to be helped in any way. Under questioning, this person suddenly admits that he is experiencing grief and anger directed at his mother: grief at the death, anger at the fact that her dying has turned him into a needy and helpless child.

The third possibility, and perhaps the most common, is that the knowledge of the evaluative significance of the death has not yet sunk in. John sort of knows his mother is dead, and sort of doesn't. He is not really assenting to propositions having to do with her central importance in his life, although she really was important in his life. He may be saying those words, but there is something in him that is resisting. Or if he assents to something, it is not to that same proposition. He may be assenting to the proposition, "Mrs. Y is dead" (his mother's proper name). Or even (if we suppose that "my mother" could possibly lack eudaimonistic evaluative content) to the proposition, "My mother is dead." What he is not fully acknowledging or taking in is the thought, "A person whom I deeply love, who is central to my life, is dead." For to recognize this is to be deeply disturbed.

This case is very close to my second case. Both reflect the fact that people dislike being helpless and passive, and therefore characteristically resist the knowledge of deaths of loved ones, or of their own illnesses. The difference will be that in my second case John has internalized the knowledge and his actions have been changed by it; in the third case, the knowledge is still being kept at bay, and to that extent has not yet influenced the pattern of his other judgments and actions.

Notice, then, that it is of crucial importance to get clear about the precise content of the thought we ascribe to the person. For if we were to make the salient thought one with no evaluative content, say, "Betty Craven is dead" (my mother's proper name),[37] we would be right to think that the acceptance of that thought could be at most a cause of grief, not identical with grief itself. Again, if we put value in without the reference to the self, saying that the content of the thought was, "Betty Craven, a most valuable person, is dead," again – we would not have a thought that we could plausibly identify with grief. The neo-Stoic claims that grief is identical with the acceptance of a proposition that is both evaluative and eudaimonistic, that is, concerned with one or more of the person's important goals and ends. We have not yet fully made the case for equating this (or these) proposition(s) with emotion: but so far it appears far more plausible that such a judgment could itself be an upheaval.

It is, and should remain, an empirical question whether one of these three possibilities must always be the case, when there appears to be

---

37 Of course the minute we insert the name of a human being there is already some evaluative content; and some moral theories would urge that this is all the value that there should properly be, in any response to any death. I shall address this in Chapters 6 and 7.

belief without emotion. If we found a large number of convincing cases that answered to none of these three descriptions, we might have reason to cast doubt on the sufficiency thesis. But these phenomena of denial and avoidance are so well recognized, and so ubiquitous, that we do not yet appear to have a group of counterexamples that would cause us to lose confidence in it.

We must now add one further element. For the Stoics, the judgments that are identified with emotions all have a common subject matter: all are concerned with vulnerable things, things that can be affected by events in the world beyond the person's own control, things that can arrive by surprise, that can be destroyed or removed even when one does not wish it. These are the person's "external goods" – external not in the sense that they must lie outside the perimeter of the person's body, but in the sense that they elude the person's complete control. They held that when one's mind took as its intentional object an element of life that the person regarded as utterly secure – such as her own virtue – then the resulting state would not be an emotion. If we call it joy, we should recognize that it is a different type of joy, one that isn't really emotional.[38]

Should we accept this further claim, defining emotions in terms of a definite subject matter? Here we come close to building surprise and change into the definition of emotion itself, a move that has recently been made by psychologist Keith Oatley and philosopher Aaron Ben-Ze'ev, but one that we will have reason to reject in Chapter 2.[39] And we also seem to compromise our methodology: for people do speak of joy at their own good character, as even Seneca acknowledges; so we are saying of a large class of experiences that people have classified them to some extent wrongly. It is a little difficult to assess the Stoics' move, since most of us do not agree with them about the fully controllable na-

---

38 See Seneca, letter 39.

39 Oatley (1992), Ben-Ze'ev (2000); see Chapter 2, section III. Particularly revealing is Ben-Ze'ev's attempt to account for the steady background fear of one's own death in terms of the change theory. He holds that all emotions involve "a *perceived change whose significance is determined by us*" (p. 16), but almost immediately states that "our possible death is always in the background of our existence: it reminds us of our profound vulnerability" (p. 16). Then, in the very next sentence, he continues as if no problem had surfaced: "This type of change expresses *our profound vulnerability* and dependence on external factors which we do not control" (p. 16). (A footnote at this point refers to the argument of the present chapter of this book.) Much though I admire Ben-Ze'ev's book, I do not find this particular move convincing.

ture of our thinking and our virtuous inclinations; we tend to think that no mental state or activity is fully under our own control. Our idea that emotions take these as objects may be influenced by this difference. But it still seems to be a kind of dogmatism to assert in the very definition of emotion that the object must be vulnerable to reversal. It would be still more dogmatic to insist that the content of an emotion-thought must record a belief that some change has actually occurred.

We can say something close to this without that dogmatism. Many of the specific emotions have vulnerability to reversal built into their own characteristic definitions. Fear, hope, pity, anger, envy, jealousy, grief – all these must take an object of the sort that the Stoics demand, since their propositional content asserts that there is change or that change is a possibility. Some varieties of joy and love are like this as well: internal to their very specific cognitive structure will be the thought of perilous fortunes, or the likelihood of change. Erotic love notoriously involves the thought of instability in this way, as the Baron de Charlus's mind reports, linking love with envy, jealousy, suffering, and astonishment. Some varieties of joy and love, by contrast, will not be like this; their cognitive structure will differ in consequence, as will their relationship to other emotions, and the experience of being in their grip. This is really what the Stoics have said already; we have simply removed the dogmatic assertion, "and these are not really emotions." (Spinoza's view is closer, since he makes intellectual love of God a real kind of love, yet lacking in some of the baneful properties of other love.)

In short, most of the time emotions link us to items that we regard as important for our well being, but do not fully control. The emotion records that sense of vulnerability and imperfect control.[40] We will see shortly how this emerges in the complex combination of circumstantial and evaluative considerations that must be present in the relevant thoughts. For now, we can observe that this means that the acceptance of such propositions says something about the person: that she allows herself and her good to depend upon things beyond her control, that she acknowledges a certain passivity before the world.

At this point, we are in a position to conclude not only that judg-

---

40 This is still not equivalent to the claim that emotions record a change that is actually thought to have occurred, as in Ben-Ze'ev's view (see preceding note).

ments of the sort we have described are necessary constituent elements in the emotion, but also that they are sufficient. For we have argued that if the emotion is not there we are entitled to say that the judgments themselves are not fully or really there. The arguments of the previous section suggested that we should view this sufficiency internally, as that of a constituent part that itself reliably causes whatever other parts there may be. For I spoke of the way in which the relevant judgments were at least a part of the identity conditions of the emotion. But we need to return to this issue now that we have elaborated the view of judging that underlies our claim, since it still may seem counterintuitive to make the emotion itself a function of the cognitive faculties (of thought, in its most general sense) rather than a nonrational movement produced in some way by cognition.

Well, what element in me *is* it that experiences the terrible shock of grief? I think of my mother; I embrace in my mind the fact that she will never be with me again – and I am shaken. How and where? Do we imagine the thought causing a fluttering in my hands, or a trembling in my stomach? And if we do, do we really want to say that this fluttering or trembling is *my* grief about my mother's death? The movement seems to lack the aboutness and the capacity for recognition that must be part of an emotion. Internal to the grief itself must be the perception of the beloved object and of her importance; the grief itself must estimate the richness of the love between us, its centrality in my life. The grief itself must contain the thought of her irrevocable deadness. Now of course we could say that there is a separate emotional part of the soul that has all these abilities. But we seem to have lost our grip on the reason for housing grief in a separate noncognitive part: thought looks like just the place to house it.

The adversary might now object that this is not yet clear. For even if we concede that emotion's seat must be capable of many cognitive operations, there also seems to be a kinetic and affective aspect to emotion that does not look like a judgment or any part of a judgment. There are rapid movements, feelings of pain and tumult: are we really to equate these with some part of judging that such and such is the case? Why should we not claim that the judgment is a cause of emotion, while identifying emotion itself with these movements? Or we might even grant that judgment is a constituent element in the emotion, and, as a constituent element, a sufficient cause of the other elements as well, and yet insist that there are other elements, feelings and movements, that are not themselves parts of the judgment. I have already begun to respond to this point by stressing the fact that we are conceiving of judging as dynamic, not static. Reason here moves, embraces, refuses; it can move rapidly or slowly, it can move directly or with hesitation. I have imagined it entertaining the appearance of my mother's death and then, so to speak, rushing toward it, opening itself to take it in. So why would such a dynamic faculty be unable to house, as well, the disorderly motions of grief? And this is not just a cheat: I am not stuffing into thought kinetic properties that properly belong to the arms and legs, or imagining reason as accidentally colored by the kinetic properties of the bloodstream. The movement toward my mother was a movement of my thought about what is most important in the world; that seems to be exactly what there is to be said about it. If anything, the movement of my arms and legs, as I ran vainly through South Philadelphia to University Hospital, was a kind of vain mimesis of the movement of my thought toward her. It was my thought that was receiving, and being shaken by, the knowledge of her death. I think that if we say anything else we lose the close connection between the recognition and the being shaken that experience gives us. The recognizing and the upheaval, we want to say, belong to one and the same part of me, the part with which I make sense of the world.

It seems, moreover, that the adversary is wrong to think of the judgment as an event that temporally precedes the grieving – as at least some of the causal language suggests. When I grieve, I do not first of all coolly embrace the proposition, "My wonderful mother is dead," and then set about grieving. No, the real, full recognition of that terrible event (as many times as I recognize it) *is* the upheaval. It is as I described it: like putting a nail into your stomach. The appearance that she is dead sits there (as it sat before me during my plane ride) asking me what I am going to do with it. Perhaps, if I am still uncertain, the image of her restored to health sits there also. If I go up to embrace the death image, if I take it into myself as the way things are, it is at that very moment, in that cognitive act itself, that I am putting the world's nail into my own insides. That is not preparation for upheaval, that is upheaval itself. That very act of assent is itself a tearing of my self-sufficient condition. Knowing can be violent, given the truths that are there to be known.

We have spoken of a judgment as an assent to an appearance: so we now have a question. Is the emotion the act of assenting, or is it a state that results from that act? The same issues arise about belief and judgment more generally, since both may persist through situations of many kinds. Although initially there may be an act of acceptance, and judgment is defined in terms of that act, there is also an ensuing state, namely of having that content inside, so to speak; one *accepts* or *assents to* that proposition continuously. It seems that emotions have exactly this twofold character: we initially assent to or acknowledge a proposition, and then there it is, part of our cognitive makeup. In grief, given our propensity to distance ourselves and to deny what has occurred, we may have to go through the act of accepting many times, before the proposition securely rests there; but all this is part of the life of an emotion, just as the initial acceptance and the ensuing retention are parts of the life of any judgment. But we should insist on two things: first, that even the initial act makes a claim – it says, yes, this is how things are; and, second, that even the subsequent retention involves the continuous acceptance of that claim, saying, again and again, yes, this is true, this is how things are.

I have spoken of truth. And it is, of course, a consequence of the view I have been developing that emotions, like other beliefs, can be true or false, and (an independent point) justified or unjustified, reasonable or unreasonable.[41] The fact of having an emotion depends on what the person's beliefs are, not on whether they are true or false.[42] So if I believe my mother to be dead and grieve, and she is not really dead, my emotion is in that sense false. We are not likely to speak of it as

41 On reasonableness, see the excellent discussion in Pitcher (1965), pp. 339–41. Pitcher notes that love, unlike other emotions, is not typically thought to be either reasonable or unreasonable, thus making the same observation that Adam Smith did about its difference from other emotions; I shall return to this in Parts II and III.

42 See the good discussion of this in Ben-Ze'ev (2000), pp. 15–16. Thus Gordon (1987), who insists on equating emotion with a certain sort of *knowledge* (and who makes it clear that he means to be distinguishing knowledge from simple belief), seems just wrong here: conviction and acceptance, not truth, are what carry the day. De Sousa's (1987) account of the "objectivity" of emotion seems to me to make a similar mistake, though in a far more subtle and elegant way. Emotions are part of my view of the world, and responsive to changes in belief in much the same way that other judgments are (though there are also some differences that I shall discuss in Chapter 4). But they are still beliefs about the world, not just about my conception of the world, and so they can be false.

"false grief," since the term "false" means both "not accurate" and "fraudulent," and in this context we standardly use it to mean "fraudulent" or "feigned." We do not want to confuse the important issue of sincerity with the issue of true or false content, and so we will call the grief "mistaken" or "inappropriate" rather than false. But the propositional content is nonetheless false.

In a different way, the judgment can be false if I am wrong about the evaluative aspects of the judgment: my emotion says (inter alia) something about mothers, namely that they have a tremendous value, and that this element too can be true or false. As I shall shortly elaborate in section V, eudaimonism has two aspects: we are saying that such-and-such is an important part of my own scheme of goals and ends, but we typically think that this is so *because* of some real value the item possesses: it is such that, without that thing (or a thing of that sort), my life would be incomplete. And in building a conception of *eudaimonia* for themselves people often seek to build in just those items about which such true evaluative claims can be made. I am not trying just to get any old conception, I am trying to get the one that values things aright. For this reason, Chrysippus plausibly said that grief (along with other emotions) contains not only the judgment that an important part of my life has gone, but that *it is right* to be upset about that: it makes a truth-claim about its own evaluations. It asserts the real value of the object, it says that getting upset is a response to something really important, not just a whim. Emotions can be true or false in that sense too. Often, trying to avoid the implication that statements about value can be true or false, we say instead that they are "appropriate" or "inappropriate." The language of appropriateness, however, confuses the issue, since things can be appropriate or inappropriate in many different ways: it doesn't single out the aspect of value-correctness that we want to single out. Chrysippus's "and it is right to get upset" does very well, and makes a truth claim of the relevant sort.[43]

43 Could an emotion mistakenly estimate the other aspect of a eudaimonistic judgment, the reference to one's own scheme of goals and ends? Certainly I can be wrong about what is important to me. But this will frequently emerge in the fact that I don't have emotions of the type I would have if such goals were important to me. I'm inclined to think that sometimes it is possible to have an emotion whose content does not accurately reflect my real scheme of ends – but that these will be cases of attempted self-persuasion, for example, talking oneself into liking or cherishing someone one really

A point commonly made about the emotions, purportedly in order to distinguish them from beliefs, is that they have a different "direction of fit": in belief, we are trying to fit our mental attitude to the world; in emotion, we are trying to make the world fit our mental attitude.[44] I think that there are several confusions in this picture. First of all, as we have just seen, emotions do attempt to fit the world – both to take in the events that really do take place, and to get an appropriate view of what matters or has value.[45] Second, they really don't try to get the world to fit them. Emotions may or may not engender desires for action, which might, if successful, make the world a better world for the *objects* of our emotions. (I shall discuss this issue further in Chapter 2.) But even when they do engender such desires: does the world thereby fit the emotions better? Fear says that there is danger at hand. If that emotion is correct, then the world right now does contain danger. If I change the world by successfully evading the danger, the emotion presumably will change accordingly. Now the world no longer contains that danger, so I don't have fear any longer. But the idea that we are trying to make the world fit the emotions suggests, oddly, that it doesn't fit them already. That was not so in the case of fear: what I was trying to do was not to make the world fit my fear, but to make it a place where fear is no longer appropriate. Fear already fit the world; that was the problem that gave rise to the desire for evasive action. Even in hope, where we focus on the good prospects, the content of the emotion is that there are these robust good prospects; and that is either true or false right now. If I make the good prospects realities, then hope will turn into joy. So I haven't made the world more like the emotion, I have changed the world and the emotion.

doesn't like, or talking oneself into grieving for someone one really doesn't love – and the emotions will have to that extent a factitious and insincere character. They can thus be called "false" in the more usual sense, as well as in the sense that their content is inaccurate.

44 For a good discussion of this idea, and a much more subtle version of the distinction, see Wollheim (1999), pp. 45–51.

45 Thus I differ from Solomon (1976), who analyzes emotions as self-created valuations that are then subjectively posited. Whatever one ultimately says about the complex question of the objectivity of value, the experience of emotion does not have this free-floating existentialist character. In grief, fear, and so on, one feels bound by the world, by the way its important items are configured. Moreover, this idea of responsiveness to reality is probably intrinsic to the emotions' adaptive evolutionary significance; see Chapter 2.

In short: the objection denies the evident fact that emotions are responsive to the way the world already is. It does not succeed in establishing any interesting asymmetry between emotions and beliefs.

V. EUDAIMONISM, INTENSITY, THE PERSONAL POINT OF VIEW

Let us now return to the topic of eudaimonism. Emotions, I have said, view the world from the point of view of my own scheme of goals and projects, the things to which I attach value in a conception of what it is for me to live well. For Aristotle, these goals typically form a system of some sort, and they are always goals that the agent, in some form, commends to others. But real people are usually not this systematic. We value things, often, without asking how all our goals fit together; sometimes they do not fit together well, and sometimes painful emotional conflicts ensue. So we should distance ourselves from this part of the ancient eudaimonist idea: emotions have to do with whatever I do value, however well or badly those things fit together.

Next, we should also insist that not all the things that I value are things that I commend to others. For Aristotle, the search for value is the search for what is good for a human being. Often this search for value in general is indeed part of the emotional life. In my love for my mother, for example, is the thought that parents are extremely important, and that people should cherish their parents if they have them. Indeed, in much grief for parents this general element is very prominent: for people think, I no longer have a chance to love and cherish my mother, and this leads easily to the wish that one had cherished her more, which is often bound up, in turn, with the thought that people who have parents should cherish them while they have them. In love of children, this general element is also very important. Before people have a particular child, they usually wish for *a child*, sometimes for a long time. So when they have the particular one, and love that one, they also usually continue to value the idea of having a child, and to think this a valuable thing in life generally.

The same thing happens, frequently, with goals and attachments of other kinds. In an attachment to one's own country, there is frequently the thought that this country has valuable things about it, and that it is a good country. When a goal is freely chosen, we can expect this element to become even more prominent: in opting for a given profession, I appraise it as containing something of value, sometimes just for me, but often for people more generally. These general thoughts come at many different levels of specificity and generality, a topic to which I shall return in section VIII.

However, these examples bring out some significant limitations of the ancient eudaimonist picture. I have already said that ancient eudaimonism overestimates the amount of order and structure in most people's schemes of goals. But in several further ways emotions diverge from the picture of a system of ends that I commend to others as valuable in a human life generally. First, my goals and ends, the things to which I attach importance, may contain some elements that I think good or valuable for myself, but do not especially commend to others. A career may seem valuable to me, and I may be able to say why, without my thinking that others have reason to pursue it. In some cases this will be because the goal is a concrete specification of a more general goal that I do commend to others. For example, I might think that everyone should have some interest in the arts, while being, myself, a passionate music lover with little interest in (and no emotion about) architecture. At the same time, internal to my passion about music are some general thoughts about the importance of art that represent common ground between myself and the lover of architecture.

We can develop this point further by speaking about the role of *specification* of general ends in a eudaimonist theory of value (and in many of our common deliberations in life).[46] In reflecting about how a human being should live, a person may commend some very general goals as good for human beings in general: for example, friendship, parental love, civic responsibility. But she will also deliberate about which more concrete specification of each of these general ends she will prefer; some of this work still involves asking which specifications are to be commended for human beings in general. At some point in the process, however, we get to items that are not commended for all human beings, but are just her own ways of realizing the general human ends in her situation and context. For example, if the general

---

46 See Richardson (1994) for the best account of this, with reference to Aristotle, but offered as an account of a process we commonly undertake in life.

goal were artistic cultivation and performance, she might realize this by playing the clarinet, but she would believe that other human beings can equally well realize it by dancing, or singing, or playing the oboe. (In fact, in this case she will actively wish that others do not *all* play the clarinet, since then the general good of musical performance could not be well realized.) The ancient eudaimonist picture does allow for this type of specification of ends; but it does not fully develop the idea.

Here, however, we arrive at a second, and more serious, limitation of the ancient eudaimonist project: people cherish and value things that they do not really think good, things that they would not be prepared to commend as good to others. Often they love a person, or a house, or a country, just because it is theirs, the one they have grown up with. At times they may actively disapprove of the person or country that they love – but, after all, it is theirs, and in some way or other they love and cherish it. And thoughts about the good may prove less powerful, in shaping a conception of importance for me, than habit and time. (I think Finland a fine nation, and in some sense I value it, on reflection, more than I do the United States. To some extent I also love it. But I still feel like a stranger there, and I have a certain love for the United States that is not at all proportional to my reflective evaluation.) Often thoughts about the good and thoughts about what I have lived with are entangled in countless ways, and it is hard for anyone to separate them.[47] Ancient eudaimonism has little to say about these complexities.

Third, it may be very important to certain emotions *not* to engage in a great deal of reflective weighing of the goodness of an object. Ancient accounts of love often seem lacking in the idea of the unconditionality of love. Whether the object of my love is a child, or a parent, or a lover, there seems to be something deficient about taking the inventory of the person's good points, as though the love is somehow based upon them. It isn't that the search for good points is totally irrelevant to love; but especially where the relationship is nonchosen, as in the love of parent for child or child for parent, it ought to take a back seat. We love the one we love, whatever bad traits they have and express. The failure to make room for this sort of unconditionality is a

47 See "Love and the Individual," in Nussbaum (1990), for some reflections on this tangle.

notorious limitation of ancient eudaimonism, to which I shall return in Part III.[48]

In short, the ancient eudaimonist framework will be a good one for thinking about the emotional life only when we acknowledge that people's sense of what is important and valuable is often messy, disorderly, and not in line with their reflective ethical beliefs.

But so far we have left out, or so it seems, the most important thing of all, something that lies deep in ancient eudaimonism but that is never explicitly recognized. Emotions contain an ineliminable reference to *me*, to the fact that it is *my* scheme of goals and projects.[49] They see the world from my point of view. The fact that it is *my* mother is not simply a fact like any other fact about the world: it is what structures the geography of the whole situation, and we cannot capture the emotion without including that element. It's not just the fact that Betty Craven has died. It's the fact that Betty Craven is *my mother*. In short, the evaluations associated with emotions are evaluations from *my* perspective, not from some impartial perspective; they contain an ineliminable reference to the self.[50]

Thus, in my grief I endow my mother with (at least) three different

---

48 See ibid., and further discussion of this element of love in Chapters 11, 12, 13, and 16.

49 We might relate this point to John Perry's famous discussion of indexicality, "The Problem of the Essential Indexical" (1979). Consider a famous example of Perry's. He is in a grocery store. He notices sugar leaking out onto the floor. He decides to follow the trail of the sugar, so that he can tell the person that a bag is leaking. He follows the trail around and around the store – and eventually realizes that it is his own grocery cart that is the source. Perry's point is that the discovery that it is *him* is not just the discovery of the name of the person; it's a different kind of discovery, one that we cannot describe without the use of indexicals themselves. And this element is crucial to explaining what he does. Perry argues: if he had said, "I came to believe that John Perry is making a mess," he would no longer have explained why he stopped and looked in his own cart. We'd have to add, "and I believe that I am John Perry," bringing the indexical back again (pp. 4–5). Following Perry, we should then conclude that emotions can't be propositional attitudes in the classical sense, where propositions are understood to be detachable from their context and to have truth value in an absolute sense, rather than just for a person at a time (p. 6). As we have seen, emotions contain some elements that are detachable; but a crucial core is not.

50 See Foot (1988), with the example of cops and robbers: what is good for one is not good for the other, and up to a point they do not contradict one another – although, as Foot also stresses, a person's scheme of values also contains general interests that are interwoven with the personal intrests. My account of the locatedness of the emotions is closely related to the distinction between "I-desires" and "non-I desires" in Williams (1973), who distinguishes aptly between the egoism/altruism distinction and the I/non-I distinction.

roles: as a person of intrinsic worth in her own right; as *my* mother, and an important constituent of my life's goals and plans; and as *a mother*, that is, a type of person that it would be good for every human being who has one to cherish (though obviously they shouldn't all cherish the same one). Only one of these three ways of focusing on my mother makes reference to me;[51] and this one, I have insisted, does not consider her a person of merely instrumental importance. And yet, this one appears to be crucial in making the difference between love and nonlove, grief and nongrief.

Once again, then: my view emphatically does not make the emotions egoistic, unless one should hold that any attachment to one's own parents, by contrast to the parents of others, is a form of egoism – a harsh doctrine. It does make them localized, and in that sense in tension with completely impartialist forms of morality. It is clear that the mixture of self-referential and non-self-referential considerations may differ in different emotions, and also in the emotions of different people. But we must emphasize that the eudaimonism of emotions does not imply that grief is not really grief for the death of the loved person. Consider this passage from Proust:

The idea that one will die is more painful than dying, but less painful than the idea that another person is dead, that, becoming once more a still, plane surface after having engulfed a person, a reality extends, without even a ripple at the point of disappearance, from which that person is excluded, in which there no longer exists any will, any knowledge . . . [52]

This emotion is still eudaimonistic: it is localized within Marcel's own life. It contains prominently and centrally the thought of a loss that looms large from the person's own viewpoint. But it sees the lost person's life as a feature of the world's landscape, and abhors the sight of a world from which that feature has been removed.

Are all emotions eudaimonistic? Do all, that is, make reference to my important goals and projects? Do all contain the self-referential element that lies at the heart of the eudaimonist structure? The most

---

51 Although, in the end, understanding why some of the other features get a grip on me may ultimately lead back to the self, as in, "Well, it's not a particularly great country, but it is the one I'm used to, the one I grew up in."

52 *Remembrance of Things Past*, III.519. References are to volume and page number in the Moncrieff/Kilmartin translation.

striking exception would appear to be the emotion of wonder, which I shall discuss further in Chapter 4. This emotion responds to the pull of the object, and one might say that in it the subject is maximally aware of the value of the object, and only minimally aware, if at all, of its relationship to her own plans. That is why it is likely to issue in contemplation, rather than in any other sort of action toward the object. Another related emotion would be reverence or awe: again, awe, for example in a religious context, is an acknowledgment of the surpassing value of the object, not just from the person's point of view, but quite generally.[53]

Wonder is sometimes an important ingredient in other emotions. In grief there is, I think, often a kind of wonder – in which one sees the beauty of the lost person as a kind of radiance standing at a very great distance from us. Describing his mourning for Albertine, Proust's narrator writes:

My imagination sought for her in the sky, at nightfall when we had been wont to gaze at it while still together; beyond that moonlight which she loved, I tried to raise up to her my tenderness so that it might be a consolation to her for being no longer alive, and this love for a being who was now so remote was like a religion; my thoughts rose to her like prayers.[54]

In this tender moment – one of the few times that Marcel gives the impression of really loving Albertine herself – we see a love that has moved not only beyond the egoism characteristic of Marcel, but also to some extent beyond eudaimonism as well, a fact well brought out by the religious imagery. It is still in the framework of a fundamentally eudaimonistic attachment, however, for it is for his Albertine, and not some chance woman, that he grieves.

In Chapters 4 and 6 I shall argue that wonder plays an important part in the development of a child's capacity for love and compassion. Children whose capacity for this response to the world is strengthened through imaginative play have a more robust capacity for nonpossessive love, and for bringing distant others into their system of goals and plans; in this way I shall qualify the eudaimonism of the account of

---

53 Wonder and awe are akin, but distinct: wonder is outward-moving, exuberant, whereas awe is linked with bending, or making oneself small. In wonder I want to leap or run, in awe to kneel.

54 *Remembrance of Things Past*, III.522.

these emotions. But I shall insist that in love and compassion the object must ultimately be seen as a part of the person's own scheme of ends: a eudaimonistic judgment must ultimately be formed in order for the emotion to occur. Wonder, as non-eudaimonistic as an emotion can be, helps move distant objects within the circle of a person's scheme of ends. We may, then, maintain the eudaimonism of the theory in a general way, holding that it is essential to the explanation of why emotions such as grief, fear, and hope focus on some events and not others, without dogmatically forcing it into a case where it seems not to play a central role.[55]

Finally, we need to discuss the issue of importance. For now that we have a fuller account of the emotions' eudaimonism, we can see that this feature also helps us to explain why some emotions seem like great upheavals, and others seem less momentous. For these *differences of intensity* themselves involve object-directed intentionality: they are explained by the importance with which I invest the object (or what befalls it) among my own goals and projects. If the importance is beneath a certain threshold, I will not have an emotion at all. The loss of a toothbrush does not occasion even a mild grief; someone who takes a paper clip off my desk does not make me even a tiny bit angry. But above that threshold, differences of intensity are occasioned by differences in the eudaimonistic evaluation. The anger we feel is proportional to the size of the harm that we think has occurred; the grief we feel is proportional to the extent of the loss. People grieve only mildly for a person who has been a small part of their lives.

Two nights ago, I went to bed thinking that Todd Martin had been knocked out of the U.S. Open (since he had lost the first two sets to a tough opponent.) I felt a little sad. When I woke up, I found out that he had won in five sets. I saw him on TV dancing around the court, and I felt a surge of joy. But of course it was a trivial sorrow and a trivial joy. While one watches a tennis match, one is intensely focused on the athlete one likes, and so an emotion can develop as one temporarily comes to think the match very important – and perhaps also

---

55 One might mention respect, too, as a non-eudaimonistic emotion, but I would disagree, since I think respect is best understood as a pattern of thought and action, rather than as an emotion.

identifies with the aging Martin, with his graying temples, so like one's own if one did not dye one's hair. But when normal life resumes, the evaluation assumes its usual low level. Todd Martin just isn't a very important part of my life.

Emotions are of course frequently disproportionate to their objects. But this is usually because the person has a skewed view of the object, seeing it as more or less important than it really is. People will often suffer greatly over trivial losses – if they are used to the things involved, or think them their due.[56] Again, they may make the object a vehicle for concerns and anxieties that come from their own lives, and thus invest it with a significance that seems peculiar – as one might do with a sports star or one's favorite team. But once again, it is the nature of the eudaimonistic evaluation that explains the intensity of the emotion.[57]

To the extent that the emotional response seems out of line with the *person's own view* of the object, or with her own assessment of what has occurred, we typically suppose that she really had a deeper concern for the object than she had realized (Proust's account of self-knowledge through emotion); or that the present object has a symbolic significance, standing for another absent object; or that there is some further hidden content that really explains her emotion. We should not be dogmatic about this, since we would then be in danger of simply waving away objections rather than replying to them. But I think that once we have the historical materials of Chapter 4 on the table, we will see that the view contains rich resources for understanding such cases, and that we really can establish that such mistakes about significance occur, and why they occur.

VI. ARE THERE NECESSARY NONCOGNITIVE ELEMENTS?

We have now argued that judgments of the requisite sort are necessary for the emotion; that they are not external causes, but constituent parts of what the emotion is; and that they are sufficient for emotion, if they

---

56 See examples in Chapter 6 where people ask for compassion in connection with trivial losses.

57 Again, wonder is exceptional: the intensity of my wonder seems proportioned only to the value I see in the object, not to its value for me in my scheme of goals and ends.

have the requisite eudaimonistic evaluative content. Now we must confront an especially difficult and delicate question: are there other constituent parts to the grief that are not themselves parts of the judgment
(the evaluative thought)?[58]

In any particular instance of grieving there is so much going on that
it is very difficult to answer this question if we remain at the level of
token-identities between instances of grieving and instances of judging.
How do we decide which of the many things that are going on contem-
poraneously with the grief are or are not parts of the grief? Since we
are talking about living sentient beings, and since having some feelings
of some type is probably a necessary condition of waking mental life
for any sentient being, we could assert that any instance of emotion,
given that it is a part of the waking life of a sentient being, has as its
necessary condition the presence of some feeling or other. But we don't
have any clear reason to say that these things are parts of the grief
itself. We do not seem to have said any more than that a pumping heart
is a necessary condition of any episode of emotion; but we would not
be inclined to say that a pumping heart is a constituent part of my
grief. And yet if we confine ourselves to a particular episode of emotion
we have difficulty finding arguments bearing on the question of
whether a given feeling or bodily process is or is not a necessary part
of its internal conditions of identity.

We have a more powerful argument – and also a deeper understanding of the phenomena – if we ask instead about the general identity
conditions for grief, and whether there are elements necessary for grief
in general that do not seem to be elements of judgment. In other words,
if these elements should be missing, would we withdraw our ascription
of grief? This is an extremely difficult question, about which we should
be open-minded and humble, and prepared to change our minds. But I
provisionally believe that the answer is that we do not find any such
elements. There usually will be bodily sensations and changes of many
sorts involved in grieving; but if we discovered that my blood pressure

58 It is here that my view differs most from that of Ben-Ze'ev (2000): his view is more
open-ended, including appraisals, feelings, and motivations into the account of emotion. Because he does not look for necessary and sufficient conditions for emotion, but
instead for prototypes, which particular cases may resemble to a greater or lesser
degree, it is difficult to compare our views, or to say how he would deal with the
problems I raise here for claims that feelings and bodily movements are necessary for a
given emotion type. To that extent, his view and mine may not really differ.

was quite low during this whole episode, or that my pulse rate never got above sixty, we would not, I think, have the slightest reason to conclude that I was not really grieving. (Quadriplegics lack altogether the usual connections between central blood pressure and heart rate regulatory mechanisms and peripheral effector mechanisms, and yet we have no difficulty thinking that such people really have emotions.) If my hands and feet were cold or warm, sweaty or dry, again this would be of no necessary criterial value, given the great variability of the relevant physiological connections.[59]

And although psychologists have developed more sophisticated so-called measures, based on brain activity, it still seems intuitively wrong of them to use them as definitive of being in an emotional state. This is recognized in other recent work where a more cautious claim is typically made: for example, that the functioning of the amygdala is a necessary condition of normal emotional activity.[60] We do not withdraw emotion ascriptions otherwise grounded if we discover that the subject is not in a certain brain state. Indeed, the only way the brain state assumes apparent importance, in such experimental work, is through a putative correlation with instances of emotion identified on other, experiential grounds. Moreover, as we shall see in the next chapter, emotions cause physiological effects: so it is extremely difficult to say which effects are consequences and which are even plausible candidates for being parts of the experience itself.[61]

We should certainly grant that all human experiences are embodied, and thus realized in some kind of material process. In that sense, human emotions are all bodily processes. But the question is, are there any bodily states or processes that are constantly correlated with our experiences of emotion, in such a way that we will want to put that particular bodily state into the definition of a given emotion-type? And here we run up against an issue well known to biological researchers:

---

59 The psychologists' term "arousal" typically refers, often quite imprecisely, to changes of this sort: see Chapter 2. Gibbard (1990), p. 131, proposes that we think of evaluations as emotions minus "physiological arousal," but the precise meaning of "arousal," and its relation to the wide spectrum of the emotions, remains unclear.

60 See, for example, Pinker (1997), pp. 371–2 and Le Doux (1996), discussed in Chapter 2.

61 Seligman (1975) shows with powerful experimental evidence that the subject's cognitive condition may actually cause further physiological states that are sometimes (wrongly, in his view) identified with emotions.

the plasticity of the human organism, or, in other words, the multiple realizability of mental states. There is plasticity within a given subject: functions previously performed in one part of the brain may be assumed by another. Even in quite large-scale ways, the brain is a remarkably versatile and plastic part of the organism: people with damage to one hemisphere can frequently replicate a function associated with that hemisphere in the other hemisphere. Given this type of plasticity, there will also be variation between subjects: a function performed in one hemisphere in subject A may be performed in the other in subject B. For these reasons, if we said that grief is always of necessity accompanied by the firing of so-and-so many neurons of such and such type, we would be likely to find hundreds of cases for which this just isn't quite right. (And of course if we add to this reservation the fact that we will ultimately recognize in nonhuman animals emotions very similar to those we find in humans, the case for inserting a specific neural activity into the definition becomes weaker still.)

It would appear that the facts that prevent us from putting the physiological description into the definition are permanent facts about the type of organism we are, and the versatility of our design. However, we can certainly say that we are ready to change our minds, if things should turn out to be otherwise. In Chapter 2 I will return to the issue of physiological explanations, arguing that research in neuroscience in many ways confirms the type of view advanced here, and offers further illumination in connection with it.

(Another issue that arises here, and which will concern us in future chapters, is that much of the philosophical/religious tradition has ascribed emotions to god or gods,* often imagining god to be a bodiless substance. Thus if we should adopt an account that makes a particular physiological process a necessary condition for an emotion of a given type, its consequence would be that all of these thinkers are talking nonsense when they make these ascriptions. We may or may not believe that their accounts are correct, but it is a heavy price to pay to adopt from the start a view that entails that they are suffering from a profound conceptual confusion. I think that they are not confused.

*For the sake of evenhandedness toward monotheists and polytheists, I reject the convention whereby we standardly find 'God' but 'gods.' I depart from this practice when discussing historical texts in Part III, in order to follow standard usage in translating them.

Whether we believe that bodiless substances exist or not, the reason it makes sense to imagine a bodiless substance having genuine emotions is that it makes sense to imagine that a thinking being, whether realized in matter or not, could care deeply about something in the world, and have the thoughts and intentions associated with such attachments. And that's all we really require for emotion. We can happily state that in human beings thought and emotion are, even necessarily are, enmattered forms, without concluding that this must of necessity be so for every emotional being. People who don't like this argument are free to ignore it, since it is not necessary for my conclusion.)

More plausible, perhaps, would be certain feelings characteristically associated with emotion. Anger is associated with a boiling feeling, fear with a chilled and queasy feeling. But here we should beware of the word "feeling," which is remarkably slippery and likely to mislead. We should distinguish "feelings" of two sorts. On the one hand, there are feelings with a rich intentional content – feelings of the emptiness of one's life without a certain person, feelings of unhappy love for that person, and so forth. Feelings like these may enter into the identity conditions for some emotion; but the word "feeling" now does not contrast with our cognitive words "perception" and "judgment," it is merely a terminological variant of them. And we have already said that the judgment itself has many of the kinetic properties that the "feeling" is presumably intended to explain. On the other hand, there are feelings without rich intentionality or cognitive content, let us say feelings of fatigue, of extra energy, of boiling, of trembling, and so forth. I think we should say about these exactly what we said about the bodily states: that they may accompany an emotion of a given type and they may not – but that they are not absolutely necessary for it. In my own grief, feelings of crushing fatigue alternated in a bewildering way with periods when I felt preternaturally wide awake and active; but it seemed wrong to say that either of these was a necessary condition of my grief.

We may want to grant here that there are some nonintentional feelings that are *frequently* associated with a given emotion: take boiling and anger, or trembling and fear. Nonetheless, it appears that here too the plasticity and variability of people (both of the same person over time and across people) prevents us from plugging the feeling into the definition as an absolutely necessary element. Many men report experiencing anger in connection with a boiling feeling; this seems to be somewhat less true among women, or among people in general, who are taught to suppress or fear their own anger. My own experience of anger is that it is associated with tension at the back of the neck, or a headache that appears the next day. This doesn't mean that I am not really angry, as the further examination of the pattern of my statements and actions would show.

There are two distinct points here. First, if we are prepared to recognize nonconscious emotional states, such as nonconscious fear of death or nonconscious anger – as the next section will argue that we should, under carefully defined circumstances – then we cannot possibly hold to any necessary phenomenological condition for that emotion-type. Second, even if we don't like totally nonconscious emotions, we should recognize that there is a great deal of variability in the feeling states people characteristically experience in connection with a given emotion-type – variability both within a given subject and between subjects. My anger exemplifies both of these points: for at times it is entirely asymptomatic; and then, the following day, it will manifest itself in a headache. In neither case does it have the phenomenology of "boiling" that so many people report.[62]

Do we get further by recognizing qualia, and saying that it's not *boiling* or *trembling* we're after, but the sui generis feeling of *anger*, which has a constancy across subjects, in something like the way that we imagine that seeing red has constancy? I don't feel that much is contributed by this move. So far as we can see, what has constancy across subjects is a pattern of thought, which is of course a type of experience. If we are to be convinced that there is anything further that

---

62 Of similar elusiveness is the concept of "affect" that is fundamental to the noncognitive account of emotion in Stocker (1996). Although Stocker announces his opposition to cognitive views of emotion, and introduces the psychological concept of "affect" as an element that will mark the difference between his view and cognitive views, it later becomes clear that the term is extremely capacious: he announces that "it is useful to have a common term for the affectivity common to emotions, moods, interests, and attitudes" (p. 20). When, finally, he insists that we should recognize unconscious affects, along with many contemporary psychoanalysts (p. 21), we seem to have lost our grip on the notion itself. Certainly it can't be a feeling, which we recognize by the way it registers in our awareness. Is it a kind of psychic energy? But what kind? And is the kind specific to each emotion-type, or is it something that distinguishes all emotions from nonemotions? Deigh (1998), reviewing Stocker's book, concludes that the term "affect" is a primitive term. I would say that if it is so understood, Stocker has not made out his case that we need to include it as a distinctive item in the definition of emotions, over and above the elements we have recognized already.

has constancy across subjects, we need to be told something about what this might be. The positing of a sui generis something seems like mere hand-waving. Besides, I shall argue later that the experience of anger is subtly inflected by cultural variation in ways that color perception is not taken to be by the partisans of qualia (although that is not to say that they are entirely correct about color either).

What concessions should we make to the role of feelings? We should grant, I think, that in typical cases emotions are conscious experiences; as with beliefs generally, the nonconscious are atypical cases, and parasitic on the conscious cases. So it feels like something to have an emotion. Much of the time, that feeling might be described as involving something that psychologists typically call "arousal"[63] and that Proust calls "upheaval" – experiences of being shaken up or in ferment. The upheaval is a part of the experience of what it is like to have those thoughts – at least much of the time. But that is not true of all cases: a lot of joy and love won't feel this way, nor indeed will grief or fear always feel this way. So this is a loose claim, which helps us to understand something, but that probably should not enter into the definitions of emotions. Far less should the more concrete feeling-states, such as trembling and boiling, enter the definition. There is just too much variation among persons, and across times in the same person, for that to be right. Even within a given culture at a given time, we have variants, as my experience of anger shows. George Pitcher puts this point extremely well:

If P comes upon Q just as Q is setting fire to P's house, and P rushes at him in a blind fury, it seems singularly inappropriate to insist that P must be having certain sensations. In fact P, in such circumstances, probably experiences no sensations of any kind, and yet he is undoubtedly extremely angry. Again, if a person's attention is too strongly diverted to other matters, he might have an emotion without having the sensations that usually go with that emotion. A young man, P, is being interviewed for an important job, and he is extremely anxious to make a good impression. One of the interviewers, Q, makes an insulting remark to P, and thereafter an observer might detect an icy tone creeping into P's voice when he addresses Q, although there are no other signs of anger. The iciness is not intentional, however,

---

63 Although this term is not consistently used: sometimes, as I have already suggested, it designates a physiological change (elevated heart rate, etc.) that may or may not have a phenomenological concomitant.

and in fact P is so intent on following the conversation and on creating a good impression, that he is not even aware of it; and he is certainly too engrossed to experience any feelings of anger. I think we might say, under these circumstances, that P was nevertheless angry with Q . . . [64]

Pitcher's analysis captures the way in which variations in circumstance and personality affect the extent to which people will experience the so-called characteristic feelings of anger and fear. (His case of the interviewee has interesting implications for women's common failure to experience the sensations of anger: so often we do feel like interviewees, subordinates who must depend on the good will of those in power over us.) If we now add cross-cultural variation to this picture, we will get even more variation. Thus, we characteristically associate grief with a quasi-sensory feeling of blackness; but in a culture such as India, where white is the color of mourning, this is less likely to be the chosen metaphor. In short: we should note the characteristic feeling-words used in connection with emotions (usually metaphorical descriptions), but we probably should not put any specific feeling-description into the definition.

Should we make an exception for pain and pleasure, saying that some emotions, such as grief, are of necessity accompanied by pain, and others, such as joy, by pleasure? Here we have, once again, the problem of the nonconscious forms; but those may rightly be seen as atypical. Even in the typical case, however, we need to know more about how pain and pleasure themselves are being conceived. On some philosophical accounts, pleasure is not a feeling at all, but a characteristic way of doing something, for example, unimpededly (to use Aristotle's definition). In that way of thinking, to think with pleasure about one's child's preciousness will not be to have some extra element, the pleasure, over and above the thinking; it will be to do the thinking in a certain way, viz., unimpededly. I am inclined to think that this is the right direction to go with the analysis of pleasure – at least, that there is no one subjective nonintentional state that is constant across our many pleasurable experiences.[65] So adding pleasure

---

64 Pitcher (1965), p. 338.

65 See also Plato's *Philebus*: Protarchus maintains that pleasure is a single nonvariegated feeling that simply has different *sources*; Socrates objects, and eventually carries the day. On all this, see Gosling and Taylor (1982), and, for one good philosophical discussion of this perpetual problem, see Gosling (1969).

to the definition of an emotion does not add an independent non-cognitive element.

Is the same true of pain? Again, this is a complex topic. There are pains that seem to be definable in purely physiological terms, or in purely nonintentional psychological terms. But is the pain we associate with grief among them? Aristotle's definitions of pain-linked emotions always speak of the "pain at . . .", suggesting that he views pain itself as an intentional state with cognitive content. I believe this is correct, in such cases. We may have nonintentional pains in connection with grief, fear, and pity. These would be dull aches and bodily feelings of nerves being painfully stimulated. But these seem like the "boiling" and the "trembling" – frequent correlates, but not necessary to the identity of the emotion. We also have a type of pain that probably is necessary for grief: namely, the pain *that an important element of one's life is gone.* But of course that is not a noncognitive element, and we have already included it in our cognitive/evaluative account, which has stressed, with Chrysippus, that such losses are bad and that it's right to be upset about them.

So we appear to have type-identities between emotions and judgments – or, to put it more elastically, looking ahead, between emotions and value-laden cognitive states. Emotions can be defined in terms of these evaluative recognitions alone, although we must recognize that some feelings of tumult or "arousal" will often accompany them, and sometimes feelings of a more type-specific kind, and although we must recall that they are at every point embodied. If we want to add this very general stipulation to the definition, we may do so, though we must add the proviso that we are talking only about the likely case, in order to retain the possibility of recognizing nonconscious emotions.[66]

VII. ARE THERE OTHER COGNITIVE ELEMENTS? IMAGINING THE OBJECT

But if we do not make these concessions to the presence of the noncognitive, there is one important alteration to the cognitive/evaluative view that we should now make. Although emotions can in a sense be defined

---

66 And also the proviso that we are talking only about humans, since we don't know anything about what feeling-states other animals have, and since we may want to hold open the conceptual possibility that a bodiless god has emotions.

by their evaluative-eudaimonistic thought content alone, the experience of emotion usually contains more than that content. It contains rich and dense perceptions of the object, which are highly concrete and replete with detail. Thus, typically, grief is not just an abstract judgment plus the ineliminable localizing element: it is very richly particular. Even if its propositional content is, "My wonderful mother is dead," the experience itself involves a storm of memories and concrete perceptions that swarm around that content, but add more than is present in it. The experience of emotion is, then, cognitively laden, or dense, in a way that a propositional-attitude view would not capture; and it is probably correct to think that this denseness is usually, if not always, a necessary feature of the experience of an emotion such as grief.

What this means is that the emotions typically have a connection to imagination, and to the concrete picturing of events in imagination, that differentiates them from other, more abstract judgmental states. Sometimes, this imagining is best understood as a vehicle for making a eudaimonistic connection with the object. If I am thinking of a distant sorrow, let us say the death of many people in an earthquake in China a thousand years ago, then I think it's likely that I won't have grief, unless and until I can make that event vivid to myself through the imagination. What that means is that I won't really succeed in caring about those people as a part of my scheme of goals and ends without such rich imagining (see Chapter 6).

But even where I already invest the object with significance, imagination is often at work, supplying more than the eudaimonistic thoughts by themselves supply. People differ, and some minds may rely on the sensory more than others; but it is probably a feature of emotions' evolutionary character (see Chapter 2) that they do typically have this sensory richness and this tendency to focus in upon the object. When I grieve for my mother, I *see* her, and the sight is, like a picture, dense and replete. That density is inseparable from the experience: in fact, it is often tiny details of the dense picture of the person one loves that become the focus for grief, that seem to symbolize or encapsulate that person's wonderfulness or salience. So human emotions are shaped by the fact that we are perceiving creatures: they derive their rich texture from those sensory abilities. There is no easy way of plugging those into a general definition of emotion, although we might simply say that grief is the acceptance of a certain content, *accompanied (usually) by* relevant acts of the imagination. These acts will be multiple and not easily summarized, but they typically involve a more intense focusing on the object than would be strictly necessitated by the propositional content.

Why does the imagination focus on some objects and not on others, and how is this selection relevant to the thought content of the emotions? Typically there will be connections in both directions: the very fact that a certain person (my mother) is necessary for my nutrition and survival will cause me, in infancy, to focus more intently on her, perceptually, than on other mothers; in this case, it appears to be the antecedent need and attachment that drives the focusing, and yet we do not need to deny that the many details one notices about a person also enrich the love we feel, and that love becomes intertwined with perceptual habits in very many ways.[67] In other cases, the striking properties of a person or thing may elicit our attention first, resulting in the formation of an emotional attachment. This often happens with emotions directed toward nature, and also, sometimes, with romantic/erotic love. (Not always: Proust's narrator stresses that the particular properties of Albertine are a matter of indifference to him, her relation to his need for maternal comfort far more important. And in general, the object rarely summons love into being without some connection to past memories and habits.) In compassion, our ability to picture vividly the predicament of a person assists in the emotion's formation, as I shall argue in Chapter 6; we may feel less emotion toward other cases that we can't similarly imagine with vividness, though they may have a similar structure. Here what the imagination seems to do is to help us bring a distant individual into the sphere of our goals and projects, humanizing the person and creating the possibility of attachment. Compassion itself will still be defined by its thought content, including its eudaimonistic content, as I shall argue in Chapter 6; but the imagination is a bridge that allows the other to become an object of our compassion.

As with feelings and bodily movements, so here: any list of the

---

67 See Chapter 4, where I mention that infants have a remarkable ability to discriminate between the smell of their own mother's milk and that of another mother's milk; this specificity informs the general relation, even as the specific attachment is shaped by the general need for milk.

"relevant" acts would have to be a long, open-ended disjunction, and the whole point is that the imaginings are highly concrete, varying with the particularity of the object and situation. Nor need acts of imagining be present in any particular *episode* of emotion; what is more likely is they are present at prominent points in its history. (And even here, as I have said, it may be that some individuals rely less than others on these sensory cues.) As I shall argue further in section VIII, we may even have grief and joy and fear that don't form part of our conscious awareness at all, so long as that is not the standard case, and so long as the propositional content persists throughout. Even when we are conscious of grief, or fear, it's not evident that we need have the rich dense imagining in every instance. It seems possible to love one's child, even consciously, while intently perceiving a symphony of Mahler, or the highway in front of one's car. And: one may be angry at someone without noticing that person very much, if at all, since one may be focusing on the damage to oneself. In that sense, some emotions have a closer connection to the sensory imagination than do others.

In many central cases, however, focus on an object through dense imaginative picturing or sensory attention is a salient element in emotional experience (and, as we shall see in Chapter 2, a likely part of what explains the emotions' contribution to survival). This feature should probably not be added to the definition of emotions, since it exhibits such great variability and plasticity; and yet it should be mentioned, since it alerts us to features of emotional development and change that we might otherwise not notice. This addition, which is a cognitive addition, helps us to understand some of the problems emotions may pose for morality, and also some of what they bring to morality.

VIII. BACKGROUND AND SITUATIONAL, GENERAL AND CONCRETE

We have now accounted for many aspects of my experience of grief: its localized character, its intensity, its imaginative dwelling on its object. But two further distinctions must now be introduced, in order to capture the multilayered texture of grief: a distinction between *general* and *concrete* evaluative judgments, and a distinction between *background* and *situational* judgments. It will be seen that these are two independent distinctions. Generality first: in my grief a number of different evaluative judgments are at work; it is difficult to disentangle them. The judgment that at least some things and persons outside the self have great importance for my flourishing; the judgment that people with certain characteristics of generosity and warmth have such importance; the judgment that one's mother has such importance; the judgment that this particular woman, whose history has been intertwined with mine in so many concrete ways, has such importance – all of these might be invoked to explain my grief, and deciding which is the most relevant will often be impossible without a broader analysis of the pattern of my judgments and actions. They are of course not mutually incompatible; indeed, the first is a sine qua non of any of the rest. In many cases several different levels will be salient. While grieving for my mother in a way that emphasized her particularity and the particularity of my history with her, I grieved also for the fact that I now had no *parent*.

But sometimes it is important to ask which level of generality[68] is most salient, in grief and in other emotions: for if one loves a person primarily as the bearer of certain properties that might be instantiated elsewhere, the pattern of one's grief, and future love, cannot fail to be different in consequence – a fact that philosophical theories of emotion obsessively exploit (see Chapter 10). This is one reason why there is something especially terrible in the death of a parent: for (despite Antigone's argument in favor of brothers) it is that death that seems the most final and irrevocable, being the death of a part of one's history that has great length and depth, to which no replacement can bear anything like the same relation.

68 Notice that I have introduced the distinction as one between the general and the concrete, rather than between the universal and the particular. I treat particularity here as a limiting case of concreteness, in the sense that the focus is still on certain descriptions – historical rather than just qualitative – that might in principle be universalized. The question of universalizability arises in two ways: I might ask whether my judgment of my mother's importance implies a judgment that for anyone similarly situated, with a similar history, the parent should similarly be loved by that person; and I might also ask whether a numerically distinct clone with all the same properties, including historical properties, should be similarly loved by me. I believe that the answer to the first question is yes, and that the answer to the second is no. The self-referential element of the emotion-thought, of course, moves us beyond the focus on the concrete description, and is part of the explanation of why we won't accept a clone of our loved one: we want the very one that has been in a close relationship with *us*.

It may remain obscure to a person which description of her object is, in fact, the most salient. When it is important to decide this, we can only inspect the pattern of our judgments and actions. In 1995, when I was deciding whether to move to the University of Chicago from Brown, I experienced, as I thought of being in Chicago, a powerful grief. What was its object? If the object was the Brown Philosophy Department, then this was a sign, perhaps, that I should not make the move: Brown was more important to me than I had been inclined to think. On the other hand, there was a good possibility that the object of the grief was a much more vague and elusive object, such as "my past" or "the years of my youth," since I had spent twenty-five years living in Cambridge, Massachusetts, before that. This highly general object, unlike the Brown Philosophy Department, was definitely not in my power to regain; so it would not have been such a good idea to stay in Cambridge simply in order to avoid mourning for twenty-five years of my past. By thinking about situations in which I experienced the grief, and considering the pattern of my other judgments and actions, I decided that the past was probably the real object of the grief, and I did move to Chicago. This case involves two distinct objects; but we proceed in the same way when we are sorting out two different descriptions of the same object.

Of equal importance is a distinction between *background* and *situational* emotion-judgments. By this I mean the distinction between evaluative judgments that persist through situations of numerous kinds, and judgments that arise in the context of some particular situation.[69]

69 The relationship between this distinction and Richard Wollheim's distinction between *states* and *dispositions* (see Wollheim [1999], pp. 6–11) is complex. For Wollheim, mental states are transient and episodic, elements in the stream of consciousness; they are always conscious and directly experienced. Dispositions are persisting modifications of the structure of our mental life, which are never experienced directly, and have no subjectivity. They have, nonetheless, psychological reality, prominently including causal properties. Often, a mental state will be an eruption of a disposition; but one might have a transient mental state (an episodic fear of snakes, for example) without having any associated dispositional fear.

My distinction between the background and the situational is, first of all, less dichotomous than Wollheim's distinction. It really suggests a continuum, since "situations" may be more or less enduring, and thus an emotion might be situational and yet relatively enduring; a background emotion is one that persists through situations of different types, and thus is more enduring than that. Another difference is that on my account, the background situational distinction does not perfectly map on to the conscious/nonconscious distinction. One may, I believe, have a situational emotion of

It is, given our analysis, the distinction between ongoing or background emotions and episodic emotions. For example, my judgment about my mother's importance persisted over time (though I need not have been conscious of it throughout that time); one's judgments about one's own mortality and the badness of death persist, in a similar fashion, throughout one's adult life, though only certain circumstances bring them to consciousness; one's beliefs about the importance of one's own bodily health, and the vulnerability of one's body to disease and injury, similarly persist, unnoticed unless a circumstance calls them into view. And these judgments, I claim, are background emotions. They are not simply dispositional; they have psychological reality, and often explain patterns of action. One loves one's parents, children, spouse, friends, continuously over time, even when no specific incident gives rise to an awareness of the love. In a similar way, many people have an ongoing fear of death that has psychological reality, that motivates their behavior in ways that can be shown, even though it is only in certain circumstances that the fear is noticed. One may be angry over time at a persisting wrong – as, for example, many women live in a state of continuous anger at the domestic injustice that is a part of their daily lives; and yet the anger will surface only in certain circumstances. One may also have background joy – for example, when one's work is going well, when one's children are flourishing, when an important relationship is going smoothly. One may be able to discern such joy in the

which one is not aware: as when someone has grief at a particular death without being aware of it (or not yet), or when one is angry at someone for some specific reason without being aware of it. (This nonconscious operation of a situational emotion is analogous to the nonconscious operation of a whole host of concrete beliefs in one's ordinary movements. Thus, when I move across my office, I have and use various concrete situation-focused beliefs about the locations of objects, of which I have no conscious awareness.) On the other hand, background emotions are not always nonconscious. A persisting love or joy may have a distinctive phenomenology, without transforming itself into a situational emotion. Lucretius plausibly argues that the background fear of death has a phenomenology all its own, the feeling of a heavy weight on the chest. On the most important issue, however, Wollheim and I agree: it is important to recognize the existence of enduring structures in the personality that have psychological reality whether or not they are conscious; emotions are among such structures.

In other respects, the complex architecture of Wollheim's book will not be investigated here; as with any highly refined and artfully constructed theory, it is difficult to get into it without seeing the whole topic from that theory's viewpoint; and it is too late in the game for me to do that.

pattern of one's actions, and yet in these cases joy frequently manifests itself in a lack of reflexive self-awareness, a complete absorption in the thing one loves.

In short, once one has formed attachments to unstable things not fully under one's own control, once one has made these part of one's notion of one's flourishing, one has emotions of a background kind toward them – on my view, judgments that acknowledge their enormous worth – that persist in the fabric of one's life, and are crucial to the explanation of one's actions, though it might take a specific circumstance to call them into awareness. Background emotions need not be nonconscious, just as episodic or situational emotions need not be conscious; but frequently they will be, since they are persisting conditions that are often unnoticed partly on account of their pervasiveness. We may also be unaware of the many ways in which they shape our situational emotions. Thus, grief at the death of a parent is often shaped, rendered more terrible, by the background fear of one's own death. One has the idea that one is helplessly standing on the edge of an abyss – and that sense of helplessness is surely colored by the sense that one is now the generation next to die.

It is tricky to admit nonconscious emotions into our account, in part because they lack the phenomenological and imaginative features that we have informally linked with our definitions of emotion-types, but in part, as well, for methodological reasons. We began identifying the phenomena by pointing to experiences of emotion, as identified by people who have them. Once we admit that we may be wrong about what we are experiencing, we seem to call into question the entire argumentative strategy. If our theory doesn't really match experiential classifications so well after all, were we then right to use an appeal to experience against partisans of other views?[70]

This would be a problem if the nonconscious cases were central or ubiquitous; and it would also be a problem if, even though not central, they were such that people could rarely be brought to acknowledge their presence and the role they play in their own experience. Classical Freudian accounts of the unconscious sometimes suffer from these difficulties. But I am thinking of the nonconscious in a much more ordinary sense, just the sense in which many of our most common beliefs

70 See also the remarks on methodology and on Griffiths (1997) in the Introduction.

are nonconscious, although they guide our actions in many ways: beliefs about cause and effect, beliefs about numbering, beliefs about where things are, beliefs about what is healthy and harmful, and so forth. We don't focus on such familiar and general beliefs every time we use them or are motivated by them. And yet, if we were asked, "Do you believe that the refrigerator is to the right of the microwave?" or "Do you believe that if you turn on the faucet the water will run?" or "Do you believe that one dollar is worth more than fifty cents?" or "Do you believe that it would be bad to drink that rat poison?" we would of course say yes. We are repositories of an indefinite number of such beliefs, and we rely on them in our actions. Indeed, if we weren't like this, if we could use only those beliefs on which we were consciously focusing, we couldn't possibly survive.

In the case of emotion-beliefs, there may at times be special reasons for not confronting them consciously, for they may be very painful to confront. This means that it may take much longer to get someone to recognize grief or fear or anger in herself than to admit to spatial or numerical beliefs. There is a resistance to the acknowledgment of one's own vulnerability that must be overcome. To that extent, the Freudian account has force (though the cases I discuss here do not involve repression in its technical sense). But if we are to recognize such background emotions, I claim, we still need good reasons for doing so. The attribution is most secure when it can be validated by the person herself, who ultimately should acknowledge that the pattern of her actions is best explained by that emotion. Short of such acknowledgment, we may point to the pattern, and say to her, "Don't you think you were angry at Z today?" or "Aren't you really afraid of that exam?" – and it is possible that we may be correct even if she refuses the ascription. But things are on a far more solid footing if she assents. This means, of course, that the methodological issue no longer poses a problem, since we are dealing with yet another case of emotion that the person identifies as such.

As can be easily seen, the background/situational distinction is logically independent of the general/concrete distinction. A general emotion will frequently also lie in the background, but it may also be situational: many emotions connected with political justice toward groups are of this sort, as is much wonder at the world and its beauty. A concrete emotion may often be situational, but it may also lurk in the background, as the highly concrete fear of one's own death does throughout much of one's life.

Both of these distinctions are logically independent of the distinction between the self-referential elements in emotion and the non-self-referential elements. The background fear of death usually includes both the highly personal thought that it is bad for me to die and the general thought that death is a bad thing; so too, the fear of a loved one's death involves fear *for that person* and also for one's own goals and projects. Situational fear and grief contain the same complex mixture of elements. General emotions are not necessarily less eudaimonistic than concrete emotions: I may focus on the importance of parental love for all human beings, or on its importance in my own scheme of goals and ends. Usually I will do both. The least eudaimonistic emotions, especially wonder, may take a very general object (the moral law), or a highly concrete object (some instance of natural beauty). (Is there background wonder? Or does wonder, as I'm inclined to think, always involve a focused awareness of some object? Wonder's non-eudaimonistic character might be relevant here: for what is especially likely to persist in the background is a structure of personal goals and plans.)

For a situational emotion to occur, it is usually necessary that the background judgment be combined with a specific judgment that situates the emotion's object in a concrete way in some actual (or imagined past or future) context. A background fear of death may become situational, when combined with a specific event in which one's vulnerability is made clear. A background anger at domestic injustice may surface as situational anger, given an event in which the woman thinks herself slighted. A pervasive jealousy about all possible rivals for the love of a certain person may be associated with an episode of particular jealousy directed toward a concrete rival.

This classification is still too crude to cover all that takes place. For example, we might find that background love gets transformed by a situation not (or not only) into situational love, but into an episode of grief. It is hard to say at what point the grief itself turns into a background emotion – since in a sense it always fixes on a particular event, and yet it may persist, sometimes conscious and sometimes unconscious, for a long time. Again, sometimes we want to say that the situational emotion is just an excuse for the surfacing of a background emotion – as happens very often in jealousy, and in domestic anger – and sometimes we want to say that it is the situation that takes priority – as when a person not in general especially motivated by anger gets angry at some particular wrong that occurs.[71] Again, we must insist that levels of generality and concreteness interweave with the background/situational distinction in many and complex ways: I may have background emotions of a highly specific sort (for example, love of my mother, or of a particular child), and situational emotions at a high level of generality (for example, anger at the situation of women in developing countries who are deprived of equal nutrition and health care).

Finally, we have to notice that some of our background emotions can be further broken down into a persisting attachment and a situational component, usually of some generality. For example, in my case of women's anger, a background attachment to one's own worth and self-respect (seen as vulnerable) is combined with a judgment that certain pervasive wrongs were taking place. In background fear of illness, again we find both attachment to one's own health and a general belief about conditions of bodily life. We might say, in fact, that the central form of a background emotion is always love or attachment to some thing or person, seen as very important for one's own flourishing – in combination with some general belief to the effect that the well-being of this thing or person is not fully under one's own control.

Many of these subtler points will occupy us in later chapters. What is important to see now is the way in which one's general conception[72] of value shapes the geography of one's emotional life, setting one up, so to speak, for the contributions of chance. The background emotion acknowledges dependence on or need for some ungovernable element in the world; the situational emotion responds to the way in which the

---

71 Notice, however, that in this case background emotions toward the thing wronged or slighted must be invoked to explain why anger surfaces.

72 I do not mean that this has to be a highly articulated or theorized conception; and indeed, frequently one would make mistakes in trying to describe what the conception is by which one guides one's actions. I mean something like an inner "evaluative grammar," some set of attachments and evaluative priorities that any person who acts and chooses, like a competent speaker of a language, has at some level, whether or not she could articulate them.

world meets or does not meet one's needs.[73] To use a very Stoic image,[74] the background emotion is the wound, the situational emotion the world's knife entering the wound.

Finally we are in a position to describe my case, trying to articulate the many different types of judgment that are at work in it. Its background judgments include the judgment that (assent to the appearance that) my mother is of enormous importance – both as a person in her own right and as an element in my life. (Indeed, the way I view her as an element in my life includes the thought of her worth in her own right.) They include, as well, the judgment that the particular relationship and history that we share has enormous importance; the more general judgment that it is very important to have and love a parent; the judgment that the human beings one loves are mortal and fragile in health; the concrete judgment that I had wronged my mother in various ways by anger and inattention; the judgment that it was possible for love to address these wrongs; and many others – corresponding to background emotions of several interweaving kinds of love, and fear, and guilt, and hope. No doubt that is only a part of the story; subsequent chapters will go into this more deeply.

These background emotions are closely associated with a whole network of beliefs and expectations at many different levels of generality, such as – the belief that it will be important to make my mother happy on her birthday and that I shall do this; the belief that she will read with pleasure the Barbara Pym novel that I gave her to read in the hospital, a novel that I do not like at all myself but know that she will like; the belief that when I next argue with her about politics it will be good not to be too hyper-logical, something she associates with a failure of love; the belief that I will talk to her on the phone in a few hours. And all the rest of a way of life.

---

73 On need and emotion, see also Kenny (1963), pp. 44–51, and Stampe (1986), pp. 167–9. Notice that it is important to distinguish the needs that I have in mind here – needs that enter into the animal's psychology in evaluative judgments – from actual needs (for example, nutritional needs) of which the animal may be unaware. Once again I insist: what is crucial for emotion is what the animal believes, not the truth of the belief. "False needs" (to use the Marxian language) are just as likely to give rise to deep emotions as are "true needs."

74 In Seneca's *Medea*, Medea notes Jason's ongoing love for their children, and observes: "He loves? Good. He is caught. There is a hole wide open for a wound." See Nussbaum (1994), Chapter 12.

We now combine this with the contribution of the chance events of the world. In the actual event, my grief was, I argued, identical to a judgment with something like the following form: "My mother, an enormously valuable person and an important part of my life, is dead." Of course, to put it this way is absurdly crude, and by now we can see that in reality we have on our hands not a single judgment, but a network of judgments at many levels of generality and specificity, some remaining in the background and some focusing on the situation, some being expectations that are frustrated by and made void by the situational judgment.[75] But what the crude formulation brings out is the way that a specific episode of grief combines a background judgment of value with a noting of the way the world is with what one values, thus combining one's ongoing goals and attachments with the perceived reality.[76]

Now that we have recognized the plurality and complexity of the judgments involved in any actual instance of grieving, the adversary, or some ally, is ready to leap in. For now, this new opponent will say, we seem to have granted as well that in any given case there is no particular proposition in this complex network that is necessary for grief. What is necessary is that a certain amount of this network remain in place, and it is by this "family resemblance" to other instances of grieving, not by strict necessary and sufficient conditions, that we seem to have identified grief. But then we can do the same thing for the nonintentional feelings and sensations: there is no particular sensation that is necessary for grief, but what is necessary is that there be some sensations within a given family. So the symmetry between thoughts and sensations seems to be reestablished; and if this has not given the old adversary everything he wanted, its jolt to my search for necessary and sufficient conditions does satisfy this sort of anticognitivist opponent.

To the new opponent I can say, first of all, that I am not persuaded that symmetry has been reestablished, even for the token instance of grieving. For I have a very good idea what sorts of concrete beliefs and judgments to look for in a case of grief, and I have a very good idea

75 Notice that both background and situational judgments have both self-referential (localized) and non-self-referential components.
76 These attachments give rise to desires and projects – and I shall say more about these motivational questions in Chapter 2.

which ones should be considered parts of the grief rather than other incidentally linked features of my makeup at the time. I do not have any such clear idea about sensations, since quite contradictory sensations seemed to me to be linked with my grief at different moments. And I think they will find that if they start to try to pin the relevant "family" down they will be inexorably drawn (despite their dislike of necessary conditions) to talk of "feelings" that are really my "thoughts" under another description, the "feelings" with rich intentional content that I described a while back.

But the really important thing of which the new opponent must be reminded is that we were claiming to find *type-identities*, not token-identities, and that our claims about the asymmetry between sensation and thought were worked out on this level. And on this level it seems to me to be unshaken. My conclusion was that in any case I have many concrete judgments, not simply the gross and general judgment, "An enormously valuable part of my life is gone." But of course my concrete judgments entail that one, and that one is the one in terms of which I would wish to identify and define grief. Even if I would not ever put the matter that way to myself, it seems to me that I do have that general judgment. (We should bear in mind that not all of the relevant judgments need be conscious.) And if I did not have that general judgment, I think I would not have grief, whatever specific judgments falling short of that I did possess. But I have argued that there is no general description of a nonintentional sensation that cites, in a similar way, a necessary condition for grieving. If this is correct, the asymmetry holds.

We can now return to the first adversary and his original motivations. For now that we have laid out the view in its entirety, we can see that it does not neglect, but in fact responds very well to, his experiential points. First, our view can explain why the emotions have heat and urgency: because they concern our most important goals and projects, the most urgent transactions we have with our world.[77] Views that make emotions cognitive without stressing that the cognitions in ques-

---

[77] This is the language used by Lazarus (1991) to describe the emotions of animals in his experimental work – on this, see Chapter 2.

tion are both evaluative and eudaimonistic have difficulty explaining urgency; mine does not. Indeed, it explains urgency better than does the adversary's view. For if there is urgency in being hit by a gust of wind, it is not after all a noncognitive urgency – the urgency, if it is there, comes not from the unthinking force, but from my thought that my well-being is threatened by that force. My view, by bringing thought about well-being right into the structure of emotion, shows why it is *the emotion itself,* and not some further reaction to it, that has urgency and heat.[78]

Second, the experience of passivity in emotion is well explained by the fact that the objects of emotion are things and people whose activities and well-being we do not ourselves control, and in whom we have invested a good measure of our own well-being. They are our hostages to fortune. In emotion we recognize our own passivity before the ungoverned events of life.

And this gives us our third answer to the adversary: the reason why in some emotional experiences the self feels torn apart (and in happier experiences filled with a marvelous sense of wholeness) is, once again, that these are transactions with a world about which we care deeply, a world that may complete us or may tear us apart. No view that makes the emotion just like a physical object hitting us can do justice to the way the world enters into the self in emotion, with enormous power to wound or to heal. For it enters in a cognitive way, in our perceptions and beliefs about what matters. Not just an arm or a leg, but a sense of life, gets the shock of grief.

A fuller answer to the adversary must, however, be given in connection with the account of emotional development to be presented in Chapter 4. One prominent reason why emotions do feel, at times, like

78 In this connection, it is now possible to respond to a point made by de Sousa (1987), who says that the major reason why emotions should not be identified with beliefs or judgments is that these can be hypothetically entertained, while emotions cannot be, are either there in all their motivating force or not there. By now, this alleged asymmetry should seem unconvincing. I may entertain any proposition without assenting to it: those with which emotions are concerned among others. But if I do not assent to the proposition, it will be just as wrong (in the nonemotion case) to say that I actually *believe* in the truth of the proposition, as it will be in the emotion case to say that I have that emotion. Entertaining the proposition that my coffee cup is red is not believing that it is red; but it is really believing, assenting, taking the proposition into oneself as true, that I am invoking to explain what emotions are.

external energies not hooked up to our current ways of valuing and appraising is that they often derive from a past that we imperfectly comprehend. We preserve in ourselves emotional material of great moment that derives from our early object relations. Often we have not scrutinized this history, and are not in a good position to say what emotions it contains. Nonetheless, these emotions continue to motivate us, and they do surface at times, sometimes with disturbing intensity, sometimes conflicting with other appraisals and emotions that pertain to our present. It is tempting, at such times, to revert to the adversary's ways of speaking – which psychoanalysis has frequently endorsed: these are drives or affective forces that really do not have an intentional evaluative content. I shall argue that this would be the wrong conclusion: we cannot explain these emotions and the way they motivate us without thinking of them as value-laden intentional attitudes toward objects.

Seeing them in this way will require us to acknowledge that the intentionality of emotions comes at different levels of sophistication and explicitness. Some emotions, even in an adult, may preserve a preverbal infant's archaic and indistinct view of the object. We therefore cannot think of all emotions as having a linguistically formulable content. This modification (which I make already in Chapter 2, in response to concerns about animal emotions) will not require us to reject any central contention of the neo-Stoic view. It will enable us to do justice to what is intuitively right in the adversary's view, as we could not do apart from a developmental account.

IX. "FRESHNESS" AND THE DIMINUTION OF GRIEF

The Greek Stoics introduce a complication into their account that we must now consider – for it arises prominently in the experience of grief. They say that a judgment, in order to be equivalent to an emotion, must be "fresh" – using a Greek word, *prosphaton*, that is used frequently of food, and also of corpses newly dead, to imply that no decomposition has set in. The point of this is to account for the sort of affective waning or distancing that takes place in grief. The suggestion is that the original proposition is retained, and that the waning must therefore be accounted for in some other way. My violent grief for my mother's death has by now grown calmer: but it seems wrong to say that I no longer believe that she is dead, and more terribly wrong to say that I no longer believe her enormously wonderful and valuable.

The adversary is ready to leap in here. For it appears that the Stoics concede that they cannot explain all the phenomena of the emotional life by appealing to cognition alone. They seem to be granting that there is something more to grieving than judgment. And mustn't this something be an irrational movement or feeling that follows laws of its own, fading while judgment remains intact? The Greek Stoics do not have a clear reply here, or if they do, it has not survived; we know only that Chrysippus said that the phenomenon of fading grief is "hard to figure out." But we need to try to figure it out, for it poses a threat to the very substance of our theory.

The real question then is: is the difference between my calmed state of August 2000 and my grief-stricken state of April 1992 a cognitive difference, or a noncognitive difference? I believe that it is a cognitive difference, but in four quite different ways. First, we have the fact that as mourning progresses the emotion is more likely to be a background emotion rather than a situational emotion, in the sense that fewer concrete situations will call it to mind. That itself means that, even while it persists, its character will alter and it will be less noticed as troubling.

Second, we must consider the place of the grief propositions in my whole cognitive organization. When I receive the knowledge of my mother's death, the wrenching character of that knowledge comes in part from the fact that it violently tears the fabric of hope, planning, and expectation that I have built up around her all my life. But when the knowledge of her death has been with me for a long time, I reorganize my other beliefs about the present and future to accord with it. I no longer have the belief that I will see my mother at Thanksgiving dinner; I no longer think of the end of a busy day as a time when I can call her up and enjoy a long talk; I no longer think of a trip abroad as an occasion to buy presents for her; I no longer expect to make happy plans to celebrate her birthday. Indeed, the experience of mourning is in great part an experience of repeatedly encountering cognitive frustration and reweaving one's cognitive fabric in consequence. I find myself about to pick up the telephone to tell her what has just happened – and then see before me that image of her lying in the hospital bed, with the tube coming out of her nose. In every area of my life in which she has played a part, I find myself expecting her to appear – and I then must work to cut short and to rearrange these expectations. This feature of grieving is discussed memorably by Proust, and is now central in the psychological literature on mourning. A vivid expression of it is found in C. S. Lewis's diary account of his mourning for his wife, Helen:

> I think I am beginning to understand why grief feels like suspense. It comes from the frustration of so many impulses that had become habitual. Thought after thought, feeling after feeling, action after action, had H for their object. Now their target is gone. I keep on, through habit, fitting an arrow to the string; then I remember and I have to lay the bow down. So many roads lead through to H. I set out on one of them. But now there's an impassable frontier-post across it. So many roads once; now so many culs-de-sac.[79]

This feature explains why the process of mourning took a different form for me than it did for my sister, for whom my mother was a regular part of each day. Although we valued and loved her equally, we did not have equal structures of expectation built up around her; and this difference, a cognitive difference, accounted for the difference in the rate at which grief began to fade. The grief thoughts remain; their relationship to other thoughts changes.

But that is not yet emotional change. I have defined emotions by their content, not by their relationship to other parts of our mental content. And I have denied that emotions should be defined in terms of surprise or change, which might involve a relation of their content to other mental contents. (I shall argue this point further in Chapter 2.) This seems right. The life of a person who has made many cognitive adjustments has less cognitive dissonance, less surprise, less frustration: but in and of itself this does not mean that there is less grief there. Mourning is in part a process of removing cognitive dissonance, but it is also a process of managing and to some extent reducing the burden of grief. So we must look elsewhere for that element of the process.

This brings us to a fundamental issue. I have said that the judgments involved in love and grief, in this and other cases, are eudaimonistic:

---

79 Lewis (1961), p. 59, discussed in Bowlby (1980), pp. 93–4. Compare Proust, *Remembrance of Things Past*, III.487: "In order to be consoled I would have to forget not one, but innumerable Albertines."

that is, they evaluate the external object or person as an important part, not of the world from some detached and impersonal viewpoint, but of the world from the viewpoint of the agent's own goals and projects. I have said that this is fully compatible with valuing the person and seeking to benefit her for her own sake; I have said that the beloved person, and the relationship of love with the person, may enter into my conception of flourishing not merely as means to my own states, but as constitutive parts of my flourishing. But it is also the case that the individuals who will be singled out for this role will be singled out on the basis of their depth in *my* life, not in someone else's, and that this sort of recognition of intrinsic worth is not easily separable (if separable at all) from the thought that without this person or relationship my own life is not complete. The thought of grief included prominently, in this way, the thought of a gaping hole in my own life.

This has implications, I think, for the analysis of mourning. First, it implies that not only the relationship of the grief-thoughts to other thoughts, but also the grief-thoughts themselves, change over time. I will still accept many of the same judgments – including judgments about my mother's death, about her worth and importance, about the badness of what happened to her. But propositions having to do with the central role of my mother in my own conception of flourishing will shift into the past tense. By now, in August 2000, it is no longer as true of me as it was in 1992 that "my mother is an important element in my flourishing"; I now am more inclined to accept the proposition, "The person who died *was* a central part of my life," and this judgmental change itself is a large part of what constitutes the diminution of grief. Some things stay constant: my judgments about her intrinsic worth, and about the badness of what happened to her, my judgment that she has figured centrally in my history. We may even say that I do not altogether remove her from my present life, since after all I have hardly ceased to write and think about her. So in one respect, my experience is still an experience of loss. But I put her into a different place in my life, one that is compatible with her being dead, and so not an ongoing active partner in conversation, love, and support. The eudaimonistic element of my beliefs has shifted, and with it the eudaimonistic aspect of my belief that I have suffered a loss. (We might add that what distinguishes normal from pathological mourning is, above all, this change of tense: the pathological mourner continues to put the dead person at the very center of her own structure of goals and expectations, and this paralyzes life.)[80]

This raises questions about identity, which are movingly discussed by Proust. For as one reweaves the fabric of one's life after a loss, and as the thoughts around which one has defined one's aims and aspirations change tense, one becomes to that extent a different person. This explains why the shift itself does not take place without a struggle: for it is a loss of self, and the self sees forgetfulness and calm as threatening to its very being. As Proust's narrator describes his first experience of equanimity after the death of Albertine: his soul, becoming conscious of happiness, began to tremble and rage like a lion who sees a snake in his cage. The snake is forgetfulness, and the lion trembles because he knows that it will get him sooner or later.[81]

Thinking about the issue of importance and centrality brings us, as well, to a second deep issue, which I can only mention here, and which will be confronted more fully in later chapters (especially Chapters 4 and 6). It would appear that there is a second difference between me and my sister, where grief is concerned: namely, that my mother did not, at the time of her death and for some years before that, play the same central role in my daily structure of goals and projects that she continued to play for my sister. This did not stem from alienation or indifference, but from geographical remoteness; nonetheless, it was true that I did not weave my life around hers in the way my sister did. I want to say, and have said, that we loved my mother equally. In one sense that is true: we ascribed intrinsic importance to her in the same way. And yet the partly eudaimonistic account of emotion I have just given seems to cast some doubt on this, suggesting that we did not just mourn differently over time, but also grieved differently from the start, and presumably, by implication, loved differently, at least where reference to our own *eudaimonia* was concerned. We did not accept the very same propositions. This issue is at the heart of many objections to the emotions, and I shall grapple with it.

But we must finally reach a fourth issue about fading grief, which derives from the qualification to the cognitive thesis that I introduced in section VII. I have said that it is typical of emotion, though not

80 See Bowlby (1980).
81 Proust, *Remembrance of Things Past*, III.455–6. On the stages of Marcel's mourning, see also III.470, 487–525, 547–8, 570, 605–9, 637, 641–2, 751.

entirely necessary, that we focus on the object in perceptual imagination, attending to many details that are not strictly relevant to the
propositional content (or that serve to concretize the particular importance of the object in a way not altogether captured in the propositional
content). But imagination fades in the person's absence. Doesn't this
mean that there is a much simpler explanation of the diminution of
grief than the one I have given? The imagination fades, and this leads
the emotion's content to shift: it is *because* I no longer see my mother
before me that I no longer make her such an important part of my life.
Such an explanation is compatible with the previous one, which appeals to a shift in the eudaimonistic propositions, and it doesn't render
the view noncognitive, since imagination is itself a highly discriminating intentional/cognitive faculty. But it suggests that cognitive activities
external to the propositional content have a dynamic role in emotional
change, influencing the shifting of the propositional content.

This is a complicated question. There is much truth in the idea that
emotions, in central human cases, need to be fortified by sensuous
perception, lose their vivacity when perception is curtailed, and can be
recalled by vivid perceptual reminders (see Chapter 6). Proust, not
implausibly, holds that we can recover our past emotional life only
through such vivid experiences. But the question now is: what is their
relationship to the judgment of salience or importance? Which comes
first, so to speak? Is it because I see this particular nightgown, or this
particular color of lipstick, that I believe that my mother is enormously
central to my life? Or is it because I already consider her at the core of
my life that I notice her nightgown with such intensity, and the sight of
that lipstick on an immobile mouth fills me with such horror? It seems
to me that there is truth in both formulations, but more truth in the
latter. It is true that the child's developing sense of its parent's centrality
is bolstered by many sensory experiences. But in the beginning, as we
shall see, the experiences are highly general, and revolve around its
own states. It is more the idea of the parent's great importance for the
child's own nutrition and comfort that causes the child to focus attention on this particular parent, than that there are characteristics of the
particular parent that makes her worthy of notice in her own right.
The child enters a situation in which it is an established fact that it will
die without certain people, and (a separate fact) that it deeply needs
their comfort; this shapes what it notices and singles out. As time goes

on, and love develops a more generous and outgoing character, the sensory recognitions will also be more complex. And of course the sheer fact of making a person a large part of one's life entails that one will spend a lot of time in the physical presence of the person, noticing the way the person looks and laying down sensory habits and memories involving that person. But once again, here it is the eudaimonistic choice that leads to the focusing, not the other way around.

Proust is right, I believe, to find in mourning (especially mourning for the death of a parent) the same direction of fit between need and sensory focusing. One misses in a primitive way what held one and gave one comfort: even when one fastens on particular details, such as the nightgown, they are complex eudaimonistic symbols of comfort and support. This suggests that it is more because the need for comfort and support fades that the sensory memory fades, rather than that the memory simply fades out on its own, causing thereby a diminution in the need for comfort and support. Both may be true to some degree; and the balance may vary in different types of relationships. But in the case of a parent's death, the Proustian account of the role of the senses has more depth. Thus, when some triggering perception reminds me of my mother's fall coat, or her way of saying "Martha," or her hairstyle – these memories are painful because they are reminders of the absence of comfort and love, rather than significant in their own right. Attached to a person other than my mother, they would mean nothing at all. They are so many signs of her. That is why they throw me back into the state of a person who has not repaired the hole in her life, who desperately needs those sources of comfort and support, and the very person whom she has loved.

We may admit, then, that fading has a cognitive dimension that is to some degree independent of the thought content, without thinking that this dimension explains very much on its own. At every point it leads us back to the thought content, and takes on significance in the light of that. Perceptual change becomes significant in large part as a corollary of the reweaving of one's needs, goals, and projects.

X. EMOTIONAL CONFLICT

The neo-Stoic view of emotion has implications for the analysis of emotional conflicts – both conflicts between emotions and other judgments and conflicts among the emotions themselves. In the adversary's view, these conflicts are viewed as struggles between two forces, simultaneously active in the soul. In the latter case we have two uncomprehending forces battling it out, like two opposing winds; in the former, we have an articulate, reasoning force doing battle somehow with such a wind – and it would appear that the only way it can keep it down is to use force, since the wind does not listen to reason. Both forces go on acting on one another, until one of them wins.

Suppose now I am grieving for my mother; I am also reading Seneca and endeavoring to be a good Stoic, distancing myself from grief with the thought that virtue is sufficient for happiness. (This is in no sense autobiographical.) The adversary's view will say that my mindless emotional part is doing the grieving, while my reason is thinking philosophical thoughts and also (somehow) trying to restrain me from grief. The neo-Stoic view would urge us, instead, to regard this conflict as a debate between recognition and denial of the importance of the loss that has occurred. At one moment I assent to the thought that an irreplaceable wonderful person has departed from my life. At another moment I deny this, saying, "No human being is worth so much concern," or "That is just a mortal human being like many others," or (if I am that morally smug), "You still have your good character, and that is all that counts." Then the thought of my mother, lying in the hospital bed as I so often saw her lying at home, returns – and I know that she is not like anyone else, and that I love her; and I assent once again to the thought that something has gone from my life that I cannot replace. (Once again: the sensuous details are reminders of significance, and come on stage to speak against the Stoic picture of value.)

The neo-Stoic view claims that this story of oscillation and shifting perspective provides a far more compelling account of the inner life of such conflicts than does the story of battle and struggle – which makes it difficult to understand how reason *could* restrain a force with which by hypothesis it could not communicate. Once we understand that the crucial cognitions are evaluative, we have no difficulty seeing the conflict as a debate about what is really the case in the world. In this rhythm of embrace and denial, this uneven intermittence of vision, we have a story of reason's urgent struggles with itself concerning nothing less than how to imagine life. To struggle against grief is to strive toward a view of the universe in which that face does not appear, luminous and wonderful, on every path, and in which the image of that lifeless form in a posture so like sleep does not stand out, like one of Charlus's mountains, above the flat landscape of daily life.

With conflicts among emotions, much the same seems true. Conflicts between fear and hope, anger and gratitude, grief and joy – these are badly explained in the adversary's way, as the battles of unthinking forces. When joy masters grief, as in my experience at the funeral, it is on the basis of certain judgments: in this case, the judgment that my mother was in certain crucial respects not gone from the world. Hope and fear contend in a more subtle way: both seem to require some uncertainty and some possibility of both good and bad outcomes, but they also differ – both (often) in their estimation of the probabilities and, more important, in what they consider salient in the pictured future. A conflict between anger and gratitude toward the same person usually revolves around assessment of harms and benefits conferred by that person, of the person's level of responsibility for these, and of their importance.

If we now consider in a more general way the passage from one emotion to another, we find that we now have a deeper understanding of why the emotions should be grouped together as a class. It is not only that fear, grief, anger, love, and the others all share certain features, the features I have tried to describe. It is also that they have a dynamic relationship to one another. Given a deep attachment to something outside one's own control, the very accidents of life, combined with that attachment to an object, will bring the person who is so attached now into intense joy, when the beloved object is at hand, now into fear, when it is threatened, now into grief, when catastrophe befalls it. When another fosters the object's good (or, to put it another way, the vulnerable aspects of the person's good) the person feels gratitude; when the other damages the object, she feels anger. When another has such a valuable object and she does not, she feels envy; when another becomes her rival with regard to such an object, she feels jealousy. In short, once she has hostages to fortune, she lets herself in for the entire gamut of the emotions, or so it seems; it will be difficult to admit some while refusing the others (although one might separate anger from the rest, if one were convinced that people never willingly do wrong). So far as the passage from one emotion to the other goes, one is in the hands of the world. In my story, hope and fear alternated, not because I wished them to alternate, but because the uncertainties of the situation produced this double thought; grief ensued not because I chose to move from hope into grief, but because an event beyond my control – given my underlying love for my mother – precipitated me into grieving. Anger was the response to the belief that the damage had a blameworthy cause – whether in others or in myself. Depression was in this case one manifestation of grief, responding to the strangeness of living in a world untenanted by that particular form. I could not have said, it seems, "I'll love my mother, but I will never have fear" – or grief, or depression, or even perhaps anger: for the reasons for those emotions were supplied by life, as it simply happened, in combination with the underlying evaluation itself.

In short, the geography of the world as seen by the emotions has two salient features: uncontrolled movement, and differences of height and depth. Think again of Proust's description of Charlus. The world of Charlus in love is compared to a landscape full of mountains and valleys, produced as if by "geological upheavals of thought"; and this differentiated landscape is contrasted with the "uniform plain" of his previous unattached life, where no idea stood out as urgent or salient, no evaluation jutted up above any other. His self-sufficient world was, we might say, very much like the world seen from the point of view of a far-distant sun, a world not yet humanized by the earthquakes of human love and limitation, which are at once comic and tragic. His new world of twisted jealousy and towering love is a more agitated world, alive as it is at every moment to small movements of thought and action in a person whom he in no way controls (and who is, besides, especially inscrutable and unreliable). And yet the narrator tells us that this world is a world "enriched" – and enriched *by the agitation itself* (*"par là même"*). This normative conclusion remains to be examined. For now, we are begining to have some idea of what it is to understand emotions as a certain sort of vision or recognition, as value-laden ways of understanding the world.

2

HUMANS AND OTHER ANIMALS

The Neo-Stoic View Revised

I. ANIMALS GRIEVING

In 55 B.C.E. the Roman leader Pompey staged a combat between humans and elephants. Surrounded in the arena, the animals perceived that they had no hope of escape. According to Pliny, they then "entreated the crowd, trying to win their compassion with indescribable gestures, bewailing their plight with a sort of lamentation." The audience, moved to pity and anger by their plight, rose to curse Pompey – feeling, writes Cicero, that the elephants had a relation of commonality (*societas*) with the human race.[1]

Flo, a female chimpanzee, died of old age by the side of a stream. Flint, her son, stayed near her corpse, grabbing one of her arms and trying to pull her up by the hand. He slept near her body all night, and in the morning he showed signs of depression. In the days following, no matter where he wandered off, he always returned to his mother's body, trying to remove the maggots from it. Finally, attacked by the maggots himself, he stopped coming back, but he stayed fifty yards away and would not move. In ten days he lost about a third of his body weight. Finally, after his mother's corpse had been removed for burial, he sat down on a rock near where she had lain down, and died. The post mortem showed no cause of death. Primatologist Jane Goodall concludes that the major cause of death had to be grief. "His whole world had revolved around Flo, and with her gone life was hollow and meaningless."[2]

---

1 The incident is discussed in Pliny, *Nat. Hist.* 8.7.20–1; Cicero, *Ad Fam.* 7.1.3; see also Dio Cassius, *Hist.* 39, 38, 2–4. See the discussion in Sorabji (1993), pp. 124–5.
2 Goodall (1990), p. 165. Goodall reports five such cases of death from grief, all involving chimpanzees under five years old at the time of the mother's death.

George Pitcher and Ed Cone were watching TV one night in their Princeton home: a documentary about a little boy in England with a congenital heart ailment. After various medical reversals, the boy died. Pitcher, sitting on the floor, found his eyes filled with tears. Instantly their two dogs, Lupa and Remus, rushed to him, almost pushing him over, and licked his eyes and cheeks with plaintive whimpers.[3]

Animals have emotions. Few who have lived closely with dogs and apes would deny this; and most researchers agree in ascribing at least some emotions to many other animals as well, including rats, the most common subjects of experimental work in this area.[4] What are the implications of this fact for the cognitive/evaluative theory of emotions?

In the previous chapter, I argued that emotions should be understood as "geological upheavals of thought": as judgments in which people acknowledge the great importance, for their own flourishing, of things that they do not fully control – and acknowledge thereby their neediness before the world and its events. I explicated this neo-Stoic view in terms of the Stoic idea of judgment as assent to an appearance. The appearances in question were value-laden, and concerned with what people see as their most important goals and projects; a lot is therefore at stake in this assenting. The best explanation of the emotions' heat and urgency, I argued, was this sort of cognitive explanation, invoking the content of (usually) eudaimonistic evaluations.

In my examples, as in the Stoics' original view, the "appearances" in question had propositional content, and I imagined this content as being linguistically formulable. *What* appears is some state of affairs in the world; but I proceeded as if that state of affairs has some handy linguistic translation that could, in principle, be made by the subject of the emotion. I said that this analysis would prove, in the end, too narrow to accommodate everything that a theory of emotion ought to accommodate.

Exactly this narrowness caused trouble for the original Stoic theory.

3 See Pitcher (1995), one of the best accounts of animal emotion, because it is not at all pretentious or flashy, but entirely dedicated to telling a detailed story of a particular pair of animals and their contribution to the emotional life of their human family.
4 See, e.g., Seligman (1975), LeDoux (1996).

Since Chrysippus understood emotions to involve the acceptance of *lekta,* proposition-like entities corresponding to the sentences in a language, it seemed to him obvious that creatures not endowed with linguistic capabilities could not have them; he concluded that popular ascriptions of emotion to animals (and young children) were based on a kind of loose and illegitimate anthropomorphizing.[5] Critics such as the Stoic Posidonius and the Platonist Galen insisted that animals obviously have fear and anger and grief. Since they agreed with Chrysippus about the capacity of animals for learning and judgment, they believed this a knock-down objection to Chrysippus' analysis of emotion as judgment. Emotions, they concluded, must be "nonreasoning movements" (*aloga pathê*), housed in a separate nonreasoning part of the soul.[6]

Both of these views are unpalatable. Chrysippus' view flies in the face of our experiences of commonality between ourselves and many animals. It also makes it impossible for us to give an adequate account of emotional development in infants and young children. Posidonius' view neglects the emotions' object-directed intentionality and their connection to beliefs about the world. But we are not forced to choose between these two views, since they share a false premise: that animals are incapable of intentionality, selective attention, and appraisal.[7]

In this chapter I ask how reflecting about animal emotions should cause us to revise the theory of Chapter 1. Animal emotion is by now the subject of a vast cross-disciplinary literature. In no sense do I pretend to offer a comprehensive account of the topic: I pursue those pieces of it that are of most importance for my question. I approach

5 On this topic, see Sorabji (1993), Labarrière (1993); Sorabji argues, however, that the denial is not fully consistent, since Chrysippus is forced to ascribe to animals perception with a complex content, involving something like predication. A view similar to that of Chrysippus has recently been defended by Averill (1980): the application of emotion-terms to animals is "primarily metaphorical and derivative" (p. 306); "most physiological theories are based on animal studies and hence are only tangentially related to human emotions" (p. 307). See also Averill (1968, 1982).

6 On the debate between Chrysippus and Posidonius, and its implications for the analysis of poetry and music, see Nussbaum (1993a).

7 On the origins of the false premise, see Sorabji (1993), which puts the blame entirely on the Stoics, and Rachels (1990). In the ancient world, Aristotle had a much more promising account of the continuity between humans and other animals, although he did not develop a clear account of animal emotion. For a summary of modern studies of primate cognition (linked to a very inadequate historical account), see Wise (2000).

the topic from two complementary angles. First, I focus on some aspects of current experimental work in cognitive psychology, where a cognitive/evaluative view has recently displaced various reductionist accounts of emotion. This work is closely connected to work in evolutionary biology, since the claim of the new cognitivists is that their account of emotion offers a superior account of the emotions' adaptive significance. But since the theory of Chapter 1 was itself based on close attention to narratives of experience, we should attempt to use the same method here as well. Although we inevitably lack first-person reports in the animal case, we can come as close to that as possible by focusing on a detailed narrative account of the emotions of particular animals, made by an observer who has unusual empathy and unusual awareness of the specific capacities of the animals in question. I find such an account in George Pitcher's biography of his dogs, Lupa and Remus.[8] This account is consistent with scientific accounts and it enables us to appreciate the contribution of such accounts from a different perspective. And it reminds us, as well, that all such scientific accounts must begin with experiences of interaction between humans and animals, and are thus only as rich as are the capacities of the scientist for observation and empathy.[9]

I shall conclude that the basic outlines of the theory advanced in Chapter 1 can still be defended in the light of the evidence concerning animals; but I shall also argue that the theory must undergo some major modifications if it is to meet this challenge, modifications that will make it more adequate as an account of human emotions as well. I hope it will emerge that a philosophical and humanistic account of the emotions, as this one is, need not be unscientific or indifferent to scientific evidence, and also that an account responsive to that evidence need not be, indeed should not be, reductionistic, or indifferent to the complex object-directed intentionality of the emotions. Having made the necessary revisions in the theory, I shall then explore some further distinctions that could not profitably be discussed at an earlier stage of the argument: distinctions between emotions and appetites, emotions and moods, emotions and desires for action.

8 Pitcher (1995).
9 See Wise (2000) for examples both good and bad. And see Introduction for further methodological discussion.

II. THE DECLINE OF REDUCTIONIST THEORIES
OF EMOTION

Psychological approaches to animal emotion have been handicapped until recently by various forms of physical reductionism that ignored, or even denied, the role of the creature's own interpretations of the world. Such views have not altogether disappeared. If we want to modify our own view in the light of the best work in psychology, we therefore need to understand the reasons for the decline of reductionist theories and the resurgence of cognitive theories. Since these cognitive theories have, in turn, been challenged from the point of view of new physiological research, research that is in some cases more conceptually subtle and sophisticated than some of the old reductionist research programs, we must see exactly what form this challenge takes, and how far it goes. My ultimate aim will be to understand what modifications experimental work really does require us to make in the theory outlined so far, and what modifications would be unnecessary concessions to lingering reductionism.[10]

Fifty years ago, most psychologists scoffed at the idea that the study of emotion was an important part of their job. In their zeal to dismiss the inner world of experience, psychologists in the grip of the newly fashionable behaviorism predicted that emotion would soon disappear from the scientific scene, as a "vague" and "unobservable" phenomenon, a relic of our prescientific past. A typical piece of the rhetoric of the period is M. F. Meyer's statement:

Why introduce into science an unneeded term, such as emotion, when there are already scientific terms for everything we have to describe? . . . I predict: the "will" has virtually passed out of our scientific psychology today; the "emotion" is bound to do the same. In 1950 American psychologists will smile at both these terms as curiosities of the past.[11]

---

10 Some of this work uses human subjects, but its aim is in general to understand the animal basis of emotional life. Typically, we find animal subjects used whenever the experimenter intends to inflict pain or distress, human subjects whenever the subject's self-report about emotional state is crucial to the experimental design. Many experiments, of course, involve neither of these elements and can be run with both types of subjects.

11 Meyer (1933), p. 300, quoted by Lazarus (1991), p. 8, and also by Hillman (1960); Hillman reproduces an extensive sample of such statements, ranging in date from the 1930s to the early 1950s.

The prophecy was not fulfilled. Indeed, recent years have seen an increasing preoccupation with emotion in psychology, and the production of works of increasing subtlety and philosophical, as well as experimental, sophistication. By now virtually all major investigators in the area grant that emotions can and should be studied by psychology, *and* that emotions are richly cognitive phenomena, closely connected with the animal's ways of perceiving and interpreting the world.[12] As Richard Lazarus remarks with irony, psychology has now fought its way back to the place where Aristotle was when he wrote the *Rhetoric* – by which he means a position in which intentionality is taken seriously and regarded as part of what any good theory must include.[13] What brought this progress (or regress) about?

The hope for the elimination of emotion from psychological discourse rested on two more general hopes: the hope for the success of radical behaviorism, which would replace all talk of the creature's own interpretive activity with talk of stimulus inputs and behavioral responses, and the hope for a successful physiological reductionism, that is, for a physiological view that would make reference to intentionality and interpretation completely eliminable. At one point during the rise of behaviorism, it was simply assumed that all "nonobservables" would soon prove to be otiose in psychological explanation, and that belief–desire explanations would be replaced by stimulus–response explanations, in which the creature's own thoughts and interpretations would be bypassed altogether, and emotion with these. Such simple models of behavior, however, kept proving to be inadequate as predictive and explanatory accounts; it came to be recognized that S–R models would have to be replaced by S–O–R (stimulus–organism–response) models of a far more complicated sort.[14] This recognition was prompted by experimental results in the area of learning, where it became clear that the animal's own view of its situation, and of the stimuli to which it was subjected, were crucial explanatory

---

12 Even those who officially deny the cognitive view – for example, R. B. Zajonc (1980, 1984) and J. Weinrich (1980), both of whom I shall shortly discuss – unofficially concede cognitivism in the language that they use to describe their own views.

13 Lazarus (1991), p. 14: "Ironically, these changes in outlook also brought us back to a kind of 'folk psychology' once found in Aristotle's *Rhetoric*."

14 An elegant brief account of this history is in Lazarus (1991), pp. 8–15, "The Retreat from Radical Behaviorism and the Rise of Cognitivism," with many references to the literature.

factors.[15] An important part of this experimental work was Seligman's work on learned helplessness, which I shall shortly describe.

At roughly the same time, philosophers effectively attacked the conceptual foundations of behaviorist psychology, arguing for the irreducibility of intentional concepts and giving reasons for finding nonintentional accounts of animal behavior inadequate.[16] Psychologists, however, often failed to acknowledge these conceptual and foundational points; they kept trying to salvage the behaviorist program until they were forced to reject it because of its predictive failures.[17] This was in retrospect a blessing in disguise: for now it is clear that the behaviorist program failed on its own terms, as an explanatory scientific theory. Thus even those who are skeptical of philosophical analysis and the contribution it can make to scientific understanding should grant that the critique of behaviorism has had force.

But the demise of simple behaviorism did not lead directly to a more complex and conceptually sophisticated approach to the study of animal or human emotion. The hope persisted, in at least some quarters, that if emotion could not be eliminated in favor of stimulus–response explanations, it might at least be reduced to some relatively simple physiological response that could then be studied without concern for the creature's own interpretations. Once again, philosophers had already argued plausibly that the attempt to eliminate intentionality from emotion rests on a conceptual confusion.[18] But such criticisms went unheeded for a long time. The research program of emotion psychology

15 See Lazarus (1991), p. 11.
16 See Kenny (1963), C. Taylor (1964), Pitcher (1965); Taylor's work deals extensively with the explanation of animal behavior. Some of this work draws on the more general work of Roderick Chisholm on intentionality: see, for example, Chisholm (1957). Chisholm attacks behaviorism in his seminal article on intentionality, "Sentences about Believing" (1956). His arguments are used in the debate by Kenny (pp. 197ff.), along with related arguments of Aristotle, Aquinas, and Brentano.
17 Lazarus (1991) is unusual in recognizing that philosophical confusions have marred much of his colleagues' work; and his arguments rely as much on philosophical as on experimental considerations. Averill and Oatley also emphasize the need for greater conceptual clarity.
18 See Kenny (1963), pp. 48–9: ". . . a bodily state is not *qua* bodily state an emotional state; for it is only if it occurs in the appropriate circumstances that we can call it an emotional state at all . . . The occasion on which an emotion is elicited is part of the criterion for the nature of the emotion." See also Pitcher (1965); Pitcher is less concerned with physiological views than with Humean views focusing on sensation; nonetheless, the arguments are valuable against such views as well.

during the 1960s and 1970s, for human and animal emotions alike, could fairly be characterized as follows:[19]

Find a set of physiological indicators of the emotion, do a validity study showing that human subjects' introspections correlate with these indicators, argue that these indicators reliably reveal the feeling of the emotion, and then enshrine these physiological indicators as the definition of the expression of the emotion in future studies.[20]

(The description is that of James Weinrich, at the time a leading young experimentalist, asked in 1980 to produce a retrospective account of recent research in the area.) This program was inspired not only by the general atmosphere surrounding behaviorism, but also by the earlier and still pervasive influence of the James/Lange theory of emotions, which had led researchers to expect a correlation between an emotion and a discernible physical state. Another influential source of physiological reductionism in emotion theory of the time was the hydraulic conception of emotion characteristic of early Freudian psychoanalysis. Since this was a less direct influence on experimental psychology, I shall not discuss it further here.

It is likely that if subjects' judgments about concrete experiences of emotion had been studied by the physiological reductionists with the systematic care with which philosophers had long been studying them, this would have called that entire research program into question. And indeed there had long been experimental thinkers who did express skepticism about the elimination of intentionality, on grounds related to those advanced in the philosophical accounts.[21] The intentional focus of an emotion on an object seemed to play an ineliminable role in subjects' identifications of what emotions they were feeling. But even though this could have been noticed in many different ways, and indeed

19 This summary is taken from Weinrich (1980), p. 125. Weinrich was at that time an evolutionary psychologist; more recently he has focused on the biology and psychology of sexual orientation. But he here gives an accurate characterization of what was going on in emotion psychology generally.

20 We may safely ignore the phrase "expression of the," since in the rest of his account Weinrich talks of defining the emotions themselves, and makes no systematic distinction between an emotion and its behavioral expression.

21 See Lazarus (1991) and Oatley (1992), both of whom give an account of the development of their own thinking and that of like-minded scientists. Mandler (1975) is another figure who contributed significantly to the resurgence of interpretive theories.

was, it took an experimental result that was on its own terms pretty unsatisfactory to stimulate the profession as a whole to investigate intentional theories once again.

In a now-famous set of experiments, Stanley Schachter and J. E. Singer[22] set out to demonstrate that people's cognitions about the situation they are in are essential elements in their self-report of their emotional state. (This work was meant to have implications for other animals as well, and was closely linked to experimental work the authors had been doing with animals.) The researchers begin by noting that for years experimenters had sought to find physiological ways to individuate one emotion from another, and had utterly failed to do so. Already in 1929, W. B. Cannon had criticized the physiological program (which he traced to the influence of the James/Lange theory of emotions) by noting that "the same visceral changes occur in very different emotional states and in non-emotional states."[23] Cannon also noted that sympathectomized animals and humans manifest emotional behavior and report emotions, even though they have no correlated physical states.[24] Subsequent experiments for the most part found no reliable correlation at all between emotional state and physiological state; those that found any physiological patterns at all found at most two different states, correlated with a wide range of emotional states. The researchers now describe somewhat quaintly the perplexity into which these results thrust a field so dominated by physiological paradigms:

Since as human beings, rather than as scientists, we have no difficulty identifying, labeling, and distinguishing among our feelings, the results of these studies have long seemed rather puzzling and paradoxical. Perhaps because of this, there has been a persistent tendency to discount such results as due to ignorance or methodological inadequacy and to pay far more attention to the very few studies which demonstrate *some* sort of physiological differences among emotional states than to the very many studies which indicate no differences at all.[25]

22 Schachter and Singer (1962).
23 Cannon (1929), p. 351, quoted in Schachter and Singer (1962), p. 379.
24 Cannon (1929), p. 350. Noting that both James's and Lange's theories would predict that such animals would be wholly without emotion, Cannon observes that the animals acted "with no lessening of the intensity of the emotional display, . . . behaving as angrily, as joyfully, as fearfully as ever."
25 Ibid., p. 397.

To this one might reply that the puzzle goes the other way: why did scientists for so long refuse to let their own insights "as human beings" influence the science they did, when they were all along relying, in some respects, on the ability of human subjects to classify emotions?

The Schachter–Singer experiments reached the conclusion that subjects' evaluative appraisals of the situation they are in are a necessary part of their emotional state, central to the identification of an emotion and to the individuation of one emotion from another. Given one and the same induced physiological condition, subjects will identify their emotion as anger if placed in a situation in which they are given reasons to be angry (e.g., at the experimenters for their insulting and intrusive questions); they will identify their emotion as happiness if put in a situation where they are given reasons to think the world is great (it's fun to play basketball), and so on. This is the familiar philosophical thesis of the irreducibility of the intentional, a thesis that has been advanced again and again in philosophy, not in a way that is hostile to scientific explanation, but in order to indicate what an adequate scientific explanation would have to include. The experimenters also hoped to show that the general state of physiological arousal induced by an epinephrine injection was a necessary condition of emotional response, but the experiment failed to confirm this result. Thus they did not even get the very weak link to a physiological condition that they had expected to get.

As has often been argued, the experiments had some serious conceptual weaknesses; and it is thus not too surprising that the results proved difficult to replicate.[26] Other antibehaviorist experimental work, for example that of Seligman, seems far more adequate in conceptual design. The primary importance of Schachter–Singer was the impetus it gave to the rising generation of researchers to try out more complex

26 See Reisenzein (1983). To the many criticisms that have been proferred, I would add that the experiment oddly confuses emotional "contagion" between stooge and subject with a shared emotional *response* to a situation. (Thus the fact that the subject comes to share the stooge's anger at an intrusive questionnaire is put down to contagion, when a more natural inference is that the stooge drew the subject's attention to features of the questionnaire that gave him reason for anger.) Furthermore, its subjects, all male undergraduates, seem to have an impoverished conception of emotion: running around throwing paper airplanes is supposed to be a paradigm of happiness. It is actually rather surprising that subjects did share the stooge's "happiness," rather than simply getting irritated at him; perhaps this too is to be attributed to the narrow subject population.

paradigms and to loosen their commitment to a simple type of physio-logical reductionism. Most psychologists abandoned the search for physiological definitions of emotional state, although some persisted for a time in the search, focusing on erotic love and its connection to bodily sexual arousal. The attempt to define love in terms of changes in penile blood volume is a bizarrely comical corner of our subject, which shows the dogmatic adherence of some psychologists to the physiological program, but since it sheds no light on animal emotions, or on the development of an adequate theory, it may be bypassed here.[27] I turn now to the views that give intentionality and interpreta-

27 See Weinrich (1980), with copious reference to the experimental literature. Weinrich announces that he studied love because he believed that the Schachter–Singer experiment had made the goal of finding a single simple physiological account of anger and fear look difficult to attain. But he believes that "genital plethysmography offers an important opportunity to study objectively an emotion of importance to anyone who has ever fallen in love" (p. 135). He hopes its success will lead to a broader research program that will ultimately encompass other emotions as well. Despite the oddities of the claims, they are worth studying because many forms of physiological reductionism contain similar errors in a less transparent and charming form.

The experimental design has an elegant simplicity. A "penile plethysmograph" is "essentially a volume-measuring device connected to a small chamber placed over a man's penis . . . In this way the degree of erection, and thus of sexual arousal, is measured directly." The vaginal plethysmograph, by contrast, "is a probe that reflects and measures light off the vaginal wall," indicating vaginal blood volume. Weinrich mentions that since this latter instrument is still under development, "there are few results for women."

The plethysmograph is, then, applied. If it proves possible for the man to have an erection while hooked up to this device, it measures the change in penile blood volume. This new measure is now taken to be the measure – not just of sexual *arousal*, but of sexual *desire*, and not just of sexual desire, but of "*the emotion*" (sometimes called "a sexual emotion" and sometimes called "being in love").

First, does the plethysmograph even measure sexual arousal? Perhaps it is a useful measure of relative sexual arousal in different circumstances in a particular subject (the use for which it was actually designed by sex therapists). Even this may be doubted. For it is well known that certain medications (some antidepressants, for example) produce increased ease in having an erection, in combination with decreased sensation and decreased ease in attaining orgasm. It would not be unnatural to describe that condition as one of decreased arousal, by contrast to one's unmedicated condition. At the same time some medical conditions, such as diabetes, impede erection without affecting sensation and orgasm. Again, it is not obvious that a man who does not have a full erection, but who has intense pleasure and orgasm, should be taken to be less aroused than he was on every occasion when he had a full erection. In short, even a single person's sexual arousal has multiple dimensions, not all of which are measured in Weinrich's philosophy.

Turning now to interpersonal comparisons of arousal, should one conclude, as Weinrich's definition would appear to entail, that a man with a larger penile blood

tion an important role in the account of what emotions are and of what role they play in animal behavior.

III. THE RESURGENCE OF INTENTIONALITY:
SELIGMAN, LAZARUS, ORTONY, OATLEY

What, then, has been established by the new nonreductionist[28] accounts, and how should their scientific findings about both humans and animals cause us to modify the account we have presented? I turn first to a study that illuminates both general issues about emotion and cognition and also some substantive issues concerning connections between depression and action. Martin Seligman's *Helplessness: On Depression, Development, and Death* is by now a classic in the field, and has been highly influential outside it, together with Seligman's later modifications of his view.[29] The work remains morally controversial,

---

volume is more sexually aroused, or more capable of arousal, than a man with a smaller blood volume? One might hesitate to draw that conclusion. Should one, moreover, grant that erection is either necessary or sufficient for sexual arousal? Weinrich himself concedes that it is not sufficient, when he mentions that "males in many species have erections when they assert dominance over other males; the relationship between this form and 'pure' sexual arousal could be clarified." One could cite more mundane examples, such as erections on waking up in the morning, erections of small infants, the well-known phenomenon of erection at death from hanging. None of these seem to me to be cases of sexual arousal, "pure" or impure. Why not? Presumably because they lack the right sort of object-directed intentionality. As for necessity, would one really want to grant that a person with an injury that makes erection impossible is incapable of arousal? That, in general, impotence is incompatible with arousal?

But if these questions cast grave doubt on the prospect of using plethysmography as a measure of sexual *arousal*, it is self-evident that they vitiate the project of using it as a measure of sexual *desire* – for all the reasons so far given, and still others. Desire is an intentional notion; so no description of a subject's nonintentional physiological state will suffice as an account of it. And the problems we had with necessity become more obvious: for if it seems plausible that a person without an erection might still be said to be aroused, it is perfectly evident that such a person may be said to have sexual desire. Among other things, Weinrich has defined away the entire problem of male impotence: for if there is no erection there is by his definition no desire, and therefore no project being frustrated, unless it is the (not negligible) project of manifesting one's masculine control. And need we even speak of defining the emotion of erotic love? Does Viagra really make men more loving, or even more in love? We must wait until a later chapter to apply the plethysmograph to Heathcliff.

28 From now on I shall use "reductionism" as a shorthand for "physiological reductionism," alluding to the type of view described in the previous sections.

29 Seligman (1975); for an "updating" of the theory, see Abramson, Seligman, and Teasdale (1978). Seligman's work has been very influential in psychology; and, unlike most

for its treatment of subject animals; I do not conceal the moral unease it causes me to describe these experiments.[30] On the other hand, the work is of remarkable rigor and insight, and it offers surprising illumination for our topic. The topic of Seligman's work is depression, in both humans and animals, and the connection of depression to the belief that one is helpless to control one's environment. Its thesis is that a belief in one's own helplessness produces depressive emotion in animals as diverse as humans, dogs, and rats; that this depressive emotion is cognitive, involving complex evaluative appraisals; and that it has complex and alarming behavioral consequences, ranging from inability to learn to sudden death.

Seligman's central experiment is as follows. Dogs are placed in a device known as a "shuttle box," with a barrier down the middle. Shortly after a signal given by a light, a shock is applied to the side of the box in which the dog has been placed. By jumping the barrier the dog may escape the shock. Dogs usually learn to do this very quickly, and are soon jumping with ease before the shock, as soon as the light goes on. We now take a group of dogs and strap them into a hammock. Shocks are applied to them, and there is nothing they can do to alter or terminate the shock.[31] After some experience of this situation of helplessness, the dogs are now placed in the shuttle box and given the same opportunities for evasive learning that led to fluent escape behavior in normal dogs. The previously helpless dogs prove unable to

work in psychology – perhaps because of its argumentative rigor – it has affected the work of philosophers; see especially Graham (1990).

30 Seligman is sensitive to criticism concerning the nature of his animal experiments, and defends himself by employing a frank anthropocentrism: "To my mind they are by and large not only justifiable, but, for scientists whose basic commitment is to the alleviation of human misery, not to do them would be unjustifiable. In my opinion, each scientist must ask himself one question before doing any experiment on an animal: Is it likely that the pain and deprivation that this animal is about to endure will be greatly outweighed by the resulting alleviation of human pain and deprivation? If the answer is yes, the experiment is justified." (p. xi). This anthropocentric justification may be adequate for rats, but hardly for dogs. If Seligman had a mediocre mind, it would be easy to conclude that the work should not be pursued. Since he has one of the few profound and excellent minds in the field, the work poses a tragic moral dilemma.

31 See Seligman (1975), p. 21, where he describes the accidental discovery of helplessness phenomena in the process of performing a different experiment on conditioning. He carefully shows how the conditions meet his definition of uncontrollability: "No voluntary response the animal made – tail wagging, struggling in the hammock, barking – could influence the shocks. Their onset, offset, duration, and intensity were determined only by the experimenter."

learn to escape. They sit languid and huddled in the box, making no voluntary response. For they have learned that voluntary responding does no good. It is only when, by dint of much effort, researchers again and again drag the whole weight of the dog across the barrier, showing it in this laborious way that escape is possible, that they begin to learn to undertake escape for themselves. Many variants on this experiment are tried, with different species, different varieties of control or noncontrol, and different sorts of uncontrolled outcomes, both good and bad.[32]

Before I describe Seligman's theory, let me note that both he and some other psychologists whose work I shall be describing in this section are confirmed representationalists. That is, they assume that the natural and best way to describe the way an animal fixes on a situation or object in the world, and to convey to their readers the fact that it is the way the world appears to the animal that has explanatory salience, is to invoke an internal mental representation. They never debate the relative merits of inner representationalism and other ways of construing intentionality. This does not seem to me to be damaging to the basic claims of their theories: one could replace the representationalist language with another account of interpretation or seeing-as, without changing much else. So for the sake of simplicity I shall present their claims in their own language, while myself remaining agnostic, as before, about representationalism.

On the basis of these experiments, Seligman argues for his theory of helplessness, fear, and depression. The theory has three components: (1) information about the contingency in question; (2) cognitive representation of the contingency in the animal; and (3) behavior.[33] It is a central part of the work to argue that the animal's behavior cannot be explained without mentioning its cognitive representations of the

32 A result that might have controversial political implications: the free gift of food to pigeons, without effort, inhibits voluntary responding when they later need to search for food. Seligman notes that this might be used in connection with criticisms of the welfare state: but of course it doesn't show that people who are given food and health care don't learn to work or strive *in some other way*; it just shows that they probably won't be good at foraging for their food, or providing for their own health care. Most of us don't teach our children to forage for food; we feed them instead. But we don't think that this makes them altogether incapable of voluntary responding, and of course it doesn't.

33 Seligman (1975), p. 47.

world, and that these representations include an idea of control or uncontrol in important matters. (This is supported experimentally by devising experiments in which subjects have false beliefs about their degree of control over the environmental contingency; these results show that it is belief and expectation, not actual controllability, that determine the outcome.)[34] The theory of helplessness constructed from these components makes three claims:

the expectation that an outcome is independent of responding (1) reduces the motivation to control the outcome; (2) interferes with learning that responding controls the outcome; and, if the outcome is traumatic, (3) produces fear for as long as the subject is uncertain of the uncontrollability of the outcome, and then produces depression.[35]

The major modification that Seligman has subsequently introduced[36] is to emphasize the importance of the subject's interpretation of the failure of control: there is a great difference, it seems, between cases in which the subject believes that the failure to control the outcome is due to an avoidable personal failure that could be corrected by more effort, and cases in which the subject feels genuinely powerless to do anything about the problem. A growing experimental literature applies these insights to various learning differences among humans – between males and females, between poor and privileged children, between racial minorities and the dominant racial group. Seligman has argued that an attitude of optimism about one's possibilities for attaining important goals is an important part of maintaining successful agency.[37]

Seligman's theory is important for our own account of the continuity between humans and animals, not only because it defends a cognitive/ evaluative view, but also because of its specific content regarding helplessness and loss.[38] How does Seligman commend his cognitivist ac-

34 Ibid., pp. 48–9.
35 Ibid., pp. 55–6. Further experiments added *predictability* and *unpredictability* to the variables, showing that where controllability remained constant, unpredictability made things worse – see the reports of Weiss (1968, 1970, 1971) on p. 118.
36 Abramson et al. (1978).
37 Seligman (1990).
38 The early focus on animals made it difficult to do justice to the prominent role of self-blame in human depression; and even in the later work, Seligman's rather optimistic take on situations of self-blame, which he thinks of as more promising because more closely connected with will and change, may neglect important elements of human self-torment.

count of helplessness against noncognitivist rivals? The book argues against three distinct opponents.

The first opponent alleges that helplessness behavior can be explained without ascribing complex value-laden learning to the animal – by supposing that while in the hammock the dog has learned some *other motor response* that competes with barrier jumping later on – for example, a response such as freezing, which may in some cases diminish the severity of the shock, whereas active responding may exacerbate it. Seligman argues against this hypothesis in three ways. First, he points out that it involves a logical difficulty: for if active responding is occasionally "punished" by shock onset, it is also occasionally "rewarded" by shock termination. Second, he shows experimentally that dogs whose muscles are entirely paralyzed with curare while in the hammock behave subsequently like the nonparalyzed subjects. Third, he points to the "passive-escape" experiment devised by S. F. Maier to rule out the opponent's hypothesis.[39] The dogs in this experiment *can* control the shock – but only by remaining completely still and passive. The opponent's response-learning hypothesis makes the prediction that these dogs will later prove the most helpless in the shuttle box; the Seligman learned-helplessness hypothesis makes the prediction that they will prove capable of learning just like other dogs who have learned that what they choose to do makes a difference. The Seligman hypothesis is experimentally confirmed: these dogs jump the barrier like normal dogs. Similar results obtain for rats.[40]

A second group of opponents allege that the reason why the dogs shocked in the hammock fail to learn to jump in the box is that they have become *adapted* to the shock or (alternatively) are simply too *exhausted* by the shocks to do anything about further shocks. Again, this is experimentally disconfirmed – largely (I am here simplifying a complex argument) by showing that severe shocks previously received do not lead to inability to learn to respond in the box if the animal retains some degree of control over escape possibilities. It is the helplessness, not the shock, that is explanatory. Moreover, adaptation to intense pain has never been demonstrated.[41]

Finally, Seligman turns to physiological explanations. He reminds us that the cognitive condition is itself enmattered, and that in that sense

39 Maier (1970); see Seligman (1975), pp. 64–5.
40 Seligman (1975), pp. 62–5.
41 Ibid., pp. 65–8.

a cognitive account does not rule out a physiological account, if we should find reliable correlations between some physiological conditions and the cognitive condition. In this sense LeDoux's recent work, which we shall discuss in section IV, suggests further development of Seligman's theory, since it offers some ways of understanding the persistence of emotional conditioning, despite relearning. (LeDoux's work, as we shall see, is in no way hostile to cognitive theories: indeed, it is explicitly cognitive in its claim that the fright message is transmitted to the auditory cortex, and involves the sensory awareness of an object as dangerous.)

Seligman then turns to the claim that helplessness behavior in animals is caused not via any cognitive representation, but *directly*, without such representations, by norepinephrine (NE) depletion alone (a view reminiscent of the view that Schachter and Singer argued against for human subjects). It proves possible to produce circumstances in which rats who have had helplessness conditioning do not have NE depletion – which is in most cases associated with this conditioning. The NE depletion view predicts that these rats will exhibit helplessness behavior; the cognitive view predicts that they will not. In an ingenious experiment by Weiss,[42] the noncognitive view was confirmed: the non-depleted rats escaped and avoided like normal rats. But when Maier, Seligman, and others attempted to replicate this result, they got a very different result: their rats failed completely to escape shock. This issue, then, remains unclear; but there are other data that the cognitive theory can explain that cannot be explained by the NE theory. First, there are many other cases in which helplessness conditioning does not produce NE depletion: and yet, helplessness behavior results.[43] Again, NE depletion is always transient; yet helplessness conditioning proves relatively permanent in rats. Finally, teaching rats or dogs how to turn off the shock, by dragging the animals through the response, can undo helplessness conditioning, although there is no reason to think that this training suddenly restores NE.[44] Other data suggests, in similar fashion, that a greater understanding of physiological phenomena will complement, and not displace, cognitive hypotheses.[45]

---

42 Weiss, Stone, and Harrell (1970); Weiss, Glazer, and Pohorecky (1974).
43 Such are cases where humans and rats receive unsolvable discrimination problems, and fail to solve subsequent problems, although they do not become NE depleted.
44 Seligman (1975), pp. 71–3.
45 Ibid., pp. 68–74.

Seligman's work is not directed to the analysis of emotion per se. He does not attempt to produce definitions of emotions such as fear and (cognitive) depression, and frequently he speaks loosely, as if the cognition and the emotion were distinct phenomena. His work is tremendously suggestive for the analysis of these emotions, and their connections with helplessness and control; it shows that animal behavior cannot be well explained without ascribing to animals a rich cognitive life, including evaluations of many sorts concerning elements in their own flourishing and their relation to those elements. It obviously explains well instances of animal grief and its occasionally devastating effects, as in the case of Flo and her young son. But the implications of experimental work for the development of *theories* of emotion in cognitive psychology have been drawn by others, rather than by Seligman himself. Theories embodying these and related insights have been advanced by Richard Lazarus, Keith Oatley, and Anthony Ortony.[46] I shall not describe the experimental data that ground them; I simply describe the theories, which converge remarkably with the neo-Stoic position.

For Richard Lazarus, emotions are "appraisals" in which an animal recognizes that something of importance for its own goals is at stake in what is going on in the environment. In other words, they are urgent transactions between an animal and its world, in which the animal takes in "news" about how things stand in its ongoing relationship with the environment.[47] We begin with the fact that animals need things from their world. They are organized systems living in an environment and adapting to it. They therefore need to attend closely to what is going on in that environment, and to assess it as it bears on their goals. Emotions are forms of intense attention and engagement, in which the world is appraised in its relation to the self.

46 Lazarus (1991), Oatley (1992), Ortony et al. (1988). Lazarus and Oatley developed elements of their views in numerous articles over the years, before summarizing them in book form; similarly, Oatley published a series of articles beginning in the 1970s: see particularly Oatley and Johnson-Laird (1987), Oatley and Bolton (1985). See also the related work of Mandler (1975) – important as a background to Oatley's work – and Fridja (1986), and the attachment theory of Bowlby, now supplemented by Sarah Hrdy's work with primates, described in Hrdy (1999). I shall discuss Bowlby and Hrdy further in Chapter 4.

47 Lazarus (1991, see pp. 16, 30, 38, 39, and passim). It will be seen that Lazarus frequently uses the word "person," focusing on the human rather than the animal case. But his is nonetheless a general theory, supported by animal data. The human side of the theory is further developed in Lazarus and Lazarus (1994).

What I propose is that to engender emotion an adaptational encounter must center on some *personal business*, as it were; it is an ongoing transaction between person and environment having a bearing on personal goals, which are brought to the encounter and with respect to which the environmental conditions are relevant . . . [T]he person must decide whether what is going on is relevant to important values or goals. Does it impugn one's identity? Does it highlight one's inadequacy? Does it pose a danger to one's social status? Does it result in an important loss? Is it a challenge that can be overcome, or a harm that one is helpless to redress? Or is it a source of happiness or pride?[48]

Individual emotions are defined with reference to particular types of relationship that may obtain between a creature and its world, what Lazarus calls "core relational themes," which specify "the personal harms and benefits residing in each person-environment relationship."[49] A taxonomy of emotions is thus a taxonomy of a creature's goals, in relation to environmental events and temporal location. Taken as a group, a creature's emotions summarize the way it conceives of its very identity in the world, its sense of what selfhood is and what is central to selfhood.

An especially useful taxonomy of both animal and human emotions, in the spirit of Lazarus's theory, has been developed by Anthony Ortony and his coauthors,[50] who hold that emotions should be classified (1) by temporal reference – direction with respect to a state of affairs or event or action past, present, or future; (2) by the self–other distinction – one appraises events as good/bad for oneself, and also as good/bad for others; and above all (3) by the good–bad distinction. Thus, for example, under emotions connected with the present fortunes of others, we have four major categories: (a) emotions that see an event that is good for another as a good thing – congratulatory and empathetically joyful emotions; (b) emotions that see an event that is good for another as a bad thing – envious and resentful emotions; (c) emotions that see an event that is bad for another as a bad thing – pity or compassion; (d) emotions that see an event that is bad for another as a good thing – spite and gloating. Notice that this taxonomy is very similar to ancient Stoic taxonomies, with the important addition of the

48 Lazarus (1991), pp. 30–1; see also p. 39.
49 Ibid., p. 39.
50 Ortony, Clore, and Collins (1988).

self–other distinction, and the addition of the past to the present and future.

Lazarus makes it clear that these appraisals are made from the creature's own point of view, on the basis of the information that it has: the "cognitive appraisals" are in that sense "subjective evaluations." But since emotions are urgent transactions, they embody a high degree of focused attention to the world. They are thus highly revealing phenomena, in more than one way. They reveal the world to the creature, the creature's deepest goals to itself, and all of this to the astute observer:

> The reaction tells us that an important value or goal has been engaged and is being harmed, placed at risk, or advanced. From an emotional reaction we can learn much about what a person has at stake in the encounter with the environment or in life in general, how that person interprets self and world, and how harms, threats, and challenges are coped with. No other concept in psychology is as richly revealing of the way an individual relates to life and to the specifics of the physical and social environment.[51]

Here, Lazarus plausibly suggests, we may locate the adaptive significance of emotions – indeed, the importance of emotions in explaining the entire phenomenon of adaptation.[52] Given their urgency, their connection with important goals, and their keenness of perception, emotions explain, more than do other types of cognition, how creatures decide to move from one environment to another, and/or to modify their goals to fit the environment. Answering his longtime opponent Zajonc (whose views I shall describe at the end of this section), Lazarus points out perfectly correctly that there is no contradiction at all between analyzing emotions as cognitive appraisals and insisting that they embody a sense of importance and urgency: "Cognition can be relatively cold when there is *minimal self-involvement or low stakes* in what is thought; cognition may also be hot or emotional."[53]

---

51 Lazarus (1991), pp. 6–7.
52 On emotion and adaptation, see also de Sousa (1987), Oatley (1992), and Gibbard (1990), pp. 132–5.
53 Lazarus (1991), p. 131; for a direct response to Zajonc, see Lazarus (1984). Lazarus is not always perfectly consistent; sometimes he insists that the cognitive appraisal *is* the emotion, sometimes he seems to make it just one constituent part among others, and sometimes he even suggests that it temporally precedes the emotion. I present the theory in the form I like best – but I also believe that it is the view that his argument actually supports, and on which he usually relies.

Lazarus notes that goals may be present to an animal in many ways: they may be supplied by biology, by society, or by a process of personal development; they may be objects of conscious reflection, or they may be deeply internalized without being conscious; appraisal may follow set patterns, or it may be done step by step in each case. Emotions need not be "rational" in the sense of being, in every case, explicit or verbal. But in another, normative sense they are profoundly rational: for they are ways of taking in important news of the world. The suggestion that we might rid ourselves of emotions or cease to be prompted by them is, as Lazarus sees, the suggestion that we should radically reorganize the sense of self that most of us have, and the sort of practical rationality that helps most of us, much as it helps other animals, to carry on our transactions with a world that helps or harms us:

To desire something and to recognize what must be done to attain it, as well as to recognize when its attainment has succeeded or failed, is to be inevitably emotional. In this way, emotions and reason are inextricably linked in an inescapable logic.[54]

Lazarus's theory is thus in all essentials the view of emotions I have defended in Chapter 1. Like that theory, it stresses that emotions are usually eudaimonistic, concerned with one or more of the creature's most important goals and projects. In fact, for nonhuman animals it seems plausible to claim that they are always strongly eudaimonistic. And like that theory, Lazurus's stresses that emotions are usually, though not necessarily, accompanied by a high degree of focused sensory attention to the object, attention that in part explains their motivational and adaptive significance.

A further issue about emotion is raised in a fine book by Keith Oatley.[55] Oatley, who has long been associated with the cognitivist line of argument in emotion theory, and who has long shown more awareness of philosophical distinctions and arguments than most psychologists,[56] argues for a general account of emotion and its adaptive advantages that lies very close to that of Lazarus. He focuses somewhat more than does Lazarus on animal evidence. There is, however, one crucial divergence, which we should now assess. Oatley revives and develops

54 Lazarus (1991), p. 468.
55 Oatley (1992). See also Fridja (1986).
56 See Oatley and Bolton (1985), Oatley and Johnson-Laird (1987).

an idea pioneered by George Mandler,[57] according to which "conflict" and "interruption" – as well as "appraisal" – are central to the analysis of emotion. To Lazarus's basic idea that emotions are appraisals of the environment with respect to the agent's important goals, Oatley adds the requirement that the cognition is of some *change* in the status of those goals. "[E]motions occur when a psychological tendency is arrested or when a smoothly flowing action is interrupted."[58] Sometimes he puts the point by saying that something must intervene from the world to prompt a change in appraisal; sometimes he speaks as if a change in appraisal can be initiated at any time by the creature itself. The final statement of the view is that emotion involves an awareness of a change in the probability of progress toward some important goal. Oatley relies in part on intuitive evidence, alleging that we experience emotions such as fear and grief at times of sudden tumult or change.

Now indeed there are many such phenomena. But the theory, focused as it is on emotions that have a close connection to action, has weaknesses in two areas: explaining some positive emotions, and explaining what I have called the background emotions. Oatley himself recognizes that joy, love, hope, and other positive emotions that do not seem to be focused on progress toward a goal are a problem for his account, since we appear to love and find joy in people and things even when they stay just as they are. His response makes the notion of "change" so elastic that it loses all explanatory value. For he says that these positive emotions represent the appraisal that some cherished plan is "progressing well."[59] His characterization of such cases is eloquent, but it diverges from his theory:

Enjoyment occurs where some overall goal is important, as with being in love. It also occurs where there is no pressing overall goal, in states where the mind is full as in listening to music, in creative activities, in play, or when social participation is more important than any end result. Being happy requires that there be no distressing reevaluations, but rather the easy incorporation of new elements into the activity.[60]

Here – apart from the confusion between making something an end in itself and having *no goal* – is a good characterization of some sorts

57 Mandler (1984).
58 Oatley (1992) p. 46.
59 Oatley (1992), pp. 46ff.
60 Ibid., p. 48.

of happy emotion. But they do not fit the theory, and Oatley admits it – "no distressing reevaluations" means, here, "no reevaluations." Even some negative emotions are not well explained in this way: we may be persistently angry over an event that is fixed and unchangeable, even one that occurred before we were born. But clearly the view doesn't even begin to explain contentment, joy, or love. (Proust does give a rather Oatleyesque analysis of love, and I shall return to it in Chapter 10; but I believe it is incomplete as an account of that emotion.) We should perhaps see this weakness not as a major weakness in the theory so far as it goes, but as a sign that the theory is a theory well suited to explaining a certain range of emotions, less well suited to others. That would be a grave weakness only insofar as it purported to offer a global explanation for all emotions, which, as I read Oatley, it does not.[61]

As for the *background emotions*, Oatley again offers no account of these. There can be on his account no persisting emotions connected with important goals that are not hooked onto a situation of change – therefore, no enduring love and attachment, no background fear of death, no compassion for people who are starving the world over just provided that they go on starving without change. Again, this is a weakness only insofar as he purports to offer an account of the whole range of emotional phenomena, which, as I read him, he does not.

Oatley's account is thus a good account of a narrower range of phenomena than my account tries to address. Its narrowness is explained largely by his focus on nonhuman animals, otherwise one of the strengths of his account.[62] For one can see that this sort of account, though incomplete for the emotions of nonhuman animals, is much more nearly complete for them than for humans. Other animals, especially those that lack a sense of temporal duration, may well have fewer background emotions than humans, and more situational emotions – although there are obvious difficulties in establishing this conclusion. They fear death only when some environmental change reminds them that it is impending; they have fewer enduring attachments

---

61 I am grateful to Oatley for correspondence on this point.

62 He also goes wrong because of the focus on *Anna Karenina*, in which sudden tumult and upheaval are indeed central. And even here, I think, he confuses suddenness in the *manifestation* of an emotion with the role of change and interruption in the genesis of the emotion itself. Emotion seems to burst through in the sudden way it does because of the repressed character of the Karenins' marriage. But that does not show us that no emotions were there before.

and are less shaped by them. They are also less likely to hold grudges, or to get angry about historical events that cannot be changed. They may not be at all capable of persisting internalized guilt about a bad action in the past, although some of them are, it would seem, capable of shame.

Nonetheless, Oatley's theory fails to explain many prominent cases of persisting animal emotion.

Consider the love of dogs for their owners, such as the persisting love of Lupa and Remus for George Pitcher and Ed Cone. Remus *manifested* his love for Pitcher on the occasion of a change in Pitcher's demeanor; but the reader of Pitcher's narrative is in no doubt that the two dogs love him steadily, and that this persisting love organizes their lives, as it does his own. Perhaps it is easier for psychologists to be confident in ascribing emotion to nonhuman animals when there is a change in the situation and they have made a sharp response;[63] but this does not mean that emotions are not present on other occasions, as Pitcher's detailed narrative convinces us. Similarly, the animals described by Seligman have pervasive emotions of fear, grief, and depression, which persist unchanging through events of many different kinds. Indeed, in these cases it is precisely the changelessness of their situation that is crucial in explaining their emotions.

On balance, however, the new intentionality-based accounts offer subtle and basically adequate paradigms for the explanation of human and animal emotion that have a striking resemblance to the type of philosophical account I have been trying to develop. We can see that a focus on interpretation and experience is in no way unscientific: indeed, it is an ineliminable part of an adequate scientific account. In fact, it would appear that the intentionality of emotions is important not only in the explanation of current animal behavior but also in the evolutionary explanation of how emotions came to have significance in animals' lives.

The only reductionist program currently influential in psychology is a program I associated in Chapter 1 with "the adversary" – the program of reducing emotions to noncognitive, nonintentional subjective feeling-states. The most influential proponent of this program is R. B.

---

63 See Lazarus (1991), p. 16, who explains interruption theories as responses to the fact that we notice such attention in other creatures more readily when there is a change.

Zajonc, who has been engaged in a long debate with Lazarus.[64] Like Lazarus's work, Zajonc's is offered as an account of the common ground between humans and other animals, however difficult it is to gain access to animals' subjective feeling states. It therefore needs examining to see whether it causes us to modify any of our contentions.

Zajonc begins with the unexceptionable contention that any good account of emotion must do justice to emotions' heat and urgency, their frequent reliance on nonverbal channels, and the fact that they frequently focus on their object in an inchoate and incompletely articulated way. These points are correct. They have been evident to all cognitive theorists who focus on animals, but they do not subvert the main contentions of intentionalist views like those of Lazarus and Ortony. Zajonc now contrasts love and other emotions with a cold intellectual sort of thinking. The position for which he actually argues is that emotion must contain an element of evaluation that explains its "heat." But without any clear argument, he concludes that in order to do justice to these phenomena we must define emotions as altogether noncognitive, rejecting Lazarus's cognitive/evaluative theory. To make matters still more perplexing, Zajonc continues to characterize emotions using heavily intentional and cognitive language, calling them "hot cognitions," by contrast to their "cold cognitive counterparts," and speaking of "affective judgments" in contrast to "cognitive operations."

I believe that to a large extent Zajonc does not really have a difference with Lazarus and Ortony: he simply uses different terminology. Once we discover that intentionality plays a significant role even in his account, we may conclude, I think, that insofar as there is a coherent account present in Zajonc, it is at any rate not one that actually upsets the main contentions of the intentionalists. He seems to be animated by the thought that the intentionalist view cannot make any room for feelings of any kind, or for the fact that emotions register in awareness. Since that is obviously not the case with Lazarus, Ortony, and Oatley, we may conclude that misunderstanding animates this debate. Zajonc's view does remind us, however, that we need to develop a flexible account of intentionality and cognition that does not focus exclusively on language.

64 Zajonc (1980, 1984); the second is answered by Lazarus (1984).

IV. NONREDUCTIONISTIC PHYSIOLOGICAL
ACCOUNTS: LEDOUX, DAMASIO

Research continues, of course, into the physiological basis of emotion, but this research tends to be far less reductionistic and far more compatible with accounts emphasizing intentionality and interpretation than work of the earlier period, when behaviorism provided the dominant research paradigm. A good example of the illumination that can be offered by a subtle nonreductionistic physiological theory is Joseph LeDoux's extremely interesting work on emotional learning and memory.[65] By producing brain lesions in rats, LeDoux has shown that a variety of distinct parts of the brain are involved in the transmission of fright signals and the laying down of an emotional habit or memory. The amygdala, an almond-shaped organ at the base of the brain, plays a very central role in the process, as do the thalamus and the auditory cortex. Notice that the theory is in that sense already a cognitive theory: the transmission of information within the animal is central to it.

LeDoux carefully avoids claiming that human emotions involve similar physiological processes; they may, but this has not yet been demonstrated. He also avoids claiming that he has found specific physiological processes that individuate one emotion from another. It would be rather difficult to make such an argument in the case of rats, where we have no independent way of labeling or categorizing the emotion and thus of establishing the correlations required. But even if certain emotions in rats correlated exceptionlessly with a particular type of physiological process, and this could be soundly established, the human case obviously offers possibilities of plasticity that make it unwise to generalize to it prematurely without direct evidence. Even in the case of the creatures LeDoux has studied, he is at pains to stress the complexity and variability of the physiology: the "establishment of memories is a function of the entire network, not just of one component. The amygdala is certainly crucial, but we must not lose sight of the fact that its functions exist only by virtue of the system to which it belongs."[66] If this is so for rats, it is all the more likely to be true in humans. Finally,

65 LeDoux (1993, 1994, 1996).
66 LeDoux (1994), p. 56.

LeDoux claims only to have uncovered some phenomena involved in fright behavior, not to have illuminated the subjective experience of the emotion of fear, in either rats or humans. LeDoux writes that he considers fear to be a "subjective state of awareness" involving reaction of the organism to danger, and that what he studies is therefore not that emotion. "Subjective experience of any variety is challenging turf for scientists."[67]

Thus LeDoux's nuanced approach supports and does not undermine the cautious attitude toward the physiological underpinnings of emotion that we have taken so far. We should certainly not eliminate the intentional account in favor of a physiological account, and we should not at this time include a particular physiological process as a necessary element in a definition of a given emotion type – although we should not rule out the possibility that such a move will in the future be supported by adequate evidence, at least for some simpler emotions, such as fear and surprise.[68] Within the limits established for his work by LeDoux himself, his results are highly suggestive for our later analyses of the chronological trajectory of emotional states. In particular, he shows that habituated fright changes the organism, and thus proves very difficult to reverse. Once animals are conditioned by a frightening stimulus, they can become unconditioned again only by a very long process of reconditioning. These findings may ultimately help us to explain the tenacity of emotional habits and their own recalcitrance to change.

Another neuroscientist whose work is nonreductionistic and can readily be joined to an intentionalistic/evaluative account is Anthony Damasio.[69] Damasio's primary concern, in *Descartes' Error*, is to convince his reader that the emotion/reason distinction is inaccurate and misleading: emotions are forms of intelligent awareness. They are "just as cognitive as other percepts,"[70] and they supply the organism with

---

67 LeDoux (1994), p. 57.
68 On "startle," see Jenefer Robinson's good discussion (1995). Robinson is mistaken only in thinking that the nonreflective, immediate, and relatively simple character that she plausibly ascribes to "startle" is incompatible with a cognitive account. To call an emotion cognitive does not, of course, entail that it is either conscious or reflective; it is just to say that it involves processing of information, and, in the case of my theory, some sort of rudimentary appraisal of the situation relative to the agent's goals.
69 Damasio (1994).
70 Damasio (1994), p. xv.

essential aspects of practical reason. They serve as "internal guides" concerning the relationship between subject and circumstances.[71] Thus his conclusions converge with those of Lazarus, though from a very different starting point. His secondary aim is to show that emotional functioning is connected with particular centers in the brain. (A further claim, that the object of all emotions is the agent's own body, is unconvincingly argued, as I shall mention later.)

The case from which Damasio starts is the sad history of Phineas Gage, a construction foreman who, in 1848, suffered a bizarre accident: an explosion drove an iron bar through his brain. Gage was not killed; indeed, he made an amazing recovery. His knowledge and his perceptual capacities were unaltered. But his emotional life was altered completely. He seemed to be like a child, with no stable sense of what was important and what was not. He was fitful, intemperate, obscene. It was as if he didn't care about one thing more than another. He seemed bizarrely detached from the reality of his conduct. So he could not make good choices, and he could not sustain good relationships with the people around him. "Some part of the value system remains," summarizes Damasio, and can be utilized in abstract terms, but it is unconnected to real-life situations.[72]

Damasio discovered a modern Gage by accident, in a patient named Elliot, who had a benign brain tumor. Elliot was weirdly cool, detached, and ironic, indifferent even to intrusive discussion of personal matters – as if such remarks were not really about him. He had not previously been this way; he had been an affectionate husband and father. He retained lots of cognitive functions: he could perform calculations, had a fine memory for dates and names, and the ability to discuss abstract topics and world affairs. After surgery to remove the tumor (which took part of the damaged frontal lobe with it), he was even less able to care about things or to rank priorities. He could stick obsessively to a task and perform it very well; but on a whim he might shift his attention and do something completely different. "One might say that Elliot had become irrational concerning the larger frame of behavior, which pertained to his main priority, while within the smaller

71 Ibid.
72 Ibid., p. 11.

frames of behavior, which pertained to his subsidiary tasks, his actions were unnecessarily detailed."[73]

On intelligence tests, Elliot showed as unimpaired. Even the cognitive tasks (sorting and so on) that are often used to test frontal lobe damage were a breeze to him. Standard IQ tests revealed a superior intellect. Two things were out of order: his emotions, and his capacity for setting priorities and making decisions. Something specific was absent from Elliot emotionally: namely, the sense that something was at stake for him in the events he could coolly narrate. "He was always controlled, always describing scenes as a dispassionate, uninvolved spectator. Nowhere was there a sense of his own suffering, even though he was the protagonist . . . He seemed to approach life on the same neutral note."[74] In other words, he had cognitions and even, in some sense, evaluations: what he lacked was their eudaimonistic element, the sense of vital projects of his own being engaged. Damasio's idea was that this failure – which clearly seemed connected with his brain damage (even Elliot himself could remember that he had been different before) explained his decision-making failure. How can one set priorities well in life, if no one thing seems more important than any other? Even though Elliot could reason his way through a problem, he lacked the kind of engagement that would give him a sense of what to do.[75]

Damasio's research confirms the work of Lazarus, Ortony, and Oatley: emotions provide the animal (in this case human) with a sense of how the world relates to its own set of goals and projects. Without that sense, decision making and action are derailed. Damasio suggests further that these operations have their seat in a specific region of the frontal lobe, the region that was known to have been affected by Elliot's operation, and which Damasio's wife has reconstructed as the likely site of Phineas Gage's brain damage. Such conclusions are extremely interesting. They do not suggest in any way that emotions are nonintentional physiological processes: indeed, the whole thrust of Da-

73 Ibid., p. 36.
74 Ibid., pp. 44–5.
75 See Ibid., pp. 46–51, where Elliot is put through a battery of decision-making tests, which require only analysis and not a personal decision, and does very well. He produces an abundance of options for action. " 'And after all this,' says Elliot to Damasio, 'I still wouldn't know what to do!' "

masio's argument is strongly antireductionistic. All cognitive processes have their roots in brain function, and this does not mean that we should think of them as noncognitive feelings. The point Damasio makes is that the same is true of emotions: they help us to sort out the relationship between ourselves and the world. But the fact that the healthy functioning of a particular area of the brain is necessary for these processes is relevant and very interesting.

Should we include this physiological information in the definition of the emotions?[76] As in the case of LeDoux's cautious conclusions, it seems that such a move would be premature. We do not have very much data, nor are we likely to acquire it, since it requires vivisection of a sort that we do not tolerate in humans and surely should not tolerate in animals – unless we have an injured subject like Elliot or Gage. We do not know how the evident plasticity of the brain with regard to at least some functions affects the "location" of emotional functioning, nor do we know how much intersubjective variation there is. (The injuries to Elliot were pretty large; Gage's as we envision them are the result of a historical reconstruction; so we cannot even compare these two cases with precision.) In the end, then, we have an illuminating set of findings that suggest a further research program; in the meantime, the functional definition of emotions seems to be on solid ground.

Damasio's third claim is that the object of all emotions is a state of the subject's own body. Thus he revives one aspect of the James–Lange view, though without that view's reductionism. On that score, however, the arguments he offers seem thin and unconvincing. Surely they do not seem adequate to explain the detachment of Gage and Elliot from all goals and attachments. It is true, of course, that all emotions involve a prominent eudaimonistic element, and thus an ineliminable indexical element (see Chapter 1): the subject is aware that it is *herself* or *himself* who has the goal or attachment in question. So in that sense an awareness of self (and therefore, often, of one's body) is a part of the ex-

---

76 For LeDoux and Damasio, it is important to note, this question is not on the table. They are working in a framework that does not even attempt to establish type–type correlations between the emotions and physiological changes; instead, they are investigating ways in which the mental more generally supervenes on the physical. But we may fairly pose the question using their results, since someone else might try to use them to postulate type–type correlations.

perience of any emotion. It does not follow from this that the emotion's *object* is the body: the object is the goal or person or thing, whatever it is, to which the subject is attending. When I grieve for my mother I am aware that she is *my* mother; I sense the grief as an absence in my being. But that does not imply that I am really grieving for myself: this is the very confusion between eudaimonism and egoism that we sought to undo early in Chapter 1. Damasio really doesn't mean to make the emotions egoistic; indeed, all his accounts of their role suggest that they involve the ascription of real value to things and persons outside the self. His claims about the body are simply inadequate to capture the richer account of emotion that he proposes in the bulk of the book.

Neuroscience, when not wedded to a reductionist program, can make richly illuminating contributions to the understanding of emotions, their intentionality, and their role in the economy of animal life. Whether they will ever produce the kind of uniformity and constancy across cases to give us reason to incorporate a concrete description of a specific type of neurological functioning into the definition of a particular emotion type remains, as yet, unclear.

V. ANIMAL EMOTION IN NARRATIVE FORM: PITCHER

Experimentalists give us reason to conclude that animals are emotional, and that their emotions, like ours, are appraisals of the world, as it relates to their well-being. We still have questions about the range of emotions of which other animals are capable: for example, about whether any nonhuman animals are capable of emotions that require causal thinking (anger) or perspectival and empathetic thinking (compassion). More fundamentally, we need some reassurance that these experimental views square with experience, sensitively observed. Many experimentalists are themselves highly empathetic observers of particular animals, and come to know their subjects well as individuals. But we have also seen that cognitive psychology has been prone to reductive and inadequate accounts of animal intelligence, accounts that were readily repudiated by people who knew and interacted with animals. This makes us want to hold the scientific accounts up against the best interpretive accounts of behavior, just as we held scientific accounts of humans up against the rich descriptions we produce from our emotional experience. We cannot turn to experience in exactly the way that we did in Chapter 1, which relied both on my detailed case history and on readers' Socratic participation, as they mined their own histories for similar material. But there is nonetheless a methodological analogue. We can turn to detailed histories of interaction with particular animals, produced with a sensitivity and imaginative power that convinces us that the writer has managed to avoid the twin pitfalls of reductionism and anthropocentrism. (And of course, as in Chapter 1, the role of such an account is to invite the reader to mine his or her experience for similar examples.) If such an account squares with the experimental theories, we will have greater confidence that the experimenters have not oversimplified – and also that the biographer is not guilty of illegitimate anthropomorphizing.[77] A classic example of such an animal biography is George Pitcher's account of the dogs Lupa and Remus, in *The Dogs Who Came to Stay*.[78]

Pitcher is a philosopher who has written influentially on the intentionality of the emotions – in that case, focusing on human examples alone.[79] The biography, however, pursues no theoretical agenda, although it displays the same observational capacities that are used to good theoretical ends in the philosophical work. In approaching the lives of Lupa and Remus, Pitcher neither withholds imaginative speculation nor uses it loosely; he is always keenly aware that he is dealing with a nonverbal creature with certain specific capacities, and his accounts of the emotions of Lupa and Remus are in consequence convincing accounts of the emotions of two specific dogs, rather than fanciful human projections. Indeed, it is Pitcher's point in this book to show that the dogs showed him aspects of emotion that he had not really understood before, or been able to exemplify in his own life – a life characterized by an inability to express love and grief, and by a perpetual undercurrent of mourning, which he traces to his mother's insistence that all bad events were to be denied. One further advantage,

77 On the importance of philosophical attention to scientific fact, see Pitcher (1965).
78 Other helpful examples are gathered in Wise (2000). A fascinating account of a rich relationship with a dog, comparable in subtlety to Pitcher's, is Barbara Smuts's account of her "friendship" with Safi, in Smuts (1999), which also contains very interesting accounts of her interactions with a troop of baboons with which she lived for a long period of time. See also de Waal (1989a, 1989b, 1996).
79 See Pitcher (1965), discussed in Chapter 1.

for me, in focusing on this account is that I knew the two dogs in question, and can therefore compare Pitcher's narrative to my own experience.

Lupa was a wild dog, used to deprivation, and probably to repeated abuse. (Even years later, she cringed at the sight of a stick in a man's hand.) Pitcher encountered her when she had a litter of puppies in a "cave" under his toolshed. He and Ed Cone decided to feed her as long as she stayed there; but she refused to approach food while the men were in view. We now arrive at a pivotal point in the story:

It was clear that she was tempted by the biscuit but that she simply could not bring herself to approach a human being. (What had she endured? How must she have been mistreated!) Each of these sessions, in which I tried to appear harmless and to be irresistibly charming, ended in the same way: after ten or fifteen minutes of weighing my blandishments, she turned and crept back to her lair.

Feeling rejected and strangely hurt, and sensing at the same time a huge vulnerability in her, I was more determined than ever to get close to her. I knew that her fear of people was altogether general, but I couldn't help taking it personally: I was the one, after all, from whom she was actively keeping her distance. I wanted to show her that though her poor opinion of mankind was no doubt warranted, I, at least, meant her no harm.

Days passed with no thaw in her massive distrust of me . . . I was sure that if it weren't for the food I set out for her, she wouldn't care whether I lived or died. Apart from the food, I was simply a nuisance, forever coming around, peering in, bothering her. She must have felt like the two potted plants in the *New Yorker* cartoon several years ago: as a glowing middle-aged woman, watering can in gloved hand, approached them, one plant said to the other, "Here we go again, yackity, yackity, yackity!"

One afternoon, when I looked into the cave, I found her, for the first time, not hidden away in utter darkness but crouching only a foot or two from where I knelt.

"Well, hello there," I said quietly, trying oh so hard not to frighten her. I scarcely dared to breathe. I wanted to reach out and touch her, but I couldn't risk it. She turned her head away, and I thought she would creep to the back of the cave, but no, she held her ground. In a moment, she began to wag her tail ever so slowly. It thumped against the side of the cave. With that gentle motion, all my defenses were instantly swept away. "Well then," I said to myself as she suddenly looked blurred to me, "I'm yours forever!"[80]

80 Pitcher (1995), p. 20–1.

This description might be a case study in Lazarus's theory. Pitcher here ascribes to Lupa emotions with a definite propositional content, connected with important goals. Her fear of humans (or perhaps of adult human males?) contains the thought that they are likely sources of pain and abuse. Her eager longing for the biscuit, which pulls against the fear, is another kind of focusing on a goal she sees as extremely good. Her hesitation is plausibly characterized as a deliberate "weighing" of the "blandishments" that Pitcher offers, in his attempts to appear "harmless" and "charming" as he offers the biscuit. She also experiences something rather like anger or irritation at Pitcher, who turns up again and again with his words, getting in the way of her feeding. Pitcher plausibly attributes causal thinking to her when he ascribes to her the thought that Pitcher's presence has interrupted her attempt to enjoy the biscuit. Finally, although Pitcher doesn't explicitly give us the content of the crucial tale-wagging, it is clear what he thinks it is: "Although most humans are to be avoided, you seem to be different." She saw Pitcher as good, and behaved in accordance with that cognition. It was this awareness that he was being seen as good that elicited Pitcher's own strong emotional response, as the animal's trust unlocked his own ability to give love, which had been compromised by his inability to mourn his mother's death – and, more generally, by his mother's implicit teaching that any sign of mourning or loss is a culpable weakness.[81] The guilt about vulnerability that had relegated his emotions to "the deep freeze" was somehow absolved by the dog's own "huge vulnerability" and her willingness to show affection despite its risks.

This is, of course, a highly human story, and one in which a human being is labeling a dog's emotions in human language. Nonetheless, we have no reason to suppose the report of Lupa's emotions to be less reliable than Pitcher's own self-report. (Indeed, we are reminded that all of our self-descriptions are similarly fallible.) As the narrative progresses, indeed, it is precisely the interweaving of reaction and counter-reaction that convinces the reader that Pitcher has gotten it right about the dog: he is not just standing at a distance, he is involved in an emotional relationship. Again and again, a tentative hypothesis is confirmed by further behavioral interactions, and the closeness and respon-

81 See ibid., pp. 7–8, 130.

siveness of the relationship the two dogs (mother and son) ultimately develop with Pitcher and Cone itself permits the dogs to cultivate complex positional emotions that researchers sometimes ascribe only to primates. The reader sees that Lupa and Remus feel love for their human friends, and even something of compassion when they suffer – as well as fear, anger, and joy of various types, associated with various specific goals and projects. During my own visits in their home, I had no doubt that Lupa felt fear of me, as a menacing outside human who had not gained her trust; that Remus felt joy when he was asked to go wake me up at 7 A.M. with a bark outside my door, and profound grief, affecting his entire life, when his mother died of old age.

Above all, as Pitcher stresses, the dogs were capable of a type of unguarded and unqualified love that humans don't always manage to have. Indeed, he offers a lot of evidence that the dogs were fully capable of valuing the two men in ways that far outran their interest in food and shelter. They showed a dejection when the men were temporarily absent, and a boisterous joy when they returned home, that showed that they had put these two men into their lives in a much more than instrumental way – still eudaimonistic, in the sense that the men were central to their scheme of goals and projects, but not simply survival-linked in the way of many of the eudaimonistic emotions of animals. Repeated stories of the dogs' loyal behavior, and their sheer joy in the presence of the two men, confirm the hypothesis that the attachment is noninstrumental. (Remember that the relationship with Pitcher began when Lupa was able to make the distinction between treating Pitcher as a mere means to her survival and treating him as something more, a trusted ally.)

Pitcher here returns to a theme of his earlier philosophical work on emotion, where he stresses that love, unlike most of the other emotions, is not based on articulable reasons, and is therefore more unconditional than the reason-based emotions.[82] He reaches that same conclusion in reflecting about Lupa and Remus:

Yes, we had many reasons for loving Lupa and Remus, but when it comes to love, reasons, as everyone knows, don't count for much. You can list a few if you try, but the list soon gives out, and you are left with what is essentially the inexplicable fact of love itself. So whatever the reasons, be-

82 Pitcher (1965).

yond all the reasons, we simply loved them with all our hearts; we perhaps even loved them – I'm not ashamed to say it – beyond all reason. And they loved us, too, completely, no holds barred.[83]

One may ask whether this account is not suspiciously anthropocentric, whether the emotion projected onto the dogs is not too similar to a type of unconditional love that Pitcher portrays his mother as not having given, or received. (Pitcher does stress that he and Cone felt both like Lupa's parents and like her children, protected by her from harm.)[84] But the fact that the dogs' love satisfies a perceived human need does not show that it was not really unconditional love. As Pitcher suggests, it is the conditionality of love that is more plausibly seen as the specifically human invention.

There's always room for skepticism about these attributions of intelligence and emotion to animals. But at this point, it is useful to remind ourselves that our attribution of emotion to other human beings itself involves projection that goes beyond the evidence. As Proust says: a real person imposes "a dead weight that our sensitivity cannot remove." Primatologist Barbara Smuts puts the point well, describing her dog Safi's response when she becomes aware that Smuts is feeling low. At those times, Safi

approaches, looks into my eyes, and presses her forehead against mine. Then, without fail, she lies down beside me, maximizing contact between her body and mine . . . As soon as I am supine, she rests her chin on my chest, right on top of my heart, and locks her gaze with mine until my mood shifts. Perhaps, a skeptic might respond, she does this simply because she's learned, first, that you're more fun when you're not feeling sad, and, second, that she can cheer you up in this way. To this I would reply: if we had human companions who behaved in much the same way, for identical motives, would we doubt their sincerity, or consider ourselves very lucky indeed?[85]

(And lest we think things are different with our own selves, let us not forget that we use a common language to describe our own inner states, and that the nature of those states is hardly transparent, even to the most patient introspection.) All of our ethical life involves, in this sense,

83 Pitcher (1995), p. 163.
84 Ibid., p. 66.
85 Smuts (1999), pp. 199–200.

an element of projection, a going beyond the facts, a use of "fancy." We should not deny that the sympathetic imagination can cross the species barrier – if we press ourselves, if we require of our imaginations something more than common routine. J. M. Coetzee's imaginary character Elizabeth Costello, a novelist lecturing on the lives of animals, points out that we are capable, with pain and effort, of thinking the fact of our own death. But then, why say that we're incapable of imagining the life of a creature of another species? "The heart is the seat of a faculty, *sympathy*, that allows us to share at times the being of another."[86]

Pitcher's account, like all particular narratives, needs to be assessed for its conformity to experimental findings. And it does, of course, agree very well with the picture of animal emotions painted by Lazarus and by Seligman, whose account of animal fear and helplessness assists us in understanding Lupa's behavior. But experimental work also needs to be assessed for its conformity to the rich data of particular animal lives. It is because Seligman and Lazarus produce an account that can make sense of stories like this that their theories seem more convincing than earlier reductionist theories. As an ally of such psychological accounts, Pitcher's narrative offers information about the capacity of dogs for causal thinking, positional thinking, and noninstrumental love that can, and should, be further tested by experimental methods.

VI. REVISING THE NEO-STOIC ACCOUNT

By looking at nonhuman animals, and by looking at ourselves as animals, we see that the neo-Stoic view is not a stranger to the animal world – indeed, that the strongest theories advanced to explain animal behavior in this area are, like the neo-Stoic view, cognitive, evaluative, and eudaimonist. But we must now summarize the modifications that the view should undergo in the process of extending it to other animals.

The animal evidence confirms the Stoic view that an emotion is an evaluative appraisal of the world. These ways of seeing will always involve some sort of combination or predication – usually of some

---

86 Coetzee (1999), p. 34. Costello's argument here is directed against Thomas Nagel's famous article, "What Is It Like to Be a Bat?" (Nagel 1979). For my view of empathy and sympathy, see Chapter 6. For further reflections about sympathy with animals, see Nussbaum (2001a).

thing or person with an idea of salience, urgency, or importance. More-over, these predications of salience are in turn combined with an as-sessment of how the goal is faring in the world. In each case, the world impinges on the animal not directly, but through these evaluative ap-praisals – which may be accurate or inaccurate, and may be modified by teaching. All of this our view contains already; but the following modifications must now be made.

First, we should insist vigorously on a fact that we have already mentioned: the cognitive appraisals need not all be *objects of reflexive self-consciousness*. Animals (and humans) can discriminate the threat-ening from the nonthreatening, the welcome from the unwelcome, without self-consciousness. Many if not most animals have something that we may call conscious awareness: that is, there is something the world is like to them, and that intentional viewing of the world is significant in explaining their actions; but this need not imply that they study their own awareness. Some of the animals we have discussed have emotions without ever having self-consciousness. We have self-consciousness, but do not always exercise it; and we can ourselves discriminate threat from nonthreat, the loved from the nonloved, with-out explicitly formulating this to ourselves in every case, or reflexively scrutinizing our own ascriptions.

What about consciousness in the simpler sense of ordinary (non-self-reflexive) awareness of an experience? I have said that humane emo-tions will at times not register at all in felt experience. Sometimes the emotion will not attain consciousness because it is part of a routine,[87] sometimes because it is a background, rather than a situational, emo-tion. In both cases, nothing in the situation has caused us to register our emotion: it doesn't feel like anythiing to us. And yet, it is often right to say that the emotion remains there, explaining what we do, just as the belief that two plus two equals four is present, explaining higher mathematical operations, even though we are not aware of it all the time. Sometimes there are more complex reasons why an emotion might motivate without reaching consciousness: the fear of death, for example, may be actively suppressed, while continuing to explain our actions.

Should we say that all this is true of nonhuman animals? Here we

87 See Lazarus (1991), pp. 151, 156.

have difficulty knowing what to say, since we do not have the type of self-report evidence that would convince us that the emotion does not reach the level of awareness (as when people deny fearing death and yet show by their acts that they fear it, or report no awareness of anger but behave in an angry manner). We infer to animal emotions by some combination of empathetic imagining and thinking about what is necessary in order to explain behavior; both strategems are fallible, and it is difficult, in any case, for such a procedure to yield the distinction between the background and the situational that we find in the human case. And yet it seems reasonable that, to the extent that animals are capable of general and temporally extended thinking, background emotions of fear, love, and anger will play at least some role in explaining what they do. I have said that Lupa and Remus loved Pitcher and Cone continuously, not only when they were leaping for joy and wagging their tails; that Lupa feared other humans continuously, not just when she was shrinking back from a touch. To the extent to which persisting attachments organize the fabric of an animal's life, explaining patterns of pursuit and avoidance, it seems right to ascribe background emotions to them. Here, then, we need not make a major modification in the account, although we should grant that some reasons for human refusal of emotion are absent in other animals.

A major change in the theory is, however, required in the area of language. The cognitive appraisals involved in animal emotions are linguistically formulable in a way, since we characterize their cognitive content by choosing the nearest plausible verbal formula. These characterizations can be loosely accurate. But this does not mean, of course, that the content actually uses linguistic symbolism, or is formulable in language without a degree of distortion. Nor does it mean that it is formulable, even with distortion, by the subject of the emotion. All of this is true not only of our emotion ascriptions to animals but also of our ascriptions to human infants and young children, and of some of our own self-ascriptions: in all of these cases, the subject may not be able to make a good (or perhaps any) verbal translation of the emotion's content, and even the best translation an observer can make will involve some degree of distortion.

Sometimes the distortion simply involves translation from one rather sophisticated medium to another. There are many kinds of cognitive activity or seeing-as in which ideas of salience and importance figure:

there are pictorial imaginings, musical imaginings, the kinetic forms of imagining involved in the dance, and others. These are not all reducible to or straightforwardly translatable into linguistic symbolism, nor should we suppose that linguistic representing has pride of place as either the most sophisticated or the most basic mode.[88] Where all emotions are concerned, we want to insist on the presence of combination or predication, and on the centrality of eudaimonistic evaluation. But we have seen that we have reason to ascribe these to totally nonlinguistic creatures; even in the human case language is far from being the only medium in which an emotion's content can register. Translations from another medium into language can be reasonably accurate. Thus, Henry James granted that his eleven-year-old character Maisie could not have used Jamesian language, and yet insisted that his words were accurate translations of acts of perception that her imagination could flexibly perform. At other times, we may feel that translations distort simply by being linguistic: thus Mahler insisted that any verbal translation of his musical ideas was distorting, since he never expressed musically what he could express in words.[89]

Sometimes, however, the distortion involves not only shifting to a new medium, but also ascribing to the emotion a level of articulateness and definiteness that it has not attained, and perhaps could not attain. This is why good animal narratives are cautious in their use of linguistic content, as Pitcher's always is. It is for this reason, too, that Lazarus and Oatley are especially cautious about cross-species comparisons, and that Averill, more cautious still, views the entire idea of such comparisons with skepticism. On the other hand, the fruitfulness of such comparisons in the work of Seligman and others[90] shows that, pursued with sufficient caution, they can yield important insights, especially by revealing an animal level of human psychology too frequently obscured by excessive emphasis on the verbal. The issue of definiteness has importance for human development: in later life we often find ourselves motivated by a sense of salience that is not only derived from early childhood but still at the level of childhood, inchoate and without clear boundaries. To bring this material to verbal or

88 See Goodman (1968).
89 See Chapter 5.
90 See also the attachment theory of Bowlby, to be discussed in Chapter 4.

other symbolic expression involves both self-discovery and self-change.[91]

What we need, in short, is a multifaceted notion of cognitive interpretation or seeing-as, accompanied by a flexible notion of intentionality that allows us to ascribe to a creature more or less precise, vaguer or more demarcated, ways of intending an object and marking it as salient.

Next, Lazarus's work on animals makes us insist, once again, on the importance of the intense perceptual focusing involved in emotion. Our intuitive arguments for this feature, presented in Chapter 1, now have support from a different source: for focusing seems important in order to explain emotions' adaptive significance. For reasons given by Lazarus, we do not want to make this a necessary condition of emotional experience, but we do want to say that it is an important feature when it does occur.

Finally, LeDoux's very interesting work on memory makes us understand the importance of remaining alert to what biology can tell us about the pathways of emotional response. There is a danger that, irritated by the grandiose claims of physiological reductionism, we may veer too sharply to the other side and fail to learn all that we can about the specific geography of emotion that biology has mapped out for a given species. As it happens, LeDoux's work is a very useful supplement to Seligman's work on helplessness, explaining why certain types of emotional conditioning prove unusually hard to undo. Over time, such discoveries and others like them may lead us to group emotions in new ways, and to understand more fully the relationship between background and situational emotions.

VII. APPETITES, MOODS, DESIRES FOR ACTION

At this point we are in a position to answer three questions that were introduced in Chapter 1: How are emotions like and unlike *bodily appetites*? How are they like and unlike *moods*? And how are they related to *action*?

Thinking about animals shows us some common ground between

---

91 There is a good account of this issue in Lear (1990).

emotions like fear and anger and bodily appetites like hunger and thirst. Both are elements of the animal's psychology that relate it to its environment; both may be both situationally focused and pervasive; both are connected with the animal's sense of its own well-being, and respond to the presence or absence of items that seem to be important to that well-being. Both contain some degree of intentional awareness – awareness both, it would seem, of the condition itself and of an object of some sort that would answer to the condition.[92] But if we begin to reflect on the type of intentionality at work in the two cases, we begin to have a sense of what separates them.

The best beginning on the problem was made by Plato, who seems to have argued as follows, in a most obscure part of the *Republic*.[93] Appetites are always directed toward a certain sort of object from which they never diverge: thirst for drink, hunger for food – and the appetite itself does not contain any further thought of the value or goodness of the object. They are, then, both *object-fixated* and *value-indifferent*. Emotions contain,[94] internal to themselves, a thought of the object's value or importance. And indeed, this thought of value is the central way the emotion has of characterizing its object; in other respects, emotions such as fear, grief, love, and anger are very flexible about the types of objects they can take. One may love people or things, one may grieve for an animal or a child – what is crucial to the emotion is the value with which the object has been invested.[95] Emotions, then, are *value-suffused* and (to some extent at any rate) *object-flexible*.

Another closely related difference pertains to origins. A bodily ap-

---

92 This might not be the case with appetites in all animals; and it would certainly be difficult to show that it was. But if in some cases appetites lack intentionality altogether, their difference from emotions is in these cases plain. I focus, therefore, on the subtler cases.

93 *Republic* IV, 435ff. The passage has been interpreted in many different ways; I give one plausible reading.

94 Plato does not speak of emotions here. The point of the passage is to show the difference between the "appetitive" and the "reasoning" parts of the soul; the account of the "spirited" part presented subsequently is probably an account of emotions, but it is notoriously underdeveloped and obscure.

95 Aristotle holds that anger must be at a particular person; he also holds that love, properly speaking, is always for a being capable of reciprocating the love. I am not clear that these claims are correct. Love may be unrequited; and it is not always for a person capable of reciprocating it. Furthermore, one can be angry at a nation, at an animal, even at nature; and one may love a poem, a painting, a cat, a city.

petite such as hunger is a *push*: that is, it arises relatively independently of the world, as a result of the animal's own bodily condition, and it is this condition that causes the appetite to represent an object that it then seeks. (One's hunger may of course be increased by the presence of appetizing food, but in general hunger is a regularly arising drive.) Emotions, on the other hand, are *pulled* into being by their object, and by the seeming importance of the object. In that sense intentionality is at their very core. (Sexual desire is highly complex, with elements of both push and pull: on the one hand it is a drive arising independently of the presence of an object, and demanding satisfaction. On the other hand, it is also pulled into being by the value of the object, and exhibits rich and selective intentionality.)

These differences have consequences for the adaptivity and flexibility of the phenomena. Because they are pushes, bodily appetites do not go away if there is no object of the right sort around. Hunger, to say the least, persists in the absence of food. Indeed, since they are value-independent drives, they do not go away even if the person is convinced that an object of the appropriate sort is actually harmful: if I am thirsty at sea, my knowledge of the danger of drinking salt water does not stop me from wanting to drink it. Emotions, by contrast, do go away when the relevant beliefs about the object and about value alter. I do not get angry when I am not aware of a wrong to which I ascribe significance; and if I am convinced that the wrong did not really take place, or was not really a wrong, my anger will go away. Of course it is difficult to alter such beliefs in a stable way, especially if they are based on cultural traditions that are learned early in life; Chapter 4 will suggest some further reasons why some emotions resist modification. But if the belief is really stably altered, the emotion alters with it.

Emotions are more flexible in another way as well. Because appetites are object-fixated, one cannot buy them off with the objects of other appetites: dry food will not satisfy thirst, nor water hunger. But love, lacking one sort of object, may find satisfaction in another. Hope, too, may shift its ground, as may fear and joy. (In such cases, since the emotions are not persisting "pushes," the reason why the emotion stays on the scene to search about for another object, if it does, is likely to be that the person has formed a general plan of life in which having someone or something to love has an important place: this place will be filled by a new concrete object.) Because the emotions are so closely connected to our sense of what has value and importance, remaking that plan will alter the objects of all emotions, and their concrete texture. Sexual desire is intermediate here as well: for it is clear that it frequently does persist in the absence of a suitable object; on the other hand, the phenomenon of sublimation – which will occupy us in later chapters – shows that it has an object flexibility unknown in hunger and thirst.

These contrasts are, so far, too simple: for appetites can be modified by teaching and habit, and can thus have at least some of the focused intentionality and value selectivity characteristic of emotions. We develop particular tastes in food and drink on the basis of learning, habit, and personal preference. Our appetites may then contain a focus on the value of certain objects, as when we long for freshly baked bread, or a fine wine. Epicurus held, plausibly, that this evaluative element in appetite is especially marked in humans, and represents the contribution of social norms and habits to our appetitive life. But animals, too, develop characteristic food preferences, and can be said to have at least some selective intentionality in their appetites. (I shall argue in the next chapter that a related difference of degree exists in emotion: specific social norms play a larger role in human than in animal emotions.) Nonetheless, this qualification does not remove the contrast between appetite and emotion: for when fresh bread is not available one's appetitive hunger can still be satisfied with something less delicious – to that extent, hunger remains fixated on food and relatively unselective. One's grief for one's mother does not, similarly, have a fixed appetitive component that can be satisfied, say, by the visit of a stranger.

These are some of the logical relations between emotions and appetites. Causal relations between the two also need investigation. The fact that animals and humans experience hunger, thirst, desire for shelter from the cold and relief from the heat, and sexual desire, is not irrelevant to the analysis of the grounds of their fear and hope and love and grief. The nature of our bodily neediness shapes our emotional geography; and appetites are signals of our neediness. Appetites signal bodily needs, and it is plausible that we will have emotions about the objects that satisfy those needs – unless, like the Stoics, we have taught ourselves not to value any external good.

The difference between *moods* and emotions is implicit in the account of emotion I have been giving, but Seligman's account of depression equips us to understand it better. Emotions always have an object, even if it is a vague object; they always invest the object with value, and involve the acceptance of beliefs about the object. It is very important to insist that emotions often do have a vague object: a fear that one's projects will come to nothing, a hope for good events, a joy in things as they are. But there is still an object there, and the emotion is still hooked into my conception of what is worthwhile and important. Moods such as irritation, gloom, elation, and equanimity lack these characteristics. In reality it is very difficult to distinguish an emotion with a vague or highly general object from a mood: one may feel generally fearful, and that will be an emotion with a vague object, if its content is that some (vague) danger is viewed as impending. It will be a mood to the extent that even that type of highly general or vague object is absent. Similarly, one may have highly general joy about how one's life is going, or how the world is, and that will be an emotion with a very general object; on the other hand, joy may be moodlike and truly objectless, a kind of euphoria that doesn't focus on anything.

The fact that these distinctions are difficult to make in many particular cases and that even the theoretical distinction is a somewhat imprecise one (at what point does an object become so vague that we should say that there is insufficient object-directed intentionality to call the state an emotion?) should not be seen as a problem for the account: for what would be a problem in an account of emotion would be an excessive rigidity or definitional dogmatism. The first responsibility of any good account is to the phenomena, and classifications that make boundaries seem unrealistically sharp or rigid are to that extent suspect.

Another problem makes this distinction even more complex. Sometimes we conceal from ourselves, or cannot retrieve, the object of an emotion. A generalized feeling may masquerade as a mere mood, and yet have a very definite object, as in Lucretius' wonderful description of the fear of one's own death, which simply feels like a heavy weight on one's chest. Here inspection of the entire pattern of one's actions will reveal, he plausibly claims, that what one is experiencing is in fact an emotion with a hidden object. On the other hand, there may well be cases with similar symptoms (of weight, anxiety, generalized discontent) that are purely moodlike, where there is no object to be uncovered.

This phenomenon may be present in the emotions of nonhuman animals as well, to the extent that their behavior is shaped by past events of which they are not currently aware. Thus Lupa experienced a generalized suspiciousness of humans that one might well call a mood that characterized her whole way of relating – and yet, on further inspection, it turns out that it was actually an emotion of fear directed at some person or persons who had abused her, as Pitcher discovered when he happened to take a stick in his hand and she suddenly quailed with fright. Again, a casual observer might read Lupa's tendency to bark at people who left the house as the sign of an irritable mood. Pitcher suggests, instead, that there was an object that he could not identify.

Seligman's work suggests a similar analysis for many cases of depression. Although there are many cases of depression that are genuine moods, caused by chemistry without the intervention of belief and unresponsive to changes in situation or belief, there are also many cases in which the general symptoms of depression are *about* something in the person's life. In particular, they are likely to focus on the belief (conscious or nonconscious) that the person is helpless in matters of great importance.[96] As Seligman has shown, this cognitive analysis is not incompatible with a physiological analysis: cognitive changes of this sort are experimentally correlated with physiological changes, frequently of great import for the creature's well-being.[97]

The conceptual distinction between emotional (intentional) and moodlike, endogenous depression is clear enough; in practice it may be extremely difficult to differentiate them. Even a case where chemical treatment yields good results for depression would not show that there was no object; it would only show that at that stage of the person's life symptomic relief was sufficient to make a real improvement. It may therefore remain obscure in a particular case whether we are dealing

96 See the related analysis in Oatley and Bolton (1985), and the impressive philosophical argument in Graham (1990), who carefully distinguishes depression with intentionality from depression without intentionality.

97 He argues that even cases of sudden death, coinciding with the time named in a curse or spell, may be explained as a result of the impact of the subject's belief in her helplessness vis-à-vis her death at this time.

with a mood or with an emotion that has a vague, or general, or hidden object.

Emotions are closely connected with *action*; few facts about them are more obvious. And yet it would be a mistake to identify them with *desires* for particular types of action.[98] Emotions direct us to an important component of our well-being and register the way things are with that important component. Sometimes this value-acknowledging, in combination with the situational perceptions and beliefs that are at hand, will straightforwardly give rise to motivations to act. Concrete fears prompt evasive action, or at least the desire for it; anger prompts the desire for retaliation;[99] love prompts desires to protect and to be with the object. But not all emotions suggest a definite course to follow. Sometimes this may be because things are well with oneself and with the object. Happy love may prompt a desire for its own continuation, and for various types of action constitutive of this continuation, but it may also express itself in no action at all, but rather in a sort of exuberant delight, or quiet contemplation.[100] Joy may inspire no desire, or simply the desire to act in some way expressive of joy – to write, to make love, to listen to the Dvorak Violin Concerto. Grief may prompt many wishes, above all the wish that the person one loves had not died.[101] But my wish that my mother had not died did not suggest a definite course of action; and running to University Hospital was not so much an action prompted by the emotion as an action whose irrational goal was to make the world other than the emotion knew it to be.

Emotions, in short, are acknowledgements of our goals and of their status. It then remains to be seen what the world will let us do about them. Desires may all contain a perception of their object as a good;[102] but not all perceptions of good give rise directly to action-guiding desires. This suggests that the tendency to explain action in terms of

---

98 See Deigh (1994) for a discussion of Davidsonian desire-based views, and a good criticism.

99 Not in every case: for one may believe retaliation to be either inappropriate or impossible (as when one is angry at some historical injustice): see C. C. W. Taylor (1986).

100 These and related aspects of emotion are especially well discussed in Taylor (1986).

101 See ibid., p. 222.

102 This observation is central in Aristotle's theory of action: see *De Anima* III.9-11 and *De Motu Animalium*, Chapters 6–11; one interesting modern treatment of this issue is in Stampe (1986).

two distinct sorts of items, beliefs or judgments and desires, needs to be made more complicated.[103] Emotions are judgments, but not inert judgments; on account of their evaluative content, they have an intimate connection with motivation that other beliefs do not; on the other hand, because they may not hook into the situation at hand in a way productive of a concrete plan of action, they are different from desires as well.

The picture of emotions and desires that I have just presented entails a considerable modification of familiar Humean models of the explanation of action – for both humans and animals.[104] On these familiar accounts, desires are hardwired in psychology, lacking in intentionality and impervious to modification. Beliefs then simply function to provide desire with information about how to attain its object. It was on this account that Hume famously held that reason is and must always be the slave of the passions.

By now we have seen three reasons to modify this account. First, it is wrong about desire: desire contains considerable intentionality and selectivity, even when we are talking about nonhuman animals.[105] Second, when we explain actions we need to mention other psychological items in addition to belief and desire: in particular, emotions, which themselves contain evaluations of the world and states of affairs in it. Such evaluations are part of emotions, and this also means that other beliefs can modify them. Third, the analysis of desire and emotion also implies that the role of belief need not be and is not simply instrumental. Because emotion and desire contain object-directed intentionality, belief need not subserve them as a slave. Belief (or some related form of predicational perception) is already in them; and other beliefs may therefore modify their cognitive content. This means, as well, that we may deliberate not only about how to get to ends that are already fixed, but also about the ends themselves – asking, for example, whether they are consistent with our other ends, how we ought to specify one of our ends more concretely, and so forth. This sort of

103 Notice that in Aristotle it is more complicated than it is in some later philosophers, who leave intentionality out of desire: for Aristotle has a complicated conception of desire's intentionality, and therefore of the logical, and not merely causal, links between belief and desire.

104 For a good account of our need to complicate the traditional Humean psychology, see Baier (1986).

105 See Quinn (1993).

deliberation takes place in animals as well. Thus Lupa deliberated about Pitcher, and finally decided to specify her concept "bad human threat" in a way that excluded him. Or, to put it another way, she decided that her initial inclusion of Pitcher under the concept "bad human threat" was inconsistent with the evidence of his gentle voice and nonthreatening manner. So the hydraulic view of action offers an inadequate account of animal behavior, just as it does of human action.

VIII. NONEMOTIONAL ANIMALS

Chapter 3 will discuss some differences between human and animal emotion that are caused by language and social variation. But there is one difference that should be mentioned now, since it is the main point of Pitcher's narrative, and his major reason for thinking that we can learn a lot about emotions from animals. This is, to put it in my own terms, that human beings appear to be the only mortal finite beings who wish to transcend their finitude. Thus they are the only emotional beings who wish not to be emotional, who wish to withhold these acknowledgments of neediness and to design for themselves a life in which these acknowledgments have no place. This means that they frequently learn to reject their own vulnerability and to suppress awareness of the attachments that entail it. We might also say (introducing a theme of Chapter 4 and of Part III) that they are the only animals for whom neediness is a source of shame, and who take pride in themselves to the extent to which they have allegedly gotten clear of vulnerability.

The issue is not simple in nonhuman animals. Seligman's work shows that an animal cannot flourish unless it believes to a certain extent in its own control and mastery. If it thinks that all its voluntary responding will bring no change in its situation, depression and even death will ensue. Never, however, does a nonhuman animal reach the point that humans frequently reach, with or without the help of philosophy: of putting all their emotions "in the deep freeze," to use Pitcher's self-description, and believing that self-respect (or, perhaps, manly pride) requires not deeply needing or trusting anything outside oneself.

By contrast, consider Lupa, with a history that justified Stoic withdrawal as amply as could any human history of abuse and jeopardy. She lived, for a time, a very Stoic dog life, attached to nobody, lurking around the Princeton neighborhood, appearing for food only when no human form was in sight. But one would not have said that she felt *pride* in her self-sufficiency and her lack of love. And perhaps this was why the simple overtures Pitcher made to her were ultimately success-ful. Unlike many human beings who have suffered, she had never formed the conception that a good or fine or worthy life required the extirpation of love. Her "huge vulnerability" was evident and not hidden. This, in turn, may be connected with the fact that she never taught herself that it was shameful to be a bodily creature, to need food and drink, to feel pain or desire. Pitcher's account plausibly sug-gests that a specifically human pride frequently blocks the achievement of unconditional love. As a boy he had learned what philosophical systems frequently justify: that it is bad to be incomplete. This led to what he describes as a "crippling inability to feel and express genuine affection or tenderness."[106] Lupa cured him of this because in her presence he was able to be like her: to let mistrust give way to trust and self-protectiveness to devotion. The account suggests that learning to be in that respect more like Lupa may be a key to the human phenomenon so often called, in philosophy, the "ascent" or reform of love. Part III will develop this suggestion.

106 Pitcher (1995), p. 66.

3

EMOTIONS AND HUMAN SOCIETIES

I. GRIEF AND SOCIAL NORMS

Tomas, a five-year-old Ifaluk boy, contracted meningitis and was co-
matose within twenty-four hours. Relatives and friends began to gather
at his parents' home. Female relatives washed the feverish body until
the efforts seemed futile; then male relatives took turns holding the
semi-rigid form, weeping as they cradled it. "At the moment of death,
a great wailing went up. The dead boy's biological mother, seated on
the floor mats near him, rose to her knees as if she had been stabbed
and pounded her fist violently against her chest. The adoptive mother
. . . began to scream and throw herself about on the ground." The
whole house was filled with crying, "from low moaning to loud,
wrenching and mucus-filled screaming to wailingly sung poem-laments,
and continued without pause through the night. Both men and women
spent tears in what seemed . . . equal measure." (The Ifaluk believe that
those who do not "cry big" at a death will become sick afterwards.)
Anthropologist Catherine Lutz found the proceedings "shocking": like
many young Americans, her only contact with death had been "the
subdued ritual of one funeral."[1]

One afternoon in Bali, Norwegian anthropologist Unni Wikan's
housekeeper, a young Balinese girl, came to her to ask for several
days off. She was smiling and laughing. Asked for her reason, she
told Wikan that she wanted to attend the funeral of her fiancé, in a
distant part of the island. Wikan immediately suspected deception:
she could not believe that this cheerful, bouncy girl had recently
suffered a major bereavement. Several days later, the girl returned,

1 Lutz (1988), pp. 125–7.

139

even more cheerful and energetic than before. Certain that she had gone on some pleasant holiday at her expense, Wikan considered dismissing the girl for lying. Talking to others, however, she discovered that the girl was telling the truth: her fiancé, whom she had loved very much, had indeed died of a sudden illness. Over time, Wikan came to understand that the Balinese believe sad feelings to be dangerous to a person's health. If you brood and let yourself grieve, you weaken your life force, and become prey to malign forces. It is therefore best to respond to loss by distracting oneself, focusing on happy events, and acting cheerfully.[2]

Human beings experience emotions in ways that are shaped both by individual history and by social norms. My own grief was shaped not only by my attachment to my mother, but also by norms about the proper way to mourn the loss of a parent. These norms, as I experienced them through my own inclinations, were unclear and to some extent inconsistent, with elements of the Ifaluk and the Balinese uneasily thrust together. One is supposed to allow oneself to "cry big" at times, but then American mores of self-help also demand that one get on with one's work, one's physical exercise, one's commitments to others, not making a big fuss. Thus I considered canceling the lecture I had been writing on the plane, out of respect for my mother and my grief. I wanted to give some sign that, only one week after the funeral, I could not go on as if everything were all right. Canceling seemed one substitute for dressing in black, an expressive gesture no longer available. But I was soon urged by friends that canceling a big lecture would be a bad thing. One doesn't defect from a commitment that way, they said, and one should be able to rise to the occasion. Besides, they said, it would be good for my psychic health to focus on something that I could control, in which I was not helpless. These contradictory instructions came, as well, from my own history, as I asked myself what my mother would have wanted of me (prolonged sadness, or so I felt), and what my father would have said (that a person of dignity carries on in the face of misfortune, head "bloodied but unbowed").[3] (These differences instantiate common gender differences in the responses of Amer-

2 Personal communication, Unni Wikan; see also Wikan (1990).
3 See Nussbaum (1998) for the association of these poetic lines with my father's view of life.

icans to sad events.)[4] At times I focused on thoughts of loss, and had periods of intense weeping; but I also prided myself on making the lecture as good as it could possibly be, tirelessly revising it, distracting myself from thoughts of grief. I felt guilty when I was grieving, because I wasn't working on the lecture; and I felt guilty when I was working on the lecture, because I wasn't grieving. The night before the lecture my hosts wanted to take me to a festive dinner, but there I drew the line. Eating a big celebratory meal seemed to me disrespectful and terrible. Some of my hosts understood these feelings, but others thought me peculiar. I ate quietly in someone's home, insisting on baked chicken with no sauce.

So far I have stressed the universality of certain human emotions. Based, as they are, on vulnerabilities and attachments that human beings can hardly fail to have, given the nature of their bodies and their world, emotions such as fear, love, anger, and grief are likely to be ubiquitous in some form. I have argued, moreover, that they are elements of our common animality with considerable adaptive significance: so their biological basis is likely to be common to all. But this does not mean that emotions are not differently shaped by different societies. The capacity for language is, similarly, common to all, and any infant can learn any language – but languages nonetheless differ greatly, both in structure and in semantics, and to some extent therefore in expressive range. We now must ask to what degree emotional repertoires also differ, and to what extent these variations are caused by societal, rather than individual, differences.

It is evident that the behavior associated with emotion differs greatly in my three cases. But it is likely that the differences run deeper, affecting the experience of the emotion itself. All three bereaved people have suffered an important loss, going to the heart of their goals and plans. But the responses to the loss take very different forms, and not only outwardly. The Ifaluk mother believes that she will be ill if she does not dwell on her grief and indulge in sad thoughts. Wikan's

4 See Nolen-Hoeksema (1990), who argues that women are more at risk for depressive illness than are men, because they tend to respond to reversals and losses by indulging in sad thoughts and picturing themselves as helpless, rather than by distracting themselves and getting on with life, a common male response. To a degree, she endorses the Balinese theory that sad thoughts make you ill.

housekeeper believes that she will be ill if she *does* indulge in sad thoughts, and therefore she tries not only to behave cheerfully but also to distract herself with happy thoughts. I oscillated between the belief that it is a sign of respect and love to the dead to focus on loss and sadness, and the belief that one should distract oneself and go about one's business, showing that one is not helpless. These differences marked not only my behavior but also my inner experience.

A cognitive/evaluative conception of emotion is neither necessary nor sufficient for the recognition of significant social variation, or, as it is frequently called, "social construction." If one held a mechanistic or hydraulic conception of emotion, it would be somewhat difficult to see how societies could mold or shape emotions in different ways, but it would not be impossible. Plato, in the *Laws*, seems to hold that emotions are unreasoning movements in the organism, and yet he offers advice to pregnant women about how to soothe and mold the emotions of their fetuses by regular rhythmic movement and other noncognitive techniques. Nor is a cognitive/evaluative view sufficient for the recognition of "social construction": for one might hold that the relevant cognitions are universal, and shaped by our common situation as vulnerable beings in a world we do not control. Or one might hold that there is significant variation among emotional repertories, but that the primary source of variation lies in the developmental history of individual children with individual parents.

On the other hand, taking up a cognitive/evaluative view makes it easy to see how society could affect the emotional repertory of its members. If we hold that beliefs about what is important and valuable play a central role in emotions, we can readily see how those beliefs can be powerfully shaped by social norms as well as by an individual history; and we can also see how changing social norms can change emotional life. This was, of course, central to the ethical program of the original Stoics, who used their cognitive/evaluative conception of emotions to show how societies might rid themselves of some pernicious forms of anger, envy, and fear. Although they themselves tended to focus on large general areas of emotional life that to some extent all societies share, their view naturally lends itself to the recognition of differences between one set of social norms and another. The Stoics did not care much about these differences, because they held the extreme view that all emotions are bad, and thus that all known societies are profoundly diseased. If one should reject that extreme view and yet still hold that there are some emotions that are socially pernicious, social variation would become of major significance. For one would then want to look and see what different societies do about emotions, and whether there are better and worse ways of constructing an emotional taxonomy. We will face these normative issues much later; but we can only face them well if we have some sense of the degree and nature of emotions' social variability.

Theorists of emotion frequently fall into one or the other of two extreme camps on this issue. Some theorists completely ignore the role of society, and treat emotional life as universal in all salient respects. This is a common position in evolutionary psychology, and in at least some work in cognitive psychology that emphasizes, following Darwin, the putative universality of facial expressions as indicators of emotion.[5] It is equally common, however, in psychoanalysis, where the role of cultural factors in shaping the developmental process is only just beginning to be discussed.[6] Psychoanalytic thinkers are usually practitioners with a culturally narrow sphere of reference. They frequently have difficulty distinguishing the universal from the local in what they observe, and often don't even raise the question. We notice local Viennese cultural patterns in Freud's patients, features of British emotional life in Bowlby's and Winnicott's patients, American styles of parenting (focused on both empathy and independence) in Mahler's and Stern's parental subjects, and so forth; but few analysts build the recognition of cultural difference into their accounts.

At the other extreme, anthropologists sometimes speak as if the emotional repertory of a society were socially constructed through and through, and as if there were few limits imposed on this constructing by either biology or common circumstances of life. At the very least, there is often a certain lack of curiosity about what this commonality might be. The tendency to present cultures as emotion-systems with

5 See, for example, Paul Ekman's influential work on facial expression, which continues Darwin's views: Ekman has published many articles on this topic, but a representative account of his view can be found in Ekman (1975, 1993, 1994) and in Ekman and Davidson (1994). Ekman does not always claim that his view shows a complete universality in emotion across cultures; but he is generally understood as having made that claim. I shall assess his view later in section IV.
6 See, for example, Kurtz (1992), Kakar (1978), Carstairs (1967). For a brief but effective early discussion of this question, see Klein (1984), pp. 247–63, especially pp. 262–3.

little overlap is exacerbated when the researcher describes a culture in general terms, ignoring the variety of its individual members. Recently more complex conceptions of culture have been emerging in anthropology, with an emphasis on plurality, conflict, and porous boundaries; these have paved the way for more balanced and nuanced accounts of a society's specific emotional range.[7]

A good account of social variation in emotion, then, should neither exaggerate difference nor overlook it – a platitude easy to endorse in theory, and far more difficult to realize in practice. As in the previous chapter, my aim in developing such an account is to show how the cognitive/evaluative view needs to be modified or supplemented. This can most effectively be done if we first reflect about some differences between humans and other animals that play a role in the social construction of emotion. We can then proceed to identify the most salient *sources* of social variation; and this, in turn, will put us in a position to describe the most common *types* and *levels* of variation.

II. HUMAN–ANIMAL DIFFERENCES: TIME, LANGUAGE, NORMS

In nonhuman animals, the capacity for *temporal thinking* – for memory, for expectation, for conceiving of a life as a temporal process with a beginning, a development, and an end – is obviously limited. These limits are different in different species, but even in dogs and primates temporal thinking plays a far smaller role than it does in the life of a normal human adult, for whom time is a background grid on which the self orients itself, and without which it cannot experience itself as a continuous self.[8] To the extent to which an animal lacks awareness of the passage of time, it must also lack a sense of habit and routine, something that is also of great consequence for the sense of self and the emotional life.[9]

To the extent that awareness of time is lacking, the capacity of other animals for *generalizing* is limited. All animals recognize at least some objects as instances of types seen before. Thus, their very ability to

7 See, for example, Lutz (1988), Briggs (1970), Turner (1998).
8 See the wonderful discussion in Proust, I.5–6.
9 This is, of course, a central theme in Proust's account of emotion; I shall discuss it further in Chapter 4.

survive requires the recognition of "food," of dangerous predators (general schemata for which are probably innate), and of members of their own species. But types of generalizing that require a sophisticated awareness of historical patterns or of social structures will elude them. Lupa and Remus could generalize about many things, including the likely structure of a day; they could therefore expect the arrival of Pitcher and Cone at a definite hour. They also had other general concepts, such as "thief" and "dangerous human," and "guest of my friends," and even "time for the guest to get up," as well as the more obvious "food" and "walk" and "sit." Nonetheless, insofar as they lacked a sense of history, they lacked the capacity for other types of generalization pertinent to their lives, for example, the notion of "being abused in childhood" or of "middle-aged man"; and many that were not very pertinent, involving political or civic affairs.

Putting these two elements together, we find that there are thoughts of potential import to emotional and moral life that nonhuman animals are unlikely to be able to form: for example, the idea of membership in a distinctive group with a distinctive history, perhaps a history of glorious deeds, perhaps a history of oppression; the idea of being a member of a species that has done great evil and can also do what is right; the idea of planning or striving for the realization of national or global justice; the idea that certain calamities are the common lot of one's species. We should not posit a sharp discontinuity between human beings and other species: recent research with chimpanzees and bonobos shows their remarkable capacity to learn a conceptual repertory, which matches that of children around the age of three or four.[10]

Animals also vary in the degree to which they have *causal concepts*; and again, most species have them to a much less marked degree than do human beings. Lupa clearly had many forms of causal thinking: she saw Pitcher as the person who fed her, she saw a stick as a likely cause of abuse, and so forth. To that extent, she could have emotions such as shame and anger, which seem to be dependent on forms of causal thinking ("he did that to me," "I disappointed him in this way"). Many animals do not have the basis for such emotions. It is, of course, difficult to tell to what extent an animal's reactions express a condi-

10 See references in the following note, and the useful summary of recent research in Wise (2000) Chapters 8–10, with references.

tioned routine, and to what extent they express a more specific cognition with real causal content. But Pitcher's history with Lupa shows, I think, that the dog was able to move from a mere association between the men's presence and the food to some thought more like, "This man has brought me food." This clearly underlay her eventual change in demeanor toward Pitcher, and her subsequent expectations, demands, and so forth. Certain causal stories, however, Lupa was unlikely to tell herself: for example, those that point to a history of oppression and abuse beginning in childhood. She is unlikely to conceive of herself as Pitcher does, as a dog who was once shamefully abused but who is now loved and cared for; certainly she did not believe that she was abused by a human because she was a dog. Nor would she, like Pitcher, trace her adult states of shyness and suspiciousness to a childhood history that explains them.

All normal humans can imagine what it is like to be in the shoes of another, and from early childhood they receive constant practice in this ability. Such perspectival thinking is fundamental to human emotional and moral life. I have argued that Lupa and Remus have this ability to a limited degree, in the sense that they do respond to cues of sadness sent by Pitcher and offer him consolation. Apes have more sophisticated forms of the ability, and are able to engage in imitative play, to recognize their images as such in a mirror, and in other ways to manifest a sophisticated awareness of positionality and self–other relatedness.[11] The degree to which a creature possesses these abilities will be fundamental to its capacity for compassion and love.

Some emotions will prove altogether unavailable to many animals, to the extent that the sort of thinking underlying them proves unavailable: hope, for example, with its robust sense of future possibility; guilt, with its keen identification of a past wrongdoer with the agent's own present self;[12] romantic love, to the extent that it involves a temporal sense of aim and aspiration, and a fine sense of particularity; compassion, to the extent that it calls upon a sense of general possibility and fellow feeling; types of shame that involve thought of a norm against

11 See de Waal (1989, 1996), de Waal and Lanting (1997), and Wise (2000), esp. pp. 152–4, comparing the performance of a chimpanzee on a test of perspectival thinking with that of an autistic child (the chimp performed much better).

12 On this, see the fine remarks of Nietzsche in *Genealogy of Morals*, Essay II, on "breed[ing] an animal with the right to make promises."

which one has measured oneself and found oneself wanting; and even some forms of anger, fear, and grief, to the extent to which they require causal and temporal judgments. Apes and dogs can have some of these, or can have them to some degree; but many animals lack them entirely.

Only humans, it seems, elaborate explicit theories of the world. Religion, metaphysics, philosophy, and science are human phenomena. But this, too, makes a great difference to the emotional life, not only by giving the human being new emotional objects (Nature, God), but also by providing a framework of understanding within which causal and temporal thinking will operate. The nature of this framework will shape the emotions. Thus anger is shaped by views about who is responsible for what, and how the causality of evil works. Fear is shaped by thoughts about what harmful agencies exist in the world, how harmful they are, and how to ward them off.

All these cognitive differences between humans and animals create differences in the concept of self, and the concept of relations between self and other. The way we see ourselves depends upon our innate cognitive and perceptual and integrative capacities, but also on our specific conceptions of temporality, of causality; on our conceptions of species and nation and family; on ideas of god, spirits, and the universe. It depends upon the degree to which we grasp our distinctness from others, and also on the degree to which we consider ourselves members of categories along with others. Animals have comparably rudimentary self-conceptions, in many cases none at all.

The emotions' eudaimonistic character rests upon a sense of the self, its goals and projects. It will therefore vary with the conception of self in each species. For all animals, some parts of the world stand out as salient, as connected with urgent needs of the self. But the human animal is much more likely to have a relatively organized and comprehensive conception of the self and its goals, much more likely to think of these goals as forming some sort of network, and much more likely to include among them persons and things at a distance, either spatially or temporally.[13] Furthermore, humans have an unparalleled flexibility in the goals they will pursue.

13 Good accounts of goal hierarchies are in Ortony et al. (1988) and Lazarus (1991). Scruton (1997) offers the following helpful formulation: "In general, the emotions of self-conscious beings have a structure which distinguishes them from the motives of animals. A self-conscious subject is aware not only of the object of a feeling, but also

From this follow a number of implications for the logic of the emotions. First, that in the human case there *is* logic in them, to an extent unknown in the rest of the animal world. Humans may form inconsistent goals and have emotions accordingly; but the awareness of an inconsistency is likely to be a reason for deliberation, self-criticism, or at least anxiety in a way that it will not be in the other species.

More generally, human emotions, unlike animal emotions, are subject to deliberation and revision in connection with general deliberation about one's goals and projects. If, like Seneca, a person believes that dignity requires depending on nothing and nobody outside himself, and yet at the same time is so passionately attached to his status and reputation that he is furious at being seated in a less-than-high place at a dinner party,[14] this is an inconsistency: for he both believes and does not believe that a certain external item is of enormous importance. Sort this out, and get your life in order, Seneca tells himself. This does not mean that it will be easy to get rid of anger, or grief, or fear, where these do not accord with our reflective sense of value: for the judgments these emotions embody may lie very deep in the personality, and be settled parts of our sense of self. But they are in principle available for deliberation and "therapy," as part of my general deliberation about *eudaimonia*. This deliberative activity is initiated in interactions with others, and is carried out in substantial measure in the context of such interactions.

Human deliberative sociability also affects the range of emotions of which humans are capable. For it permits the object of an emotion to be a group: the city or country or nation itself, and possibly even the whole of humanity – abstractions of which no other animal is capable. Some social and interactive emotions involve complicated forms of reciprocity that are peculiarly human: thus animals may have attachment, but few will have love in the sense in which Aristotle defines it, that is, as requiring mutual awareness, mutual good intentions, and reciprocity.

---

of himself as its subject. He therefore *puts himself into* his emotion, and expresses himself through it. To a varying extent, his emotions are artefacts of his own devising, and grow from thoughts not only about the object, but also about the subject. Hence self-conscious emotions are liable to corruption in ways which are unknown in the animal kingdom. They can become narcissistic, sentimental, bathetic . . ." (pp. 347–8).

14 See Seneca, *De Ira*, III.36 ff.

And since humans are more fully social, they are also more fully capable of being *alone* – therefore of the exhilaration of solitary contemplation, of awe before the silence of nature, of peaceful solitary joy at the air and light that surround them, also of loneliness, of the gloomy horror that can seize one in the middle of a forest, in whose shadows one finds images of one's own death. It seems likely that the capacity to be alone (even in the presence of others) is fundamental to human emotional development, and an important determinant of adult human emotional relationships.[15]

In short, in an ethical and social/political creature, emotions themselves are ethical and social/political, parts of an answer to the questions, "What is worth caring about?" "How should I live?"[16]

At the same time, however, human emotions at times go beyond their eudaimonistic framework, in a way that animal emotions more rarely do. Thus, it seems likely that few if any nonhuman animals experience wonder and awe, emotions that, as I argued in Chapter 1, depart from the focus on one's own scheme of goals and projects.

Language, I have said, is not everything in emotion: emotions can be based on other forms of symbolic representation. But the fact of language does change emotion. The fact that we label our emotions alters the emotions we can have. (So much is presumably true of those apes who have learned American Sign Language.) We do not simply apply terms to antecedently organized items. In the process of labeling, we are also frequently organizing, bounding some things off from others, sharpening distinctions that may have been experienced in an inchoate way. From then on, we experience our emotions in ways guided by these descriptions.

A person who does not know the emotional "grammar" of his or her society cannot be assumed to have the same emotional life as one who does know this "grammar." To be able to articulate one's emotions is *eo ipso* to have a different emotional life. This does not mean that one cannot fear without being able to name one's fear, and so forth; I have said that there are many reasons why an emotion, espe-

---

15 See Winnicott (1965), to be discussed in Chapter 4.
16 I do not mean to deny that some revisability is in principle present in the emotions of some higher animals as well: but it would have to be assessed on a species-by-species basis, in connection with the creature's ability to form and reevaluate general plans and goals.

cially a background emotion, might remain unconscious, in a person who could readily recognize and label the emotion in the right circumstances. But a person who never develops fluency with the emotion words at all, and with the criteria for their application, is likely to be different "inside" from the person who does.

This sheds light on a complicated problem. For there is a good deal of research showing that, in our society, males are far more likely than are females to be inept at labeling their emotions. They tend not to know what evaluative/situational criteria to look for; and whatever does not manifest itself in the form of a strong physiological feeling, they have trouble naming.[17] This does not appear to be true in societies in which males are socialized to pay more attention to these things,[18] nor is it by any means true of all men in American society; so we should probably not think of it as a biologically based gender difference. It is more likely to be explained by the fact that American boys spend a great deal of time playing sports together, whereas girls are more likely to spend time talking about people together. In any case, one might be tempted to take the view that these males actually have all the same emotions, but just don't know how to talk about them. This view is appealing, since it offers the hope of discovery, of "opening up," and thus of mutual understanding. But if, as seems more philosophically plausible, the real conclusion to be drawn is that such men really do not have exactly the same "inner" life, or experience exactly the same emotions, then the prospects for understanding are less rosy.

All these differences – but especially those connected with labeling and deliberation about the good – give us reason to look at the role played by society in constructing emotions. Animals have emotions about other animals with whom they share a society; but human societies transmit practices of emotion labeling and normative evaluation

17 See Pennebaker and Roberts (1992) for some very interesting findings and a comprehensive bibliography. Their conclusion is that males and females label the same emotion via different criteria: males by attending to their respiration, heart rate, etc., females by attending to the situation, their reasoning about it, etc. It would be better, I think, to say that the females succeed in naming *fear* and *anger* and *love*, whereas the males are attaching those terms to physiological states that might or might not be correlated with those emotions, and thus showing their ignorance of the "grammar" of the emotions.

18 See, for example, Briggs (1970), Lutz (1988); and consider the meticulousness of emotional labeling among Romans influenced by Stoicism, for whom Epictetus' injunction to watch over oneself as over an enemy led to practices of obsessive self-scrutiny – on which see Foucault (1986).

that actually enter into the content of the emotions their members will have.[19] The thesis of "social construction," in its most plausible form, is the thesis that these practices, in their specificity, make a difference to a society's emotional repertory.[20]

III. SOURCES OF SOCIAL VARIATION

Human life has some invariant features that are dictated by the nature of our bodies and of the world in which we live. We are physically weak among the species, and cognitively mature at an early age, while we are still physically helpless. (In the next chapter we will see that these features produce some constant general patterns of emotional development.) There are many things that are really dangerous to us, and which we therefore have good reason to fear, assuming that we are attached to our own survival, as we innately are. Thus it would be a remarkable society that contained no fear, and a highly unsuccessful one. But certain specific fears are also ubiquitous, and dictated by our animal heritage: the fear of snakes, for example, appears to be innate and based on perceptual schemata that have adaptive significance. Fears of thunder and lightning, of sudden loud noises, of large animals – all of these are, once again, ubiquitous and highly functional.[21] (It is now thought that children all pass through a long sequence of fears,

19 An odd consequence of Wise's (2000) convincing case for seeing chimpanzees and bonobos as capable of many types of human thinking – roughly, the level of a three-to four-year-old child – is the thought that this potential is most fully realized when apes live among humans and are socialized and taught by them. What research would appear to show is that these apes have capacities that their own educational and social practices do not fully tap.

20 The claim that emotions are "socially constructed" has been advanced in cognitive psychology by James Averill (1980, 1982), whose work is extremely rigorous and well-argued; see also Lazarus (1991); in anthropology, a beginning was made by the influential work of the late Michelle Rosaldo – see, for example, Rosaldo (1980, 1984), and Schweder and LeVine (1994); see also Harré (1986) for a representative collection of recent work. Two anthropological studies that have greatly impressed me along these lines are Briggs (1970), a remarkable account of the Ifaluk, an Eskimo people who eschew anger and aggression, and Lutz (1988), an account of a Polynesian community, with a substantial theoretical discussion. This work has close connections to the historical and "genealogical" work on sexual desire in Foucault (1985, 1986); and see also Halperin (1990).

21 See Pinker (1997), pp. 386–8, referring to studies of snake fear by D. O. Hebb and Mark Hauser. Spiders are also universally scary; other fears that appear to have a universal basis are fears of darkness, large animals, deep water, confinement. These are all circumstances that really did spell danger to our ancestors.

and that most are eventually mastered after being activated.[22] Thus a child who fears large dogs would be a child who had never unlearned a fear with an innate basis, not a child who had learned an atypical fear.) Similarly, all known societies contain some varieties of anger, hope, and grief. Strong attachments to parents or caretakers are also ubiquitous, as are the early bases of imaginative empathy and social compassion.[23]

What features of societal difference might plausibly be invoked in arguing for intersocietal differences in the emotional life? First, there are *physical conditions*. Some societies face danger from the elements on a much more regular basis than do others. Lutz plausibly argues that Ifaluk culture – an island culture based on a fishing economy – is especially preoccupied with the dangers of nature, and that its emotional repertory has developed in response to this preoccupation. Some face hostile enemies more regularly than do others. Thus a young Roman under the Empire would be taught that his task in life was to beat down all the barbarian enemies of Rome, and this would inform his emotional development and response. Some societies, and groups within societies, have opportunities for leisure that others do not. This, again, will shape the range of emotions that will be developed and expressed: certain sorts of highly self-conscious romantic love seem to require a relatively unharried middle-class or even aristocratic life. Some people live crowded together and others spend a good deal of time in solitude. Thus Finnish people intensely cultivate and prize emotions connected to the solitary contemplation of the forest, one's own smallness and insignificance in the face of monumental nature; the conditions for these specific experiences are unknown in Calcutta. Some need to cooperate closely in order to survive at all, while others may go their own way, pursuing self-directed projects. The Utku Eskimos studied by Jean Briggs needed fine-tuned cooperation at all times in order to hunt enough food to live, in the inhospitable climate; they therefore could not afford hostility that would have done little harm in the old American West, with its wide-open spaces for people to avoid each other.

Second, societies differ in their *metaphysical, religious, and cosmological beliefs*. The fear of death, which in some form is ubiquitous,

22 See Marks (1987).
23 See Chapters 4 and 6.

will be powerfully shaped by what one thinks death is, and whether one believes there is an afterlife. The Hindu theory that we should renounce selfish urges and desires shapes the emotional lives of people who believe it, and even their practices of child rearing.[24] The belief that an enemy's curse can cause death shapes emotional life so profoundly that, as Seligman has shown, it may produce a sense of extreme helplessness resulting in sudden death.

Grief is deeply affected by these metaphysical differences. Although people who have a confident belief in an afterlife still grieve for the deaths of loved ones, they usually grieve differently, and their grief is linked to hope. Not so the Ifaluk, for whom any death tears a hole in the fabric of the community, jeopardizing its safety. The Balinese theory of the vital force and its enemies shapes Balinese grief, teaching people to view it as a dangerous threat to health. So too, in somewhat related ways, does the American theory (of Protestant European origin) that one can conquer all contingencies through work: grieving is thus sometimes felt as a sign that one is not making sufficient effort. (An idiosyncratic offshoot of this view is found in the metaphysics of Christian Science, whose members believe that bodily disease is caused by personal deficiencies in religious willing. This view leads to a radical denial of grief.)

Practices also shape emotional life, usually in ways that are closely connected to physical conditions and metaphysical beliefs. For example, practices of child rearing differ in significant ways, probably with significant effects on emotional development. Chinese infants are typically encouraged to be immobile. Their limbs are tightly wrapped; styles of interaction discourage initiative and promote peace. American children, by contrast, are given a lot of stimulation and encouraged to move; their limbs are free. Again, a typical Indian infant is constantly carried by its mother on her hip during the first months of life, and is given the breast on demand; at the same time, the mother spends little time talking to her child or interacting with it, frequently because she has other children and tasks to attend to, also because her dwelling is likely to be highly porous, with people from her extended family and village moving in and out.[25] American infants, by contrast, usually have long periods of physical separation from the mother's body, and fre-

24 See Kurtz (1992).
25 Kurtz (1992), Kakar (1978), Carstairs (1967).

quently cry before feeding; at the same time, the mother interacts a lot with the infant, smiling and talking – partly because she spends long stretches of her time alone with the infant, in a single-family dwelling where privacy is the norm, and is less likely to have many other children to attend to. All of these differences influence development, though the nature of these influences is hard to pin down.

Weaning practices, once again, vary greatly. American mothers usually wean gradually, after the child is well accustomed to solid food. Utku children are weaned abruptly in favor of the newborn baby: they suddenly find themselves turned away from the breast and see another child in their place. Briggs not implausibly connects this difference to the intense sibling jealousies that characteristically erupt.

In later childhood we also find large cultural differences. Utku children are permitted to display aggression against siblings in ways that shocked Briggs, because of the Utku theory that children do not have reason, or the ability to control their passions. American parents tend to expect more control, believing that children are capable of control. American children generally see their mothers daily throughout their childhood. The Indian male child, by contrast, is often moved suddenly, at around the age of six, from the constant company of his mother to a male world where he rarely sees the mother. Similarly, British children of the upper classes are frequently sent quite suddenly from the sheltering atmosphere of the nursery to boarding school at the age of eight, a world that is (still) usually single-sex and highly hierarchical. Again, we may expect that these differences have some impact on emotional development, although, again, it is difficult to isolate these factors and to say precisely what their influence is.

In all cultures, practices of child rearing mark at least some differences between boys and girls, although the degree and nature of these differences will vary across cultures and individuals. The practice of training males for separation from the mother, and females for continuity with the mother's domestic function, profoundly shapes gender development in many societies.[26]

It is extremely important not to generalize prematurely about such cultural practices. Any cultural group, studied in sufficient detail, exhibits many different practices, even in these familiar areas of child

26 See Chodorow (1978).

development. (Male–female differences, for example, are too rarely studied with the care that they deserve.)[27] Amy Halberstadt's studies of American children from different ethnic and economic backgrounds shows a wide range of family styles in the areas of communication and expressiveness – as we would naturally expect, since we are used to the fact that people we know are different from one another, WASP families different from Jewish families, and so forth. Some families talk a lot and some do not; some tell each other what is on their minds, others bottle up grievances.[28] We should not make the mistake of thinking that members of a distant culture, especially one as vast and diverse as India, for example, are more homogeneous than we take members of our own culture to be. Many generalizations that are made about "the Indian child," however suggestive, rest on a very small sample and don't adequately reflect cultural, religious, or regional differences – or differences of sex, since all the studies have focused exclusively on boys.[29] Briggs's study of the Utku and Lutz's of the Ifaluk are different because they have attempted to examine all individuals, albeit within a very small population; the studies carry conviction in part because they do point to significant differences among families and individuals.

Language differences probably shape emotional life in some ways, but the role of language has often been overestimated, and it is very difficult to estimate it correctly. For example, we should not make the common error of supposing that if there is no single term in a language for an experience, that experience must be lacking. This is just as wrong as the idea that if a word is the same the experience is likely to be the same. Aristotle already pointed out that certain patterns of virtuous conduct that he could clearly describe and exemplify from his culture had no one-word name in his language. This "namelessness" probably has some significance. For example, the fact that there was no name for a moderate disposition of character with regard to anger and retaliation (Aristotle has to co-opt the concededly imperfect term "mildness," *praotês*) probably reflects the fact that his culture placed an unusually high value on retributive conduct, and spoke about it far

27 See Kurtz (1992).
28 Halberstadt (1991); see also Parke et al. (1992).
29 See Kurtz (1992), pointing out that the studies that have given rise to the sweeping hypotheses of Carstairs and Kakar rest on a handful of scattered observations.

more than about mild conduct. Nonetheless, his audience was expected to recognize what "mildness" was, and that "mildness" was not quite the right term for it (because even the "mild" person will take revenge when his family is damaged).

So too with emotion terms. The fact that Greek and Roman cultures have many fine-grained words for different varieties of anger shows us that they were unusually preoccupied with that emotion. But once we read their definitions we can understand how they were individuating the kinds, and recognize examples of these kinds in our own world. Thus it would take further argument to show that the presence of a large number of distinct words really made a difference in the emotional life itself. Cicero points out that Latin has only a single word for love, *amor*, whereas Greek has a plurality of terms; and yet he expects his readers to be familiar with the different types of love identified by the Greek discussions: they are just different subtypes of *amor*, to be marked off by further qualifying words.[30]

Language is most revealing as a source of difference when we find a culture classifying together things that we would usually classify apart. Thus Lutz shows that the Ifaluk word for love, *fago*, is also the word for compassionate care for the weak, sadness at the lot of the unfortunate, and so forth. It thus covers part of the territory of "compassion," and yet it is the central term for personal love. Lutz plausibly argues that Americans focus on romantic love as the paradigm case of "love," while the Ifaluk focus on maternal nurturance and, more generally, on meeting the basic needs of another, as the paradigm experience of *fago*. This probably reveals (or helps to constitute) at least some difference in the emotional life. Americans probably do think of romantic love as more central in their conception of what life is about than do the Ifaluk, and their emotional experience varies accordingly. Language, of course, doesn't shape these differences by itself: in this case, we can understand the difference as growing largely out of differences in physical condition. A society that is preoccupied with bare survival may have less time for romantic love than a prosperous society, and is more likely to focus on compassionate care for vulnerability as a core experience. But it is plausible to think that the culture's vocabulary does also shape, to some extent, its members' sense of what is salient in experience.

30 Cicero, *Tusculan Disputations*, IV.

Finally, and perhaps most important of all, *social norms* pertinent to the emotional life vary. If emotions are evaluative appraisals, then cultural views about what is valuable can be expected to affect them very directly. Thus a culture that values honor highly, and attaches a strong negative value to the slighting of honor, will have many occasions for anger that an equality focused culture such as that of the Utku will not have. The Stoics were correct to think that the more one values external goods that are not stably within one's control, the more occasions one has for all sorts of emotions, such as fear, grief, anger, envy, jealousy, and hope. (As Seneca said, "You will cease to fear, if you cease to hope.") Societies have different normative teachings with regard to the importance of honor, money, bodily beauty and health, friendship, children, political power. They therefore have many differences in anger, envy, fear, love, and grief.

IV. TYPES AND LEVELS OF VARIATION

First and most obviously, the criteria for the appropriate *behavioral manifestation* of emotions such as fear and anger are socially taught, and may vary considerably from society to society. The Ifaluk learn to "cry big" at a loss, the Balinese to smile and appear cheerful, the English to manifest composed restraint.[31] Cathy Lutz found Ifaluk wailing shocking, but an American might also be shocked by British decorum. To the Utku, Western people are childish in their volatile expression of anger and sorrow; they are said to be an uncontrolled and bad-tempered race. To a Finn, the happy greeting of an American runner, smiling on the path, seems an intrusion bordering on hostility: one does not behave with merry joy in the forest, and one certainly does not invade the contemplative space of another person.

In some cases, we should probably imagine that emotional experience remains very similar, and that it is only the outward manifestation that is different. As we can tell from literature, letters, and personal friendships, British and American grief are probably not very dissimilar, although the rules for public manifestation are somewhat different. In other cases, the behavioral rules probably alter the experience itself.

---

31 The public response to the death of Princess Diana shows that these norms are changing – but not for the upper classes.

Finns certainly do experience profound joy, but the merry casual joy of the outgoing exuberant American, who waves at a fellow runner, is a type of joy that may be unavailable to people who have learned to be extremely shy and introverted, and who associate the forest with profound thoughts about helplessness and the shortness of life. Few Finnish emotions are casual or easily tapped.[32] This makes an experiential difference.

Paul Ekman's research on facial expression, following Darwin, suggests that certain facial expressions are cross-culturally recognized as signs of anger, fear, disgust, surprise, joy, or sadness. Less conclusively, he also shows a cross-cultural tendency to display such expressions, in the appropriate circumstances. (For example, even Japanese subjects who quickly inhibited manifestation of one of the classic expressions showed, when observed without their knowledge, a momentary tendency of the mouth toward making the expression.) What exactly does this research show?

I have to admit to a brain deficiency here, because I don't always find it easy to recognize the emotions of the subjects in these photographs; insofar as I do recognize some of them, they tend to look like the contortions of children making faces, not like expressions that a real person would have. And I have a tendency to wonder whether what I'm seeing is the habitual pattern of frown lines in the face of an older person who might be perfectly happy at that moment, or an expression of an actual sadness. But let us bypass these worries and stipulate that the research does show what Ekman claims it does. What would this itself show? It would show that there is probably some underlying evolutionary basis to some emotional behavior and signalling. It does not show, of course, that this cross-cultural part is central to emotion-behavior in a given culture, or that a person could not be recognized as having the emotion in question without it. It also does not show that the tendency in the direction of a given kind of facial behavior could not be effectively overridden by social teaching – as the manifestations of sadness expected by Wikan were overridden, in her employee's behavior, by teaching that such expressions were dangerous. And of course it does not show that the facial expression in

---

32 For eight years I spent one month every summer in Finland, and I still return there almost every year.

question cannot be assumed by someone who doesn't have the emotion in question. That's what deception is all about.

Moreover, as Paul Griffiths points out, Ekman's research claims something far out of line with the data when it claims to show that *emotions* are universally experienced. For the research deals exclusively with the behavioral manifestation of (some) emotions (what Griffiths calls the "output" side), and with only a part of that behavioral manifestation. It does not deal at all with the emotions' content, or with the ways people interpret situations as calling for a particular emotion.[33] It thus has nothing to say about universality in occasions for anger, or grief, or fear. Those are matters of interpretation and belief, and the studies confine themselves to behavior and recognition of behavior.

Thus the claim of behavioral universality can be accepted in the case of some emotions, without at all compromising a case for cultural variation. A second type of variation is social variation in the *judgments about the worth of an entire emotion category*. Briggs's Utku Eskimos teach that anger is always inappropriate, because it is always inappropriate, at least for an adult, to care deeply about slights and damages. Although they do backslide, and certainly do experience anger,[34] the Utku always feel it to be a sign of immaturity, which infantilizes the possessor. Adults should put away such childish things. In this, if not across the board,[35] they are true Stoics. Although it is difficult for the anthropologist to get at the distinction between displaying and having an emotion, Briggs's argument is convincing on this point, since she was careful to engage in prolonged conversation with her family about norms of human goodness. Especially revealing was their discomfort at the incident in the Bible in which Jesus drives the money changers out of the temple. As good Christians they had to endorse this, but they really had trouble fitting it into their normative picture of Jesus' character (not just his public demeanor). Their explanation: he did scold the money changers, but not out of anger – he did it in

---

33 Griffiths (1997), Chapter 3.

34 Briggs's findings are misreported in Pinker (1997), who attacks the view that the Utku "have no word for anger and do not feel the emotion" (Pinker, pp. 364–6). Briggs describes at length a complex set of terms for various types of angry emotion and behavior, finding at least five terms in the language that refer to angry emotion (Briggs, [1970], pp. 328–37).

35 They are permitted to have strong attachments that are associated with longing, loneliness, even grief.

order to improve them, since they were being "very bad, *very bad*, and refusing to listen to him."[36] In general Jesus is praised for his lack of anger. (Briggs noted that the Utku, ashamed of being angry, gave their dogs unusually severe punishments – not admitting to anger, and treating the punishment as a form of training. Nonetheless, she plausibly saw in the striking harshness a back-door outlet for emotions of anger and frustration that could not be acknowledged to one's fellow humans.)

Contrast the attitude toward anger in the Rome described by Seneca, where it was expected that a truly manly man would be extremely attached to his honor and therefore eager to get angry at any slight or damage. Anger is classified in both Greek and Roman Stoic taxonomies as a pleasant emotion directed at the future, because of the pleasure of contemplating revenge. This is a specific cultural idea. Even though modern Americans are closer to the Romans than to the Utku in violent behavior, our norms about the appropriateness of anger are much more ambivalent. In years of polling my classes as to where they would categorize anger along the Stoic good–present, good–future, bad–present, bad–future axes, I have found not one student (apart from experts in Stoicism) who classified anger in the good–future category, as the Greek and Roman philosophers all do. Our Christian heritage has at least some impact on our view about anger, if not always on our actions.

Such differences in normative judgment affect experience itself. For an Utku, being angry will be hooked up to shame and the feeling of diminished adulthood; for a Roman, it will be hooked up to a feeling of manly pride, and to a quasi-erotic excitement, as he prepares to smash the adversary. Americans are raised with conflicting signals, and different Americans are raised differently, with gender differences being especially prominent among the sources of variation. As a child I learned to find anger terrifying, and came to believe that it meant that I would do something irrevocably destructive; as I mentioned in Chapter 1, this means that I rarely experience it directly, but discover its presence through headaches, patterns of behavior, and so forth. My audiences, especially the males in them, report that they experience anger as a painful sort of boiling or exploding; this is still quite far

36 Briggs (1970), pp. 331–2.

from the Greco-Roman view that anger is a terrific and delightful thing, dripping "sweeter than honey" before the heart.[37]

So too with other emotions. We may expect the experience of erotic love in a society that has internalized the Augustinian view of original sin to be very different from the experience of love in a society that has no such teaching. People often do learn to feel ashamed of and troubled by their own arousal, and this affects the experience of both sex and erotic love. Similarly, again, the Balinese judgment on grief – that it is dangerous to the health – affects experience as well as behavior. My father's view that one should not be bowed down by life made his grief rather close to Balinese grief, and very different from the grief of someone who believes it right to enter fully into the experience of helplessness and hopelessness.

Societies may also differ more subtly in their normative judgments about an emotion type, simply by giving an emotion greater or lesser prominence. It is evident that modern America gives romantic/erotic love an unusual degree of prominence among the cultures of the world, a fact stemming from a long Western European heritage. And love is a different experience when it is believed to be a central source of meaning in life. The Ifaluk certainly experience romantic love, but that is not what they think life is primarily about: it is about basic material stability and survival.

In a remarkable comparative study of child-rearing practices, Stanley Kurtz suggests that Western romanticism affects the early behavior of (middle-class) mothers and children in America, through romantic norms of closeness and fusion. He observes that an American mother will typically gaze often into her baby's eyes, smile, respond – creating, over time, a richly responsive interpersonal world.[38] A typical mother in India,[39] by contrast, will carry her baby on her hip, letting it feel the solidity of her bodily presence, but rarely looking into its eyes, as she goes about her chores. Even when the child is at the breast, eye contact is much less elaborate than in the American case. She gives the child a sense of material stability and security, but seems less interested in

---

37 Aristotle, *Rhetoric* II.2, quoting Homer. Aristotle does not deny that anger is painful: he holds that it has both aspects.

38 See also Stern (1977, 1985).

39 Here again I note the need for more data, and for a recognition of the tremendous cultural variety within that nation.

cultivating an intensely personal kind of loving interaction with it. (To some extent, as we have seen, these differences are the product of family size and physical circumstances.) Kurtz's own conclusion is that American practices lead to exaggerated expectations of perfect intimacy and harmony that cause difficulties in later romantic life; Indian practices seem to him more sensible and realistic.[40] But whatever normative judgment one makes, one can see how our cultural idea that romantic love is necessary and central may color many aspects of the emotional life, and indeed may shape its very foundations.

All five of our sources of emotional variation play a role in these differences of normative judgment. Physical conditions shape the Utkus' desire to distance themselves from anger, the American leisured life that focuses so much on love, the Ifaluk life that has more room for compassion than for romance. Metaphysical beliefs (or their absence) shape the Balinese distaste for grief, the American connection between love and salvation. Practices and routines also contribute, as when a mother looks into her infant's eyes because that is what she has seen others do, or a Roman threatens an adversary because that is the way things are done in his social set. Language probably plays some role: thus the absence of a special term for romantic love, and the fact that the term *fago* is taught in connection with core experiences of nurturance and need fulfillment, may help explain why the Ifaluk don't share the American belief that romantic love is the center of the universe. And finally, of course, social norms – about what all people in a culture should be like, about what men and women should be like, about what different social classes should be like – pervasively shape judgments about categories of emotion, either for society as a whole or for particular social actors.

Next, societies impart different views about the *appropriate objects for an emotion*, views that, again, shape experience as well as behavior. The doctrine of "reasonable provocation" in the Anglo-American criminal law embodies social norms about the occasions on which a "reasonable man" will get violently angry. These include the adultery of a spouse (but not of a fiancée) and a blow to the face (but not a boxing of the ears).[41] Although judges know well that people got violently

---

40 Kurtz (1992).
41 See Kahan and Nussbaum (1996), pp. 306–8.

angry at many other provocations, the assumption behind the doctrine is that social norms should guide norms of sentencing: the well-brought-up person responds with violence to some provocations only. Today the doctrine remains, but the objects have changed. A man's wife is no longer taken to be his property; therefore adultery is no longer imagined as "the highest invasion of a man's property," and the claim of violent anger at adultery is less likely to win a criminal defendant a conviction for manslaughter rather than murder. New objects of proper anger have, however, been added to the menu: in particular, the anger of a battered woman against her abuser.

These are differences within a single society; there are also intersocietal differences. Romans approved a far larger menu of objects for extreme, even murderous, anger than do modern Americans. Seneca examines himself at the close of every day, thinking of the anger he has felt at slights at a dinner party, being put in the wrong seat, and so forth. And his *On Anger* is full of stories of trivial provocations that arouse murderous responses – the idea being that these are what the society teaches as acceptable, although the reader is supposed to see them, ultimately, as unacceptable. Anger is also often taught differently to different social actors. Many studies show that angry and aggressive behavior by American boys is subtly encouraged or at least little discouraged, where similar behavior by girls is sharply discouraged. We can easily find similar differences in the objects of fear, pity, and other central emotions.

The appropriate objects of grief might be thought to be rather uniform in all cultures that think grieving to be appropriate at all; but even here there are differences. Cathy Lutz suggested to her Ifaluk hosts that the death of a very elderly woman was not so bad, since it would "put her out of her misery" – thus expressing an American judgment that has much currency, though it is far from universal. The Ifaluk were shocked and even incredulous: "the death of a person of any age tears a hole in a wide-ranging network."[42]

Finally, *emotion taxonomies* themselves vary across societies. I have said that all known societies have some variety of the major emotion-types: love, fear, grief, anger, jealousy, envy, compassion, and some others. But even at the level of the big generic categories we do not find

42 Lutz (1988), p. 110.

a perfect one-to-one correspondence across cultures, since cultures organize in different ways the elements that individuate emotions from one another. Thus Ifaluk *fago* contains elements both of personal love and of compassion, the core idea being a nurturing attitude focused on the object's neediness or vulnerability. Cultures that connect love with the high value or specialness of the object, more than with its neediness, cannot connect the two emotions in the same way: to that extent, the list I just gave of the "big generic categories" is a sectarian list. Similarly, one may doubt whether the anger that the Romans classified as good/future is exactly the same generic emotion as the anger that my students uniformly classify as present/bad.

If this is so at the generic level, it is much more likely to be so at the level of particular species. The precise species of guilt and shame about the sexual body that many Christian cultures experience and cultivate has no precise equivalent in ancient Athens, since Athens lacked the Christian metaphysical belief in original sin. Species of erotic and romantic love are especially various, even within the Western tradition. Ancient Greek *erôs* is not mutual: it is an intense erotic longing for an object, which includes the thought of possession and control of the object. It is explicitly contrasted with *philia*, a type of love that need not be sexual (although it may be), and that centrally involves reciprocity and mutual benefit; also with *agapê*, a selfless and usually nonsexual benevolent love.[43] Although a language without a plurality of love words could articulate these distinctions (and Latin authors try, using only the term *amor*), the conceptual contrasts both represent and shape, it seems, real contrasts in experience: a Greek does not expect erotic love, as such, to pursue mutuality. (Contrast the modern American conception of erotic love, with its heavy emphasis on mutuality and reciprocity.) Again, medieval courtly love has some distinctive features that were not present in ancient Greece and that probably could not be present in modern America: the idealization of the female object, seen as chaste and unapproachable; the paradigm of selfless devotion to and risk in the service of this perfect being. Modern American conceptions of love contain features of ancient *erôs* and of courtly love, but they are also powerfully shaped by romantic paradigms of

---

43 But consider the topless courtesan called "*Agape*" on an early red-figure vase: see Dover (1989).

love as a ceaseless striving culminating in death or extinction. Most other societies would be seen to contain similar layers of historical complexity and interweaving, if we understood them well enough.

V. AMERICAN DEATH

To put all these elements together, let us now closely examine one complex example, dissecting its cultural and personal elements. And let us continue with the example of grief, which we have followed as a central case in this chapter as well as in Chapters 1 and 2. In Chapter 5 and in Part III I shall discuss the expressive content of various powerful and original works of art. But creative artists are frequently cultural outsiders; in this case, one part of my interest in the works I select is in their portrayal of the outsider, and the outsider's gaze. In order to focus on the issue of "social construction" in its daily force, we need, then, a popular and "inside" work, one whose emotion depictions have appealed to a mass audience in its own culture and elicited strong emotions from it. I therefore choose the ending of the film *Terms of Endearment,* a classic Hollywood tearjerker whose story of premature death makes American audiences cry.

Let us recall the plot briefly. Deborah Winger plays the daughter of Shirley MacLaine, a well-to-do Texas widow known for her charm and graciousness. Winger has left home to marry a college professor, moving from Texas to Iowa. Her husband is not very hardworking or successful; while she cares for their two boys on a small income, he has affairs with students. Eventually the marriage breaks up. Soon after, Winger discovers that she has breast cancer. She has throughout the film maintained a very close relationship with her mother, so she goes home to stay with her, taking the children; it is there that she hears the medical news. Meanwhile, MacLaine, long imprisoned by her sense of decorum, has had an affair with an outrageous and unreliable ex-astronaut, played by Jack Nicholson. He has broken up with her because he cannot commit himself to marriage.

Winger ends her life in a modern urban hospital. An actress of tremendous vitality, she looks preturnaturally beautiful and strong during these final scenes, like a horse chained up, and this somehow heightens the effect of the premature death. She is visited by all the people who care for her, and all maintain their composure, as does she, although her misery and her hatred of dying are evident. (Her voice wobbles, but she does not break down.) Even her no-good husband turns up and tries to make amends, in a flat and affectless manner that tells us that he has not become a better or stronger person, but also that he was not evil to begin with, only weak. Finally, to the surprise of all, the astronaut turns up, pretending, as usual, not to care about what is happening. Outside the hospital, he and MacLaine have a conversation that makes it clear that he is now willing to commit himself to her.[44]

In a climactic scene, the two young boys now enter their mother's room for the last time. They are trying to remain composed, but each reacts to the situation in a characteristic way: the affectionate younger son with hugs and some tears, the difficult older son with an angry stony silence. Winger views it as her job to say something helpful to the boys that they will remember for life. To the older son, who won't speak to her, she says in a loud and emotional voice, "I know that you love me." Barely restraining her own tears, she says that years from now she wants him to remember that she knew that. Then she hugs the little boy again, and says in a softer voice, with a wobble in it, "There. I think that went very well. Don't you?" These are her last lines, and this is the point at which the audience usually weeps most profusely.

As I shall later argue, the audience's emotions when responding to such a work rely on acts of empathetic identification in which we consider the events depicted as "the sort of thing that might happen" to ourselves or our loved ones (Aristotle's words). Let us now dissect the grief depicted in the film, and, at the same time, the audience's response of grief to the film, asking to what extent its elements are universal and to what extent they display particularly American (and also regional) features.

At one level, the story is a tragedy of a cross-culturally recognizable sort. Premature death from disease has been a staple of tragic fiction through the ages, as it is a staple of real life, and the death of a young woman is a classic focus of audience grief, from Euripides' *Alcestis* to Puccini's *La Bohème*. This death is in that genre. But its specific *physi-*

---

44 So far as this movie is concerned: for in the sequel, *The Evening Star*, he evidently has not committed himself to her, and has continued his flings with younger women. I have not read the Larry McMurtry novels on which the two films are based, so I cannot tell you what happened.

cal circumstances are shrewdly chosen to tap specifically American fears. These people need not fear starvation, or human sacrifice, or even tuberculosis. Breast cancer, however, is the great fear of young American women, and a young woman stricken this way without warning taps especially powerful fears in an American audience. It is indeed the sort of thing that might happen.

The construction of grief in the film also draws on common American *metaphysical and cosmological beliefs*: the absence of secure faith in the afterlife, the sense that breast cancer is a mysterious nemesis stalking young women, the belief in medicine and hospitals as the great lifesaving forces (if anything is), the quasi-psychoanalytic belief that the boy will suffer psychic damage if he is allowed to believe that his aggressive wishes have contributed to his mother's death. Grief is enacted through characteristic American *practices*: death takes place in an immaculate hospital under a doctor's supervision, and the impressively modern exterior of the building reveals that MacLaine has gotten the best possible care for her daughter. All parties behave with the decorum required by the medical setting. Nobody looks at or touches the corpse, and the audience is not permitted to see it.

Finally, *social norms* enter in: first, in the construction of the heroine as an appropriate object of sympathy. It is significant that Winger, unlike Mimi or Violetta, is a mother. Like these two operatic heroines, she has had a complex erotic life, and the audience recalls with romantic approval her affair with a lonely businessman, movingly portrayed by John Lithgow. But it is also important that the affair has ended, and that Winger throughout shows herself to be devoted above all to her children. She ends her life in the company of mother and children, with her ex-husband on the margins and her lover nowhere in sight – restored to chastity, or its American equivalent. This makes her available to American audiences as an attractive and unproblematic dead person. One imagines that a French or Italian director would have told the story with greater ambiguity and darkness, and might not have caused the extramarital lover to disappear. (To a degree, the gambit is problematic even in American normative terms, since Lithgow is clearly the most interesting man in the film.)

In the death scene itself, yet other norms are evident: norms of forgiveness, of pluck and courage, of maternal care, of continuing life in the face of loss (MacLaine and the astronaut). It is very important that Winger, in death, is beautiful, energetic, courageous, focused on her children, and continuously loving, rather than depressed and despairing; that the astronaut surrenders his macho self-protectiveness at the time of crisis; that a resolution to the difficult mother–son relationship is projected, and the son's freedom from crippling guilt allegedly guaranteed.[45] The victory of forgiveness over anger, and of love over guilt, displays a characteristic American optimism.

Some of these norms are universally American: but the film has also made regional points about sensitivity and care for others, marking these attitudes as characteristic of the South and Midwest. (To a salesgirl's claim that she didn't know she was treating Winger rudely by mocking her inability to pay, Lithgow memorably replies, "Then you must be from New York.") The film thus appeals to its audience to respond with the emotions of the American heartland, not those (if they have them) of the snooty and insensitive urban elite. Finally, of course, the film depicts its emotions as arising out of a personal history that is in some ways highly particular: the love of mother and daughter has unusual texture, humor, and depth, and the daughter's way of meeting death is seen as drawing on the internalized resources of her mother's dauntless strength.

These elements construct a scene of grief that is in some ways universal, but also recognizably all-American. The *behavior* of the characters is obviously altogether different from the behavior of the Ifaluk mother and the Balinese housekeeper; it is even somewhat different from that of the East Coast university professor working on her lecture. The characters all share certain *norms about grief itself* – that it is appropriate and good, but should not be allowed to spill over too much into the conduct of one's life, and certainly should not blight the personal search for happiness. (The boy must be freed from guilt; MacLaine must get married to Nicholson.) These norms are not sui generis, but they are recognizably American, of a piece with other aspects of American optimism and individualism. The film's *norms about the appropriate occasions and objects of grief* are in some ways universal, since in all cultures the death of a young person from illness is an appropriate occasion for grief, if anything is. But as I have said,

---

45 Again, for the purposes of this film only: *The Evening Star* shows that he has a difficult life.

the choice of breast cancer has special cultural significance, and the film's choice to focus on the death of a young person shows its determination to avoid cultural controversy: Americans often have uncomfortable ambivalence about the deaths of parents. There are also gender norms: it is all right for the little boy to be weepy, but older males cannot shed tears.

In short, the various cultural notions cannily manipulated by the film give the generic emotion of grief a setting and a tonality that are highly specific, making it an inner experience that is not quite like the experience one would have in Bali, or Gjoa Haven – or even in New York.

VI. CULTURE AND UNDERSTANDING

Culture provides a crucial part of the explanation for an individual's emotions, and the cognitive/evaluative theory is well equipped to illuminate this aspect of the emotional life. But social constructionists frequently suggest several more ambitious theses: that cultural forces leave no room for individual variety and freedom; that they make the details of a personal history aetiologically unimportant; that they create mutually inaccessible worlds. By now we have reason to question all these claims.

The claim of mutual incomprehensibility is, of course, belied by the very act of sensitive culture description, and by the long history of imaginative receptivity that precedes any good anthropological emotion-study. Both Lutz and Briggs found much about the people they studied initially opaque. Nor did time altogether dispel mystery: Briggs remained baffled by the moodiness and inconsistency of her Utku host Inuttiaq. But, as she also realized, people are mysterious and inconsistent, and some more so than others. When she got to the point of treating Inuttiaq as a person, rather than as a cultural text, she could allow him to be as mysterious as any of her Western friends, and not consider this a failure of method.

Both biology and common circumstances, I have argued, make it extremely unlikely that the emotional repertories of two societies will be entirely opaque to one another. It is no surprise that cross-cultural communication often focuses on generic experiences that derive from this common situation. Thus the works of Sophocles and Euripides cross cultural boundaries with tremendous power, since they focus on myths of loss and family conflict that are easily recognizable to other cultures. Homer's *Iliad* has been used successfully in treating Vietnam War veterans who suffer from postcombat trauma – because its stories of rage and fear are recognizable across cultural differences. So too the *Mahabharata*, which attracted huge audiences when presented in New York by an international cast, in a production by Peter Brooks intended to underline the work's human universality. Jean Briggs found that Italian opera provided a valuable common ground between Western and Utku emotion-concepts. Since the Utku in general, and Inuttiaq in particular, were great lovers of Verdi and Puccini, moments in the works could be used to discuss specific emotions. Inuttiaq's favorite was *Il Trovatore*, which he called "the music that makes one want to cry."[46] The world of a New York theater audience is of course enormously far from the world of the ancient Indian epic, and the world of Verdi's mythical Italianate Spain far from the simple life of the Utku hunters. But at another level, grief for the loss of a mother and thoughts of revenge against those who have damaged her are not in the least foreign to any society.

Some forms of life are, as such, unavailable to us. Thus medieval courtly love is not a live option in the present day, since we cannot share the metaphysical beliefs and practices necessary to sustain it. We can understand it reasonably well through literary and historical imagining, but we can imagine *ourselves* in that world only at a very general and partial level, focusing on ideas of sacrifice, idealism, devotion, and the "gentle heart" that are still available to us. In the same way, some contemporary emotion-concepts may prove unavailable to us, in the sense that we cannot well imagine what it would be for us to have these concepts. I think, however, that there are very few cases of this kind, once we understand the logic behind another culture's emotions at a deep enough level. Although I do not intend to enter deeply into anthropological debates about the universality of rationality, I am convinced, with Donald Davidson, that the very act of interpretation requires assuming that things make sense, and thus that communication presupposes something like a common rationality.[47] In just this way,

46 Briggs (1970), p. 154.
47 Davidson (1984).

the Balinese idea of the vital force looks at first blush strange and superstitious – until we recall that we believe something very like that about the effect of stress on the immune system. There usually will be reasons of habit and deep personal history that prevent us from actually taking on a different set of emotion-concepts, but they do not seem unimaginably foreign or uninhabitable.

As for individual variety and freedom, some social constructionist accounts err in this area, sometimes under the influence of Michel Foucault – who, whatever his genius, was not terribly interested in individual diversity.[48] We should not go as far as psychoanalyst Donald Winnicott, who wrote that cultural differences can be studied simply "as an overlap of innumerable personal patterns."[49] Culture itself has an explanatory role to play: the fact that something is a widely endorsed cultural norm gives people a reason for following it that is not reducible to an overlap of individual endorsements. Nonetheless, Winnicott is right to stress that culture only exists in the histories of individuals, that individuals vary greatly, and that the existence of diverse personal patterns creates spaces for diversity in the culture itself. People usually see this where their own culture is concerned. They intuitively understand it to be highly variegated – not a power machine that stamps out a series of identical humans like so many cookies from a cookie cutter, but a scene of vigorous debate and considerable diversity, where these very features create spaces within which the individual has at least some room to move around. They are also intuitively aware that individual parents are the first and in some sense the primary medium of culture transmission, and that culture is transmitted only when it enters the life of the individual child. Individual parents and individual children vary greatly, and parents have at least some latitude to choose what elements of culture will enter the lives of their children.

When we consider other societies, especially distant societies, we do not always remember these facts. We tend to speak of "the Utku view of anger," or, more absurdly (given the size and diversity of the society), "the Indian view of the child." And we do not always grant to

48 Foucault (1985, 1986) conflates different sorts of Greek and Roman texts, from different social classes, geographical locations, and religious and philosophical backgrounds, to produce a single unified picture for each epoch.
49 Winnicott (1965), p. 15.

others prerogatives we usually take for granted in ourselves – of criticism, change, and the conscious shaping of moral development.[50]

This brings us back to the eudaimonistic character of the emotions. The cognitive/evaluative view implies that emotional content is itself part of a creature's pursuit of flourishing. Given the fact that human beings deliberate ethically about how to live, it implies that emotions are part and parcel of ethical deliberation. If we see emotions as impulses, we will think that we can educate or change them only by suppression. Thus Kant thought that virtue must always be a matter of strength, as the will learns to keep a lid on inappropriate inclinations, rather like a good cook holding down the lid on a boiling pot. But in daily life, we more often endorse a different picture: we believe that emotions have an intentional content, and that people can do a good deal to shape the content of their own, and especially of their children's, emerging emotions.[51] Thus the recognition of "social construction" should lead to a recognition of space and freedom, rather than the reverse.

An American who spends time with the Utku and judges that Utku ideas about anger are valuable cannot simply go home and turn America into Gjoa Haven.[52] Her stance toward America and toward herself will be very much like that of Seneca toward Rome – that of a social critic who can try to shape the course of the moral development of the next generation, even while struggling with her own deeply implanted cultural impulses. But she certainly need not judge that she has a fate that dooms her to (what she thinks to be) excessive anger. As her conception of *eudaimonia* changes on reflection, so too her emotions may gradually alter – although their deep roots in childhood make alteration a gradual and partial matter. Perhaps more important, she can consciously shape her interactions with children, transmitting the norms that she reflectively endorses.

Indeed, a great advantage of a cognitive/evaluative view of emotion is that it shows us where societies and individuals have the freedom to make improvements. If we recognize the element of evaluation *in the*

---

50 See Winkler (1990) for a discussion of these issues in the treatment of ancient Greek norms.

51 On the prevalence of this view in the Anglo-American legal tradition, see Kahan and Nussbaum (1996).

52 My example is hypothetical. Briggs, though originally American, has lived and taught in Canada for years; nor does she make the normative judgments I explore here.

emotions, we also see that they can themselves be *evaluated* – and in some ways altered, if they fail to survive criticism. Social constructions of emotion are transmitted through parental cues, actions, and instructions, long before the larger society shapes the child. We teach children what and whom to fear, what occasions for anger are reasonable, what behavior is shameful. If we believed that racial hatred and aggression were innate, we could at best teach children to suppress these impulses. But according to the cognitive/evaluative theory, there would be no racial hatred if there were not certain perceptions of salience – that people with different skin color are threatening, or dangerous, or evil. By shaping the way children see objects, we contend against these social conventions.

The recognition of "social construction" does entail a recognition that our emotions are made out of elements that we have not made ourselves. This, of course, any view of emotion would have to grant, one way or another. But the social constructionist view says that many, at least,[53] of these elements are of a particular sort: they are intelligent pieces of human normative activity, of the sort that can in principle, within certain limits, be changed by more intelligent human activity.

A plausible view of social construction must make room both for cross-cultural intelligibility and for human freedom. One further constraint must now be mentioned. Any plausible such view must do justice to the narrative history of the individual personality, as its distinctive emotional traits are laid down extremely early in interactions with individual parents, siblings, and other caretakers. It is surely true that no parent is an island free from culture, and social constructionists have offered psychoanalysts valuable reminders of this fact. The way a child is held, nursed, talked to, all involve the influence of culture. But a fundamental aspect of treating a person as a person is the recognition that an infant has a separate history in a separate body, intertwined with other specific individuals in a history of great depth and intensity. Only from such a history does an infant come to be a member of a larger social group. Here Winnicott is absolutely right: "[T]he clue to social and group psychology is the psychology of the individual."[54] To that fundamental aspect of our topic I now turn.

---

53 This qualification points back to the recognition of some innate bases for certain fears. But note that this research grants that these proto-fears can be unlearned: in that sense, even such emotions are social, resting on social confirmation of the innate tendency.
54 Winnicott (1965), p. 15.

4

EMOTIONS AND INFANCY

I. THE SHADOW OF THE OBJECT[1]

That night in Trinity College, when I dreamed about my mother, I saw her looking as she did when I was a child of two or three. In the intensity of my anxiety and love, I called her Mommy, a name I had not used since childhood. When, later, I saw her lying dead in the hospital bed, I saw, too, the many times that I had seen her lying asleep at home, in just that position, with just that lace collar around her neck.[2] And even as my dream of her contained a desperate wish for her life and health, it also contained an anguished wish that I might give her some special happiness (in the dream, by saying something to please her that no one else had thought to say) – perhaps because that memory of her youthful face lay very close to two other memories, my earliest persisting memories from childhood.

In one, I am playing with some older children, who are experimenting by poking a stick into a hole in the ground into which some insects have been flying. Suddenly a fierce cloud of wasps swarms up out of the ground. The older children vanish. Terrified and totally bewildered, too small to run, I wail as loudly as I can, as the wasps sting me again and again. My mother runs to me from the garden, where she has been

1 This phrase originates in Freud's "Mourning and Melancholia" ("Thus the shadow of the object fell upon the ego . . ."). It is taken as the title of Bollas (1987), to be discussed later in this chapter.
2 This perception is shaped, in turn, by the emotional impact of Dickens's description of Steerforth in *David Copperfield*, as David "saw him lying with his head upon his arm, as I had often seen him lie at school" – a description of the corpse that quotes an earlier description of the living man. When I saw how my mother's posture in death was so like her characteristic posture in life, that sentence came into my mind, and I could describe the scene in no other way.

working, sweeps me up in her arms, and carries me home. I recall the feeling of rescue and comfort that came over me as she ran with me in her arms and I clung to her neck like a small monkey. This feeling of holding is with me at many times, especially when I am working by myself and when I am with someone I love.

In the other picture, I am in the garden with her. I am very angry with her – I think because she is working and not paying attention to me. As she bends over to dig around a marigold, I bite her on the thigh. What I remember is the horrible black and bitter sensation of my own internal badness, of powers of destruction surging out of me that I had not known were there, a cauldron of corrosive liquid. I wept for my own blackness, my imperfect love. In my Trinity College dream, she looked just as she had looked that day in the garden – she was even wearing her gardening shorts; and I tried to please her. Then, when I awoke, I began to interrogate myself, asking whether my absence that day in Dublin was not at some level a kind of retribution for her early separateness in the garden. My grief therefore contained, as well, an anxious dialogue between the defense and the prosecution, between rational arguments assuring me that I had had no reason to expect a sudden complication, and voices of guilt, which accused me.

Emotions, in short, have a history. In this case, it would not be possible to have an adequate understanding of my grief without grasping it as one strand in a history of deep love, of longing for protection and comfort, of anger at the separate and uncontrolled existence of the source of comfort, of fear of one's own aggression, of guilt and the desire to make reparations. The grief itself bears the traces of that entire history; those other emotions, lurking in the background, give it its specific content and cognitive specificity. And this is true not only of the later history of an early childhood relationship. For new objects of love and anger and fear bear the traces of earlier objects; one's emotions toward them are frequently therefore also, in both intensity and configuration, emotions toward one's own past.

Proust's narrator, waking up in the night, feels a primitive longing for comfort that derives from his early childhood. In an attempt to mother himself, he presses his cheeks "tenderly" against the "comfortable cheeks" of his pillow, "as round and rosy as the cheeks of our childhood" – and thinks that it will soon be morning. "Soon someone will come to his aid. The hope of being comforted gives him the courage to suffer."[3] He now has a dream:[4] sexually aroused, he sees a woman before him, and imagines that it is she who has caused his pleasure and his desire. He feels the warmth of his body mingle with hers; he feels the warmth of her kiss on his cheek, he feels his body pressed down by her weight. As he attempts to "become one with her,"[5] he awakes.

By placing this dream near the opening of the *Recherche*, Proust draws our attention to what will be one of the narrative's central themes: the continuity of later loves with a childhood history of need and longing. The woman seen by Marcel is an adult woman, as he, both as dreamer and in the dream, is an adult man. And yet, even as his attempt to comfort himself before sleep contained images of childhood comfort, so here his longing bears the trace of a small child's longing: the strange woman kisses him on the cheek like a mother, and her posture, weighing him down, combines sexuality with the solidity and comfort of a maternal embrace. His ardent desire is for his body to "meet up with" the warmth of hers, to become fused with her. We know from this point on that what he will later call the "general form" of his loves points backwards toward the past, toward the solitary anxieties of the child who longs passionately for his mother's goodnight kiss, that "concession to my misery and my agitation" – and views her arrival with "utmost pain," since it is a sign that she will soon be departing.[6] His insecurity and longing for comfort, his greedy desire to be held and immobilized[7] – all this will mark his relationship with Albertine as surely as it here marks his dream of the unknown woman. Years later, needing Albertine's comfort and reassurance, he accuses her of lesbianism and tells her that he can no longer love her – all in order to bring about the tender scene that ensues, so deeply desired, so unsatisfactory, in which she holds him still in her arms, and licks slowly

---

3 Proust, *Du côté de chez Swann* (Paris; 1954 Gallimard edition), p. 10. The translations are my own. The Moncrieff/Kilmartin version oddly mutes the theme of comfort, rendering "lui porter secours" by "look after him."

4 Strictly speaking, the entire narrative is in the *imparfait*, and the experience of waking in the night is said to be followed sometimes by sound sleep, sometimes by nightmares of "childish terrors," and sometimes by this dream of erotic tenderness.

5 Here I follow Moncrieff/Kilmartin rendering of "mon corps . . . voulait s'y rejoindre."

6 *Du côté*, p. 21, my translations.

7 One of the desired effects of the mother's embrace is to blot out disturbing stimuli from the world around him; I go on to discuss this further.

with her tongue the lips that refuse to open.[8] Albertine is the victim of this history; for it is thanks to his past insecurity, as he here acknowledges, that he can never really attend to her as a person in her own right and can therefore never really love her.[9]

The Stoics, categorizing emotions, omitted the past as a temporal category. Their taxonomy made no place for emotions directed at past events. More important, they also failed to give prominence to the way in which past events, especially events in infancy and childhood, influence present emotions. Here their too-intellectual brand of cognitivism prevented them from fully comprehending the specific cognitive content of the emotions. Much the same is true, I believe, of some prominent recent attempts to defend a cognitive account of emotion in philosophy, which sever emotions from their past and depict them as fully and reliably determined by present input about one's current situation.[10]

I shall argue, by contrast, that in a deep sense all human emotions are in part about the past, and bear the traces of a history that is at once commonly human, socially constructed, and idiosyncratic.[11] I have

8 Proust, (Moncrieff/Kilmartin), II.863.

9 See *Sodome et Gomorrhe* (II.857–8 in the Moncrieff/Kilmartin translation), where the narrator ascribes to himself (in my own translation) "that binary rhythm that love adopts in all those who lack sufficient confidence in themselves to believe that a woman could ever love them, and also that they could really love her. They know themselves well enough to be aware that in the presence of the most varied women they would experience the same hopes, the same fears, would invent the same stories, would say the same words; and thus they know that their emotions and actions are not in a close and necessary relation to the loved woman, but pass by her side, brush up against her, surround her like the tide that crashes along the rocks – and this awareness of their own instability increases still further their conviction that this woman, whose love they so much desire, does not love them . . . [T]his fear, this shame, bring about the counter-rhythm, the ebb tide, the need . . . to take back the offensive and to regain esteem and control." I shall discuss this passage further in Chapter 10.

10 Some forms of modern cognitivism do include emotions, such as guilt and regret, which take a past object; my objection is to their failure to consider how present emotions are colored by the past. This dimension of emotions is omitted by both Lyons and Gordon, though not by de Sousa, whose account of "paradigm" scenarios leaves room for the introduction of the complexities of an individual history, though his book (1987) does not focus on that issue in the way I shall here. The absence of the past in Gordon's account is one reason why he has such difficulty distinguishing his computer from a person. Similarly Solomon, in thinking of the emotions in terms of existential value-positing, omits the past as a determinant of the present personality. (Sartre would surely have rejected the ideas I am developing as a form of bad faith that masks from us the extent of our freedom to posit value.) In another area of the subject, Pinker (1997) also has difficulty distinguishing the human being from a computer.

11 See the similar observation in de Sousa (1987), Chapter 8.

spoken of emotions as urgent transactions with a changing environment. I have argued in Chapter 2 that we can understand both human and animal emotions to involve such transactions, mediated by a value-laden intentionality. Chapter 3 has added a social dimension to the account, while acknowledging that the social is always mediated by complex and highly varied personal processes. I shall now turn to those processes, building on the "common account" of human and animal emotions presented in Chapter 2, but focusing on human development. Understanding emotions developmentally will help us to complete the description of the revised neo-Stoic view. At that point, we will be in a position, too, to understand why some objections to cognitive views of emotion have force, and to argue that the present view is not vulnerable to such objections, precisely because of the way in which it incorporates a developmental dimension.

I shall argue, then, that adult human emotions cannot be understood without understanding their history in infancy and childhood. For this history will bring to light both the responsiveness of the emotions – their appropriateness to the life of an incomplete creature in a world of significant accidents, their connections to the development of practical reason and a sense of self – and their frequent lack of responsiveness, their rigidity before present objects as they project the images of the past upon them. The child Marcel, in his mother's absence, amuses himself with a magic lantern that projects onto his wall images of his favorite stories, so that he sees his room as if illuminated by the presence of Golo and Bluebeard. Emotions are often like that magic lantern, coloring the room one is actually in with the intense images of other objects, other stories. This feature of emotion can lead into insight and deep love, as when childhood thoughts about the feelings of one's parents enable a person to understand the needs and wishes of an adult love, and childhood confidence in the parents' reciprocating love enables her to love an adult partner without suspicion. Not all failures to respond to the present evidence are normatively bad: no adult love would be possible without a degree of trust that goes beyond the evidence. But the same feature of emotion can also lead, as it does in the adult Marcel, to the absence of particular perception and love – or to a love that is the mask for a profound egoism, turned in on its own insecurities. When he sees the present through the lens of the past, he proves unable to accept any love that he cannot control.

Clearly, then, any assessment of the emotions that intends to raise normative questions – as I shall in Parts II and III – must investigate these developmental issues. We must ask, first, whether there are features of the typical human child's history that make its emotions intrinsically problematic from the ethical viewpoint, and, more generally, from the point of view of practical rationality. Second, we must ask whether there are other features of typical emotional development that offer assistance to ethics. Finally, we must examine sources of variation in development, individual and social, asking how and to what extent it is possible to encourage developmental patterns that are more supportive and less subversive of ethical norms.

Investigating these issues will also help us to refine further the account of emotions sketched in Chapter 1, revising further the simple Stoic cognitive analysis of emotion. I shall argue that the cognitive content of emotions arrives embedded in a complex narrative history, without mentioning which one frequently cannot give an account of the full specificity of the emotion itself. I shall try to articulate these complexities here, sketching a general account of the roots of emotion in infancy and childhood that should also help us in analyzing particular emotion histories and understanding their variety. I shall put forward both a genetic thesis and a causal thesis: both that the emotions of later life make their first appearances in infancy, as cognitive relations to objects important for one's well-being, and also that this history informs the later experience of emotion in various specific ways. I shall then argue that these findings explain why emotions, though in their origin and in many ongoing functions adaptively rational, may frequently also be irrational in the sense that they fail to match their present objects, as they project the images of the past upon them. This rigidity has consequences, as well, for any attempt to become ethical or to produce children who are ethical; and I shall examine contrasting developmental patterns with a view to a set of highly general ethical aims. An investigation of these normative issues will suggest an important role for the imagination, and thence for narrative art, in the understanding of emotion, and in emotional development itself.

My account of the development of emotion will be a philosophical account; I am neither an empirical psychologist nor a psychoanalyst. But the developmental aspects of the emotional life have been little treated by the philosophical tradition (although there are passages of deep insight in both Lucretius and Spinoza, on which I shall draw). Literature and psychology contain much that illuminates a philosophical account. Proust, here as elsewhere, will therefore play a major role in my account. Among the modern psychoanalysts I am most influenced by Donald Winnicott and the earlier theorists of the "object-relations" school, whose concerns complement and flesh out a neo-Stoic theory.[12] Psychoanalysis has recently become more closely allied to experimental work than it was in its early years; two eclectic figures provide valuable links between clinical data and experimental studies: John Bowlby, with his insightful studies of attachment and loss,[13] and Daniel Stern, with his experimentally informed reconstructions of the earliest stages of infancy and the infant's object world.[14]

The narrative I shall construct, focused on themes of ambivalence and omnipotence, is informed by the work of all of these thinkers, especially by Proust and Winnicott, but it is essentially a philosophical development of the account of Chapter 1, an attempt to complete the articulation and revision of the neo-Stoic theory, before making the transition to normative analysis. Its aim is both to show how thinking about infant development helps us to construct a more complex and subtle view than is sometimes found in cognitive/evaluative accounts of emotion, and also, at the same time, to show how starting from a cognitive account of the sort I have been developing gives us an illumi-

---

12 Among the object-relations theorists, I have been especially influenced by the work of W. R. D. Fairbairn (1952), as well as by Winnicott (1965, 1986). Among more recent writers, I find valuable the account of the inchoate and archaic content of early cognitions, and of the longing for wholeness, in Christopher Bollas (1987); and the account of the questionable results of the pursuit of control and completeness in Nancy Chodorow (1978). Finally, concerns about the role of shame and its relationship to infantile narcissism are persuasively developed in Andrew Morrison (1989); although Morrison follows the self-psychology school of Heinz Kohut, rather than the object-relations school, in this case the two schools are very close in emphasis, and complement one another.

13 Bowlby (1982, 1973, 1980). Bowlby's attachment theory is now supplemented and confirmed by Sarah Hrdy's work with primates; see Hrdy (1999). Bowlby's work is, like Fairbairn's, of considerable importance for Chodorow's account; and Bowlby, unlike the more orthodox psychoanalysts, has been influential in cognitive psychology – especially in the work of Lazarus and Seligman; Oatley is unusual in cognitive psychology insofar as he draws on both Fairbairn and Bowlby – and also on the related anthropological work of Lutz. Bowlby's attachment perspective has continued to be fruitful in contemporary experimental work: see the very interesting defense of the perspective, and review of the literature, in Lopez and Brennan (2000).

14 Stern (1977, 1985, 1990).

nating angle from which to view some of the traditional concerns of developmental psychology and psychoanalysis.

It has become fashionable in the United States to sneer at psychoanalysis. In part this dismissive attitude results from the fact that Americans are generally impatient with complexity and sadness, and tend to want a quick chemical fix for deep human problems. People who have that view of life will not have reached Chapter 4 of this book anyway, so I shall not attempt to address them here. There are, however, people who admire humanistic approaches to life when they are presented in literary or philosophical form (Proust, Plato), but who still react with suspicion to any mention of the names of Klein, Fairbairn, and Winnicott. In part, I believe, their skepticism stems from a view that these figures are pretend scientists, and simply don't measure up to a model of science set by the natural sciences. To them I simply want to say that I myself treat these figures as humanistic interpretive thinkers, very closely related to Proust and Plato, whose work gains texture and depth through having a clinical dimension – and, in the case of Daniel Stern and Bowlby, also an experimental dimension.[15] And I would ask them to consider the possibility that Winnicott's perspective on human beings may be even more illuminating, ultimately, than that of Proust, whatever his genius, because Winnicott is simply a saner and more responsive person, more genuinely interested in human variety and interaction.

II. THE GOLDEN AGE: HELPLESSNESS, OMNIPOTENCE, BASIC NEEDS

Human beings, like the other animals, are born into a world that they have not made and do not control. After a time in the womb, during which needs were automatically met, they enter the world, making, as Freud put it in the passage that is this book's epigraph, "the step from an absolutely self-sufficient narcissism to the perception of a changing external world and the beginnings of the discovery of objects." Human infants arrive in the world in a condition of needy helplessness more or less unparalleled in any other animal species.

15 It is important that Winnicott, unlike most other analysts, saw healthy children most of the time, since he was a pediatrician; so his sample is not skewed by the self-selection of patients who turn to psychoanalysis for treatment.

What they encounter is both alarming and delightful. As Lucretius puts it: the infant, helpless and weeping from the disturbance of birth,

like a sailor cast forth from the fierce waves, lies naked on the ground, without speech, in need of every sort of life-sustaining help, when first nature casts it forth with birth contractions from its mother's womb into the shores of light. And it fills the whole place with mournful weeping, as is right for someone to whom such troubles remain in life. (5.222–7)

A "gentle nurse" now calms the child with calm talk and caresses – as well as nourishment.[16] The poet bleakly remarks that the rougher, better-equipped wild animals have no need of such soothing (229–30) – a claim not altogether true, as we have seen and shall see, but relatively true. The prolonged helplessness of the human infant marks its history; and the early drama of its infancy is the drama of helplessness before a world of objects – a world that contains both threatening things and good things, the things it wants and needs. The infant's central perception of itself, Lucretius suggests profoundly, is as an entity very weak and very powerless toward things of the greatest importance. Freud, noting the same facts, comments that "we cannot endure the new state of things for long, [so] that we periodically revert from it, in our sleep, to our former condition of absence of stimulation and avoidance of objects."

But the infant is not altogether helpless. For from the first there are agencies in the environment that minister to its needs, supplying what it cannot supply for itself. These agencies therefore take on an intense importance in the infant's inchoate and as yet undemarcated awareness of the world. Its relationship to them focuses, from the first, on its passionate wish to secure what the world of nature does not supply by itself – comfort, nourishment, protection.

Lucretius presents a picture, not a theoretical account. But we may

16 Some of the cultural biases of psychoanalysis are shown here: for Lucretius, with his own Roman upper-class bias, never supposes that the comforting and nourishing figure will be the infant's own mother, whereas all psychoanalysts with the exception of Chodorow – and Bowlby in some later work – simply assume that it will be. Recent thinkers in the attachments tradition are much more flexible, taking cognizance of the findings in evolutionary biology that show that a certain degree of flexibility in attachment relations (an ability, for example, to thrive in day care) is crucial for a species that is going to survive. If human infants were hardwired to require a single mother attending them at all times, they acknowledge, the human species would not have survived (personal communication, Kelly Brennan; see also Hrdy [1999]).

extrapolate an account from it. The resulting picture will differ in several ways from classic Freudian and Kleinian psychoanalytic accounts. The central difference is that the Lucretian picture makes the drama of infancy have little to do with sexuality per se, little even with pleasure per se, and nothing at all to do with innate aggression, as Klein would hold. (I shall return to this important issue later.) Instead, the drama has everything to do with what the ancient world called "external goods" – with the infant's relationship to objects of high importance. As we have seen, this is just the account of emotional development in animals on which cognitive psychologists have been converging. Both experimental and psychoanalytical work, as we shall see, gives it further support. Now, therefore, as I focus more closely on several aspects of the Lucretian infant, I shall begin to draw on some of this modern material.

Lucretius' description points to three distinct facets of the infant's neediness, each of which appears to be irreducible to any of the others. If we consider these in turn, we will have a starting point for talking about the infant's emotions, which will be its recognitions of the importance of these external items. First and most obvious is the "need of every life-sustaining help," the basic bodily need for nourishment and care, communicated to the infant through its appetites of hunger and thirst. This has been emphasized in all discussions of infancy, and needs little further comment here. If we focus on the infant's evolving perceptions, we will see this need as both Lucretius and the modern psychologists present it – as a felt need for the removal of painful or invasive stimuli, and for the restoration of a blissful or undisturbed condition.

The connection of this restoration with survival is important to the evolutionary account of the infant's development, and thus to the evolutionary significance of its developing emotions – as we have seen in reflecting about animal emotions. But this connection is not part of the infant's own subjective awareness. The infant's subjective perception of hunger is well captured by Daniel Stern in his metaphorical reconstruction of the "hunger storm" at the center of the child's being, which explodes within, giving rise to pulsing currents of pain, until the arrival of food calms the storm.[17] It is fascinating to see Stern, in his effort to

17 Stern (1990), pp. 23–43.

capture in words the quality of the preverbal child's experience, drawn to the very images of "storm" and "calm" that Epicureans characteristically use to capture the ways in which we are troubled by hunger and relieved by its gratification.[18]

These felt needs, as the infant's ability to perceive definite objects and to become aware of its own boundaries develops – and it is now clear that it begins to develop remarkably early in the first months of life[19] – gives a central importance in the infant's "object world" to that or those object(s) who are perceived as the agents of this restoration of the world. Whether it is mother, father, nurse, or some other caretaker or caretakers who plays or play the primary role here, this restorative agency will at first be experienced by the infant not so much as a distinct object, but as a process of transformation through which the infant's own state of being is altered. For this reason Bollas speaks of the caretaker as a "transformational object," and perceptively remarks that much of a human being's subsequent history bears the imprint of early longing for this object, in the form of a desire for a "second coming" of that shift toward bliss, and for an object that can be its vehicle.[20] Still in a state of "infantile dependence,"[21] the infant can do little to control the arrival of the transformational process, and its sudden arrivals and disappearances mark the infant's world as a chancy and unpredictable one, in which the best things arrive as if by lightning, in sudden penetrations of light and joy.

Consider a myth that plays a central role in ancient accounts of

18 See, for example, Epicurus, *Letter to Menoiceus*, 128: as soon as a creature achieves a state free of disturbance or pain, "the entire storm of the soul is undone." Cf. Lucretius II. 1 ff.: happy is the person who watches others storm-tossed on the waves, while he himself is safe on the shore.

19 See Stern (1985), Chapter 3; (1990), pp. 23–43. Stern's vivid depiction of the infant of six weeks, an attempt to encapsulate the current state of research in developmental psychology, ascribes to the infant perceptions of definite forms in space that stand out from others, and of patterns of sound, touch, and light that mark off one region from another. Between eight and twelve weeks, the infant becomes aware of the face, and begins to make eye-to-eye contact, treating eyes as "windows" to events of crucial significance for its world. By four months, the infant has highly complex social interactions with the closest people in its world, and has begun to be able, in part through awareness of its own voluntary responses, to demarcate self from nonself in a reliable way.

20 Bollas (1987), pp. 13–29.

21 Fairbairn (1952) uses this term by way of contrast with "mature dependence," in which one acknowledges one's need of others but also recognizes and accepts their separateness; I shall return to this topic, and to the way in which Fairbairn connects it with a bold social-political thesis.

emotion. It is, I think, best seen as an imaginative attempt to recreate this world of infancy. This is the well-known story of the Golden Age – an age in which people do not have to do anything for themselves, to labor, to act, to move here and there. For the earth itself brings forth nourishment exactly where they are. Rivers of milk and honey spring up out of the ground; in the mild climate there is no need for shelter. The people of this age, Hesiod remarks, lack prudential rationality – presumably because they have no need of thought. They live in a state of blissful totality. Stoics who repeat the story add that in this age "crime is far off":[22] there is no aggression, because everything is complete. What this myth describes is the omnipotence of the infant, its sense that the world revolves around its needs, and is fully arranged to meet its needs.

But of course, as our Lucretian image lets us see, the infant's experiential world is from the very start unlike the world of the Golden Age. Perhaps, as Freud observes in our epigraph, rudimentary prebirth experiences give the infant a true Golden Age: hooked up securely to the sources of nourishment and comfort, the infant is indeed in a state of blissful totality. But birth disrupts all that, as Freud says, bringing the infant into a world of objects, in which it must depend on external things and persons for its survival. Thus, although at times the infant's world is a Golden Age world, these times alternate with times when the world is hungry, distressed, and in discomfort.[23] The Earth does not give everything automatically, and the infant's world of sudden transformations is felt from the start as chancy, porous, full of uncertainty and danger. For this reason, the infant has a sense of its own helplessness, which gives rise to a need for comfort and reassurance that is not reducible to its basic bodily needs. Lucretius' image suggests this already, with its account of the nurse, who both feeds the child and calms it with soothing words and caresses.

Early psychoanalytic accounts of infancy reduced all needs to needs for bodily gratification.[24] A fairly early exception was Winnicott, whose concept of "holding" incorporates nutrition, sensitive care, and the

22 See Seneca, *Medea*, 329–30.
23 I choose these odd locutions – making the subject the infant's experience-world rather than the infant – to remind the reader that the infant does not yet, in the first eight weeks of life, begin to experience itself as a definite subject. Compare Stern (1990), Chapter 3.
24 See the summary in Bowlby (1973); Chodorow (1978), p. 72ff., contains a good account of the issue.

creation of a "facilitating environment." As Winnicott remarks, a reasonably supportive "facilitating environment" is one in which the omnipotence of the infant (which is also to say, its total helplessness, which explains its demand to be at the center of attention) is met and acknowledged. Through an identification with the infant, the caretaker or caretakers know what it needs, and supply those things: not only food, but also sensitive interaction and comfort. Bowlby shows, similarly, that we should think of the need for security as a distinct need, and think of the infant's attachment to its caretaker or caretakers as having these two distinct aspects, which may in principle be separated. Experiments with monkeys suggest, he argues, that animals who are well fed from a hard prickly mechanical device still need to cling to something soft and comforting and to be caressed. If this need is not met, the infant grows up with severe behavioral disabilities; it fails to develop the kind of confidence in its environment that makes normal cognitive functioning and acting possible.[25] And if this need is met, but by a figure who is not identical with the source of nourishment, the monkey will attach itself far more firmly to the comfort source than to the nourishment source. Given the choice between a hard mechanical food source and a soft cuddly non-nourishing object, the monkeys spend a very short time getting the necessary food from the food source, the rest of the time clinging fast to the soft cuddly object.[26] Bowlby makes a very convincing case for seeing the need to be held and comforted as a part of our common primate heritage, highly adaptive in evolutionary terms as a source of protection from danger. Clinging is a pervasive feature of infant primate life; the main difference in the human case is that the human infant is so physically immature at birth that it cannot initiate contact on its own, but must rely on the agency of its sources of transformation. As Winnicott says, "The infant who is being held . . . is not aware of being preserved from infinitely falling. A slight failure of holding, however, brings to the infant a sensation of infinite falling."[27] This acute helplessness makes much room in its life for uncertainty, anxiety, and rage.

25 Again, I note that these experiments are morally controversial, since some of them did produce psychotic monkeys who were unable to lead a normal life.
26 Bowlby (1982); and on attachment as a basic element in primate behavior, see Hrdy (1999).
27 Winnicott (1965), p. 113.

Thus Proust's narrative of the self-comforting that precedes sleep gets at something that is deep not just in human life but in the development of animals as well. The need for *"soulagement"* against the painful intrusive stimuli of a strange world is an independent and very powerful need, in some ways even more powerful, as a bond between infant and adult, than the bond of nourishment. As biologist Sarah Hrdy puts it, "Human infants have a nearly insatiable desire to be held and to bask in the sense that they are loved."[28] Through holding, the infant becomes willing to live in the world, develops the conviction that the world is sufficiently benign, despite its dangers,[29] to support its own active efforts. The idea that one is not completely helpless, that one's demands will meet some response from the environment, is an essential foundation of all learning. In early infancy, when action is more or less impossible, the passive experience of receiving comfort removes the incipient sense of helplessness. In the light of this, Bollas's picture of the "transformational object" acquires new depth and complexity: for this object now does far more than minister to bodily need. It makes a world worth living in.

Many accounts, whether experimental or clinical, assume that care will be given primarily by a single figure, who is assumed to be the mother (although Winnicott stresses that this is a generic term, intended to include fathers as well, insofar as they play the standard maternal role). Experimental evidence shows that infants can recognize a particular caretaker almost immediately: at only three days, an infant is already able to discriminate the smell of its own mother's milk on a breast pad from the smell of another mother's milk, and will turn to its own mother.[30] In general, the ability to recognize a particular caretaker and to develop a strong and exclusive attachment is a surprisingly early and pervasive feature of primate life.[31] But the object of the infant ape's affections may be its mother, or a male, or another

28 Hrdy (1999), p. 493.

29 Bowlby persistently downplays the dangers, suggesting that an infant who is properly cared for by its mother will see the world as perfectly benign and have no anxiety. This is implausible – and, as I shall argue, it would also mean disaster for the child, who needs to learn how to get around in the actual world.

30 Stern (1985), p. 39.

31 Bowlby (1982); he observes that this ability is also evident in birds, but that here it has no evolutionary signficance for the human case, since birds and humans diverged at the point of common reptile ancestry, where there seems to have been no such ability.

female, or even a human researcher – who may be either female or male.[32] Bowlby speaks at times as if the reliable presence of the child's own mother is essential for good emotional health, and he seems to suggest that any other child care arrangement is a dangerous thing for very young children. But his data show something much weaker: that human infants, like those of other primates, need security and stability in their environment, and need, for this purpose, the ability to recognize and enjoy the comfort of one or a small number of reliably caring individuals.[33] As our knowledge both of primate cultures and of other human cultures expands, Sarah Hrdy points out, we have come to see that secure attachments may be nourished in many different ways; children raised by multiple caretakers can be just as secure, or "if anything more so," than children raised by a single mother.[34]

As the relationship between child and caretaker(s) develops, it is important that the caretaker(s) show sensitivity to the child's particular rhythm and personal style, which Stern calls a "dance."[35] The balance between indifference and intrusiveness, attention and the giving of space, must be struck in the right way, or the result will be an inability to trust. Winnicott plausibly argues that this balance can be best struck by a person who has a good imagination and who is able to identify with the child in fantasy.[36] Stern's photographic studies of mother–

---

32 See in this connection Bowlby's story of Dr. Z, who, during the absence of the researcher originally in charge of a young chimpanzee, became that ape's favored and beloved object from then on.

33 See Chodorow (1978); Hrdy (1999), pp. 485–581; Lopez and Brennan (2000). Hrdy points out that the idea of a "critical period" of bonding immediately after birth has long since been revised: data show that such "imprinting" occurs in sheep, but that primates are far more flexible. In human subjects, where the mother is not already at risk for abandoning her child, a period of separation after birth does no harm (pp. 486–8). The mother-separated children studied by Bowlby are of three sorts: children displaced to the country because of the war, children who suffered an early bereavement, and children of poor families who were in institutions because of the mother's need to work. All three situations deprived the children of stable and constant care. Surprisingly, Bowlby never considers the fact that in the England of his time, privileged children were rarely raised by their own mothers – and yet presumably the constancy of the nursery relationship led to an outcome different from those he describes.

34 Hrdy (1999), p. 495, speaking of the Aka and the Efé, "where infants from birth are passed among multiple caregivers with whom they become very familiar and are quite at ease."

35 Stern (1977); see especially the chapter "Missteps in the Dance."

36 Kurtz's account of large Indian working families reminds us, however, that a familiar middle-class American norm, where the mother spends much of the day cooing to her

child interactions reveal the subtle interplay of eyes and face that characterize most such relationships – and also show how the relationship can go awry, through excessive intrusiveness, overstimulation, or depressive neglect.[37]

I now turn to the third aspect of the Lucretian child's experience. It is introduced by the beautiful phrase "into the shores of light," *in luminis oras*. This phrase lets us see that the world into which the child arrives is radiant and wonderful, claims its attention as an object of interest and pleasure in its own right. (Later on, in the context of describing our fear of death, Lucretius speaks of the pain with which people leave "the sweet light of life," *dulcia lumina vitae*.) The wonder and interest of the world are too little stressed by psychoanalysts, who are usually stricter Epicureans than Lucretius himself, portraying the infant's basic tendencies as directed toward the removal of pain and disturbance alone.[38] But Aristotle got it right: the interest in cognitive mastery is a part of human infants from the start of life. Thus Stern, drawing on recent experimental work, stresses the infant's intense interest in cognitive stimulation and its surprisingly mature early ability to make distinctions.[39] It is now clear, for example, that extremely young infants seek out intensity of light, and turn their attention to the brightest or most intense stimulation in their world that is not actually painful.[40] This tendency is extremely valuable in helping it begin to sort out the world. In a related way, Winnicott draws attention to the importance of the child's creative impulse, its delight in initiating imaginative activity.

Indeed, quite apart from this evidence, we need to posit an original need for cognitive distinction-making, and an original joy in sorting

baby, is not necessary for psychic health, and may even at times conduce to excessive intrusiveness: see Kurtz (1992). (On the cover of the book is a photograph, taken by Kurtz, of a mother sitting on the ground cleaning lentils, while her baby, on her back, looks over her shoulder and another young child plays on the ground at her feet.)

37 Stern (1977).
38 Lear (1990) appears to be an exception, since he speaks often of the sufficient lovability of the world, and even argues that there are signs of this view in later writings of Freud.
39 Stern (1985, 1990).
40 See Stern (1990), p. 17ff., where the infant stares with fascination at a patch of sunlight on the wall, and, in Stern's metaphorical recreation, the sunlight is a moving, dancing magnet drawing the child's attention – until the child, seeking new stimulation, turns to the exploration of the adjacent patch of wall.

out the world, in order to explain why infants get going and pursue projects of their own in the uncertain world. For if the only positive value with which they invest items in their environment is instrumental value toward the removal of some negative condition, then it should be as Epicurus says: when once pain and disturbance is undone, "the animal has no need to go off anywhere."[41] But animals initiate projects of their own. In human animals the independence from mere self-protection of curiosity, cognitive interest, and wonder is especially apparent, and essential to explain initiative and creativity.

III. EARLY EMOTIONS: "HOLDING," LOVE, PRIMITIVE SHAME

Where in all of this do we find emotions? At first, as I have said, the infant has no clear sense of the boundaries of self and other. It experiences mysterious transformations, and it does not yet trace them to a distinct external origin. We have the roots of the emotions already, in the inchoate sense that some processes of profound importance to one's being are arriving and departing in a way that eludes control. Emotions are recognitions of that importance coupled with that lack of full control. This means that they develop gradually, as the infant becomes more and more cognizant of the importance of the transformations to its being, and of the fact that they arrive, so to speak, from outside. When they are traced to a definite agency, and when that agency is to some extent distinguished from the self, the emotions will be provided with an object. The earliest emotions are likely to be fear and anxiety, when the transformation is temporarily withheld, joy when it is present, and increasingly, as time goes on, a kind of hope for its blissful arrival.[42] Love is not yet fully present, insofar as the infant is as yet unable to conceive of the caretaker as a whole person with a separate career in space and time. But a kind of rudimentary love and gratitude are involved in the awareness that others aid it in its attempts to live (Spinoza's definition of love). At the same time the infant has an incip-

---

41 Epicurus, *Letter to Menoeceus*, 128, on which see Nussbaum (1994), Chapter 4.
42 Cf. Wittgenstein (1967), p. 469: "One might observe a child and wait until one day he manifests hope; and then one could say 'Today he hoped for the first time'. But surely that sounds queer! . . . And why queer? . . . Well, bit by bit daily life becomes such that there is a place for hope in it."

ient kind of wonder and delight at parts of the world that are not related to its own states. These parts of the world include persons and parts of persons, toward whom wonder and gratitude may be profoundly interwoven.

At this point (in the first few months of life) the infant has no clear sense of external objects as persisting continuous wholes, nor of itself as a distinct whole and persisting substance; its thoughts about objects and about self are less definite. Insofar as emotion has an object it may be a region of the world, or, a bit later, a part or stage of the caregiver, not the caregiver as a complete person.

How are these emotions connected to the child's appetites? The fact that an infant is a needy appetitive creature, whose earliest and most intense news of the world comes in part from its own appetites, is a central part of the story of its developing emotions. Many of its most intense concerns revolve around getting fed, and at first its anxiety and its hunger are hard to distinguish, a general turbulence that seeks pleasure in the Epicurean sense, an absence of disturbance and pain. On the other hand, the need for security and holding is distinct from the need for appetitive gratification; this distinctness manifests itself increasingly, as the child becomes increasingly aware of sources of comfort in its world. Nor, I have argued, is the pursuit of cognitive mastery reducible to appetite satisfaction. But this pursuit provides the child's inner life with emotions, such as wonder, that are nonegoistic and even, to some degree, non-eudaimonistic; it also infuses the structure of the other emotions, giving object relations a noninstrumental and even non-eudaimonistic aspect from the start, and allowing the child to take its own emotional states as objects of curiosity.

If gratitude is present in a rudimentary form, in the thought that others aid it in its efforts to live, then, by the same token, anger should be present in a rudimentary form, in the thought that others sometimes fail it in its efforts to live. As Spinoza stresses, a dependent being who sees itself as such will experience both love and anger toward the agencies on which it depends. The infant does not yet understand, however, that love and anger are directed toward the same source. Indeed, its uncertainty about the boundaries of self and other may make it unclear about whether the source of frustration is in or outside of itself. It may develop a vague sense that there are bad and good agencies that are somehow parts of its own self, and it may confusedly direct anger against these parts as well as outward, or fail to make this distinction.[43] Such ambivalence may possibly arise in the lives of some nonhuman animals; but the human child's unique combination of cognitive capacity and bodily incapacity gives rise to an equally unique emotional complexity.

Anger understood in this way is not an innate instinct of destruction: it is a reaction to one's life situation.[44] As Fairbairn, Bowlby, and other object-relations theorists argue, we have no need to introduce a destructive instinct to explain infant behavior, and much reason, in the infant's primary clinging and comfort-seeking behavior, to refuse to introduce it. On the other hand, the process of development entails many moments of discomfort and frustration. Indeed, some frustration of the infant's wants by the caretaker's separate comings and goings is essential to development – for if everything were always simply given in advance of discomfort, the child would never try out its own projects of control.[45]

On the other hand, the infant can hardly be in a position to comprehend this grand design. Its posture is one of infantile omnipotence,[46] in which the entire world revolves around its wants. Any failure on the part of the caretaker to fulfill those wants will lead to reactive anger, as if (to put it in prematurely complex terms) some right of its own had been slighted.[47] Another way of putting this point is Seneca's: in the Golden Age "crime is far off," and greed and anger are absent – because the world operates to fulfill people's every want in advance. But, as we have insisted, our world is not and never was that world. The child's evolving recognition that the caretaker sometimes fails to bring it what it wants gives rise to an anger that is closely linked to its

43 This is the basic idea behind the elaborate accounts of "introjection" and "splitting" in Kleinian psychoanalysis; the basic idea, if not all of the elaborate superstructure, is endorsed by Fairbairn as a reasonable way of making sense of the rudimentary nature of emotions at this stage.

44 Contrast Klein (1984, 1985) on the death instinct; she derives this idea from Freud (1920).

45 See also Bollas (1987), p. 29: "Transformation does not mean gratification. Growth is only partially promoted by gratification, and one of the mother's transformative functions must be to frustrate the infant." Compare Seligman (1975) on the importance of learning that voluntary responding can control the environment.

46 This is well captured in Freud's famous (if sexist) phrase, "his majesty the baby" – endorsed minus the gender narrowness by both Fairbairn and Bollas.

47 Fairbairn (1952), p. 171ff.

emerging love. Indeed, the very recognition that both good things and their absence have an external source guarantees the presence of both of these emotions[48] – although the infant has not yet recognized that both take a single person as their object.

This anger will soon produce a crisis in the infant's life. But we can already observe that the nature of parental[49] holding itself affects the child's situation as the crisis approaches. Winnicott draws attention to the way in which holding that is "good enough" permits the child to be at one and the same time omnipotent and utterly dependent, both the center of the world and utterly reliant on another.[50] The parents' (or other caregivers') ability to meet the child's omnipotence with suitably responsive and stable care creates a framework within which trust and interdependence may thus gradually grow: the child will gradually relax its omnipotence, its demand to be attended to constantly, once it understands that others can be relied on and it will not be left in a state of utter helplessness. This early framework of steadiness and continuity will provide a valuable resource in the later crisis of ambivalence. On the other hand, to the extent that a child does not receive sufficiently stable holding, or receives holding that is excessively controlling or intrusive, without space for it to relax into a relationship of trust, it will cling, in later life, to its own omnipotence, demanding perfection in the self and refusing to tolerate imperfection either in object relations or in the inner world.

These ideas receive a fascinating development in the fragment of a lengthy analysis by Winnicott posthumously published under the title *Holding and Interpretation.*[51] The patient B, a young male medical

---

48 See Spinoza's account of love and hatred, to be discussed in Chapter 10.

49 Here and elsewhere I will sometimes use this term without qualification, but it should be understood that I refer to the child's primary caregivers, whether or not they are its parents.

50 See Lopez and Brennan (2000) and Hrdy (1999) for the same points established experimentally, using a Bowlby-inspired attachments theory.

51 Winnicott (1986), with a piece of the early part of the analysis, published as an article in 1972, appended to the text. The patient was nineteen at the time of the beginning of his first analysis; he was referred by his mother, herself in analysis with Winnicott. He made a good recovery. Eight years later Winnicott wrote to the mother to inquire about B's progress; he interviewed her, and she described the pathologies in her own maternal care that she had by then discovered in her own analysis. Some time later the young man, now a medical intern, had a breakdown and was hospitalized. Winnicott looked him up, and the patient began analysis a week later. During the last six months of the analysis, Winnicott wrote down his extensive notes after five crucial sessions,

student, suffered from an inability to be spontaneous or to express any personal thought. In the presence of others, he could not initiate either conversation or activity, and he was found extremely boring. The petrified and lifeless persona he presented to others was an attempt to maintain omnipotent control over his inner world, by constant vigilance over language and thought.

During the analysis, it emerged that B had suffered from rigidly anxious and unresponsive parenting in early life.[52] His mother required perfection of herself, and interpreted any neediness on the part of the infant as a signal that she had not achieved the desired perfection (which she saw as commanded by a quasi-paternal idealized husband).[53] (Winnicott notes that the mother's tendency to idealize her husband implied that she did not love him. "[N]ot being concerned with a real person, she emphasized the quality of perfection.") As B makes contact with these memories of a holding that was stifling, the patient gradually becomes aware of his own demand for perfection in everything – as the corollary of his inability to permit himself to be a needy child. Because his mother wanted perfection (which he felt as a demand for immobility and even death), he could not allow himself to be dependent on, or to trust, anyone. "Imperfect for me means being rejected," he finally tells Winnicott. And then: "I feel that you are introducing a big problem. I never became human. I have missed it."[54]

---

stating that, though difficult, it was not impossible to remember what had transpired. Fourteen years after the completion of the second analysis, Winnicott wrote to B to ask how he was doing; he had done well in both life and work.

52 Winnicott (1986), p. 10: the patient's symptom was a fear of annihilation as a result of satisfaction itself, as if, once he finished feeding, he had no way of knowing that the good things would ever come again. The interpretation of B's early life that was developing in the analysis was confirmed by Winnicott's interview with his mother, during which she told Winnicott about material she had discovered in analysis with another analyst. As she reported to Winnicott during their interview, she became aware of a rigid demand for perfection in her maternal role and of a refusal to tolerate the separate life of the child: she understood perfection as a kind of death of the child, in which he would have nothing more to demand. Notice that B's mother is in many ways similar to George Pitcher's mother, as he describes her in Pitcher (1995), and produces some of the same emotional problems in her son: see Chapter 2.

53 The mother emerges as an anxious but by no means passive figure: one gets the impression that she is flamboyant. In his last letter to B, responding to the news of the mother's death, Winnicott writes, "She was indeed a personality."

54 Winnicott (1986), p. 96.

Signs of humanness were rejected by his mother, who, because of her own anxiety, was pleased only by a quiet perfect baby.

Already in the first months, then, the character of parental care and "holding" shapes the child's attitude toward its own human neediness – either creating the sense that human neediness is all right, and that its helpless body is a source of pleasure and concern – or, on the other hand, sending the message that perfection is the only tolerable state and that anything else will be repudiated.

In our terms, what has happened to the early emotions of this unfortunate man? First, the dynamics of both love/gratitude and anger have been thrown off by his inability to trust that he is being held, that his mother wants to hold and care for a dependent needy baby. A feeling of "infinitely falling" lurks in the background. This feeling gives rise to an especially intense anger, and a possessive love that brooks no human reality. (In this the patient resembles Proust's narrator.) The patient so fears his own anger that he frequently makes himself fall asleep. As Winnicott says to him, "there is very great hostility wrapped up in this sleepiness."[55] Second, for this reason the play of wonder and curiosity has been arrested: the creativity that grows in a context of trust and holding has never matured, and the patient's way of presenting himself is stilted, rigid, entirely impersonal. In a personal relationship, imperfect things might happen, but the patient's way "makes it all impersonal, and there is no excitement or anger or elation, and I do not want to get up and hit you."[56] This rigid impersonality, in turn, marks his relations to other people: one constant feature of the analysis is the patient's inability to describe his wife or any other person, and his frequent inability to use people's Christian names.[57] Winnicott tells the patient that in a real personal relationship there is an element of "subtle interchange": this was lacking in his early relationship with his mother, and his sleepiness expresses hopelessness about finding such a relationship anywhere. The patient responds with real excitement: "I

---

55 Ibid., p. 172. See also p. 163: "The difficulty is the fear of the anger."
56 Ibid., p. 123.
57 See ibid., p. 96: "I do not know if I could describe her. I have tended to assume you are not interested in her as a woman. Also I always have a difficulty in describing people. I never can describe a personality, the colour of people's hair, and all that sort of thing . . . I am always reluctant to use Christian names . . ."

must have been aware of the idea of a subtle interchange because I recognize that I have been looking for just something like that, without really knowing it." Winnicott points out that he has just been achieving it: "We are both engaged in this matter of subtle interplay. I think that the experience of subtle interplay is pleasurable to you because you are so vividly aware of hopelessness in this respect." The patient responds: "I would go so far as to say that it is exciting." Love, concludes Winnicott, means many things, "but it has to include this experience of subtle interplay, and we could say that you are experiencing love and loving in this situation."

Finally, we notice that there is another primitive emotion that dominates this patient's entire existence: it is the emotion of shame, connected to the very fact of his own humanness. All infant omnipotence is coupled with helplessness. When an infant realizes that it is dependent on others, we can therefore expect a primitive and rudimentary emotion of shame to ensue. For shame involves the realization that one is weak and inadequate in some way in which one expects oneself to be adequate.[58] Its reflex is to hide from the eyes of those who will see one's deficiency, to cover it. If the infant expects to control the world, as to some extent all infants do, it will have shame, as well as anger, at its own inability to control.

Notice, then, that shame is far from requiring diminished self-regard. In a sense, it requires self-regard as its essential backdrop.[59] It is only because one expects oneself to have worth or even perfection that one will shrink from or cover the evidence of one's nonworth or imperfection. To the extent that all infants enjoy a sense of omnipotence, all infants experience shame at the recognition of their human imperfection: a universal experience underlying the biblical story of our shame at our nakedness. But a good development will allow the gradual relaxing of omnipotence in favor of trust, as the infant learns not to be ashamed of neediness and to take a positive delight in the playful and creative "subtle interplay" of two imperfect beings. Winnicott's patient's mother, instead, believed that all that was not perfect was worthless, and that her child was worthless just by virtue of being a child and wanting to be held and comforted. "Imperfect for me means being

58 For fundamental discussions of shame, see Morrison (1989), Piers and Singer (1953).
59 See the perceptive discussion in Deigh (1996), pp. 226–47.

rejected." His crying, his demands to be fed, all these signs of his human nakedness were so many signs of worthlessness in her own eyes. The good feeding, as he understood, would be one that blotted him out completely. (Thus he dreams of being smothered by his mother's hair.) "There is only one way of achieving anything," he concludes, "and that is by perfection."[60]

B therefore becomes obsessed with the way in which others will look at him, wanting them to see him as perfect, and knowing that if they see the real him they will not see perfection.[61] His rigidity, his unwillingness to express himself, are attempts to maintain omnipotent control over his inner reality, so that he need not feel the shame of allowing his needy dependent self to emerge. Sleep is a defense against anger — but it is also the reflex chosen by his shame lest some human part of himself be revealed. A baby asleep is a good and perfect baby, and this is what his mother had wanted. Shame, then, causes the real vulnerable self to hide, the robotic and inauthentic "false self" to come to the fore. Recognizing that he had also expected perfection in Winnicott, and prompted by the analyst's gentle reminder that this idea is a defense against anxiety, the patient remarkably states, "The alarming thing about equality is that we are then both children and the question is, where is father?"[62] Here he arrives momentarily at a position of trust and playful holding that many children attain in infancy.[63]

This case shows us the extent to which the infant's ambivalent relation to its own lack of omnipotence can be shaped for better or worse by interactions that either exacerbate primitive shame or reduce it. A primitive shame at one's weakness and impotence is probably a basic and universal feature of the emotional life. But a parent who takes delight in having a child who is a child, and who reveals in interacting with the child that it is all right to be human, eases the ambivalence of later object relations; B's mother so exacerbated primitive shame that the real man was obliged to go underground, his place to be taken by a simulacrum, or by prudent sleep. "A feature of excitement," says B,

60 Winnicott (1986), p. 97.
61 See ibid., where he describes wanting women to look at him as a perfect lover, and giving up in despair when he realizes that he is seen as human.
62 Ibid., p. 95.
63 Compare ibid., p. 147, where the patient gets angry at Winnicott and says he is like "the ogre of childhood play." Winnicott expresses pleasure: "So you have been able to reach play with me, and in the playing I am an ogre."

"is irritation that it is not private . . . I have always had a difficulty that in sexual relationship with a girl there is no privacy, because there are two people. It is undesirable."[64] (Proust would, perhaps, agree.)

Shame, of course, comes in many forms. Any ideal to which one holds oneself has shame as its permanent possibility. What I have termed "primitive shame" – the demand for perfection and the consequent inability to tolerate any lack of control or imperfection – is a specific type of shame, closely connected with narcissism, or infantile omnipotence. I have said that all human beings very likely have this emotion in some form. Doubtless, too, it is renewed and deepened by awareness of one's own mortality, when that awareness comes. Nobody wants to be condemned to die, and everyone would like to exert control over death; yet, of course, we are all powerless to do that. In that way the body may come to be a primary focus of primitive shame, as the seat of our inability to master the world and to go on living. But if these developments are in some form universal, B's history shows an exaggerated and paralyzing hypertrophy of both shame and the narcissism (demand for omnipotence, grandiosity) that is its counterpart. As Morrison nicely expresses the point, "Thus, shame and narcissism inform each other, as the self is experienced, first, alone, separate and small, and, again, grandiosely, striving to be perfect and reunited with its ideal."[65]

By focusing on B, whose shame was closely related to his mother's demand for perfection, we have so far concealed other sources of individual and social variation in primitive shame. Psychoanalytic accounts of these issues typically focus on the role of parents, although they do not always exclude other variables. But we can easily see that there are many issues that might contribute to a hypertrophy of the sense of shame. One issue is physical disability.[66] C, a child of my acquaintance, combined precocious cognitive gifts with a right hemisphere dysfunction that affected spatial perception, motor coordination, and the ability to adjust to new physical surroundings. We might say that C is doubly human: more cognitively able at an early age than

64 Ibid., p. 166. Compare the experimental data in Lopez and Brennan (2000), concerning the relationship between early attachment problems and inability to tolerate ambiguity and uncertainty, particularly in romantic life.

65 Morrison (1989), p. 66. See also Wurmser (1981), with numerous detailed clinical studies; Chapter 1 has the title, "Shame, the Veiled Companion of Narcissism."

66 Compare Lopez and Brennan (2000) on the influence of a variety of life events on the development of secure attachments.

most humans, and much more physically helpless. The extent of this discrepancy was striking: C learned to read before the age of two, and learned to tie her shoelaces at the age of eight. IQ tests showed, similarly, off-the-chart gifts in verbal and conceptual skills, mild retardation in spatial and physical skills. To the infant C, the world is more than typically alarming; it impinges on her in ways that she cannot control, and, with her highly acute cognitive capacities, she is especially keenly aware of these impingements. This is a set-up ripe for the development of an unusual degree of shame about one's capacity for mastery. Cognitive gifts help, and the drive to cognitive mastery was unusually strong in C. One day Henny Wenkart, an authority on the teaching of reading who knew C's mother, gave the mother a copy of a reading instruction manual she had just published. On its cover was a picture of the author, sitting and reading with a young child. C, just under two, already fluent in the alphabet, kept coming to her mother with this book, which clearly fascinated her. "Teach me, Mommy, she kept nagging," – and then, when her mother capitulated – "I'll be Henny Wenkart, and you be the child." This game continued until, after a very short time, C could carry on reading on her own. Notice the significance of C's choice of roles: she wanted to be the teaching adult, in control of the cognitive process, rather than the vulnerable child she felt herself to be. Reading was for her a passport to that ideal of control. When asked, at age six, to make up a story about the creation of the world, she wrote that the world was created from a book. And indeed, for her, this was so.

But all that cognition can do is insufficient to dispel the accurate perception that one cannot move the way other people move, cannot find one's way from here to there the way other people do, cannot learn to ride a bicycle, and so forth. All human bodies are limited, and all give rise, in that sense, to some shame. But a body that is relatively so much more limited than others disproportionately gives rise to shame. So shame, present for C already, grew in her life in a virtually unavoidable way. The fact that peers tease uncoordinated children only exacerbated her problem. Thus, as with any disability, the biological and the socially constructed interact in an extremely complex way.[67]

In C's case, then, we see an etiology of shame different from that of

---

67 See the excellent account of this interaction in Bérubé (1996), a moving account, by a social constructionist literary critic, of the life of his son, born with Down Syndrome.

B. Nor did it lead to the same result, since C had many more emotional resources than B, formed richly loving relationships, and had a rich inner world of imagination and creativity. Nonetheless, exaggerated shame caused her pain. More generally, in a world made for the normal, any child who is in any way non-normal is at risk for shame hypertrophy, particularly if the culture is intolerant of difference, as most cultures, especially child cultures, are.

Another source of difference in shame may come from the fact that cultures impose different ideals on different children. In some cultures, for example, males may be expected to show perfect control and mastery to a greater extent than females – in a way that produces at least some of B's rigidity and inability to play or engage in "subtle interplay." Elsewhere, little boys may be encouraged to play and explore the environment while little girls are treated as future brides and carefully guarded as they lead an indoor life. (When I encountered such girls in rural Rajasthan, India, they proved rigid in their attitude toward schooling, and had a very hard time learning to tell stories and engage in imaginative play.)[68] Thus we need to think resourcefully about the issue of primitive shame, seeing the many different types of influences that may combine to augment it.

So far, then, we see emotions – not formal acceptances of propositions, but inchoate cognitive appraisals – arising out of the infant's developing awareness of the uncertainty of the good and its own lack of omnipotence. Now I shall argue that emotions, so construed, are essential to the development of practical reason and the sense of self; that they bring problems to the moral life, but also substantial resources without which that life would be drastically incomplete.

IV. DISGUST AND THE BORDERS OF THE BODY

There is another related emotion that we must now consider: the emotion of disgust.[69] Disgust arrives somewhat later than primitive shame; it seems to be absent from children until the time of toilet training; so

---

68 See Nussbaum (2000a), Chapter 1.
69 See Nussbaum (1999b) for a more extended analysis, and related social/legal reflections.

in considering it we are to some extent getting ahead of our developmental account, which is still focused on the first two years of life. But because disgust has a close relationship to shame's concerns about bodily insufficiency, and because in later chapters these links will prove important, we must introduce it now; in Part III we shall carry the story further.

Disgust appears to be an especially visceral emotion. It involves strong bodily reactions to stimuli that often have marked bodily characteristics. Its classic expression is vomiting; its classic stimulants are vile odors and other objects whose very appearance seems loathsome.[70] Nonetheless, important research by psychologist Paul Rozin[71] has made it evident that disgust has a complex cognitive content, which focuses on the idea of incorporation of a contaminant. His core definition of disgust is "[r]evulsion at the prospect of (oral) incorporation of an offensive object. The offensive objects are contaminants; that is, if they even briefly contact an acceptable food, they tend to render that food unacceptable."

Rozin does not dispute the idea that disgust may well have an underlying evolutionary basis; but he shows that it is distinct from both *distaste,* a negative reaction motivated by sensory factors, and (a sense of) *danger,* a rejection motivated by anticipated harmful consequences. Disgust is not simple distaste, because the very same smell elicits different disgust reactions depending on the subject's conception of the object. Subjects sniff decay odor from two different vials, both of which in reality contain the same substance; they are told that one vial contains feces and the other contains cheese. (The real smells are confusable.) Those who think that they are sniffing cheese usually like the smell; those who think they are sniffing feces find it repellant and unpleasant. "It is the subject's conception of the object, rather than the sensory properties of the object, that primarily determines the hedonic value."[72] In general, disgust is motivated primarily by ideational factors: the nature or origin of the item and its social history (e.g., who

70 By "classic," Rozin and I mean both that these are ubiquitous occasions of disgust and also that these are the central paradigm cases to which people typically turn in explaining disgust or why a particular thing is disgusting.

71 Rozin has published many articles on aspects of disgust, but a comprehensive account of his views is in Rozin and Fallon (1987).

72 Ibid., p. 24, n. 1.

has touched it). Even if subjects are convinced that ground dried cock-roach tastes like sugar, they still refuse to eat it, or say it tastes revolting if they do.

Nor is disgust the same as (perceived) danger. Dangerous items (e.g., poisonous mushrooms) are tolerated in the environment, so long as they will not be ingested; disgusting items are not so tolerated. When danger is removed, the dangerous item will be ingested: detoxified poisonous mushrooms are acceptable. But disgusting items remain dis-gusting even when all danger is removed. People refuse to eat sterilized cockroaches; many object even to swallowing a cockroach inside an indigestible plastic capsule that would emerge undigested in the sub-ject's feces.

Disgust concerns the borders of the body: it focuses on the prospect that a problematic substance may be incorporated into the self. For many items and many people, the mouth is an especially charged bor-der. The disgusting has to be seen as alien: one's own bodily products are not viewed as disgusting so long as they are inside one's own body, although they become disgusting when they leave it. Most people are disgusted by drinking from a glass into which they themselves have spit, although they are not sensitive to saliva in their own mouths. The ideational content of disgust is that the self will become base or con-taminated by ingestion of the substance that is viewed as offensive. Several experiments done by Rozin and colleagues indicate that the idea involved is that "you are what you eat": if you ingest what is base, this debases you.

The objects of disgust range widely, but Rozin has confirmed exper-imentally that "all disgust objects are animals or animal products," or objects that have had contact with animals or animal products – a major source being contact with "people who are disliked or viewed as unsavory." It is difficult to explain why plant products (apart from decayed or moldy specimens) are not disgusting,[73] but research suggests that the movitating ideas have to do with our interest in policing the boundary between ourselves and nonhuman animals, or our own ani-mality. Hence tears are the one human bodily secretion that is not

---

73 Some people find okra disgusting, and it has been suggested that this may be because it has what seems like a mucous membrane and thus strikes them as animal-like. This reaction seems less prevalent in cultures where okra is typically stir-fried so as to lose its mucosity (it is, for example, a staple, in this form, of Indian cuisine).

found disgusting, presumably because they are thought to be uniquely human, and hence do not remind us of what we have in common with animals.[74] Feces, snot, semen, and other animal bodily secretions, by contrast, are found contaminating: we do not want to ingest them, and we view as contaminated those who have regular contact with them. (Thus "untouchables," in the Indian caste system, were those whose daily function was to clean latrines; oral or anal reception of semen, in many cultures, is held to be a contamination and a mark of low or base status.) Insofar as we eat meat without finding it disgusting, we typically disguise its animal origin, cutting off skin and head, cutting the meat into small pieces.[75]

Rozin tentatively concludes that the core idea in disgust is a belief that if we take in the animalness of animal secretions we will ourselves be reduced to the status of animals. We can extend this thought by adding, along lines suggested by Rozin's research, that we also have disgust reactions to the spoiled or decaying, which, on this picture, would make us mortal and decaying if ingested. Disgust thus wards off both animality in general and the mortality that is so prominent in our loathing of our animality. Indeed, we need to add this restriction in order to explain why some aspects of our animality – for example, strength, agility – are not found disgusting. The products that are are the ones that we connect with our vulnerability to decay and to becoming waste products ourselves. Thus in all cultures an essential mark of human dignity is the ability to wash and to dispose of wastes. (Rozin points to analyses of conditions in prisons and concentration camps that show that people who are forbidden to clean themselves or to use the toilet are soon perceived as subhuman by others, thus as easier to torture or kill.[76] They have become animals.)

A prominent feature of disgust is the idea of "psychological contam-

---

74 Rozin and Fallon (1987), p. 28, citing Sherry Ortner.
75 Ibid., citing research by A. Angyal. When we do not disguise the meat – roasting a whole lamb, eyes and all, on a spit, or serving a pig with the head intact and an apple in its mouth – there is typically an air of macho bravado attaching to the gesture, as when hunters display the head of a quarry as a trophy, expecting to shock and a little disgust the faint-hearted. (In that sense, the famous and much-discussed *Playboy* "beaver hunters" cartoon strikes deep to the roots of misogyny, with its picture of a woman splayed across the roof of the hunters' car in the manner of a deer.)
76 Rozin and Fallon (1987), citing T. Despres. For more examples of this tendency, and its negative relation to empathy and compassion, see Chapter 6.

ination." The basic idea is that past contact between an innocuous substance and a disgust substance causes rejection of the acceptable substance. This contamination is mediated by what Rozin, plausibly enough, calls laws of "sympathetic magic." One such law is the law of *contagion*: things that have been in contact continue ever afterwards to act on one another.[77] Thus, after a dead cockroach is dropped into a glass of juice, people refuse to drink that kind of juice afterwards. A second is "similarity": if two things are alike, action taken on one (e.g., contaminating it) is taken to have affected the other. Thus, a piece of chocolate fudge made into a dog-feces shape is rejected, even though subjects know its real origin; subjects also refuse to eat soup served in a (sterile) bedpan, or to eat soup stirred with a (sterile) flyswatter.

These reactions are at one level irrational; and they display an error that mars many emotions: the object is identified, it would seem, at the wrong level of generality, and thence linked with objects from which it is crucially different. But while we can call this tendency irrational if we like, we must recognize that it is in two ways quite functional. In evolutionary terms, overgeneralization about what objects to avoid no doubt served to steer our ancestors more successfully away from truly dangerous items. As Nietzsche long ago said, a species that refused to overgeneralize, investigating each particular object precisely before any generalization, would probably have perished long since.[78] And even in contemporary terms, it appears that a firm and overgeneral bounding off of the self from the disgusting serves to reassure the self about its own solidity and power. That is why disgust tends to spread itself so promiscuously over people and groups, as we shall see.

Disgust appears not to be present in infants during the first three years of life. It is taught by parents and society. This does not show that it does not have an evolutionary origin; many traits based on innate equipment take time to mature. But it does show that with disgust, as with language, social teaching plays a large role in shaping the form that the innate equipment takes. Usually this teaching begins during toilet training; ideas of indirect and psychological contamination are usually not firm until much later. Both parental and social teaching are involved in these developments. (The disgust levels of

---

77 This law has a positive side, in our eagerness to possess or even just to touch objects that have been the property of celebrities, to sleep where they have slept, etc.

78 Nietzsche, *The Gay Science*, 111–12.

children correlate strongly with those of their parents,[79] and disgust objects vary considerably across cultures.)

Disgust, as Rozin says, is an especially powerful vehicle of social teaching. Through teaching regarding disgust and its objects, societies potently convey attitudes toward animality, mortality, and related aspects of gender and sexuality. Although the cognitive content and aetiology of disgust suggest that in all societies there are likely to be certain primary objects of disgust – feces and other bodily fluids – societies have considerable latitude in how they extend disgust reactions to other objects, which objects they deem to be relevantly similar to the primary objects. Thus, although it seems right in a sense to say that there are some "natural" objects of disgust, in the sense that some broadly shared and deeply rooted forms of human thinking are involved in the experience of disgust toward primary objects, many objects become objects of disgust as a result of highly variable forms of social teaching and tradition. In all societies, however, disgust expresses a refusal to ingest and thus to be contaminated by a potent reminder of one's own mortality and animality.

Our child, then, absorbs from toilet training and related social teaching some definite attitudes toward her own bodily wastes and toward other related substances. Disgust plays a valuable role in motivating the avoidance of genuinely harmful substances, and it does appear to have an evolutionary basis: so it would not be wise or perhaps even possible to bring up a child to lack it altogether, although both parents and societies can surely exercise great influence over its intensity and its manifestations. In this way, another root of conflict arises in the child's life: for her own body now seems to her problematic, the source of vile substances. She learns to some extent, in some way, to cordon herself off against the decaying and the sticky in herself, and she comes to see herself in a new way as a result. A ubiquitous reaction to this sense of one's own disgustingness is to project the disgust reaction outward, so that it is not really oneself, but some other group of people, who are seen as vile and viscous, sources of a contamination that we might possibly keep at bay. As we shall see in Part III, misogyny has been an especially potent instance of these projection reactions, as have anti-Semitism and loathing of homosexuals. For now, however,

79 See Rozin et al. (1984).

our child, as she becomes toilet trained and moves into her peer group, will start thinking about cooties, and who has them. By the age of six or so, she will target other children who are in some way different, saying that they have cooties. She will make paper cootie-catchers, and pretend to catch disgusting bugs on the bodies of these children. In that way, she will create an in-group and an out-group, the out-group serving to reassure the in-group that they are one step further away from being disgusting (oozy, sticky, decaying) themselves.

With disgust as with primitive shame, our ambivalence about our bodily makeup, its helplessness and its connection to mortality and decay, color the emotions of the child's developing social life, sowing the seeds of some tenacious moral and social problems.

V. PLAYING ALONE, THE AMBIVALENCE CRISIS, AND THE MORAL DEFENSE

We now return, however, to our somewhat younger child.[80] The people of the Golden Age were, as Hesiod puts it, *nêpioi* – infantile, lacking speech and reason. This condition fit their blissful environment. For they did not need to learn to protect themselves, to farm or search for food, to form societies, even to speak. They did not even need to learn to move from here to there: for just as they were, they were complete. Closely connected to this is the fact that they are without the emotions of the ordinary infant. It is not only anger that they lack, lacking frustration; they also fail to have that infant's joy, insofar as they fail to conceive of the objects that fulfill their needs as external, and the transformations as taking place from outside their own wishes. And of course fear and anxiety will be absent from a life that knows no threat of pain.

It was all right for the people of the Golden Age to be emotionless, since that condition was suited to the world in which they lived. But in our world emotions are needed to provide the developing child with a map of the world. The child's emotions are recognitions of where important good and bad things are to be found – and also of the

---

80 Ages given for the recognition of ambivalence vary widely, from the second half of the first year to several years later; I shall be thinking of the crisis as occurring when the child is around two, but I don't think that the precise age is very important for the overall account.

externality of these good and bad things, therefore also of the boundaries of its own secure control. Fear and joy and love and even anger demarcate the world, and at the same time map the self in the world, as the child's initial appraisals, prompted by its own inner needs for security and well-being, become more refined in connection with its own active attempts at control and manipulation, through which it learns what good and bad things are parts of its self, or under its control, and what are not. Among these external good and bad things it also learns that some are inert objects and some are endowed with their own agency. A child who does not learn fear is a child at risk; even anger is, I have suggested, a valuable effort to seize control and to assert the integrity of damaged selfhood.[81] This emotional demarcation is adaptively valuable, teaching the child the importance of its boundaries, and rescuing it from a sense of helpless passivity before the world.

The infant we imagined had an inchoate awareness of self as various transforming processes, of others as parts or agents of such processes. As emotions and efforts at voluntary control develop in tandem, the picture of a substantial self develops more and more, as that of a container with boundaries, fortified against but also seeking the aid of the external world. Of course the self never is self-sufficient; and the images that the Stoics like to use – images of roundness, hardness, impermeability – are not only inaccurate images but also quite dangerous images for someone whose life is carried on in a world full of actual dangers and urgent needs for goods. Winnicott's patient B learned such ideas of the self: the tightly controlled impermeable persona, the body asleep. One task of this phase of development will be to accept images that permit trust and vulnerability.

On the other hand, it seems to be essential to the child's growing ability to think and to act that it think of itself as a relatively enduring and stable thing in a not-too-hostile world, and that it become confident that it can achieve things on its own. It is at this stage that Winnicott revealingly introduces the concept of the child's ability to

---

81 In this connection, Aristotle's insistence that anger is not over just any damage, but always over something felt as a "slighting," begins to seem deep rather than narrow. For anger is not a reaction to just any bad event, but to one touching on what the person perceives as his or her sphere of value, things she would like to have go well and to some degree control. Thus the prompting event always has an aspect of invasion, the response an aspect of self-vindication and the affirmation of one's own boundaries.

"be alone in the presence of mother," occupying itself with its own projects rather than constantly seeking comfort. His idea is that the sense of the self, and especially any inner depth or creativity in the self, require a sense of safety that is not always being reinforced by the physical holding of a caretaker.[82] In order for this sense of safety to emerge, the child must be able to feel held even when not being physically held: she[83] must come to feel that the environment itself holds her. At first, this environment is supplied by the presence of the parent, available in case of need but not making demands. Secure in that presence, the infant can relax and turn inward, discovering her own personal life. As time goes on, real physical aloneness is increasingly possible: but, as Winnicott stresses, physical aloneness is not sufficient for "the capacity to be alone," which requires trust and confidence, and the ability to be preoccupied with one's own thoughts and one's inner life. (Only in analysis did B acquire the sense that he could be alone, since previously his inner world had been an object of shame.)[84] The personal kind of aloneness is always inherently relational: someone else is always there, and it is from the shadow of the early holding object that creative aloneness derives its richness. "A large number of such experiences form the basis for a life that has reality in it instead of futility."[85] This is the basis of the memory I recorded at the opening of this chapter, in which the thought of my mother holding me was continuous with later feelings of personal joy and reflection.

Another valuable concept Winnicott introduces is that of the "transitional object," such as a blanket or stuffed animal, through which the child assuages her need for reassurance without needing to seek the presence of the parent. She thus increasingly becomes – as in Proust's narrative of adult sleep – her own parent and her own reassurance. Both the concept of playing alone and the concept of the transitional

---

82 Winnicott (1965), pp. 29–36.

83 At this point, it seems necessary to supply the child with a gender, since I shall go on to mention gender differences in development.

84 Winnicott (1965), p. 126: the patient says that he feels that "the barrier" is "almost broken through," and that this means that he is no longer so worried about how to occupy the time: he doesn't feel the same pressure to fill it up by "idle chat," and he is more willing to sit with nothing to do. Winnicott replies: "You are telling me that for the first time you might be able to be alone, which is the only satisfactory basis for making relationships."

85 Winnicott (1965), p. 34.

object give a crucial role to imagination. Just as the parent exercises imagination in responsively meeting the child's needs, so now the child plays at being her own solace, imagining a safe world in the absence of visible sources of safety.

To a certain extent, then, the child's emotions, if things go well, evolve in relation to an environment that is relatively stable, which provides spaces for the development of wonder and joy, as well as stable love and gratitude. But of course no such environment is completely stable, nor can it be, if the child is to learn to be active and independent. Caretakers must come and go, support the child and allow her to fend for herself, so that, through her evolving emotions of fear and joy, she will learn how to get around in the world. So the child is always inhabiting a world that is both safe and dangerous, aware of herself as both hard and terribly soft, both able and unable to rely on receiving nourishment and security from her caretakers. This intermittance of care, and the intermittance of safety that results, is an essential part of becoming able to live.

Before long a time comes when the child, further cultivating her imagination of absent possibilities, recognizes that the very same objects who love and care for her also go away at times and attend to other projects, heedless of her demands. Even as she gradually forms the conception of herself as a definite persisting substance, so she realizes that her caretakers or parents are such substances, that she depends on them, and that they are not in her control. This means that love and anger come to be directed to one and the same source. As Bowlby puts it: "Thus love, anxiety, and anger, and sometimes hatred, come to be aroused by one and the same person. As a result painful conflicts are inevitable."[86]

This is a pivotal stage in the child's emotions. For she now really has love for the first time – if we think of a recognition of the separateness and independence of the object as a requirement of real love. But this love is colored in its very genesis by a profound ambivalence. (This ambivalence seems not to be present in the attachments of young animals of other species, who are far less physically helpless and also far

---

86 Bowlby (1973), p. 253. This stage is a central focus of object-relations psychoanalysts, including Fairbairn and Bollas. Klein already gave a good account of this phase, although she was, I think, in error to explain it with reference to an innate "death instinct" of aggression.

less capable of these integrative perceptions.) Still unable to accept the separate life of the caretaker, still intensely needy even while more cognitively mature, the child feels that very separateness as a cause for furious anger. Anger, which previously was inchoate rage directed at the frustrating processes or parts of the world, now becomes full-fledged and takes a person as its object, seeing the person as a blame-worthy agent of damage. This anger, as Bowlby correctly emphasizes, is itself ambivalent, for it is mixed up with the wish of love to incorporate and possess the needed object, and the anger itself may be used as a device of control.

In consequence, next to anger we now also have on our hands the emotion of jealousy – the wish to possess the good object more completely by getting rid of competing influences, the judgment that it is very bad that there should be these competing influences and that it would be good for them to vanish from the earth. And jealousy, which has the caretaker as its focus, is next-door to envy, which takes as its focus the competing objects who for a time enjoy the caretaker's favor – especially other siblings, and the lover or spouse of the primary caretaker – or their love for one another, if both are primary. In envy the child judges that it would be a good thing for her to displace the competing objects from their favored position.

It is here, as Fairbairn convincingly argues,[87] that we should locate the Oedipus complex. For at this early stage, rather than finding an emotional drama that revolves altogether around specifically sexual needs and aims, we seem to find instead a more inclusive family of emotions connected with the child's desire to possess and control, her inability to renounce omnipotence. We find jealous hatred of those who compete with her for the attention of the one(s) she loves, and whom she wishes to possess completely; and we also find the envious wish to displace those competitors from their favored positions. Rather than being about sex per se, this drama is about the infant's object relations more generally – her need for sustenance, security, and love, her un-

---

87 See especially Fairbairn (1952), p. 175, where he notes that the child may have ambivalent relationships of love with both parents, and then may "constitut[e] the Oedipus situation for himself" by focusing on the exciting aspects of one parent and the rejecting aspects of the other. In drawing this constructed situation together with other forms of envy and jealousy, I am, however, going well beyond Fairbairn, who still stays more or less within orthodox psychoanalytic confines in his account.

willingness to accept the separateness of the source of these good things, and her primitive shame at the fact of her own needy incompleteness.

It is difficult to say precisely where sexuality itself fits into this drama, and I believe it is not possible to make convincing arguments on this score in universal terms. In all cultures, of course, sex can figure as an element in the competition, as sexual needs and sexual intimacy remove the beloved object from the infant's control. And the infant's own nascent sexuality can become a device through which she seeks to compete with her rival or rivals. Beyond this, however, a great deal depends upon culture: on the degree to which dwelling patterns have made the infant aware of sexual activity, on the intensity of the bonds within the family unit, and on the degree to which culture and the individual family have saturated the child's experience with intimations of sexuality.[88] We should not assume that the intense and often highly eroticized bonds of the Western nuclear family are ubiquitous, and Stanley Kurtz's work on India has given us at least some reason to think that they are not.[89] Similarly, the fact that ancient Greece knew nothing of the Oedipus complex is best interpreted not as a failure to grasp what lay at the roots of their own experience, but as a sign that they had different patterns of emotional development (almost never seeing their fathers, for example), in which jealousy and envy took slightly different forms.[90] In the case I have described, my intense and eroticized love for my father was an extremely important part of the picture somewhere along the line. It would be difficult to say (and certainly memory does not say) whether my anger at my mother in the particular case was occasioned by competition for her attention against other distractions (her gardening, my father), or whether it also involved an element of competition with her for the attention of my

88 Proust draws our attention to these facts by pointing out that Marcel's mother's idea of a good bedtime story for an anxious boy of around twelve is George Sand's *Francois le champi*, a sentimentalized tale of virtual incest in which a foundling infant is raised by a young wife whose boorish husband he later displaces. The novel contains scenes that closely resemble scenes that Marcel enacts with his mother or other women; and it ends with an incestuous triumph, as Francois actually marries the woman who raised him. Just as Francois, at age twelve, implores his guardian for a goodnight kiss and, receiving it, weeps tears of bliss, so too Marcel learns to demand a maternal kiss, and to experience a temporary cessation of anxiety.

89 Kurtz (1992).

90 See Nussbaum (1993c).

father. But both sorts of anger could certainly be found in my child-hood. What I am claiming, however, is that the most powerful and to some degree universal element in this phase of development is ambiva-lent love/anger, attended by shame and envy. Whether and to what extent these emotions are sexual in the narrow sense, or involve a specifically sexual jealousy, will vary across societies and individual cases.[91]

This jealousy and anger grow out of the asymmetry of need that characterizes the child's relationship with her caretakers:[92] for the child now realizes that she depends almost totally upon a person or persons who do not need her at all, who can walk away at any time, leaving her immobilized and helpless, and who indeed at times choose other relationships. The object of Oedipal envy is, then, anything that com-petes with her own need. Very often this may indeed be the other parent, but it may equally well be siblings, or any person or activity to which the caretaker is passionately devoted. The object of Oedipal shame will be the child's own needy self, seen as insufficient for the omnipotent control of the object. Shame and envy are closely con-nected, since primitive shame involves the judgment that anything short of perfection is hideous, and this entails that any life in which the child shares the good object with others is unacceptable. The child can re-nounce envy only if she is able to tolerate living in a world in which others make demands on the good object, and these demands are granted legitimacy. But these demands will not be given legitimacy if the situation of being partial and incomplete is itself felt as shameful, and perfect control is the only acceptable goal.

Another way of putting this is to say that the "subtle interplay" characteristic of mature love permits the other to be independent, and takes delight in that independence; it thus works in favor of the re-nouncing of envy. But "subtle interplay" will be rejected by the child who is profoundly in the grip of the demand for perfection, since only a complete manipulation of the object will stave off shame. (To antici-

---

91 There is also the issue of age: object-relations theory posits ambivalence at an earlier stage of development than the original Freudian Oedipus complex; one will then have to ask what the child could be aware of, and how. Winnicott recognizes both a two-person relation of ambivalence at a very early age, and a triangular relationship of jealousy/ambivalence at a later age.

92 On the asymmetry of need, see Bowlby (1982), p. 196, and Chodorow (1978).

pate a theme of Chapter 8, Proust's narrator is never so happy as when he has turned real people into literary characters, thus succeeding in the primitive wish to incorporate and control the good objects. It is only toward literary characters, he tells us, that we can have love without jealousy and envy. He can love real people without jealousy only when they are asleep.)

Before we describe the "ambivalence crisis," let us recall some resources the child has by now acquired to meet it. First, she has nascent love and gratitude, now directed toward a whole object. If early holding has been successful, she has developed an increasingly subtle interplay with the object, which contains elements of trust and willing self-exposure. Second, she has curiosity about the world, combined with wonder and love of what is seen. Third, through her capacity to be alone and her play with transitional objects, combined with the subtle interplay she has developed with her caretaker, she has a nascent ability to imagine. In particular, by this time she is likely to be able to imagine the suffering of the good object. I knew that my bite had hurt my mother; I learned this by the kind of exercise my capacities got in periods of both solitary and interactive play, as I sang songs and told stories involving the experiences of others. (The impulse of wonder and the ability to imagine another's pain work closely together, since wonder turns the child outside herself to involve her with lives she doesn't know.) This development of imagination requires that the child not be unduly focused on primitive shame, an emotion that paralyzes play and cultivates rigidity.[93]

Consider again Winnicott's patient B. He had to make himself sleep so that he would not show any playfulness, or weakness, or anger. This pathological situation resulted from his inability to be imperfect, which paralyzed all three of the resources I have just described. He could not be alone or play. Preoccupied with being seen as imperfect, he had to go into hiding. Nor did he have much wonder and delight at the world: he could not attend to people as interesting in their own right, because he was so busy hiding his true self from discovery. Finally, his nascent capacities for love and gratitude were also stifled, since he could not trust another to see him, and therefore could not develop with them

---

93 Disgust also inhibits empathetic imagining: not in general, but in relation to the experience of any person who becomes its object.

the subtle interplay that is characteristic of love. As we shall see, this meant that he lacked resources for an adequate confrontation with the ambivalence crisis.

Let us now describe the crisis, as it might occur in a child who has had a more fortunate development. It is nonetheless a painful and terrifying crisis. First, the child feels the pain of frustrated need itself, and the corrosiveness of the accompanying anger. But, given that the child now knows that the object of her anger and the object of her love are one and the same, awareness of her angry wishes will also bring the pain of guilt, an emotion that is now felt for the first time. My memory of biting my mother is as vivid as it is because of the tremendous upheaval occasioned by this early experience of guilt – which involves the judgment that there are parts of oneself that are very bad, and have done bad things. My horrible feelings arose out of the awareness that the very person who had saved me from the wasps was the one whom I had bitten; this meant that my own love was tainted with badness. Finally, there will also be a powerful emotion of primitive shame, reflecting the fact that one has been imperfect, and thus fallen short of one's aims and wishes, which continue to retain traces of infantile omnipotence. The degree and nature of this shame will vary with the extent to which the child's first relationships have prepared her to take delight in her own humanness.

At first it may be impossible for the child to accept the co-presence of goodness and badness in herself, or to conceive of any way in which the badness can be discharged. This complex situation leads to grief, and to what Klein revealingly calls "the depressive position," a position that is at least temporarily that of psychological helplessness.[94] For the child has in a very real sense experienced a profound loss – of the totality of its world of bliss, of the pure goodness of the object of its love, of the full attention and love of that object, and, finally, of its own full goodness and purity. The world is no longer a golden world punctuated by moments of external danger. Danger is now seated at the heart of love, and of oneself. At first, it would seem that there is nothing to be done about this situation; one is, quite literally, helpless before the nature of one's wishes.

94 On this stage the observations of Klein (1984, 1985) are especially valuable.

On the other hand, the child now has resources to meet this crisis. She has gratitude and love, which involve wishing well to the parent who cares for her and holds her, and a subtle interplay with the parent's expressions of concern. She has wonder and curiosity about the parent as an independent part of the world, which already renders her love partly noninstrumental and even, to some extent, noneudaimonistic. And she has the ability to imagine the parent's pain (indeed, this ability explains why her suffering and guilt are so intense). These capacities suggest a strategy, which she will increasingly follow: to wipe out bad things with good things, damage with loving deeds. A crucial part of this strategy of "reparation" is the acceptance of proper boundaries to one's demands, as the child understands, and shows increasingly in her acts, the fact that she lives in a world in which people other than herself have legitimate demands, in which her own needs are not the center of the universe. In other words, catapulted into a kind of rudimentary thought by the pain of having injured someone she loves, the child comes up with the ideas of justice and reparation. Gratitude and wonder already turn the child outward to some extent. But it seems plausible to suppose that much of the intensity and urgency of its transactions with others is fueled by the sense that something very bad must be atoned for; and this means that the very badness itself can be made a source of good.[95]

What is remarkably suggestive about this line of thought is that it shows that the ambivalence of human love – which might at first be thought to be a bad feature of our difference from the animals – may also be an important source of the intensity and creativity of human love, the terrifying moment of discovering one's own impurity the source of a genuine turning outward toward the recognition of another person's needs.

As Fairbairn perceptively notes, this rudimentary moral idea that one can pay back the bad with the good comes as an enormous relief to the child, who would otherwise be condemned to live with the awareness of a kind of limitless badness in herself. He speaks of the so-called moral defense as follows:

95 This is a very important contribution of Klein (1984, 1985), whose powerful intuitive grasp of human situations here goes beyond the limitations imposed by some aspects of her theoretical structure.

It is obviously preferable to be conditionally good than conditionally bad; but, in default of conditional goodness, it is preferable to be conditionally bad than unconditionally bad. If it be asked how it comes about that conditional badness is preferred to unconditional badness, the cogency of the answer may best be appreciated if the answer is framed in religious terms; for such terms provide the best representation for the adult mind of the situation as it presents itself to the child. Framed in such terms the answer is that it is better to be a sinner in a world ruled by God than to live in a world ruled by the Devil. A sinner in a world ruled by God may be bad; but there is always a certain sense of security to be derived from the fact that the world around is good . . . and in any case there is always a hope of redemption. In a world ruled by the Devil the individual may escape the badness of being a sinner; but he is bad because the world around him is bad. Further, he can have no sense of security and no hope of redemption. The only prospect is one of death and destruction.[96]

In other words, morality, by limiting a child's badness, defends the child against being devoured by it. It makes the child have a feeling of safety and protection from harm, and permits the child to renounce wishes for complete control of the object, and the envy and jealousy that attend those wishes. From this point on, the child agrees to live in a world in which others make legitimate demands and one's own desires have appropriate boundaries. If one oversteps those boundaries, one must pay a penalty; and insofar as one forms aggressive wishes toward others, one must struggle to limit the damage these wishes do, and to repay the objects of aggression by creative and benevolent efforts. But because those moral demands rescue the child from helplessness and depression, they are at the same time welcome demands. Moral guilt is so much better than shame, because it can be atoned for, it does not sully the entirety of one's being. It is a dignified emotion compatible with optimism about one's own prospects. The structure of morality thus performs a "holding" function for the child, giving her a feeling of safety. In this sheltering structure she can play and exert herself. Unlike Winnicott's patient, she need not put herself to sleep for fear of murdering someone. Indeed, a good cycle now ensues: because she has accepted moral demands, she agrees to renounce envy and

---

96 See Fairbairn (1952), pp. 65–7, esp. pp. 66–7. Winnicott has a similar account of the origins of morality, which also invokes, as has mine, the trust occasioned by early "holding": see Winnicott (1965), pp. 73–82, 93–105.

jealousy; but to the extent that she is able to renounce these, she has less ambivalence and less occasion for guilt.

Notice that this story of the origin of morality gives morality itself a particular character. Morality protects the intrinsic worth of persons and their dignity, at risk from the damaging effects of the child's internal aggression. It is nonegoistic and focused on the intrinsic worth of objects outside the self; it sets limits to self-interest and enjoins respect for the legitimate activities of others. But it is also infused by love and wonder, and thus it is not a gloomy authoritarian morality. Indeed, morality performs the holding function of a loving mother (if we may use Winnicott's proviso, that this "mother" may also be the father playing a "maternal" role). Rather than making a forbidding and stifling demand for perfection, it holds the child in her imperfection, telling her that the world contains possibilities of forgiveness and mercy, and that she is loved as a person of interest and worth in her own right. She therefore need not fear that her human imperfection will cause the world's destruction.[97] And because she is not stricken by annihilating shame at her imperfection, she will have less need for envy and jealousy, emotions that express her desire for omnipotent control of the sources of good: in this way, too, a benign cycle is established.

The "moral defense" does not always take this form, as we have seen. In Winnicott's patient, morality had the visage of an ideally perfect father in whose eyes his mother and he both judged themselves to be shamefully imperfect. The perfection of the imagined father strengthened primitive shame, and prevented the child from understanding the potential for "holding" and mercy inherent in human love. Because nobody in the environment had any capacity for flexibility or mercy toward human frailty, and because nobody had the slightest interest in imagining the experiences of another, the child's ambivalent feelings became a source of unbearable anxiety, which never quite metamorphosed into a guilt that could be atoned for. Because he had to be perfect, he could not see his imperfection as anything that might be forgiven; he probably didn't even see it as a bad *deed* that he had

97 Winnicott (1965), notes that this idea of a good and merciful parent can frequently be associated with a corresponding idea of God: "man continues to create and re-create God as a place to put that which is good in himself, and which he might spoil if he kept it in himself along with all the hate and destructiveness which is also to be found there" (p. 94).

done, but instead as an inexorable badness covering his whole self. Shame, not guilt, was thus his primitive response: hiding, and shutting down. He had no way of coping with his own anger, and so he simply refused to go through the struggle most children fight with their anger and envy. "I see now," B concludes, "that there can be value in a struggle later when things have gone well at the beginning . . . To sum up, my own problem is how to find a struggle that never was."[98] The moral crisis felt like a death sentence, and he made himself die. Winnicott says he is "cluttered up with reparation capacity" because he has not yet found the anger "that would indicate the use of the reparation phenomenon."[99] In consequence, he of course became utterly incapable of morality, since morality involves the use of reparation capacities, respect for the humanity of another person, and regard for the other's neediness.

Notice that my account gives an important role to both shame and guilt; but it sees guilt as potentially creative, connected with reparation and the acceptance of limits to aggression, whereas shame, at least shame of the primitive sort, is a threat to all possibility of morality and community, and indeed to a creative inner life. Guilt can, of course, be excessive and oppressive, and there can be a corresponding excessive focus on reparation, one that is unhealthily self-tormenting. On the other side, shame of a specific and limited sort can be constructive, motivating a pursuit of valuable ideals. But in their role at this pivotal stage of a child's life, shame, with its connection to narcissism, would appear to be the emotion, of these two, that poses the bigger danger to development. I connect this suggestion with the idea that one of development's central tasks is the renunciation of infantile omnipotence and the willingness to live in a world of objects. Guilt is a great aid in this task, whereas shame threatens to undermine it entirely.[100]

In a lecture on "Morals and Education," Winnicott suggests that religious systems of morality harm development if their central focus is on original sin rather than on goodness, and if they neglect the human conditions for the growth of trust and "belief in," which include a central role for love and holding. "Actually moral education does not

---

98 Winnicott (1986), p. 165.
99 Ibid., p. 29.
100 On shame and guilt, see, more generally, G. Taylor (1985), Piers and Singer (1953), Morris (1971).

work," he concludes, "unless the infant or child has developed in himself or herself by natural developmental process the stuff that, when it is placed up in the sky, is called God."[101] (Winnicott's criticism does not pertain to one religious system rather than another, or lead us to prefer one religion to another. The contrast he makes is internal to all of the major religions, in all of which we find interpretations that emphasize perfect obedience, and versions that emphasize flexibility and mercy.)

In the light of our account we can flesh out this suggestion further. Any strong emphasis on the badness of human imperfection, any strengthening of primitive shame through the image of a perfect and intolerant parent, may exacerbate the child's moral crisis to the point of producing moral death. On the other hand, a merciful "holding" encourages the child to combat her aggression with reparative efforts. For this to happen, it seems important that the parent understand herself as imperfect, and nourish in the child a sense of delight in the sort of "subtle interplay" that two equally human figures can have. This can be done, for example, by showing delight in the child's playfulness and creative efforts. But creating a relationship that builds the child's love of the human in herself and in others requires giving up a certain type of safety, namely, that to be found in the type of rigid system in which a perfect and merciless father prescribes all duties from on high. As B says: "The alarming thing about equality is that we are then both children, and the question is, where is father?"

B's is an extreme case. But we should note that many familial and cultural norms contain elements of the demand made by B's mother, the demand to be without need, the demand not to be a child. Such a demand, Nancy Chodorow argues, is implicit in the developmental history of males in many cultures of the world.[102] Taught that dependence on mother is bad and that maturity requires separation and self-sufficiency, males frequently learn to have shame about their own hu-

---

101 Winnicott (1965), pp. 93–105, at p. 94. Winnicott may be wrong to treat belief in original sin as the target. The real target is a belief that it is impossible to achieve redemption through one's own reparative efforts; a view of original sin may or may not be coupled with that idea.

102 But note that, insofar as some cultures treat girls as marriage material from an early age and carefully guard their purity, they may also be deprived of the ability to play and be interdependent – albeit in a quite different way, with a focus on renunciation of their own agency: see my earlier remarks about girls in Rajasthan.

man capacities for receptivity and play, whereas females are more likely to get the message from their parents that maturity involves a continued relation of interdependence, and that emotions expressing need are appropriate. In the light of our discussion of B, we can now see that the males Chodorow describes will frequently, like B, though less extremely, both hide their need for others and avert their gaze from their own inner world, not mapping it with care. This can become a vicious bad cycle, as unscrutinized and undeveloped emotions remain at an infantile level and are therefore felt to be all the more shameful, all the more out of step with the controlling adult self who appears. Winnicott's theory of the "false self" and Bollas's related account of the "normotic personality" inform us that such people may function well up to a point, frequently using intellectual competence to conceal neediness, while the needy emotional elements lie dormant, lacking love and cultivation.[103] This can lead to a situation of helplessness like, though less extreme than, B's, as the needy elements are inarticulate, unable to make demands. This condition is highly correlated with depressive illness in later life. In other words, many people receive a type of emotional development that puts them on the road to B's situation, with its lack of the capacity for "subtle interplay," although few suffer B's complete emotional impoverishment.

We must now return to disgust, which also poses dangers for morality. The threat posed by disgust differs from the threat posed by primitive shame, although both take as their focus aspects of our imperfection and lack of control. Whereas shame remains focused on the self, disgust spreads outward. The parts of the self that are disgust's focus are found disgusting after they leave the body, and the wish of disgust is to remove them, to expel them from the sphere of the self. This wish typically issues, as we have seen, in magical projections of the disgust properties onto people or groups who from then on become a device by which people create more secure boundaries between themselves and aspects of their own animality and mortality. These vehicles of the disgusting are rarely if ever the child's own parents or her closest circle: for that would not accomplish the desired cordoning off. If your cootie-catcher finds cooties on your mother, they are probably already on you

103 Winnicott (1965), pp. 140–52, Bollas (1987), pp. 135–56. Bollas notes that such a person can frequently be recognized by his inability to read and comment on a poem.

too. So the disgusting people are typically people who are different, and who can be avoided as bearers of the contagion of slimy animality.[104] Disgust poses a threat not to morality itself, then – one can have a type of moral system while treating certain people as vehicles of disgust; but it does pose a threat to the idea of the *equal* worth and dignity of persons that is a very important part of any morality that most of us would favor. Primitive shame and disgust are, however, closely linked, in the sense that both spring from an unwillingness or inability to accept one's actual situation as a needy animal, mortal and highly dependent on others. One might say without exaggeration that the root of disgust is primitive shame, the unwillingness to be a needy animal. Of course all human beings have some primitive shame, and probably could not function without it; disgust, too, is ubiquitous and in some ways functional. But in both cases the hypertrophic forms are not inevitable, and it is in these forms that these emotions pose a particular threat to morality.

Once again, development creates different paths for disgust, and these paths are often correlated with gender. In his ambitious study *The Anatomy of Disgust,* William Miller, analyzing disgust's content as I have here, closely links disgust to misogyny and the male's longing to distance himself from the slimy products of his own body, ultimately from his own animality and mortality.[105] The woman becomes disgusting and slimy because she is the vehicle of the man's semen. She becomes, by projection, the bearer of all those animal characteristics from which the male would like to dissociate himself. Although Miller at times suggests that this gender difference in disgust is inevitable, there should surely be no doubt that it is social, and closely connected to teachings concerning ambition and control. And societies vary considerably in the extent to which they encourage such projection reactions.

104 One of the irrationalities in disgust is its association of dirt with nonhuman animals – for nonhuman animals are, on the whole, much cleaner than humans. But the associations, I have argued, are symbolic, aimed at shoring up the sense of power and invulnerability of a dominant group. Similarly impervious to reality was the belief of upper-caste Hindus in India that they were clean and "untouchables" dirty. In actual fact, as Gandhi discovered while working to prevent the spread of a cholera epidemic, the lower castes had cleaner surroundings, since they defecated at some distance from their dwellings, while the upper castes, who frequently used the gutters outside their windows for this purpose, were at high risk of infection.
105 Miller (1997), discussed extensively in Nussbaum (1999b).

Klaus Theweleit's remarkable *Male Fantasies*,[106] a detailed study of an elite corps of German soldiers after World War I, finds in the writings of these soldiers a hypertrophy of disgust misogyny, in which the clean, virtually mechanical body of the soldier is strongly contrasted with the sticky polluted bodies of the women from whom they were born and into whom they ejaculate. One of his significant findings is that, while at some level the bodies of all women and perhaps especially one's mother are objects of disgust, at the level of conscious conceptualization there is a sharp splitting – wives, mothers, and nurses being represented as pure and "white," prostitutes and working-class women as sticky and disgusting. So in that sense the disgusting remains "other," and it is always possible to imagine removing it from the world the way one flushes away feces or disposes of spoiled food. We can see, even before embarking on our discussion of compassion in Part II, that disgust is thus likely to pose a particular threat to compassion, or at least to any form of it that extends it to human beings generally, without hierarchy or discrimination.

As we see, then, a view of emotional development reveals some problems that emotions, as acknowledgments of neediness and incompleteness, contain for morality; they also reveal rich resources for morality. Indeed, the story strongly indicates that without emotions morality could not come into being, and that it relies on them continuously for sustenance.

A view of what morality should be like and a view of psychological health are mutually supportive, though each also needs to be supported by independent arguments. When we see that a particular sort of moral system aids and abets primitive shame or conduces to the stifling of "subtle interplay," we have at least some reasons to be skeptical about that system. At the very least, we have reason to wonder about its transgenerational stability, since it seems likely to produce people like B, who shut down morally and cannot find access to their reparative capacity. But we may also make a deeper criticism: that such miral systems harm elements of the human being that need support and sustenance. When, on the other hand, we see that a morality that incorporates a large role for flexible judgment and mercy supports the child in her ambivalence crisis, reinforcing her sense that the world is

106 Theweleit (1987, 1989).

worth living in despite her own badness, this gives us some reasons for being interested in that moral view. At the very least, it is likely that such a view can replicate itself stably across the generations, producing people who continue to inhabit and endorse it. And we may also give the view a deeper sort of praise, saying that it is gentle and supportive toward vulnerable parts of the personality that badly need support.

Similarly, if a moral view encourages children to project their disgust reactions onto vulnerable people and groups, we may wonder about that system from the psychological viewpoint: for, as Theweleit's study shows, people who cannot abide their own animality and learn to fantasize their bodies as pure machines are telling lies to themselves, and sustain a brittle and difficult existence. If, on the other hand, we discover that a moral view insists on equal respect for all persons and therefore teaches children that it is wrong to single out a group as the disgusting ones, because we are all equally moral and animal, we will suspect that this view is psychologically promising, because it tells no lies and does not require children (and adults) to live lives of brittle self-deception.

From the other direction, when we see that "holding" and the capacity for imaginative play support the renunciation of envy and the acceptance of the legitimate demands of others, we have reasons to think them important and attractive parts of child development, over and above the reasons given in the account of development itself. When we see that an upbringing like B's, with its stress on perfection and primitive shame, produces a person who cannot respect or attend to others as ends in their own right, we have additional reasons for being critical of such an upbringing, over and above those given in B's sad developmental history itself. Similarly, when we see that a type of toilet training that does not encourage a hypertrophy of disgust, and later parental efforts to inhibit the projection of disgust onto other children and groups, are supportive of a just society that accords respect to all persons, then we have reason to support that type of development, over and above the psychological reasons that have been mentioned. When we see that the developmental history of the German officers studied by Theweleit produced people whose rabid anticommunism and anti-Semitism were the vehicle of a hypertrophic and in origin misogynistic disgust, we have reason to shun that sort of child development even if it had otherwise appeared to be conducive to happiness.

In this way, the developmental story I have presented seems well suited to one broad type of ethical view, one that is both merciful and committed to equal respect. We might still select a morality of the sort that I have characterized as rigid and lacking in mercy, if we were convinced that other powerful arguments supported it. But if we did select such a normative view, we would need to beware of the strains it imposes on the human child, and the possibility that these strains would produce not perfect morality, but moral collapse. Again, we might still prefer the social norms of gender described by Chodorow, or even the male education of Theweleit's officers, if we should conclude (*per impossibile,* as I believe) that they promote social justice and general well-being in ways that we could independently justify (though surely one prominent aspect of general well-being ought to be the health of individuals). But we would then still need to beware of the strains that they impose on the personalities of individuals, and on the needs of individuals for the "subtle interplay" that is an essential ingredient of love.

VI. "MATURE INTERDEPENDENCE" AND THE FACILITATING ENVIRONMENT

Winnicott and Fairbairn describe a norm of health, which is said to be the condition in which this story of emotional development culminates in a person who has not suffered some unusually disturbing blow. Fairbairn revealingly uses the term "mature dependence," rather than "independence", and contrasts this with the young child's "infantile dependence."[107] In infantile dependence the child perceives herself as terribly needy and helpless, and her desire is to control and incorporate the sources of good. In mature dependence, by contrast, which from now on I shall call "mature interdependence," the child is able to accept the fact that those whom she loves and continues to need are separate from her and not mere instruments of her will. She allows herself to depend upon them in some ways, but she does not insist on omnipotence; and she allows them, in return, to depend in certain ways

---

107 Fairbairn (1952); compare Winnicott's use of the terms "absolute" and "relative" dependence.

upon her; she commits herself to being responsible for them in certain ways.

Although this acceptance is never achieved without anger, jealousy, and envy, the story of maturity is that at a certain point the child will be able to renounce envy and jealousy along with other attempts to control, and will be able to use the resources of gratitude and generosity that she has by now developed – and developed in part on account of her guilt and sorrow – to establish the relationship on a footing of equality and mutuality. She acknowledges that she will always continue to need love and security, but sees that this can be pursued without a jealous attempt to possess and control. It is only at this point, Fairbairn stresses, that adult love is achieved, since love requires not only the recognition of its object's separateness, but also the wish that this separateness be protected.

Analysts sometimes speak as if health were a rather easy thing to achieve. Proust's narrative of the "intermittences of the heart" gives us a valuable reminder of the tensions and ambivalences of the adult human emotional life, and therefore of the enormous achievement represented by what Fairbairn so calmly describes as health, which may require a continuous struggle against the desire for perfection and totality. Behind the increasing competence and maturity – and, indeed, the mature and generous love – of a "normal" human adult lurks much that the Stoics and Proust correctly describe, in an inchoate and often preverbal form that is therefore, while cognitive, especially impervious to reasoning and argument – a seething jealousy, a demand to be the center of the world, a longing for bliss and comfort, a desire to wipe the competing object off the face of the earth – any of which may be very ill-suited to some of the adult's chosen plans and projects. The ambivalence crisis is never completely resolved, and reparation remains a lifelong task.

This being the case, we should not ask about the "facilitating environment" for development by looking to the family circle alone (even in its cultural context). To the extent that it ignores roles and institutions, object-relations psychoanalysis has shortcomings as an account of emotions and the imaginative capacities they involve. People cultivate emotions in larger social and political groupings, and they need to learn the types of imagination and empathy suitable to those interactions. Chapter 6 will describe those processes and the role of institutions in them. At this point in the account, however, we should acknowledge that political institutions and systems of law are also part of the facilitating environment for the development of all the emotions of a citizen – and we now need to ask, at least in a preliminary and general way, what features such an environment might need to have, if it is to be capable of supporting the adult's continued search for health.

Once again, any such political view would need to be well supported by independent arguments; but we can at least get some general sense of the "fit" between a certain account of the personality and a certain set of institutions. At the very least, seeing this "fit" will help us to address issues of stability, showing us that certain sorts of institutions can replicate themselves over time through the personality, and that others cannot.[108] But we have independent reasons to prefer institutions that support individuals in their efforts to develop their capacities for love and reparation, since these are "primary goods" that any just political system should support.[109]

Of necessity these remarks must be sketchy; they will receive further development in Chapter 8. I begin with some suggestive remarks by Fairbairn. Invited in 1935 to lecture on the relationship between psychoanalysis and communism, Fairbairn decided to construct an argument about the political view suggested by his psychology of mature interdependence, acknowledging that it was highly speculative. Just as the mature psyche, he argues, is one that accepts the other's separate (and imperfect) will and life, and seeks to foster that – while still accepting the fact of mutual dependence – so too, a political life governed by that sort of maturity will be a liberal one, in which individual choice and autonomy are protected and fostered, and people agree to the Millean condition of the maximum liberty that is compatible with a like liberty for all. In this respect, he acknowledges that communism (as then practiced) fares very badly. On the other hand, he also holds that the child's development away from infantile dependence and toward mature interdependence involves the renunciation of exclusive and local loves and the acceptance of ever-broader forms of community, governed by reciprocity and mutual care. "Mature dependence"

108 See Rawls (1971). I pose the question he poses, using a somewhat different account of moral development.
109 See the list of "central human capabilities" in Nussbaum (2000a) and elsewhere.

involves a recognition of the parent's separateness and liberty. But by the same token it involves the recognition that others have a claim on the parent – more generally, that others have needs and have, like oneself, a right to the good things of life. Thus, while communism must be rejected because of its assault on liberty, some forms of democracy should also be criticized for being excessively nationalistic and ethnocentric. Ultimately, he argues, a full recognition of human interdependence should lead in the direction of internationalist humanism and away from local, tribal, religious, and ethnic particularism. (Thus he defends something like Kant's idea of a global federation of free republican states.)

Fairbairn does not dwell on material need: but it is easy to take the argument one step further, with help from Winnicott. Mature interdependence requires acknowledging the imperfection of the human body, and its needs for material goods; it also involves renouncing the wish of envy to monopolize the sources of good. We might then suggest that mature dependence entails the determination to pursue the fulfillment of basic material needs for all citizens, granting that all have rights not only to liberty but also to basic welfare. All are allowed to be children, in the sense that all are permitted to be imperfect and needy, and an essential part of regard for the humanity in them is to attend to the "holding" of those needs and the creation of a political "facilitating environment." Thus a norm of psychological maturity also suggests a norm for public life, a commitment to the meeting of basic needs, or, to put it differently, to support for a group of basic human capabilities. I have defended this view of the goal of political organization elsewhere, with independent arguments. At this point, we can see that such a view supports psychological health, as I have described it. It is also well suited to replicate itself stably over time, since its leading ideas support the formation of personalities that are likely to be intensely concerned with the needs of others, and thus to support for its leading ideas.

Facilitating environments are created, then, not only by individual parents, but also by customs, institutions, and laws. Institutions can express the view that we are all people who exercise initiative and creativity on a footing of equality; or they can express the view that there is a perfect patriarch who denies to the child the right to be alone. (B comes up with this idea on his own, on the last day of analysis, when he is about to leave Winnicott: "The great master, Freud, the Pope, Stalin: the acceptance of dogma is something that takes the place of father.")[110] They can express the idea that need is a sign of shameful failure, or they can express the idea that need is a normal part of being human. Finally, they can express the idea that our aggressions can never be redeemed, or they can express the idea that we may make reparation for our aggressive wishes and acts. In thinking about material need, political structure, the choice of a system of punishment – in all these areas we should ask what capacities of the personality different institutions support, and to what extent this gives us reason to choose one set over another.

We can give one more example of how such deliberations might go, by thinking about punishment. In childhood, an essential goal of punishment, according to the view I have developed, must be to support the child's reparative capacities. Punishments will do this best, my argument indicates, if they do not strengthen primitive shame, which undercuts the reparative capacity. The child should be encouraged to feel guilty, since that is a moral emotion appropriate to what she has done. But she should not be encouraged to have shame at her imperfection, as B did, since this will be likely to create rigidity and terror in the personality, causing the reparative capacities to go underground. This means that the punishing parent should treat the child with dignity and not mock her, since this will give the message that "imperfection means being rejected." The parent should choose a method that strengthens the child's confidence in her reparative capacities, what Winnicott calls her "growing confidence that there will be oportunity for contributing-in."[111] For example, this might involve a period of separation from the family context, followed by a reintegration, as the child is allowed to make reparation for what she has done.

Public punishments have to meet many demands that parental punishments do not. They must be chosen with an eye to protecting society from violent offenders, and also with an eye to deterring crime. So anything we say here will represent only a part of what must be considered. Nonetheless, the view that I have developed gives us some reasons

110 Winnicott (1986), p. 186. Winnicott points out that B avoids naming him, and that he probably wants to name him, since Winnicott has been both a mother and a father figure in the analysis, and he wants to establish independence by defying him.
111 Winnicott (1965), p. 77.

for skepticism about the current revival of interest in "shaming penalties" for offenses such as drunk driving, soliciting prostitutes, and so on.[112] Societies that use shaming penalties to mock criminal offenders reinforce primitive shame at the frailties of the human being. In the case of the particular offender, this may prove psychologically damaging; it may even produce a moral shut-down like B's, as a crippling anxiety about imperfection paralyzes the ability to attend to others as worthwhile in their own right. In society generally, shaming others contributes to a merciless rigidity such as that characteristic of the B family, in which one was either the father or one didn't deserve to be on the face of the Earth. What we want is more like what B found with Winnicott, a society in which all are children, needy and fallible, and all respect one another as of interest and value in their own right. In dealing with a criminal offender (of the kind, let us suppose, who does not pose an immediate threat to the safety of others), society can perform the function of a parent who "holds" the child despite its imperfection, by allowing an offender to display and strengthen reparative capacities, in community service, conferences between offender and victim,[113] and so on. This should have healthier effects for the individual, strengthening his confidence in his capacity to contribute to society; and it should also lessen the amount of anxiety and hiding in society generally, given that we do not say that "imperfection means being rejected." In general, the argument of this chapter is that most people have too much shame already; what they need is to develop confidence in their capacity to make reparation.[114] We recall, too, that it was B's mother's anxiety that led her to persecute and stifle her infant; and we can guess that as people jump on the shaming bandwagon, their own anxiety will exacerbate their aggressive and persecutory tendencies toward others. Again, we still might choose such punishments for other reasons – if, for example, they were shown to have a deterrent effect vastly superior to others. But we should do so in the light of a knowledge of the strains that they are likely to impose on the personality.

112 See Kahan (1996).
113 See Braithwaite (1999).
114 There are other reasons for being skeptical of shaming: in particular, it is difficult to calibrate the quantity of punishment to the quantity of the offense. See J. Whitman (1998), E. Posner (2000).

VII. THE NEO-STOIC VIEW REVISED AGAIN

I have argued that the childhood history of emotions shapes adult emotional life: that the emotions of adult life originate in infancy, and that this infantile history shapes their adult structure in powerful ways. Cognitive views that leave out infancy cannot explain the way in which the emotions of adult life bear the shadows of earlier objects. Neither, I have argued, can noncognitive views. The difference between B and a more fortunate man, archaic though it is, is still at root a cognitive difference, a difference in one's perceptions of value and salience, a difference in the narratives of need and dependency one has come to accept.

We can now understand more deeply, however, some of the motivations underlying opposition to a cognitive/evaluative view. The emotions of the adult life sometimes feel as if they flood up out of nowhere, in ways that don't match our present view of our objects or their value. This will be especially true of the person who maintains some kind of false self-defense, and who is in consequence out of touch with the emotions of neediness and dependence, or of anger and aggression, that characterize the true self. We should remember that in Winnicott's terms the "false self" is a matter of degree, and that we all have one to some extent, if only the polite social veneer we use to mask our deeper emotions.[115] But for many people the conscious valuations of daily life serve also as a mask worn in the presence of oneself; deeper emotions persisting from childhood operate, and motivate, in ways that the person may not consciously understand. When these emotions manifest themselves, or when their motivating activity is made clear, the person may well feel as if forces of a noncognitive kind were pushing her around: for the cognitive content of these emotions may not be available *to her*, and even to the extent that it is available it may have an archaic and infantile form. Moreover, it may not match at all the thoughts about the value of objects that she is aware of having. And she may stick to her view despite her conscious thoughts and the evidence before her.

Thus, R may be carrying around a great deal of anger against paren-

---

115 Winnicott (1965), pp. 140–52, esp. p. 143: "In health: The False Self is represented by the whole organization of the polite and mannered social attitude, a 'not wearing the heart on the sleeve,' as might be said."

tal objects without recognizing that she has anger at all, and she may even, like Winnicott's B, have a very strong determination not to allow anger into play, for fear of the destruction that might ensue. R may think of herself as someone who wishes all of her objects well, and she may actually wish them well. If she should become aware of murderous anger against them, this might seem to her like being possessed by an alien force, and she might easily form the view that energies of a noncognitive type were pushing her personality around. But she would not be right. We can see that we would not fully understand her anger unless we understood its intentional content; thinking of it as merely impulsive, we do not see that she wants to kill a parent, and thus we miss what really explains her actions.

Or take Q, a more healthy personality, who has found ways of atoning for aggressive wishes through reparation, and who has developed at least some confidence that she can overcome love by hate. Such a person does not allow a false self to push all primary emotions from the scene; and yet, in her intense focus on creative or reparative efforts, Q may not be fully aware that anger and guilt toward parental objects is a crucial part of her motivation, essential to the explanation of her intense need to make reparation. To the extent that she becomes aware of her anger, she too may feel that it is like an alien force: for precisely what she is doing in her reparative efforts is to make herself into a person who produces good for others. And yet we would not have a complete account of her motivation if we were to treat the anger as an alien impulse, failing to note its intentional content.

Take, finally, P, a man who has been raised as the males described by Chodorow are raised: taking pride in self-sufficiency, believing that he has no need of anyone. Like many such males, P continues to have intense needs for holding that will manifest themselves under certain circumstances, and are crucial to the full explanation of his actions. On the other hand, he may have a very strong interest in not identifying those needs as part of him, since he is ashamed of them. When they erupt, he will think: "Who is this needy child? Certainly not me." And he may form the view that emotions don't at all manifest the way the person views his objects; indeed, they may seem to him like invading and obtuse forces that resist seeing things the way the personality sees them. Nonetheless, in such a case we see that the intentionality of early object relations is a crucial part of explaining how he will act. It is important both to see that his love has an early object and also that the emotion's intentionality has remained at an archaic level, rather than getting further development through "subtle interplay" and creative imagining.

In short, the phenomenology of the adversary's view is appealing precisely because it does capture the dissonance that many of us feel between what we are aware of intending and what we suddenly find ourselves experiencing under certain circumstances. These may be differences of kind, as when we are aware of goodwill and experience sudden anger; or they may be differences of degree, as when we think we have a mild emotion toward someone and suddenly discover a very strong emotion. The past wells up in us, in ways that surprise the deliberately intending self. But once we see that it is the past that so wells up, and not some shot of adrenalin, we also see that we cannot understand it without getting at the intentional content that is proper to it. The difference of kind is ultimately explained by the fact that infantile emotion toward a beloved object has somehow come to take this present object as its occasion or symbol; the difference in degree is explained by the fact that the present object, not terribly important in my scheme of goals and ends, somehow represents an early object of great centrality. A cognitive view will be obtuse if it does not make room for such archaic and infantile cognitions and for their present force; but a noncognitive view cannot do justice to the way in which the past wells up, to the intense attachments to early objects that are manifest in it.

Thus my cognitive view, by including a developmental dimension, makes room for the mysterious and ungoverned aspects of the emotional life in a way that many such views do not. This has consequences, as well, for the picture of character the view will support. All cognitive views of emotion entail that emotions can be modified by a change in the way one evaluates objects. This means that for such views virtue need not be construed (as Kant construes it) as a matter of strength, the will simply holding down the brutish impulsive elements of the personality. Instead, we can imagine reason extending all the way down into the personality, enlightening it through and through. If a person harbors misogynistic anger and hatred, the hope is held out that a change in thought will lead to changes not just in behavior but also in emotion itself, since emotion is a value-laden way of seeing.

Clearly this view has important implications for moral education, in the area, for example, of emotions toward members of other races and religions: we can hope to foster good ways of seeing that will simply prevent hatred from arising, and we don't have to rely on the idea that we must at all times suppress an innate aggressive tendency.

Some such views suggest that emotional change will be a relatively easy matter: thus Aristotle gives the aspiring orator instructions for taking anger away, by presenting the objects of anger in a new light. If, say, we understand that the Persians have not really wronged us, we will stop being angry at them. But of course life is not always like that. Some angers may indeed shift directly with a new account of the facts; many do not. Again, some hatred and disgust toward groups can be prevented from arising by a good moral education; and yet, hatred seems to arise again and again, despite our best efforts, as if it had some deeper root in the personality.

Seeing this recalcitrance in emotion may then make us doubt the cognitive account: if persuasion doesn't bring change directly, and if our efforts at moral enlightenment don't eradicate prejudice, this must be because we are dealing with something other than evaluative thought. I have already addressed this point in Chapter 1, pointing out that many nonemotional thoughts are also resistant to change, particularly thoughts that are formed early in life, and in which we are deeply invested through reliance and habit. Emotion-thoughts involve, in addition, a stronger kind of investment, for they concern elements of our conception of well-being. Surely the Stoics already showed that the emotional life is hard to change: their cognitive view implied only that there was a task to be undertaken, not that this task could be easily accomplished; perhaps it could not be completed at all. Similarly, among modern writers on virtue, Iris Murdoch has stressed the long and patient effort of vision, the painstaking inner moral work, that is required if we are to change our ways of seeing people we fear, or hate, or resent. Precisely because such matters are both habitual and important to us, change will not be easy.

My view, however, goes further than these views, which ascribe the difficulty of emotion change to habit and the early roots of the relevant cognitions. For my view suggests that we may be quite ignorant of what our emotion-cognitions are, and also that we may have a lot invested in not changing them. For B, seeing himself as perfect/shamefully imperfect was not just a habit to be addressed by behavioral therapy. These ways of seeing himself were not fully conscious: they emerged into full awareness only in the analysis. Moreover, so much of his life had been organized around them that any change brought a sense of large-scale upheaval: in that sense, one's own character becomes an object of attachment, and poses resistance to alteration. Where early moral development is concerned, my account suggests that we are never dealing with a purely benign picture, into which hatred will enter only if we put it there. The roots of anger, hatred, and disgust lie very deep in the structure of human life, in our ambivalent relation to our lack of control over objects and the helplessness of our own bodies. It would be naive to expect that projections of these negative emotions onto other people will not take place – although we may certainly hope to moderate their number and intensity.

My view, then, urges us to reject as both too simple and too cruel any picture of character that tells us to bring every emotion into line with reason's dictates, or the dictates of the person's ideal, whatever that is. Given human ambivalence and neediness, and the emotions that have grown out of that, this is simply not a sensible goal to prescribe; and prescribing an unachievable norm of perfection is the very thing that can wreak emotional havoc, as B's case shows us. If Aristotle's view entails that the good person can and should demand emotional perfection of herself, so that she always gets angry at the right person, in the right way, at the right time, and so forth, then Aristotle's view is tyrannical and exacts of us more than humanity can deliver.[116]

One way of bringing this out clearly is to refer to a criticism of Aristotle – and of modern Aristotelians – made by the late H. Paul Grice, the distinguished philosopher of mind and language. In a lecture delivered in the early 1980s at the Princeton Ancient Philosophy Colloquium, Grice claimed that Aristotle has "a Prussian view" of human life. "I cannot lie in the sun," Grice said, "simply because I want to." Everything, he said, has to be justified by its role in *eudaimonia*. This was a shocking claim: Kant, of course, is usually taken

---

116 Notice that Kant, by contrast, is less harsh toward the vicissitudes of passion. If we do the right thing with reluctance, or perform our duty with little sympathy, Kant will not think the less of us, so long as we were using every means in our power to do the right. For Kant thinks that some things just can't be helped, and he is inclined to be merciful to the deficiencies of the passional personality.

to be the Prussian one, both literally and figuratively, and Aristotle the sunny Hellene. Grice was arguing that it should be seen the other way around: Aristotle exercises surveillance over every aspect of life, whereas Kant lets the passions go, so long as they don't interfere with the will.

Now of course the response to this – which Aristotelians were ready enough to give – is that an Aristotelian view can, as Aristotle's does, make ample space for virtues of playful friendly association, and we can easily defend lying in the sun as a virtuous deed on some such conception. The virtuous agent will be the one who chooses *and desires* to lie in the sun at the right time, in the right way, for the right reasons, and so forth. But Grice's point remains: the sheer wish to do some things *not* for a reason, and the merciful willingness to cease interrogating oneself about the appropriateness of one's motives and passions, are given no place at all in Aristotle's conception.[117] Kant is less "Prussian" than Aristotle in two crucial respects: (a) once duty is fulfilled, I can do other permissible things as I like; and (b) my duty does not extend to the formation of appropriate desires in the area of sunbathing. It was Epictetus, not Aristotle, who said, "Watch over yourself as over an enemy lying in wait." And it is the Stoic tradition that develops to the most extreme point the idea of zealous critical surveillance over desire and emotion (including the extirpation of the latter where possible).[118] But there is something like this in Aristotle, too, albeit more cheerfully expressed. To this extent, my neo-Stoic view of emotion, by providing the emotions with a history, has already diverged from normative Stoic ethics, and even from Aristotle: for already in my psychological account I provide the basis for condemning those normative approaches as excessively violent toward human complexity and frailty.

---

117 A valuable discussion of this issue, apropos of the relationship between Dostoyevsky's *Notes from Underground* and the Aristotelian view of motivation, was given in a Ph.D. dissertation by Eunice Belgum, (Harvard, 1976). Because of her untimely death, this material remains unpublished.

118 As Seneca's *De Matrimonio* puts it, "The wise man loves his wife by judgment (*iudicio*), not by passion (*adfectu*): he controls the desire for pleasure, and is not easily led to intercourse." Kant is, again, less rigorous: even though sexual desire, in his view, always leads to the objectification and use of persons, it is vain to try to reform it: instead, we simply hedge it round with an institution (as marriage is, in his view) that guarantees mutual regard and noninstrumental treatment.

VIII. IMAGINATION AND NARRATIVE

We have had several occasions to refer to narrative and to imaginative play. This theme needs further development, since it is fundamental to our later inquiries into love and compassion. Emotions, we now can see, have a narrative structure. The understanding of any single emotion is incomplete unless its narrative history is grasped and studied for the light it sheds on the present response. This already suggests a central role for the arts in human self-understanding: for narrative artworks of various kinds (whether musical or visual or literary) give us information about these emotion-histories that we could not easily get otherwise. This is what Proust meant when he claimed that certain truths about the human emotions can be best conveyed, in verbal and textual form, only by a narrative work of art: only such a work will accurately and fully show the interrelated temporal structure of emotional "thoughts," prominently including the heart's intermittences between recognition and denial of neediness.

Narrative artworks are important for what they show the person who is eager to understand the emotions; they are also important because of what they do in the emotional life. They do not simply represent that history, they enter into it. Storytelling and narrative play are essential in cultivating the child's sense of her own aloneness, her inner world. Her capacity to be alone is supported by the ability to imagine the good object's presence when the object is not present, and to play at presence and absence using toys that serve the function of "transitional objects." As time goes on, this play deepens the inner world; it becomes a place for individual creative effort and hence for trusting differentiation of self from world. Winnicott speaks of artistic activity, therefore, as a type of "potential space," sacred to the individual, that mediates "between baby and mother, between child and family, between individual and society."[119] Notice that it is only because the mother herself has cultivated her own "potential space" that she is able to imagine the experience of her child and to respond appropriately to its needs: so imagination is a crucial part of the reproduction of healthy character, and hence of a society's transgenerational stabil-

---

119 Winnicott, in Rudnytsky (1993). See also the essays by Bollas and Milner in the same volume.

ity. The "subtle interplay" between baby and parent is crucially mediated by play with narratives and images, as the child too becomes able to imagine another person's experience.

During the ambivalence crisis, narrative play provides the child with several distinct benefits. First of all, spending time in narrative play has already given her ways of understanding the pain that her destructive wishes would inflict on others, and therefore of taking their full measure. At the same time, narratives have given nourishment to curiosity, wonder, and perceptual delight, strengthening her ability to see other people in noninstrumental and even non-eudaimonistic ways, as objects of wonder in their own right. This assists her in her own reparative efforts. Furthermore, this same wonder and delight give her ways of relating to her own sometimes frightening and ambivalent psychology: she becomes interested in understanding it, rather than fleeing from it and pushing it underground in the manner of B. This project of understanding, in turn, militates against depression and helplessness, feeding her interest in living in a world in which she is not perfect or omnipotent. Finally, and perhaps most important, by dressing imperfection in a pleasing and playful shape, narrative play can undercut primitive shame at all that is human, helping a child to attain a certain forbearance and even joy about the lives of imperfect beings.[120] If I am right, that development in turn contributes to the struggle of love and gratitude against ambivalence, and of active concern against the helplessness of loss.

120 See Nietzsche, *Gay Science* 107: art saves us from nausea at human life by giving us a good will toward things that we have made. We can relax the demand for omnipotence and perfection because we find that we enjoy something that is fully human.

INTERLUDE

"Things Such as Might Happen"

Narrative play, I have argued, provides the child with a "potential space" in which to explore life's possibilities. Like the transitional objects – stuffed animals, blankets, dolls – with which children learn to comfort themselves in the absence of the mother, stories, rhymes, pictures, and songs people the world of the child with objects that she can manipulate as symbols of the objects in real life that matter most to her. As Winnicott says, the transitional object is itself a symbol, and the child's play with it is an early example of artistic creativity. Frequently the child acts out stories with her stuffed animals – so there is a tight interweaving between the symbolic physical object and the symbolic aesthetic object. Through symbolic activity, the child cultivates her ability to imagine what others experience, and she explores the possibilities of human life in a safe and pleasing manner. At the same time, she cultivates her ability to be alone, and deepens her own inner world.

I shall return to the child's use of narrative in Chapter 6, discussing the relationship between narrative play and the acquisition of compassion. But we now need to open up several more general questions about artistic activity and emotion. Literary works will be important to the normative part of my account in Part III – along with one musical work. In the chapter that concludes Part I, I have chosen to focus on music. There are several reasons for this choice. The topic is of great intrinsic interest, and is of particular interest to me. Furthermore, in focusing on music we have an opportunity to display the merits of the account of emotion that we have been developing, showing that it helps us to solve some problems that other accounts cannot solve. A focus on music will also assist us in making some further refinements in the account. Finally, the topic of music and emotion, though recently more often discussed than it was for some years, remains a relatively neglected topic in aesthetic theory; I therefore need to indicate what my approach to it is, since I shall be speaking of music as well as literature in Part III.

At this point, however, I need to prepare the way for that analysis by saying something more general about emotional expression and response in connection with works of art. Some accounts of musical emotion get bogged down by not thinking about how these issues arise, and are resolved, in the other arts. Certain questions have sometimes been treated as insoluble, as putting an end to discussion – questions such as: "How can we have real emotions when listening to a musical work if there is no real-world object for those emotions to be about?" "If the negative emotions of sadness, grief, fear, and so forth that we experience in response to music are real emotions, why ever would we seek them out deliberately?" "If in grasping the expressive content of music we are acquiring new cognitive content, doesn't this mean that we are just using the music as a tool of understanding?"[1] But these questions are less often regarded as discussion stoppers in the analysis of literature; a long tradition, beginning from Aristotle, has addressed them, and they have generated valuable constructive analyses. It will be useful to place my account in this context.[2]

The very form of a literary work of art can be rich in emotionally expressive content. To focus on the example of ancient tragedy, the tragic genre contains, in the very form of its plots and the actions of its characters, what Aristotle calls "the pitiable" and "the fearful": that is, material that is appropriately perceived (by an attentive and suitably educated reader or spectator) with those emotions. For in its very structure it represents good people coming to grief in important ways through no fault of their own, and this is part of the content of pity, or, as I shall be calling it, compassion.[3] (Fear is felt both for the

---

1 The first question is ubiquitous: see especially Levinson (1990) for a probing discussion; the second is especially well treated by Levinson (1990), who is one of the few to offer a constructive answer; the third is the impasse from which Budd (1985) does not seem to be able to extricate himself, in order to come up with a positive account.

2 I am offering here a compressed account of positions for which I have argued elsewhere: see Nussbaum (1986, 1992).

3 For discussion of the various English and Greek terms, see Chapter 6. As we shall see (Chapter 6), Aristotle and I differ to some extent concerning the rest of the analysis: but

characters, as bad things are impending, and for oneself, as one reflects on the possibilities they show for human life in general.) The characters may also have and express various emotions, and to the extent that spectators, in some local part of the work, identify with one or another character, they will also experience those emotions, sharing Philoctetes' anger and desolation, or the devastation of Oedipus when he discovers what he has done; to the extent that they are encouraged to identify with a perspective that is detached from that of a given character, they may have a range of reactive emotions toward the character: compassion for Philoctetes' suffering, anger at Odysseus' manipulative use of him, fear for Oedipus' impending downfall. But the pitiable and the fearful are not simply local: they are embedded in the overall structure of the form, through the particular type of identification and sympathy with the hero that the form itself cultivates. We might, using Wayne Booth's valuable terminology, which we shall introduce more fully in Chapter 5, call this perspective that of the *implied author*, the sense of life that animates the work taken as a whole. That perspective is frequently modeled, in tragedies, by the reactions of the tragic chorus, who encourage a certain range of reactions toward the unfolding plot.[4] The sense of life running through such works, in other words, is that of someone who looks at the reversals and sufferings of reasonably good people with both compassion and fear.

The perspective of the implied author typically operates on multiple levels, from the concrete to the highly general. On one level, we see the sufferings of Philoctetes with compassion for a world in which this good and admirable man suffers unbearable pain. More generally, we think of acute physical suffering and have compassion for those in its grip. On a still more general level, however, we are encouraged to think of his sufferings as "things such as might happen," and thus to consider, in a more general way the vulnerability of human beings to reversals and sufferings. These more general perspectives are, themselves, multiple; they permit of numerous different spectatorial options.

this is the area of agreement. For me, these judgments will be sufficient for pity or compassion only in conjunction with what I call the *eudaimonistic judgment* – that the people and what happens to them are part of what is important to my well-being. Dramas awaken that sort of concern through the focus on similar possibilities, which I shall shortly discuss.

4 Not always, of course: sometimes a chorus has a particular personality from which the spectator implicitly detaches herself.

One spectator might focus on bodily pain, another on deception, another on the general vulnerability of human life to unexpected reversals.

This general perspective invites spectators, in turn, to have emotions of various types toward the possibilities of their own lives. Seeing events as general human possibilities, they naturally also see them as possibilities for themselves. Thus, seeing Philoctetes' plight they may experience fear for their own pain, or for the possibility of manipulation and abuse; grief at similar disasters that have overtaken people they love; anger at people in their own world who use other people as tools. Again, these emotions operate on multiple levels of generality and specificity: I might connect Odysseus' manipulation of Philoctetes to some bad political events in my immediate environment, as Greek tragedies were often connected to democratic decision making. Or I might just think in a more general way about the possibility that I or my loved ones might suffer manipulation and abuse. I might think of the specific possibility of being afflicted with a very painful illness; or I might just fear unexpected reversals and difficulties.

Finally, spectators may also have reactive emotions toward the sensibility of the implied author, both concrete and general. Sometimes these reactions betray the fact that the work is being rejected: thus, one might react with anger, or boredom, or amusement to a tragedy, if one simply thought it badly done, or expressive of trivial or wrongheaded sentiments. But insofar as the work is accepted by the spectator, the reactive emotions will be sympathetic responses: sympathy, for example, with states of fear and grief expressed in the work as a whole – or, perhaps, a sympathetic anger against a world in which such terrible things can be permitted to happen. In tragedy, such sympathetic emotions are usually very difficult to distinguish from the emotions felt from the perspective of the "implied author," given that the latter perspective is already one of compassion. But often the two perspectives are distinct. If I follow Sappho's excruciating account of the pain of erotic jealousy, I may enter the perspective of the implied author (which is identical to that of the speaker) and feel that emotion; but, again, I may simply react with sympathy to the torments so vividly recorded. These reactive emotions, again, operate on multiple levels: I may have sympathy for the character Sappho; for women whose same-sex love is thwarted by conventional courtship and marriage; for unhappy love in general. And depending on how my own life is positioned toward these possibilities, I will have a corresponding range of emotions toward my own erotic possibilities.

We have, then, the following levels and types of emotion:

1. Emotions toward characters: (a) sharing the emotion of a character by identification, (b) reacting to the emotion of a character.
2. Emotions toward the "implied author," the sense of life embodied in the text as a whole: (a) sharing that sense of life and its emotions through empathy, (b) reacting to it, either sympathetically or critically. These emotions operate at multiple levels of specificity and generality.
3. Emotions toward one's own possibilities. These, too, are multiple and operate at multiple levels of specificity and generality.

All of these emotional responses (with the exception of those that involve a rejection of the work) are built into the work itself, into its literary structures. Thus it involves no neglect of the literary form to conclude that a work is rich in emotive content; indeed one cannot well describe the form or structure of a tragic work without mentioning this.

What is the connection between these formal structures in tragedy and the actual emotions of a spectator? A plausible claim is that the formal structures are such as to arouse certain emotions in a spectator who is such as the work demands, who watches with absorption, following the beckonings of the form. Not all spectators at Sophocles' *Oedipus* would feel pity for Oedipus and fear for themselves. As Wayne Booth says, there is frequently a gulf between the implied reader (or spectator) and the real reader (or spectator). Real spectators are often distracted and inattentive. As Aristophanes notes in *Birds*, many spectators of ancient tragedy, "bored with tragic choruses," are really thinking about how nice it would be to be able to fly away home like a bird, to enjoy food, or sex, or excretion.[5] But the implied spectator – who is also the real spectator, when that person is sufficiently attuned to the work – will feel a range of emotions connected to the presence of the "pitiable" and the "fearful" in the plot. As I have said, there are numerous options for the spectator, particularly in negotiating levels of

---

5 *Birds* 785–97, trans. Halliwell, in Halliwell (1997).

generality, and connections between the work and one's own life; thus no single "correct" experience is built into the form – rather, it offers a range of possible experiences.[6]

I have said that the "potential space" of aesthetic activity is a space with which we investigate and try out some of life's possibilities. In responding to a tragedy with pity and fear we are grasping certain urgent claims, not only about the characters but also about the world and about ourselves: not only that Oedipus is coming to grief through no fault of his own, but also that it is possible for a good person to come to grief in this way, and that it is possible for us to do so. In this way, the reader or spectator of a literary work is reading or watching the work, but at the same time reading the world, and reading her own self. The work is, in that sense, as Proust puts it, an "optical instrument" through which the reader may focus on certain personal realities.[7] The cognitive grasping is not produced by the emotional experience, it is embedded in it. And the cognitions, while in a certain sense detachable from the work – for one might realize certain things about one's life without seeing a tragedy, and one might preserve the knowledge that tragedy promotes after the experience is past – are still about the work and are responses to the work. Even when they pertain to one's own life, they involve a grasp of the work's specific literary structures. Indeed, this is what makes tragedy so important in our lives, that its forms are well suited for generating experiences that cut through the dullness of everyday life and show us something deep about ourselves and our actual situation.

In this way, as Aristotle stressed, poetry is "more philosophical" than history.[8] History tells us what has happened one time: but this may not show us anything interesting about our own possibilities, if the event is idiosyncratic. Literary works, by contrast, show us general plausible patterns of action, "things such as might happen" in human life. When we grasp the patterns of salience offered by the work, we are also grasping our own possibilities.

In what has been said, we have an answer to the question about

6 See Oatley (1999a, 1999b) for a good account of dialogues between a work and readers of different types.
7 Proust, III.1089: "For it seemed to me that they would not be 'my' readers but the readers of their own selves . . ." See further in Chapter 10.
8 *Poetics*, Chapter 9.

negative emotions. For we seek out painful literary experiences, as Aristotle argued, for the understanding of self and world that they offer. While the understanding itself is painful in content – for it is always painful to recognize that one is a needy and limited creature – it is, on the other hand, a valuable and a pleasant thing to acquire understanding.[9] The aesthetic activity, which takes place in a safe and protected "potential space" where our own safety is not immediately threatened, harnesses the pleasure of exploring to the neediness and insufficiency that is its object, thus making our limitations pleasing, and at least somewhat less threatening, to ourselves. Exercising this sort of understanding preserves us from a hard arrogant feeling of self-sufficiency that would in many ways mar our dealings with others in life. Such experiences increase our understanding of our own emotional geography; they also "allo[w] us to partly reassure ourselves in a non-destructive manner of the depth and breadth of our ability to feel,"[10] keeping our personality in an open and permeable condition. As Aristotle remarks, if one has an "overweening disposition," a *hubris-tikê diathesis*, one will not feel pity. Tragedies construct a spectator who does not have a *hubristikê diathesis*, who is open to emotional experiences having to do with the sufferings of others, and who is therefore (other things being equal) somewhat better prepared to relate to fellow human beings on a basis of mutuality. We thus have a fourth type of emotion to add to our list of spectatorial emotions: joy or pleasant emotion at coming to understand something.

For this reason, Proust compares novels to experiences of grief or other profound emotions in real life: "[c]ertain novels are like great but temporary bereavements, abolishing habit, bringing us once more into contact with the reality of life, but for a few hours only . . ."[11] Our habits screen from us our real situation – our neediness, our love for uncontrolled objects, our vulnerability. A novel, like a bereavement, shows us the truth of our situation – though only briefly, in a way that is quickly eclipsed by the "oblivion" and the "gaiety" of daily routine.

Are the spectator's emotions real emotions? Obviously enough, they do not all have a concrete real-world situation in our own lives as their object, although some do. And this makes a difference to their intensity

9 See Halliwell (1992) for an excellent account of Aristotle's position.
10 Levinson (1990), p. 326.
11 Proust, III.569.

and their duration. On the other hand, although we remain aware that Oedipus' story is a fiction, our emotions do in two ways address themselves to the real world: by taking general objects as well as the concrete fictional object, and by taking ourselves as objects. We are aware that the immediate tragedy is that of a fictional character; and yet we are also aware that these are possibilities for all human beings, hence the story of our own situation in the world. Thus in having pity for Oedipus we also have pity for all who suffer disaster in a relevantly similar way. In having fear for his predicament, we have fear that we ourselves may possibly suffer a similar reversal.

Putting things this way allows us to see how the emotions can be genuine and not simply playacting,[12] and also how they can have the cognitive content of the real-life emotion.[13] Pity has the content, "Someone who is (right now) important to me is suffering undeserved misfortune." This content is deployed at two levels: at a concrete level, these thoughts take Philoctetes, the fictional character, as their intentional object; to this extent, the spectator retains a simultaneous awareness that the person exists in a fictional world and not in the real world. At a more general level, however, pity takes as its intentional object the unjustified suffering that is really in the world, the suffering that makes us attend to Philoctetes' story and see it as plausible. Similarly, at one level we fear lest Oedipus come to grief; at another level, we fear for things "such as may happen in life," to ourselves and to those about whom we care. If the work were not held to life in this way, by threads of plausibility, it could not engross us emotionally as it does. We see this when we read a work that is unsuccessful: we don't have real emotions when we haven't managed to care about the story as "the sort of thing that might happen."

Consider another genre built around negative emotions: the horror film.[14] It is tempting to think that our emotions at such films could not be real terror or anxiety, or we would not seek out such experiences. But things are more complex. Once again, I would argue that these films have power and interest precisely to the extent that they are able

---

12 See Levinson's apt critique of Walton in Levinson (1990), pp. 316–17.

13 Levinson holds that they contain only the affective and not the cognitive aspect of emotions: as I shall argue in Chapter 5, this position is unnecessarily defensive, and does not correspond to his own analyses of musical emotion.

14 See the excellent cognitive analysis of horror movies in Freeland (2000).

to make us relate to the events as "thing such as might happen," constructing real emotions that operate in the four ways I have identified. When I watch Hitchcock's *Psycho*, at one level (1) I fear for Janet Leigh as she stands in the shower. I know well that danger stalks her – or, if I know the film already, I know very concretely that she will soon be bleeding into the drain. In fearing for her, I retain awareness that she exists in fiction, and that no person in my real world is currently so threatened. But of course the reason why this moment in the film has such mythic power is that it is "a thing such as might happen." The female body is always vulnerable to rape and assault. While I fear for Leigh, then, I am also aware of (2) the vulnerability of women to such violations. (I may have these emotions on several different levels of generality, thinking of all women, or of American women, and so on.) If I am a woman, I will also (3) think of my own body and its possibilities. If I am not, I will think of the bodies of women I care about.

On all these levels I have real fear. My fear for Leigh is concrete, but leads to no action, since I am aware that she lives in a fictional world. My fear for women in America is directed toward the real world; it leads to no particular action right now, but it does prompt a type of concern that might in principle lead to action. My fear for myself is, again, directed toward the real world, and prompts a type of concern that might in principle lead to action.

The way Hitchcock constructs the crucial episode plays on our own multiple attention, as we both follow the plot and investigate our own bodily vulnerability. We see the woman's secure trusting demeanor, as she stands naked in the shower. And we are able to see, as she does not, the threat that approaches her. In a safe context, we allow ourselves to investigate a fear that at some level accompanies us everywhere we go. What we want from such works is the opportunity to explore these fears in a context of immediate safety.

Because we are in a context of safety, we are also encouraged to have a range of reactive emotions: (1) sympathy for Leigh and rage at the predator who stalks her; (2) sympathy for women who are raped or assaulted and rage at their attackers.

But things are still more complex, since the film actually constructs for its viewer a disturbing double identification. Through his characteristically voyeuristic and aggressive use of the camera, Hitchcock places the viewer in the position of the danger that stalks the heroine. In this way he also brings viewers into contact with their own sadism and persecutory aggression. The camera itself makes us accomplices to aggression, as does the structure of the genre itself: both awaken our desire for mayhem and blood. One evident reason for Hitchcock's power is his uncanny ability to investigate the most uncomfortable aspects of infantile emotion. We both wish Leigh well and want to see her slashed, both identify with her and persecute her. In the process we become aware of our own aggression toward cherished objects. These experiences would lack power if we were not investigating our own psychology and the possibilities it contains.

Finally, in this case as in the case of tragedy, we have (4) the exhilaration and delight of learning something about ourselves, disturbing though this knowledge in some respects is.

Does such an approach to fictional works, as being about ourselves and our inner world, lead to a neglect of their form? Not in the least. For it is precisely in virtue of its formal features that such a work succeeds in constructing emotions about one's own possibilities; nor would any account of the form of such a work be complete if it did not link it to human possibilities. Aristotle's *Poetics* is in a sense a work about tragic form. But its account of the form involves discussing pity and fear, because the structure of a tragic drama is built around the evocation of these emotions.

The greater danger is that such an approach, focused as it is on general human possibilities, might lead to a disregard of historical and cultural context. One sometimes encounters the view that a tragedy, or a musical work, expresses grief, or joy, timelessly and universally, in a way that does not require the interpreter to be educated in a particular aesthetic or cultural tradition. In Chapter 5 I shall argue against such an approach, claiming that the expressive characteristics of a musical work cannot be decoded without considerable knowledge of the musical tradition in question, and the oeuvre of the composer. The same is evidently true of literary works, although at a very general level their representations of common human events may sometimes enable them to elicit emotion across wide divides of space and time.

Are we simply using the work as a tool of our own understanding, if we attend to it as an exploration of "things such as might happen"? I see no reason why this should follow. Any work that is sufficiently rich in structure and content to elicit deep emotional responses will also elicit admiration and wonder for its own complexity of design. I have said that wonder and delight are crucial ingredients in the process of aesthetic play; as elsewhere in life, they invest these processes with a noninstrumental and even to some extent a non-eudaimonistic character. And because the work is itself a symbol of cherished objects in our world, it will to some extent, like any other transitional object, also elicit the emotions of love and gratitude that we have for such objects.

Some works of art will elicit only wonder and delight, without tapping our more eudaimonistic emotions. This is evidently true of some works of visual art and of music, and of some literary works as well, those that please primarily by sophistication of form and do not purport to explore human concerns with time, death, love, and other eudaimonistic issues. By contrast, there are some entire literary genres that could not function at all without rich eudaimonistic connections to their audience: tragedy, romance, melodrama, the realist novel, and some types of comedy. This helps us to give a more general reply to the charge of neglect of aesthetic value: we cannot explain how these genres function, without mentioning the ways in which they relate to the audience's concern with the shape of human possibility.

5

MUSIC AND EMOTION

I. EXPRESSION AND THE IMPLIED LISTENER

Music has deep connections to our emotional life. So much has been granted by most philosophers who have addressed the topic.[1] But the nature of those connections is difficult to describe. Some of the difficulties have been compounded by deficiencies in the conceptions of emotion with which some philosophers of the past have approached the question. I shall argue that my own conception leads to progress. I shall be guided by three writers who (in substantial agreement with one another) seem to me to offer the most promising leads toward an adequate view: Marcel Proust, Paul Hindemith, and Gustav Mahler.[2]

I approach this topic neither as an expert in the theory or history of music nor as an expert performer, but rather as an amateur music lover whose emotional life is profoundly influenced by musical experiences. Given both the limits of my ability and the context of this chapter within my larger project, my aim is not, and could not be, to provide a complete theory of the complicated topic of musical emotion. It is, instead, to indicate how an emotion theory of the type I have been developing would approach the topic, and how it might help to illuminate issues that have proved difficult to address. I believe that the best way for me as an amateur to approach these issues is to focus on a

---

1 Among the most significant and interesting contemporary attempts to connect a general analysis of emotion with the analysis of musical emotion are Budd (1985), Levinson (1990), Ridley (1995), and Scruton (1997). I have learned a lot from all of these, and I shall not be able to engage here with all the aspects of their theories that would be worthy of extensive comment. Some major recent philosophical accounts of emotion – for example de Sousa (1987), Lyons (1980), Gordon (1987) – are silent about music.
2 Proust (1982), Hindemith (1961), Mahler (1979).

single composer whom I love and in connection with whose works I have intense emotional experiences. I have therefore chosen to focus on Mahler (to whom I shall return in Chapter 14); a welcome dividend of this choice is that an analysis of his theoretical remarks can be closely linked to an examination of his musical practice. In applying the view, I shall focus on the first and final songs of the *Kindertotenlieder*, which will allow me to connect the musical analysis to the discussion of grief that has been a prominent feature of all of the preceding chapters.

This chapter has the title "Music and Emotion." That rubric subsumes two apparently different issues: the emotions of the listener, and the expressive properties of the music itself. I shall address both issues, and ultimately connect them; but it seems important at the outset to keep them apart. On the one hand, we ask how we are to understand the emotions we experience when we listen to music: are they "real" emotions or not? What emotions are they? Whose emotions are they? What is their intentional object and their content? On the other hand, we ask about our ascriptions of emotional properties to the music itself: what are we really doing when we say that the last movement of Beethoven's Violin Concerto is joyful? That Mendelssohn's *Hebrides* Overture contains an expression of hope?[3] That the Scherzo of Mahler's Second Symphony expresses a sardonic disgust with everyday life? We make these judgments with confidence that such ascriptions tell us something about the music. We also make finer discriminations than these, ascribing to musical works different subspecies of a single emotion. For example, I feel that I have gotten at something about the music itself, not just about my idiosyncratic responses, when I say, comparing the final movements of the Beethoven and Dvorak Violin Concertos, that both express a passionately exuberant sort of joy, but that the joy in the former is a more reflective, more stable, and in a sense more active sort of joy, the joy in the latter a darting volatile giddy elation. Again, if we compare the *Liebestod* of Wagner's *Tristan* to the final duet, "Pur ti miro pur ti godo," from Monteverdi's *L'Incoronazione di Poppea* (and we can do so, I claim, in abstraction from the semantic content of the text, though not, perhaps, in abstraction from the fact that the instruments that perform it are human

---

3 See "Hope in the *Hebrides*," in Levinson (1990), an excellent account of the work and the issue.

voices), we can say that both express sexual passion, and that both express the triumph of passion over moral rules – but in very different ways. The *Liebestod* expresses unending, unresolved tragic longing in which bodily joy is always at a distance; the Monteverdi duet expresses complete absorption in sensuous delight and is, in effect, an extraordinary musical depiction of lovemaking.[4] The question is, what does all of this come to? And are we really saying anything of value about music when we say things like this?

The two questions cannot be answered in isolation. Any persuasive account of the ascription of emotional properties to the music must mention the experiences of listeners, including the ways in which the music is ultimately experienced as about them and their emotional life. But we should not conflate the questions unreflectively from the start. For as listeners we have many actual responses that are not connected in any deep way to the structures of the music itself: if I am very tired, I may feel exhaustion rather than joy when listening to the Beethoven; if it reminds me of a train of thought leading to a person about whom I have complicated emotions, I may find myself feeling those emotions rather than the emotions embedded in the sweeping and soaring lines of the music. We therefore should not begin from the simplistic position on expression that is most familiar from Tolstoy's *What Is Art?*,[5] according to which the expressive properties of the work are just the responses that it evokes in any chance listener, regardless of that listener's attentiveness, musical education, or familiarity with the work. Any good analysis of the expressive properties of music must ground itself in the specifically musical properties of the work; an analysis that too hastily cashes out expression in terms of average audience reaction will be bound to fail at this task.

A beginning of progress can be made, I think, by considering a set of distinctions familiar from the analysis of literature. In analyzing a literary work, Wayne Booth has argued, we need to keep separate two

---

4 In this area, a remark made by Felix Mendelssohn seems apt: "a piece of music that I love expresses thoughts to me that are not too *imprecise* to be framed in words, but too *precise*. So I find that attempts to express such thoughts in words may have some point to them, but they are also unsatisfying" (quoted in Ridley [1995], p. 116). Certainly few if any verbal depictions of sensuous delight have the specificity of the Monteverdi, and few verbal depictions of tragic erotic longing the specificity of the Wagner.

5 Tolstoy (1962). As I point out in note 11, Tolstoy's position, though frequently understood as a naïve and mistaken description, actually involves a complex prescription.

authorial figures: the *implied author*, which is to say the voice or presence or sense of life that animates the work taken as a whole; and the *real-life author*, the person with all of his or her daily life, lapses of attention, and much else that does not figure in the work. Both of these figures must be distinguished, in turn, from the *narrator* of the work and various other characters in the work, all of whom may express views of the world that are at odds with the sense of life embodied in the work as a whole. On the side of the reader, we have a similar distinction: between the *real-life reader*, who may be attentive or distracted, preoccupied with emotions from her own life rather than from the work, and so forth; and the *implied reader*, that is to say, the readerly response that is invited in the work's very structure.[6] Booth argues that the real-life author and the real-life reader are of little concern to us when we ask what patterns of desire and emotion are built into the literary work: our concern should be with the implied author and the implied reader. We should ask not about the daily meanderings of attention and desire in the real-life author, we should ask about the sense of life that animates this text. And we should talk not about what a randomly chosen person just happened to think or feel, but about what sort of thinking and feeling is built into the form. (The implied reader is closely linked to, if not identical to,[7] the implied author, and novelists such as Charles Dickens and Henry James frequently draw attention to this fact, speaking of themselves as re-readers of their own work.)[8]

In music, a similar set of distinctions seems essential. On the side of the composer, we have a distinction between the varied emotions of the composer during everyday life, and the sense of life of the musical work, with its emotional structures.[9] Within the work there may also

6 Booth (1983, 1988).

7 The relation is not always one of identity, for an implied author may draw attention to the fact that the implied reader may be living in a time or a culture distinct from his own. See, for example, the ending of Dickens's *Hard Times*, in which the authorial voice, addressing the reader, speaks of "our two spheres of life" as distinct scenes for political action.

8 See Richard Wollheim's similar observation about the way in which painters occupy the position of the viewer during the process of painting – in Wollheim (1987).

9 This distinction is well captured in Ridley (1995), who develops a very interesting way of speaking of the "implied author" – the sort of personality expressed in a musical work. Although he carefully distinguishes this personality from that of the real-life composer, he mentions that some works of music criticism that ascribe the expressive

be analogues to the literary figures of narrator and characters: that is, subportions of the work that express a sense of life out of keeping with the work's overall sensibility. This will happen most obviously in opera or in an explicitly programmatic work, as when Richard Strauss depicts his hero's enemies; as when Prokoviev satirically depicts pompous arrogance or foolish love. But it may also happen in a more abstract work, as when Mahler depicts the shallow docility of conventional society in a subportion of the Scherzo of the Second Symphony, a movement whose overall stance (see Chapter 14) is one of sardonic detachment.

On the side of the listener, we have the point of view that the music invites the listener to occupy – what Jerrold Levinson has aptly called "the point of view of the music." We also have various more local positions within the music that the listener might choose to occupy, in identifying with one of its "characters." And finally, of least interest to us, we have the actual emotions of this or that listener, who may be distracted, attending badly, ignorant of the work's structure, and so forth.

In what follows I shall connect the question about the music's expressive properties to the notion of the "implied listener," the emotional structures built into the music itself. But the implied listener is also the real listener when the listener listens well, following the beckonings of the form with sufficient education and attunement.[10] For this reason the question of expressive properties is intimately related to a question about the listener, when that question is asked not in Tolstoy's way, but in a way that looks for responses that are embedded in the music itself.[11]

properties of the music to the real-life composer may not be hopelessly flawed – they may just have chosen a slightly careless or elliptical way of talking about the implied composer (in his terms, the personality expressed in the work) (see esp. pp. 174–5, 188–91). I would add that the implied composer is, typically at least, some part or parts of the real-life composer, so it should not surprise us that these compressed ways of speaking should occur. Ridley has a properly qualified and complicated discussion of this relation on pp. 188–91.

10 There is more than one way of doing this: see especially the discussion that follows here of a likely alternation between empathetic and sympathetic perspectives, and of the flexibility musical works allow in terms of levels of specificity and generality.

11 It should be said that Tolstoy, here, is not simply naive or confused. For he really is interested not in the implied listener, who follows the lead of the form, but in what will move real listeners, regardless of their social class, education, familiarity with the

II. A DILEMMA AND THREE RESPONSES

The basic dilemma is this. On the one hand, music seems to be profoundly connected to our emotional life, indeed perhaps more urgently and deeply connected to that life than any of the other arts. It digs into our depths and expresses hidden movements of love and fear and joy that are inside us. It speaks to us and about us in mysterious ways, going "to the bottom of things,"[12] as Mahler put it, exposing hidden vulnerabilities and, so to speak, laying our souls open to our view. "A burning pain crystallizes," writes Mahler of his experience as conductor/listener of his own work.[13] Proust's narrator speaks of music's revealing "what richness, what variety lies hidden, unknown to us, in that vast, unfathomed and forbidding night of our soul . . ."[14] It seems natural to speak this way about music, and we shall see that this impulse has often been followed, by theorists who agree about little else. Furthermore, these examples indicate already that there may be an especially close connection between music and emotions as described in my theory: for these accounts of music connect it to the perception of urgent needs and vulnerabilities that are often masked from view in daily life.

On the other hand, it also seems plain that music usually does not contain evident representational or narrative structures of the sort that are the typical objects of concrete emotions in life, or even in literary experience.[15] So it is less than obvious how it *can* be about our life, or how the emotions it arouses can be real emotions with a definite intentional content.

This problem is clearly posed in a letter from Mahler to his sympathetic correspondent Max Marschalk. Mahler begins and ends the letter by giving Marschalk one of his several programmatic descriptions

---

music, and so forth: for he wishes to use music as a bridge to universal sympathy. So for him it is no good pointing out that the implied listener of a Beethoven symphony is a leisured and musically well-educated person, that we cannot ask about the expressive properties of a Beethoven symphony by asking what emotions it arouses in a serf working in the fields. He is all too aware of this, and it is, for him, a point against Beethoven.

12 Mahler (1979), p. 201, letter to Marschalk December of 4, 1896.
13 Mahler (1979), p. 346, letter to Bruno Walter of December 19, 1909.
14 Proust (1982), I.380.
15 See the good treatment of this question in Scruton (1997), Chapter 5; and see also Walton (1988).

of the "plot" of the Second Symphony, according to which each movement concerns a particular stage in a hero's life and death. He gives Marschalk a detailed description of the emotions of the implied listener. But midway through this description, Mahler expresses exasperation with the whole enterprise:

We find ourselves faced with the important question how, and indeed *why* music should be interpreted in words at all . . . As long as my experience can be summed up in words, I write no music about it; my need to express myself musically – symphonically – begins at the point where the *dark* feelings hold sway, at the door which leads into the 'other world' – the world in which things are no longer separated by space and time.[16]

For Mahler there is clearly no paradox in asserting both that music concerns our inner world and that it is not really translatable into words. I believe that he is correct. But to many people the verbal expression of emotion seems natural and unmysterious, the expression of emotion through other symbolic forms unnatural and questionable. Such a person might feel that there is a deep puzzle about Mahler's position: for how can he continue to assert the 'aboutness' of music while denying resolutely – if intermittently (since he keeps producing programs of his symphonies) – that it has any story or subject that we can describe?

A long-standing theoretical controversy about music and emotion begins from this point. We find three warring positions, which can be schematically characterized by setting out the following argument:

1. Music does not embody (or cause)[17] linguistically formulable cognitive attitudes.
2. Linguistically formulable cognitive attitudes are necessary constituents of emotions.
3. Music cannot embody (or cause) emotions.

To put things very simply, Position A accepts premises 1 and 2, and therefore accepts the conclusion. Positions B and C begin from a denial of the conclusion, which they take to be self-evidently false, and

16 Letter to Marschalk of March 26, 1896, in Mahler (1979), pp. 178–9; this segment of the letter is also cited in Cooke (1988), and I here follow Cooke's translation rather than that of Wilkins and Kaiser in the Mahler/Martner volume.
17 In what follows, I try to keep my two original questions theoretically distinct, since the theorists whom I shall discuss do not necessarily connect them as I connect them.

therefore a reductio of the argument. Position B gets rid of premise 2, taking up a noncognitive view of emotion to explain how music can in fact contain emotions. Position C gets rid of premise 1, discovering in music a language-like structure out of which propositions can be formed; it is therefore able to retain a propositional-cognitive view of emotions while denying the conclusion. Position A was the position of the Greek Stoics;[18] in modern times its most influential and able defender has been Eduard Hanslick.[19] Position B was elaborated by the dissident Stoic Posidonius in the ancient world;[20] in modern times, in different ways, it has been held by Arthur Schopenhauer,[21] Suzanne Langer,[22] and, recently, by Jerrold Levinson.[23] The somewhat eccentric Position C is defended by Deryck Cooke in his book *The Language of Music*.[24] Let us examine each of the positions in more detail, in order to understand the impasse to which their defects bring us.[25]

The Greek Stoics, holding the propositional view of emotion that I described and (with some reservations) defended in Chapter 1, also noticed that music is considered to be a major source of emotional experience, and that music itself is frequently characterized using emotional terms. That was as true during the third century B.C. as it is now. But there was a difference: most of the the *mousikê* that they encountered was textual. From hymns and dirges and marching songs to tragic choruses, poetry and musical accompaniment went hand in hand. This enabled them to accept my three-step argument while still acknowledging the evident fact that *mousikê* both contains and arouses emotions. For, they said, it is the text that does the work, and the text contains cognitive structures sufficient to house (and to elicit) emotions as their view described them. If I weep when I hear a tragic Achilles singing a dirge for Patroclus, it is not on account of anything in the musical

18 See Nussbaum (1993a); I there accepted the Stoic position, and now regret this.
19 Hanslick (1986). See also Kivy (1980, 1990).
20 See Nussbaum (1993a).
21 Schopenhauer (1969), Vol. I, section 52.
22 Langer (1951, 1953).
23 Levinson (1990), especially "Negative Emotions in Music."
24 Cooke (1959).
25 The impasse is eloquently and rigorously set out in Budd (1985), who begins by defending a belief-based conception of emotion and at the same time casting doubt on the conclusion of Hanslick's negative argument. He then goes on to work out devastating criticisms of Schopenhauer, Langer, Cooke, and others – with the result that he himself can see no positive view emerging from the wreckage.

accompaniment: it is on account of my grasp of the story, my identification with the characters, my belief about what is happening to them.
It is in virtue of these same narrative features, and these alone, that the
dirge as a whole expresses grief.

Modern theorists of the Stoic persuasion have not had such an easy
time solving the problem of musical emotion. For they are forced to
acknowledge that we are moved by purely instrumental music and
ascribe emotional properties to such music. But a version of the Stoic
position has still been vigorously defended by Eduard Hanslick, in his
influential work *On the Musically Beautiful* (1854). Hanslick begins
with a vigorous defense of our second premise: emotions are based
upon beliefs and individuated in accordance with beliefs, which must
have a complex conceptual structure:

What, then, makes a feeling specific, e.g., longing, hope, love? Is it perhaps
the mere strength or weakness, the fluctuations of our inner activity? Certainly not. These can be similar with different feelings, and with the same
feeling they can differ from person to person and from time to time. Only
on the basis of a number of ideas and judgments (perhaps unconsciously at
moments of strong feeling) can our state of mind congeal into this or that
specific feeling. The feeling of hope cannot be separated from the representation of a future happy state which we compare with the present; melancholy compares past happiness with the present. These are entirely specific
representations or concepts. Without them, without this cognitive apparatus,
we cannot call the actual feeling "hope" or "melancholy"; it produces them
for this purpose. If we take this away, all that remains is an unspecific
stirring, perhaps the awareness of a general state of well-being or distress.
Love cannot be thought without the representation of a beloved person,
without desire and striving after felicity, glorification and possession of a
particular object. Not some kind of mere mental agitation, but its conceptual
core, its real, historical content, specifies this feeling of love. Accordingly, its
dynamic can appear as readily gentle as stormy, as readily joyful as sorrowful, and yet still be love. This consideration by itself suffices to show that
music can only express the various accompanying adjectives and never the
substantive, e.g. love itself. A specific feeling (a passion, say, or an affect)
never exists as such without an actual historical content, which can only be
precisely set forth in concepts.[26]

26 Hanslick (1986), p. 9. See the interesting comments on this passage by Scruton (1997),
pp. 165–8.

This admirably clear and, so far as it goes, accurate account of the cognitive content of emotions leads Hanslick to the conclusion that the so-called expressive properties of music are really only metaphors for structures that are peculiarly musical. He seems to be assuming that the type of precise conceptual and judgmental structure he has in mind can be embodied only in a medium that can represent definite historical particulars, and he is probably requiring language for the purpose, although he does not make this requirement explicit. (He would probably allow that a tragic drama could embody and cause real emotions.) Deeply gripped by the thought that music is music and nothing else, that its structures are distinct from linguistic propositions, he can understand the habit of calling music "sad" or "joyful" only as a metaphorical way of characterizing these sui generis forms, above all dynamic and rhythmic forms. He has little to say about the basis for the metaphorical transposition, although he does seem to allow, as in the passage cited, that music can represent some of the usual kinetic attributes of passions.

As for the listener's emotions, he does allow that these occur, as a subjective response to some of these dynamic features; but he does seem to deny that they are in any deep or intrinsic way connected with the point of view of the music itself – an anthropomorphism to which he would no doubt be resolutely opposed. For these emotions are based on idiosyncratic personal psychological factors, and so cannot, he feels, be part of the analysis of the musical work itself.[27] The beauty of music, he concludes, is "a specifically musical kind of beauty . . . a beauty that is self-contained and in no need of content from outside itself, that consists simply and solely of tones and their artistic combination."[28] In a memorable assertion of this autonomy, he argues that if anything about a person's inner world is expressed in a musical artwork, it is "an inner singing, not a mere inner feeling."[29]

Hanslick's clear argument poses a profound challenge to anyone who wants to say that music is, after all, about our life and our inner world. For it starts from a strong and (up to a point) correct conception of emotion, and also from the important recognition that musical struc-

27 See Hanslick (1986), p. 45ff. Kivy (1980) takes a similar line on p. 30. See the good criticism by Ridley (1995), pp. 123–6.
28 Hanslick (1986), p. 28.
29 Hanslick (1986), p. 47.

tures are not translatable into linguistic structures. On the other hand, he has too hastily denied something without which it is difficult to explain why music has the importance that it does for us. He cannot explain why it is a more or less universal view of composers and listeners that these ascriptions are not merely metaphorical, that there is some way in which music does indeed speak about the inner world. Nor can he explain why certain so-called metaphorical ascriptions of emotion are apt and others are not – why it would be weird to call the last movement of Beethoven's Violin Concerto sorrowful, or the first movement of Mahler's Second an expression of light-hearted joy. These ascriptions are not merely arbitrary, or based upon idiosyncratic states of mind; they are rooted in the music itself.[30]

The holders of Position B begin from the obvious fact of music's emotional expressiveness, and unravel the dilemma by taking up a view of emotion that makes it possible to see how emotion could be quite literally in music. The earliest holder of such a view was the dissident Greek Stoic Posidonius, who, criticizing the older Stoics for their neglect of the purely musical element in *mousikê*, located the problem in their cognitive conception of emotion, which did not permit them to see that, or how, music could either express or inspire emotions. As we saw in Chapter 2, he argued that emotions are in fact not judgments or recognitions at all, but "unreasoning movements" in a part of the personality common to all animals and altogether distinct from the cognitive part. These movements may vary in rhythm and speed, and thus many different qualities may be exemplified. Music has these same possibilities, and thus can contain emotion in a quite literal sense.

Modern defenders of this type of view have added little to Posidonius' basic argument. For Arthur Schopenhauer, music is connected as is no other art to the "Will," that is, the force of erotic striving that propels us on into life and manifests itself in various emotions, above all those connected with love and sexuality. Music represents the surgings of this inner force, "the many different forms of the will's efforts, but also its satisfaction by ultimately finding again a harmonious interval."[31] For this reason, its effect is more immediate and more profound

---

30 This should not be taken to imply that they are "natural" and precultural, any more than the claim that ascriptions of emotion to a poem are rooted in the poetry itself would imply that poetry's ability to arouse emotion is precultural.

31 Schopenhauer (1969), I.260.

than that of other arts: for "these others speak only of the shadow, but music of the essence."[32]

Schopenhauer tries to handle the obvious absence of situational beliefs from music by arguing that music represents emotions in an abstract and general way, without embodying them in particular situations:

Music does not express this or that particular and definite pleasure, this or that affliction, pain, sorrow, horror, gaiety, merriment, or peace of mind, but joy, pain, sorrow, horror, gaiety, merriment, peace of mind *themselves*, to a certain extent in the abstract, their essential nature, without any accessories, and so also without the motives for them. Nevertheless, we understand them perfectly in this extracted quintessence.[33]

The difficulty is, however, that this does not really answer Hanslick's argument (or an argument of Hanslick's sort, since Schopenhauer's work predates Hanslick's). Hanslick convincingly claimes that one cannot identify either the general form of these emotions or their particular manifestations without beliefs and concepts. Schopenhauer responds, to this extent plausibly, that music may lack highly specific situational objects, but contains general objects. But then Hanslick will rightly respond that even a general emotion has object-directed intentionality and requires some belieflike content, even if of a highly general kind. Schopenhauer's conception of the Will prevents him from giving an adequate account of this content. Will is a force of erotic striving totally lacking in selectivity, awareness, and intentionality. Thus music, in representing the Will, can, it appears, represent no form of intentionality at all.[34]

There is something right in Schopenhauer's position. What is right is the recognition that music is intimately linked with our deepest strivings and most powerful emotions. This aspect of music he feels deeply, and in that sense his response to music is more complete than Hanslick's. Schopenhauer is also right to think that music takes an object that is both more general and less demarcated than the objects of situational emotions in daily life.[35] His view is a major antedecent of

---

32 Ibid., I.257.
33 Ibid., I.261.
34 See Budd (1985) for an effective criticism of this aspect of Schopenhauer's argument about music.
35 See the good discussion of this aspect of his view in Scruton (1997), pp. 364–7.

the views of music as dream that I shall defend in the next section. One might even argue that Schopenhauer's view that Will is altogether non-cognitive does not disable the position completely: for he says, after all, that music represents Will in the form of an idea, and all ideas have at least some cognitive content. What is wrong with the view lies more in what it says about Will and its lack of intentionality than in what it says about music; but in any case it cannot give a satisfactory account of the relation of musical structure to emotional structure.

Because Schopenhauer's view has a great deal of depth and plausibility, versions of it keep being resurrected, without some of its metaphysical baggage, by writers on art who are lovers of music and wish to give music a special place among the arts. Two of the most influential of these are Suzanne Langer and Jerrold Levinson. For Langer, music contains forms symbolic of the dynamic patterns of human feeling – which she takes to be an inner activity whose form can be comprehended without reference to intentionality. For Levinson, who is persuaded that beliefs are necessary for emotions, music cannot represent or cause[36] the whole of an emotion. But it can represent, and also cause, the kinetic and affective side of emotion. Levinson treats this "affective side" as necessary for the complete emotion, causally independent of belief or judgment, and sufficient without belief or judgment to identify the emotion.

But the trouble with all of these views is that Hanslick is correct. Judgment, or some intentional activity very like judgment, is necessary for emotion; and emotions can be individuated only with reference to their characteristic cognitive/intentional content. Because Langer omits intentionality from her account, she is led to make very peculiar claims about emotions (far less interesting than the corresponding claims of Schopenhauer). As Roger Scruton correctly describes her position:

The emotions are portrayed as sensations might be portrayed: as consisting of crescendos and diminuendos, surges and releases, tensions and plateaux; and these peculiar 'formal' features are then isolated as the *things that matter* in our emotional life. As though loving someone mattered because of those

---

36 Levinson keeps these two issues firmly apart, but he adopts parallel positions on the two, in separate articles: "Music and the Negative Emotions" and "Hope in the *Hebrides*." And he provides an interesting account of the connection between them, through his concept of the point of view of the music. This point of view, however, need not be identified with that of an imaginary subject: see Scruton (1997), pp. 350–3.

inner rushes of blood to the heart (if that is how it feels) and not because the person himself matters a million times more![37]

Levinson, more sensitive to the cognitive content of musical emotions, makes no such crude claims. Instead, when he tries to give an account of a complex piece of music and its emotional content, he simply veers away from Position B toward a more cognitive view of emotion. Thus, in his very impressive analysis of Mendelssohn's "Hebrides" Overture in connection with the emotion of hope, he is continually drawn toward cognitive language to explain how music can embody hope – only to take it away again with the left hand, so to speak, reminding the reader that it is not really the cognitive part of hope that we are considering, but only its "affective side."

In the light of the difficulties encountered by Positions A and B, it is tempting to think that the solution must lie in denying premise 1, and holding that music can indeed contain, and cause, beliefs. I think that the solution to the dilemma does indeed lie in this general area. But a great deal depends on whether we then make the further move of insisting that these beliefs have to be formulable in something like a language. For such an account of music as language will run the risk of ignoring specifically musical forms, and will thus lie open to Hanslick's eloquent reminder that music is music and nothing else. Such an account has recently been produced, by Deryck Cooke, the scholar who produced the excellent performance version of Mahler's Tenth Symphony and who has written eloquently on Mahler and other composers. In his 1959 book *The Language of Music*,[38] Cooke attempts to produce a musical lexicon that would specify the emotional meaning of the basic elements of Western music. He tries to show that certain sound patterns have universal emotional significance: the major fifth, for example, is associated with joy around the world.

There are many problems with this project. First, as Malcolm Budd has pointed out, it does not really make music into a language, since the "lexicon" contains semantic items only and not rules for their combination into larger utterances.[39] Second, it takes no account of the

---

37 Scruton (1997), p. 166.
38 Cooke (1959); a valuable account and criticism of Cooke is in Budd (1985), p. 122ff. See also Ridley (1995), pp. 42–4.
39 Budd (1985), pp. 122–3.

cultural and historical specificity of musical expression, the fact that grasping the expressive properties of a work requires hearing it in its historical context, in its relation to previous works in its genre and in the oeuvre of the composer. The central psychological claims are both too crude to help us with a complicated work such as a Mahler symphony, and almost surely false. Music may be universal in the sense that people widely separated by language and culture can learn to love the same music. It is not universal in the sense that this response is automatic or without effort. The expressive content of Japanese or Indian music is utterly baffling, at first, to Western ears; so too is that of a Mahler symphony to someone who has never heard any other symphony. Tolstoy was correct to say that certain folk tunes have an ease of expressive access that complex symphonic works do not – and in that sense have a greater universality just on account of their simplicity, in the same way that street signs are more easily read than the novels of Henry James. And it is obvious, too, that certain sophisticated works are easier to enjoy than others: thus Verdi's *Il Trovatore* was loved by Briggs's Utku leader Inuttiaq, who found its emotions highly accessible,[40] – as do many Americans who have little formal training in music. Schoenberg's *Moses und Aron*, by contrast, is more or less unavailable to the untrained listener. But the fact that certain works are relatively easily decoded does not imply that there is no learning required, or that the code is universal.

On the other hand, to say that the music-as-language view fails is not to say that we are left with a bitter choice between Position A and Position B. For by now we are aware that there are forms of cognitive/ intentional activity, embodying ideas of salience and urgency, that are not linguistic. And not coincidentally, the very same decades during which behaviorist views about emotion were replaced, in psychology, by cognitivist views also saw the dominant "musical behaviorism" – the position that music learning and musical activity can be explained by appeal to stimuli and responses, without mention of cognitive activity – replaced by "musical cognitivism," the view that music acquisition and musical functioning do involve complex cognitive functions at levels of sophistication that increase with development. In a fascinating book entitled *Music as Cognition*, Mary Louise Serafine constructs for

40 See Briggs (1970) p. 154, discussed in Chapter 3.

music the analogue of the Lazarus–Seligman antibehaviorist argument, showing that children's acquisition of musical abilities cannot be explained without ascribing to them complex forms of cognitive functioning.[41] At the same time, interpreters of music have become increasingly willing to ask questions about how peculiarly musical forms express complex views of the world – showing, by producing convincing interpretations of particular works, that a cognitive analysis of musical content need not involve any neglect of the formal and specifically musical properties of the music. As Mahler said long ago in writing to a ten-year-old girl who had asked him why such a large orchestra is necessary these days: certain emotional ideas seek a specific musical form. As "ever deeper and more complex aspects" of the emotional life become a subject matter for music, the form of music and the means by which it is made will evolve also.[42]

We need to remember two facts, too rarely borne in mind. First, language is a medium of representation. When we express the content of an emotion in words, we are already, in many cases, performing a translation of thoughts that did not originally take an explicitly verbal form. Sometimes there is relatively little distortion in making this translation, but sometimes, as Chapters 2 and 4 have stressed, there is relatively great distortion. Second, music is another form of symbolic representation. It is not language, but it need not cede all complexity, all sophistication in expression, to language.[43] So it is not obvious why we think that there is a greater problem about expressing an emotion's content musically than about expressing it linguistically. We think this way because we live in a culture that is verbally adept but (on the whole) relatively unsophisticated musically.[44] But there is no reason to think that we are stuck with the choice between translating music into language and adopting the "nonreasoning movements" view. That is the move one makes if one is hooked on language, so to speak, so used to thinking in linguistic terms that one cannot imagine that any other symbolic structure might possibly be able to contain rich expressive

41 Serafine (1988).
42 Mahler, letter to Gisella Tolney-Witt of February 7, 1893, in Mahler (1979), p. 147.
43 This is well seen in Goodman (1968), who otherwise has little to say about music.
44 When W. E. B. Du Bois set epigraphs before the chapters of The Souls of Black Folk, he chose musical motifs from the blues – indicating that African-American culture, while lacking (for obvious reasons of linguistic dispersal at the time of slavery) a common literary tradition, had, powerfully, a sophisticated common musical tradition.

possibilities. All three positions err by accepting the exclusive disjunction – "either linguistically formulable or noncognitive." Chapters 2 and 4 have already argued that this disjunction is inadequate. The inclusive view of cognitive appraisal developed there indicates a way out of the impasse.

What we need, then, is an account that preserves the cognitive and symbolic complexity of musical experience, while refusing to treat the music as a mere means to a cognition that is extramusical in nature.[45] Such an account must do justice to our intuition that music has an intimate connection with our emotional depths – indeed, a connection that may have, among the arts, a special intensity and urgency. But it must show how the emotional material is embodied in peculiarly musical forms. It must allow us to distinguish the expressive properties of a musical work from the responses of the implied listener, but also to connect these in a perspicuous way. And finally, it must do justice to the historical and cultural variety of musical expression.

III. MUSIC AS DREAM

Let us now return to Mahler's phrase characterizing his experience as conductor/listener of his own work: "A burning pain crystallizes." And let us join to it Mahler's claim that the expressive world of his symphonic writing begins at a point at which the narrative power of words leaves off, "at the point where the *dark* feelings hold sway, at the door which leads into the 'other world' – the world in which things are no longer separated by space and time." Of course these phrases tell us much that is specific to Mahler's music and its particular expressive range; but they also go to the heart of our issue. For what is claimed is that in the music itself – and, in consequence, in the experience of the listener who positions herself in the way that the music demands – intense and one might say highly concentrated emotions are embodied, but emotions that do not inhabit the daylight world of distinct physical objects and clearly comprehensible narrative structures. Music is not vaguer than literature: indeed, the suggestion is that it may have a more direct and powerful access to the depths of our emotions just in virtue of its "otherness." But it does not represent objects or tell a story in

45 This point is well put in Budd (1985).

the way that a work of literature does; in consequence our responses to it are the crystallizations of general forms of emotion, rather than reactions to the doings or sufferings of characters who inhabit, like us, the daily world of space and time. This fact seems to be in some way connected with the emotional potency of music, its ability "to get to the bottom of things, to go beyond external appearances."[46]

In connection with such thoughts, it has been natural for some of the most profound writers on musical emotion to describe the expressive content of music as dreamlike, our reactions before it like the experiences we have in dreams. In the same letter in which he speaks of the burning pain, Mahler speaks of "this strange reality of visions, which instantly dissolve into mist like the things that happen in dreams."[47] We find the same comparison in Proust, who speaks of the Vinteuil sonata as embodying the "very essence" of an "intimate sadness," in the form of "actual ideas, of another world, of another order, ideas veiled in shadow, unknown, impenetrable to the human intellect."[48] Like Mahler, he connects this otherworldiness in music, its difference from daily linguistic structures, to its ability to express the depths of the emotional world: "I wondered whether music might not be the unique example of what might have been – if the invention of language, the formation of words, the analysis of ideas had not intervened – the means of communication between souls."[49]

This account of musical expression as dream receives extensive theoretical elaboration in Paul Hindemith's *A Composer's World*.[50] Musical emotions, he argues, lack the daily-life narrative coherence of our everyday emotions, and also of the emotions we have as readers of literature. They follow one another in rapid and sometimes surprising succession; they seem to lack rootedness in specific events and in the usual sequencing of events in space and time; they grow and fade with a bewildering rapidity. In all of this they are like dreams or certain sorts of memories; they have the characteristics of compression, multi-

46 Mahler (1979), p. 201, letter to Marschalk.
47 See also his reference to the composer as "a second self active in sleep" (Bauer-Lechner [1980], p. 150), and the claim that his music is "never concerned with the detailed description of an *event*, but at most with that of a *feeling*" (Mahler [1979], p. 172).
48 Proust, I.379–80.
49 Ibid., III.260. See Nattiez (1989) for a fascinating account of the role of music in Proust's own compositional technique.
50 Hindemith (1961), pp. 27–53.

ple reference, illogical order, displacement, and rapidity that we associate with our experience of dreaming. In short, we have in musical experience "a phantasmagoric structure of feelings that hits us with the full impact of real feeling."[51]

Hindemith's further development of the idea goes astray. He can see no way in which such reactions could be embedded in the musical form itself, since he has already committed himself to the view that musical form must be apprehended by the intellect alone. And his view of intellect is far narrower than our view of "cognition": he connects intellect with analysis and the apprehension of form, not with evaluative judgments about our own urgent concerns. Being unable to bring the emotional and the intellectual together, and being unable to conceive of musical structure as more than accidentally emotional, he describes these emotions as emotions of the real-life listener, connected with that listener's own idiosyncratic history and thus in no way built into the musical work itself. He cannot make use of our distinction between the implied listener and the real listener, since he denies that musical form as such has anything emotional built into it. Thus he is compelled to focus on the varied experiences of real-life listeners of every sort, and to validate all of their inconsistent reactions as equally correct, while nonetheless holding that the emotional response is what gives the music its meaning. (In an amusing and possibly self-referential example of this variety in response, he writes, "there are people in whom Gilbert and Sullivan operettas arouse only feelings of boundless desolation and despair.")[52]

It is revealing that Hindemith finds an impasse here: for Hindemith's music frequently does appear to get bogged down in an obsessive intellectualism and to have difficulty working human emotion into musical form. His unsuccessful setting of Walt Whitman's "When Lilacs Last in the Dooryard Bloomed" shows this difficulty plainly. The subject calls for deep emotional expression, but the musical structures self-consciously direct attention to their formal sophistication, rather than hooking up with the ideas of grief and mourning suggested by the text.

51 Hindemith (1961), pp. 45–6.
52 Hindemith (1961), p. 40. Compare other examples of this sort in Ridley (1995), pp. 144, 147. Ridley criticizes both Kivy (1980) and Hindemith for their reduction of emotional expression to mere association, pp. 123–6.

Proust has a similar difficulty, for opposite reasons. In the conviction that it is only when intellect is put aside that we achieve veridical perceptions that can later be ordered and grasped by the mind, he too separates the expressive elements of the music from its cognitively graspable structure. Where emotion is concerned, he focuses, as does Hindemith, on the contingent patterns of association that make listeners of different sorts have very different emotions.[53] These difficulties show us our task: to follow the lead of the suggestive image of musical emotion as dream, without losing our grip on the idea that what embodies the dream material is the form of the music itself. Mahler alone of the three, not surprisingly, gets it right, holding repeatedly that "content and form are indissolubly blended,"[54] that the pain and sorrow of life is actually *in* the music itself, in a sui generis and, strictly speaking, untranslatable form. The 'aboutness' of the work is not at odds with its formal sophistication: for, as he puts it, "To me 'symphony' means constructing a world with all the technical means at one's disposal."[55]

The image of music as dream brings us to an important fact: music is not the language of habit. When we go about our daily business, language is the form of symbolic representation on which we overwhelmingly rely. For this reason, the linguistic expression of feeling must use a medium that is in many ways shopworn, or blunted – by our habitual use of the words themselves, by our habits of narration, by our very at-homeness in a world of narration and verbal representation. Language is, on the whole, a medium of exchange, a useful tool of communication that is frequently abased by its toollike use. This is why the task of the literary artist (and especially the poet) requires calling cognition back to the language itself, to the texture of word and phrase.[56] But however well this is done, it remains difficult for language to bypass the intellectual defenses we have developed as we cope with the world, and to have access to emotion in its most acute and urgent form. And since language has a complex syntactic and semantic structure, it will be especially difficult for language to capture without

53 See Proust (1982), I.227ff. – the famous account of the Vinteuil sonata.
54 Bauer-Lechner (1980), p. 37.
55 Mahler, in Bauer-Lechner (1980), p. 38.
56 Thus Helen Vendler writes that nothing counts as literary criticism if the criticism would be just as true of a paraphrase.

distortion the primitive and extremely intense emotions of childhood, which remain deep in the personality in archaic and not fully propositionalized form.

Now music[57] is not, as such, primitive or archaic. Nor is the inner world that music expresses lacking in complex intentionality and content. Here Schopenhauer's view has major shortcomings. But Schopenhauer was onto something profound when he suggested that music is especially well-suited to express parts of the personality that lie beneath its conscious self-understanding. Music can bypass habit, use, and intellectualizing, in such a way that its symbolic structures seem to pierce like a painful ray of light directly into the most vulnerable parts of the personality. Lacking the narrative and objectual structures to which we are accustomed in language, it frequently has an affinity with the amorphous, archaic, and extremely powerful emotional materials of childhood. And it gives them a sharpening, an expressive precision, what Mahler calls a *crystallization*, that they did not have when covered over by thoughts, in their still-archaic form. One enters the "dark world," in which language and daily structures of time and causality no longer reign supreme; and one finds the music giving form to the dim shapes of that darkness.[58] Another way of expressing the point is that music seems to elude our self-protective devices, our techniques of manipulation and control, in such a way that it seems to write directly into our blood. Its very indefiniteness, from the point of view of the propositional use of language, gives it, frequently, a superior definiteness in dealing with our insides.[59] This connection between musical experience and the absence of intellectual control or manipulation means that the experience of the implied listener is at one and the same time one of

57 I do not mean to rank the classical music of the West above other traditions of great depth and sophistication – the African-American blues/jazz tradition in particular, and the musical traditions of India and many other cultures. As an enthusiastic listener to jazz and an enthusiastic reader of Gunther Schuller's fine analyses, I would like to be in a position to talk about the expressive content of jazz, but feel musically ill-equipped to do so.

58 Mahler on the experience of listening to his Second Symphony: "The whole thing sounds as though it came to us from some other world" (Mahler [1979], p. 158).

59 Cf. Mahler, in Bauer-Lechner (1980) p. 46: "All the most important things are almost impossible to pin down." Proust (1982) argues that music, by showing us the needines and the variety that exists hidden in our souls, is "more determinate" than language (III.379, 387). For a revealing comparison of Mahler to Proust see Adorno (1992), p. 145.

intensely focused cognitive activity and also one of amazing passivity: hence Mahler's remarkable images of the musical experience as feminine and feminizing, as that of being "played on by the spirit of the world."[60]

Such a view of music might now easily go astray, by suggesting that there is something "natural" about the language of music, that we can recognize the emotions it expresses without cultural education and a specifically musical training. Aaron Ridley's excellent analysis of musical expression, one of the most interesting constructive proposals in recent years, does not altogether avoid this danger.[61] Although Ridley carefully avoids and plausibly criticizes Cooke's view of music as universal language, his own positive analysis relies on the power of music to evoke the experience of the human voice and human movement: among the expressive features of music, prominent are "those that share qualities of sound with the human expressive voice and qualities of movement with human expressive behavior."[62] Although this is not altogether wrong, and at least some of music's expressive elements may be as cross-culturally communicative as behavioral and vocal gestures, Ridley surely either underestimates the opacity of music to someone not trained in a particular musical culture, or overestimates the cross-cultural expressive opacity of voice and bodily movement – presumably the former, because the problem of cultural difference plays no significant role in his account. It is certainly true that gestures and vocal cries are not perfectly transparent – and yet I am far more likely to be able to "read" a Japanese person's cry of distress or the exuberant joy of a child from Tamil Nadu than I am to decipher without prolonged study the emotions of grief and joy that are expressed in Japanese and South Indian music. Music (at any rate formally composed music) is more akin to poetry than it is to daily gesture and movement: its emotional power is inseparable from a compressed and formally intricate use of the media of expression, in such a way that only the most superficial understanding, if any, is available to those ignorant of the poetic (musical) tradition in question. We readily grant that poetry has specifically poetic ways of expressing emotion, and that these ways are internal to a given poetic tradition. Why should we be so reluctant to grant that

60 La Grange (1973), p. 274.
61 Ridley (1995).
62 Ridley (1995), p. 117.

there are also specifically musical ways of expressing emotion, and ways specific to a particular musical tradition? The expressive content of a formal structure is given by its place in a communicative tradition. Thus in what follows I shall use the analogy of tragic poetry, assuming as I do so that we are dealing with a spectator (listener) who has the requisite upbringing to appreciate a complex cultural work produced in the form in question.

Finally, we must add a point well made by Roger Scruton: there is an important distinction to be drawn between the general atmosphere of a musical work and the emotions it expresses. A work may have a general atmosphere of jollity, for example, without expressing it: "An expressive work does not merely possess a certain atmosphere: it has a content, upon which it meditates, and which it sets before us in articulate form."[63] When we interpret a literary work we look for emotions that are germane to its content, not just for any emotion that seems to be in the atmosphere it creates – emotions to which it draws the listener's attention, around which its structure is organized, not just any emotions that are in the vicinity; so too with music, however difficult it is to get clear about the distinction between content and atmosphere.[64]

IV. MUSIC AND HUMAN POSSIBILITIES

Let me now try to express these ideas in the terms of my account of emotions – granting, as I do so, that to verbalize the nonverbal is to engage in a halting process of translation. I have suggested that literary artworks are "transitional objects": objects toward which we have rich emotions, but which we see, at the same time, as symbolic of other

---

63 Scruton (1997), p. 155, referring to Nelson Goodman's exemplification theory of expression.

64 Scruton's example: Percy Grainger's *Shepherd's Hey* is a jolly work, the overture to *The Bartered Bride* expresses jollity. He gives another example that doesn't seem to work: he says that the prelude to act 3 of *Tristan und Isolde* expresses emptiness (right), but that the choruses from John Adams's *Death of Klinghoffer* are "an empty work of music." If I understand Scruton here, he is expressing contempt for the Adams work, and thus saying that it doesn't succeed in expressing much of anything; but that seems to be rather different from saying that it has a general atmosphere of emptiness without expressing emptiness. The difficulty of imagining a work that has such an atmosphere without expressing emptiness may indicate that the distinction is more useful for some emotions than for others.

objects and events. When we have emotions of fear and pity toward the hero of a tragedy and his reversal, we explore aspects of our own vulnerability in a safe and pleasing setting, apprehending general possibilities for human life, "things such as might happen." In the process, I have argued that the spectator has emotions of the following types:

1. Emotions toward characters: (a) sharing the emotion of a character by identification, (b) reacting to the emotion of a character.
2. Emotions toward the "implied author," the sense of life embodied in the text as a whole: (a) sharing that sense of life and its emotions through empathy, (b) reacting to it, either sympathetically or critically. These emotions operate at multiple levels of specificity and generality.
3. Emotions toward one's own possibilities. These, too, are diverse and operate at multiple levels of specificity and generality.
4. Emotions of exhilaration and delight at coming to understand something about life or about oneself.

I now claim that musical artworks may play this same role, with the differences that I have described. Music can contain symbolic structures of urgency and salience. Musical works are somehow able – and, after all, this "somehow" is no more and no less mysterious than the comparable symbolic ability of language – to embody the idea of our urgent need for and attachment to things outside ourselves that we do not control, in a tremendous variety of forms. This ability, like the expressive ability of tragic language, is the product of complex cultural histories; we need to be educated in the particular tradition in question, in order to take up the position of vulnerability that the music makes available to us. But, within a given tradition, to a listener educated in that tradition, a musical work may present symbolic structures every bit as complex as linguistic propositions, and embody analogous visions of salience and dependency, for the listener's acknowledgement or acceptance.

Thus, to continue with the Mahler example, the work may both contain structures in which a burning pain is crystallized and construct an implied listener who experiences that burning pain. Or – to use his description of the emotional structure of a part of his Second Symphony – it may contain forms that embody the acceptance of the incredible remoteness of everything that is good and fine, and, in virtue of these very forms, construct a listener who has this experience of desolation: "One is battered to the ground." It may contain forms that embody the hope of transcending the pettiness of daily human transactions – the acceptance of the possibility of that transcendence – and, in virtue of these structures, construct an implied listener who is "raised on angels' wings to the highest heights."[65]

But there are also some crucial differences between musical works and tragedies. For musical works, as we have said, do not contain the narrative representational particularity that tragic dramas do. To some extent there may be a narrative coupled with the music, as in opera or song, or in music with a stipulated programmatic content. But insofar as we are considering the expressive possibilities of the music itself, we must acknowledge that these do not make available to the listener any analogue of Philoctetes and Oedipus, or of their plight. The implied listener may still have some emotions that fall into our first category: for local stretches of the work may function in a characterlike way, expressing, for example, a foolishness or hollowness or bombast, or the triviality of daily life, or a sweet passivity; and the listener may both share the emotions of those local stretches of the work and (invited by the overall structure and expressive content of the music) have reactive emotions (scorn, contempt) toward them. But most of the listener's emotions will fall into our second and third categories: they will be emotions directed at general human possibilities (reversal of fortune, happy love) toward which the music gestures. At times, listeners will share the emotions built into the forward movement of the work (longing for happiness, dread of disaster); at times they will also react sympathetically toward those elements (with sympathy for a cataclysmic disaster, with pleasure at the happy conclusion of longing).

At the same time, listeners will have various related emotions toward their own lives and the possibilities they contain. Our image of music as dream already builds in the idea of compressed references to one's own life prospects, and these may be pursued at multiple levels of specificity and generality, with the relevant emotions.

Finally, listeners will have, typically, the exhilaration of discovery

65 Mahler (1979), p. 158.

and self-discovery. This pleasure, the pleasure of expanding our own personalities, is a major part of the explanation for why we seek out painful musical experiences.

In virtue of what could musical forms possibly "build in" such emotions as longing for happiness or dread of disaster? Here we should not altogether reject Ridley's suggestion that some similarities to the sounds of the human voice and the movements of human behavior may play a role in anchoring listener emotion. One could say something like this about the rhythms of poetry as well. But by far the greater part of the work, here as with poetry, is done by a system of expressive conventions that the listener must simply learn. Only a crude poem has an expressive content confined to dynamic and rhythmic features that are available to someone who has no education in poetry. Thus, Vachel Lindsay's "The Congo" imitates the rhythms of African dance, and there is not much more to say about its expressive content. To read a sonnet of Shakespeare well, by contrast, one must know the English language thoroughly and with subtlety, and one must understand the form of the sonnet and the traditions of expression within it. So too with music. It is possible to say some very vague things about the ways in which rhythms embody emotional dynamics, stress patterns notions of salience, upward and downward movement emotional risings and fallings, dynamic and kinetic variation the related emotional traits. But even these vague things are probably not universal; and any really persuasive reading of the expressive content of a complex musical work must focus, like the interpretation of a tragic drama or a lyric poem, on the work in detail, situating it in its historical context of traditions of expression. It must talk not simply of such very general features of dynamic, rhythmic, and melodic structure, but also of the expressive use of orchestration, of relationships to other musical works – all of which is even more obviously embedded in a particular time and tradition.

The listener, educated in the musical tradition of the work, attends to musical forms that are suffused with patterns of salience. Occupying the point or points of view constructed for her by the music, she follows its emotional development, sharing in the emotions it constructs. At times, too, stepping aside from the point of view of the music and contemplating that structure, she reacts emotionally to the "story" laid out there. What are the intentional objects of her emotions? When the emotions are of the first sort (toward localized char-acterlike features of the music), their object is the musical structure, seen as symbolic of some elements of human life, or of persons of a certain sort (the artist's enemies in Strauss, the herdlike people who are like the fish listening to St. Anthony in Mahler). Such emotions are most likely to arise when the work has a certain narrative definiteness imposed upon it by a text or program, although, as already suggested, it can happen locally without this.[66]

When the emotions are of the second sort, inasmuch as the musical forms gesture toward certain general human facts and possibilities – the emptiness of a life without love, the struggle to overcome pettiness – the listener's emotions will take those general human possibilities as their objects, at different levels of generality. Sometimes she will partic-ipate empathetically in the emotional trajectory of the work (having desolation, or fear), and sometimes experience sympathy for those who experience desolation or fear. The listener is frequently invited to shift back and forth between the empathetic and sympathetic perspectives, just as the spectator at a tragedy may at times share the fear or grief of the characters and at times feel compassion for their plight.[67] More-over, the music itself may contain this sympathetic perspective: this is particularly common in opera, which, like Greek tragedy, has ways of expressing reactive emotions that are not identical to the emotions of the characters.[68] Thus the emotions of the listener toward the patterns of salience in the musical work, and the general human possibilities to which they are directed, are complex and heterogeneous, and admit of some latitude and creativity on the part of the spectator.

66 See, for example, the interesting discussion of characterization in Mahler in Adorno (1992), p. 51.

67 See Scruton (1997), pp. 145, 354–66, for an eloquent and valuable account of the sympathetic dimension of musical experience. See also Ridley (1995), pp. 129–34. Ridley ultimately recognizes both what I have called the empathetic and what I have called the sympathetic dimensions of the response. He holds that through music we "grasp the dominant character of a different affective life" and thus "experience that character," seeing the world as it would look to someone with that character (pp. 161–3); but he also appears to hold (in no way inconsistently) that we sometimes react, as well, with sympathy or whatever other emotion is prompted, to that character as we experience it (pp. 137, 164).

68 See Scruton (1997), p. 366. Following Wagner, he compares the music of an opera to the chorus of a Greek tragedy: "The music stands proxy for the listener himself, expressing not the emotions of the characters, so much as a sympathetic response to them."

The emotional content of music typically remains in some ways more general than that of many literary artworks. Here we find the truth in Hanslick's remarks.[69] In literary works we typically find the emotional material concretely situated, and connected to specific characters, a setting, and so on – all of which may be more or less isomorphic to people and events in our lives. Hanslick apparently thought that emotions had to have highly concrete objects, and that played a role in his negative conclusions regarding music. But we have seen that emotions can in fact have highly general objects, and also objects whose form is vaguely specified.[70] I may fear the many different ways in which disaster may befall me; or grieve for all that has been lost and that will not come again; or rejoice at the way the world is. I have suggested that the absence of concrete narrative elements in music sometimes allows it to be more, not less, precise in its relation to the amorphous material of the inner world. But just as in the world of the young child the emotions themselves have an indefinite character because they are not yet linked to the perception of concrete objects, so too with music it will at times be difficult to demarcate one emotion clearly from another, or to say precisely what the emotion's object is. This does not mean, however, that there is no such content or that we cannot say (as best we can in words) what it is.

We should be careful to say what generality means here and what it does not. Although a musical work may contain no concrete narrative and represent no concrete person whose emotions the work depicts (the pain of Philoctetes, for example), and although its emotional trajectory

---

69 See also Walton (1988) p. 356ff.
70 See Ridley (1997), pp. 31, 136; he prefers to think of the emotions as objectless, whereas I think that, although there are indeed genuinely objectless moods (and music may embody these), there are also many emotions that have a highly general object (fear of unnamed and unnamable dangers, hope for something good), and that music very often embodies these. Because Ridley holds that music expresses only objectless emotions, he concludes that it can never embody emotions such as "grief, humiliation, shame" – all of which he believes to be object-dependent in a way that fear and anger are not (p. 169). I question this: on my view, primitive shame can take just as vague an object as a generalized dread of future possibilities. So too can grief for the loss of omnipotence, or innocence – the grief of the child who has discovered her own aggression. We should, however, concede that some *species* of these emotions, and other emotions as well, require some kind of textual concretization before they can be definitely expressed in music.

may be in that sense general (a possibility for anyone), its emotional content itself may be highly specific, and certainly in no way vague or vacuous.[71,72] It may express a type of pain, for example, unlike any other, or an erotic sweetness that words would try to capture in vain. Thus while the absence of named particulars makes for a certain sort of generality, there may at the same time be particularity such that the longing we hear could only be *this* sort of longing (the longing embodied in this Mahlerian phrase, for example). When Wagner and Mahler express longing, they do it so differently that it would be the height of obtuseness to think of their works as embodying a common general form of human longing. The listener, assuming the point of view of Mahler's specific expression of longing in a given passage, sees human possibilities from that viewpoint; or, sympathetically, she responds to the presence of such painfully exposed longing in her world. Even when the music is accompanied by a text or program, the music (as we shall shortly see in the case of Mahler) may be more definite in certain ways than the text, making the emotional movement precise in a way that the text by itself does not. Thus the text of the same poem may be set by different composers with altogether different expressive outcomes.

At the same time, again like the spectator at a tragedy, the listener is also "reading" her own self, her own inner world, and her own possibilities – and sometimes more directly, since the music interposes no represented fictional intermediaries to distract her, and no texture of habitual language to make everything seem worldly or daily. Her focus on her own life does not entail that she is simply using the music as a tool for her own personal ends. Here again, her emotions may have different levels of specificity and generality – anger at a specific instance of obtuseness, fear for disaster of some nameless type. Again, this allows for flexibility and creativity on the part of the spectator.

Finally, wonder and delight are also mingled in her response, and these emotions take the musical work as their intentional object and value it for its own sake. In fact, it is precisely because artworks can

---

71 Walton (1988), p. 357, argues correctly that at some point, great generality turns into vacuity and we lose interest; and he holds that music may express some aspects of emotions with greater detail and specificity than the other arts.

72 Walton puts it well when he says that music may lack reference to a definite *subject*, but may have all the specificity of a very detailed predicate (ibid., p. 359).

arouse these non-eudaimonistic emotions that they are also valuable media of self-exploration: they make a process that would otherwise be painful wonderful and delightful.[73]

The spectator's emotions are, then, real emotions, of a complex sort. They include emotions such as fear and pity and grief assumed through empathy with a perspective or perspectives embodied in the work; sympathetic emotions responding to the presence of those structures in the work; closely connected emotions about human life in general and about her own possibilities; and, finally, emotions of wonder and delight that take the artwork itself as their object. We do not think that this combination is so mysterious when the experience of a tragedy is at issue. We should not think it mysterious in the case of a symphony, or a song cycle.

As with literature, so too with music: not all works arouse deep emotion. Some works are just fun, or interesting for their intricacy of structure, or wonderful in themselves without deep pertinence to the inner world. Music is perhaps somewhat more free to create such purely formal works than is literature, although to conclude that a given musical work is lacking in emotional content would be a delicate endeavor, involving a close study of the tradition, the composer's oeuvre, and the expressive capacities of the form in its historical setting. When I hear classical Indian music, I hear it purely formally; but I also know that its forms are linked with a rich expressive range, and that someone who can occupy adequately the position of the "implied listener" at such a performance, as I cannot, would have emotional responses and would apprehend the work as relating to general human possibilities.

But since I have said that little work of interest can be done in the abstract, I shall turn for the remainder of this chapter to a reading of two short musical works of enormous emotional power, the first and final songs of Mahler's *Kindertotenlieder*, or songs on the deaths of children. I shall not always hammer home the details of my theory, but instead attempt to offer convincing readings of the emotional content

---

73 Thus my answer to the challenge of Kivy (1980), p. 23, as to why one would ever submit oneself to a genuinely painful experience, is the same as Aristotle's, and closely related to some of the points made in Levinson, "Negative Emotions." Ridley (1995), pp. 150–4, speaks of "the bracing sense of satisfaction that comes from knowing, or finding, that one is up to it."

of the songs and their musical form, letting the theoretical claims emerge from these. Nor shall I end with any theoretical summary, for I want to let the readings speak for themselves, and to end the chapter on that note. It is necessary to bear in mind that language can function here only haltingly, often through the use of metaphor.

V. THE *KINDERTOTENLIEDER*: LOSS AND HELPLESSNESS

How can music contain the most terrible grief of all, the grief of a parent at the death of a child? The concerned listener will, I think, readily agree that Mahler's *Kindertotenlieder* do so; and yet my question must be *how* they do so. Precisely what emotional content is expressed by the songs of the cycle as it develops, and in virtue of what musical structures is it possible for the songs to have this expressive capability? (Possible, therefore, for the songs to arouse this range of emotions in a listener who succeeds in occupying the point of view of the music?)

It may appear to be unfair, at this point in my argument, to select musical works that have a textual component. For then, one might object, it is all too easy to get clear about the emotional trajectory of the songs – but only by relying on the text as a crutch. I believe that this would not be a good objection. For one thing, Mahler repeatedly insists – and this seems to be true – that the expressive power of his music calls for words as a final elaboration, but is independent of the verbal element.[74] We should see text and music, then, as parallel and intimately intertwined expressions of an inner world, or perhaps even the text as the epiphenomenon of the music. And indeed, the presence of the text will give us a very good way of separating the specifically musical contribution to expression from the textual contribution.

We may grant that the subject matter of the text locates the emotions of the music, giving them a specific intentional object: the deaths of children. In other ways too, the text orients the music, and of course music and words do form a remarkable unity – it would be a strange misinterpretation to write about the music without recognizing the ways in which it sets the text. Nonetheless, we can grant this while still

74 See, for example, Mahler (1979), p. 212.

insisting that the expressive power of the work does not reside in the text alone, and that the music has its own independent contribution to make to the work's emotional trajectory. I believe that it will emerge that the emotional trajectory of Mahler's music is in all sorts of ways underdetermined by the content of Rückert's text; in some ways it may even work against the most plausible reading of the text in its religious context. And throughout it has a subtle and altogether determinate structure that renders its expressiveness more various and deep than that of the text.

I can begin my argument by talking about the important interpretation of the song cycle by Donald Mitchell in *Songs and Symphonies of Life and Death*, the third volume of his magisterial work on Mahler.[75] Mitchell's is a remarkable achievement, from which I have learned much. His observations about the harmonic and dynamic structure of the cycle, about its expressive use of orchestration, and about the deployment of various specific motives within the songs show, it seems to me, a deep understanding of Mahler's compositional technique. And there are in his analysis passages of haunting beauty – for example, his description of the entrance of the piccolo toward the end of the fifth song:

In this particular instance it is not at all far-fetched to think of it as a piercing ray of *light*, penetrating the chromatic coils and darkness of the storm and magically initiating the process of dispersal.[76]

And yet, it seems to me that Mitchell's overall interpretation – in particular his reading of songs 1 and 5, which will be my focus – is profoundly flawed. And by attempting to show why I think he is so wrong about the emotional trajectory of these two songs I can perhaps begin to make clear how, in my view, these musical forms manage to embody a determinate emotional content.

The cycle sets five poems of Friedrich Rückert (1788–1866), depicting the response of a grieving father to the deaths of his two

---

75 Mitchell (1985), pp. 75–143. See also La Grange (1995), pp. 825–46; Russell (1991). The details of Russell's interpretation of the imagery of light and dark in the cycle (which I discovered only in the last stages of revision of this chapter) are often very revealing, although I disagree with the overall interpretation of the cycle, which he shares with Mitchell.

76 Mitchell (1985), pp. 83.

children.[77] (Two of Rückert's children in fact died of scarlet fever in 1833, and the poems were written shortly afterward.)[78] Mitchell's general account of the first song, "Nun will die Sonn' so hell aufgeh'n," is as follows. The song contains a dialogue between grief and consolation, embodied musically in a dialogue between wind textures (with voice) and string textures. At first, grief alone is on the scene; the messages of consolation then enter with the reference to the sun, which Mitchell understands as "the symbolic image of mitigation . . . the sun that will rise again and gladden the heart."[79] The light of this consoling sun slowly gains the ascendancy as the song progresses, new elements of "light" being progressively added, in the form of the late entrances of the flute and the higher strings. The expressive meaning of this development is the progressive assuagement of sorrow in the heart of the grieving parent. It is Mitchell's view that, so far as the poetic text and the natural trajectory of the song's expressive development are concerned, the song should end with the utter victory of consolation and the sun. That this manifestly does not happen he cannot deny – but he interprets the song's conclusion as merely uttering some residual doubts. And he believes that even these doubts are inserted by Mahler only for dramatic purposes, in order that the cycle should have somewhere further to go.[80]

Song 5, "In diesem Wetter," begins, according to Mitchell, with another agonized outburst of grieving, the storm within the parent's heart echoing the storm that (in the words of the poem) rages outside, as the children are carried to their funeral. Focusing on the remarkable moment at which the glockenspiel, silent since song 1, reenters, along

---

77 See the appendix to this chapter, pp. 293–4, for German texts and English translations of songs 1 and 5.

    Luise, the youngest of Rückert's six children, contracted scarlet fever the day after Christmas 1833, when she was three years old, and died on New Year's Eve. Her five-year-old brother Ernst then contracted the illness and died on January 16. Three other children contracted the illness but survived. The poems used for the first three songs were written about Luise's death; only the fourth and fifth songs refer explicitly to both children. On the composition of the poems, their publication, and their quality, see Russell (1991), pp. 28–53; La Grange (1995), pp. 825–6.

78 The poems were published only after Rückert's death, in 1872, although they were circulated in manuscript among Rückert's friends during his lifetime. The collection contains a total of 425 poems, from which Mahler made his selection of five. See Russell (1991), pp. 24–39.

79 Mitchell (1985), p. 93.

80 Ibid., pp. 93–5.

with the piccolo – a moment to which I shall return – he argues that the expressive function of the child's bells is to "cut off the torrential storm of anguish"[81] and to prepare the way for consolation. The piccolo's "laser beam" then disperses the clouds of grief, the bells become "divested of their funereal associations and emerge as serene heralds of the concluding lullaby."[82] The transition to D major now "confirm[s] the attainment of eternal peace . . . The whole cycle moves into the lengthening shadows, out of the light and into – this time – a *benign* darkness."[83]

Now Mitchell is correct, I believe, in his suggestion that the point of view of the music is throughout the point of view of the grieving parent, or, more generally, of a person who has suffered a great loss. His interpretation, furthermore, corresponds to a plausible interpretation of the Rückert text, as it would easily be heard in its Christian context, where the parent would be seen as calling himself to the duty of self-consolation. (Thus Rückert did not even see fit to publish the poems in his lifetime.) But I shall argue that this message of benign consolation, satisfying though it may be, is not at all the emotional message that these two songs contain: Mahler's own relation to grief, shaped by the heritage of Romanticism, undercuts the commonplace sentiments of this simple reading of the text. The musical setting reveals darker interpretive possibilities, still compatible with the poems' semantic content.

The Mitchell reading must contend, from the start, with Mahler's own comments about the work, which he evidently thought almost too painful to hear. He told Natalie Bauer-Lechner how sorry he felt "for himself that he had to write these songs, and for the world which would one day have to listen to them."[84] This remark is at least difficult to square with the idea that the work brings a gift of consolation to those afflicted with suffering. He also told Guido Adler that if his own daughter had already died by that time, he could not possibly have

81 Ibid., p. 80.
82 Ibid., pp. 83, 84.
83 Ibid., p. 84. Contrast the account of this ending (somewhat more accurate, in my view) in Cooke (1988), p. 77: ". . . and finally the peace and haven the children have found in spite of the storm – a haven of eternal sleep rather than the paradise of the Fourth Symphony. The nihilism of the Sixth Symphony had intervened before the song was composed."
84 See La Grange (1995), p. 829.

written such a work – suggesting, again, that it is a dark and terrible work, not one that helps the heart of the grieving.[85] And so, I shall argue, it is.

I shall argue that the first song expresses the isolation of personal grief and pain within the exuberant and indifferent life of nature, which by contrast seems not at all consoling but callous, falsely sweet, and sinister. In the final song, new dimensions of the parent's grief are explored – in particular, a kind of hammering anxiety that half believes that it still must be possible to do something about the situation, and a ferocious guilt that strikes again and again because the children are being destroyed and nothing *is* being done about it. This anxiety and guilt are then resolved – in a sense: but not into consolation. The illumination of the piccolo beam, the bell's devastating stroke, bring the knowledge of utter helplessness, of the eternal finality of loss, and the irreparable character of guilt.

As I have said, with Mitchell, the music invites the listener to assume, throughout, the posture of the grieving parent. The world is seen entirely from that viewpoint; no posture of detachment is offered within the music for an observer, or for an observer's sympathy. Thus, although emotions of sympathy toward that parent are always a theoretical possibility in the view I have developed, the music appears to make no place for them here, so compelling and so perilous is the listener's identification with the grieving persona (both character and implied author). Thus the listener's emotions will be the emotions of one who sees the world from such a perspective and meditates on her own possibilities in such a light.

We must begin with some general remarks about the overall structure of the cycle. Its character is indeed in a marked sense cyclic, and the first and fifth songs are especially closely linked, both harmonically and dynamically. The first song begins in d minor, and ends with a transition to D major; the second, third, and fourth songs explore c minor and E-flat major; but in the fifth we return to d minor – with a final "resolution," once again, in D major – signalled by the reentry of the glockenspiel, another recapitulatory element summoning our memories of the material of song 1. In effect, the parent's grief does not progress to any new place; after the intervening process of wishful

85 Ibid.

memory of the children's eyes (song 2), the jumpy and futile searching for the child's face in the doorway (song 3), the impossible hope that the children have only gone for a walk and will soon return (song 4) – all this expressed by the departures into new keys – the cycle of grief returns full circle, and the parent is left alone with the abrupt fact of mortality. This by itself should begin to cast doubt on Mitchell's highly progressive reading of the cycle. But this remains unclear, since he puts much of the weight of progress on the transition inside each song between d minor and D major, which we have yet to explore.[86] In dynamic terms as well, the cycle is cyclical: beginning with the solitary voice of the oboe, building gradually to a dynamic climax within the fifth song – and then dropping abruptly back to end with a delicate pianissimo, but in the strings this time, the winds being for the most part silent. This, we might say, is a return with a difference – and I shall argue that it expresses the transition from active grieving to the sense of utter helplessness.

Let us now consider the first song.[87] [Reader: if at all possible, listen to the Kathleen Ferrier/Bruno Walter recording, now reissued on compact disc by EMI.]

We hear first the oboe, plaintive,[88] broken, earthy, sounding in isolation out of the air,[89] its convoluted chromatic movement, descending and ascending, accompanied by the descending movement of the horn. As the voice enters, the texture is still extremely spare: the strings and harp, and also the flute and clarinet are altogether silent. The impression is that of a mind tormenting itself, biting into itself in silent isolation, after a night of utter sleeplessness. The message of light and hope suggested in the words "Nun will die Sonn' so hell aufgeh'n" ("now will the sun rise up as brightly") is contradicted by the move-

---

86 Mitchell (1985) himself observes, and indeed stresses, the cycle's cyclical features: p. 75ff.

87 Although in general I do not acknowledge specific suggestions made by friends and colleagues, whom I generally thank at the end of the book, I make an exception here to acknowledge my great gratitude to Edward Cone for his very generous and detailed comments on an earlier draft of this section of the manuscript, without which my amateur efforts would have been still more amateurish. I shall also acknowledge several particular points that I owe to Cone's suggestions.

88 Mahler marks "*klagend*" over the oboe part here.

89 Cf. Mitchell (1985), p. 92.

ment of the music, which does not rise up, but rather descends; which is not bright and confident, but blunted and hesitant.

What Mitchell calls the "dialogue" now begins, as the strings and the harp enter for the first time, and the swelling and soaring vocal line suggests the rising of the sun – again against the grain of the words, "als sei kein Unglück die Nacht gescheh'n" ("as if no misfortune had happened during the night"). It is one of the remarkable features of the orchestration of the cycle to destabilize the listener's relation to the strings. Accustomed on the whole to hear strings as "normal," as human and warm, as the bearers of human thought and emotion, the listener is here subtly wrenched from that habitual posture, as winds and horns, with their jerky movement and their brooding chromaticism, take up the function of personal expression, and the strings, and with them the otherworldly and oddly cloying sound of the harp, the function of expressing nature's soaring beauty and soothing rhythmic regularity – set over against, and blankly indifferent to, the personal point of view. It is at this point, I believe, that Mitchell's misreading begins: for, determined to find in the song a message of reconciliation, he finds an opportunity in the traditional association of string sounds with warmth and light. But the point is this: when one is biting into oneself in the most intense grief, it is a bitter misery to see things go on in their ordinary way around one. The strings here must be heard, so to speak, from the oboe's and the voice's point of view – and the harp, so frequently associated with the otherworldly and extrahuman, gives us our tip. If there is sweetness here, it is the sweetness of the *Erlkönig*. The sun is rising and light begins to flood the world – for everyone but the one who has lost a child in the night.

This reading[90] is shortly confirmed. For as soon as strings and harp and voice reach a temporary resting place – apparently in the key of D major (bar 16) – the glockenspiel enters, with its inexorable high stroke, repeated six times, in three rhythmic pairs, to remind us that the funeral of a child is at hand. The glockenspiel plays a central role in the cycle. As Mitchell says, it is at one and the same time the funeral

90 See Adorno (1992), p. 7: ". . . Mahler's symphonies plead anew against the world's course. They imitate it in order to accuse . . . Nowhere do they patch over the rift between subject and object; they would rather be shattered themselves than counterfeit an achieved reconciliation."

bell tolling and – in its difference from the larger tubular bell that is more often used with funereal significance – the toy bell used by a child at play, thus a memory of the carefree and happy life of the child and of the parent at play with the child.[91] In this way the music expresses the fact that the stroke of loss just *is* the weight of happiness, viewed as past. The stroke of this small bell, then, puts a stop to the indifference of the string-and-harp world, ushering back the oboe, and the second strophe, as the horn now assumes the oboe's burden of mourning.

The second strophe follows the expressive pattern of the first – with a gradual advance on the part of the malign false blandness of nature, as the second violins are now added to the violas and cellos. Following upon the swelling exuberance of the conclusion, "scheinet allgemein" ("shines neutrally"), the oboe cuts in as if in a protest against the onward march of the light, with a variation on its initial melody more bitingly intense in its chromaticism (bars 41–4); at the conclusion of this outburst, the glockenspiel sounds again – this time, sounding only one stroke to the bar,[92] as if it lacked the energy to strike the second stroke, like something running down – the toy, the little life.[93]

At the opening of the third strophe the voice – now addressing to itself the words "Du musst nicht die Nacht in dir verschränken" ("you must not enfold the night within yourself") – takes up its own melody, in inverted form, accompanied by the oboe with the original form of the melody.[94] The inversion of the grief melody represents the voice's attempt to conquer its own grief – the official sentiment of the text; but the oboe, persisting with the melody's original form, insists that this effort is in vain.[95] As if in response to this struggle in the human world, the first violins now enter, pianissimo but soaring, "mit grossem Ausdruck," asserting the pitiless triumph of the light – and the arpeggios of the harp snatch the child out of the parent's arms into the world of natural process and decay, as the swelling vocal line ascends and broad-

91 Mitchell (1985), p. 78, with n. 25.
92 Very oddly, Mitchell (1985) who is on matters of musical detail usually so precise, claims that the glockenspiel always sounds in patterns of two strokes on two crotchets (p. 78). Both this passage and bars 84–5 (in other words, two of the four glockenspiel passages in the song) are ignored in this claim.
93 I owe this suggestion to Edward Cone.
94 See Mitchell (1985), p. 104.
95 I owe this point to Edward Cone.

ens, celebrating the drowning capacities of the "ew'ge Licht." It is impossible not to feel that the usual polarities of light and darkness are being reversed here, both verbally and musically, the strings and the "ew'ge Licht" being not benign but indifferent, merciless, the drowners of small lives, the darkness of oboe, bassoon, and horns expressing the human intensity of love and grief. The climax swells out, beyond the reach of the voice itself:[96] its highest point is reserved for the orchestra alone, as violins and flutes dip and soar.

At this climactic point the little bell returns, summoning the listener back to the darkness with three pairs of strokes, as in its initial entrance. The vocal line begins the final strophe: "Ein Lämplein verlosch in meinem Zelt" ("In my tent a small lamp went out"). The melody is slightly varied – it breaks, slipping down from a to g, in such a way as to turn the second syllable of *verlosch* into a disyllable (or even, in Kathleen Ferrier's remarkable performance, a trisyllable) – the stammering, stumbling weakness of grief. The horn repeats the falling movement. And now, the forces of nature assume control, and the voice greets them with the words, "Heil sei dem Freudenlicht der Welt" – "Hail to the joyous light of the world" – an entrance marked by Mahler as sung "mit Erschütterung" ("with utter devastation").[97] Even the oboe is co-opted into the string–harp group this time, echoing the violins' ascending melody. The voice repeats its greeting to the daylight. The little bell rings on the offbeat: a pair of strokes on the third and fourth beats of bar 83, a single stroke on the third and fourth of bar 84. The other instruments now fall silent.

The little bell sounds once more, alone, its painful memory of joy sounding in the void, with a high and inexorable stroke.

Let us now consider the fifth and final song of the cycle. This song, with its intensely biting chromaticism, its dizzying spurtings and flashings, is marked by Mahler "mit ruhelos schmerzvollen Ausdruck"

---

96 See Mitchell (1985), p. 93; and for a very convincing account of this section as a development section, see pp. 105–7.

97 See the apt comment of Russell (1991), p. 75: "The mood evoked by the words *Heil sei dem Freudenlicht der Welt!* is not one of joyful acceptance . . . A final lack of resolution is suggested by the cadential process itself, with its avoidance of a fully articulated V-I cadence."

("with restless, pain-filled expression"). The external storm, in which the dead children are being carried off to their funeral, is also an internal storm of anguish. Nothing has been resolved: with the return to d minor, after the vain searchings for hope that inhabit the middle songs, we are back where we started, but with a new intensity of agony. The chromatic melody gives the impression of something sharp and malign digging or burrowing its way into one's flesh.[98] The hard hammering rhythms, punctuated by sudden whizzings and flashings, suggest forces of great brutality and indifference, forces that seem to be hacking the children limb from limb. The listener, occupying the point of view of the music, which is also the point of view of the parent, is at one and the same time the spectator of brutality, as the children are dismembered, and also the scene of the brutal assault, as the hammering blows reach down into the parent's own insides, as the children are pounded and hammered inside the parent's own body.

The emotional movement of the song is, first of all, a movement of acute and terrible anxiety. Something dreadful is happening to a most important part of the parent's life, and the parent seeks, in agony, for some control, some escape from the helplessness. This agonized and fearful searching is in the musical structure itself, and the listener, accepting the form, is inhabited by those emotions. But it is, I want to argue, not only anxiety that the music here expresses: it is also guilt, guilt and shame. The message of the text, again and again repeated, is this: something terrible is happening to my children, I never would have allowed this terrible thing to happen, but it is happening anyhow, and I am powerless to do anything about it. However, this message is already teetering on the edge of self-torment: for what is it to be a parent but to be boundlessly responsible for the safety and well-being of one's children? To stand between the children and the terrible things? I suggest that the music itself, with its relentless self-biting and self-hammering texture, pushes the text over that line: the parent is not just anxiously (and vainly) seeking for escape, but is also punishing herself for not finding such an escape.

Insofar as the focus of self-torment is on powerlessness to protect, we might call the emotion shame – and it gestures toward a primitive shame at the sheer helplessness of a human being in the sweeping all-

98 On the melody, see Mitchell (1985), pp. 80–1.

powerful world of nature. To be a parent is to wish to be omnipotent, and to regain infantile omnipotence: one is supposed to be able to prevent death and harm. Thus the realization of the parent's own finitude is shameful and a reminder of the more fundamental shame attached to being merely human. Insofar as the parent imagines that the failure to protect is culpable, the emotion may be called guilt. In the music the two are closely linked, and it would be difficult to individuate them very precisely. I claim, however, that, given the fixing of context performed by the text, one may legitimately hear this shame and guilt in the agonized self-hammering textures of the music, even where Rückert's words do not plainly put them.

At one point, an escape route opens: for at bars 40–2 the vocal line wrests the music a round from d minor to B-flat major, briefly asserting the vigilance of parental care: "I feared that they would become ill." All too briefly – for in the falling halftone of bar 44, the hope is abandoned: "Those are only idle thoughts now."

And in effect we might say that the parent not only envisages being hammered by the blows that destroy the children; the parent, in taking up the point of view of the music, also participates in the infliction of the blows. That is the deepest point of the guilt that is present in this music, the thought that one has oneself, by one's failure to find escape, committed an aggression, that the children's blood that is spurting out in the orchestral spoutings has been shed by one's own hand.

At this point a biographical detail might be tentatively mentioned. Rückert's son was named Ernst. Mahler had a younger brother named Ernst, who died at the age of fourteen. (Before Mahler's birth his parents had lost another child, their first, named Isidor.) Theodor Reik suggests, not implausibly, that the Rückert poems revived for Mahler the memory of his parents' double bereavement. Some of his remarks to Natalie Bauer-Lechner indicate that he was preoccupied by the memory of past loss, as well as by fear for the loss of his own children. Reik then suggests that such memories are made more difficult by the unconscious envy and jealousy children often feel at the death of a sibling.[99] Mahler is identifying with his parents' grief, but also recalling, with guilt, his own ambivalence. If we accept this suggestion (and even if we do not accept it as a specific biographical detal), we may hear in the

99 Reik (1953), p. 315.

music not only the parent's guilt at failure to save the children, but a child's guilt at aggressive wishes that have now had their unexpected fulfillment. In that sense the "parent" really is participating in the infliction of the blows upon the child: for the parent is also an envious child whose aggressive fantasies have become all too powerful. We do not need this conjecture to hear guilt in the music: but it gives the presence of aggression and guilt a further dimension.

Now I want to confront the moment on which Mitchell is so eloquent, and on which he most bases his case for a consolatory reading of the cycle as a whole. The chromaticism and the pounding intensity of the storm reach a climax in bars 85–91, "Man hat sie hinaus getragen, ich durfte nichts dazu sagen" ("They carried them out, I couldn't say anything about it"). As the vocal line descends from c to b natural, and from b to b flat, the strings and horns, joined now by timpani, reach a fortissimo climax. All of a sudden there is a hush. A broken phrase from the clarinets, accompanied by horn and drums – and then suddenly two strokes from the glockenspiel, on a, "invading" the d minor harmony.[100] These strokes are accompanied by a high a on the piccolo, piercing, as Mitchell says, like a sudden ray of light, but a cutting ray, like a laser beam – and also by an octave on the harp, and a harmonic on the cellos. The storm music intervenes briefly, only to be silenced again by the sound of the bell – six pairs of bell strokes in all. And now the transition to D major arrives, and with it the rocking soothing music from the strings that is marked by Mahler, "Slowly, as in a lullaby." The vocal line now sings a sweet high remote melody, accompanied by the gentle rocking of the strings, and by the celesta, often associated in Mahler with remoteness and otherworldliness. The winds have for the most part fallen silent (the oboe, that most human of instruments in Mahler's orchestral vocabulary, is not heard from again). "In diesem Wetter, in diesem Saus, in diesem Braus" ("In this weather, in this storm, in this tumult") – and now a marked chord from the harp – "They sleep, as if in their mother's house" – and the voice soars upward like a star. The string–celesta–voice–harp group continue to the conclusion of the vocal line, which reaches an apparently serene cadence on d. The last fifteen bars are purely orchestral,

---

100 See Mitchell (1985), pp. 90–1, 83.

the rocking movement becoming fainter and more distant, finally to die away.

Is there resolution here? And does the transitional moment signal an escape from anguish into consolation and the thought of a benign darkness sheltering the child? Such a fantasy would also assuage shame and guilt, since it would tell the parent that nothing bad has become of the children, and thus no parental failure has harmed them.[101] We must admit, I think, that the consolatory reading is compatible with the poetic text – is perhaps even suggested by it, given Rückert's piety.[102] But the question is, what does the music itself express?

Here we are confronted by an interesting technical anomaly.[103] The song ends in the ostensible tonic key, D. But this ending seems false and unjustified: as Edward Cone writes, "it has no right to." At the words "von keinem Sturm erschrecket, von Gottes Hand bedecket," the music strongly implies a modulation to the key of the dominant, A. The resolution back to D at "sie ruh'n" therefore sounds like a temporary resting place in the subdominant of A. Yet the modulation to A is never completed, and we are thus left with the alternative of having to accept D as the tonic, a solution that Cone describes as "unsatisfactory." On Mitchell's reading of the cycle, we would have to accept this unsatisfactory conclusion as a mistake on Mahler's part. On my read-

101 Odd in this regard is the interpretation of Russell (1991), pp. 111–12: having insisted that the storm is really the image of internal psychological states (p. 102), he now takes that telling observation back, in order to make the end of the cycle into a real resolution: "As psychological science tells us, grief and depression are both often the symptom of an anger turned inwards: here, the anger is at last turned outwards, in the dramatic outburst of a storm, and the result, in nature as in human nature, is that the cataclysm is followed by calm. The emotional storm runs its course; the heart is at last at peace and receptive to consolation." He cites as parallel the last movement of the Fourth Symphony (p. 111) – a comparison that does not inspire confidence, at least in me, since I think that the sweetness of that movement is highly complex, and not exactly what it might seem on first hearing.

102 Rückert was not an entirely conventional Christian: a professor of Oriental languages, he had an abiding interest in Eastern mystical religion. One distinct possibility is that he is blending thoughts of Christian heaven with thoughts of the absorption of the individual into the general movement of the universe, a thought that represents, in both Buddhism and Hinduism, a benign idea of escape from suffering. Mahler approaches such ideas in *Das Lied von der Erde*, in his own complicated way – but in *Kindertotenlieder*, I claim, the world is not illusory but real, and the tragedies it presents are final and insoluble.

103 I owe this point to Edward Cone.

ing, we will be able to see it as deliberate – Mahler's way of showing that the protagonist really doesn't acccept the apparent comfort offered by the words. As Cone writes, "If the children were really in God's hand, they would come to rest in the key of A major!"

We should also consider the role of the piccolo, which, as Mitchell and I agree, plays a crucial role in bringing the song to a conclusion. The piccolo actually enters much earlier in the song, when, beginning in measure 5, it anticipates and then later twice doubles (35ff., 56) the vocal line on "Nie hätt' ich gelassen die Kinder hinaus." In other words, it is the voice of the parent's own anxious self-torment. Furthermore, well before the bell itself tolls at the climactic moment, the piccolo introduces the high a, with three drawn-out a's, while the voice continues to sing "nie hätt' ich gesendet die kinder hinaus" (77ff., number 7 in the score). It is as if the a sounds first during the storm, while the parent is still in the grip of anxious self-torment, and then finally very clearly as the storm dies down. All this suggests that the a represents the parent's own knowledge of death: the piccolo, which has been so closely associated with the vocal line, begins to express the final static awareness of loss, eventually, in a moment of silent clarity, to be joined by the funeral bell.

Immediately prior to the bell, the music has been expressing an increasingly desperate fear and anxiety, accompanied by guilt. But the other face of fear is hope: to fear a terrible outcome is, in most cases at any rate, to believe the outcome to be uncertain, to think that one's own desperate strugglings might still achieve something.[104] Fear, like hope, like love, extends outward toward the world, attaching itself to uncertain outcomes there. At this point, I want to say, the parent is still distracting herself with "idle thoughts," and has not really accepted the finality of what has happened. The piercing light of the piccolo, the little bell of death – sounding together with the harp, whose sinister sweetness recalls us to the fact that the child is not in this world – these bring, I claim, the knowledge of death, and therefore of utter helplessness. In acknowledging those sounds, sounding together, in taking them in, or rather in sounding them – since, as I have argued, the piccolo is a voice from within the parent's own mind – the parent acknowledges that there really *is* nothing to be done about it, no hope

104 On this see Aristotle, *Rhetoric* II.4 ff.

of safety for the children, no hope of an exit from helplessness for the parent. Instead of love, fear, hope extending outward, opening the parent to the world, there is now a closure of the self into a world without love.

The escape from minor to major is now found – but not by the vocal line. Instead, the sickly sweetness of harp and celesta sweep the children into the indifferent world of nature, where they are being taken care of all right, and rocked all right, but surely not by the hand that ought to have rocked them and that passionately desired to do so. For the children it is a sleep not of comfort but of nothingness. For the parent, it is the knowledge of the impossibility of any loving, any reparative effort. The oboe, voice of active love, has fallen silent. The voice, immobilized by helplessness and a now irreparable guilt, falls silent. The world of the heart is dead.[105]

APPENDIX: TEXTS AND TRANSLATIONS OF SONGS I AND 5

Text of "Nun will die Sonn' ":

Nun will die Sonn' so hell aufgeh'n
Als sei kein Unglück die Nacht
  gescheh'n.
Das Unglück geschah nur mir allein.
Die Sonne, sie scheinet allgemein.

Du musst nicht die Nacht in dir
  verschränken,
Musst sie ins ew'ge Licht versenken.
Ein Lämplein verlosch in meinem Zelt,
Heil sei dem Freudenlicht der Welt.

Now the sun is going to rise, as bright as if nothing bad had happened in the night.
The bad thing happened only to me;
The sun sends light out neutrally.

You must not fold the night into yourself,
You must drown it in eternal light.
In my tent a small lamp went out.
Hail to the joyous light of the world.

---

105 Compare these words of Theodor Adorno's – apropos of the finale of the Seventh Symphony, but they have relevance here too:
  "Mahler was an unconvincing yea-sayer (*war ein schlechter Jasager*). His voice falters . . . when he himself practises that dreadful concept of overcoming, . . . and composes as if joy were already present in the world. His vainly jubilant movements unmask jubilation, his subjective incapacity for the *happy end* [in English in the text] itself denounces it" (Adorno [1992], p. 137, but in the translation given in La Grange [1995] p. 824).

Text of "In diesem Wetter":

In diesem Wetter, in diesem Braus,	In this weather, in this tumult,
nie hätte' ich gesendet die Kinder hinaus,	I would never have sent the children out,
man hat sie getragen, getragen hinaus.	they have been carried, carried out.
Ich durfte nichts dazu sagen.	I could say nothing about it.
In diesem Wetter, in diesem Saus,	In this weather, in this storm,
nie hätt' ich gelassen die Kinder hinaus.	I would never have let the children out.
Ich fürchtete, sie erkranken,	I feared they would fall sick,
das sind nun eitle Gedanken.	those are now vain thoughts.
In diesem Wetter, in diesem Graus,	In this weather, in this horror!
nie hätt' ich gelassen die Kinder hinaus.	I would never have let the children out.
Ich sorgte, sie stürben morgen,	I worried that they would die tomorrow.
das ist nun nicht zu besorgen.	That is nothing to worry about now.
In diesem Wetter, in diesem Graus!	In this weather, in this horror,
nie hätt' ich gesendet die Kinder hinaus.	I would never have sent the children out.
Man hat sie hinaus getragen,	They have been carried out.
ich durfte nichts dazu sagen!	I could say nothing about it!
In diesem Wetter, in diesem Saus, in diesem Braus,	In this weather, in this storm, in this tumult
sie ruh'n als wie in der Mutter Haus,	they are sleeping as if in their mother's house,
von keinem Sturm erschrecket,	frightened by no storm,
von Gottes Hand bedecket,	sheltered by God's hand,
sie ruh'n wie in der Mutter Haus!	they are sleeping as if in their mother's house!

PART II

COMPASSION

6

COMPASSION: TRAGIC
PREDICAMENTS

I. EMOTIONS AND ETHICAL NORMS

The child we imagined in Chapter 4 now has many emotions: joy at the presence of good things and fear of their absence; anger at the sources of frustration and gratitude for aid and comfort; shame at her inability to control the sources of good; envy of competitors and guilt at her own aggression; disgust at the slimy and the decaying; wonder at the beauty of the world. By now we can see how these emotions support the child's ability to act, as they mark off patterns of salience and urgency in her surroundings; we also see how they may support generous and beneficent action. But we also see a darker set of connections. The urgent needs of infantile dependency can engender a paralyzing shame, accompanied by destructive resentment that puts later ethical development at risk. The child's intense involvement with nearby objects risks impeding general social concern in later life. The intensity and ambivalence of the child's attachment to its first objects may distort the perception of other objects she will soon encounter. Disgust's repudiation of animality can eventually lead to destructive forms of social hierarchy. None of these problems threatens the account of emotion as value-laden recognition: for it is from evaluation that they all arise. They do, however, make us wonder to what extent emotions are rational in a normative sense, that is, suitable for guiding good adult deliberation.

Chapter 4 began to address normative issues, suggesting a mutually supportive relationship between an account of emotional health and a normative ethical view that stresses imagination, reciprocity, flexibility, and mercy. These connections, I said, should not be pressed too far. A normative ethical view needs independent support; and psychology shows us as many problems for ethics as resources for its implementation. But a persuasive psychological account can at least help us to a better understanding of those problems and those resources.

At this point, however, and for the rest of this book, I shall pursue a different, though related, question: what positive contribution do emotions, as such, make to ethical deliberation, both personal and public? What reasons do we have to rely on people's emotions, rather than on their will and on their ability to obey rules? Why should a social order cultivate or appeal to emotions, rather than simply creating a system of just rules, and a set of institutions to support it? Such questions are sometimes posed, in political theory and law, without much prior analysis of emotions and without sorting out competing theories of their structure and development. It is my hope that the theory worked out to this point will prove a valuable resource in posing them clearly and getting plausible answers. Here again I follow the Stoics, who understood that normative reasoning about emotions would be only as convincing as the account of emotions it employed. Chrysippus thus devoted three books of his work *On the Passions* to the theory, and the fourth book to normative matters.

The Stoics' normative ethical theory relies heavily on their analysis of emotions as value judgments; we could not understand how emotions could possibly be removed from human life without seeing them in the way this analysis recommends. There is, however, no converse implication: we can accept the Stoic analysis (or a development of it) without at all accepting their normative thesis that the emotions are always bad guides and should be completely removed from human life. Much the same is true of the relationship between Part I of this book and Parts II and III: the later parts rely heavily on the analysis of emotions given in Part I, but that earlier analysis does not imply the conclusions reached here. (It could not, of course, insofar as it is a development of the Stoic theory, which was combined with a quite different normative account.) Nor will Parts II and III offer a complete defense of a normative ethical theory: the normative suggestions in these parts are intended to be both incomplete and general, compatible with more than one total ethical theory.

One could imagine many ways of using the material of Part I to raise normative questions. In keeping with my belief that these questions are best raised through a detailed focus on each emotion in turn, rather than by generalizations about emotions as a class, I have chosen to investigate just two cases of particular importance, by following two distinct, though related, strands in the tradition of Western philosophical debate about emotion. I turn first to the emotion most frequently viewed with approval in the tradition, and most frequently taken to provide a good foundation for rational deliberation and appropriate action, in public as well as private life. This is the emotion that I shall call *compassion*, though, as we shall see, several different terms have figured in the debates about its proper role. In this chapter I shall investigate the cognitive structure of compassion, drawing on analyses in Aristotle, Adam Smith, and Rousseau. I shall examine the resources for good that this emotion has seemed to contain, and also some impediments to its benign operation. In Chapter 7 I shall then reconstruct a philosophical debate about the proper role of compassion in social life that goes all the way back to Plato's attack on the tragic poets; it continues in modern thinkers, including Smith, Rousseau, Kant, Schopenhauer, and Nietzsche. I shall argue that this debate has frequently been misunderstood in contemporary thought, and that a correct understanding will help us see what we ought to say about contemporary issues. Finally, in Chapter 8 I shall describe some specific ways in which a society pursuing justice might legitimately rely on and cultivate compassion, and suggest some ways in which it might deal with the impediments to compassion's ethical work supplied by shame, resentment, envy, and disgust.

But we will still have left unaddressed the more intense and more problematic emotions of the personal life, which itself both shapes public choice and is shaped by it. To that extent we will not have given a full answer to our questions about emotion's role in a good human life, even in its public dimension. To explore these normative questions further, I then turn, in Part III, to a different strand in the philosophical tradition: the tradition of proposing a reform or "ascent" of (erotic) love, in order to convert the most urgent and potentially ambivalent of our emotions into a constituent of the good and reasonable life. Thus we might say that Part II treats the most normatively attractive and promising case, Part III a difficult case, but one of central importance for any normative role that emotions may play. In the process, the account will continue to be attentive to several emotions that seemed normatively problematic, even from the limited perspective of Part I: envy, shame, and disgust. These emotions will figure in the account as impediments to the development of compassion, and as insidious poisoners of the normative potential inherent in love.

One way of understanding the structure of the ensuing argument is to think of the structure of the self and its concerns. In thinking of emotions as eudaimonistic evaluations, I have pictured a self as constituted (in part at least) by its evaluative engagements with areas of the world outside itself.[1] Thinking of things in this way, we may now notice a bifurcation in the emotions. Some expand the boundaries of the self, picturing the self as constituted in part by strong attachments to independent things and persons. Love and grief are paradigmatic of such emotions; and, as we shall see, compassion pushes the boundaries of the self further outward than many types of love.[2] Some emotions, on the other hand, draw sharp boundaries around the self, insulating it from contamination by external objects. Disgust is paradigmatic of such an emotion. It still makes evaluative judgments about the importance of uncontrolled objects for the person's own flourishing: but these judgments are typically negative, and the project of disgust is to keep them away. Thus disgust might be said to be the emotion of an unachieved and anxious Stoicism: the disgusted person still cares about mortality and the body, but is trying very hard to reach an undisturbed condition. The intense and excessive shame that I have called pathological shame partakes, as well, of this boundary-drawing character: although it contains an acknowledgment of the weakness and insufficiency of the self, it wishes to conceal that weakness and to restore a condition of omnipotent control over objects. Like disgust, it contains the judgment that weakness and need are bad things, to be kept at bay. And, as we have already seen, shame and disgust are frequently linked to a hatred that seeks the total obliteration of the threatening object.

Parts II and III ask, then, how and whether ethical agents can live with the facts of their own interdependence and incompleteness – venturing out into the world and engaging evaluatively with it – without

---

1 I have learned a great deal on this matter from thinking about Charles Larmore's important work on the self. (That does not mean that he would agree with any of the specific claims about emotions made here.)

2. I am grateful to Keith Oatley for discussion of this point. See Oatley and Jenkins (1992), p. 58.

being stifled by shame, disgust, and hate. The Stoics recommended *apatheia*, the emotionless condition, because they thought that no non-Stoic life could be free of these reactive emotions and the evils they bring. The possibility of a non-Stoic ethics, in which there is some positive role for the guidance of emotions, depends on our answering their question differently.

A note on terms. The emotion I shall be describing in Part II seems to be a ubiquitous human phenomenon. Descriptions and analyses ranging from the theoretical accounts of Aristotle and Rousseau to the sociological data presented in Candace Clark's excellent book *Misery and Company*[3] remain remarkably constant across place and time. To put it simply, compassion is a painful emotion occasioned by the awareness of another person's undeserved misfortune. Compassion, in some form, is also central to several Asian cultural traditions.[4] Moreover, there is strong evolutionary evidence that compassion has played a central role in group selection; and related ethological evidence that it plays a central role, irreducible to that of egoistic reciprocity, in primate species, and in our own.[5] But there is more than the usual degree of verbal confusion in the English language concerning what to call the experience I have just defined. "Pity," "sympathy," and "empathy" all appear in texts and in common usage, usually without clear distinction either from one another or from what I am calling "compassion." "Pity" has recently come to have nuances of condescension and superiority to the sufferer that it did not have when Rousseau invoked *pitié*, and still does not have when "pity" is used to translate the Greek tragic terms *eleos* and *oiktos*. I shall avoid it here because of those associations.[6] "Empathy" is often used, as I shall later use it, to designate an

---

3 Clark (1997).
4 See Kupperman, in Marks and Ames (1995).
5 See Sober and Wilson (1998), de Waal (1996).
6 It is worth remarking, however, that "pity" has standardly and consistently been associated with the undeserved character of a misfortune, and thence with potential issues of justice; compassion occasionally has a looser usage, taking in the sufferings of creatures who are not imagined as agents, deserving or undeserving. There are perhaps not just terminological differences here, but subtly different phenomena; I shall use the term "compassion," but my analysis shall focus on the standard cases where compassion is linked to undeserved misfortune, and is thus coextensive with pity, in its older use.

imaginative reconstruction of another person's experience, without any particular evaluation of that experience; so used, obviously, it is quite different from and insufficient for compassion; it may not even be necessary for it.[7] But psychologists and psychoanalysts sometimes use the term "empathy" to mean some combination of imaginative reconstruction with the judgment that the person is in distress and that this distress is bad.[8] So used, it comes close to being compassion, although it still might not be identical to it (if, for example, we conclude that one may have compassion without imaginative reconstruction). I shall use "empathy" in a way that clearly distinguishes it from "compassion": empathy is simply an imaginative reconstruction of another person's experience, whether that experience is happy or sad, pleasant or painful or neutral, and whether the imaginer thinks the other person's situation good, bad, or indifferent (separate issues, since a malevolent person will think the other's distress good and her happiness bad). Finally, "sympathy" is frequently used in British eighteenth-century texts to denote an emotion equivalent to what I call "compassion." Contemporary authors often follow this usage: thus Candace Clark's research into the emotion is all conducted using the term "sympathy." If there is any difference between "sympathy" and "compassion" in contemporary usage, it is perhaps that "compassion" seems more intense and suggests a greater degree of suffering, both on the part of the afflicted person and on the part of the person having the emotion. People who are wary of acknowledging strong emotion are more likely to admit to "sympathy" than to admit that they feel "compassion."[9] But "sympathy," as standardly used today,[10] is very different from "empathy": a malevolent person who imagines the situation of another and takes pleasure in her distress may be empathetic, but will surely not be judged sympathetic. Sympathy, like compassion, includes a judgment that the other person's distress is bad.

We can see that there is a little more difficulty here than in many other cases about identifying the extension that the definition is to

---

7 For the history of the term "empathy," see Wispé (1987).

8 See examples in Eisenberg and Strayer (1987), Batson (1991).

9 It is also possible that "compassion" has a closer connection to concern and subsequent action than does sympathy: in terms of my later analysis, that sympathy lacks the eudaimonistic judgment, at least in some cases.

10 Not so in Smith, who associates the term "sympathy" with contagion of feeling: see note 11.

cover. But the fact that literary, philosophical, psychological, and sociological accounts are in remarkable agreement in the descriptions they give helps us to believe that the search for an account is not a waste of time.

A source of further complexity – but also a source of kinship holding the terms together – is the fact that in the philosophical tradition they are translated and retranslated in many different ways. Words in one language that may initially have had different connotations from those in another get drawn toward one another by the practice of philosophical translation and discussion over the years. Thus Greek *eleos* and *oiktos* get rendered into classical Latin by *misericordia*, and both of these into Italian by *pietà*, into French by *pitié*. All of these, in turn, are translated into English by *pity* – although the British moral philosophers of the eighteenth century also at times use *sympathy* to allude to the classical tradition in question.[11] In German, meanwhile, *Mitleid* is the word most commonly chosen to translate the Greek, Latin, and French words, although *Mitgefuhl* also occurs. Although *Mitleid* may initially have slightly different associations from some of the words in the family, it gets pulled toward them by philosophical practices. English can at times render *Mitleid* (literally) by *compassion*, a word with its own (medieval) Latin history, which I shall not discuss here. The interchangeability of the two English words in philosophical contexts is noted already by Hobbes in *Leviathan*, chapter 6: "*Griefe*, for the Calamity of another, is PITTY; and ariseth from the imagination that the like calamity may befall himselfe; and therefore is called also COMPASSION, and in the phrase of this present time a FELLOW-FEELING" (1991, p. 43). Nietzsche is aware of all of these complexities, since he comments on Greek and French texts sometimes using the German vocabulary (when he wants to insist on the fact that *Mitleid* means a double amount of *Leid*, pain), sometimes the French word (when he wants to scoff at Rousseau and the democratic tradition).[12]

11 Smith is clearer, using *pity* and *compassion* for our pain at the sorrows of another, *sympathy* for the more general tendency to have fellow feeling with "any passion whatever" in another person (Smith [1976], p. 10).
12 In thinking about who Nietzsche's opponents are, we need to be aware that *pitié* is not common as a central ethical term in nineteenth-century texts: in Comte, Renan, etc. one tends to find, instead, phrases such as *sentiments fraternels* and *fraternité*. Rousseau's usage, with its strong links to the Greco-Roman tradition, seems not to have survived the Revolution.

In short, the most sensible way to proceed is to give clear accounts of each term one uses and to be consistent; in the case of historical texts, we must ask to what extent their analyses are shaped by their choices of terms.

II. THE COGNITIVE STRUCTURE OF COMPASSION

Philoctetes was a good man and a good soldier. When he was on his way to fight with the Greeks in the Trojan War, he had a terrible misfortune. By sheer accident he trespassed on a sacred precinct on the island of Lemnos. As punishment he was bitten in the foot by the serpent that guarded the shrine. His foot began to ooze with foul-smelling pus, and the pain made him cry out curses that spoiled the other soldiers' religious observances. They therefore left him alone on the island, a lame man with no resources but his bow and arrows, no friends but the animals that were also his food.[13]

Ten years later they come to bring him back: for they have learned that they cannot win the war without his bow. The leaders of the expedition think of Philoctetes as simply a tool of their purposes. They plan to trick him into returning, with no sympathy for his plight. The chorus of common soldiers, however, has a different response. Even before they see the man, they imagine vividly what it is like to be him, and they enter a protest against the callousness of the commanders:

> For my part, I have compassion for him. (*oiktirô nin egôge*)
> Think how
> with no human company or care,
> no sight of a friendly face,
> wretched, always alone,
> he wastes away with that savage affliction,
> with no way of meeting his daily needs.
> How, how in the world, does the poor man survive? (169–76)

As the chorus imagine a man they do not know, they stand in for the imaginative activity of the audience, for whom the entire tragic drama is a similar exercise of imagination and compassionate emotion.

The drama strongly suggests that this emotion is linked with benefi-

---

13 I narrate Sophocles' version of the story. In the lost versions by Aeschylus and Euripides, we know that the island was inhabited.

cent action, as the chorus, having seen Philoctetes with compassion, begin to question the plot against the suffering man, imploring their young leader to grant his wish and send him home. Their speech of urging begins with the words, "Have compassion on him, lord" ("*oik-tir', anax*," 507). Philoctetes himself relies on this connection when he asks for aid: just before pleading to be sent home, he says:

Save me, have compassion for me (*eleêson*),[14,] seeing that all mortal life lies open to risk and terrible affliction:[15] good things can happen, but the opposite can also happen. The person who is outside of suffering ought to look out for terrible affliction, and when someone's life is going well, then above all he should watch out, lest he be ruined unawares. (501–6)

The connection determines the shape of the plot: for it is when the young commander Neoptolemus feels for the first time the tug of compassion, witnessing an attack of Philoctetes' pain, that he repudiates his own deceitful conduct and returns the stolen bow to its rightful owner. Philoctetes, blinded by pain, asks, "Where are you, my child?" (805) – and Neoptolemus replies, "I have long been in pain (*algô palai*), grieving for your suffering" (806). He gives his location in the world by naming his emotions. The distress by which he locates himself is ethical distress: when Philoctetes refers to the discomfort his affliction causes others, Neoptolemus says, "Everything is discomfort, when someone leaves his own character and does what is not fitting" (902–4). And at last, when it is time to sail with the stolen bow, he says, "A terrible compassion (*deinos oiktos*) for this man has fallen upon me" – comparing his emotion to the sudden afflictions mentioned by Philoctetes, which fall upon mortals unawares. The affliction of compassion prompts a decision to treat Philoctetes justly and humanely.

Philoctetes' story displays the structure of compassion, drawing attention to the elements of its cognitive structure that are stressed in standard theoretical accounts. It is useful to begin with the fine analysis given by Aristotle in the *Rhetoric*, which has guided the subsequent philosophical tradition. Aristotle's analysis is continuous with less sys-

---

14 I have not been able to find a significant difference between *eleos* and *oiktos*; their interchangeable use in the play seems governed more by poetic considerations than by considerations of sense.

15 In the Greek, *deina pathein*. The repetition of *deina* below does not explicitly include *pathein*, but I have translated both as "terrible affliction" to indicate the repetition.

tematic earlier treatments in Homer, the tragic poets, and Plato; it is taken over, in most respects, by defenders of compassion such as Rousseau, Schopenhauer, and Adam Smith, and by opponents of the emotion such as the Greek and Roman Stoics, Spinoza, Kant, and Nietzsche.[16] Finally, the very same elements are stressed in many contemporary psychological accounts and in Candace Clark's analysis of current American beliefs. As I follow Aristotle's account, I shall also assess it in the light of the subsequent tradition, and criticize it in view of my own developing argument.[17]

Compassion, Aristotle argues, is a painful emotion directed at another person's misfortune or suffering (*Rhet.* 1385b13 ff.). It has three cognitive elements. It seems to be Aristotle's view that each of these is necessary for the emotion, and that they are jointly sufficient. Apparently he thinks that the pain itself is caused reliably by the beliefs: he calls it "pain at . . . the misfortune one believes to have befallen another," and gives the aspiring orator advice about how to induce or remove it, by inducing or removing the beliefs. Later we will have to ask (both on Aristotle's behalf and on our own) whether the pain is a necessary element of the definition, over and above the cognitive elements. For now, however, we may begin with the fact that the cognitive elements are, at the least, among the constituent parts of the definition: the pain of pity is distinguished from the pain of grief, or fear, only by the type of cognition it involves.

The first cognitive requirement of compassion is a belief or appraisal[18] that the suffering is serious rather than trivial. The second is the belief that the person does not deserve the suffering. The third is the belief that the possibilities of the person who experiences the emotion are similar to those of the sufferer. (I shall later argue that this

---

16 I discuss Aristotle's account in Nussbaum (1986), Interlude 2, and also in Nussbaum (1992), Nietzsche's in Nussbaum (1993b). See also the very perceptive analysis of both Aristotelian and tragic pity in Halliwell (1986).

17 Although Aristotle's Greek term, *eleos*, is usually rendered as "pity," I shall continue to translate it as "compassion," as seems more appropriate to the nuances of the two English terms.

18 Aristotle uses the participle of the verb "appear"; in Nussbaum (1994), Chapter 3, I argue that this does not entail that he is thinking of *phantasia* as contrasted with judgment or belief. In fact, he regularly uses belief-words interchangeably with appearance-words.

third element is not strictly necessary, and that another as yet unspeci-
fied element is.) Let us examine each Aristotelian element in turn.

Take seriousness first. Compassion, like other major emotions, is
concerned with value: it involves the recognition that the situation
matters for the flourishing of the person in question. Intuitively we see
this quite clearly. We do not go around pitying someone who has lost
a trivial item, such as a toothbrush or a paper clip, or even an important item that is readily replaceable. In fact, internal to our emotional
response itself is the judgment that what is at issue is indeed serious –
has "size," as Aristotle puts it (1386a6–7).

What misfortunes are taken to have "size"? Once again, not too
surprisingly, there is remarkable unanimity about core instances across
time and place. The occasions for compassion enumerated by Aristotle
are also the ones on which tragic plots, ancient and modern, most
commonly focus: death, bodily assault or ill-treatment, old age, illness,
lack of food, lack of friends, separation from friends, physical weakness, disfigurement, immobility, reversals of expectations, absence of
good prospects (86a6–13). Candace Clark's study of appeals to compassion in America[19] includes the same elements – adding some variants
specific to contemporary life:

When I looked at what had triggered sympathy, I discovered dozens of
plights. The inventory encompasses all of those enumerated in blues lyrics
(e.g., poverty, a partner's infidelity, death of loved ones). It includes illness
(including "functional" or behavioral illnesses such as alcoholism and drug
use), physical or mental disabilities or deformities, injury, and pain. The
respondents also mentioned war trauma, sexual abuse, physical abuse, crime
victimization, disaster victimization (e.g., by earthquakes, hurricanes, or airplane crashes), homelessness, infertility, divorce (or loss of "partner"), discrimination (e.g., in jobs or housing), political victimization (e.g., liberties
abridged by tyrannical government), role strain (e.g., single parenthood),
unwanted pregnancy, physical unattractiveness, car accidents, car trouble,
house trouble (e.g., leaky roof), insensitive parents, ungrateful children, so-

---

19 This part of her account focuses on both interview data and the annual listing by the
New York Times of its "Neediest Cases," whose descriptions of "debilitating plights"
involving "death, mental and physical illness, disability, poverty . . . loneliness" show
that our sense of tragedy is not discontinuous with that expected from the audience of
the *Philoctetes*.

cial ostracism, loss in competition (e.g., sports or job), depression, fear, public humiliation, accidental embarrassment, fatigue, bad judgment, ruined vacations, boredom, and discomfort (e.g., enduring heat, cold, or traffic jams).[20]

Apart from the fact that (as Clark stresses) Americans today tend to include more relatively mild predicaments in the list of "plights" than they did formerly, the list she presents is remarkably similar to Aristotle's – and to Rousseau's, and to Smith's. Even though her list includes more items, she insists that this is because they are seen as having "size," not because "size" is not considered important:

For a person to be considered unlucky, his or her plight must fit prevailing standards of direness – that is, it should be considered sufficiently harmful, dangerous, discrediting, or painful . . . Moreover, the plight must be bad and unlucky for those with the person's particular set of gender, age, social class, and other characteristics. (82)

One interesting difference between Aristotle's list and the "plights" enumerated as dire by Clark's subjects is that various forms of political injustice and oppression play a more central role for Americans than they do in Aristotle's account. But even this is not a general historical/cultural difference. For in omitting this occasion for emotion Aristotle has neglected central cases of Greek tragic compassion, where slavery and loss of citizenship are pivotal; even in Philoctetes' case, the fact that he had suffered undeserved political injustice is as important as are his isolation and his pain.

We may conclude that societies (and individuals) vary to some degree in what they take to be a serious plight; they vary, too, in the level of damage required before something is taken to be a serious plight.[21] Moreover, changes in the shape of life construct new predicaments: obviously enough, car and airplane crashes were not on Aristotle's list. Nonetheless, the central disasters to which human life is prone are remarkably constant; constant as well is the fact that people take these disasters to be central.

An important question now arises: from whose point of view does

---

20 Clark (1997), p. 83.
21 Here Clark's use of the term "sympathy" may be significant: it is hard to imagine that her subjects would have described themselves as having "compassion" for people caught in traffic.

the person who has compassion make the assessment of "size"? Consider the following two examples. Q, a Roman aristocrat, discovers that his shipment of peacock's tongues from Africa has been interrupted. Feeling that his dinner party that evening will be a total disaster in consequence, he weeps bitter tears, and implores his friend Seneca to pity him. Seneca laughs. R, a woman in a rural village in India, is severely undernourished, and unable to get more than a first-grade education. She does not think her lot a bad one, since she has no idea what it is to feel healthy, and no idea of the benefits and pleasures of education. So thoroughly has she internalized her culture's views of what is right for women that she believes that she is living a good and flourishing life, as a woman ought to live one. Hearing of her story and others like hers, workers in the province's rural development agency[22] feel deeply moved, and think that something must be done.

What these examples bring out is that people's judgments about what is happening to them can go wrong in many ways. Suffering and deprivation are usually not ennobling or educative; they more often brutalize or corrupt perception. In particular, they often produce adaptive responses that deny the importance of the suffering; this is especially likely to be so when the deprivation is connected to oppression and hierarchy, and taught as proper through religious and cultural practices.[23] On the other hand, people can become deeply attached to things that on reflection we may think either trivial or bad for them; their suffering at the loss of these things may be real enough, even though the onlooker is not disposed to share in it. Compassion takes up the onlooker's point of view, making the best judgment the onlooker can make about what is really happening to the person, even when that may differ from the judgment of the person herself.

Adam Smith makes this point powerfully, using as his example a person who has altogether lost the use of reason. This, he argues, is "of all the calamities to which the condition of mortality exposes mankind . . . by far the most dreadful." It will be an object of compassion to anyone who has "the least spark of humanity." But the person affected does not judge that his condition is bad – that, indeed, is a large part of what is so terrible about it:

22 For these and similar cases, see Chen (1983), Chen's paper in Nussbaum and Glover (1995), and Nussbaum (2000a).
23 See Nussbaum (2000a), Chapter 2, with references to the literature on this question.

But the poor wretch . . . laughs and sings perhaps, and is altogether insensible of his own misery. The anguish which humanity feels, therefore, at the sight of such an object, cannot be the reflection of any sentiment of the sufferer. The compassion of the spectator must arise altogether from the consideration of what he himself would feel if he was reduced to the same unhappy situation, and, what perhaps is impossible, was at the same time able to regard it with his present reason and judgment.[24]

In short: implicit in the emotion itself is a conception of human flourishing and the major predicaments of human life, the best one the onlooker is able to form.

This is another way of putting our familiar point that the object of compassion is an intentional object – interpreted within the emotion as he or she is seen by the person whose emotion it is.[25] Therefore, as with any emotion, it may also happen that the person who has the emotion is wrong about what is going on, and the suffering person is right. Many judgments about the suffering of others are skewed by inattention, or bad social teaching, or by some false theory of human life. Seneca does not have compassion for Q, and here he is probably correct. As a Stoic, however, he would also refuse compassion to R, because he would judge that hunger and lack of education are not very important. Most of us will think him wrong, and to the extent that we do, we will be more likely to have compassion for R. Compassion, or its absence, depends upon the judgments about flourishing the spectator forms; and these will be only as reliable as is the spectator's general moral outlook.

The judgments of the sufferer are not altogether irrelevant to pity,

24 Smith (1976), p. 12, from which the two previous citations are drawn as well. Smith goes on to talk of a mother's pity for the suffering of her infant, as yet unable to understand the difficulties of its situation, and of our pity for the dead. Contrast Rousseau (1979), who holds that "the pity one has for another's misfortune is measured not by the quantity of that misfortune but by the sentiment which one attributes to those who suffer it" (p. 225). Blum (1980), p. 510, follows the Rousseau position, where what he calls "compassion" is concerned; he distinguishes "pity" from "compassion," arguing that the former involves a degree of distance and condescension to the sufferer. This may be right about some current nuances of usage, but not about the history of their philosophical use; nor would it be right to suppose that approaching the predicament of another with one's own best judgment, rather than the sufferer's, need involve condescension. I would say that there is condescension in suspending one's own reflection, and true compassion in trying to get things right.

25 Aristotle registers this point by insisting that compassion, like other major emotions, relies on the "appearances" and beliefs of the person whose emotion it is.

where these differ from the personal judgments of the pitier: for the onlooker may judge that the sufferer is right to accord importance to a certain sort of loss, even though she herself does not do so. For example, a wind player whose lip becomes even slightly injured may judge the suffering to be of tremendous size, and I may have compassion for him on that account, even though I myself would find a similar injury trivial. But this is because, at a more general level, I validate the judgment of the sufferer: for I agree with him that it is a terrible thing to be deprived of one's career and one's mode of expression, whatever it is, and I see his injury as such a deprivation. My compassion revolves around the thought that it would be right for anyone suffering a loss of that sort to be very upset. On the other hand, the wind player will be right to laugh at me if I complain a great deal about a minor injury to my own lip: for the very thing that would mean loss of career to him means no such thing to me, and it is this general description that validates the judgment of "size." Human beings have different ways of specifying the content of the major constituents of human flourishing: but unless the onlooker can bring the suffering back to one of these major components, as she conceives of things, she will not have the emotion.

Sometimes the relationship between onlooker and sufferer may militate against an independent judgment of "size." Often love takes up the viewpoint of the loved person, refusing to judge a calamity in a way different from the way in which the beloved has appraised it. Other circumstances, too, may suggest evaluative deferral. For example, if I know that a group in my society has suffered greatly in ways that I, a privileged person, have a hard time understanding, I may choose to take the estimate of misfortune offered me by qualified members of that group. But even in such cases I am, in effect, making a judgment of my own: namely, the judgment that the other person's estimate of "size" is the one I shall go by.

Now I turn to *fault*. Insofar as we believe that a person has come to grief through his or her own fault, we will blame and reproach, rather than having compassion. Insofar as we do feel compassion, it is either because we believe the person to be without blame for her plight or because, though there is an element of fault, we believe that her suffering is out of proportion to the fault. Compassion then addresses itself to the nonblameworthy increment. This comes out very clearly both in

Aristotle's account and in the poetic material on which he bases it. *Eleos*, he insists, sees its object as "undeserving (*anaxios*)" of the suffering.[26] Such undeserved suffering appeals to our sense of *injustice* (1386b14–15). He adds that for this reason the emotion is more likely to be felt toward people who are seen as in general good (1386b6–8): for then we will be more likely to believe that they do not deserve the bad things that befall them.[27] But it is not inconsistent with his account to have compassion for people for things they do out of their own bad character or culpable negligence – so long as one can either see the suffering as out of all proportion to the fault *or* view the bad character or negligence as itself the product of forces to some extent excusably beyond the person's control.

This point about desert is strongly emphasized in Homeric and tragic appeals for compassion. When the suffering is plainly not the person's fault, as in Philoctetes' case, the appeal for compassion need not be preceded by argument. But where there is a possible disagreement about culpability, the appeal to pity comes closely linked with the assertion of one's innocence. Throughout the *Oedipus at Colonus*, Oedipus insists on the unwilling nature of his crimes – in order to hold the emotions of the characters (and of the audience). Similarly, Cadmus, at the end of Euripides' *Bacchae*, joins to his admission of wrongdoing a claim that the god, by inflicting "unmeasurable sorrow, unbearable to witness" (1244) has exceeded the just penalty.[28] Only this justifies, it seems, his claim to compassion from the other characters (1324); the audience is being asked to share those judgments and that emotion.[29]

---

26 *Rhet.* 1385b14, b34–86a1, 1386b7, b10, b12, b13; *Poetics* 1453a4, 5.

27 He adds that if one believes that people in general are pretty bad, one will rarely have compassion, for one will be inclined to believe that they deserve the bad things that happen to them. In saying this, however, he ignores the importance of the causal connection between the person's badness and the *particular* thing for which he or she suffers: even bad people will get sympathy for a particular reversal if it is clear that it is not their fault. Such connections are sometimes in fact ignored – as when people who despise homosexuals view AIDS as a punishment for their alleged bad way of life; but the logic of compassion requires the person who withholds it to posit some sort of causal link; such links are often supplied by views of divine punishment.

28 *Endikôs men, all' agan*, 1259; and *epexerchêi lian*, 1346.

29 On the connection thus made between compassion and the Aristotelian notion of *hamartia*, see Nussbaum (1992), Halliwell (1986), and, for a superlative study of the word and its connection with blame and innocence, Stinton (1975).

A significant further step is taken in Sophocles' *Trachiniai*. Hyllus insists that the tragic predicament of Heracles was caused by the negligence (*agnômosunê*) of the gods. This being the case, it is appropriate for the human actors to have compassion for his plight – it is "an object of compassion for us (*oiktra men hemin*)." But it would not be appropriate for the gods to have compassion, since it was their fault: instead the events are "an object of shame for them (*aischra d'ekeinois*)." So compassion requires blamelessness not only on the part of its object, but also on the part of the onlooker. It would be simply hypocritical to weep over a plight that you yourself have caused. In other words, the onlooker has to see the disaster as falling on the person from outside, so to speak; and she will be unable to do this if she believes either that the person has caused it or that she herself has caused it.[30]

These ideas are developed in a fascinating way in Clark's study of contemporary American attitudes. Her subjects all feel sympathy only for plights caused by "bad luck" or "victimization by forces beyond a person's control" (84). And "[a] plight is *unlucky* when it is *not* the result of a person's willfulness, malfeasance, negligence, risk taking, or in some way 'bringing it on him or herself' " (84). Such assessments, of course, are profoundly influenced by prevailing social attitudes. Clark finds that Americans are not very tolerant of ambiguity: they tend to place events "either in the realm of inevitability, chance, fate, and luck or in the realm of intentionality, responsibility, and blame" (100). In order for emotion to occur, they need to be able to conceive of the event as something that simply strikes someone, as if from outside: they use terms such as "befalls," "besieges," "ails," "struck," "hit her like a ton of bricks." Where it appears that agency makes some difference, they are unwilling to see any admixture of external bad luck. Thus Clark finds that Americans are on the whole less ready than Europeans to judge that poverty is bad luck, given the prevalence of the belief that initiative and hard work are important factors in determining economic success. Similarly, Americans have been slow to judge that sexual assault is a "plight," even if it is clearly a wrongful act against the woman, because they retain attitudes suggesting that the

---

30 For further discussion of Hyllus's speech, and Bernard Williams's interpretation of it, see Nussbaum (2001b).

woman "brought it on herself" – by walking alone in a dangerous place, for example. On the other hand, alcoholism and drug abuse are surprisingly likely – and more likely than in previous generations – to be seen as things that "fall on" the person through no fault of her own.[31]

This cognitive element of the emotion is, then, highly malleable. The rhetoric of "sympathy entrepreneurs" such as politicians and journalists can make a considerable difference to public emotion. Sociologist Michele Landis has argued, for example, that Roosevelt was a brilliant rhetorician of compassion during the New Deal, when he got Americans to think of economic disaster as something that strikes people from outside through no fault of their own, like a flood or a dust storm. Even the term "the Depression" was a masterstroke, with its links to hurricanes ("a tropical depression") and ensuing flash flooding.

We often have compassion for people whose "plights" are in large part of their own creation. A parent, for example, may feel compassion for the mess an adolescent child has gotten into, and yet think that it is the child's own fault. Still, when we have such thoughts, we are, I believe, making a two-stage judgment. In one way, it is the child's own fault; and yet the condition of adolescence, which is not her fault, brings with it a certain blindness and a liability to certain types of error. For these sorts of errors, culpable though in one way they are, we also have compassion; we would not in the same way feel compassion for errors that do not seem to be a part of the predicament of adolescence. Thus, we are likely to feel compassion for a teenager who has been arrested for drunk driving, but not for one who has tortured and killed a dog. The latter does not seem to be a part of any kind of "bad fate," even the bad fate of being sixteen.

Compassion requires, then, a notion of responsibility and blame. It also requires, as we can now see, the belief that there are serious bad things that may happen to people through no fault of their own, or beyond their fault. In having compassion for another, the compassionate person accepts, then, a certain picture of the world, a picture according to which the valuable things are not always safely under a

---

31 See Clark, Chapter 3, describing responses to a questionnaire about several examples of "bad luck," including a sexual assault and a job loss due to alcoholism. For the general evolution of attitudes on women's responsibility for sexual assault, see Schulhofer (1998).

person's own control, but can in some ways be damaged by fortune. As we shall see in Chapter 7, this picture of the world is profoundly controversial. Nobody can deny that the usual occasions for compassion occur: that children die, that cities are defeated, that political freedoms are lost, that age and disease disrupt functioning. But how important, really, *are* these things? To what extent are important human goals really at the mercy of fortune?

Let us now turn to the third requirement of compassion, as Aristotle and the poetic tradition understand it. (My account will depart from Aristotle at this point.) This is a judgment of *similar possibilities*: compassion concerns those misfortunes "which the person himself might expect to suffer, either himself or one of his loved ones" (1385b14–15). Thus, Aristotle adds, it will be felt only by those with some experience and understanding of suffering (1385b24 ff.); and one will not have compassion if one thinks that one is above suffering and has everything (1385b21–22, b31). This fact is repeatedly stressed in poetic appeals to compassion: thus Philoctetes reminds his visitors that they, too, may encounter uncontrollable pain. To Achilles, who is slow to identify his lot with that of ordinary mortals, Homer's Priam points out the vulnerability he shares with them through the old age of a beloved father (*Iliad* 24). In the *Odyssey,* Antinoos' belief in his own immunity from reversal (the state of mind that Aristotle perceptively calls a "hubristic disposition") apparently suffices for his refusal of compassion to Odysseus, disguised as a beggar.

This element in compassion is the focus of the marvelous discussion of that emotion in Rousseau's *Émile.* Drawing his account from the classical tradition, Rousseau takes as his epigraph Dido's statement from the *Aeneid*, "Not inexperienced in suffering, I learn how to bring aid to the wretched." He argues, agreeing with Aristotle, that an awareness of one's own weakness and vulnerability is a necessary condition for *pitié*; without this, we will have an arrogant harshness:

Why are kings without pity for their subjects? Because they count on never being human beings. Why are the rich so hard toward the poor? It is because they have no fear of being poor. Why does a noble have such contempt for a peasant? It is because he never will be a peasant . . . Each may be tomorrow what the one whom he helps is today . . . Do not, therefore, accustom your pupil to regard the sufferings of the unfortunate and the labors of the poor from the height of his glory; and do not hope to teach him to pity them if he considers them alien to him. Make him understand well that the fate of these unhappy people can be his, that all their ills are there in the ground beneath his feet, that countless unforeseen and inevitable events can plunge him into them from one moment to the next. Teach him to count on neither birth nor health nor riches. Show him all the vicissitudes of fortune.[32]

Both Rousseau and Aristotle insist, then, that compassion requires acknowledgment that one has possibilities and vulnerabilities similar to those of the sufferer. One makes sense of the suffering by recognizing that one might oneself encounter such a reversal; one estimates its meaning in part by thinking what it would mean to encounter that oneself; and one sees oneself, in the process, as one to whom such things might in fact happen. This is why compassion is so closely linked to fear, both in the poetic tradition and in Aristotle's account.[33]

As I observed earlier, this judgment of similar possibility requires a demarcation: which creatures am I to count as sharing possibilities with me, and which not? If it really is true that I will have compassion only to the extent that I see the possibilities of others as similar, this means that the emotion will depend on my ability to see similarities between myself and others. Aristotle insists that the similarity should be not to my own possibilities alone, but to those of my loved ones as well – a plausible addition, given that this is a prominent way in which we make sense to ourselves of disasters befalling people of different age, for example, or different gender.

Here we arrive at another place where social and familial teachings play a powerful role, and errors may easily occur. The beings who are likely to be seen as similar to myself or to my loved ones will probably be those who share a way of life, those whom society has marked as similar. Rousseau argues that acquaintance with the usual vicissitudes of fortune will make it impossible for Émile (who does not inhabit a diseased society) to exclude the poor, or members of the lower classes, since he will know that people lose money and status all the time, and their political entitlements. But he also tells us that in his own society many people sever themselves in thought from the possibilities of the lower classes: nobles and kings therefore lack compassion for those

---

32 Rousseau (1979), p. 224; I have altered Bloom's translation in several places, in partic-ular substituting "human being" for "man." I have retained "pity" for *pitié*.
33 See *Rhetoric* 1386a22–8, 82b26–7; *Poetics* 1453a5–6; for discussion, see Halliwell (1986) and Nussbaum (1992), pp. 274–5.

beneath them. In a similar way, in our own society, juries often have a hard time sympathizing with the life story of a criminal defendant who is very different from them in class and background; they have even more difficulty if they are provided, at the same time, with a "victim impact" statement from people who are more similar to them.[34] All kinds of social barriers – of class, religion, ethnicity, gender, sexual orientation – prove recalcitrant to the imagination, and this recalcitrance impedes emotion.

Finally, the species boundary usually proves difficult to cross in emotion, since the possibilities of another creature for good or ill are opaque to us. Spinoza takes this difference in emotional nature to justify indifference to the suffering of animals.[35] Most major theorists of compassion also draw the species boundary firmly, focusing on human ills alone. Rousseau, by contrast to many, feels that Émile will naturally judge the lot of small animals as similar to his own, and will learn compassion best if he begins by focusing on their sufferings.

Why are similar possibilities important? Is the judgment of similarity on a par with the judgments of seriousness and of fault – that is to say, is it a necessary constituent part of the emotion, a part of its very definition? Or is it only a helpful epistemological device, a way of getting clear about the significance of the suffering for the life of the person who has it? The point made by Aristotle and Rousseau seems to be that the pain of another will be an object of my concern, a part of my sense of my own well-being, only if I acknowledge some sort of community between myself and the other, understanding what it might be for me to face such pain. Without that sense of commonness, both Aristotle and Rousseau claim, I will react with sublime indifference or mere intellectual curiosity, like an obtuse alien from another world; and I will not care what I do to augment or relieve the suffering. Spinoza supports this, when he links his denial that humans and animals have a "similar nature" with the judgment that it is all right to cause animals pain. What should we make of this claim?

34 See Bandes (1997), discussed further in Chapter 8.
35 Spinoza, *Ethics*, Part IV, Proposition 37, Scholium I: "I do not deny that beasts feel; I am denying that we are on that account debarred from paying heed to our own advantage and from making use of them as we please and dealing with them as best suits us, seeing that they do not agree with us in nature and their emotions are different in nature from human emotions."

One can see that a certain sort of stranger cannot help being indifferent and unconcerned: for if he or she has no experiential sense of the importance of these matters, it will be hard even to grasp that suffering *is* suffering, and hard not to be clumsy or callous in dealing with it in consequence. But need this be so? Is this just a point about the limitations of understanding? Could we imagine a divine or perfect being feeling compassion for the sufferings of mortals without an awareness of sharing the same possibilities and vulnerabilities? Frequently, in the classical tradition, the gods are depicted as obtuse and lacking in compassion; this lack is connected to their lack of vulnerability. To a being who cannot feel more than temporary or trivial discomfort, the appalling suffering of a Heracles will be hard to see correctly.[36] But gods (and godlike humans) sometimes do have compassion: Zeus weeps for the death of Sarpedon; the Christian god feels ceaseless compassion for the errors and sufferings of mortals; the Buddhist who has successfully escaped from personal vulnerability and pain experiences compassion for the sufferings of those still fettered. Such cases are tricky to estimate: for usually in one or another way they do after all fulfill Aristotle's requirement that the person acknowledge similar vulnerability, "either himself or one of his loved ones." In pitying Sarpedon, Zeus pities his own son, for whom he also grieves; this personal vulnerability gives him a basis for more general pity of those dead in the war. The Christian god is vulnerable in a similar way, suffering agony and death both in his own person and in the person of his son. The boddhisatva has experienced the ills that he pities, even if by now he no longer expects to do so. Furthermore, the attachment to the concerns of the suffering person is itself a form of vulnerability: so a god, in allowing himself to be so attached, renders himself to a degree needy and non-self-sufficient, and thus similar to mortals. Religious conceptions such as those of Epicureanism, Stoicism, and Platonism, which imagine the godlike condition as strictly self-sufficient, also deny compassion to the godlike.

Must this be? What is really at issue here, it would seem, is the eudaimonistic character of the emotions, as I have defined them. I have argued that in order for grief to be present, the dead person must be seen, and valued, as an important part of the mourner's own life, her

36 See Nussbaum (1992), Winnington-Ingram (1980).

scheme of goals and projects. Similarly, in order for compassion to be present, the person must consider the suffering of another as a significant part of his or her own scheme of goals and ends. She must take that person's ill as affecting her own flourishing. In effect, she must make herself vulnerable in the person of another. It is that *eudaimonistic judgment*, not the judgment of similar possibilities, that seems to be a necessary constituent of compassion. For that judgment to occur, it is not strictly necessary that she focus on the other person's relation to herself. A truly omniscient deity ought to know the significance of human suffering without thinking of its own risks or bad prospects, and a truly loving deity will be intensely concerned for the ills befalling mortals without having to think of more personal loss or risk. (For such a deity, all humans are already children or loved ones, part of its scheme of goals and ends.) But human beings have difficulty attaching others to themselves except through thoughts about what is already of concern to them. Imagining one's own similar possibilities aids the extension of one's own eudaimonistic imagination.

The recognition of one's own related vulnerability is, then, an important and frequently an indispensable epistemological requirement for compassion in human beings – the thing that makes the difference between viewing hungry peasants as beings whose sufferings matter and viewing them as distant objects whose experiences have nothing to do with one's own life. Such a judgment is psychologically powerful in moving other people into one's own circle of concern. Even when we feel compassion for animals, whom we know to be very different from ourselves, it is on the basis of our common vulnerability to pain, hunger, and other types of suffering that we feel the emotion. Even when we feel compassion for precisely those aspects of an animal's suffering that are unlike our own – for example, their lack of legal rights, their lack of power to shape the laws that affect their lives, or (in some cases) their lack of understanding of what is happening to them – it is most often on the basis of a sense of shared vulnerability to pain that we extend our sympathy. We think, how horrible it would be to suffer pain in that way, and without hope of changing it.

This fact explains why so frequently those who wish to withhold compassion and to teach others to do so portray the sufferers as altogether dissimilar in kind and in possibility. In *The Destruction of the European Jews*, Raoul Hilberg shows how pervasively Nazi talk of

Jews, in connection with their murder, portrayed them as nonhuman: either as beings of a remote animal kind, such as insects or vermin, or as inanimate objects, "cargo" to be transported. (Later we shall see how disgust aids that project, bounding off the sufferers from their tormentors.) When by surprise an individual sufferer was encountered in a manner that made similarity unavoidably clear, one frequently saw what philosopher Jonathan Glover, reflecting on a wide range of cases of genocide and evil, calls a "breakthrough," in which the seriousness of the suffering was acknowledged and pity led to shame and confusion.[37] Sometimes the catalyst of a breakthrough is simple physical proximity. Sometimes it is the the reminder of a similar type of family life.[38] Sometimes it may even be sexual desire. A remarkable moment of that kind is shown in the film *Schindler's List*, when the Nazi camp commandant confronts the beautiful Jewish housemaid. As she stands in her basement room trembling in her slip, he graps her chin, stares violently into her eyes, and asks, in some strange agony of conscience, "Is this the face of a rat?"[39]

In short, the judgment of similar possibility is part of a construct that bridges the gap between the child's existing goals and the eudaimonistic judgment that others (even distant others) are an important part of one's own scheme of goals and projects, important as ends in their own right. Equipped with her general conception of human flourishing, the spectator looks at a world in which people suffer hunger, disability, disease, slavery, through no fault of their own. She believes that goods such as food, health, citizenship, freedom, do matter. And yet she acknowledges, as well, that it is uncertain whether she herself will remain among the safe and privileged ones to whom such goods are stably guaranteed. She acknowledges that the lot of the beggar might be (or become) her own. This leads her to turn her thoughts

---

37 See Hilberg (1985); Glover (1999), pp. 81, 345–8.
38 Glover (1999), p. 346: Rudolf Höss records how the sight of women and children caused men working in the crematoria to think of their own families. Christopher Browning (1992), p. 113, describes a man who refused to take part in the shooting of Jews " '[b]ecause there were children among the Jews we had brought and at the time I myself was a father with a family of three children.' "
39 Rousseau insists that Émile is ready to learn compassion only when budding sexual desire has already turned his thoughts outward toward others. He appears to be wrong about the development of compassion; and desire may lead to objectification as well as to the humanization of the object. Nonetheless, a humanizing effect is also possible.

outward, asking about society's general arrangement for the allocation of goods and resources. Given the uncertainty of life,[40] she will be inclined, other things being equal, to want a society in which the lot of the worst off – of the poor, of people defeated in war, of women, of servants – is as good as it can be. Self-interest itself, via thought about shared vulnerabilities, promotes the selection of principles that raise society's floor.

It is through this set of ideas that compassion is standardly connected, in the tradition, to generous giving. Once again, generous giving could take place without the prudential thoughts of similarity, if the person already cared intensely about the good of the recipients. But the prudential thoughts do frequently assist in this process, as we shall see shortly (section IV).

Compassion, then, has three cognitive elements: the judgment of *size* (a serious bad event has befallen someone); the judgment of *nondesert* (this person did not bring the suffering on himself or herself); and the *eudaimonistic judgment* (this person, or creature, is a significant element in my scheme of goals and projects, an end whose good is to be promoted). The Aristotelian *judgment of similar possibilities* is an epistemological aid to forming the *eudaimonistic judgment* – not necessary, but usually very important.

Finally, let us recall that, like all emotions directed at living beings, compassion frequently either contains or is closely linked to a non-eudaimonistic element of *wonder* (see Chapter 1, section V). In viewing Philoctetes with compassion, as worthy of concern and help, I also consider him as a human being, and I see that humanity itself with an emotion that is likely to be, at least in part, non-eudaimonistic; but the non-eudaimonistic element of wonder strongly reinforces or motivates my eudaimonistic concern. Similarly, when I see with compassion the beating of an animal, a wonder at the complex living thing itself is

---

40 Rousseau remarks that the emotion develops most easily where people live highly unstable political lives: thus the Turks, he alleges, are "more humane and more hospitable" than Europeans, because their "totally arbitrary government . . . renders the greatness and the fortune of individuals always precarious and unsteady" (1979, p. 224). One would not wish to draw normative political conclusions from this dubious observation. I have already argued that the perceptions of people who are inured to suffering and ill-treatment are very likely to be deformed by that experience – as Rousseau himself later argues. Maximizing the awareness of risk and vulnerability is not a morally valuable strategy – see Chapters 7 and 8.

likely to be mixed with my compassion, and to support it. (Thus we rarely have compassion for the deaths of creatures, such as mosquitos and slugs, toward whom we do not have wonder.) Wonder's role varies in different cases of compassion, and it is always hard to say whether we ought to see it as a part of the emotion itself, or as a different emotion closely associated with it. (I am inclined to the latter view.) But I think that wonder does often play a very important role in marking the world for our concern, and thence in directing our attention to the sufferings of its members. It shapes, in that way, our conception of *eudaimonia*.

What is the relationship of the cognitive elements to the emotion itself? It is natural to ask at this point whether one could not have all of the judgments without having the painful emotion. One might grant the necessity of these judgments without granting that they are sufficient for having the full emotion[41] – still less, that the emotion itself is a certain sort of acknowledgment of their truth. I see a stranger in the street. Someone tells me that this woman has just learned of the death of her only child, who was run over by a drunken driver. I have no reason not to believe what I have been told. So: I believe that this woman has suffered an extremely terrible loss, through no fault of her own. I know well that I myself might suffer a similar loss. Now I might at this point feel compassion for the woman; but then again, I might not. As Adam Smith says, giving a similar example, the fact that she is a stranger might make it difficult for me to picture her suffering; or I might simply be too busy and distracted to focus on what I have been told.[42] Doesn't this show that I can, after all, have all of the judgments without the emotion?

Notice, however, that the person does not in fact have all of the cognitive elements of compassion, as I have defined it: for she lacks the *eudaimonistic judgment*. She does not see the woman as an important part of her own scheme of goals and projects. Often the judgment of similar possibilities will suffice to value the person as a

---

41 As in Chapter 1, at this point in the argument sufficiency may be imagined either causally – these judgments produce whatever other constituents are also necessary for compassion – or by saying that these judgments are the only constituents there are. In both cases, however, we are considering the judgments as among the constituents of the emotion, each necessary to its being the emotion it is. I shall go on to argue that there are no further constituents that we should recognize as necessary in compassion.

42 Smith (1976), pp. 17–18.

part of one's circle of concern; but in this case that common psychological connection has not been made, probably because the person is a stranger; or the person might be distanced from the self in some other way. Furthermore, in this case it is not entirely clear that she even thinks the suffering a serious bad thing; she may know that for the woman it is bad, but it is not clear that she has affirmed its serious badness from her own viewpoint. A sadistic torturer knows that his victim's suffering is bad from the victim's point of view, but from his own point of view it is a good thing. In our example, the woman's suffering is probably not seen as either good or bad – because the eudaimonistic judgment is lacking. Here we see how closely the judgment of size and the eudaimonistic judgment are related. If the judgment of size relies on the onlooker's point of view, it will fail if the onlooker is just not very concerned with the fate of the suffering person one way or another.

Another way in which compassion may fail is connected with immaturity: one may have the judgments on authority, and yet not understand their true significance. Rousseau describes an Émile who has suffered himself, and who has it on good authority that others suffer too. He sees gestures indicative of suffering, and his teacher assures him that they mean in the case of others what they would in his own. But, Rousseau claims, he does not really believe or judge that this is so, until he has become able to imagine their suffering vividly to himself – at which point he will also suffer the pain of *pitié*. "To see it without feeling it," he writes, "is not to know it."[43] By this he means something very precise: that the suffering of others has not become a part of Émile's cognitive repertory in such a way that it will influence his conduct, provide him with motives and expectations, and so forth. He is merely paying it lip service, until he can perform the thought experiment that is, in Rousseau's view, sufficient for being disturbed.

To cast doubt on my claim that the three cognitive requirements are sufficient for the emotion, we need, then, a different kind of example, one where it is clear that the judgment of size is not just parroted but comprehended, and where it is clear that the eudaimonistic judgment has been made. So let us imagine that my own child, an important part

43 Rousseau (1979), p. 222.

of my scheme of goals and ends, has just suffered a serious loss. I know that it is serious, and I know that it was not her fault. Is it possible for me to have all these judgments and yet to fail to have compassion for her plight? Only, I would say, in a case similar to my case of delayed mourning in Chapter 1, where I simply haven't yet taken in what has happened. I may be able to say the words, but their significance has not sunk in. This means, however, that the belief itself has not become a part of my cognitive repertory, in such a way that it will affect the pattern of my other beliefs and my actions. In other words, the example does not show that some noncognitive element, such as an ache or a pain, is required in addition to the three judgments.

But what about the case of an omniscient and invulnerable god – or even a boddhisatva, who has succeeded in severing himself from personal vulnerability to pain? Couldn't such a being have all the judgments involved in compassion without having the upheaval of the painful emotion itself? What this question reveals is that I have arrived at my result only because I have not seen compassion as strictly entailing a judgment of similar possibilities. For Aristotle, such beings would not have compassion; according to my account they do. In my account, unlike his, compassion does not entail personal vulnerability, although the recognition of personal vulnerability is extremely important, psychologically, in getting imperfect humans to have compassion for another person's plight. This means, too, that compassion is not linked to personal fear in my account, as it is in Aristotle's: one may have compassion for another without having anything at all to fear for oneself – although, again, in imperfect humans this link will usually prove psychologically valuable, in promoting concern.

One might then object that what the nonfearful and nonvulnerable person has is not the painful emotion itself, but just some distanced version of it, and that my three judgments are sufficient for, and constitute, that distanced attitude – let us call it humane concern. They are not, perhaps, sufficient for the upheaval of compassion itself. Now there may be some cases where we do want to say that a self-sufficient being has humane concern and not compassion: the Stoic sage is like this, and perhaps, in some interpretations, the boddhisatva as well. But the sage really does not share my three judgments, because he denies that the vicissitudes of fortune have "size." Marcus Aurelius gives us a good image: we are to think of the sufferings of others as like the sufferings of a child who has lost a toy – they are real enough, and worthy of our concern, but only in the way that we'd console a child, not because we ourselves think that the loss of a toy is really a large matter. If, instead, we imagine a self-sufficient being who really does care deeply about the vicissitudes of fortune, and who really does think that they are a big thing – the Christian and Jewish images of God, for example – then I think we do want to say that the three judgments are sufficient – not merely for humane concern, but for the upheaval of the emotion itself. Such a being, though not vulnerable to upset personally, has become vulnerable to upset in the person of another. That is how such a being differs from the Stoic sage.

If the cognitive elements are both sufficient for compassion and constituent parts of it, we still need to ask, as always, whether there are other necessary elements as well. Here again, the response will have to be, what might those other elements be? I shall assume that in Chapter 1 we have ruled out the possibility of a general type/type correlation between a given emotion and a specific physiological state, and that we have also cast a great deal of doubt on the claim that feelings of a determinate kind always arise in the case of any given emotion, as constituent parts of it. But that possibility needs to be considered here once again, in the following way. Aristotle mentions pain in his definition: compassion is a particular type of pain. And it seems natural to describe the experience this way. Indeed, the pain seems crucial to compassion's motivational role. But what is this pain? Is it something over and above the thought that something very bad is happening and that it matters for one's scheme of goals and projects? On the one hand, we are strongly inclined to say yes, it is something more. It is a disturbance, a tug at the heartstrings. But that doesn't quite solve our problem, because we know by now that thoughts are some of the most disturbing things there are.

First of all, we must ask whether the pain is being imagined as just a fluttering or a spasm, only contingently or causally linked to the thoughts, or whether it is itself so closely linked to the thoughts that we might call it the affective dimension of the thought, a pain "at the thought of" the bad thing, as Aristotle puts it. If it is the former, a knot in the stomach or a lump in the throat, then, here as elsewhere, it seems implausible to require that any particular such pain be present in order to ascribe compassion to someone. People are extremely variable in the modes in which they experience their emotions physically, and even phenomenologically. Even if every compassionate person has *some* pain or other, it would surely be arbitrary and wrong to require any particular type of such pain. And the possibility of nonconscious compassion makes us still more skeptical: for surely it is possible to have compassion and not be aware of it – if one is not reflecting on one's own emotions, or if one has been led to suppose that real men don't have such soft sentiments. Then one could well have and be motivated by the thoughts, without being in any noticeable phenomenological state.

If, however, by "pain" we mean something more organic to the thoughts, that is, if the very character of this pain cannot be described without ascribing to it the intentionality embodied in the thought, then it is not clear after all that it is a separate element. At the very least it looks as if a pain of that sort – Aristotle's "pain at" the thought of someone's suffering – is reliably caused by the thought, and does not have much, if any, causal independence. Once we begin to think harder about how to define such a pain, moreover, it appears that it does not have much conceptual independence either: not any old throbbing or tugging will do, but only the sort that is "about" or "at" the misfortune. It is mental pain directed toward the victim that we want, not some obtuse physical spasm; but what is this mental pain, if not a way of seeing the victim's distress with concern, as a terrible thing? Perhaps we could call it the affective character of the thoughts: but the notion of "affect" is notoriously slippery and vague, and it is unclear whether we have really succeeded in defining a truly separate element.[44] In short: if we do discover a separate element in the notion of pain, to the extent that it is separate from the cognitive material it also seems to be too various to be a necessary element in the definition. To the extent that it is closely tied to, or even an element in, the cognitive material, we probably haven't succeeded in introducing a separate element. Certainly, when we are trying to ascertain whether Émile has learned compassion or not, we are satisfied by the evidence of a certain sort of imagination and thought, a certain way of viewing the distress of others. We don't inquire whether in addition he has a throbbing or an

---

44 See my remarks on Stocker (1996) in Chapter 1, note 62.

aching. This suggests that we really do not think that pain in that sense is a further necessary element.

III. EMPATHY AND COMPASSION

I have said that compassion is distinct from empathy, which involves an imaginative reconstruction of the experience of the sufferer. Now we must investigate the connection. First of all, how does empathy itself operate? This has occasioned a good deal of debate in the philosophical tradition. Does one actually think, for the time being, that one *is* oneself the sufferer, putting oneself in his or her own place? [45] Does one imagine one's own responses as *fused* in some mysterious way with those of the sufferer? [46]

Such cases might possibly occur. More often, however, empathy is like the mental preparation of a skilled (Method) actor: it involves a participatory enactment of the situation of the sufferer, but is always combined with the awareness that one is not oneself the sufferer. This awareness of one's separate life is quite important if empathy is to be closely related to compassion: for if it is to be for *another*, and not for oneself, that one feels compassion, one must be aware both of the bad lot of the sufferer and of the fact that it is, right now, not one's own. If one really had the experience of feeling the pain in one's own body,

45 This view is endorsed by Smith (1976) early in his account: "By the imagination we place ourselves in his situation, we conceive ourselves enduring all the same torments, we enter as it were into his body, and become in some measure the same person with him, and thence form some idea of his sensations . . ." (p. 9). This is inconsistent with his observation about the case of the brain damaged person, and is corrected by his later observation that the relevant viewpoint is that of the judicious spectator, not that of the sufferer, which may be ill-informed.

46 This seems to be the view of Schopenhauer, *Preisschrift über das Fundament der Moral* (trans. Payne, 1995), p. 143 (my translation here): Compassion requires "that in *his* pain as such I directly feel, with suffering, *his* pain as I otherwise feel only my own, and on that account want his good directly, as I otherwise want only my own. This, however, requires that in a certain manner I should be *identified* with him, that is to say, that the entire *distinction* between me and that other person, which is the basis for my egoism, should be, at least to a certain extent, removed." On the other hand, Schopenhauer also distinguishes the identification involved in compassion from a pathological kind that "arises from an instantaneous deception of the imagination [whereby] we put ourselves in the position of the sufferer, and have the idea that we are suffering *his* pains in our person." Thus the type of fusion he has in mind remains somewhat unclear.

then one would precisely have failed to comprehend the pain of another *as other*.[47] One must also be aware of one's own *qualitative difference* from the sufferer: aware, for example, that the person with a lip injury is a bassoon player, as one is not oneself; that this Philoctetes has no children, as one does oneself. For these recognitions are crucial to getting the right estimation of the meaning of the suffering for the suffering person. What is wanted, it seems, is a kind of "twofold attention,"[48] in which one both imagines what it is like to be in the sufferer's place and, at the same time, retains securely the awareness that one is not in that place. It is this sort of twofold attention that is most commonly described as "empathy" in the psychological and psychoanalytic literature, in discussing both the analyst's empathy with the patient and the patient's own capacity for empathy. Obviously enough, if the analyst thought she was the patient, or that she was fused with the patient, this would be not empathy but a dangerous delusional response; the same is true of a lover's empathy for her partner, or a parent's empathy for her child.

This account of empathy makes it clear that empathy may be inaccurate.[49] As Proust says, a real person poses "a dead weight that our sensitivity cannot remove" (I.91, my translation). Only in fiction is the mind of another transparent. The empathetic person attempts to reconstruct the mental experience of another, and if she does this too crudely she will probably not get credit for empathy at all, just as a person who cannot move her feet in a one-two-three rhythm will not get credit for waltzing. But even a generally capable imagination may get things wrong – perhaps by projecting itself too insistently into the other person's mind, perhaps through sheer ignorance.

How is empathy, so construed, related to compassion? Clearly, it is not sufficient for compassion. First of all, one may have empathy with joyful or placid experiences, and compassion, as I have defined it, requires its object to be (thought to be) in a bad state. But even where

---

47 See Cavell (1969), "Knowing and Acknowledging." An excellent account of this element of empathy is given by John Deigh in his article "Empathy and Universalizability," in Deigh (1996), pp. 175–6; Deigh contrasts empathy with a type of emotional identification that is associated with the loss of a sense of oneself as a distinct person.

48 This term is introduced by Richard Wollheim (1980, 1987) to describe the way in which the spectator of an artwork is simultaneously aware of the represented object and of the fact of representation

49 See Kohut (1981b).

bad events are present, empathy does not suffice for compassion. Actors may have great empathy with characters in various types of bad predicaments, without having any particular emotion toward them. They may consider their characters to be wicked, and undeserving of compassion; or they may just think, this is a fictional character and it doesn't make sense to have any emotion at all toward her. In ordinary life, too, people may have considerable empathetic understanding of someone for whose suffering they refuse compassion. Seneca can empathize with Q, understanding well what makes Q shed such bitter tears, and reconstructing that suffering in his imagination – after all, these are the emotions of his own former life – without having any tendency to have compassion for Q: his Stoic judgments about seriousness preclude that emotion.

In quite a different way, one may judge that the suffering is serious without considering it to be a *serious bad thing*: thus a torturer may be acutely aware of the suffering of the victim, and able to enjoy the imagining of it, all without the slightest compassion, for he regards the pain of the sufferer as a great good for him, and he believes that his purposes matter and that those of the victim do not.[50] More generally, enemies often become adept at reading the purposes of their foes and manipulating them for their own ends: once again, this empathy is used egoistically, denying real importance to the other person's goals. In a different way, a child may have a limited empathy for a parent's suffering without yet believing that the parent is a separate person whose purposes matter; thus the gap between empathy and compassion may result from infantile narcissism.[51]

One may, again, empathize with someone to whom one refuses compassion on grounds of fault: as a juror, for example, I may come to understand the experience of a criminal without having compassion for the person's plight, if I believe him both responsible and guilty.

And of course one may fail to have compassion because one withholds the eudaimonistic judgment: one does not view the person as an

---

50 See Kohut (1981b), p. 540: "I did not write about empathy as associated with any specific emotion such as, in particular, compassion or affection. It may be motivated by and used in the service of hostile-destructive aims." See also Deigh (1996), pp. 174–7.

51 See Deigh (1996), p. 177, insisting on the importance of a developmental conception of empathy.

important part of one's scheme of goals and ends. A different type of empathetic torturer, for example, may comprehend the victim's suffering without thinking it especially important, for bad or for good. More commonly, we may briefly participate in the experience of another person whom we have met or whose life story we read, without sufficient concern or regard to generate compassionate emotion. The type of empathy prompted by people telling their life stories on daytime TV, for example, rarely leads to genuine compassion: it is too fleeting, too much prompted by curiosity and sensationalism, to engender real concern for the person involved.

If empathy is not sufficient for compassion, is it even necessary? Some philosophers have claimed that it is. [52] But this assertion seems dogmatic. We often have compassion for creatures whose experience we know we can never share: most compassion with animals has this feature.[53] And compassion for human beings from very different national or racial backgrounds frequently has this feature as well: one is aware that the other person's experience is remote, and that one can hardly begin to reconstruct it. Richard Wright wrote that in creating Bigger Thomas he had deliberately set out to repel the reader's empathy: he is a dark and alarming character, and we never feel confident that we have reconstructed his experience in our minds – although we may still have compassion for his plight. Furthermore, we may not need empathy if we have some other good source of understanding: for example, we may have it on good authority that the person's suffering is serious, and be moved accordingly, even without having a lively imagination.[54] Similarly, images of a compassionate god need not endow that god with empathy (or even imagination), since divine omniscience might offer other routes to knowledge of the sufferer's predicament.

And yet there is something correct in the contention that empathy is psychologically important as a guide. Usually, without it, we are likely to remain obtuse and unresponsive, not even knowing how to make sense of the predicament we see. It is a very important tool in the service of getting a sense of what is going on with the other person,

---

52 See Blum (1980), who subsequently changed his mind about this; and Piper (1991).
53 See Snow (1991, 1992).
54 Here one might think of Bob and Fanny Assingham in James's *The Golden Bowl*: he has no imagination, but he can "get the tip" from her, and be moved accordingly.

and also of establishing concern and connection. So it underwrites (if in a non-necessary way) both the judgment of size and the eudaimonistic judgment. Sometimes it does so simply by drawing my attention vividly to the other person's predicament and its size: I have concern for her simply because my attention has now been directed to her, when previously it was not. At other times, it probably operates to produce concern by inviting the judgment of similar possibilities – which, as I have said, is often connected to the formation of the eudaimonistic judgment. By reconstructing in my own mind the experience of another, I get a sense of what it means for her to suffer that way, and this may make me more likely to see her prospects as similar to my own, and of concern in part for that reason.

Evidence of a connection between empathy and compassionate emotion is significant, in both the psychoanalytic and the experimental literature. Heinz Kohut, the leading theorist of empathy within psychoanalysis, resists the attempts of some followers to inflate its role: he insists that empathy is limited, fallible, and value-neutral. Moreover, he stresses that for the infant it is not the mother's empathy that is important, but her helping actions. Nonetheless, he stresses (on the basis of his extensive clinical experience) that empathy (when reasonably well done) is a valuable guide to accurate responding, an "informer of appropriate action" – appropriate not in the ethical sense, but just in the sense of conforming to the person's aims, whether these are beneficent or malevolent.[55]

C. Daniel Batson, whose experimental work shows a strong link between compassion and helping behavior (see section IV), also gives empathy a significant role in producing compassion.[56] Batson's experiments typically involve two groups of subjects, both of which hear a narrative of a person in distress. One group is discouraged from having compassion, by instructions asking them to attend closely to the tech-

55 See Kohut (1981b), p. 543.
56 Batson (1991). A note on terms: Batson uses "empathy" in a way that is equivalent to my use of "compassion" – as he himself announces on pp. 86–7, saying that he means to describe what the tradition has called "sympathy" or "compassion," but prefers the term "empathy" as less "moralistic" than "compassion" and less confusing than "sympathy," which may be linked with thoughts of emotional contagion, which is not what he means to describe. When he wants to describe what I call "empathy," he uses terms such as "perspective-taking," or says that the subjects were instructed to assume the perspective of the person whose story they were about to hear.

nical aspects of the broadcast. The other group is urged to imagine the experiences and feelings of the person in the story: this is viewed as a device for encouraging compassion. An alternative device in some experiments, interestingly enough, is to make subjects aware that they are very similar to the person in the story: for example, that they have written similar things about their hopes and fears for themselves on a questionnaire. What Batson typically finds is that both the judgment of similar possibilities and the exercise of empathy produce self-reports of compassionate emotion. This is not what he was testing: he was looking for the relationship between compassion and helping. But there is sufficient material in the experimental reports to see that there is also a strong relationship between empathy (or, alternatively, the judgment of similar possibilities) and compassionate emotion. If empathy is not clearly necessary for compassion, it is a prominent route to it.

Batson told subjects stories about people who were very similar to themselves – usually other undergraduates at the University of Kansas.[57] Is it plausible to think that empathy would play an important role in compassion where the object of compassion is very different from oneself, and difficult to understand? We can pursue this question by thinking, again, of my two apparent counterexamples. Even though Bigger Thomas is constructed in order to repel a facile empathy, ultimately the novel does offer its white reader at least a limited empathy with Thomas, far more empathy than this same reader would be likely to achieve were she to run into Thomas on the streets of Hyde Park in Chicago, where the novel is set. And this empathy is relevant to the emotions she will feel at his predicament: seeing how his shame and rage are the products of forces beyond his control informs her judgment of fault. It would be officious to claim that we have a perfect empathetic understanding of people whose lives are very different from our own – or, for that matter, even of those who are close to us, such as our own parents, or our children. But without an attempt at empathy we would surely be less likely to have appropriate compassion, or to take any actions that might be associated with this emotion.

57 Even when he wanted to get students to think of someone very different from themselves – in order to refute the claim that mental merging was taking place – the most different he was willing to get was an undergraduate at a rival campus of the state university, Kansas State University! (See Batson et. al. [1997].)

As for the claim that we have compassion for members of other species despite our awareness that we entirely lack empathy with them, that, again, is less clear than it at first appears. The genesis of the movement for the humane treatment of animals in Great Britain relied heavily on narratives that offered at least a limited empathy with the predicaments of animals cruelly treated: the novel *Black Beauty* is one example of the great importance of empathy for compassion. Obviously that novel anthropomorphizes the horse in many illegitimate ways: so we know that the empathy it offers is flawed. But it is not altogether flawed, especially where it deals with physical pain. It seems clear that we are much more likely to have appropriate compassion for the pain of animals if we are able at least to try hard to reconstruct their experience of the bad things we do to them.

In short, empathy is a mental ability highly relevant to compassion, although it is itself both fallible and morally neutral.

Does empathy contribute anything of ethical importance entirely on its own (when it does not lead to compassion)? I have suggested that it does not: a torturer can use it for hostile and sadistic ends. On the other hand, it does involve a very basic recognition of another world of experience, and to that extent it is not altogether neutral. If I allow my mind to be formed into the shape of your experience, even in a playful way and even without concern for you, I am still in a very basic way acknowledging your reality and humanity (or, in the case of an animal, its capacity for complex experience). The empathetic torturer is still evil. But there is another, deeper type of evil: the utter failure to recognize humanity. As Kohut put it, in a speech given shortly before his death:

Empathy serves also, and this is now the most difficult part – namely, that despite all that I have said, empathy, per se, is a therapeutic action in the broadest sense, a beneficial action in the broadest sense of the word. That seems to contradict everything I have said so far, and I wish I could just simply bypass it. But, since it is true, and I know it is true, and I've evidence for its being true, I must mention it. Namely, that the presence of empathy in the surrounding milieu, whether used for compassionate, well-intentioned therapeutic, and now listen, even for utterly destructive purposes, is still an admixture of something positive. In other words, there is a step beyond an empathy-informed hatred that wants to destroy you, and [this is] an empathyless environment that just brushes you off the face of the earth. The dreadful experiences of prolonged stays in concentration camps during the Nazi era in Germany were just that. It was not cruelty on the whole . . . They totally disregarded the humanity of the victims. They were not human . . . That was the worst.[58]

In short, there is something worse than the empathetic villain. Consider Hannibal Lecter's treatment of Clarice Starling in *The Silence of the Lambs*. Although Lecter's intentions toward Clarice are entirely malign, and although he might easily be imagined eating her, nonetheless, in his very effort to reconstruct the workings of her mind there is a basic human respect. The evil of utter dehumanization seems worse: for Jews, or women, or any other victim to be treated as mere objects whose experience doesn't matter may perhaps involve a more profound evil than for them to be tortured by an empathetic villain who recognizes them as human.

Some human beings deny the recognition of humanity across the board. Such is the case, for example, with the psychopathic killer who is the protagonist of Joyce Carol Oates's novel *Zombie*. Oates shows how the inability to empathize at all with others is closely linked, in the life of this character, to a total lack of awareness that he is doing wrong in killing a human being. In discussing her novel, Oates has said that she set out to show how basic an ingredient of humanity this imaginative ability is.[59] Empathy may not be strictly necessary for recognizing humanity in others: it is at least conceivable that a beneficent god would treat human beings respectfully and well without it. It is at least conceivable that we could recognize distant others as human without it. But typically we will be right to find a person without empathy frightening and psychopathic. We will suspect this person of an incapacity to recognize humanity.

In short, empathy does count for something, standing between us and a type of especially terrible evil – at least with regard to those for whom we have it. The habits of mind involved in this exercise of imagination make it difficult to turn around and deny humanity to the very people with whose experiences one has been encouraged to have empathy. Thus the Nazis, as we have noted, went to great lengths (as

58 Kohut (1981a), p. 530.
59 Personal communication, Joyce Carol Oates, 1997.

did German culture more generally) to portray Jews as a separate kind, similar to vermin or even inanimate objects. This device obstructed the judgment of similar possibilities, as I have argued, obstructing compassion by that route. But it obstructed compassion by another route as well, by blocking empathy. When, unexpectedly, empathy did arrive on the scene – whether through desire or through some personal experience that tapped its roots – the result was a breakdown in the mental mechanism that sustained moral denial. Thus many Germans constructed for themselves, in effect, a double life.[60] Brought up to have empathy for those they recognized as human, they led lives of cultivated imagination with those people; toward those whom they killed and tortured, they denied the very recognition of humanity.

IV. COMPASSION AND ALTRUISM

Compassion is frequently linked to beneficent action. Given my analysis, it is easy to see how this link might be thought to occur. If one believes that the misfortunes of others are serious, and that they have not brought misfortune on themselves, and, in addition, that they are themselves important parts of one's own scheme of ends and goals, then the conjunction of these beliefs is very likely to lead to action addressing the suffering. It may not do so, if there is no available course of action that suggests itself. But if there is, it will be difficult to believe that the compassionate person really does have all three judgments, if she does not do something to address the victims' vulnerability.

Is the helping prompted by compassion really altruistic? Given the fact that compassion is frequently accompanied by the judgment of similar possibilities, isn't it a kind of self-interested reasoning after all? I give to Mary because I expect that I may be in need some day, and I want other people to give to me. On my account, however, a compassionate person does not help a beggar simply because he or she does literally think that he may shortly be in a similar position. Entertaining that thought, feeling one's own vulnerability, is an important route to the emotion for many people; but the emotion itself acknowledges the pain of another separate person as a bad thing, because of what it is doing to that other life. The compassionate person remains fully aware

60 See Lifton (1986), Chapter 19.

of the distinction between her own life and that of the sufferer, and seeks the good of the sufferer as a separate person, whom she has made a part of her own scheme of goals and ends. (Even children are perfectly aware that giving food to a beggar would not improve one's own lot were one to become a beggar oneself – unless the practice were made a general law.)

It is tempting to say at this point that this account is unilluminating, because all it says is that if one is concerned for others one will be motivated to do things that show concern. We haven't really seen any extra element supplied by emotion itself: it's the eudaimonistic judgment that is doing the work. What's the point of the emotion, when all we need is that judgment? This objection crumbles on closer inspection. First of all, the objector must grant that we need not only the eudaimonistic judgment, but also the other two judgments, if the motivations to help are to follow. I may have all the concern in the world for my child, but I won't be motivated to bail her out if I think her plight is trivial, and I probably won't be so motivated if I think that she brought it on herself – unless I think that she is too young or weak to be held fully responsible for her actions, or unless I see her foolishness as part of a developmental stage that all children inevitably go through. So what we are saying is, why do we need compassion, when we can just rely on the three judgments? But I have argued that the three judgments are sufficient for compassion – so the objector is really saying, why do we need compassion when we can just rely on compassion? If the objector replies that compassion is not just these judgments but something else, a kind of pain, we have already dealt with that point: yes, it is usually very painful to see the plight of a person one cares about, but insofar as that pain is relevant to beneficent motivation, it is probably not an element separate from the three thoughts. To the extent that it is separate, it would appear not to be necessary for the emotion.

What the objection is really getting at, I think, is that compassion as I have described it already involves a significant quasi-ethical achievement: namely, it involves valuing another person as part of one's own circle of concern. This may be done consistently or inconsistently, and it may embrace some people rather than others – so in that sense compassion in and of itself is not very closely linked to a good ethical theory. As I have said, all three judgments might contain defects from the point of view of such a theory. But some work is already done in the emotion itself: the emotion itself sees another person in a way that is highly relevant to morality. I think that what the objector is saying is: then it's no surprise if compassion is connected with ethically good things like helping, for we've plugged ethics into the account already. What the objector thought we were doing was to conjure an ethical attitude out of something nonethical. Instead, we are conjuring ethics out of ethics. And there's nothing surprising about that.

Yes indeed, we are conjuring (a limited) ethics out of (a limited) ethics. What the objector wants to know is, how do we get to ethics in the first place? I have given only tentative and partial answers to that question, by describing the helping roles played by the judgment of similar possibilities, the exercise of empathy, and the elusive element of wonder at human (and animal) life. These are surely important parts of any good answer to the question of how children become capable of compassion. But remember that my account of a child's emotions, unlike many others, does not imagine that people are completely egoistic from the start. Infants have concern about items in the world, in some ways from the very beginning of life – in the wonder and curiosity that leads them outward to explore objects, in the sheer interest they have in examining a human face and interacting with that face, in their need for attachment, not entirely reducible to other, more egoistic needs. So for my account the problem is not how to plug other things and persons into a fundamentally egoistic system; it is, instead, how to broaden, educate, and stabilize elements of concern that are already present – and in particular how to build a stable and truly ethical concern for persons, who are also objects of need and resentment and anger. By the time compassion comes on the scene, some of this work has been done already, and parents are already seen with love, guilt, and a desire to make reparations, as well as with the wonder with which a child from the start greets the human face. The achievement represented by compassion is thus new only in the sense that the child now becomes able to move beyond a narrow circle and to have intense concern with (at least some) lives that are distant or not directly related to the self. But compassion does not have to appear magically out of nowhere: it is a direct outgrowth of proto-ethical elements in responding that are already present.

Here, though with much caution, we may mention recent work on the evolutionary basis of compassion. There are many reasons to avoid evolutionary theorizing: there is a great tendency in the surrounding culture to overread the data, and to draw from them normative implications that they do not have. But if we remember that evolution can show at most a tendency, not something that must be, and if we also remember that tendencies no more suggest what a norm should be than they suggest what a good normative structure has to contend against, then we may get some help in understanding how psychological mechanisms actually work by thinking about their evolutionary basis. As we have mentioned in Chapter 2, there is a good deal of evidence for compassion in at least some higher animals. More pertinently, Frans de Waal has made a powerful case for finding compassionate emotion and related altruistic behavior in animals closely linked to us, that is, chimps and bonobos.[61] Elliott Sober and David Sloan Wilson have made a powerful argument for the evolutionary advantages of altruistic behavior in terms of a theory of group selection. While that theory remains controversial, Sober and Wilson have given a powerful and philosophically sophisticated account of the limits of evolutionary explanation, its complex relationship to psychological and philosophical explanation, and its interdependence with cultural explanation. Given the precise and compelling nature of their overall enterprise, their conclusion that the most likely evolutionary story involves positing both egoistic and altruistic psychological mechanisms has a solidity that few findings of the type have achieved.[62] We may, then, cautiously conclude that there is a reason why empathy typically leads to compassion and thence to helping rather than to sadistic torturing: we have psychological mechanisms that tend in that direction, when suitably activated by developmental cues.

Is it in fact true that compassion motivates altruistic behavior? This is an empirical question, and in principle it can be tested. There are a number of difficulties in the way of testing it: the difficulty of finding anything helpful to do, when a predicament is severe; the difficulty of telling precisely why the person is performing the helpful action; the difficulty involved in defining compassion itself, and in deciding what role in it is played by empathy, and by the judgment of similar possibilities.

---

61 See de Waal (1996); and a related discussion, with a wide range of references, in Wise (2000).
62 Sober and Wilson (1998).

The question has been extensively studied in recent psychological research, especially by C. Daniel Batson.[63] Batson's experiments do show a very strong connection between compassion and altruistic behavior. Batson has focused intelligently on the problem of separating egoistic from altruistic motivation, and to my mind he succeeds in showing that the helping behavior is not explainable on the basis of egoism. He has also shown convincingly, I think, that the helping behavior is not to be explained by the hypothesis that the helper imagines being merged with the person helped.[64] He avoids the problem of predicaments where there is nothing helpful to do, by studying only artificially constructed scenarios where there is something obvious, and not too taxing, for the subjects to do, such as donating to a fund to help the victim, or helping a fellow student study for an exam.

Batson's accounts of egoistic and altruistic motivation are quite rigorous, as are his experiments aimed at separating genuine altruism from subtle forms of egoism, such as the desire to avoid unpleasantness, or the desire to feel good about oneself. What is less satisfactory about Batson's experiments, for our purposes, is his account of what is being tested. As I have mentioned, Batson portrays himself as producing two groups of subjects: a "high-empathy" group and a "low-empathy" group. Since by "empathy" he means (as he tells us) what philosophers typically mean by "compassion, tenderness, and the like," what he is really doing is producing a compassionate group and a noncompassionate group – and then seeing how the emotion affects helping. But he does not define the emotion itself with any rigor, nor does he have altogether satisfactory ways of ascertaining its presence. Typically he asks for self-reports of emotional states – as he is aware, a fallible strategy. But his main way of separating the two groups of subjects is by the instructions that they are given. Some subjects, as we have seen, are told to attend closely to the technical elements of a broadcast – and those subjects are labelled "low-empathy" on the basis of this instruction alone (although he also notes that these subjects typically rate themselves low on emotion). Other subjects are instructed to take the perspective of the person in the broadcast and to imagine her feelings – and these subjects are called "high-empathy" just on that

63 Much of Batson's research is well summarized in Batson (1991); see also Sober and Wilson (1998) for detailed analysis.
64 Batson et al. (1997), replying to Cialdini et al. (1997).

account (although he also notes that they do self-report high on compassionate emotion). Now of course few University of Kansas undergraduates are likely to be empathetic torturers; most are likely to share a view about what important predicaments are, and about who is responsible for what, that makes the transition from empathy to compassion easy – especially when the narrative they hear is rigged to accentuate elements of seriousness and nondesert. But still, whether or not they have compassion as I have defined it is not altogether clear, on the basis of what Batson has asked them. We'd also like to know more about the subjects' level of concern with different types of people, and whether this changed during the experiment.

In any case, what the experiments show is that subjects who were urged to relax and use their imaginations when hearing a story of distress reported both greater emotion and a greater willingness to help the victim than did subjects who were urged to remain detached and "objective." It would seem, then, that people who attend to the distress of another in a manner sufficient for compassion have motives to help that person.

At this point, it is valuable to compare the altruism constructed by compassion with the account of the moral point of view offered by John Rawls in *A Theory of Justice*.[65] Rawls himself invites the comparison, stating that he has attempted to model benevolence in an artificial way, by combining prudential rationality with constraints on information. Replying to Schopenhauer's critique of Kant for omitting compassionate emotion from the motivational equipment of the good ethical agent, Rawls says that this combination gives us, in effect, a model of the very thing that Schopenhauer thought superior to Kantian rationality. Rawls prefers the combination of self-interest and ignorance to the combination of compassion and information, because he believes that his own strategy generates more definite results. But he acknowledges a very intimate relationship between the two strategies.

The parties in the Original Position, prudentially rational, are asked to select principles that will shape their society, knowing all of the relevant general facts but not knowing where in the resulting society they will themselves end up. One of the things that they do not know is their own personal conception of the good; but they do know that

65 Rawls (1971); see also Rawls (1980) for elaboration.

there is a plurality of such conceptions, and they also operate with an account of "primary goods," such things as liberty, opportunity, income, and wealth, which they suppose to be of importance in any plan of life that one might choose. Rawls famously argues that ignorance about where they will end up being placed in society will lead them to want principles that raise the floor: they will consider the position of the least well-off with special attention, and design the economic structure of the society in such a way that inequalities will be tolerated only if they raise that position.

Notice, then, that what Rawls has done is to withhold the eudaimonistic judgment (and, indeed, the eudaimonistic perspective)[66] and to try to generate results out of the judgment of similar possibilities plus prudential self-concern, by withholding information. In the classic cases of compassion, one is asked to imagine that the lot of the beggar might become one's own; but frequently that appeal fails (as with Rousseau's kings), because one simply knows (or believes) that it cannot. Knowledge of one's own place makes the judgment of similar possibilities insufficient, unless one adds a robust concern for the well-being of others. At this point, as Rawls is aware, compassion gives few definite results without a normative theory: with which people should one be concerned, and how much?

Another difference between the two constructs is that Rawls supplies his parties with a definite list of primary goods. These goods are closely related to the classic lists of the occasions for compassion, not surprisingly; but we have seen that compassion's objects may vary with people and societies. We would need a clear normative theory of which goods are worth caring about, and how much, in order to get any definite social result from compassion.

Finally, Rawls's account has a definite theory of desert and nondesert: people don't deserve advantages they derive from their race, or class, or sex, or any such "morally irrelevant" characteristic; more controversially, they also don't have claims of basic justice to advantages they derive from their talents. Once again, compassion in and of

---

66 Here there is a deep difference between Rawls and Smith, who always retains the eudaimonistic perspective, but asks the spectator to focus on the misfortunes of others without considering the effects on one's own situation (apart from one's friendly concern for the others). Smith's project is the one I am attempting here: compassion values others as part of one's own eudaimonistic project.

itself presupposes no definite theory of these matters, and is thus compatible with a wide range of different social results.

In short, compassion makes thought attend to certain human facts, and in a certain way, with concern to make the lot of the suffering person as good, other things being equal, as it can be – because that person is an object of one's concern. Often that concern is motivated or supported by the thought that one might oneself be, one day, in that person's position. Often, again, it is motivated or supported by the imaginative exercise of putting oneself in that person's place. I have claimed that, other things being equal, the compassionate person will acquire motivations to help the person for whom she has compassion. But to get anything out of this that has significance for normative ethics we would need to combine compassion with a plausible normative theory of proper concern, of the important predicaments, and of desert and responsibility.

V. IMPEDIMENTS TO COMPASSION: SHAME, ENVY, DISGUST

At this point, then, it is important to return to our developmental account, asking what difficulties it suggests for the formation of correct judgments in these areas, and also what resources it offers for a fruitful ethical development of concern. Let us focus on the eudaimonistic judgment, the judgment that others are part of my circle of concern. I have said that frequently the psychological mechanisms of empathy and thought about similar possibilities assist the extension of concern to others who are distant from me. Nonetheless, the movement of imagination that might lead to compassion can be blocked in several ways. One impediment, Rousseau argues, is supplied by social distinctions of class and rank (and, we could easily add, distinctions of religion, race, ethnicity, and gender). These distinctions impede compassion when they are given a sharp social form, because they make it difficult for people to see their own possibilities in the sufferings of another. This difficulty will be present in all social systems that categorize people and set them apart from one another; but, as Rousseau says, it will be especially keen in situations of hierarchy, where a privileged group defines its prospects as vastly superior to those of the inferior, and even gets to the point of thinking of itself as invulnerable.

Social institutions, then, construct the shape compassion will take. Tocqueville argued that there were greater possibilities for compassion in the American democracy than in any other nation he had seen, because institutions placed people sufficiently close to one another that they could see their own possibilities in the plight of other, and be moved in consequence.

Rousseau insists that in any setting, however unpromising, the judgment of similar possibilities has the advantage of truth on its side. The misfortunes to which compassion commonly responds – deaths, wounds, losses of loved ones, losses of citizenship, hunger, poverty – are real and general. They really are the common lot of all human beings. Thus the kings who deny that the lot of the peasant could be theirs are deceiving themselves. It could be. No human being is exempt from such things – for

[h]uman beings are by nature neither kings nor nobles nor courtiers nor rich. All are born naked and poor, all are subject to the misfortunes of life, to difficulties, ills, needs, pains of all sorts. Finally, all are condemned to death. That is what the human being really is, that from which no mortal is exempt . . . Each may be tomorrow what the one whom he helps is today.

In short, the person who refuses compassion to the stranger's need on the grounds of his own safety is telling lies. The tendency of the human imagination to respond vividly to the spectacle of pain is a device that leads in the direction of overcoming these lies. Thus, "[t]o the man who thinks," Émile's teacher continues, "all the civil distinctions disappear." We will later ask how such adequate thinking might be cultivated.

But how and why do we get these hierarchically ordered groups, whose presence impedes compassion and promotes self-deceptive thinking about one's own possibilities? If we do not at least pose this question, we will not know enough to begin thinking well about normative issues. This is a huge topic, and not one for philosophy alone to undertake. What I shall say here will therefore be at best suggestive and partial. But it seems worth saying something, on the basis of my account in Chapter 4. I have argued that envy and resentment toward competitors are an inevitable, and, in a sense, not unhealthy aspect of a child's developing object relations. But, in talking about Winnicott's patient B, I have said that the ambivalence of early object relations does not lead forward to creativity and loving action if the child is gripped by an excessive demand for perfection – accompanied by a paralyzing shame at all that is human in himself. We may now notice that shame of this sort acts as a barrier to compassion. Incapable of getting outside the self, B was incapable of concern, and also of the imaginative play that could have established and nourished concern. Other people did not have reality for him. The appeal to help someone who is suffering would fall on deaf ears – all attention being devoted to a paralyzing sense that one had better shore up one's own system of control. As object-relations analyst Otto Kernberg says of such patients, whom he calls pathologically narcissistic:

These patients present an unusual degree of self-reference in their interactions with other people . . . and a curious apparent contradiction between a very inflated concept of themselves and an inordinate need for tribute from others. Their emotional life is shallow. They experience little empathy for the feelings of others . . . These patients experience a remarkably intense envy of other people who seem to have things they do not have or who simply seem to enjoy their lives. . . . They are especially deficient in genuine feelings of sadness and mournful longing; their incapacity for experiencing depressive reactions is a basic feature of their personalities. When abandoned or disappointed by other people they may show what on the surface looks like depression, but which on further examination emerges as anger and resentment, loaded with revengeful wishes rather than real sadness for the loss of a person whom they appreciated . . . At the very bottom . . . lies [an image] of the relationship with external objects, precisely the one against which the patient has erected all these other pathological structures. It is the image of a hungry, enraged, empty self, full of impotent anger at being frustrated, and fearful of a world which seems as hateful and revengeful as the patient himself.[67]

In short, such people have not been able to become human. Like B, they have missed it. Because they cannot tolerate anyone else's having something, they experience intense envy. Because they are unable to experience loss and grief, they convert any setback into resentment. Indeed, the very reality of another person's existence threatens their control. Because they want no rivals for control of the world, they

67 Kernberg (1985), pp. 227–9, 233.

refuse both empathy and the judgment of similar possibilities. It is obvious enough that such a person will not have compassion.

Kernberg, like Rousseau, points out that the fiction of omnipotence is never successfully maintained. The attempt to maintain it is an exhausting struggle; and sooner or later life itself reveals the lie:

If we consider that . . . the individual must eventually face the basic conflicts around aging, chronic illness, physical and mental limitations, and above all, separation, loss, and loneliness – then we must conclude that the eventual confrontation of the grandiose self with the frail, limited and transitory nature of human life is unavoidable.[68]

But he emphasizes that this kind of "deathbed" realization is no cure for the personality, which has peopled the world with lifeless objects, and will have to live in the solitude that it has made.

These are extreme cases. But many normally functioning people have these traits, to a degree that undercuts empathy and compassion, and promotes self-deceptive thinking about one's own vulnerability. Such people include both males and females, but we have reasons to think that the tendency is often connected with common patterns of male development. In Chapter 4 we have already spoken about possible sex differences in development, in connection with this demand for control. And several different recent analyses of misogyny have traced it to this very type of rage for control, a narcissistic refusal to tolerate the reality of something different from oneself, especially if it is at the same time a reminder of one's bodily vulnerability. Elizabeth Young-Bruehl, whose complex study of the psychological origins of prejudice stresses the importance of seeing the multiple origins and structures of social prejudice, holds that sexism is particularly closely linked to narcissism, through the inability to tolerate the existence of the mother as separate, rather than a part of the child himself and subject to his control.[69]

Both Klaus Theweleit and Andrea Dworkin show graphically, through historical and literary materials, that this denial frequently involves a denial of one's own vulnerable and embodied self. Thus they link pathological narcissism to general facts of infancy, seeing them as exaggerated or perverse developments of deeply shared human difficul-

68 Kernberg (1985), pp. 310–11.
69 Young-Bruehl (1996), p. 132.

ties. Because a child aiming at omnipotence does not accept the soft, fleshy, fluid aspects of himself, which are so many signs of weakness and mortality, these must be repudiated from the self, in a violent gesture of differentiation and subordination. What Theweleit's *Freikorps* officers loathe is "mire," "slime," "swamps," "floods," "stench" – all, he plausibly argues, metaphors for the female body, and ultimately for the vulnerable aspects of their own. They then project these loathed attributes onto various groups of social enemies, by subordinating whom they achieve a vicarious victory over their own humanity. The wish of such a personality is given expression in Ernst Jünger's fantasy of the new German male body:

These are the figures of steel whose eagle eyes dart between whirling propellers to pierce the cloud; who dare the hellish crossing through fields of roaring craters, gripped in the chaos of tank engines . . . These are the best of the modern battlefield, men relentlessly saturated with the spirit of battle, men whose urgent wanting discharges itself in a single concentrated and determined release of energy.

As I watch them noiselessly slicing alleyways into barbed wire, digging steps to storm outward, synchronizing luminous watches, finding the North by the stars, the recognition flashes: this is the new man . . . A whole new race, intelligent, strong, men of will . . . A thousand sweeping deeds will arch across their great cities as they stride down asphalt streets, supple predators straining with energy. They will be architects building on the ruined foundations of the world.[70]

This fantasy of male omnipotence – steel replacing flesh, will effacing need – shows how close the connection can be between false omnipotence and aggression, that "single concentrated and determined release of energy" that blots out the reality of other people. How shameful, to be merely human: this is what the new male body states in its very demeanor.[71] We see this text as pathological because we know that Jünger was admired by Hitler and was an influential figure in creating the atmo-

70 Jünger, *Kampf als inneres Erlebnis*, quoted in Theweleit (1989), pp. 160–1.
71 Compare Hitler, quoted in Glover (1999), p. 337:
    My pedagogy is hard. What is weak must be hammered away. In my fortresses of the Teutonic Order a young generation will grow up before which the world will tremble. I want the young to be violent, domineering, undismayed, cruel. The young must be all these things. They must be able to bear pain. There must be nothing weak or gentle about them. The free, splendid beast of prey must once again flash from their eyes.

sphere that led to the rise of Nazism.[72] But we ought to ask ourselves: how far is it, really, from what many of our fellow citizens pursue every day? And how easy is it to differentiate these pathological cases from the general facts and tendencies of human life out of which they grow?

Closely linked to shame, in this reaction, is disgust. To Theweleit's officers, the very things that represent vulnerability and mortality – stickiness, stench, liquidity, ooze – are seen as disgusting. And if we now return to the interrupted narrative of Chapter 4, we see that disgust, which always serves the purpose of setting us at a distance from our own animality and mortality, easily takes as its object other persons and groups, who come to represent what is avoided in the self. So powerful is the desire to cordon ourselves off from our animality that we often don't stop at feces, cockroaches, and slimy animals. We need a group of humans to bound ourselves against, who will come to exemplify the boundary line between the truly human and the basely animal. If those quasi-animals stand between us and our own animality, then we are one step further away from being animal and mortal ourselves.

Thus, throughout history, certain disgust properties – sliminess, bad smell, stickiness, decay, foulness – have repeatedly and monotonously been associated with, indeed projected onto, groups by reference to whom privileged groups seek to define their superior human status. Jews, women, homosexuals, untouchables, lower-class people – all of these are imagined as tainted by the dirt of the body. The stock image of the Jew, in anti-Semitic propaganda, was that of a being disgustingly soft and porous, receptive of fluid and sticky, womanlike in its oozy sliminess, a foul parasite inside the clean body of the German male self.[73] When Jews were depicted in fairy tales for children, they were standardly represented as disgusting animals who had these same prop-

72 Jünger himself was a nationalist and conservative, but never became a member of the Nazi Party. Some of his writings have been read as containing veiled criticisms of Hitler, although this interpretation is disputed. In any case, he certainly helped to create the atmosphere in which Hitler rose to power.

73 See Otto Weininger, *Sex and Character*, pp. 306–22: ". . . some reflection will lead to the surprising result that Judaism is saturated with femininity, with precisely those qualities the essence of which I have shown to be in the strongest opposition to the male nature." Among the Jewish/feminine traits explored here is the failure to understand the national State as the aim of manly endeavor: thus Jews and women have an affinity for the ideas of Marxism. They also fail to comprehend class distinctions: they are "at the opposite pole from aristocrats, with whom the preservation of the limits between individuals is the leading idea" (p. 311).

erties. [74] Lice, vermin, viruses bearing disease – all these were common images.[75] Thus for Hitler (and not only for him), the Jew is a maggot in a festering abscess,[76] hidden away inside the apparently clean and healthy body of the nation.

Disgust was further mobilized in the Nazi campaign of extermination. Repeatedly, Nazis made Jews do things that would further associate them with the disgusting. They were made to scrub latrines – even, in one case, with their *tefillin* (sacred prayer bands) – thus, in the spectator's mind, linking the thought of Jewish worship to the thought of filth.[77] They were deprived of access to toilet facilities so that they had to squat in the open. Primo Levi described the reaction:

The SS escort did not hide their amusement at the sight of men and women squatting wherever they could, on the platforms and in the middle of the tracks, and the German passengers openly expressed their disgust: people like this deserve their fate, just look how they behave. These are not *Menschen*, human beings, but animals, it's as clear as day.[78]

Thus the Germans forged the will to carry out the atrocities.

Similar disgust properties are traditionally associated with women, as receivers of semen and as closely linked, through birth, with the mortality of the body. Otto Weininger made this idea explicit: the Jew is a woman.[79] (Jewish women, accordingly, were doubly disgusting, hyper-animal beings who exercised a fascinating allure but who had to be warded off.)[80] And women in more or less all societies have been

---

74 See the remarkable exhibit of such children's books in the Historisches Museum in Berlin. Similarly, "untouchables," in the traditional Indian caste system, were viewed as quasi-animals, soiled by the pollution of the animal aspects of their betters.

75 See examples in Glover (1999), pp. 338–9.

76 Hitler (1969), p. 53: "Was there any form of filth or profligacy, particularly in cultural life, without at least one Jew involved in it? If you cut even cautiously into such an abscess, you found, like a maggot in a rotting body, often dazzled by the sudden light – a kike!"

77 See Glover (1999), p 342, quoting from William Shirer, *Berlin Diary*.

78 Levi, *The Drowned and the Saved*, quoted in Glover (1999), p. 342.

79 For a valuable treatment of these aspects of disgust, see the essays "Repulsion" and "Dirt/Death" in Dworkin (1987). For further discussion of Otto Weininger's virus, see Chapter 14, section VI.

80 Unpublished paper by Rachel Nussbaum, based on research on the Jewish woman in anti-Semitic novels of the 1920s and 1930s. Weininger also has this idea: if the Jew is a woman, the Jewish woman is accordingly the most sensual and bodily, the "odalisque." There are related stereotypes of black women.

vehicles for the expression of male loathing of the physical and of the potentially decaying. Taboos surrounding sex, birth, menstruation – all these express the desire to ward off something that is too physical, that partakes too much of the secretions of the body. In his recent book on disgust, legal theorist William Miller describes these male attitudes toward women as inevitable aspects of male sexuality, although he also views them as connected with political discrimination against women.[81] Because the woman receives the man's semen, she "is what she eats" (whether in the sense of oral or vaginal incorporation); she becomes the sticky mortal part of him from which he needs to distance himself.

Consider, finally, the central locus of disgust in today's United States, male loathing of the male homosexual. Female homosexuals may be objects of fear, or moral indignation, or generalized anxiety; but they are less often objects of disgust. Similarly, heterosexual females may feel negative emotions toward the male homosexual – fear, moral indignation, anxiety – but again, they rarely feel emotions of disgust. What inspires disgust is typically the male thought of the male homosexual, imagined as anally penetrable. The idea of semen and feces mixing together inside the body of a male is one of the most disgusting ideas imaginable – to males, for whom the idea of nonpenetrability is a sacred boundary against stickiness, ooze, and death. The presence of a homosexual male in the neighborhood inspires the thought that one might oneself lose one's clean safeness, that one might become the receptacle for those animal products. Thus disgust is ultimately disgust at one's own imagined penetrability and ooziness, and this is why the male homosexual is both regarded with disgust and viewed with fear as a predator who might make everyone else disgusting. The very look of such a male is itself contaminating – as we see in the extraordinary debates about showers in the military. The gaze of a homosexual male is seen as contaminating because it says, "You can be penetrated." And this means that you can be made of feces and semen and blood, not clean plastic or metal flesh.[82] (And this means: you will soon be dead.)

---

81 Miller (1997), Chapter 6. I discuss Miller's view further in Nussbaum (1999b).
82 Thus it is not surprising that (to males) the thought of homosexual sex is even more disgusting than the thought of reproductive sex, despite the strong connection of the latter with mortality and the cycle of the generations. For in heterosexual sex the male imagines that not he but a lesser being (the woman, seen as animal) receives the pollution of bodily fluids; in imagining homosexual sex he is forced to imagine that he himself might be so polluted. This inspires a stronger need for boundary drawing.

We should not deny that each form of prejudice is both internally multiple and distinct from other forms. And yet we find a thread running through many forms: the intolerance of humanity in oneself. This refusal, connected with shame, envy, disgust, and violent repudiation, turns up not only in misogyny but in other prejudices to the extent that they share the logic of misogyny. It would then seem that a central challenge for a society that wants to teach a broad and appropriate compassion is to combat the mechanisms underlying these hypertrophic versions of shame and disgust, producing people who can live with their humanity – not easily, for it is not likely that that ever would be easy, but in some way or other.

I think that this, indeed, was Rousseau's idea, when he said that Émile would learn compassion without hierarchy if his teacher taught him to focus on the common vulnerability of all human beings. "Thus from our weakness," he concludes, "our fragile happiness is born." Surrendering omnipotence is essential to compassion, and a broad compassion for one's fellow citizens is essential to a decent society. And yet, by depicting Émile as simply learning all of these things without strain once he reaches the age of puberty, Rousseau denies a depth and complexity to the problem that his own narrative reveals. Despite Book IV's injunction to have compassion for all human beings, there is certainly at least one human being for whom Émile never shows compassion: his consort Sophie, whom he never tries to understand and whom – in Rousseau's unpublished conclusion to *Émile* – he eventually cruelly repudiates.[83] The tragic conclusion to their union is not what *Émile* itself projects, and yet Rousseau found that he could write their future no other way. This acknowledgment of the incompatibility between male dominance and compassion so troubled Rousseau that he could neither publish nor destroy it.

VI. COMPASSION AND TRAGEDY

Compassion, then, rests on a highly unstable basis. It is not unreliable merely in the way that Rousseau states, dependent on institutions that create a diseased sense of inequality in human worth. It is unstable in a different and deeper way as well, dependent on struggles within the

83 For discussion of this fascinating text, see Okin (1979).

personality that are difficult to wage and uncertain in outcome. Chapter 8 will ask to what extent social institutions can assist in its development; Part III will address the deeper roots of the struggle, asking whether it is possible to disentangle love from shame and disgust.

Our account does not simply show us problems, however. It also shows resources that the personality can call upon to contend against these problems. One, clearly, is the development of the love, concern, and guilt that we have hypothesized in the (non-pathologically narcissistic) child's relation to parents: for these experiences cement outward-looking concern, and provide her with powerful motivations to extend herself in helping behavior of many kinds. Another is the ability to mourn a loss, which (again, absent pathological narcissism) is a way of expressing and further developing concern about others, and also a way of acknowledging one's own mortality.

In fact, we can without exaggeration say that the child's entire emotional life is a way of acknowledging her non-omnipotence. In this sense the emotions as a group make an extremely fundamental contribution to morality, by undermining the narcissistic wishes that appear to be so deeply implicated in prejudice and aggression. Finally, the ability to take the perspective of another, present from the start of a child's life, and present in higher primate species as well, proves a fundamental source of other-directed concern and emotion.

In Chapter 4 I have argued that the arts, by nourishing the ability to look on human finitude with delight, assist the personality in its struggle with ambivalence and helplessness. Now, thinking about compassion, we may extend this point. The narratives to which we would naturally turn for a development of compassion through the arts are narratives of tragic predicaments, prominently including classic tragic dramas themselves – for example, the story of Philoctetes, who suffers terrible suffering through no fault of his own. We can easily see that such works of art promote compassion in their audience by inviting both empathy and the judgment of similar possibilities. They also work more directly to construct the constituent judgments of compassion, the judgment of seriousness and the judgment of nondesert. Moreover, they typically have normatively plausible and helpful views of these things: tragedies do not revolve around a shipment of peacock's tongues, but around predicaments that we all ought to see as having "size." They assist our evolving judgments of "size." And they typically reveal in a compelling and plausible way the limits of human control over and responsibility for the disasters that bring good people low.

Finally, albeit in a fictive way, tragedies promote concern for someone different from oneself, through the compelling resources of poetry and drama. Although it is of course possible for tragedies to support the view that certain groups or classes are not fully human, and thus not worthy of the spectator's compassion, it is significant that they tend, on the whole, to be in advance of their surrounding cultures in recognizing the similar humanity of different groups of vulnerable humans. Thus the highly hierarchical and misogynistic society of ancient Athens created tragedies involving subtle forms of sympathy for the sufferings of women; the slaveholding United States created *Uncle Tom's Cabin,* the animal-exploiting society of Victorian England created *Black Beauty.* Tragic fictions promote extension of concern by linking the imagination powerfully to the adventures of the distant life in question. Thus, while none is per se eudaimonistically reliable, tragedies are powerful devices promoting the extension of the eudaimonistic judgment.

Moreover, if the arts in general make human vulnerability pleasing, tragic dramas (and other works describing tragic plights) encourage pleasure of the most difficult type: the pleasure of contemplating our mortality and our vulnerability to the worst disasters in life. The tragic spectator, as long as she plays that role in the way that the drama constructs it for her, will not be afflicted by pathological narcissism or a paralyzing shame at her failure to be omnipotent. Nor, as the story of Philoctetes shows, will such a spectator be afflicted with disgust at human suffering. When Neoptolemus becomes a compassionate spectator of Philoctetes' plight, he utterly lacks the reaction of disgust that apparently caused the Greeks to leave him on the island. He has no reaction at all to the much-described foul stench of the wound, but simply views Philoctetes as a suffering friend. The ability to imagine suffering has gotten in ahead of the need to cordon oneself off from suffering. So too with the spectator: she finds herself looking unabashed at an outcast who was left alone because he was apparently intolerable to be with. And she is made fully aware that in so befriending Philoctetes she is befriending those elements of his life that belong to her own as well. In fact, she befriends herself.

With Neoptolemus, then, she participates joyfully in a world in which she does not control the sources of all good, and affirms it as a world worth living in. As Nietzsche writes in *The Birth of Tragedy*, art proves "a saving sorceress, expert at healing" (*BT* 7), permitting the spectator to view her own life and her own body as pleasing in their very vulnerability, the "erring, striving, suffering individual" as a mask for the (mortal) power of Dionysus (*BT* 10). Nietzsche's idea was that this experience helps people to embrace their own lives.[84] Sophocles' (closely related) idea – and my own – is that it helps them to embrace the lives of others.

84 Nietzsche, of course, was a great enemy of pity, and we shall discuss some of his arguments in the next chapter. But his defense of the tragic experience, in this early work, appears somewhat at odds with the more Stoic spirit that inspires his middle-period attacks on pity.

7

COMPASSION: THE
PHILOSOPHICAL
DEBATE

I. COMPASSION AND REASON

Compassion is controversial. For about twenty-five hundred years it has found both ardent defenders, who consider it to be the bedrock of the ethical life, and equally determined opponents, who denounce it as "irrational" and a bad guide to action. These opponents have strongly influenced the rhetoric of contemporary debates about the emotion. Contrasts between "emotion" and "reason" are ubiquitous in the law, and in public life generally – particularly where appeals to compassion are at issue. These contrasts are seldom drawn with clarity. We are rarely told whether "irrational," as applied to emotion, means "not involving thought" or "involving thought that is in some way substandard and bad." In the process, we frequently encounter traces of the historical debate – but in an unclear and degenerate form. For this reason it seems worthwhile to study the historical debate closely, assessing it in connection with our evolving theory of compassion. It will turn out, I believe, that most of the contemporary opponents of compassion do not share the philosophical position with which they appear to ally themselves.

To set the stage, let us consider the way in which the attack on compassion as "irrational" has figured in one recent legal debate. In a jury instruction case[1] (concerning the same rules for sentencing under which O. J. Simpson would have been sentenced, had he been convicted), Justice O'Connor argues that "the sentence imposed at the penalty stage should reflect a reasoned *moral* response to the defendant's background, character, and crime rather than mere sympathy or

[1] *California v. Brown*, 479 US 542–3 (1987).

emotion." The assessment of penalty, she continues, is a "moral inquiry" and not "an emotional response" – assuming without argument that these are two utterly distinct categories. Justice Brennan, too, holds that "mere sympathy" must be left to one side.

Nor is this depreciation confined to the opponents of emotion. For Justice Blackmun, while urging that compassionate emotion has a valuable and ineliminable role to play in criminal sentencing,[2] still accepts the contrast between emotion and reason-based moral judgment, saying that although the reaction of the juror "at times might be a rational or moral one, it also may arise from sympathy or mercy, human qualities that are undeniably emotional in nature." This puts him in a weak and apologetic position, one that seems unlikely to persuade. More recently, Justice Thomas has assailed appeals to compassion that focus on the disadvantaged background of a criminal defendant, suggesting that such appeals are irrational because of their failure to give people sufficient credit for agency and responsibility (see Chapter 8, section II).

Much the same is true of quite a few legal and economic theorists who argue for some measure of reliance on emotion in public reasoning: again and again, one finds "empathy," "sympathy," and even "passion" in general contrasted with "reason" or "rationality," in a way that inevitably puts the advocates of emotion on the defensive from the start, given the normative connotations of the term "rational."[3] What they end up saying, it seems, is that there are certain elements of the personality that do not clarify or enrich the understanding,[4] that are in and of themselves pretty unreliable and substandard –

2 *Ibid.*, at pp. 561–3. A further problem with Blackmun's opinion, from the point of view of the tradition, is that it speaks of the juror's "sympathy or mercy," thus conflating the emotion with a nonemotional attribute of judgment of which the antiemotion tradition approves.

3 See Massaro (1989), Henderson (1987); Gewirtz (1988), one of the most eloquent defenses of the role of emotion in law, still speaks of "the nonrational emotions." A more careful defense of emotion in law, which does not fall into this trap, is Minow and Spelman (1988). On the side of economics, Frank (1988), though entitled *Passions within Reason*, does not in fact locate passion within reason, but consistently treats emotions as irrational forces that may nonetheless have valuable consequences.

4 This is not true of Gewirtz, who writes the interesting sentence, "But while the nonrational emotions can distort, delude, or blaze uncontrollably, they have worth in themselves and can also open, clarify, and enrich understanding" (Gewirtz [1988], p. 1050). It is hard to see why Gewirtz should call an element that can "open, clarify, and enrich understanding" "nonrational," unless he is using the language of rationality in a purely

but that we should rely on them anyway in certain legal contexts. It is no wonder that critics of compassion such as Richard Posner find this a weak position, an invitation to let into the law whatever brutish and undiscriminating forces happen to be around.[5]

Both sides in this debate fall short because they fail to examine this strong opposition between compassion and reason. The claim that compassion is "irrational" might mean one of two things. It might mean that compassion is a noncognitive force that has little to do with thought or reasoning of any kind. This position, as Chapter 6 has argued, cannot bear serious scrutiny. On the other hand, it might mean that the thought on which compassion is based is in some normative sense bad or false thought; this is in fact what the serious anticompassion tradition holds. But to hold this, as we shall see, one must defend a substantive and highly controversial ethical position, one that has been defended by Plato, the Stoics, Spinoza, and, in some respects, Kant, but one that very few of the contemporary opponents of the emotion would actually be prepared to endorse (though I think Justice Thomas might). In this way, a more precise analysis of the emotion and the historical debate about its normative role can clear the ground for a more adequate contemporary approach.

II. THREE CLASSIC OBJECTIONS

The pro-compassion tradition has assumed that many of life's misfortunes do serious harm to "undeserving" people. But for Socrates, a good person cannot be harmed.[6] And Socratic thinking about virtue and self-sufficiency inaugurated a tradition of thought that opposes compassion, as a moral sentiment unworthy of the dignity of both giver and recipient, and based on false beliefs about the value of external goods. According to this tradition, whose most influential exponents are the Greek and Roman Stoics, the most important thing in life is one's own reason and will – what the Roman Stoic Epictetus calls

descriptive and non-normative sense, meaning by it something like, "not concerned with the maximizing of individual satisfactions."

5 See also the treatment of emotion in Posner (1992): here, emotions seem to be treated as completely impervious to reasoning and argument.

6 Plato, *Apology* 41D, cf. 30DC; on this see Vlastos (1991), and my review in Nussbaum (1991).

one's "moral purpose" (*prohairesis*). This faculty of moral choice is the possession of all humans, and its virtuous use is always within our power, no matter what the world does. Moral purpose is a source of human equality: it is the possession of male and female, slave and free. Its dignity outshines all circumstantial differences and renders them trivial. Vastly superior in dignity and worth to any other good thing, it suffices all by itself, well used, for a flourishing life. Thus the only way to be damaged by life with respect to one's flourishing is to make bad choices or become unjust; the appropriate response to such deliberate badness is blame, not compassion. Blame, unlike compassion, respects the primacy of moral purpose in each person, treating people not as victims and subordinates but as dignified agents. As for the events of life that most people take to be occasions for compassion – losses of loved ones, loss of freedom, ill health, and so on – they do, of course, occur, but they are of only minor importance.[7]

Thus compassion has a *false* cognitive/evaluative structure, and is objectionable for that reason alone. It acknowledges as important what has no true importance. Furthermore, in the process compassion insults the dignity of the person who suffers, implying that this is a person who really needs the things of this world, whereas no virtuous person has such needs.[8] (Kant calls this an "insulting kind of beneficence, expressing the sort of benevolence one has for an unworthy person.")[9] If one respects the faculty of moral purpose in a human being, one will not feel compassion, for one will see that faculty as a source of equal human worth, undiminished by any catastrophe. If we include the judgment of similar possibilities, compassion also frequently insults the dignity of the person who gives it: it is an acknowledgment that her

---

7 It appears that for Socrates they can affect the *degree* of one's flourishing, though not flourishing itself: see Vlastos (1991). The Stoics refuse to admit even this much.

8 See the extensive development of this line of argument in Nietzsche: especially *Dawn* 135 ("To offer pity is as good as to offer contempt"); *Zarathustra*, "On the Pitying." Nietzsche actually makes three related points here: (1) pity denigrates the person's own efforts by implying that they are insufficient for flourishing; (2) pity inappropriately inflates the importance of worldly goods; (3) pity has bad consequences, undermining self-command and practical reason.

9 Kant, *Doctrine of Virtue*, 35, Akad. p. 457, trans. Ellington. Kant's entire argument in this passage is very close to, is indeed appropriated as a whole by, Nietzsche, a fact that ought to give pause to those who think Nietzsche's view cruel or proto-Fascist. The two add a further argument: that pity adds to the suffering that there is in the world, by making two people suffer rather than only one (Kant, ibid.; Nietzsche, *Dawn* 134).

own most central prospects may be brought low by fortune.[10] As Kant puts it, adopting some aspects of the Platonic/Stoic position, "Such benevolence is called softheartedness and should not occur at all among human beings."[11]

This position on compassion becomes the basis for Plato's assault on tragedy in the *Republic*.[12] The good person, he argues, will be "most of all sufficient to himself for flourishing living, and exceptionally more than others he has least need of another . . . Least of all, then, is it a terrible thing to him to be deprived of a son or brother or money or anything of that sort" (387DE). Accordingly, speeches of lamentation and requests for compassion, if retained at all, must be assigned to characters whom the audience will perceive as weak and error-ridden, so that these judgments will be repudiated by the spectator.[13] The Stoics take this line of thought further, insisting that the true hero for the young should be Socrates, with his calm, self-sufficient demeanor in misfortune, his low evaluation of worldly goods. Tragic heroes, by contrast, should be regarded with scorn, as people whose errors in evaluative judgment have brought them low. (Epictetus defines tragedy as "what happens when chance events befall fools.") This Stoic position on compassion and value is taken over with little change by Spinoza, and seriously influences the accounts in Descartes, Smith, and Kant.[14] It is given an especially complex and vivid development in the thought of Nietzsche, whose connection to Stoicism has not, I think, been sufficently understood.[15]

---

10 See Nietzsche, *Dawn* 251 (called "Stoical"), 133; *Zarathustra* IV, "The Sign."

11 Kant, *Doctrine of Virtue*, 34, Akad. p. 122.

12 See Nussbaum (1992) for a detailed analysis.

13 Thus they are to be ascribed to "women, and not very good women at that, and to the inferior among men." See Nussbaum (1992) for subtle differences between Books II–III and Book X on this point; and for Stoic developments, see Nussbaum (1993a). See also Halliwell (1984, 1989).

14 Descartes tries to bind a middle ground, granting that any noncallous person will feel compassion for the suffering of others, but claiming that the strong and magnanimous person will feel it in a way that does not so prominently involve the judgment of similarity: the sadness of such compassion is not bitter, and is rather like the experience, he says, of the tragic spectator (*Les Passions de l'âme*, Art. 187). Smith approves of compassion up to a point, but thinks that all emotions must be strictly kept in bounds by a rather Stoic sort of "self-command." For Kant's complex position, see the following discussion.

15 I analyze the Stoic roots of Nietzsche's position on pity, and draw some new interpretive consequences, in Nussbaum (1993b). An important new development in Nietz-

It is important to see that the motivation underlying the repudiation of compassion is at its root a strongly egalitarian and cosmopolitan one. Although the pro-compassion tradition, in its Rousseauian incarnation, can claim to be a champion of egalitarian-democratic ideas, using compassion to motivate a more equal distribution of basic resources, the opponents claim that their own stance is the one that more appropriately respects human equality, and the infinite worth of human dignity that is its source. To the pro-compassion tradition, differences in class and rank create differences in the worth or success of lives. To grant this much, the anti-compassion position holds, is to grant that the world and its morally irrelevant happenings can in effect forge different ranks and conditions of humanity. The believer in equal human worth should not acknowledge this: she should take her bearings from that basic human endowment that is not unequally distributed, and she should honor that equal basic endowment by treating that, and that only, as the measure of a life. To suggest that there is anything we could add to a human being's moral faculties that would either augment or diminish their value is to suggest that people are not truly equal in value. The Stoic repudiation of compassion can easily look like mere hard-heartedness or repressiveness; but it expresses, at its core, this idea of the dignity of humanity.

Similarly, the most shocking aspect of Stoic "indifference" – the injunction not to be upset at the deaths of loved ones, including even one's own children – should be seen as closely linked to the Stoics' egalitarian cosmopolitanism. All human beings are equal in worth, and we are fundamentally not members of families or cities, but *kosmopolitai*, members of the "city-state of the universe." This means that we should have equal concern for all; and that equal concern is incompatible with special attachments to kin. We may appropriately give our own family members or fellow citizens a disproportionate measure of our concern and energy, because that is the post where life has placed us, and it would be ineffectual to attempt to do good in all places. But we should recognize that this organizational issue, not some special

sche's line of attack is that, following (in different ways) both ancient Cynicism and contemporary Romanticism, he holds that most of the standard occasions for pity are not only not really bad for people, but are actually good: loneliness, hardship, poverty, chastity, are all favorable conditions for philosophical creation. See especially *Genealogy of Morals* III.8, and *Will to Power* 910 (1968).

value in one's own family, or ration, is what justifies the disproportion-ate investment.[16] The Greek Stoics went further, holding that the very existence of the family jeopardizes proper concern, breeding jealousies and hostilities; children should be raised communally.[17]

Notice that Stoic impartiality is independent of Stoic indifference. One might insist on equal concern for all human beings without deny-ing that the world's damages are significant and important. Such a modified Stoic could make a place for compassion, provided that it was evenly distributed. Thus the Stoic attack needs to say more about why, given the nature of the emotion, this is an unlikely result.

In addition to charging compassion with falsity in judgment, then, the classic attacks make two further objections. The first concerns the partiality and narrowness of compassion; the second concerns its con-nection to anger and revenge. Compassion, the first argument goes, binds us to our own immediate sphere of life, to what has affected us, to what we see before us or can easily imagine. Because the imagination plays such an important role in it, it is subject to distortion through the unreliability of that faculty. But this means that it is very likely to present an unbalanced picture of the world, effacing the equal value and dignity of all human lives, their equal need for resources and for aid in time of suffering. This argument, first introduced by the ancient Stoics, is given an especially vivid form by Adam Smith, who argues that to rely on "pity" as a social motive will, on this account, produce very unbalanced and inconsistent results:[18]

Let us suppose that the great empire of China, with all its myriads of inhabitants, was suddenly swallowed up by an earthquake, and let us con-sider how a man of humanity in Europe, who had no sort of connexion with that part of the world, would be affected upon receiving intelligence of this dreadful calamity. He would, I imagine, first of all, express very strongly his sorrow for the misfortune of that unhappy people, he would make many melancholy reflections upon the precariousness of human life, and the vanity of all the labours of man, which could thus be annihilated in a moment . . .

16 I present here a schematic version of the Stoic position, which does not fit all thinkers. This argument about the justification of particular ties is adopted by Smith (1976), "On Universal Benevolence."

17 See Schofield (1999); and, on the complex doctrine of *erôs* that goes with this view of family, see Nussbaum (1995b).

18 Smith (1976), p. 136; see the excellent account of these aspects of Smith's thought in Coase (1976). See also Posner (1990), pp. 411–13.

And when all this fine philosophy was over, when all these humane sentiments had been once fairly expressed, he would pursue his business or his pleasure, take his repose or his diversion, with the same ease and tranquillity, as if no such accident had happened. The most frivolous disaster which could befal himself would occasion a more real disturbance. If he was to lose his little finger to-morrow, he would not sleep to-night; but, provided he never saw them, he will snore with the more profound security over the ruin of a hundred millions of his brethren, and the destruction of that immense multitude seems plainly an object less interesting to him, than this paltry misfortune of his own.[19]

In short: broaden the emotion as we may through education, compassion remains narrow and unreliable. It takes in only what the person has been able to see or imagine, and its psychology is limited by the limitations of the sensory imagination. As we saw in Chapter 6, Smith believes that empathy is extremely important in generating compassion. If that is so, and if empathy for the similar and the near at hand – or for whatever report has managed to make "interesting" – is easier, then compassion will partake of that unevenness. But this means that it is an insufficient, and even a dangerous, moral and social motive.

Finally, the classic attack examines the connection between compassion and the roots of other more objectionable emotions. The person who feels compassion accepts certain controversial evaluative judgments concerning the place of "external goods" in human flourishing. She accepts the idea that tragic predicaments can strike people through no fault of their own, and that the losses people thus suffer matter deeply. But a person who accepts those judgments accepts that children, spouse, citizenship, and other externals all really matter for human flourishing. This means that she allows her own good to rest in the hands of fortune. And to admit one's own vulnerability to fortune is to have all the raw material not only for compassion, but also for fear and anxiety and grief; and not only for these, but for anger and the retributive disposition as well. What Stoic analyses bring out again and again is that the repudiation of compassion is not in the least connected with callousness, brutality, or the behavior of the boot-in-the-face tyrant. In fact, in this picture it is compassion itself that is

---

19 As Smith's editors note, this passage may recall Hume . . . *Treatise*, II.iii.13: " 'Tis not contrary to reason to prefer the destruction of the whole world to the scratching of my finger."

closely connected with cruelty. The person who has compassion for another acknowledges the importance of certain worldly goods and persons, which can in principle be damaged by another's agency. The response to such damages will be compassion if the damaged person is someone else; but if the damaged person is oneself, and the damage is deliberate, the response will be anger – and anger that will be proportional to the intensity of the initial evaluative attachment.

In short, this tradition claims that the soft soul of the compassionate can be invaded by the serpents of resentment and hatred. When Seneca writes to Nero reproving compassion,[20] he hardly aims to encourage Nero in his tendencies toward brutality. On the contrary: his project is to get Nero to care less about insults to his reputation, about wealth and power generally. This, Seneca argues, will make him a more gentle and humane ruler. But not only is this project not hindered by the removal of compassion, it demands it, because it demands the removal of attachments to external goods. So long as Nero, that budding actor who loved to sing the role of Agave in Euripides' *Bacchae*, indulges in tragic weeping over the vicissitudes of life, so long is he not to be trusted with the fate of his people. Cruelty, according to Seneca, is not the opposite of compassion. It is an excessive form of retributive anger, which, in turn, is simply a circumstantial inflection or modality of the same evaluative judgments that have, in other circumstances, compassion as their inflection.[21] So compassion is cruelty's first cousin; the difference between them is made by fortune.

This line of argument is developed vividly by Nietzsche, who argues, with the Stoics, that a certain sort of "hardness" toward the vicissitudes of fortune is the only way to get rid of the desire for revenge. The "veiled glance of pity," which looks inward on one's own possibilities with "a profound sadness," acknowledging one's own weakness and inadequacy – this glance of the compassionate is, he argues, the basis of much hatred directed against a world that makes human beings suffer, and against all those, in that world, who are not brought low, who are self-respecting and self-commanding: "It is on such soil, on swampy ground, that every weed, every poisonous plant grows . . .

---

20 Seneca, *On Mercy*; the term is *misericordia*.
21 See *On Anger* and *On Mercy*; the argument is discussed in Nussbaum (1994), Chapter 11.

Here the worms of vengefulness and rancor swarm."[22] Or, as Zarathustra puts it, "The spirit of revenge, my friends, has so far been the subject of man's best reflection: and where there was suffering, one always wanted punishment also."[23]

This Stoic insight is now developed further in an account of the original motives for punishment, itself indebted to Stoic antecedents.[24] Nietzsche argues that punishment is a form of exchange, in which the injured party is paid back for his pain and suffering by the pleasure of inflicting suffering on the original wrongdoer, and by the additional pleasure of being allowed to "despise and mistreat" the person who has at one time had him in his power (*Genealogy* II.5–6). This way of seeing things frequently leads to cruelty, as the one who has been put down by the offense revels in the chance to put the offender down. "And might one not add," he comments, "that, fundamentally, this world has never since lost a certain odor of blood and torture?" (II.6) In certain ways, Nietzsche prefers this simple revenge morality to a morality based on the idea that the human being is, as such, worthless and disgusting (II.7). But, like the Stoics, he is quick to point out that the interest in taking revenge is a product of weakness and lack of power – of that excessive dependence on others and on the goods of the world is the mark of a weak, not of a strong and self-sufficient, human being or society. The compassionate person is as such a weak person.

But if compassion is in this way bound up with the inclination to revenge, and if the task of a strong society is to contain and control the inclination to revenge, then one might well conclude that society has reasons to extirpate compassion in its citizens, young and old, rather than fostering it. One might have thought that the containment of revenge is a prominent theme in the tragic tradition, almost as prominent as the themes of the fragility of fortune and the value of compassion.[25] But if the anti-compassion tradition is right, tragedy breeds revenge even while it appears to argue against it; the real elimination

---

22 Nietzsche, *Genealogy of Morals* (trans. Kaufmann), III.14.
23 Nietzsche, *Thus Spoke Zarathustra* (trans. Kaufmann), "On Redemption."
24 Especially, perhaps, to Seneca's *On Anger* – see Nussbaum (1994), Chapter 11.
25 On this see Posner (1988), who finds the tragic tradition a valuable source of insight into the control of revenge, and its unsuitability as a principle of social order.

of revenge requires the banishment of the tragic poets from the city. And if the city is to be a city of law, and if it is a particular job of the legal system to make certain that revenge does not carry the day, then one might well conclude that a legal system will have especially strong reasons to avoid tragic compassion, and to discourage citizens from basing their judgments on it.

III. MERCY WITHOUT COMPASSION

What will the attitude of the good and self-sufficient person be toward the misfortunes of others? Here we arrive at an area of considerable complexity in the anti-compassion position. When others suffer the losses that are usually taken to be occasions for compassion, the good Stoic will, of course, not have compassion for them. Her paramount sentiment will be one of respect for the dignity of humanity in each and every human being, no matter how unfortunate; and she will therefore respect the sufferer, seeing his or her virtue and will as in principle sufficient for flourishing life. Insofar as the sufferer falls short of virtue, especially by adopting an inappropriate attitude toward her own misfortune, grieving and calling out for compassion, the Stoic will be critical. Epictetus urges a tough, mocking attitude. One should try to get the sufferer not to moan about fortune in this undignified way, but to take charge of herself and her life. "Wipe your own nose," Epictetus tells the passive pupil. Marcus Aurelius, gentler, urges a lofty parental attitude: think of the person who is moaning about fortune as like a child who has lost a toy. The suffering of this child is real enough, and one should console her – remembering all the while, of course, that it is childish to care so much about a mere toy (V.36).

Such a noncompassionate person will be concerned in some ways with the material side of life. She will give benefits to others, and she will do so without selfish holding back, since she herself does not need these things. This point is repeatedly stressed in the anti-compassion tradition, in particular by Seneca (in *On Benefits*). But this willingness to benefit, at least in the Stoics and in Spinoza, comes about not because these goods are seen as important, but because they are seen as unimportant. Indeed, one of the great merits this tradition sees in its moral position is that it ascribes all true value to things concerning which there could not possibly be bitter competition among persons.

As Spinoza puts it, "The highest good of those who pursue virtue is common to all, and all can equally enjoy it."[26] (Nietzsche, in his characteristically extreme way, goes a step further: the true philosopher will be delighted to get rid of all worldly goods and to live in utter poverty and loneliness, leaving the goods of the world for others – for he will know that this sort of suffering actually increases his capacity for philosophical excellence.)[27] But this means that the commitment to secure material goods to those who do happen to like them rests on a fragile foundation, and is at every step constrained by the anti-compassion person's feeling that they should not have liked those goods so much. I shall return to this point.[28]

The wise person of the anti-compassion tradition is not always "hard." Believing that the only serious harms that befall others are the harms that they have caused themselves through their folly and wrongdoing, the Stoic nonetheless believes that it is extremely difficult to be good. He therefore faces the benighted condition of most mortals – including their incessant demands for compassion – with concern for their development and well-being. Not angered on account of his own personal damage, not feeling himself dragged down by the bad acts of another, he will be free to ask what corrections and instructions, even what punishments, are most likely to do good for the wrongdoer's life as a whole, and for society as a whole. Seneca argues in *On Anger* and *On Mercy* that this is the right way to defeat the retributive attitude – by rising above the cares that support it. The punishments of the wise person will be free from the harshness and cruelty that he connects with ordinary vulnerability. They will be as judiciously selected as are a doctor's prescriptions; and frequently they will be merciful.

Mercy is defined as the inclination of the judgment toward leniency in selecting penalties: the merciful judge will often choose a penalty milder than the one appointed in law for the offense. This bending or waiving of punishment will frequently be preferred by the good person, Seneca argues, for several different reasons. First, it is expressive of his own strength and dignity: it shows that he does not need to inflict pain in order to be a whole person. Second, it displays understanding of the

---

26 *Ethics*, Part IV, Proposition 36. This good, of course, is knowledge.
27 For references, see note 15 to this chapter.
28 For the damage that this position does to Cicero's political thought, and, thence, to the foundations of modern thought about transnational duties, see Nussbaum (2000c).

difficulties of human life, which make it almost impossible not to err in some respect; it displays, too, the awareness that the punisher is himself an imperfect person, liable to error. Third, it is socially useful, since it awakens trust and mutual goodwill, rather than fear and antagonism.[29]

What we see here, in effect, is a translation of the cognitive structure of compassion into the terms appropriate to the anti-compassion tradition's conception of the self-sufficiency of virtue. For in Senecan mercy, we have, as in compassion, an acknowledgment of the difficulties and struggles peculiar to human life – in this case, struggles to perfect one's own moral purpose – coupled with an acknowledgment that one is oneself a fellow human being of the one who receives mercy. But compassion took as its focus chance events that virtue does not control; in giving these importance it told lies (so the Stoic claims) about the human good. Mercy, by contrast, takes as its focus the uphill struggle to be virtuous and to perfect one's moral purpose. It places the accent in the right place, as the anti-compassion tradition sees it, and ascribes importance to what really has importance. It still says, as compassion does, that to live well is difficult for a human being, and that it is highly likely that a person who makes reasonably good efforts will come to grief somehow. But compassion focuses on occasions where the coming to grief, was not the person's fault. According to its opponents, there are no such cases, since either there is no real coming to grief, or it is the person's fault. Mercy focuses on fault, and refuses – as Seneca emphasizes repeatedly – ever to let the person off the hook for that fault. Mercy is mitigation in sentencing, not a verdict of not guilty. Mercy simply says, look, I don't need to hurt you; and you were probably having a tough time being good, since it is very hard to be good. So, like a good doctor or a good parent, I am going to tell you firmly that you are bad, but punish you lightly.

It is in this lofty, affectionately parental attitude – combined with a deep respect for the dignity of humanity in each person – that the Stoic tradition finds a cement that will, they claim, hold society together far better than compassion, inspiring a mutual gentleness not tinged with fearfulness or a gnawing sense of personal need. One of the most eloquent defenses of this social vision can be found in Nietzsche's

29 On these arguments, see further in Nussbaum (1994), Chapter 11; and "Equity and Mercy" in Nussbaum (1999a).

Genealogy of Morals, following the passage on pity and revenge that I have already discussed. Nietzsche now argues that in a strong and self-sufficient person or society, the interest in retribution will gradually overcome itself in the direction of mercy:

As its power increases, a community ceases to take the individual's transgressions so seriously, because they can no longer be considered as dangerous and destructive to the whole as they were formerly . . . As the power and self-confidence of a community increase, the penal law always becomes more moderate; every weakening or imperiling of the former brings with it a restoration of the harsher forms of the latter. The "creditor" always becomes more humane to the extent that he has grown richer; finally, how much injury he can endure without suffering from it becomes the actual measure of his wealth. It is not unthinkable that a society might attain such a consciousness of power that it could allow itself the noblest luxury possible to it – letting those who harm it go unpunished. "What are my parasites to me?" it might say. "May they live and prosper: I am strong enough for that!"

The justice which began with "everything is dischargeable, everything must be discharged," ends by winking and letting those incapable of discharging their debt go free: it ends, as does every good thing on earth, by overcoming itself. This self-overcoming of justice: one knows the beautiful name it has given itself – mercy; it goes without saying that mercy remains the privilege of the most powerful man, or better, his – beyond the law.[30]

Like Seneca, Nietzsche stresses that mercy does not deny that wrong-doing has taken place; it does not rewrite the law concerning offenses. Justice is still there intact in the merciful deed: but, springing from a powerful and secure nature, from the self-respect of that nature and its respect for others, it is able to waive the pleasure of retribution and "overcome itself" in the direction of gentleness.[31]

The debate over compassion constructs, in effect, two visions of political community and of the good citizen and judge within it. One vision is based upon the emotions; the other urges their removal. One sees the human being as both aspiring and vulnerable, both worthy and insecure; the other focuses on dignity alone, seeing in reason a bound-

---

30 Nietzsche, *Genealogy of Morals* II.10.
31 See also *Dawn* 202, where Nietzsche deplores the custom of turning to the courts for revenge, and speaks of "our detestable criminal codes, with their shopkeeper's scales and the desire to counterbalance guilt with punishment." Here he goes further than in the *Genealogy,* wishing to do away with penal institutions altogether, replacing them with reformative "medical" institutions.

less and indestructible worth. One sees the central task of community as the provision of support for basic needs; bringing human beings together through the thought of their common weakness and risk, it constructs a moral emotion that is suited to supporting efforts to aid the worst off. The other sees a community as a kingdom of free responsible beings, held together by the awe that they feel for the worth of reason in one another; the function of their association will be to assist the moral development of each by judgments purified of passion. Each vision, in its own way, pursues both equality and freedom. The former aims at equal support for basic needs and hopes through this to promote equal opportunities for free choice and self-realization; the other starts from the fact of internal freedom – a fact that no misfortune can remove – and finds in this fact a source of political equality. One sees freedom of choice as something that needs to be built up for people through worldly arrangements that make them capable of functioning in a fully human way; the other takes freedom to be an inalienable given, independent of all material arrangements. One aims to defeat the selfish and grasping passions through the imagination of suffering, and through a gradual broadening of concern; the other aims to remove these passions completely, overcoming retaliation with self-command and mercy. One attempts to achieve benevolence through softheartedness; the other holds, with Kant, that this softheartedness "should not be at all among human beings." One holds that "it is the weakness of the human being that makes it sociable."[32] The other holds that weakness is an impediment to community, that only the truly self-sufficient person can be a true friend. We see that the debate between the friends and enemies of compassion is no merely formal debate concerning the type of thought process or the type of faculty that should influence choice in public life. Nor is it a debate between partisans of reason and partisans of some mindless noncognitive force. It is a substantive debate about ethical value. Now we must adjudicate that debate.

IV. VALUING EXTERNAL GOODS

The historical debate does not provide a full response to the Stoic objections, because the defenders of compassion do not grapple with

---

32 See Rousseau (1979), p. 221; as elsewhere I substitute "human being" for "man."

their opposition in a sustained manner. The anti-compassion tradition was for centuries the dominant tradition in the history of Western philosophy, as Nietzsche plausibly states. So great is the influence of this Stoic tradition that even Adam Smith, in some respects an eloquent defender of the public role of compassion, ends up denigrating all emotional softness rather harshly, in the highly Stoic section of his work dealing with the virtue of self-command.[33] Similarly, *The Wealth of Nations* is profoundly influenced by the view that poverty does not diminish human dignity. Again, in international morality and law, the influence of Stoic cosmopolitanism, through Cicero, on thinkers such as Grotius and Kant runs deep, shaping contemporary views about duties of material aid.[34] Whereas the anti-compassion tradition exhibits great continuity and unity of argument, the pro-compassion tradition is more scattered, including novelists as well as political theorists, psychologists as well as philosophers; its members are not on the whole clearly aware of one another's arguments.

Before we turn to the debate itself, we should bear one fact in mind. The anti-compassion tradition does indeed consider this emotion (and indeed, in the case of Spinoza and the Stoics, all other emotions) to be irrational in the normative sense; it does indeed construct a sharp, and prejudicial, opposition between emotion and reason. But it does so in a rather different way from the way in which emotion and reason are sometimes contrasted in modern legal and political discussions. The severe tradition does not deny that emotions are full of thought. In fact, insofar as its members follow the Stoics, they hold the strong cognitive position on emotion that I have been trying to defend in a modified form.[35] What is wrong with compassion (like other emotions) is not that it is not discerning and aimed at truth. What is wrong with

33 Smith (1976), pp. 237–62, which contrasts the "rules of perfect prudence, of strict justice, and of proper benevolence" with the passions, which "are very apt to mislead him; sometimes to drive him and sometimes to seduce him to violate all the rules which he himself, in all his sober and cool hours, approves of." I think that it is difficult to make a consistent whole of Smith's position on the passions. The earlier chapters of the work defend passion as a form of perception that is highly responsive to reasoning and, it seems, at least partly constituted by reasoning; there Smith seems to be influenced more by Shaftesbury and perhaps Aristotle than by the Stoics.
34 See Nussbaum (2000c).
35 This is true of all the Stoics and Spinoza; it is true of Epicurus and Plato with some qualification; it is not true of Kant, whose position on emotion is an odd amalgam of Humean positive analysis and Stoic normative analysis.

it is that it latches onto false beliefs. It is irrational not in the way that
hunger is irrational, but in the way that a belief in the flatness of the
earth is irrational: false, based on inadequate evidence, cultural prejudice, false premises, and bad argument; it is therefore capable of being
set right by true premises and good arguments. That is why, in the
thought of the Stoics and Spinoza, it is philosophy that can liberate the
human being from bondage to emotion. This would not have been the
case had emotion been an ineluctable animal force.

Many modern opponents of emotion, however, do not distinguish
clearly between the claim that emotion is noncognitive and the claim
that it is irrational in the Stoic sense. They get considerable mileage out
of the long philosophical tradition that opposes emotion to reason,
relying on the authority of this tradition rather than on argument for
the appropriateness of the contrast. And yet they do not endorse the
traditional meaning of the contrast, a meaning inseparable from this
tradition's controversial moral position on the worth of external goods.
It is not clear that they could endorse the anti-compassion tradition in
its authentic form, without rendering their own position far more controversial than it appears to be.

Let us now ask how the friend of compassion should answer its
opponents' charges. First and most basic is the charge of *falsity*: compassion ascribes to chance misfortunes an importance they do not really
possess, insulting, in the process, the dignity of both its receiver and its
giver. It should be replaced by respect for the indestructible dignity of
the sufferer's humanity.

The first thing we should say in response to this charge is that it is,
so far, much too blunt. For why are we forced to make an all-or-
nothing choice between having compassion for a suffering person and
having respect for that person's dignity? Why can't we make distinctions, having compassion in connection with the wrongs luck has
brought her way and at the same time having respect and awe for the
way in which a good person will bear these ills with strength? We do
not have to say that the person's moral humanity cancels out the loss
in order to respect humanity when we see it. Nor do we need to say
that the virtuous use of our moral faculties is sufficient for human
flourishing in order to admire excellence as the Stoics wish us to do.
Indeed, it is difficult to know what we would be admiring in such a

case if we did take the Stoic position that the loss was not a serious loss. For then, where would the fortitude be in bearing the event with dignity? Tragedy elicits wonder at human excellence not by showing its heroes untouched by the deaths of children, by rape, war, and material deprivation,[36] but precisely by showing how these horrible things do cut to the very core of the personality – and yet do not altogether destroy it.

There is something important in the Stoic position. The worth of humanity should elicit respect, even when the world has done its worst; and the excellent use of one's human faculties should elicit admiration, even when circumstances do not cooperate. The Stoic ideal of equal humanity, fundamental to Enlightenment political thought, does place many constraints on proper compassion, instructing us not to give the accidents of life undue importance in any of our dealings with others, including our responses to their misfortunes. It tells us that we must not interpret differences of material circumstances as negating a fundamental human similarity, which is a proper foundation for moral claims. On the other hand, compassion itself standardly includes the thought of common humanity, insofar as it comes joined with the judgment of similar possibilities: in this way it appears to be an ally of respect, not its enemy. And the respect we have for the equal humanity of others should, it seems, lead us to be intensely concerned with their material happiness, not indifferent to it. The fact that a certain individual is a bearer of human capacities gives that person a claim on our material concern, so that these capacities may receive appropriate support. We do not properly respect those capacities if we do neglect the needs they have for resources, or deny that hardships can deprive human beings of flourishing.

Nor are we prevented from respecting the dignity of each human

36 Tragedies typically do not focus on the loss of fortune or status, since the real hero does not attach the excessive value to these things that many people do, as I go on to discuss; at the other extreme, they also rarely focus on deprivation so extreme that it deprives people of the chance to act and think well – extreme hunger, for example; for tragedies must contain action and poetic speech. But this does not imply that extreme hunger is not one of the most acute of tragedies. Short of this, tragedy frequently does concern itself with material deprivation – consider, for example, the plight of Philoctetes, in which both the pain of his illness and the need to forage for food are continually stressed.

being if we grant, as we must, that the failure of external support can affect a person's capacity for virtue and choice itself, if it occurs early enough in a process of development, or is sufficiently prolonged. The Stoic would like to believe that no experience of worldly helplessness can touch us, that we are never victims – and that this is our dignity. Modern followers of the Stoics frequently make a similar move, insisting that the portrayal of certain people or groups as victims is inconsistent with respecting their agency. But we can acknowledge the extent to which we are at the world's mercy – the extent, for example, to which people who are malnourished, or ill, or treated with contempt by their society have a harder time developing their capacities for learning and choice – even ethical choice – without denying that our basic capacities and our agency deserve respect and sustenance, just by being there in whatever form. Indeed, it is only when we have noticed that and noticed how these capacities need support from the material world, and therefore exert a claim against our own comfort and effort, that we have appropriately respected them.

In another way as well, the attack is too blunt. For it takes an all-or-nothing position on the importance of external goods for flourishing: either compassion all over the place, or no compassion at all. But the pro-compassion tradition is not prevented from judging that some occasions for compassion are illegitimate, and based upon false evaluations. As I have said, compassion takes up not the actual point of view of any and every sufferer, but rather the point of view of an onlooker who appraises the seriousness of what has happened. The normative suitability of this emotion, as of fear and grief and anger, depends on whether the person gets the appraisals right, using a defensible theory of value. Thus compassion should not be given to my Roman aristocrat who misses an evening of peacock's tongues, no matter how much he minds this. On the other hand, compassion should be given to the person who is unaware of the extent of her illness or deprivation because of mental impairment or the social deformation of preferences. The pro-compassion tradition is preoccupied with getting the theory of value right, criticizing those who attach inappropriate importance to money, status, or pleasure. (Both Aristotle and Rousseau make this critique central to their thought.) This tradition agrees with Nietzsche that people should not find weakness everywhere they turn, or moan about any and every loss; to a great extent, they should make the best of what life brings their way, relying on their own inner resources.[37] On the other hand, it is no use denying that some losses are worth weeping about – and these include some that the sufferer herself may not even notice.

We might say that the Stoic objector depicts the person who needs the goods of fortune as a type of pathological narcissist: incapable of respecting others because she is boundlessly needy and wrapped up in her own demands. But of course we need not imagine the needs of the compassionate as boundless: the child we imagined in Chapter 4 had made a fundamental developmental step when she allowed others their legitimate demands on her, and relinquished, with mourning, her own aim to have absolute control. Indeed, we can turn the criticism around: it is actually the Stoic agent who more closely resembles the pathological narcissist, in her inability to mourn, her rage for control, her unwillingness to allow that other people may make demands that compromise the equanimity of the self. I shall pursue these suspicions in Part III.

Is the Stoic's sweeping position on external goods even consistent? It is very difficult to see how there can be an ethical theory at all if there is no value attached to any external good: for morality seems to be all about arranging for the appropriate distribution of those things. Courage, justice, moderation – all these virtues deal with our need for externals; that is why, as Aristotle said, we cannot imagine needless gods having the virtues. If Stoics give any advice at all for this-worldly behavior, it has to be because they consider something valuable. Stoic ethical theory, notoriously, tries to deal with this question through the theory of the "preferred" and "dispreferred" indifferents: things that nature has set us to pursue and that it is therefore reasonable to pursue, provided that no impediment intervenes. But the theory holds that we are never to invest these things with real value, or to think of them as

37 For this as Aristotle's position, see Nussbaum (1986), Chapter 11, and Nussbaum (1992). Aristotle stresses that a person may be "dislodged" from *eudaimonia* by chance reversals of a very severe sort; nonetheless, even in such catastrophes, the person's nobility may still "shine through" in the way misfortune is borne: and he will use the material of life as well as possible. Thus he will merit our respect (*Nicomachean Ethics* I.11).

necessary for our *eudaimonia*. This theory has real problems justifying difficult or risky courses of action, which seem to require a greater investment in the world than the letter of the theory can deliver.

Sometimes, therefore, Stoics seem to go further in the direction of valuing the external than their theory really permits. Thus, Seneca urges the slave-owner to treat the slave with respect, to renounce physical cruelty and sexual abuse – conceding, apparently, that these things, albeit external to virtue, do matter. Other Stoics, similarly, risked their lives for political liberty – again, apparently granting that this matters. Ultimately, it would appear that the Stoics are not only inconsistent when they ascribe value to these things while denying that they do so; they are also incoherent, in the sence that they draw the line in an arbitrary place. Why object to cruelty and not to the institution of slavery itself? Why object to sexual abuse and torture, and not to social conditions that keep people in a state of hunger and poverty?[38] To pursue the twistings and turnings of the Stoic reply to such charges would take us far from our topic; let it suffice to say that they do not seem able to reply without heavy reliance on a teleology of nature and a notion of divine commandment.

The friend of compassion may add that if we need a decent theory of value to guide us, compassion, as standardly exemplified and taught in tragic drama, has a pretty good theory to offer. The standard occasions for compassion, throughout the literary and philosophical tradition – and presumably in the popular thought on which the tradition draws – involve losses of truly basic goods, such as life, loved ones, freedom, nourishment, mobility, bodily integrity, citizenship, shelter. Compassion seems to be, as standardly experienced, a reasonably reliable guide to the presence of real value. And this appears to be so ubiquitously, and without elaborate prior training. Perhaps this is because compassion has an evolutionary history that connects it to attempts by our species to respond well to predicaments affecting the entire group. Perhaps it is, instead, because all societies have conceptions of the good that do attach value to such losses, and because

---

38 This is the part of Stoic theory that has had deep influence on international law, through Cicero's distinction of duties into two classes. We still believe that torture must be stopped, even if it is in another country, but that hunger can be allowed to continue; in accepting this (I would say arbitrary and indefensible) division in our duties, we are following the Stoics. See Nussbaum (2000c).

parents communicate these values to their children early in their developmental history. In any case, it is because of its intimate connection to a true "core theory" of value that compassion so often subverts ambitious false theories of value, as in my account of "breakthroughs" of Nazi rationalizations about the meaning of the suffering inflicted on Jews. When W. H. Auden wished to describe the human obtuseness he saw around him in Europe in the late 1930s, he wrote:

> Intellectual disgrace
> Stares from every human face,
> And the seas of pity lie
> Locked and frozen in each eye.

The poem connects these two failures: intellectual obtuseness is intimately bound up with the freezing of the imagination, "pity" with the possibility of an accurate vision of value. The connection is a contingent one, but it appears to be deeply rooted.

One further distinction can now be drawn. The anti-compassion tradition suggests that the pitier is too enamored of the idea that people are victims of circumstance, too inclined to see that state of weakness as a good thing. By encouraging strong attachments to the "goods of fortune" the pitier encourages people to be needy, and this is problematic. But in fact the defender of compassion is not bound to embrace as good any and every sort of human neediness and dependency. I have just argued that some forms of felt neediness derive from inappropriate evaluations, and that they should therefore, as the Stoic says, be altered. But even with respect to those "external goods" that are endorsed by the compassionate person's own reflection as of enormous importance for flourishing, this person is not required to wish on people the maximum vulnerability. There are ways of arranging the world so as to bring these good things more securely within people's grasp: and acknowledging our deep need for them provides a strong incentive for so designing things. Obviously there are some important features of human life that nobody ever fully controls; one cannot make oneself immortal, one cannot will that one's children should be healthy and happy, one cannot will oneself happiness in love. But nonetheless, differences in class, race, gender, wealth, and power do affect the extent to which the sense of helplessness governs the daily course of one's life. The compassionate person need not think it a good thing that people should experience painful vulnerability every day with respect to their daily food, that citizens should every day feel their political freedom to be in jeopardy, that relationships of friendship and love should be jeopardized by tensions produced by hierarchies of race and gender. These are all instances of vulnerability; but it would be a ludicrous travesty of the pro-compassion position to say that all vulnerability is a good thing. The pitier does not wish to keep diphtheria around just so that Rückert's children will have a special poetic vulnerability to disaster that gives the audience of Mahler's *Kindertotenlieder* a moving experience of compassion. To the extent that a type of disaster is eliminated, compassion for the sufferers of that disaster will disappear; and the pro-compassion position is perfectly entitled to say that this is a good thing.[39] To make these discriminations, compassion needs to be combined with an adequate theory of the basic human goods: but there is no reason to assume that it must have a bad such theory.

This response suggests a further point. It is a commonplace that women tend to be more emotional than men. This commonplace, however, is vague and uninformative, without further elaboration. It would seem that two quite different things are going on when we discover (to the extent that we do) that women's lives are dominated by grief, and fear, and deep personal love, and compassion, to a greater extent than are the lives of men. The first underlying factor is a difference in appraisal. The moral education of women in many societies cultivates, to a greater extent than does the moral education of men, the high evaluation of personal relationships of love and care that are the basis for most of the other emotions; men, by contrast, are often encouraged to follow a more Stoic norm, seeking separateness and self-sufficiency. Where these differences are concerned, we should simply ask what the correct theory of value is; that correct theory (which presumably would include at least some high valuation of some external goods) should be taught to all, and will give all a basis for some compassion, both given and received.

The second underlying factor is altogether different: the lives of women in many parts of the world are socially and materially shaped

39 Such a development does not make Mahler's work incapable of arousing emotion; it simply shifts the content of the "things such as might happen" thought. Instead of thinking that the death of children from diphtheria is a possibility for me, I need only think that the death of children – or, indeed, of loved ones – is such a possibility.

so that, with respect to the very same external goods, they have less control and greater helplessness. Unequal access to food and medical treatment, to political privileges, to control over the course and outcome of a marriage[40] – all of this is a basis for fear and grief, and for the onlooker's compassion. In this case, the unequal vulnerability should not and need not be endorsed as good by the friend of compassion.

But is it good to raise the floor of security? One common form of the anti-compassion position holds that this makes society inefficiently soft and indulgent. When good things are guaranteed completely independently of people's efforts, this discourages effort. Societies will produce more energetic citizens if they leave them to fend for themselves in important matters. This position needs careful scrutiny, and no doubt in some areas of economic life it makes an important point. But, once again, as a general objection to central cases of compassion it is far too crude. It is true that only a bad parent will give a child everything she asks for, since that would undermine the development of effort and strength of purpose. In Chapter 4, we insisted that loss and frustration are inevitable parts of appropriate development. On the other hand, there are many things that no good parent would expect a child to get on her own. It may well be true that my daughter, who has always been well fed without having to look for her food, would be a bad forager if she were suddenly thrust into a situation in which she had to hunt for food on her own. So would I. But I am sure that this does not make it a bad thing that I fed her regularly, as my parents fed me. I see no merit at all in spending a lot of time foraging for food, an activity that certainly impedes the development of other important human capacities. We may think of the task of society in a similar way. Society is a bad "parent" if it gives everything on demand in a way that discourages the development of effort across the board. On the other hand, this does not make it a bad thing for society to concern itself with the provision of the necessary conditions for any meaningful functioning. In fact, there are many sorts of vulnerability and need that do nobody any good, and some things, therefore, for which any good society should not ask its members to forage. Society expresses concern for the active development of citizens' higher capacities when it does

40 See, for example, Sen (1990).

support their health, nutrition, and education, when it does not force them to fight for their political freedom[41] – when, in general, it focuses on the provision of the basic goods that are the most common objects of compassion in central cases.[42]

In short, what is needed is a subtle and multifaceted inquiry into human flourishing and its material and social conditions, asking what things are important, and how far they can be secured to people without losing what makes them important. The pro-compassion person claims that it is her side of the debate that is equipped to conduct this inquiry, since her opponent is debarred from it by his dogmatic insistence that none of these things is of any importance at all. And she makes a further claim: her opponent, lacking a sense of the interdependence of human beings and their natural world, cannot make sense of something that he himself holds to be of fundamental importance, namely benevolence.

No member of the anti-compassion tradition expresses indifference to benevolence. Indeed, Stoics and their followers typically hold that one of the virtues of their position is that it promotes benevolence by minimizing competitive grasping for goods. If people respect themselves as self-commanding beings, complete in themselves, they will be less inclined to define themselves in terms of money and status, and therefore free to give generously to others. Seneca distinguishes carefully between the lofty reason-governed benevolence of the Stoic and the soft, needy giving characteristic of compassion. Spinoza makes much of the way in which removal of emotional need will minimize destructive competition. Kant speaks in a Stoic voice when he says that when we get rid of pity, that "insulting kind of benevolence," we will still be able to think of the needs of others with "an active and rational benevolence." This benevolent disposition will include an active attempt to understand the situation of another – what Kant calls *human-*

---

41 Pace Nietzsche, who makes the ludicrous claim that guarantees of freedom of speech and press undermine "the will to assume responsibility for oneself," making people "small, cowardly and hedonistic" (see *Twilight of the Idols*, "Skirmishes," 38). He concludes: "The highest type of free men should be sought where the highest resistance is constantly overcome: five steps from tyranny, close to the threshold of the danger of servitude . . . The people who had some value, *attained* some value, never attained it under liberal institutions: it was great danger that made something of them that merits respect." This is precisely the position that we should not adopt.

42 See Nussbaum (2000a).

itas practica and *Teilnehmende Empfindung* – but will repudiate the softhearted commiseration characteristic of compassion (*Mitleid*, *Barmherzigkeit*), which "can be called communicable (like a susceptibility to heat or to contagious diseases)."[43]

The question is, however, what sense such Stoic-affiliated thinkers can make of the need for benevolence, when they hold the dignity of reason to be complete in itself. They are right to say that Stoicism reduces competitiveness, and in that sense makes benevolence easier; but it seems at the same time to rob benevolence of its point. If people can exercise their most important capacities without material support, this very much diminishes the significance and the urgency of that support. The original Stoics at this point invoke teleology: Zeus's providence has made each person's survival naturally an object of concern to him, and it is therefore appropriate to concern oneself with the "goods of nature" when nothing else interferes, even though, strictly speaking, they have no true worth.[44] But Kant and other modern Stoics can help themselves to no such religious picture; so the status of benevolence in their theories becomes problematic. We are put on our guard when Kant expresses himself as follows:

It was a sublime way of representing the wise man, as the Stoic conceived him, when he let the wise one say: I wish I had a friend, not that he might give me help in poverty, sickness, captivity, and so on, but in order that I might stand by him and save a human being. But for all that, the very same wise man, when his friend is not to be saved, says to himself: What's it to me? i.e. he rejected commiseration.[45]

Kant here follows the Stoic tradition in insisting that there is no good way to register emotional distress at the present misfortune of another. So long as disaster is merely impending, the Stoic may move under the guidance of "prudent caution" to ward it off. But there is no good affect corresponding to present distress: one simply should say, "What's it to me?"[46] Kant now immediately tries to salvage the motivational foundations of benevolence by insisting that, since active be-

---

43 Kant, *Doctrine of Virtue* 34, Akad. p. 456–7, Ellington trans. p. 121.
44 On the difficulties of interpreting the Stoic position here, see Lesses (1989), and further references in Nussbaum (1994), Chapter 10.
45 Kant, *Doctrine of Virtue* 34, Akad. p. 457, Ellington trans. pp. 121–2.
46 On the Stoic doctrine of the *eupatheiai*, or good affects, see Nussbaum (1994) Chapter 10.

nevolence is a duty, it is also a duty to seek out circumstances in which one will witness poverty and deprivation:

Thus it is a duty not to avoid places where the poor, who lack the most necessary things, are to be found; instead, it is a duty to seek them out. It is a duty not to shun sickrooms or prisons and so on in order to avoid the pain of pity, which one may not be able to resist. For this feeling, though painful, nevertheless is one of the impulses placed in us by nature for effecting what the representation of duty might not accomplish by itself.[47]

This fascinating passage shows us as clearly as any text the tensions of the anti-compassion position, when it tries to defend benevolence. In what spirit, we may ask, does the Kantian visit places "where the poor are to be found"? In a truly Stoic spirit, performing a moral duty with no thought of the universality and importance of human need, no thought of his own personal similarity to the sufferers? But then what will the sight of this misery mean to him, and how will it inspire benevolence? Won't he be likely to have some contempt for these people, insofar as they are depressed at their lot? Won't he want to remind them that "a good will is good not because of what it effects or accomplishes, . . . it is good only through its willing, i.e. good in itself"?[48] He might then reflect, gazing at them, that

[e]ven if, by some especially unfortunate fate or by the niggardly provision of stepmotherly nature, this will should be wholly lacking in the power to accomplish its purpose . . . yet would it, like a jewel, still shine by its own light as something which has its full value in itself. Its usefulness or fruitlessness can neither augment nor diminish this value. Its usefulness would be, as it were, only the setting to enable us to handle it in ordinary dealings or to attract to it the attention of those who are not yet experts, but not to recommend it to real experts or to determine its value.[49]

And won't he then say to himself: I am a real expert, and I see here, in this place where the poor are to be found, not the squalor itself, not the poverty, but the pure light of human dignity, which has full value in itself and cannot possibly be increased by my gifts?

For Kant, this cannot be the complete response of the good person.

---

47 Kant, *Doctrine of Virtue* 35, Akad. p. 35, Ellington p. 122.
48 Kant, *Grounding for the Metaphysics of Morals*, section 1, Akad. p. 394, Ellington p. 7.
49 Kant, *Grounding*, section 1, Akad. p. 394, Ellington trans. pp. 7–8.

Duties to promote the happiness of others have fundamental importance in Kant's ethics. Because they are not supported by any teleological scheme, they play a fundamentally different part for Kant from their role in Stoic ethics. That is, while the Stoic can promote happiness without thinking the goods of fortune important (saying that the good person is simply following Zeus's command in distributing these things), Kant must ascribe some real importance to them. But this means that he must accept as true at least some of the propositions that the Stoics denounce as false, propositions that prove sufficient for compassion. It will be true of the good Kantian agent that, while respecting human dignity, he also believes that people may suffer serious calamities through no fault of their own. And this really means that such a person will have compassion.

Nowhere in Kant's ethics does he give analyses and definitions of the passions. Surprisingly enough – influenced as he is by both the Stoic and the Spinozistic tradition, as well as by Rousseau – he never states what he takes to be the cognitive ingredients of compassion, or indeed of anger or fear. Instead, influenced, it would seem, by the Pietism of his social context, he treats all these passions as if they derived from a prerational nature and were fundamentally impulsive and noncognitive in character. This creates problems for his moral thought in other areas as well: for example, in *Perpetual Peace*, his acceptance of the innate and impulsive character of anger and hatred limits the proposals he can make for its containment or reform.[50] Consistently with this position, he understands virtue not in the Aristotelian way, as involving a reasonable shaping or enlightening of the passions, but in a suppressive or oppositional way, as involving the mastery of emotions and other sensuous inclinations.[51] He argues, in fact, that virtue presupposes "apathy" (Stoic *apatheia*), by which he means the condition in which "the feelings arising from sensible impressions lose their influence on moral feeling only because respect for the law is more powerful than all of these feelings together" (408). The "true strength of virtue is the

---

50 See Nussbaum (1997b).
51 See, for example, Akad. p. 407: "Two things are required for internal freedom: to be master of oneself in a given case (*animus sui compos*), and to be lord over oneself (*imperium in semitipsum*), i.e., to subdue one's emotions (*Affekten*) and to govern one's passions (*Leidenschaften*) . . . Therefore, insofar as virtue is based on internal freedom, it contains a positive command for man, namely, that he should bring all his capacities and inclinations under his authority (that of reason)."

mind at rest . . . That is the state of health in the moral life; emotion, on the contrary, even when it is aroused by the representation of the good, is a momentarily glittering appearance which leaves one languid" (409).

In the case of compassion, Kant's apparent solution to the tension between his Stoicism and his non-Stoic interest in external goods is to invoke compassion as a motive fortunately planted in us by nature in order to bring about what the representation of duty might not. Given that natural fact about us, it is our duty to cultivate that emotional motive by placing ourselves in circumstances naturally suited to arousing it. Thus compassion becomes a requirement of duty: "to make use of this susceptibility for furthering an active and rational benevolence is . . . a particular, though only conditional duty, which goes by the name of humanity (*Menschheit*), because here man is regarded not merely as a rational being but also as an animal endowed with reason" (p. 456). It is therefore an indirect duty to develop our "natural (sensitive) feelings for others, and to make use of them as so many means for sympathy based on moral principles" (p. 457).

But if the motives connected with compassion are required for benevolence, and in consequence a part of our duty, isn't this more than an accident of human psychology? Kant's position seems to be that compassion is just an internally unintelligent indicator, a bell that goes off in the presence of suffering, conditioning us to recognize suffering as a morally relevant feature of a situation. But such a mechanism seems much too crude to do the work that Kant needs it to do. A bell ringing doesn't tell us what the relevant feature of the situation is, or help us to recognize that feature in new situations. In order for the passion to help solve the problem of moral discernment, it has to have intelligence and selectivity. Kant needs the intentional content of the passion, its complex evaluations, in order to tell the onlooker what is going on here, and why it matters. These evaluations are profoundly non-Stoic, and would require him to confront more fully than he does his own difference from Stoicism. Because Kant treats the passion as noncognitive, he is never forced to explore the extent of his difference from the Stoics on softheartedness, and he can speak as if he agrees with the wise man when, in reality, his position is very different. His own complex and ultimately non-Stoic view would have been better served by accepting the cognitive view of compassion and admitting that the onlooker needs compassion's judgments of the worth of external goods for animal-rational human beings. Without these evaluations, he will be like a Martian onlooker, and only some external commandment – with which the Stoics can supply him, but Kant cannot – would make him intervene.

Kant's failure to endorse as good the evaluations embodied in compassion derives from his general noncognitive view of the passions. But it has, as well, another source, which is more cognitive in nature. Kant has a deep conviction that there is something humiliating in being the recipient of compassion. He holds that respect and self-respect require distance and not too much loving concern; on the other hand, the principle of practical love enjoins closeness and attentive concern. Kant believes that these two moral forces can be balanced, but that they do pull the good moral agent to some extent in contradictory directions:

... we regard ourselves as being in a moral (intelligible) world in which, by analogy with the physical world, the association of rational beings (on earth) is effected through attraction and repulsion. According to the principle of *mutual love* they are directed constantly to approach one another; by the principle of *respect* which they owe one another they are directed to keep themselves at a distance. Should one of these great moral forces sink, "so then would nothingness (immorality) with gaping throat drink up the whole realm of (moral) beings like a drop of water" ...

It seems that this conception of our relation to one another, unlike the arguments we have already considered, does pose problems for the cognitions associated with benevolent compassion: for we are warned that we will insult the other person's separateness and agency if we step too close. But this warning can be heeded by the friend of compassion, who is not required to treat its recipient intrusively or condescendingly. As we have already argued, compassion can coexist with respect for agency. Indeed, it is only when we see to what extent need for external goods is involved in the development of agency itself that we have the deepest possible basis for respecting and promoting human freedom.

Nietzsche's view encounters a problem about beneficence similar to Kant's problem, and more acutely. For Nietzsche, unlike Kant, insists on the complete unity between our bodily and our spiritual natures, insisting that the human being is an animal who dwells entirely in the world of nature. He appears to endorse the tragic position that the world can intervene in our flourishing in very fundamental ways. But then it is especially odd that in his critique of compassion he refuses to conclude that human beings need worldly goods in order to function. In all of his rather abstract and romantic praise of solitude and asceticism, we find no sign of the simple truth that a hungry person cannot think well, that a person who lacks shelter, basic health care, and the other necessities of life is not likely to become a self-expressing philosopher or artist, no matter what her innate equipment.

Indeed, Nietzsche repeatedly asserts the false romantic view that suffering, including basic physical suffering, ennobles and strengthens the spirit: "it almost determines the order of rank *how* profoundly human beings can suffer" (*Beyond Good and Evil* 270). It therefore "becomes regard for the 'general welfare' not only not to lessen suffering, but perhaps even to increase it – not only for oneself but also for others" ("On Ethics," 1868).[52] In *Ecce Homo*, the answer to the lovely chapter title "Why I Am So Wise" has much to do with pain and hunger, as Nietzsche attributes the profundity of his philosophy to physical illness and nutritional disorder. *Dawn*, for example, was produced by "that sweetening and spiritualization which is almost inseparably connected with an extreme poverty of blood and muscle" ("Wise," 1). In a fragment of 1887 (*Will to Power* 910), Nietzsche wishes that others too will enjoy the improving nobility of bodily suffering: "To those human beings who are of any concern to me I wish suffering, desolation, sickness, ill-treatment, indignities . . ."

Nietzsche, in short, takes up the extreme and absurd position that the absence of external goods is an improving test for the spirit. Strong spirits survive, and weak spirits go under. This position keeps coming back to plague political thought, and has not been repudiated in our own time. Once again we should insist: the plausible idea that people need some incentives if they are to exercise their effort well does not imply that they should have to "forage" for their daily food and struggle for their basic political freedoms. What is more, Nietzsche, the apostle of the body and of an enmattered view of the spirit, is the last

---

52 Cf. also *Will to Power* 1030: "a full and powerful soul not only copes with painful, even terrible losses, deprivations, robberies, insults; it emerges from such hells with a greater fullness and powerfulness; and, most essential of all, with a new increase in the blissfulness of love."

person who should be saying such things. His romanticism and his materialism are fundamentally at odds.[53]

And because Nietzsche does not consistently grasp the fact that if our abilities are physical abilities they have physical necessary conditions, he does not understand what the democratic and socialist movements of his day are all about. The pro-compassion tradition, as developed by Rousseau, made compassion's thought about external goods the basis for the modern development of democratic-egalitarian thinking. Since Nietzsche does not get the basic idea, he does not see what Rousseau is trying to do. And thus, invoking Epictetus, Spinoza, and Kant as his mentors, he can proceed as if it does not really matter how people live from day to day, how they get their food. Thus again, having concluded that the absence of political liberty is a confirming test to the truly strong spirit,[54] he is able to dismiss J. S. Mill as a "flathead" (*Will to Power* 30) and as a "respectable but mediocre Englishm[a]n" (*Beyond Good and Evil* 253), capable only of an English "narrowness, aridity, and industrious diligence." He pronounces that "[t]he highest type of free men should be sought where the highest resistance is constantly overcome: five steps from tyranny, close to the threshold of the danger of servitude."[55] Meanwhile, his fictional imagining of the "higher men" and the prophet who educates them takes place at a level of social and material abstractness that makes Rousseau's and Mill's issues simply disappear from view. Who provides basic welfare support for Zarathustra? What are the "higher men" doing all the day long?[56] What are other people doing who have therefore no chance to become "higher men"? What are the conditions of political freedom in the city of the Motley Cow? The reader does not know, and the author does not seem to care. This happens not

---

53 At *Will to Power* 367, Nietzsche seems to see the point: "*My kind of 'pity.'* – This is a feeling for which I find no name adequate: I see it when I see precious capabilities squandered . . . Or when I see anyone halted, as a result of some stupid accident, at something less than he might have become."

54 Nietzsche, "Skirmishes of an Untimely One," *Twilight of the Idols* 38.

55 Ibid.

56 On Nietzsche's romanticism, and his interest in human pride and self-realization, see Posner (1988), pp. 146–8. Even though, as Posner suggests, Nietzsche is simply not interested in the economic side of life, he does criticize socialist and democratic movements, and should have been more willing to engage in the kind of economic thinking that would show him what they were all about.

from cruelty, but from Stoicism. Nietzsche's Stoicism is on a collision course with his respect for the needs of the embodied human being.

V. PARTIALITY AND CONCERN

I turn now to the objection about partiality. Here we have a serious objection to compassion that does not assail the worth of its basic evaluative commitments, an objection that is pressed not only by the Stoic–Kantian tradition, but also by the Utilitarian tradition, which takes the importance of human suffering as primary, and by some members of the pro-compassion tradition as well. The objection, as Adam Smith makes it, does not deny that compassion is a valuable emotion, based in central cases on true beliefs. The problem is that each of its judgments needs to be equipped with a correct ethical theory. The judgment of seriousness needs a correct account of the value of external goods; the judgment of nondesert needs a correct theory of social responsibility; the eudaimonistic judgment needs a correct theory of proper concern. The problem is not simply that societies frequently teach false theories in these areas: that would not give us reason to turn from compassion to a more abstract system of rules, since those too might embody error. The problem is that the psychological mechanisms by which human beings typically arrive at compassion – empathy and the judgment of similar possibilities – typically rest on the senses and the imagination in a way that makes them in principle narrow and uneven.

We should grant that there is a major issue here. The objector has correctly identified a serious problem in compassion-based reasoning. We see this problem, for example, in any approach to social welfare that relies on individual philanthropy; such approaches typically produce uneven and at times arbitrary results. We see the difficulty even more clearly when we focus on aid to people in other nations: for typically people find it difficult to extend their compassion that far, encompassing people whom they do not know and whose sufferings (as Adam Smith put it well) they cannot long find interesting.

We can make the objection stronger by bringing in our own observations about shame and disgust. It is highly likely that people will learn compassion under circumstances that divide and rank-order human beings, creating in-groups and out-groups. The emotional factors that produce such divisions are too deep-seated to be easily eradicated. But they create boundaries to compassion that are also difficult to eradicate. Thus if we rely on compassion we may well reinforce hierarchies of class, race, and gender.

Notice that this objection, unlike our first objection, is not exactly an objection to compassion itself: it does not say that people should not have compassion. It says, instead, that compassion requires an appropriate education in connection with a correct theory of concern; and that, even then, people so rarely extend their compassion evenly and appropriately that it would not be good to rely upon it too much.

Just as we should concede that compassion needs a correct theory of the importance of various external goods, so too we should concede that it needs a correct view of the people who should be the objects of our concern. While there is reason to think that we more often than not get it right about the importance of various external goods, there is reason to think that we are more unreliable about the people who should be the objects of our concern. I have suggested that the central cases of compassion involve a notion of common humanity – so here, as with the evaluation of basic goods, we seem to be on the right track, whether on account of culture or of biology. But it is very easy for the promising notion of common humanity to be derailed by local loyalties and their associated rivalries, obtuseness, and even hatred. This unevenness has its source in the other emotions that surround compassion, and also in the psychological mechanisms themselves that standardly undergird the emotion.

We ought to make some serious concessions to this argument. We should concede, first, that an education in proper compassion needs to be designed with these problems in view. In the next chapter I shall discuss ways in which moral education can address them. We should also concede that the argument gives us reason to rely a good deal more on appropriately informed political institutions than on the vicissitudes of personal emotion. But this does not mean that we should not consult emotion in the process of designing the institutions. In the next chapter I shall give some examples of ways in which the structure of institutions can embody the insights of a properly educated compassion, so that we do not need to rely too heavily on the vicissitudes of the compassion of individual people.

But why, then, should we rely on the emotion at all, rather than going directly to the appropriate principles and institutions? And why appeal to the compassion of citizens at all, rather than urging them to follow the correct rules?

If the account of development that I have sketched in Chapter 4 is at all plausible, people do not get to altruism without proceeding through the intense particular attachments of childhood, without enlarging these gradually through guilt and gratitude, without extending their concern through the imagining that is characteristic of compassion. Compassion is our species' way of hooking the good of others to the fundamentally eudaimonistic (though not egoistic) structure of our imaginations and our most intense cares. The good of others means nothing to us in the abstract or antecedently. It is when it is brought into relation with that which we already understand – with our intense love of our parents, our passionate need for comfort and security – that such things start to matter deeply. The imagination of similar possibilities that is an important mechanism in human (if not necessarily in divine) compassion does important moral work by extending the boundaries of that which we can imagine; the tradition claims that only when we can imagine the good or ill of another can we fully and reliably extend to that other our moral concern.

Hierocles, a perhaps nonorthodox Stoic of the first and second centuries A.D., has a vivid metaphor for this process. Imagine, he says, that each of us lives in a set of concentric circles – the nearest being one's own body, the furthest being the entire universe of human beings. The task of moral development is to move the circles progressively closer to the center, so that one's parents become like oneself, one's other relatives like one's parents, strangers like relatives, and so forth.[57] In other words, to demand from the start equal concern, or any other normatively good type of properly ranked concern, is unrealistic; no human mind can achieve this. One has to build on the meanings one understands, or one is left with an equality that is empty of urgency – what

---

57 See the discussion in Long and Sedley (1987), p. 349. The job of a reasonable person is to "draw the circles somehow towards the centre," and "the right point will be reached if, through our own initiative, we reduce the distance of the relationship with each person." Adam Smith also proposes evening out one's concern through imagination, but finds it implausible that one could do this by building up the importance of the distant; he prefers to cut down the importance of the close (Smith [1976], 139ff.). Neither the Stoics nor Smith propose a complete evening out, since they attach importance to close personal and family ties.

Aristotle, attacking Plato's removal of the family, called a "watery" concern all around.[58] Fairbairn's goal of "mature dependence" requires a gradual movement outward from the intense dependency of child-hood; it is subverted by the absence of such concern. Compassion's psychological mechanisms promote this movement.

This point is brilliantly developed in Dickens's portrait of the Utili-tarian upbringing of the young Gradgrinds, who, lacking in intense particular attachments, end up being totally unable to comprehend the needs of people at a distance, or to invest human lives and the external goods that support them with a human worth and significance. Their minds and hearts become thoroughly listless, lacking in any motiva-tional energy for good; and one political proposal seems very much like another, since they have no ability to imagine or feel what is at stake.[59] Rather than being energetically impartial – their father's origi-nal aim – they are, instead, both empty and blind. Moreover, as the collapse of both Tom and Louisa shows, the goal of producing a balanced adult personality, capable of good deliberation and energetic concern for others, is very much undercut by stunting the early emo-tions, which, so stunted, may return later in more dangerous and unbalanced forms.

We can see the same point in a darker light by thinking again about the morality of Nazism. As Jonathan Glover has argued in the material I examined in Chapter 6, a basic sort of compassion for suffering individuals, built on meanings learned in childhood, sometimes breaks through even the most carefully constructed layers of ideology and rationalization – most easily when the potential victim is physically present, and/or when some reminder of one's love of one's own children or family serve to connect the victim to one's own life. These elemen-tary emotions appear to be the most reliable part of the personality, when theory has been massively distorted. As Rousseau suggests, there is something quasi-natural about our tendency to have compassion for the sufferings of those close to us, in the sense that the emotion is likely to arise in some form in all human beings and to steer us to at least some genuinely moral connections. By contrast, an abstract moral the-ory uninhabited by those connections of imagination and sympathy

58 *Politics* II.4. For excellent accounts of Aristotle's views, see Sherman (1989) and Price (1989).
59 See Nussbaum (1995a).

can easily be turned to evil ends, because its human meaning is unclear. Thus, as Glover also shows, there were Nazis who said, perhaps sincerely, that they believed themselves to be following the precepts of a Kantian morality of duty. Certainly a rule-based morality, unanimated by the resources of the imagination, can too easily become confused with a submissiveness to cultural rules, or to rules handed down by authority.

A further literary example will illustrate this point. In Theodor Fontane's novel *Effi Briest*, Instetten, a successful civil servant who has married a much younger wife, discovers years later that she has had an affair during the early days of their marriage. Because he can think of moral decision only as a process of following social rules, he proves unable to allow his distant instincts of love and forgiveness to come forward. He insists that he must do what is required of a man in his situation. He shoots the rival, banishes the wife, brings up his child to lack all love for her mother, and finds his own life increasingly hollow and pointless. Before Effi's untimely death, she says to her parents that her husband acted as well as he could – for a man who had never really felt love.

In a very interesting article by Julia Annas, Instetten has been invoked as an example of the limitations of Kantian morality.[60] This seems not quite right, for he clearly follows a social code of honor more than any truly moral principle. But his failure does show what is wrong with bringing people up to live by rules alone rather than by a combination of rules with love and imagination. Imagination is of no use without a moral code of some sort; Effi's own failure makes this point clearly. But it is also true that compassion guides us truly toward something that lies at the core of morality, and without which any moral judgment is a ghastly simulacrum. In that way, Effi, though inconstant and flawed, has a connection to the core of what is important in life that Instetten lacks. And the novel's moral center, in a paradoxical sense, is the faithful dog Rollo, who knows only sympathy and love, and whose loyalty remains uncorrupted by either Effi's ambition or Instetten's false values of honor and shame.[61] In short: compassion does not supply a complete morality; far from it. But there is

60 Annas (1984). I am unable to do justice here to the subtlety of Annas's argument.
61 Thus the novel's conclusion is reminiscent of the argument of George Pitcher's book, discussed in Chapter 2: dogs have much to teach us about unconditional love.

reason to trust it as guide to something that is at the very heart of morality.

In a sense, the developmental argument begun in Chapter 4 and continued here speaks already about adult rationality, by talking about the production of a person capable of "mature dependence." Furthermore, since moral development is never complete, the process of "drawing the circles somehow toward the center" is one that takes a lifetime. But we can also make the argument in a nongenetic way, holding that the judgments characteristic of compassion are essential for the health of a complete adult rationality.

Theories of rationality neglect this insight to their cost. Economic accounts of human motivation as based on rational self-interest have recently been criticized, both in philosophy and in economics itself, on the grounds that such accounts fail to do justice to the way in which good reasoning ascribes value to the lives of others, distinguishing between their instrumental role in one's own life and their flourishing itself. A leading example of such criticism is Amartya Sen's famous lecture "Rational Fools,"[62] which argues that we cannot give either a good predictive account of human action or a correct normative theory of rationality without mentioning the sympathetic concern people have for the good of others, as a factor independent of their concern for their own satisfactions. For people very often sacrifice their own interests and well-being, and in many cases even their lives, for the well-being of those they love, or for good social consequences that they prize. They also stand by commitments and promises that they have made, even when to do so requires major personal sacrifice. One cannot, Sen argues, explain the behavior of loving members of families, or of soldiers who give their lives for their country, or of many other decent and unselfish acts, without pointing to patterns of action that are uneconomic – and this seems correct.[63] Batson's ex-

62 In Sen (1982); Sen's views will be further discussed in Chapter 8, section VII.
63 Notice that the family altruism to which Sen alludes is not the "altruism" assumed in standard economic models, which is really a kind of instrumental dependency, contingent on the bond's serving the good of the agent in some way. On the sympathetic decency of many ordinary people, and for many examples of the sort of behavior Sen has in mind, see the remarkable account of rescuers of Jews in Nazi Europe in Oliner and Oliner (1988).

perimental work and the evolutionary account of Sober and Wilson have given further support to his contention. Finally, Clark's elaborate account of the operations of compassion in daily life shows that even Americans – who might justly be suspected of being more like *Homo economicus* than many other people – are motivated by compassion in all sorts of ways, even when they believe that other Americans are not.[64]

But one cannot fully articulate Sen's own more complex predictive and normative theory of reasoning without prominently including the emotions in which parts of that reasoning are embodied. He himself stresses that compassion (his preferred term is "sympathy") is actually a prominent motive in the rational conduct he describes; and the judgments about the sufferings of others that he ascribes to his rational agent are the very ones that we have identified as sufficient for compassion. Indeed, we might conclude, thinking about the contrast between Dickens's Utilitarian children and Sen's more completely rational agents, that compassion itself is the eye through which people see the good and ill of others, and its full meaning. Without it, the abstract sight of the calculating intellect is value-blind.

We should not conclude from these observations that formal economic models of human conduct are useless and that we should rely on the impressions of the heart alone. The partiality objection shows us that we should not depend on the vicissitudes of personal emotion, but should build its insights into the structure of rules and institutions. Similarly, we need formal models for the purposes of description and prediction, and there is no reason at all why they cannot be built upon a richer theory of human motivation.

In short: we should not let the truth in the partiality objection lead us to turn away from compassion as an ethical guide. It must be combined with an ethical code, but it supplies something that lies at the heart of any good ethical code, without which rules and principles are dangerously blind. The right solution to its partiality problems is to work on compassion's developmental history, trying to get the three judgments right through appropriate education and institutional design. I shall return to this issue in the following chapter.

---

64 Clark notes that men, in particular, often make this claim, describing themselves as more sympathetic than most people.

VI. REVENGE AND MERCY

We now face the argument about revenge, which seems difficult for the friend of compassion to answer. For it tells her that she cannot have a form of reasoning that she prizes without also taking on attitudes that she herself views with alarm. All the major pro-compassion philosophers are also deeply worried about anger and revenge. Aristotle insists that the virtuous disposition in the area of retaliation is called *praotês*, mildness of temper; and he insists that the virtuous person will be more likely to err in the direction of deficient than of excessive retributive anger: "For the mild person is not inclined to retribution, but rather to sympathetic understanding" (*Nicomachean Ethics* IV.5, II26a2–3). Interestingly enough, then, he does not just deny that building in a role for compassion commits him to a robust interest in revenge, he even suggests that the sympathetic understanding characteristic of compassion offers an antidote to revenge. Let us see how this connection might work.

First of all, the defender of compassion can insist once again that the opponent's picture of her position is far too crude. For just as she is not committed to saying that any and every calamity is an appropriate occasion for compassion, so too she is not committed to saying that any and every damage, slight, or insult is an occasion for retributive anger. By far the largest number of the social ills caused by revenge concern damages to fortune, status, power, and honor, to which the defenders of compassion standardly do not (except to a very moderate degree) ascribe true worth. A brief perusal of Seneca's *On Anger* bears out this claim. For although once in a while he does represent anger over a damage that an Aristotelian would think serious, far more frequently he shows powerful and pampered people committing acts of violence over trivial slights – a slave's breaking of a cup, a host's less-than-attentive treatment, a subordinate's less-than-fawning subservience. None of this is the subject matter of tragedy. And when we get our concerns adjusted, our occasions for intense anger will be fewer. Descartes' account of the compassion of the generous person is right at home here: for the person he depicts has confidence in his own worth and virtue, and therefore, though he does feel compassion, he lacks the instability characteristic of someone who depends in every way on the external goods of fortune.

In short, we should simply deny that the excesses of anger give us reason to remove it. We should boldly tell the Stoics that anger is sometimes justified and right. It is an appropriate response to injustice and serious wrongdoing. Indeed, extirpating anger would extirpate a major force for social justice and the defense of the oppressed. If we are worried that anger may spill over onto inappropriate objects, we should focus on that problem, not try to remove anger completely. And if we are worried that angry individuals may inappropriately turn to personal revenge, rather than accepting legal solutions, once again, we should focus on that problem, rather than trying to extirpate anger altogether.

We can add that the conceptual symmetry between compassion and retributive anger is less perfect than the opponent makes it out to be. For any serious human suffering not caused by the sufferer's own fault is an occasion for compassion. But for anger to get going, we require, in addition, the thought that the damage was willingly inflicted by an agent, and that this agent acted in an inappropriate and unfair way.[65] Many occasions for compassion do not meet these requirements. Deaths of loved ones from illness or accident, famines, natural disasters – all will be occasions for anger as well as compassion only to the extent that we think that they ought to have been prevented. Sometimes we do think this about a disaster; but often we do not. We may be inclined to anger anyway, as a way of seizing control of a situation in which we feel helpless. But if the anger has no plausible blameworthy object, it will not get very far, and we should be highly critical of any anger that is based on false beliefs about agency.

This leaves us with the general Stoic point, reinforced by Spinoza's remarkable analysis of emotional ambivalence,[66] that the very view of the world that makes a conceptual space for compassion includes, by definition, strong attachments to external objects and therefore leaves a conceptual space for revenge. But we have already said that many of the legitimate interests of the anti-compassion moral tradition can be met by a theory that is far less extreme than the original Stoic normative theory, and that we have many reasons to adopt a less extreme

---

65 On the many ancient analyses of anger that make this point, see Nussbaum (1994), Chapters 7 and 11. For an excellent modern treatment, see Murphy and Hampton (1988).
66 See Chapter 10 of this volume.

theory. This should make us conclude that the bare conceptual connection between compassion and revenge is not sufficient to warrant the extirpation of the attachments leading to compassion. What we should focus on, instead, is how to channel emotional development in the direction of a more mature and inclusive and less ambivalent type of love. Compassion itself, by extending the agent's concern to people with whom she is not in a relation of painful dependence, makes a powerful contribution toward that development.

Furthermore, when we move the outer circles closer to the self, as an education in proper compassion urges, our inclination to favor projects of revenge toward these distant people, should we even have such projects, will be likely to diminish. Through this channeling of concern we will become concerned for others as for members of our own families, and see any damage befalling them as a damage to ourselves as well. Thus if we are justifiably angry with them, as we frequently will be, we will have reasons to handle the dispute without destruction. Compassion, and the empathy that is its frequent precursor, show the significance of vindictive acts for those who suffer them: by moving these victims closer to us, it makes us think twice before undertaking such acts. A spectator who had seen Euripides' *Trojan Woman*, right at the time of the decision to kill all of the male citizens of Melos and enslave all of the women and children, would become less likely to support such a policy – for she would see the revenge from the point of view of these suffering women and children, and would prove unable to dehumanize them in her thought. As I have already argued, compassion cuts through the dehumanizing strategies that are frequently enlisted in the service of cruelty of many kinds. It thus qualifies the motive to take revenge and forges an alliance among all human beings.

We may go further, returning to the point I stressed in responding to the partiality objection. Relationships between people that are mediated only by rule and not by empathy frequently prove more fragile in times of hostility, more prone to a dehumanizing type of brutality.[67] Again and again, the literature on violence indicates that the personality that is deficient in empathy is a danger to others. If one cannot house the other person in one's imagination, one has much less reluc-

---

67 See, again, Glover (1999).

tance to do something terrible.[68] To the authoritarian personality – rule-following and rigid – theorists of genocide have typically counter-posed a "liberal" personality, one that can allow the self to be entered by the reality of another person's life.[69] Of course, people may be empathic toward some and not toward others – there we have, again, the partiality objection, which has real force. But if one is standardly empathic toward a person, it is much less likely that one will be brutal toward that very person. Empathic torturers such as Hannibal Lecter are far rarer than people whose imaginations are blunted, who simply refuse the acknowledgment of humanity.[70]

Let us now return to the topic of law. I have said that anger need not be connected with an inclination to take personal revenge: instead, the interest in punishing the offender can be channeled by the legal system. Indeed, this idea is a deep part of the tragic tradition itself. As an attentive spectator of tragedies and reader of novels, the pro-compassion person will have recognized that private revenge is an especially unsatisfactory, costly way to effect the punishment of offend-ers, one that usually simply ensures that the exchange of damages will perpetuate itself without limit. Out of his interest in a punishment that is balanced and contained, that does not poison the entire climate of social life, he will develop a keen interest in systems of law and the legal codification of offenses and punishments.[71]

At the conclusion of Aeschylus' *Oresteia*, the Furies are not banished from the city: instead they are civilized, and made a part of Athena's judicial system. Now called Eumenides, for their kindly intentions to-ward the people of Athens, they cease to snarl, to crouch like dogs, to sniff for blood. But they do not cease to demand punishment for crime: and in that sense to place them at the heart of the judicial institutions of the city is to announce that these dark forces cannot be cut off from the rest of human life without impoverishing it. For these forces are forms of acknowledgment of the importance of the goods that crime may damage.[72] In that sense, compassion and revenge do go hand in

---

68 See Lifton (1986), Hilberg (1985).
69 See Adorno et al. (1950).
70 See also Vetlesen (1994) and, on the psychology of genocide in Bosnia, Vetlesen (1997).
71 On this see Posner (1988), who perceptively suggests that this is one of the most important contributions of literature to the law.
72 See Gewirtz (1988) and Posner (1988).

hand: for compassion understands the significance of a wrong, and of the victim's suffering. It therefore demands of the legal system some appropriate acknowledgment of the meaning of that suffering, and of the fact that it was unjustly inflicted.

Now we can return to the topic of mercy. The anti-compassion tradition was proud of its ability to render punishments that were merciful, not vindictive, dictated by thought about the good of society and the good of the offender. It connected the ability to be merciful with a lofty detachment from the ills of human life. It urged that without that detachment one will have the unseemly spectacle of weak and anxious people tearing one another limb from limb. But things are not so simple. For mercy is, in a sense, an anomaly in a Stoic system of justice. Mercy does differ from compassion: for it presupposes that the offender has done a wrong, and deserves some punishment for that wrong. It does not say that the trouble the offender is in came to her through no fault of her own. Nonetheless, as our analysis has revealed, it has much in common with compassion as well – for it focuses on obstacles to flourishing that seem too great to overcome. It says yes, you did commit a deliberate wrong, but the fact that you got to that point was not altogether your fault. It focuses on the social, natural, and familial features of the offender's life that offer a measure of extenuation for the fault, even though the commission of the fault itself meets the law's strict standards of moral accountability. In order to do this, it takes up a narrative attitude toward the offender's history that is very similar to the sympathetic perception involved in compassion. It follows the offender's whole history in considerable detail, scrutinizing it for extenuating features.[73] Sometimes these features will prove to be so central to the commission of the offense that we may after all judge that the offender should not be found guilty – if, for example, we find evidence of delusion or insanity. At many other times, however, this same process of sympathetic scrutiny will allow us to convict the offender and to assign some penalty – but will move us to lighten the penalty, as we take note of the severe obstacles

---

73 This is not meant in any way to rule out compassion for the victims of crime; in "Equity and Mercy" (in Nussbaum [1999a]) I discuss this issue further, arguing that the impact of crime on the victim is pertinent to the placing of the offense in a particular class of offenses, and that the discretionary consideration of the offender's story that may result in mercy should take place at a separate and later stage.

this person faced, on the way to becoming the sort of person who could commit that offense.

It is likely[74] that this merciful attitude is at odds with the norms of the original Greek Stoics, focused as they were on the strict dichotomy between what is up to us and what is not. It represents an attempt on the part of Seneca and the Roman Stoics to respond to an Aristotelian tradition in which compassion and mercy are very closely linked in the way that I have suggested – through the sympathetic imagining of the possibilities and obstacles that the other person's life contains. Seneca does not endorse compassion, because he does not give up the Stoic idea that what really bears down on people from outside is no occasion for weeping. But it becomes very difficult to see how he can avoid recognizing compassion as appropriate in some circumstances, given that he so stresses the obstacles to good action created by the circumstances of life. The very exercise of imagination that leads to mercy seems closely linked to compassion – the only difference being that mercy still judges that the offender meets some very basic conditions of responsibility and blame. But it seems to be Seneca's view that the fact that the offender got to be immoral and blameworthy was not fully that person's own doing – so at that earlier stage, compassion creeps, unnamed, into Seneca's account.

Mercy, in short, is no special virtue of the anti-compassion tradition, as its partisans sometimes seem to suggest. It is perfectly at home in the pro-compassion tradition, so long as that tradition does not take up the position that people are never to blame for any of the wrongs that they do, that everything bad is the result of luck. But no sensible expositor of the tradition has taken that view. And, in a way, mercy is more at home in the pro-compassion tradition than in the rival camp: for compassion invites the sort of close narrative scrutiny of particular lives that is likely, as well, to reveal extenuating circumstances in cases where there is culpability. The somewhat lofty detachment of the Stoic is less likely to reveal such circumstances, unless, like Seneca, he is so interested in the obstacles to good action that he verges close to compassion.

The friend of compassion has had to qualify her position in many ways under pressure of the opponents' challenges. Compassion will be a

---

74 See "Equity and Mercy" (Nussbaum 1999a).

valuable social motive only if it is equipped with an adequate theory of the worth of basic goods, only if it is equipped with an adequate understanding of agency and fault, and only if it is equipped with a suitably broad account of the people who should be the object of an agent's concern, distant as well as close. These judgments must be engendered through a good developmental process. On the other hand, compassion supplies an essential life and connectedness to morality, without which it is dangerously empty and rootless. In central cases, well represented in Greek tragedy, compassion embodies correct evaluations, and directs our concern to all who share with us a common humanity. Learned in childhood relationships, these connections are important in making morality discerning rather than obtuse. Thus compassion is a needed complement to respect, without which, as Kant holds, benevolence will be likely to be lacking in energy (but for more cognitive reasons than those that Kant gives). We should not attempt to produce a good society through the motive of compassion alone, since it is only within the limits of reason, so to speak, that compassion proves worthwhile rather than quirky and unreliable. On the other hand, so constrained, it provides an extremely important bridge from the child's narrow and self-referential concerns to a broader moral world.

One final concession must be made to the Kantian challenge. This is, that we should be on our guard lest the invitation to weep over the distress of others should motivate self-indulgent and self-congratulatory behavior, rather than real helpfulness. People can all-too-easily feel that they have done something morally good because they have had an experience of compassion – without having to take any of the steps to change the world that might involve them in real difficulty and sacrifice. Greek tragedy existed in a culture in which the objects of tragic compassion were rarely given relief and almost never justice. At the worst, the experience of tragic contemplation can even involve an aestheticizing of the person's plight that has a most unwholesome moral character. This does not mean that compassion by itself has bad tendencies; it means that people are frequently too weak to keep their attention fixed on a course of action, and that a momentary experience is frequently much easier for them than a sustained commitment. This gives us reasons to insist on going beyond compassion and to focus, as does Kant, on action and institutions.

On the other hand, we must also recall Aristotle's reminder that an action is morally virtuous only when it is done with the correct motives. Helping others without love of mankind and without compassionate concern for their situation has some moral value. But if we follow Aristotle rather than Kant in thinking that the moral emotions themselves can be cultivated and made part of a good character, we will feel that the grudging way in which an unsympathetic person performs these duties is morally incomplete. If we imagine the man whom Kant describes, in whose heart nature has placed little sympathy, and who is "by temperament cold and indifferent to the sufferings of others" (*Grounding*, Akad. p. 398), we should not conclude, as does Kant, that this is an unfortunate but morally irrelevant trait. We should conclude that this person is morally incomplete, insofar as he is the product of a moral development that has not sufficiently attended to the value of the lives of others. His vision of the human world is skewed. The freezing of the "seas of pity" is, after all, a precursor of "intellectual" – and hence moral – "disgrace."

COMPASSION AND
PUBLIC LIFE

I. COMPASSION AND INSTITUTIONS

How can the public culture of a liberal democracy cultivate appropriate compassion, and how far should it rely on this admittedly fallible and imperfect motive? In this chapter I shall leave aside the many roles that compassion may play in personal and community relationships of many kinds and focus on its connection to the political structure of a state that is both democratic and liberal. This means that I shall also leave aside the specific content compassion may have in connection with the different conceptions of value and ultimate meaning that citizens of such a nation may hold – religious conceptions, secular conceptions of many kinds. I shall focus only on its role in connection with a constitutional and legal structure that can be expected to be endorsed by citizens holding a wide range of different religious and secular views.

In terms of contemporary philosophical categories, then, I shall be examining compassion in connection with a form of *political liberalism*, a political conception that attempts to win an *overlapping consensus* among citizens of many different kinds, respecting the spaces within which they each elaborate and pursue their different reasonable conceptions of the good.[1] Why should such a conception deal with emotions at all, it might be asked? The answer is, plainly, that any political

---

1 Here I follow Rawls (1996); for my own particular form of political liberalism in connection with basic constitutional principles, see Nussbaum (2000a). For the most part, I shall also focus on what Rawls calls the "basic structure of society," that is, the basic constitutional order, the society's basic scheme of institutions, rights, and so forth. In talking about the media and about criminal justice, I shall broaden the scope of my concern; but these matters lie very close to the basic structure, and can be seen as essential to its establishment and maintenance.

conception needs to concern itself with citizens' motivations, both in order to ensure that the conception is feasible in the first place – does not impose impossible strains on human psychology – and also in order to ensure that it has a decent chance of being stable over time. It therefore needs a "reasonable political psychology," as Rawls says, one that is general enough to win broad approval and yet definite enough to assure us that our conception is not fatally flawed from the point of view of human motivation.

In order to pursue the issue of compassion in this way, we need to ask how many of the ideas so far advanced rest on controversial theoretical doctrines (for example, those of psychoanalysis) that we could not expect all citizens to share. In Chapter 4 I did advance them with reference to such doctrines; so people might reasonably wonder how far they could be made the basis for public proposals in a pluralistic society. It seems to me clear, however, that the general ideas about shame, omnipotence, and disgust that I have defended can be put forward without any specific psychoanalytic theoretical backing, simply as humanly plausible ideas, which holders of the different comprehensive doctrines can interpret in their own way. Indeed, the psychoanalytic doctrines (as I remarked in the Introduction) have themselves been treated as humanistic interpretive ideas, on a par with the insights of Proust, Sophocles, and other writers of imaginative literature; and I don't think people would object to the use of insights from such writers in a public setting, so long as they were sufficiently discussed and debated. The ideas about empathy, compassion, and altruistic behavior that I advanced in Chapter 6 are, similarly, part of an emerging consensus that includes experimental psychology, evolutionary biology, and other, more humanistic and interpretive disciplines; so we might reasonably expect these views, too, to be shared by people who would otherwise differ. In Part III, we shall in fact see interpretations of ideas about shame, disgust, compassion, and omnipotence from a variety of different comprehensive perspectives, including those of Augustine, Dante, Mahler, Emily Brontë, and Walt Whitman. All of these thinkers were concerned with issues of omnipotence and shame, and with the victory that love and compassion might possibly win over both shame and disgust. If that is so, it gives us some confidence that our project is on the right track, even for public purposes. Walt Whitman was correct, I think, in his suggestion that there is a "public poetry" about the emotions that can be made the basis for the public culture of a pluralistic democracy.

How, then, is it possible to promote appropriate compassion in such a society, and what would a compassionate society look like? Given that there is reason to think that compassion gives public morality essential elements of ethical vision without which any public culture is dangerously rootless and hollow, how can we make this compassion do the best work it can in connection with liberal and democratic institutions?

Given our acknowledgment that even appropriate compassion is unreliable and partial, we must approach the issue of compassion on two levels: the level of individual psychology and the level of institutional design. The insights of an appropriate compassion may be embodied in the structure of just institutions, so that we will not need to rely on perfectly compassionate citizens. This idea is used both by Smith (with his idea of the compassion of the "judicious spectator") and by Rawls, who creates an artificial model of an appropriately constrained benevolence via the Original Position. This ideal of moral benevolence is the lens through which we see how institutions and basic political principles should be designed.

The insights of the compassionate imagination may be embodied in laws and institutions at many different levels and in many different ways. As with Rawls's imagining of the human need for primary goods in the Original Position, they may be involved in the construction of the basic structure of society and the choice of its most basic distributional principles. They may also be involved in legislation at a more concrete level: in the creation of a tax code and a welfare system, in the creation of levels of offense and punishment in the criminal law, in democratic deliberation about human inequality at many different levels – and, finally, in reflection about the duties of rich nations toward poorer nations, in promoting both political and economic well-being. Since in all of these areas compassion by itself supplies nothing concrete until it is tethered to a view about basic goods, we must return to this issue, as we do in section III, when we will have a definite conception of basic goods to work with. Chapter 6 permits us, however, to say in a general way that compassionate institutions are intensely concerned with tragic predicaments and their prevention.

If institutions were really molded in accordance with compassion's insights, embodying the point of view of a compassionate spectator with an appropriate view of the good and of responsibility, would this not make compassion itself superfluous? Kant argued that there is room for compassionate personal giving only "owing to the injustice of government, which introduces an inequality of wealth that makes beneficence necessary" (*Doctrine of Virtue*, Akad. p. 454). This point goes back to Aristotle's dispute with Plato: for Aristotle objected that in the ideal city, where there was no private ownership and therefore no inequality of property, there would be no room for the moral virtue of generosity. Against this idea, Kant's point is a forceful one: what need do we have for these moral virtues themselves, if their role in human life is simply to correct a bad state of affairs and if we can and should correct the bad state of affairs antecedently, by means of laws?

We can answer that we are unlikely to live under perfect institutions, and that even if excellent institutions should come into being, they will need support from people in order to be stable. We must, therefore, rely on compassionate individuals to keep essential political insights alive and before our eyes. Political systems are human, and they are only good if they are alive in a human way. If we produced an excellent social welfare system and yet dead, obedient, authority-focused citizens, that would be a failure no matter how well the system worked. It would not prove stable; nor would it accomplish the goal of political society, which is to enable citizens to search for the good life (both in and outside of the political sphere) in their own way.[2] As Whitman says: "To hold men together by paper and seal or by compulsion is no account, / That only holds men together which aggregates all in a living principle, as the hold of the limbs of the body . . ."[3]

There are many civic roles, moreover, that require broad discretion of their actors – so even in a fully just society we need compassionate judges and jurors. We can add, furthermore, that many of the ills to which compassion responds cannot be cured by justice. Death, accident, loss of love – not even the most perfect society can prevent such things from befalling its citizens (although it is always important to ask to what extent defective social arrangements may be at work in the

2 Thus, in my view, as in Rawls's, politics is not just for the sake of politics, but for the sake of the good life.
3 "By Blue Ontario's Shore," 9.130–31.

actual deaths and accidents we see). To that extent we will continue to need compassion as an appropriate response and as a motive to attend with concern to the needs of our fellows, a motive that needs recognition in the design of the political conception and in the education of citizens. Even though good institutions cannot prevent old age and death, they can address the needs of the elderly, those who care for the elderly, and the bereaved relatives. But this will not happen if we do not cultivate in citizens a compassionate understanding of the weight and meaning of these predicaments.

The relationship between compassion and social institutions is and should be a two-way street: compassionate individuals construct institutions that embody what they imagine; and institutions, in turn, influence the development of compassion in individuals. As both Rousseau and Tocqueville show, empathy and the judgment of similar possibilities are profoundly influenced by the ways in which institutions situate people in relation to one another: sharp separations impede these mechanisms, and similar situations promote them. Similarly, institutions teach citizens definite conceptions of basic goods, responsibility, and appropriate concern, which will inform any compassion that they learn. Finally, institutions can either promote or discourage, and can shape in various ways, the emotions that impede appropriate compassion: shame, envy, and disgust.

II. VICTIMS AND AGENTS

The first topic our "reasonable political psychology" should address is a prevalent confusion in public thinking that can be dispelled by careful thought about compassion and its public role.

Compassion requires the judgment that there are serious bad things that happen to others through no fault of their own. In its classic tragic form, it imagines that a person possessed of basic human dignity has been injured by life on a grand scale. So it adopts a thoroughly anti-Stoic picture of the world, according to which human beings are both dignified and needy, and in which dignity and neediness interact in complex ways. To admit that a person really can be laid low by life seemed to the Stoics a negation of human dignity, and of the equal worth of all human beings. The perspective of classic Sophoclean compassion says no: the basic worth of a human being remains, even when the world has done its worst. But this does not mean that the human being has not been profoundly damaged, both outwardly and inwardly.

The society that incorporates the perspective of tragic compassion into its basic design thus begins with a general insight: people are dignified agents, but they are also, frequently, victims. Agency and victimhood are not incompatible: indeed, only the capacity for agency makes victimhood tragic. In American society today, by contrast, we often hear that we have a stark and binary choice, between regarding people as agents and regarding them as victims. We encounter this contrast when social welfare programs are debated: it is said that to give people various forms of social support is to treat them as victims of life's ills, rather than to respect them as agents, capable of working to better their own lot.

We find the same contrast in recent feminist debates, where we are told that respecting women as agents is incompatible with a strong concern to protect them from rape, sexual harassment, and other forms of unequal treatment. To protect women is to presume that they can't fight on their own against this ill treatment; this, in turn, is to treat them like mere victims and to undermine their dignity. For Katie Roiphe, for example, "the image that emerges from feminist preoccupations with rape and sexual harassment is that of women as victims,"[4] an image that reinforces an antiquated perception of women as frail and helpless. Betty Friedan, similarly, criticizes the rape crisis movement: "Obsession with rape, even offering Band-Aids to its victims, is a kind of wallowing in that victim state, that impotent rage, that sterile polarization."[5] Naomi Wolf decries a "victim feminism" that "[c]harges women to identify with powerlessness."[6]

We are offered the same contrast, again, in debates about criminal sentencing, where we are urged to think that any sympathy shown to a criminal defendant on account of a deprived social background or other misfortune such as child sexual abuse is, once again, a denial of the defendant's human dignity. Justice Thomas, for example, went so far as to say, in a 1994 speech, that when black people and poor people are shown sympathy for their background when they commit crimes,

4 Roiphe (1993), p. 6.
5 Friedan (1981), p. 362.
6 Wolf (1993), p. 136.

they are being treated like children, "or even worse, treated like animals without a soul."[7]

Interestingly, we do not take this attitude in all areas. Even if we believe that people are capable of much resourcefulness under adversity, we still hold that law should protect them against many of life's ills. We all know that writers and artists are capable of extraordinary resourcefulness and cunning when their freedom of speech is suppressed by a brutal regime: and yet we do not hold that we are undermining their dignity, or turning them into soulless victims, when we defend strong legal protections for the freedoms of speech and press, protections that make it unnecessary for them to struggle against tyranny in order to publish their work. Some people have held this: Nietzsche, we recall (see Chapter 7, section III), wrote that liberties of speech and press undermine "the will to assume responsibility for oneself," making people "small, cowardly, and hedonistic." But we do not accept Nietzsche's view about liberty. Legal guarantees, we think, do not erode agency: they create a framework within which people can develop and exercise agency.

Again, we do not believe that strong law enforcement in the area of personal property turns property-holders into victims without dignity. Laws protect citizens from theft and fraud; these laws are backed up by state power, in the form of a police force supported by tax money. Nonetheless, we usually do not hear arguments that such uses of public money turn property owners into victims. Even though we are of course aware that people are sometimes capable of fighting to defend their homes and their possessions, we think it's a lot better for law and the police to get involved, so that people don't have to spend all their time fending off attack, and can get on with their other business. Often, Americans support even stronger protections for personal property, without thinking that in that way they are turning property owners into helpless victims. Those who support a repeal of the capital gains tax, for example, do not hold that this handout from the government would turn investors into victims without honor. Even though they are aware that investors are quite capable of doing pretty well even at the current level of taxation, they do not regard this legal change as dimin-

7 "Justice Thomas Blames 'Rights Revolution' for Increase in Black Crime," *Chicago Tribune*, May 17, 1994.

ishing agency or pushing people into the category of soulless animals. If, then, we hear political actors saying such things about women, and poor people, and racial minorities, we should first of all ask why they are being singled out: what is there about the situation of being poor, or female, or black that means that help is condescending, and compassion insulting?

Sophoclean tragedy helps us to pursue this issue further. When we see Philoctetes with compassion (see Chapter 6), we see him as a victim: someone who suffers serious undeserved misfortune. And so, commonly, do we see a host of other tragic characters: women who get raped in wartime, little children who are sold into slavery, men who lose their families or see their loved ones being raped, and so on. When we see them as victims, we are seeing something true about them and about life: we see that people can be harmed on a large scale, in ways that even the best efforts cannot prevent. As Philoctetes suggests, this gives people of good will strong incentives for doing something about such disasters, and bringing relief to the afflicted.

And further, Philoctetes suggests that the victim shows us something about our own lives: we see that we too are vulnerable to misfortune, that we are not any different from the people whose fate we are watching, and we therefore have reason to fear a similar reversal.

But isn't this treating people as passive rather than active? Is this victim role compatible with being seen as an agent? Entirely compatible, as we see from Philoctetes' story. We see him as a victim, in the sense that we see his loneliness, his poverty, his illness as things that he did not bring upon himself. But we also are led by the play to see him as capable of activity of many kinds. We hear him reason, we see his commitments to friendship and justice. Seeing that he is unable to be active in some parts of his life is fully compatible with observing that in other ways he remains very active. Seeing his basic human capacities, we are led to admire the dignity with which he confronts the ills that beset him, and to notice the yearning for full activity that he displays even in the most acute misery.

Nor should we accept the simplistic contrast between agency and passivity on which the objection relies, all dignity being placed in our agency, and passivity being seen as always shameful. After all, it is precisely the refusal to accept passivity (and the emotions that are the marks of our need for the world of objects, toward which we are in some respects passive) that we have criticized as pathological narcissism, noting that such narcissism can be extremely common in societies that excessively prize manly strength and invulnerability. So we should say: Philoctetes' dignity lies both in his capacity for activity and in his needy passivity. When Odysseus regards his bodily infirmity as contemptible and disgusting, signs of a subhuman status, the chorus and, ultimately, Neoptolemus see dignity even in his attack of pain, and refuse to see his neediness as license to exploit him.

It is precisely this combination of dignity (in both activity and passivity) with disaster out of which the tragic response is made. If we saw the hero just as a worm or an ant, a pathetic low creature grovelling in the mud, we would not have the intense concern we do have with the forces that have inflicted suffering on him. Sophocles, in fact, is at great pains to show Philoctetes' suffering as fully human: even when he screams out in unbearable pain, his cry is metrical. It is shown to be a human cry of pain. What inspires our compassion (and also our self-interested fear) is in fact this combination of humanity and disaster. It is because we respect human agency and passivity in Philoctetes that we come to hate the forces that bear down upon him, and we think that something ought to be done about them. It is precisely because Philoctetes is shown to be capable of a human use of his faculties that Neoptolemus eventually shrinks from treating him like an animal or a thing. Tragedy shows us that disasters do strike at the heart of human action: they don't cause just superficial discomfort, they impede mobility, planning, citizenship, ultimately life itself. On the other hand, when we see that such a disaster strikes a human agent, it is then that we feel the sense of tragic compassion: for we don't want humanity to be wasted, or even callously pushed around.

Tragedy asks us, then, to walk a delicate line. We are to acknowledge that life's miseries strike deep, striking to the heart of human agency itself. And yet we are also to insist that they do not remove humanity, that the capacity for goodness remains when all else has been removed.

A modern exemplification of this delicate balance is John Steinbeck's portrait of the Joad family in *The Grapes of Wrath*. As the novel progresses, the family is hit by an escalating series of disasters, natural and man-made. (And the natural strike so hard largely on account of defective man-made structures.) Having lost their home, the Joads (and the other migrants around them) gradually lose, as well, the basic conditions of orderly daily life, as shelter, food, civil society, and justice are denied them again and again. The reader of the novel is asked to see that these miseries are undeserved, and that they go deep, creating conditions that are an affront to human dignity. And yet – this, of course, is Steinbeck's central theme – they do not remove dignity, which is found more surely in a poor person's gift to another poor person than in the luxuries of middle-class life. The world of the poor, as Steinbeck depicts it, is rich in love, friendship, and spirituality; it also contains orderly norms and a code of mutual aid. The poor people are never too stricken to take thought for the equal or greater needs of others. In the novel's famous conclusion, a cold and malnourished young woman who has just given birth to a stillborn baby offers her breast to a starving stranger. Thus the novel indicates that ethical values of care and love remain alive when the world has done its worst.

Sophocles and Steinbeck make our issue too simple, by focusing on heroes who have and retain a good character and good intentions throughout their misfortune. We know, however, that disaster can strike earlier and harder than this, affecting people's very ability to form plans and aspirations, affecting their ability to be good. Justice Thomas insists on the Sophoclean distinction between desert and non-desert. We may have sympathy for misfortunes that are utterly undeserved, but when people commit crimes, and do so with hostile intent, it is condescending not to blame them and hold them fully responsible. To treat them as if they could not help it negates their human dignity and treats them like "children" or "animals without a soul." We can see, however, that things are not always so clear. In the first place, even a noble Sophoclean character may engage in acts that are crimes from the point of view of society. Steinbeck makes this point repeatedly, when he shows the Joads committing various illegal acts: violating parole, burying the dead without paying the state fee, lying in order to get into California, engaging in subversive labor organizing, even committing homicide. And yet we are led to see all of these acts as the most reasonable responses to their tragic predicament.

Steinbeck's perspective is close to that of Aristotle in the *Poetics*. Aristotle insisted that the hero should not be shown as falling through wickedness, or deep-seated defect of character. But he actually preferred plots where the bad consequences come about through a chain

that involves a mistake of some kind being made by the leading character, sometimes an innocent mistake but sometimes at least partly
blameworthy.[8] His general attitude toward such errors was that we
should be forgiving to people who go wrong, seeing the difficulty of
judging well in circumstances of great complexity. Even basically good
people go wrong; a forgiving attitude may be appropriate to the general
frailty and weakness of human judgment.[9] In judging a person's blameworthy errors in a forgiving spirit, we record that we ourselves are not
perfect in judgment, even when we have the best intentions.

But of course even Steinbeck and Aristotle make this issue much too
simple, by treating good character as relatively impervious to the blows
of fortune. Steinbeck depicts the Joads as saintly paragons of moral
virtue. But we know that deprivation – at least when encountered at an
early age – does not usually produce paragons. Some types of deprivation are personal, related to unfortunate family histories or physical
problems; the cases of B and C in Chapter 4 illustrate the depth to
which these factors can influence emotional development. In many
cases, however, the deforming influences are social – encountered either
because society teaches a deformed view as the proper norm (as in the
material from Theweleit's study that we considered in Chapter 6), or
because society oppresses certain groups, deforming their well-being.
Steinbeck suggests that such oppression is, if anything, improving to
the personality: his poor people are kinder and more insightful than his
rich people. But suffering is not typically ennobling; more often it can
deform or maim the personality. Richard Wright's *Native Son* offers a
more truthful look at the way in which aspiration and emotion are
deformed by economic deprivation and social hierarchy. We are not
supposed to see Bigger as innately bad; the rage and shame that make
him a criminal are themselves the artifacts of racism. Even though these
factors ultimately become part of him, we can also view them as tragic
calamities that come upon him from outside, through no (original) fault
of his own.

8 Although in some ways the plot of *The Grapes of Wrath* conforms to this norm, in the
   sense that the crimes the hero commits are responsible for his downfall, the whole plot
   is orchestrated so as to bring disaster after disaster on the heads of all of the protagonists, mistaken or not; in that way, the novel also resembles a tragedy such as Euripides'
   Trojan Women, which does not conform to Aristotle's normative remarks about mistake
   and plot.
9 See "Equity and Mercy," in Nussbaum (1999a).

Sophoclean tragedy imagines an adult, with character already formed, and then imagines the world doing its worst. But, as Wright's novel suggests, we may push the tragic perspective back to an earlier stage and see a child, not bad by nature, getting hit from without by stigma, inequality, and poverty, forces that weigh down aspiration and deform hope. It would indeed be condescending to treat all criminals with such backgrounds as not guilty by reason of insanity. On the other hand, it seems right for society to acknowledge its own share in creating the personality of a criminal such as Bigger, by a compassionate response to his alarming and forbidding personality.

Thinking about tragic predicaments, in short, gives us a very general orientation toward the miseries of modern life, helping us to avoid some confusions that plague contemporary debates about welfare, gender, and crime. Concerning welfare, we should begin by observing that all Americans in countless ways receive financial assistance from the government, and are highly dependent on that assistance. State money and state power support laws without which most of us would not know how to live: laws protecting public order, private property, the ability to make a binding contract, freedoms of assembly, worship, speech, and press, protecting citizens against assault and violence. Of course people could learn to live without the expenditure of public money protecting those rights, but as a society we have decided that we think human activity is worthy of a basic concern that involves protecting these rights, as prerequisites of meaningful human functioning.

Let us now think about poverty, and welfare reform. There are of course many complex empirical question in this area, and this is why every society must experiment and try out many programs and policies to see what effects they have. It's not evident that direct relief is the best way to promote flourishing lives, and we should explore alternatives. But there is one thing that we should not say. We should not say that financial assistance directed at providing basic food, child welfare, and other prerequisites of meaningful human life is a way of dehumanizing people or of turning them into subhuman victims. Human beings can struggle against all sorts of obstacles; frequently they succeed. But middle-class parents typically reveal in their own lives the belief that young children should not be hungry or neglected, that they should have the basic necessities of life provided to them so that they can develop their agency richly and fully. It is strange that we so often speak differently about the poor, suggesting that cutting off basic social support is a way of encouraging agency in poor mothers and children, and of improving their character, rather than a way of stifling agency, or of stunting it before it gets a chance to develop. If we do respect human dignity and the capacity for action, we owe them a chance to develop and flourish.

Just this connection between dignity and luck was made by the late Justice Brennan, in one of his most memorable opinions, in *Goldberg v. Kelly* (1970), a case that established that welfare rights could not be abridged without a hearing:

From its founding the Nation's basic commitment has been to foster the dignity and well-being of all persons within its borders. We have come to recognize that forces not within the control of the poor contribute to their poverty . . . Welfare, by meeting the basic demands of subsistence, can help bring within the reach of the poor the same opportunities that are available to others to participate meaningfully in the life of the community . . . Public assistance, then, is not mere charity, but a means to "promote the general Welfare, and secure the Blessings of Liberty to ourselves and our Posterity." (397 U.S. 264 [1970])

It is certainly legitimate, and even desirable, for states to experiment with different welfare strategies. But something more sinister is currently in the air, a backing away from the "basic commitment" to dignity and well-being that Brennan finds, plausibly, at the heart of our traditions.

Think now of women who demand more adequate enforcement of laws against rape and sexual harassment. They are asking the state to do something about this problem. Are they therefore asking to be treated as people who have no ability to stand up for their rights? Of course not. Women do manage to struggle against sexual harassment. Most working women of my generation have done so – sometimes with relatively little damage to their careers, sometimes with great damage. But the question is, is this a struggle women should be required to wage? Or do we think that a woman's dignity demands that she not have to fight this struggle all the time, that part of the respect we owe to a woman as an agent is to let her get on with her work in an atmosphere free from such intimidation and pressure? It seems plausible that women will be more productive agents in the economy and in their homes, with these pressures minimized.

Finally, when we think about crime and criminals we need to get beyond the simple dichotomy between treating as responsible and treating with compassion. It is perfectly consistent to treat a criminal such as Bigger Thomas as fully responsible for his crimes, and yet to acknowledge with compassion the fact that he suffered misfortunes that no child should have to bear. Only when we acknowledge this do we take the full measure of the cost of social hierarchy and economic deprivation. Steinbeck gives the rich an easy time, really: for he shows that all injustice can produce is unhappiness. If we understand that injustice can strike its roots into the personality itself, producing rage and resentment and the roots of bad character, we have even deeper incentives to commit ourselves to giving each child the material and social support that human dignity requires. A compassionate society, in the sense suggested by Sophoclean tragedy, is one that takes the full measure of the harms that can befall citizens beyond their own doing; compassion thus provides a motive to secure to all the basic support that will undergird and protect human dignity.

III. GETTING THE JUDGMENTS RIGHT

A compassionate society might still be an unjust society. It might weep about the fact that taxes cause people to miss out on luxury goods such as peacock's tongues. And it might fail to weep about the Joads, forced into destitution by the absence of a social safety net. It might blame the poor for their plight and fail to blame those who exploit them. And, as in Steinbeck's society, its institutions might show concern only for a narrow elite, while ignoring the plight of the laboring classes. By allowing Sophoclean tragedy to be my guide, I have given my imagined society a definite set of judgments in the three areas where judgments can go wrong: seriousness, blame, and the extent of concern. But at this point we must confront these judgments directly. For we want not just any and every type of compassion, but, so to speak, compassion within the limits of reason, compassion allied to a reasonable ethical theory in the three areas of judgment. I have argued that if compassion is there, even in a distorted form, we have an ethical core to work with, a promising imaginative basis for the extension or evening of concern.

But now we need to ask how a society of the type we are considering, a constitutional liberal democracy, might promote appropriate judgments and, thence, appropriate emotion.

Candace Clark's study, which we considered in Chapter 6, shows that modern Americans have reasonable judgments in the area of *seriousness*, judgments that pretty closely track the judgments implicit in Sophoclean tragedy, and in Aristotle's account of the cognitive basis for compassion. (Clark points out that a very similar list is implicit in the lyrics of blues music, an important observation to which I shall return in section IV.) Rousseau suggests that there are innate psychological mechanisms that make us attend with concern to the standard tragic predicaments, understanding these as possibilities for ourselves. Whether this is right or wrong – and surely there are many reasons to think it right, at least in key areas such as death and illness – human beings everywhere do indeed have a keen interest in death, loss of loved ones, illness, loneliness, political oppression, and the other standard tragic cases. If compassion begins, as it usually does, with the intense attachment children have to parents and other relatives, it is not surprising that death and illness would come to be its foci very early on.

Where Clark's Americans seem to be least reliable, from the point of view of most standard ethical theories, is in their inclusion of (what seem to be) relatively trivial plights on the sympathy list: traffic jams, boredom, ruined vacations are not quite as outrageous as peacock's tongues, but we feel that it is wrong to be terribly upset by such things. As Clark points out, judgments of seriousness are frequently comparative and tacitly employ a baseline: because others don't have to endure X, I shouldn't either. So it's not too surprising that in a wealthy and comfortable society such as our own, the relatively trivial is elevated unduly, just because we expect to have these trivialities. What seems to be required, then, is an account answering to the venerable question of the value of various "external goods": which ones are really important, and at what level?

A pluralistic liberal society should refrain from advancing a fully comprehensive view of the good that would give a complete answer to this question. Instead, the answering will have to be done by the many different comprehensive views of the good that citizens will hold, both religious and secular. These views are bound to differ in the importance that they attach to such externals as money, love, and even health. But such a society may also expect a convergence on certain basic goods, which, at some specificable level, should be available to all citizens. Constitutional guarantees of basic rights and liberties, for example, tell citizens (and ask them to agree) that these enumerated items are so important that a loss of any one of them would be especially tragic. The level at which a tragic loss is thought to occur must typically be set incrementally, through a process of judicial interpretation. Our evolving doctrine of religious nonestablishment and free exercise tells citizens, for example, what situations count as imposing a "burden" on someone's free exercise of her religion, and what situations do not. Many nations understand economic and social entitlements in the same way: a good constitution should specify a basic social minimum that should be available to all citizens.

My own view is that a liberal political society is best advised to describe its basic entitlements as a set of *capabilities,* or opportunities for functioning, in a number of particularly important areas. In other words, such a society should guarantee to all citizens a basic set of opportunities for functioning, in some central areas of human life that are likely to prove important for whatever else the person pursues. (Pluralism is respected by providing opportunities or capabilities, and then allowing citizens plenty of room to choose whether to function in accordance with the opportunities they have.) I cannot here say more about the justification for the list, either in general or with regard to each of its specific constituents. Thus, it will look like just a list, although there is in fact much more to be said about how it is grounded and articulated.

According to the theory I have been developing, then, every society ought to guarantee its citizens a threshold level of the following capabilities:[10]

The Central Human Capabilities

1. **Life.** Being able to live to the end of a human life of normal length; not dying prematurely, or before one's life is so reduced as to be not worth living.

2. **Bodily Health.** Being able to have good health, including reproductive health; to be adequately nourished; to have adequate shelter.

10 See Nussbaum (2000a) for the theoretical development of this idea.

3. Bodily Integrity. Being able to move freely from place to place; to be secure against violent assault, including sexual assault and domestic violence; having opportunities for sexual satisfaction and for choice in matters of reproduction.

4. Senses, Imagination, and Thought. Being able to use the senses, to imagine, think, and reason – and to do these things in a "truly human" way, a way informed and cultivated by an adequate education, including, but by no means limited to, literacy and basic mathematical and scientific training. Being able to use imagination and thought in connection with experiencing and producing works and events of one's own choice, religious, literary, musical, and so forth. Being able to use one's mind in ways protected by guarantees of freedom of expression with respect to both political and artistic speech, and freedom of religious exercise. Being able to have pleasurable experiences and to avoid non-beneficial pain.

5. Emotions. Being able to have attachments to things and people outside ourselves; to love those who love and care for us, to grieve at their absence; in general, to love, to grieve, to experience longing, gratitude, and justified anger. Not having one's emotional development blighted by fear and anxiety. (Supporting this capability means supporting forms of human association that can be shown to be crucial in their development.)

6. Practical Reason. Being able to form a conception of the good and to engage in critical reflection about the planning of one's life. (This entails protection for the liberty of conscience and religious observance.)

7. Affiliation.
A. Being able to live with and toward others, to recognize and show concern for other human beings, to engage in various forms of social interaction; to be able to imagine the situation of another. (Protecting this capability means protecting institutions that constitute and nourish such forms of affiliation, and also protecting the freedom of assembly and political speech.)
B. Having the social bases of self-respect and non-humiliation; being able to be treated as a dignified being whose worth is equal to that of others. This entails provisions of non-discrimination on the basis of race, sex, sexual orientation, ethnicity, caste, religion, national origin.

8. Other Species. Being able to live with concern for and in relation to animals, plants, and the world of nature.

9. Play. Being able to laugh, to play, to enjoy recreational activities.

10. **Control over One's Environment.**
A. Political. Being able to participate effectively in political choices that govern one's life; having the right of political participation, protections of free speech and association.
B. Material. Being able to hold property (both land and movable goods), and having property rights on an equal basis with others; having the right to seek employment on an equal basis with others; having the freedom from unwarranted search and seizure. In work, being able to work as a human being, exercising practical reason and entering into meaningful relationships of mutual recognition with other workers.

My idea is that all citizens should have a basic threshold level of each of these capabilities, the level to be set by internal political processes in each nation, often with the contribution of a process of judicial review.

As can be seen, the capabilities list corresponds closely to the Sophoclean and Aristotelian lists of tragic predicaments, and that is no accident. Even where the list focuses on disabilities to which women are especially vulnerable, it tracks a long tragic tradition of focusing on this special vulnerablity. (Aristotle did not mention rape, but Greek tragedy is preoccupied with it, and not just as a violation of male property rights.) Having a set of constitutional guarantees like those on this list, or based upon them, citizens would be informed from the beginning of life that there are certain entitlements that are particularly central, and deprivation of which is particularly tragic. Thus the judgment of seriousness is taught by institutions and the guarantees they afford. There are some tragedies whose prevention or removal could not plausibly be put on such a list: even in the most supportive society, people will still die, fall ill, have discord in their personal relations, suffer the indignities and pains of old age. So this list is not a complete education for the judgment of seriousness. But it is a way of informing that judgment.

The list shapes the judgment in a particular way: for what it tells citizens is not only that certain calamities are particularly grave, but also that they are unjust, wrong. No citizen should have to suffer them, and all have a basic entitlement not to suffer them. As in Philoctetes' case, there is room not only for grief, but also for indignation. Sometimes (for example, when a child is beaten, or a woman raped) the appropriate targets of this anger will be individuals, and the solution (insofar as there is one) will lie in institutions of corrective justice. But if institutions do not provide such a citizen with recourse and support, the institutions, as well, are defective. Other tragedies are entirely the result of institutional failure, as when the freedom of the press is not adequately protected, or when there is no adequate system of public education. Even when there is an element of natural necessity in the tragedies that citizens suffer – as with illness and premature death – we should not conclude prematurely that defective political arrangements are not involved. We really cannot say, without trying for an indefinitely long time, how much illness and misery we are capable of preventing. Thus, instead of resigning ourselves to tragic necessity, we should react by asking what we can do so that such tragedies are less likely to happen again.

Public institutions can also teach the judgment of seriousness in the other direction, dealing with the problem evident in Clark's survey. Just by not including a certain item on the capabilities list, the state is already suggesting that it may not be as central (at least for public purposes) as many others.[11] But the state can go much further in suggesting that some losses are not serious. A system of graduated taxation, for example, encourages citizens not to moan and groan if they do not have all the luxury goods they might have had without the tax. A consumption tax on luxury goods accomplishes the same purpose more directly. In some cases, the state more directly suggests that a certain good or practice is not important. Seat belt laws suggest that it's not a tragedy to lose the freedom to drive unbelted; restrictions on tobacco products suggest that the loss of the opportunity to smoke in a restaurant is not the loss of a basic entitlement. Such judgments may always be disputed; my point here is simply that institutions and laws shape the judgment of seriousness in multiple ways.

The judgment of *nondesert* is also shaped by laws and institutions. The civil and criminal law, of course, embody complex standards of personal responsibility for predicaments of various sorts. More generally, public policies toward the predicament of a group can decisively affect the perception of its role in incurring the predicament. As Clark notes, Americans are particularly prone to simplistic judgments in this

---

11 To forestall an objection, I do not name religion as a single capability, but not because I think it less central; rather, it is included as a specification of capabilities of several different sorts, in the areas of expression, association, and affiliation. See Nussbaum (2000a), Chapter 3.

area; often, at least, they tend to see economic hardships as deserved, by a failure of will or effort. As Chapter 6 has noted, public policy during the Depression countered that facile perception, treating the disaster like a natural calamity that struck people from outside, and for which they were not to blame. Current thinking about welfare may be reversing this shift, making it easier, once again, to see poverty as a failure of will. In other areas, too, changes in law change judgments. Changes in rape law over the past forty years, for example, have made it less easy to see rape as something a woman "brings on herself" by provocative attire, or by just walking alone at night, or by failure to use "utmost resistance" to an attack. Sexual harassment laws, again, change the judgment that women are "asking for" the harassment they experience, simply by being in a workplace as attractive women. My purpose here is not to defend a specific view in these areas as the correct one (although the capabilities list shows that I do have definite views about these issues, which I defend elsewhere). My purpose is only to show the extent to which laws and institutions shape the judgment of responsibility, for better or worse.

The judgment that goes wrong most often, and most dramatically, is the *judgment of the proper bounds of concern*, or what I have called the *eudaimonistic judgment*. (As I have argued, this judgment is closely linked to, and supported by, the *judgment of similar possibilities* and the process of empathetic imagining.) There is no agreement, to put it mildly, concerning what level of concern people owe to different groups of human beings with whom their lives are in different ways intertwined: their families, their fellow citizens, the human beings of the world. But there is a pretty general agreement that we usually are too narrow in our sympathies. Adam Smith's critique would be accepted by most people today, I think, as a good criticism of their own unreliable compassion. Most widely accepted comprehensive ethical views, whether religious or secular, urge people to have wider spheres of concern than they are thought to have already: to cross boundaries of race, or class, or religion, or even nationality. Many, unfortunately, also encourage people in some ways to narrow their concerns, to prefer members of their own religion or group, and often to despise and reject certain other groups.

Let us stipulate that a reasonable set of judgments in this area, for the public culture of a pluralistic liberal democracy, would involve an extension of something like equal respect and concern to all citizens of whatever race, sex, class, or ethnic origin. While such concern for one's fellow citizens is not incompatible with giving one's own family or group a special measure of concern, it may be incompatible with certain ways of using one's resources. Certainly, to withdraw concern altogether from any group of fellow citizens is a moral failing from the point of view of the public political conception, and one especially grave when it is linked to long-standing prejudice and discrimination. Thus public policy will be justified in taking measures to bolster appropriate concern – especially in areas where it has been lacking.

More controversially, let us also stipulate that the citizens of a pluralistic liberal democracy should have a good deal more concern than do most Americans currently for the fate of human beings outside their own national boundaries. They should know something about what plights they face, and they should have at least some concern for the relief of those plights. They should understand that many of the problems to be faced by politics are shared problems, requiring shared transnational solutions. Again, this is in no way incompatible with having a special type and level of concern for fellow citizens. But the blank ignorance and emotionlessness with which news of happenings in distant parts of the world is often greeted by Americans is a moral failure, let us stipulate, from the point of view of the public political conception. These two stipulations seem reasonable, and minimal, starting points for the discussion that follows. Those who disagree can apply the analysis, mutatis mutandis, to their own conception of proper eudaimonistic judgments.

Once again, we see that law and public policy shape such eudaimonistic judgments in many ways. As Rousseau and Tocqueville insisted, a regime that makes people equal before the law and that empowers all citizens in certain basic ways will encourage compassion to turn its sights outward. By situating people close to one another, the regime makes it easier to see one's plight in the plight of another. Affirmative measures designed to empower a previously oppressed group may be important devices in breaking down an old barrier. Thus, at the time of Indian independence, the disdain that upper-caste Hindus had learned to feel for previously so-called untouchables could not be counteracted by formal equality alone. Years of habitual contempt required sterner measures. The elaborate affirmative action schemes for these castes propelled them into economic and political life in ways that did not depend at first on the compassion or good will of others; later, having established themselves in these new walks of life, they could more easily become objects of a broadened compassion. Our extremely uneven and unreliable compassion for people outside our national borders can be traced, in large part, to the absence of any effective institutional structure that would situate us together in a common form of life – although, obviously enough, we can and sometimes do recognize our own possibilities in their tragic predicaments.

One topic on which laws and institutions are dramatically reshaping our eudaimonistic judgments is the proper treatment of the mentally handicapped.[12] Several generations ago, a child with Down Syndrome, for example, would have been seen simply as "a mongoloid idiot"; later, perhaps as "a retarded child" or "a Down Syndrome child." Now, many such children interact with their peers in integrated schoolrooms, and have a chance to be known by a proper name,[13] to be seen as a particular individual. Michael Bérubé's story of his son Jamie, born with Down Syndrome, is in part a story of family love. But it is very centrally a story of laws and institutions: in particular, the Individuals with Disabilities Education Act, which ensures every child an appropriate education in the "least restrictive environment" possible. Such policies make possible "mainstreaming" – not the ideal option for each such child, but an option that shifts the landscape for all mentally disabled children, by redefining the landscape of children with whom "normal" children make contact in everyday life. When children see a wider range of behavioral and cognitive functioning in their classrooms, they are less likely to demonize these children as disgusting outcastes. Mitchell Levitz, a young man with Down Syndrome who wrote his own story, put it this way: "It is really about how much love and compassion that you have. That's what really counts about values."[14] But that compassion, as he knows, is not spontaneous: it is shaped by social and legal structures.

At the same time, laws and institutions shape our sense of the more

---

12 See Bérubé (1996) and Nussbaum (2000e).

13 The Convention on the Rights of the Child states that every child has the right to a proper name.

14 Levitz and Kinsgley (both men with Down Syndrome) (1994), quoted in Bérubé (1996), p. 251.

intimate attachments, and of their proper relation to those that are more distant. Legal definitions of the family, and laws regulating family life, shape in many ways our perception of what those attachments are, and how the concern we have there is related to broader concern for fellow citizens of our nation and the world. Public arrangements (or lack of them) for the care of children, the disabled, and the elderly, once again, shape the type of compassion we will have for predicaments befalling people who give care, or who receive it.

While societies shape the judgments that form the cognitive content of compassion, they also shape those emotions that I have identified as powerful impediments to compassion: envy, shame, and disgust. Envy is powerfully and obviously shaped by a public scheme of justice, and by the messages it sends to people about basic entitlements. A society that teaches all citizens that they have the right to have all of the capabilities on my list, and that makes good on its guarantees, might be expected to have relatively little envy concerning these things, at any rate, and concerning what is required to support them. [15] As for the inequalities that remain, because they have been defined (rightly or wrongly) as less central to flourishing, less potentially tragic, they are to that extent less likely to be the objects of envy, since envy requires the thought that the object enjoyed by another is of significant value.

Disgust, we have said, exists in every known society, and every society teaches it in many informal ways. But societies have great latitude concerning the extent to which they call on disgust in public policy: whether they permit citizens' reactions of disgust to be the sole or primary reason for rendering a practice illegal, as with sodomy laws and the current U.S. obscenity laws; whether they allow a defendant's disgust for the victim to mitigate the crime, as in the "homosexual provocation" defense to manslaughter; whether they allow jurors' disgust at a grisly homicide to be a relevant aggravating factor. I have suggested that disgust is a particularly unreliable and suspect motive in public life, connected, as it is, with the human desire to be nonanimal. Its links with misogyny, anti-Semitism, and other forms of group hatred throughout history give us still more reason to be suspicious of its public role.

---

15 Similarly, Rawls has claimed that in the society shaped by the two principles of justice, there will be no envy concerning the primary goods of life and their distribution.

When, moreover, we consider the specific cognitive content of disgust, the emotion's relevance to law is most unclear. Anger and indignation rest on reasons concerning harm – to the self or to others. If the judgments are right and the harm is significant, it seems reasonable to think that law should take a hand in preventing and deterring it. Disgust, by contrast, rests on judgments having to do with fantasized contamination of the self. Aside from the problem that the fantasies involved are frequently magical and involve no genuine harm, the problem with making these judgments a basis for law is that the most direct and appropriate solution to feeling "grossed out" by a person of a type one does not like is to walk away – not to abridge that person's liberties, much less to use violence against him.[16]

Beyond not using disgust as a basis for law, societies may discourage the harmful projection reactions involved in disgust, by portraying the groups that are their current object in terms that make no appeal to disgust. Jews were depicted in Nazi literature as disgusting, vile insects, or vermin; instead, a society dedicated to justice can promulgate positive images of minorities, and make sure that these minorities are seen in positions of public trust. If a *dalit* (former "untouchable") holds a position of political influence, this at least undermines the tendency to view him or her as a slimy slug, no better than excrement.

But if the real issue underlying disgust is the fear and loathing people have for their animal bodies and their own mortality, then a society that wants to counteract its damages must go further, addressing the body itself, and our anxieties about it. Since Walt Whitman made this thought the central principle of his art, I shall postpone my discussion of this issue until Chapter 15.

As for primitive shame, many of its damages lie deep in the child's early history; but many can at least be mitigated by social policies addressing human weakness and infirmity. The way in which a society cares for its dependent members, whether infants or the elderly or the physically or mentally handicapped, communicates to all citizens a view about human weakness and its relation to human dignity. A society will be most likely to decrease the influence of primitive shame on its public life if it conveys the idea that there is nothing shameful about having a human body subject to all the vicissitudes of time, age,

16 I argue this all in detail in Nussbaum (1999b).

weakness, and illness. Young people should be urged to see such bodies (whether in their peers or their elders) with respect and friendship, rather than with the contempt and aggression that so frequently accompany shame about one's own possibilities. The pathology described by Theweleit is very much alive in American society, particularly in our cultivation of a body image of perfect muscular power and hardness (in both women and men). It can be counteracted in a variety of ways, both institutional and rhetorical. Social services supporting care for the infirm and the elderly give their lives (and the lives of caregivers) new dignity in the public culture. A culture that publicly supports care for extreme physical and/or mental dependency as a primary social good no longer pretends that its citizens are all independent rational adults – as liberal social contract theory sometimes seems to do. It acknowledges the neediness of every person, and the fact that all of us begin and many of us end our lives in a state of extreme dependency.[17] Recent efforts to support the dignity of the mentally and physically handicapped (mainstreaming, support for appropriate education) similarly ask us to view weakness and infirmity without shame or disgust.[18]

IV. IMPLEMENTING RATIONAL COMPASSION: MORAL AND CIVIC EDUCATION

In talking about the three judgments, I have already mentioned some ways in which a society may promote more adequate compassion. There are many areas of public life in which this analysis yields concrete recommendations. By selecting a few that appear to be central, we can illustrate the way further deliberation about compassion's role might proceed. Of course all such discussions must remain sketchy in the context of this investigation, focused as it is on the emotions themselves.

If we are persuaded that appropriate compassion is an important ingredient of good citizenship, then we will want to give public support to procedures by which this ability is taught. This means not only cultivating appropriate judgments in the three areas, but also strengthening the psychological mechanisms – empathy and the judgment of

17 See Kittay (1999), who effectively criticizes John Rawls's assumption that citizens are "fully cooperating members of society over a complete life."
18 See Bérubé (1996) for an eloquent account of these policies and their importance.

similar possibilities – that support the extension of concern. Much of this will and should be done privately, within families. But every society employs and teaches ideals of citizenship, and of good civic judgment, in many ways. And there are some concrete practical strategies that will in fact support an education for compassion.

First of all, public education at every level should cultivate the ability to imagine the experiences of others and to participate in their sufferings. The abilities that Dickens's Mr. Gradgrind denigrated as useless "fancy" and "wonder" will not displace the calculative and fact-gathering uses of intelligence that he favored; but they will form an alliance with them, enabling our pupil to see the human meaning of facts that might otherwise have seemed remote. This means giving the humanities and the arts a large place in education, from elementary school on up, as children gradually master more and more of the appropriate judgments and become able to extend their empathy to more people and types of people.

There is nothing trivial or obvious about this: the humanities and the arts are increasingly being sidelined in education at all levels. We should not say that they contribute only to the formation of citizens: for there are many other ways in which they enrich human life and understanding. We should, however, insist that they do make a vital and irreplaceable contribution to citizenship, without which we will very likely have an obtuse and emotionally dead citizenry, prey to the aggressive wishes that so often accompany an inner world dead to the images of others. Cutting the arts is a recipe for the production of pathological narcissism, of citizens who have difficulty connecting to other human beings with a sense of the human signficance of the issues at stake.

In the child's first stories, rhymes, and songs, there is already exercise for the imagination of the inner world of another. In "fancy," the child learns to endow strange forms with life and need. And since these games are enacted, often, in the presence and with the aid of the objects of the child's most intense attachments, they borrow from these some of their light and mystery.[19] Think of the song that begins, "Twinkle,

---

19 A particularly fine example of this is Dickens's *David Copperfield*: David's habits of story-telling, being connected with the experience of his mother's love for him and of his for her, become infused with that presence, and the intensity of that love. For a more general discussion of rhymes and songs, see Nussbaum (1995a).

twinkle, little star, how I wonder what you are." In learning such a song, the child develops further her already present sense of wonder – a sense of mystery that mingles curiosity with awe. The child wonders about the little star. In so doing, she learns to imagine that a mere shape in the sky has an inner world, in some ways mysterious, in some ways like her own. She learns to attribute life, emotion, and thought to a form whose insides are hidden from her. As time goes on, she does this in an increasingly sophisticated way, learning to hear and tell stories about animals and humans. These stories interact in complicated ways with her own attempts to explain the world around her, and her own actions in that world.

She sees many personlike shapes in her world. At this point she might decide to treat them like machines, refusing to ascribe to them the pain and joy she attributes to herself; or she might simply shut down, thinking nothing at all about what might be behind that shape. Many people go through life in this way. As we have seen, there is a type of pathological narcissism that does refuse to ascribe reality to others – as the result of a paralyzing demand for omnipotence and control. Such people, revealingly enough, typically do not appreciate or in some cases even understand narrative literature.[20] But a child who has been prepared by early wonder and the cultivation of the imagination, and who is psychologically able to have concern about people outside herself, will greet the shape of another human person with those narrative habits. She will attribute to this shape thoughts and feelings that are in some ways like her own, and in some ways strange and mysterious. She will form the habit of empathy and conjecture, as she tries to make out what this other shape is feeling and thinking. She will become good at decoding ways in which different circumstances shape those insides. Around the same time, she may also be encouraged to notice the sufferings of living creatures with a new keenness: the sight of blood, the deaths of animals,[21] the distress of parents and friends, will become sources of disturbance.[22] Typically, this empathy

20 See Bollas (1987).
21 See Rousseau (1979), p. 222.
22 Thus adult projects of moving others to have concern for animals would do well to cultivate or revive these childhood experiences of concern, which are frequently eclipsed in adulthood by teachings that human beings are the only sources of intrinsic value. See Nussbaum (2000a), Wise (2000).

will be accompanied by good wishes toward the object, if the child has received a basically loving upbringing; but ambivalence is never absent, and aggressive wishes need continually to be curbed by her incipient desire for reparation. Teachers need to be alert to these complex dynamics.

As the child's mastery of the rudiments of her society's emotion vocabulary grows, two new things happen. First, she becomes ready to be exposed to stories that display the vulnerabilities of human life more plainly, and in a more distressing light, than did her first stories. She can be confronted with the vivid image of human calamities of many types.[23] She can become acquainted with illness, death, slavery, rape, war, betrayal, loss of country. And it is psychologically important that she become acquainted with such things through stories that enlist her participation, convincing her of the urgency of their perceptions of importance. No mere recital of facts can achieve this.

It is now time to return to Sophocles. For it is here that the ancient Greeks located the enormous educational importance of tragic drama. Tragedy is not for the very young; and it is not just for the young. Mature people always need to expand their experience and to reinforce their grasp of central ethical truths. But to the young future citizen, tragedy has a special significance. For such a spectator is learning compassion in the process. Tragedies acquaint her with the bad things that may happen in a human life, long before life itself does so: it thus enables concern for others who are suffering what she has not suffered. And it does so in a way that makes the depth and significance of suffering, and the losses that inspire it, unmistakably plain – the poetic, visual, and musical resources of the drama thus have moral weight. By inviting the spectator to become intensely concerned for the fate of the tragic hero, and at the same time portraying the hero as a worthy person, whose distress does not stem from his own deliberate wickedness, the drama sets up compassion; an attentive spectator will, in apprehending it, have that emotion. The Greeks cultivated compassion

---

23 See Rousseau (1979), p. 224: "Let him see, let him feel the human calamities. Unsettle and frighten his imagination with the perils by which every human being is constantly surrounded. Let him see around him all these abysses, and, hearing you describe them, hold on to you for fear of falling into them. We shall make him timid and cowardly, you will say. We shall see in what follows, but for now let us begin by making him humane."

COMPASSION AND PUBLIC LIFE

primarily through drama; a contemporary child can learn these same mythic stories, or their modern equivalents.

To some extent, this is simply a continuation of earlier learning through myth and story; but we should seek out works that acquaint the young reader with a wide range of possible calamities, and of valuable things vulnerable to calamity. The specialness of literary language – or, as we shall see, of music and accompanying lyrics – is well equipped to cut through inattention and to promote both intense concern and acknowledgment.[24] But the most decisive move beyond early learning comes in the apprehension of a common humanity. As we have seen in discussing Sophocles, tragic stories are obsessed with the delineation of the possibilities and weaknesses of human life as such, and with the causes of the primary human difficulties. They pose delicate questions about the roles of necessity and of human weakness in constructing the plights that human beings experience. Some are the result of fate, some of defective political arrangements. Some, as in Philoctetes' case, combine elements of both. While they ask their spectators to ponder the origins of these plights, they also demand an extension of concern. Greek dramas moved their spectators, in empathetic identification, from Greece to Troy, from the male world of war to the female world of the household. Although all the future citizens who saw ancient tragedies were male,[25] they were asked to have empathy with the sufferings not only of people whose lot might be theirs – leading citizens, generals in battle, exiles and beggars and slaves – but also with many whose lot could never be theirs – such as Trojans and Persians and Africans, such as wives and daughters and mothers. Contemporary tragic stories are analogous exercises of extended sympathy.

The extension of empathy required of an ancient Greek spectator is remarkable, given the extremely hierarchical, male-dominated charac-

---

24 See Rousseau (1979), p. 231, about the danger that the young person would become hardened to the sight of suffering: "The object is not to make your pupil a male nurse or a brother of charity, not to afflict his sight with constant objects of pain and suffering, not to march from sick person to sick person, from hospital to hospital, and from the Grève to the prisons. He must be touched and not hardened by the sight of human miseries . . . Therefore, let your pupil know the fate of man and the miseries of his fellows, but do not let him witness them too often."

25 Women were probably present, although there continues to be controversy about their presence and their numbers. But of course they never would be citizens; thus their connection to the deliberative aspects of tragedy is quite different.

ter of Athenian society. A young male spectator is asked to see the distresses of human life from points of view that include those of young women who are raped in wartime, queens who are unable to enjoy the full exercise of power on account of their gender, a sister who must violate all the conventional norms of a woman's life to behave with courageous piety. In short: he is acquainted at one and the same time both with the similarity of women to himself and with the astonishing difference of their lot. Becoming a woman in thought, he finds that he can remain himself, that is to say, a reasoning being with moral and political commitments. On the other hand, he is confronted with the fact that this group of able people face disaster in ways, and with a frequency, that males do not, on account of their powerlessness. In the bleakest of cases, such as the *Trojan Women* of Euripides, the entire drama is a construction of helplessness, as nothing the women do has the slightest power to affect their lot, as rape, enslavement, the murder of children come their way with the inexorability of the sun, and the language of grief is the only voluntary response that appears to be still within the women's control.

We should construct similar exercises in the extension of the imagination for our citizens. This means asking what groups they are likely to understand easily, and what groups might need more mental exercise before empathy can take hold. The old canard that the Nazis were very compassionate, weeping sensitive tears over the classic works of German literature, misses this fundamental point. The imagination faces obstacles, wherever society has created distinctions. These obstacles are not automatically overcome by stories of universal humanity, for frequently these function to cast doubt on the equal or full humanity of the group that is "different." While weeping over the sorrows of Werther, young Germans were presented with images of Jews as subhuman animals, or disgusting and dangerous predators. So it is no surprise that they led, as Robert Jay Lifton argues, a double life, sympathetic and responsive toward their families and friends, brutal toward those they imprisoned and killed. It is all very well to say that Philoctetes' story could in principle serve as excellent preparation for understanding the experiences of Jews in Nazi Germany, or, even more pertinently, of African-Americans in our own society. Like Philoctetes, Jews and African-Americans have been outcasts and have suffered from the loathing and contempt of those in power. It is no accident that

Ralph Ellison's *Invisible Man* sets itself, in many ways, in the mythic tradition of the Philoctetes story.[26] But, as Ellison knew, what the reader had to become able to do was to imagine the experiences of an African-American, a task for which Greek tragedy was not sufficient preparation, given the specific obstacles to empathy across racial lines in American life.

To promote empathy across specific social barriers, we need to turn to works of art that present these barriers and their meaning in a highly concrete way. The realist social novel is one such genre: it connects its reader to highly concrete circumstances other than her own, making her an inhabitant of both privileged and oppressed groups in these circumstances. In that way, it exercises the muscles of the imagination, making people capable of inhabiting, for a time, the world of a different person, and seeing the meaning of events in that world from the outsider's viewpoint. The reader of Richard Wright's *Native Son* encounters rich liberal Mary Dalton's wish that she could know how "your people" really live – at a time well after she has herself crossed "the line" in participatory imagination, entering Bigger Thomas's enclosed, enraged world. Such a reader understands some crucial social differences more clearly than the spectator at a drama of Sophocles, and is led to focus on the difference between the vulnerabilities common to all human beings and those constructed for the powerless by the empowered. None of this will produce appropriate compassion without correct ethical judgments: but works such as *The Grapes of Wrath* and *Native Son* inspire an empathy closely linked to reasonable judgments of seriousness, nondesert, and extended concern. We need similar incentives and guides to imagine well the experiences of the mentally disabled, and of nonhuman animals – concerning whose suffering literature has always played a valuable galvanizing role.[27]

By focusing on literature I do not mean to suggest that the education I describe should neglect musical works, which can often be powerful sources of compassionate imagining – both in general and as related to particular groups. Candace Clark is surely correct when she claims that blues music seems to most Americans to express broadly shared perceptions about disaster and survival; but it also, surely, educates Ameri-

---

26 See Nussbaum (1999c).
27 On the uncertainties of empathy and compassion as guides to issues of animal entitlement, see Nussbaum (2001a).

cans about the specific experience of African-Americans, their concrete sufferings and their resourceful agency in suffering. In the international women's movement, similarly, music is among the most powerful resources for understanding (especially given that many of the most deprived women are illiterate); it creates resources for communication of a specific sense of tragedy, even while offering a fellowship that resourcefully combats the predicament.

In short, an education for compassionate citizenship should also be a multicultural education. Our pupil must learn to appreciate the diversity of circumstances in which human beings struggle for flourishing; this means not just learning some facts about classes, races, nationalities, sexual orientations other than her own, but being drawn into those lives through the imagination, becoming a participant in those struggles. One ingredient in this education will certainly be the study of political, social, and economic history; but another equally important ingredient will be contact with works of literature and other artworks that involve the spectator in the significance of the events of history for human individuals. To promote empathy in this way does not commit us to cultural relativism, to the view that every culture is equally good, or to any sort of hands-off attitude toward cultural criticism. In fact, the compassionate spectator is always attempting to compare what she sees with her own evolving conception of the good, and her compassion needs always to be tethered to the best account of the good she can find. I have argued, however, that empathetic imagining is an extremely valuable aid to the formation of appropriate judgments and responses.

It cannot be emphasized too strongly that what I am advocating, what I want from art and literature, is not erudition; it is empathy and the extension of concern. High art may be presented in such a way as to encourage elitism, or smugness, or disdain for the ordinary. And there are works of high art that discourage compassion for their characters (or some of them) and promote smugness or prejudice.[28] On the other hand, art that does not have extraordinary merit as art may, as Tolstoy saw, be capable of inspiring sentiments of brotherhood and compassion.[29] I do not follow Tolstoy in thinking that a compassionate citizenry should turn away from art that has educational prerequisites

28 For many examples, and a valuable set of evaluative criteria, see Booth (1988).
29 Tolstoy (1962).

that are not met by all the society's members; for I believe that there is a prima facie and general correlation between artistic merit and the ability to engage the personality at a deep level. The fact that Sophoclean tragedy inspires compassion for human suffering and the fact that it is great and powerful poetry are not independent facts: it is the poetic excellence that conveys compassion to the spectator, cutting through the habits of the everyday. It is not so easy for just anyone to construct a story that will move the heart. On the other hand, works that are powerful at a specific time in relation to a specific problem may not endure, and in that sense appear to be less great as art than other works. *Uncle Tom's Cabin*, one of the most influential of American novels, can hardly be read today; someday, perhaps, *Native Son* will share its fate. Nonetheless, such works, in their own time, still play an important part in my imaginary curriculum, because they help us to overcome mental obstacles to full political rationality (within which I include rationality in emotion).

Recognizing this role of the arts has one more substantial public consequence. It means acknowledging that the arts serve a vital political function, even when their content is not expressly political – for they cultivate imaginative abilities that are central to political life. This would give us special reasons for supporting the arts, and for giving artistic expression a high degree of protection from the repression that so often threatens it. If the sort of citizen we want participating in public deliberation has the robust and independent imagination of the lover of art, then we will need to protect the independence of the arts themselves from the interference of moralisms, both religious and secular, that have always borne down upon them.[30] This point was grasped as early as Periclean Athens. For Pericles, in his Funeral Oration, praised the love of artistic excellence for which his city was famous, and connected this love with the production of a certain sort of independent and passionate citizenry.[31]

V. THE ROLE OF THE MEDIA

We have spoken about education in schools. But obviously television and the other mass media are also potent educators of citizens, and

30 For telling examples of this, see Posner (1992), de Grazia (1992).
31 See Thucydides, II.42 ff.

can nourish empathy or obtuseness, appropriate or inappropriate compassion. To some extent the issues parallel the curricular issues: for we want media that do not marginalize the arts and humanities, media that nourish the ability to imagine and to have empathy. Moreover, television has tremendous power to influence empathy and the judgment of similar possibilities with regard to minorities and people in other countries. Its choices of images and roles, in news stories, advertising, and drama, will have important consequences for citizens' moral abilities, for better or worse. It is reasonable to demand media that do not cultivate disgust with or dehumanization of groups with whom citizens have to deal, or the kind of misogynistic loathing of softness that is so frequently linked with dehumanization of others. Just what the consequences of these observations should be for legal regulation or even industry regulation will be a matter of controversy among those who agree with this basic position. I do not intend to embark on that controversy here. But it is obvious that in countless ways the demands of a sane and decent public life do and should influence the ways in which racial issues and many others are presented.

If we think not just about empathy but about getting the judgments right, we can see that the media have considerable power in that regard as well, portraying calamities as more and less grave, unhappiness as striking from without or as produced by culpable lack of effort, people of different degrees of proximity as worthy of our concern. Furthermore, the media are a deliberative tool: in addition to presenting a variety of reasonable conceptions of the three judgments, they may and should also promote good deliberation about what conception we want to adopt.

All of these issues arise for the classroom as well. But there is one salient asymmetry between the media and the classroom: their relative vulnerability to market pressures. Universities and schools are not as independent as they should be: in many cases, at least, the financial bottom line influences what courses can be offered and who can be hired to teach. But relatively speaking there is great freedom to teach what one likes in a school or university. Once the department and the position exist, a teacher is usually pretty free to assign works that seem suitable. Thus, reasonable demands for the inclusion of more material concerning minorities, women, and non-Western cultures can be answered without much difficulty, if the will is there.[32] Television and print media are far less free, far more pressured to justify their choices by reference to short-term market standards. Rarely is time even given to cultivate an audience for a potentially challenging type of programming, as would be required if, for example, we wanted to produce a cultivated awareness of difficulties faced by women or poor people in South Asia, or Africa, where we're usually so deficient in background information that we cannot empathize easily, and tend to get bored as a result.

It is difficult for television to fulfill any of the social purposes I have described, so important to the education of citizens, if it is constantly held hostage to market standards and the people involved are unwilling to accept a loss for the public good. A number of solutions suggest themselves, ranging from the corporate grants that already underwrite some risky public programming, to informal guidelines and standards for the industry, mandatory public interest programming, and subsidies for national broadcasting. I am inclined to think that all of these must be tried, but that an effective solution cannot be found without the last. Citizen pressures can be expected to improve things where national minorities are concerned; and they have, where the portrayals of African-Americans, women, and gays and lesbians are concerned. They can also be expected at least to raise issues about the role of violence in the media and its negative relation to compassion. But where our deplorable ignorance of other nations is concerned, it seems to me that only independent, well-financed public media can creatively address the problem. In any case, thinking about empathy and compassion will help us to pursue these difficult issues further.

VI. POLITICAL LEADERS

We should demand political leaders who display the abilities involved in a reasonable and appropriate compassion – who show not just mastery of pertinent facts about their society and its history, but also the ability to take on in imagination the lives of the various diverse groups whom they propose to lead. This ideal of the leader of a democracy as the poetic inhabitor of all its varied lives has been most eloquently developed in the work of Walt Whitman, to which I shall

---

32 See Nussbaum (1997a) for an account of how colleges and universities have done this.

return in Chapter 15. In "By Blue Ontario's Shore," one of the central works in which Whitman articulates this ideal, he argues that laws and institutions are insufficient to hold a democracy together. The imagination of poets is also required:[33]

> To hold men together by paper and seal or by compulsion is no account,
> That only holds men together which aggregates all in a living principle,
>   as the hold of the limbs of the body or the fibres of plants.

> Of all races and eras these States with veins full of poetical stuff most
>   need poets, and are to have the greatest, and use them the greatest,
> Their Presidents shall not be their common referee so much as their
>   poets shall.

> (Soul of love and tongue of fire!
> Eye to pierce the deepest deeps and sweep the world!
> Ah Mother, prolific and full in all besides, yet how long barren,
>   barren?)[34]

The opening of this passage is somewhat prosaic; its conclusion shows the passion that the poetic imagination should supply – eye and soul and tongue powerful enough, emotionally keen enough, to pierce into all the lives in the world, and to chronicle their joy and their suffering, the fruitfulness of well-being and the barrenness of exclusion. It is in this way that the poet can become "the arbiter of the diverse," "the equalizer of his age and land,"[35] showing "the like love" for all the nation's classes, ages, and races.[36]

In one way, this is a continuation of my previous point: for it is a defense of the role of the artistic imagination in the education of citizens. But it is also a call for an appropriately compassionate leadership. The leader who for Whitman embodied that idea was, of course, Lincoln, "the large sweet soul that has gone."[37] And it is above all Lincoln's ability to imagine the situation of the slave, and to lead the country through to the end of the era of slavery, that is the focus of his love. In one of his sparest and most moving tributes to the dead president, he writes:

33 See the longer account of Whitman and the judge in Nussbaum (1995a).
34 Whitman, "By Blue Ontario's Shore," ll. 129–36.
35 Ibid., l. 141–2.
36 Ibid., l. 193.
37 Whitman, "When Lilacs Last in the Dooryard Bloom'd," l. 72.

This dust was once the man,
Gentle, plain, just and resolute, under whose cautious hand,
Against the foulest crime in history known in any land or age,
Was saved the Union of these States.[38]

I believe that Whitman is correct to find in Lincoln an exemplar of
the way in which compassion can illuminate the conduct of public life;
and an examination of the way in which compassion informs Lincoln's
judgment helps to support the argument I have made in this chapter
about the complex relationships between compassion and righteous
indignation, compassion and mercy. Many of Lincoln's public statements, especially toward the end of his life, make it clear that he took
compassion for the situation of the slave to entail indignation against
those who continued to defend the institution, especially when they
proclaimed high-minded moral motives at the same time.[39] On the
other hand, his determination to consider the lives of all those involved
with a sympathetic narrative attitude led him, while condemning injustice, to advocate mercy. This combined attitude is nowhere better exemplified than in the Second Inaugural Address:

Both read the same Bible, and pray to the same God; and each invokes His
aid against the other. It may seem strange that any men should dare to ask
a just God's assistance in wringing their bread from the sweat of other men's
faces; but let us judge not that we be not judged . . . With malice toward
none; with charity for all; with firmness in the right, as God gives us to see
the right, let us strive on to finish the work we are in; to bind up the nation's
wounds; to care for him who shall have borne the battle, and for his widow,
and his orphan – to do all which may achieve and cherish a just, and a
lasting peace, among ourselves, and with all nations.[40]

We notice, first, Lincoln's compassion for the suffering of the slaves,
whom his imagination invests with a humanity equal to that of the

38 Whitman, "This Dust Was Once the Man," written in 1871 (quoted in its entirety).
39 Approached by two southern women whose husbands were being held as prisoners of
war, and told that the husbands should be released because they were religous men,
Lincoln replied: "You say your husband is a religious man; tell him when you meet
him, that I say I am not much of a judge of religion, but that, in my opinion, the
religion that sets men to rebel and fight against their government, because, as they
think, that government does not sufficiently help *some* men to eat their bread on the
sweat of *other* men's faces, is not the sort of religion upon which people can get to
heaven!" (December 6, 1864, cited in Lincoln [1992], pp. 319–20).
40 In Lincoln (1992), p. 321.

oppressors. This leads him to have indignation against the oppressors, whose actions he in no uncertain terms condemns. And yet he announces his determination not to be retributive or punitive: "judge not that we be not judged" is the utterance, I think, of mercy rather than exculpation. He means not, don't say that this was wrong, but withhold the punitive and vindictive attitude that could all too easily animate people at this time. This reading is borne out by the famous conclusion of the speech, which renounces malice while remaining firm in the right. The imagination of compassion itself conduces to a merciful view of the offender. And remarkably, in the final sentence, the two warring sides become one and indistinguishable – all are simply those "who have borne the battle," and compassion is extended equally to men and women and children or both sides. One can find no better example of the way in which the poetic imagination does indeed create a unity in the disparate, seeing common human interests and sufferings across the sharpest of divisions.

One may only hope that this example will inspire renewed thought of compassion and common humanity at the present time. If Candace Clark's study is valid, Americans are highly responsive to "sympathy entrepreneurs," who define for the general public norms of appropriateness in the areas of seriousness, responsibility, and extent of concern.[41] Although such entrepreneurs come in many forms – journalists, civic awareness groups, artists and musicians – political leaders are such entrepreneurs inevitably. What they say (and institutionally recommend) about welfare, race, and other pertinent issues cannot help but contribute to public attitudes that shape the boundaries of compassion.

VII. ECONOMIC THOUGHT: WELFARE AND DEVELOPMENT

The compassionate imagination provides information essential for economic planning, by showing the human meaning of the sufferings and deprivations different groups of people encounter. The friend of appropriate compassion need not and should not propose to substitute emotion for modeling. Instead, one may urge that formal economic models

41 Clark (1997), pp. 84–93.

take account of compassion's information. Let me now describe more concretely what I mean by this, giving an example from the economics of welfare and development.

Formerly, when the well-being of a nation was measured by development agencies, following the lead of development economists, by far the most common strategy was simply to list GNP per capita. This crude approach does not tell us much about how people are doing: it does not even describe the distribution of wealth and income, much less investigate the quality of lives in areas not always well correlated with wealth and income – such as infant mortality, access to health care, life expectancy,[42] the quality of public education, the presence or absence of political liberties, the state of racial and gender relations. What development planners need to know about the overall "political economy" of a nation is far more than such approaches tell us, even where economic planning in the narrow sense is concerned. For they need to know how the economic resources of the nation are or are not supporting human functioning in these various different areas, and how they might do so more effectively.

For these reasons, economist Amartya Sen has argued that the focus of welfare and development economics should not be resources as such, as if they had some value in themselves, but the role of resources in supporting the *capabilities* of human beings to function in important ways.[43] As I mentioned earlier, I have used the capabilities approach to develop a theory of basic constitutional guarantees that should be made good for all citizens. Meanwhile, the same approach has had a major influence on the ways in which international agencies measure welfare. The series of *Human Development Reports* published since 1990 by the United Nations Development Programme, under the auspices of the late Mahbub Ul Haq, have presented information about well-being in a plural form, stressing the human meaning of economic measures for the ability of citizens to function in certain central areas. The idea is that development is a human matter. Rather than treating the economy

---

42 These may appear to be well correlated with GNP per capita, if one considers only gross contrasts, such as those between Europe and North America on the one hand, and the poorer regions of Africa on the other. But if one breaks things down more finely, large and significant discrepancies begin to appear; for many examples of this, see Sen (1984), Drèze and Sen (1989).

43 Sen's major papers are collected in Sen (1982, 1984); see also Sen (1985, 1987), and, on gender inequalities and capability, Sen (1990, 1995).

as an engine that has a life of its own, one should look to see what it does for people of different kinds, in different areas of their lives.

There is an intimate link between this approach to quality of life measurement and the concepts of empathy and compassion developed here. For the point that Sen has continually made, against liberal views that focus on resources, is that we do not have information enough to tell us how these resources are working, unless we see them at work in the context of human functioning. In other words, we must imagine the whole picture of a life. But when we do so, we see that individuals have widely varying needs for resources, if they are to attain a similar level of capability to function. A person in a wheelchair needs more support in order to become mobile than a person without this disability. A large and active person needs more food in order to be healthy than a small and sedentary person, and a pregnant or lactating woman more than a nonpregnant woman. Groups that have been disadvantaged with respect to education may need special educational investments to attain the same level of capability. Plural capability-based measures give the same type of rich human information that a good novel gives us, stimulating us to think empathetically about the possibilities of people in many different nations and of groups within nations. Whether such empathy will promote compassion on the part of insiders or outsiders is a further issue; it will depend on our judgments of seriousness, responsibility, and appropriate concern. And if compassion is the result, the question of appropriate action will be yet a further question; its answer will depend on our view of transnational duties, and of the proper role of the state. What is important to say here is that the imaginative exercise itself, and the emotion itself, provide information without which no informed decision about allocation can be made.[44] This is why Sen and I placed a section from Charles Dickens's *Hard Times* as the epigraph to our volume on *The Quality of Life*: we wanted to emphasize that traditional economics needs to be infused with the information, and the emotional responses, supplied by "fancy."

In Chapter 7, moreover, I have endorsed Sen's much broader argument, concerning the importance of compassion or sympathy for a complete economic notion of rationality.[45] Imagined without compas-

---

44 See the Introduction to Nussbaum and Sen (1993).
45 Sen (1982); see section III of this chapter.

sion for others, *Homo economicus* is certainly not a norm to which we should aspire. Nor, Sen argues, is he even a good description of the way in which most of us think and choose. Incorporating emotion in this way does not mean abandoning the aim of modeling human action scientifically; it does mean that science must be responsive to the facts of human psychology – facts that are also good things, as I have argued, without which rationality in the normative sense is incomplete. Presumably economics wants not only simplicity, but also, and above all, truth.

VIII. LEGAL RATIONALITY: EQUALITY, CRIMINAL SENTENCING

We began Chapter 7 with a controversy about compassion's role in the law. By now we should have seen that this debate has been constructed in a highly misleading way. Compassion is not "irrational" in the sense of "impulsive" or "lacking thought." Nor, in central cases, is it normatively irrational in the sense of being based on bad thought, as the Stoics charged. On the other hand, it is admittedly fallible and easily led astray: so we need to ask how we could avail ourselves of its best, rather than its worst, possibilities. The fallibility of compassion should not induce us to omit it entirely from legal deliberation, any more than the fallibility of belief should cause us to omit all beliefs. But – especially since in the law we cannot easily embody all that we want in institutional structures, and individual actors will continue to exercise broad discretion – we must ask how we can promote compassion of the appropriate, rather than the inappropriate, type.

What I have already said in this chapter has many implications for legal and judicial rationality: for lawyers and judges are fruits of a system of civic education, and will need to have to a high degree whatever virtues of civic rationality that system cultivates. They are also concerned with issues of human welfare, and will want to use the sort of deliberative rationality that is best equipped to handle welfare issues. They are also, some of them, leaders, to whom my argument about the importance of a compassionate leadership clearly applies. This means, I think, that it is especially important for judges and future judges to acquire the kind of information my imaginary curriculum for citizenship will offer – not just collecting many facts about the diverse ways of life with which he or she is likely to come in contact, but entering into these lives with empathy and seeing the human meaning of the issues at stake in them.[46] Through that curriculum – which can and should be reinforced through instruction in law schools – the future judge will be especially likely to discern the various kinds of unequal treatment that certain people and groups have experienced.

There are many ways in which this insight might be pursued; let me briefly discuss just two areas: the understanding of equality and inequality, and the judgment of criminal defendants.

In reflections about equal protection of the laws, we frequently come upon a spurious type of formal symmetry that masks an underlying inequality. Consider the famous Supreme Court case, *Loving v. Virginia,* which struck down laws prohibiting miscegenation. In 1958, Mildred Jeter, a black woman, and Richard Loving, a white man, were married in the District of Columbia in accordance with its laws. They then returned to Virginia, their state of residence, establishing their home in Caroline County. In October 1958, a grand jury issued an indictment charging the Lovings with violating Virginia's ban on interracial marriage. After pleading guilty to the charge, they were sentenced to one year in jail; the judge suspended the sentence on condition that they leave the state for at least twenty-five years. In his opinion, he stated that:

Almighty God created the races white, black, yellow, malay and red, and he placed them on separate continents. And but for the interference with his arrangement there would be no cause for such marriages. The fact that he separated the races shows that he did not intend for the races to mix.

Taking up residence in the District of Columbia, the Lovings went to court, challenging the constitutionality of Virginia's anti-miscegenation laws. In 1966, the Virginia Supreme Court upheld the constitutionality of the laws; the Lovings appealed to the U.S. Supreme Court. The state's central argument was that the law does not violate equal protection because the two races suffer equal and symmetrical disadvantages from the prohibition. Thus the statutes "do not constitute an invidious discrimination based upon race." On June 12, 1967, in a unanimous decision, the U.S. Supreme Court ruled such laws unconstitutional, arguing that they were clearly intended to uphold

46 See Posner (1992) for effective criticism of judges for not doing this, especially in cases involving homosexuality.

White Supremacy, and that there is "patently no legitimate overriding purpose independent of invidious racial discrimination which justifies this classification." The Court stated explicitly that the mere fact of a law's equal and neutral application does not mean that it does not constitute "an arbitrary and invidious discrimination."

A democracy could try to construct equality out of laws and institutions alone, without an education of the heart and the imagination. It could simply command citizens to respect the equal rights of those different from themselves, and not to interfere with their legitimate activities. But such a regime of formal equal protection is fragile, as the *Loving* case shows us. When people approach an issue of equal protection externally and formally, without using their imagination to try to understand the human meaning and impact of the laws in question, they are apt to be obtuse about equality, taking formal neutrality to be sufficient for equal protection and missing the role played by hierarchies of race and gender in denying citizens the truly equal worth of the protection of the laws.

Consider the famous account of legal neutrality given by Herbert Wechsler in "Toward Neutral Principles of Constitutional Law." Wechsler begins unobjectionably, arguing that judges need criteria that are not arbitrary or capricious, "criteria that can be framed and tested as an exercise of reason and not merely as an act of willfulness or will." They should be able to articulate their reasons in public, and should not function simply as a "naked power organ." As his argument continues, however, it becomes clear that Wechsler takes the demand for principled neutrality to entail standing so far back from the experience of the parties, and the human meaning of the facts, that hierarchy and subordination cannot be seen. In particular, criticizing the reasoning and evidence in *Brown v. Board of Education*, he argues that judges deciding cases relating to "separate but equal" facilities should refuse themselves concrete empathetic knowledge of the special disadvantages faced by minorities and the asymmetrical meaning of segregation for blacks and whites, in order to ensure that their principles are applied without political bias:

[T]he separate-but-equal formula . . . was held to have "no place" in public education on the ground that segregated schools are "inherently unequal," with deleterious effects upon the colored children in implying their inferiority, effects which retard their educational and mental development.

I find it hard to think that the judgment really turned upon the facts.

Rather, it seems to me, it must have rested on the view that racial segregation is, in principle, a denial of equality to the minority against whom it is directed ... But this position also presents problems ... In the context of a charge that segregation *with equal facilities* is a denial of equality, is there not a point in *Plessy* in the statement that if "enforced separation stamps the colored race with a badge of inferiority" it is solely because its members choose "to put that construction upon it"? Does enforced separation of the sexes discriminate against females merely because it may be the females who resent it and it is imposed by judgments predominantly male? Is a prohibition of miscegenation a discrimination against the colored member of the couple who would like to marry?

For me, assuming equal facilities, the question posed by state-enforced segregation is not one of discrimination at all. Its human and its constitutional dimensions lie entirely elsewhere, in the denial by the state of freedom to associate, a denial that impinges in the same way on any groups or races that may be involved ... In the days when I was joined with Charles H. Houston in a litigation in the Supreme Court ... he did not suffer more than I in knowing that we had to go to Union Station to lunch together during the recess. (Wechsler 1959, pp. 32–4)

Writing in 1959, one year after the marriage of Mildred Jeter and Richard Loving, Wechsler claims to state both the constitutional and the human meaning of various laws mandating separation of groups. But in his distance from the facts his judgments have an obtuse, Martian character. Had Wechsler tried to imagine the lunch incident in the manner of a novelist, considering the meaning, for Houston, of knowing that he could not lunch with Wechsler in a downtown restaurant, he would quickly have seen that the meaning of that denial of the freedom to associate is strongly asymmetrical – for Wechsler, an inconvenience and (as he elsewhere notes) a source of guilt; for Houston, a public brand of inferiority. Nor, clearly, is it Houston who chooses to "put that construction upon it": it is quite obviously the social meaning of the norms mandating separation, here as in the cases of education and marriage. This the Court in *Loving* saw correctly. From Wechsler's lofty distance from the human experience of discrimination, he fails to notice perfectly articulable and universalizable principles that do include the asymmetrical meaning of segregation and the history of segregation as stigma. His failure of imagination is especially evident in the two rhetorical questions with which he concludes his paragraph. He evidently thinks it absurd that the law would object to the separation of the sexes, and he appears to think that if women do complain about it, this is just a manifestation of political or personal resentment. And to wrap it all up, as if offering a reductio ad absurdum of the entire strategy in *Brown*, he says that it can't possibly be that anti-miscegenation laws constitute discrimination against "the colored member of the couple." Well, why not? What justifies this dismissal of the issue? It is not the view articulated by the Virginia judge in *Loving*, that separation of the races is fitting and proper: for Wechsler clearly thinks it improper, a denial of the freedom to associate. It would appear, then, that his own espousal of a formal ideal of neutrality as the only principled way to handle politically divisive issues has led him astray: any law framed in a verbally neutral manner, he thinks, cannot possibly be discriminatory.

Here is where the imagination should step in, giving the judge an informed understanding of the human meaning of the separation in question. It seems highly unlikely that a graduate of my imagined curriculum for citizenship would have made this error: for she would have been encouraged to imagine situations of hierarchy and to appreciate their human meaning. She would have no tendency to suppose that this pursuit of fairness requires her to stand at a lofty distance from the social realities of the cases before her. Indeed, she takes true neutrality to require a searching examination of those realities, with imaginative participation, looking in particular for evidence that certain groups have suffered unequal treatment and therefore need more attention if they are to be shown a truly equal concern.

From both judges and jurors, then, we should demand both empathy and an appropriate compassion as ingredients in the mastery of the human facts before them. This compassion must be tethered to the evidence and constrained by institutional factors. (Elsewhere I have argued that Adam Smith's idea of the judicious spectator provides a useful model as we think of these constraints.) And yet it must be there, or many pertinent facts of cases involving inequality and deprivation of basic goods will not be correctly described, much less assessed.[47] The design of judicial institutions leaves latitude for flexibility and for individual interpretive and normative reasoning. There are good reasons

---

47 See Nussbaum (1995a) for discussion of a recent sexual harassment case in which the lower court judge was overruled on the findings of fact because he omitted consideration of the asymmetry of power.

for leaving this latitude: for no document can contain instructions so precise and so unambiguous that it will settle every problem in advance, and even to try to do this would no doubt conduce to a baneful rigidity in the law. But once the latitude is there, we need judges who exemplify rationality; if my argument is correct, this means that we need judges who are properly emotional.

If we now turn to the role of compassion in the assessment of a criminal defendant, we find that the issues are highly complex. Compassion per se is neither good nor bad. It must be appropriately tethered to reasonable judgments in the three areas, and it must overcome the most pressing obstacles to correct understanding that exist in a particular social situation. I have argued in Chapter 7 that appropriate judicial compassion is merciful. The good judge or juror understands that all human beings are fallible, and that the difference between criminal and juror or even judge is frequently made by personal and social circumstances. In this chapter I have said, further, that a general social goal should be to promote an appropriate understanding of the extent to which the criminal may be formed by social and parental factors that "strike" from without, in much the same way that misfortune strikes the object of Sophoclean compassion, albeit earlier. In the Anglo-American tradition of criminal sentencing we find this idea connected with a common possibility of mitigation in sentencing. The merciful narrative attitude is taken to be a way of acknowledging the humanity of the wrongdoer, and doing justice to one's own.

In 1976, defending the role of a fully particularized narrative in the criminal sentencing process, the U.S. Supreme Court wrote in *Woodsor v. North Carolina*:

A process that accords no significance to relevant facets of the character and record of the individual offender or the circumstances of the particular offense excludes from consideration in fixing the ultimate punishment of death the possibility of compassionate or mitigating factors stemming from the diverse frailties of humankind. It treats all persons convicted of a designated offense not as uniquely individual human beings, but as members of a faceless, undifferentiated mass to be subjected to the blind infliction of the penalty of death. (428 U.S. 280, 303 [1976])

The judge who holds himself aloof from the criminal, like Rousseau's kings holding themselves aloof from their subjects, will fail to understand the "diverse frailties" that lead people to commit crimes. Acknowledging these frailties creates a community between judge and criminal; the judge's willingness to accord significance to the circumstances of an individual human life shows that he is not treating the offender as subhuman or irretrievably alien.

It is sometimes alleged that the supporter of a role for empathy and compassion in the law must, on pain of inconsistency, support all appeals to compassion. Thus legal theorist Paul Gewirtz argues that if we admit the narrative of the victim's life story at the penalty phase, and the compassion that this narrative evokes, we must also admit victim impact statements, in which the victim's family and friends testify to their sufferings as a result of the crime.[48] Some positions on compassion may have that implication, but mine does not. I have emphasized that compassion is a highly fallible motive, and that what we want to cultivate is appropriate compassion based on reasonable judgments. I have also said that we need to ask ourselves what the particular obstacles to appropriate compassion are in our society. More narrative is not always better. Sometimes narratives may impede understanding of people who are different from ourselves. They are likely to do this, for example, if they lead our minds to focus with sympathy on the sufferings of people who are more like ourselves, when that suffering has been caused by someone unlike. As I have insited, compassion can be blocked by a sense of distance and unlikeness; this distance can also be reinforced by narratives that bind the listener's imagination to people closer to home. In an excellent article, Susan Bandes argues convincingly that the introduction of victim impact statements in the sentencing process often impedes sympathetic understanding of the history of the criminal defendant, because it gives the jury an object of sympathy who is likely to be more like them.[49] This can make them feel that they need not do the imaginative work necessary to understand the defendant's history – and yet a long tradition in the criminal law, as I have just suggested, argues that this is a central task for the jury at the penalty phase. I agree with Bandes that the defender of narrative at the penalty phase is not obliged to support victim impact statements as well, since her defense of penalty phase narratives is not

48 Gewirtz (1988).
49 Bandes (1997).

based on a general preference for narrative. It is based on specific arguments having to do with the need to be fair to the defendant. She can consistently argue that anything that impedes a fair judgment about the defendant is inappropriate at the penalty phase. She may also point out that any information about the victim that is relevant to the assessment of what the defendant has done has already been presented at the trial; the introduction of further information about the victim's family is just an excuse to whip up vindictive sentiments against people who are already powerless. Moreover, there is the familiar problem that the process treats victims unequally, giving more sympathy to those who have surviving families who can appear to tell a mournful tale. We should reject that sort of unequal plea for sympathy for the same reason that Socrates refused to bring his wife and children into court: because it is irrelevant to the issues before us at the penalty phase. So more narrative is not always better: we have to ask what we need to know, and what the barriers are to our knowing it. We should introduce empathy-inducing narratives for specific reasons in order to address specific deficiencies in understanding.

But one thing we should not do – encourage the jury to view a defendant with disgust, or even to consult disgust as a reaction relevant to the assessment of the penalty. Recently, legal theorist Dan M. Kahan, having defended penalties that shame, has turned to the defense of shame's cousin, disgust, urging us to consult this "uncompromising" moral sentiment when we assess the acts of criminals. Disgust, writes Kahan, is "brazenly and uncompromisingly judgmental,"[50] indeed "necess[ary] . . . for perceiving and motivating opposition to cruelty."[51] Kahan's argument focuses, in particular, on cases in which a jury is asked to consult reactions of disgust in order to determine whether a homicide is "especially heinous, atrocious, or cruel,"[52] a determination that many state statutes make relevant to the potential applicability of the death penalty. A salient example is a Georgia statute that permitted a person to be sentenced to death if the offense "was outrageously or wantonly vile, horrible and inhuman."[53] We can easily see that this sort

50 Kahan (1998), p. 274.
51 See ibid. (1998).
52 Language from the Oklahoma statute in question in *Maynard v. Cartwright*, 486 U. S. 356, 108 S. Ct. 1853 (1988).
53 *Godfrey v. Georgia*, 446 U. S. 420, 100 S. Ct. 1759, 64 L. Ed. 2d. 398 (1980).

of language, while not explicitly mentioning the term "disgust," invites jurors to consult their disgust reactions when considering aggravating circumstances. It is plausible enough to think that here disgust plays a central and also a valuable role, in identifying an especially heinous class of homicides.

The first and most obvious problem with this, the problem that the Court has repeatedly noted, is that this language is so vague that it virtually ensures that the death penalty will be applied in "an arbitrary and capricious manner." Such was the holding in *Godfrey v. Georgia* concerning the Georgia language. "There is nothing in these few words, standing alone," the Court wrote, "that implies any inherent restraint on the arbitrary and capricious infliction of the death sentence. A person of ordinary sensibility could fairly characterize almost every murder as 'outrageously or wantonly vile, horrible and inhuman.' "[54] Similar was the finding in an Oklahoma case in which a unanimous Court found the statutory language "especially heinous, atrocious, and cruel," unconstitutionally vague, offering insufficient guidance to the jury. What has emerged as constitutional is a "limiting construction" or set of such constructions that gives jurors a far more concrete description of aggravating circumstances: felony murder, for example, and murder with torture.[55] But if we have such descriptions, we can leave disgust to one side; we really don't need it to tell us whether torture was used. And the emotion clearly doesn't correctly identify the class of murders that are typically understood to involve aggravating circumstances. Many felony murders will not typically elicit the reaction of disgust: for example, the shooting of a bank officer during a holdup will standardly be found very bad, but rarely disgusting. On the other hand, some murders that seem disgusting to many jurors may not involve constitutionally defined aggravating circumstances: the Court is surely right that many jurors will react with disgust to many if not all murders, when bloody or gory circumstances are precisely described. Bloodiness and goriness are the usual eliciters of disgust. But many especially vile murders lack these features, and many murders that have these features are vile only in the sense that any murder is vile.

---

54 Ibid. at 428–9, 100 S. Ct. at 1764–1765.
55 See *Maynard v. Cartwright*, 1859.

There is also a problem about the type of disgust that places the murderer in a class of heinous monsters more or less outside the boundaries of our moral universe. For the further away from ourselves we place him (or her, but it is almost always a him), the less obvious it is that this is a moral agent at all, and the less obvious it consequently is that this person deserves the penalty we reserve for fully responsible agents. No matter how we define insanity for legal purposes, when we turn someone into a monster we immediately raise the issue of sanity. Aristotle already held that certain individuals (for example, Phalaris, who boiled people in cauldrons) are so weird that they are not even vicious, because we think that such extreme pathology shows that someone isn't really a chooser of ends at all. No matter what psychological concepts we use, we have a hard time avoiding a similar difficulty, when we try to combine a strong ascription of moral responsibility with an account appealing to disgust at the alleged monstrousness of the person's deeds. Perhaps this difficulty can be solved; but it needs to be squarely faced. Disgust, far from shoring up the moral borders of our community, may actually make them harder to police.

But my argument in Chapters 4 and 6 suggests a deeper point. Frequently, I have argued, our disgust at a group signals a desire to cordon ourselves off from something about ourselves that this group represents to us. This diagnosis is especially clear in the areas of misogynistic and homophobic disgust, but I believe that it applies to our response to evil as well. We very often tell ourselves that the doers of heinous wrongs are monsters, in no way like ourselves. This tendency plays a strong role, for example, in writing and reading about the Nazis and the Holocaust. The tremendous enthusiasm for Daniel Goldhagen's recent book,[56] in both Germany and the United States, cannot easily be explained either by its novelty or by its quality: for its main ideas are not new, and even if one admires it one must acknowledge that there are many excellent books on this topic. What does explain the outpouring of interest, I believe, is the desire of many people (including present-day Germans, who are carefully exonerated by Goldhagen) to believe that the culture that gave birth to the horrors of Nazism was a monstrosity, an aberration. Unlike other books that stress the commonness of the evil deeds of Nazi perpetrators (in different ways, Hannah

56 Goldhagen (1996).

450

Arendt, Christopher Browning),[57] or books that stress the role of cultural ideology in building a Nazi mentality (in different ways Raul Hilberg,[58] Omer Bartov[59]), Goldhagen's book argues that the Germany that produced the Nazis was sui generis, a "radically different culture" to be viewed "with the critical eye of an anthropologist disembarking on unknown shores."[60] These people were not shaped by factors that can easily be replicated in other times and places, and they were not acting out deeply shared human capacities for destruction. They were unique, disgusting monsters. We are nothing like this, and we could not possibly create anything like this.[61] When we see the Nazis in this "anthropological" way, whether in works of history or in films and novels, we are comforted: evil is outside, alien, has nothing to do with us. Our disgust creates the boundary: it says, this contamination is and must remain far from our bodies. We might even say, in this case again, that we call disgust to our aid: by allowing ourselves to see evil people as disgusting, we conveniently distance them from ourselves.

By contrast, when we see Nazis depicted without disgust, as human beings who share common characteristics with us – whether the emphasis is on the capacity of all human beings for evil or on a universal submissiveness to distorting ideologies – this is alarming, because it requires self-scrutiny, warning us that we might well have done the same thing under comparable circumstances. It alerts us to the presence of evil (whether active or passively collaborative) in ourselves, and requires us to ask how we might prevent similar phenomena from materializing in our own society. We have to confront the fact that we might become them; but this means that in a significant sense we already are them – with the fearfulness, weakness, and moral blindness

57 Browning (1992), stressing the role of ordinary human reactions such as yielding to peer pressure, the desire not to be thought cowardly, not to lose face, etc.
58 Hilberg (1985), stressing the psychological importance of a deliberate ideologically motivated treatment of Jews as similar to vermin, or even to inanimate objects.
59 Bartov (1991), stressing the role of ideology in creating a group capable of carrying out atrocities. See also Bartov (1996).
60 Goldhagen (1996), p. 15.
61 See Omer Bartov's "Ordinary Monsters," a review of Goldhagen, in *The New Republic*, April 29, 1996, 32–8, which sees the falsely comforting message of Goldhagen's work as a possible reason for its enthusiastic reception despite its scholarly faults. See further in *The New Republic* the exchange between Goldhagen (December 23, 1996) and Bartov and Browning (February 10, 1997); also Bartov's review of *The Concentration Camp* by Wolfgang Sofsky (October 13, 1997).

that go to produce such evils. Because this response is so much more psychologically troubling and politically challenging than the response elicited by Goldhagen, it is not surprising that Goldhagen's book has been embraced with warm approval. It permits us to forget the atrocities that U.S. military officers perpetrated in Vietnam, the atrocities perpetrated against slaves and Native Americans (not to mention Jews, who were hardly well treated, even if they were not exterminated) in our own history. No, monsters cause evil, and that sort of evil could only happen over there.[62]

I believe that a similar thing happens when we are urged to react with disgust to the criminal acts of a murderer. We are being urged to see that person as a monster, outside the boundaries of our moral universe. We are urged precisely *not* to have the thought, "there, but for . . . go I." But in reality, it seems likely that all human beings are capable of evil, and that many if not most of the hideous evildoers are warped by circumstances, both social and personal, that play a large and sometimes decisive role in explaining the evil that they do. If jurors are led to think that evil is done by monsters who were just born different, are freaky and inhuman, they will be prevented from having thoughts about themselves and their own society that are highly pertinent, not only to the equal and principled application of the law, but also to the construction of a society in which less evil will exist. If we classify murders as involving "aggravating circumstances" by some reasoned account – for example, by enumerating aggravating conditions such as torture and felony murder – we permit such useful thoughts to come forth and not to be stifled: for such a classification requires us to ask why we think torture is bad, and to reflect about the strong social reasons we have for seeking to deter it. (Emotions of indignation will frequently be connected with such a reflective process.) If we classify by disgust, I would argue, we stifle such thoughts and comfort ourselves where comfort is not due. Disgust, once again, is an

---

62 See Bartov, "Ordinary Monsters," pp. 37–8: "We are left with the thesis that the Germans were normally monsters, and that the only role of the Nazi regime was to furnish them with the opportunity to act on their evil desires . . . Goldhagen is actually appealing to a public that wants to hear what it already believes. By doing so, he obscures the fact that the Holocaust was too murky and too horrible to be reduced to simplistic interpretations that rob it of its pertinence to our own time." For discussion of these issues I am grateful to Rachel Nussbaum.

impediment to correct public choice, and to reasonable compassion. In this case it is also an impediment to reasonable self-criticism, whereas the judgment of similar possibilities promotes a healthy self-criticism.

Compassion, then, is far from being the entirety of public rationality, even when it is appropriately informed by definite theories corresponding to each of its constituent judgments. But it does play a valuable role in many aspects of public life, informing citizens' understanding of the human meaning of catastrophes of many types. (So too, clearly, does appropriate anger, which is closely linked to compassion when the misfortune is caused by human agency.) Disgust and primitive shame, by contrast, while probably ineliminable from society and functional in some ways, offer nothing valuable to public deliberation, and even undermine it by setting up two classes of human beings, the high and the low.[63] All emotions are not equal.

Here we arrive at another advantage of the cognitive theory that I have been advancing: for it enables us to show why all emotions are not equal. Noncognitive theories typically speak of "emotion" and "passion" as if there were just one thing; and really, in such views, there is basically just one type of (unintelligent, impulsive) force, that moves now in one way, now in another. A cognitive theory can ask about the specific content of the emotion in question: how reliable it is, how linked with various possibilities of self-avoidance and self-deception, how easily perverted. The theory tells us that before we approve of any specific instance of emotion, we will need to know the specific judgments it involves: thus no emotion is good or reliable as a type. Even if there are many valuable instances of compassion (or grief, or fear, or anger), in which the judgments are true, there are also many inappropriate instances, in which the judgments are false and the circle of concern inappropriate.[64] On the other hand, if no emotion is per se morally good, there may be some that are per se morally suspect, whose

63 I argue this in more detail in Nussbaum (1999b), going through a series of distinct legal issues, including the law of obscenity, sodomy laws, and the homosexual provocation defense.
64 Is love per se good? Obviously this very much depends on one's specific views about love of various types; therefore the question must be postponed until Part III.

cognitive content is more likely than not to be false or distorted, and linked with self-deception. Such is the argument that I have made about disgust and primitive shame. (We might make related arguments about envy, though not about anger.) Some emotions are at least potential allies of, and indeed constituents in, rational deliberation.

ASCENTS OF LOVE

LADDERS OF LOVE

An Introduction

I. LOVE AT BALBEC

The band of girls approaches on the beach, their features indistinct. As they grow closer, Marcel's gaze fastens on "a girl with brilliant, laughing eyes and plump, matt cheeks, a black polo-cap crammed on her head, who was pushing a bicycle with . . . an uninhibited swing of the hips" (I.850). Their insolence and daring dazzle him. For a brief moment he sees the dark girl's eyes beneath her cap, sees a "smiling, sidelong glance, aimed from . . . an inaccessible, unknown world wherein the idea of what I was could certainly never penetrate" (I.851). It is at this moment that love begins, inspired by the sign of a hidden life:

If we thought that the eyes of such a girl were merely two glittering sequins of mica, we should not be athirst to know her and to unite her life to ours. But we sense that what shines in those reflecting discs is not due solely to their material composition; that it is, unknown to us, the dark shadows of ideas that that person cherishes about the people and places she knows – the turf of race-courses, the sand of cycling tracks over which, pedalling on past fields and woods, she would have drawn me after her, . . . the shadows, too, of the home to which she will presently return, of the plans that she is forming or that others have formed for her; and above all that it is she, with her desires, her sympathies, her revulsions, her obscure and incessant will. I knew that I should never possess this young cyclist if I did not possess also what was in her eyes. And it was consequently her whole life that filled me with desire; a sorrowful desire because I felt that it was not to be fulfilled, but exhilarating because, what had hitherto been my life having ceased of a sudden to be my whole life, being no more now than a small part of the space stretching out before me which I was burning to cover and which was composed of the lives of these girls, it offered me that prolongation, that possible multiplication of oneself which is happiness. (I.851–2)

Albertine stands out from the group not for her beauty – for all of the girls seem beautiful; not for her defiance – for they all seem bold and dangerous; it is because he sees the light in her eyes, and this light is a sign of a life unknown, ungoverned, that he yearns to join to his own.

Since Proust's account of love has been central to this project from the start, I return to it here. And since ensuing chapters will describe love's ascent to the clear light of understanding, we must begin with the pain and tumult of these "upheavals of thought" from which both Marcel and the Baron, in their different ways, so earnestly desire to escape. For the prospect of happiness is only a brief and momentary aspect of Marcel's passion. Immediately after seeing the girls, he is "sick with despair" (I.855) at the thought that he may not be able to find them again, and this despair – alternating with stretches of boredom when he feels secure in his possession of Albertine – charts the whole course of his love. Albertine is both outside of him, impossibly distant, unpossessable, and inside of him, an internal object that disturbs what is deepest in his sense of life. When, years later, she leaves the little train near Balbec with an ambiguous remark that awakens his jealousy, his own life seems to be departing with her:

But this movement which she thus made to get off the train tore my heart unendurably, just as if, contrary to the position independent of my body which Albertine's seemed to be occupying a yard away from it, this separation in space, which an accurate draughtsman would have been obliged to indicate between us, was only apparent, and anyone who wished to make a fresh drawing of things as they really were would now have had to place Albertine, not at a certain distance from me, but inside me. She gave me such pain by her withdrawal that, reaching after her, I caught her desperately by the arm. (II.1153–4)

Albertine is and is not inside him. He has to reach out and grab her by the arm – and yet, he does so because he is reaching after a piece of himself and his own life. In love, pieces of the self go out into objects that the lover does not control. But this means that the object also goes inside the self, creating upheaval in the inner world:

What a deceptive sense sight is! A human body, even a beloved one, as Albertine's was, seems to us, from a few yards, from a few inches away, remote from us. And similarly with the soul that inhabits it. But if something brings about a violent change in the position of that soul in relation to us, shows us that it is in love with others and not with us, then by the beating of our shattered heart we feel that it is not a few feet away from us but within us that the beloved creature was . . . [T]he words, "That friend is Mlle Vinteuil" had been the *Open sesame*, which I should have been incapable of discovering by myself, that had made Albertine penetrate to the depths of my lacerated heart. And I might search for a hundred years without discovering how to open the door that had closed behind her. (II.1165–6)

But the presence of such an ungovernable external person in the depths of the heart makes the heart itself unstable and unkind. Marcel, possessed by anxiety and tormented by Albertine's ungovernable will, has no room in his life for either friendship or justice. His life becomes obsessively focused on projects of jealous possession, which aim at putting him back in control of his own existence.

II. A DISEASE AND ITS CURE

Any investigation of the emotions' contribution to ethics, even a partial one such as this, must confront the ambivalence and excess of erotic love. It is all very well to argue that a particular type of compassion is a valuable ethical resource. That is an easy case, since compassion is less closely linked than many emotions to the ambivalent struggles of early childhood. So the qualified defense of compassion in Part II has given us no general argument supporting the ethical worth of a life rich in personal emotion. But our argument is even more seriously incomplete than this: for it appears that we have not yet really even rebutted the Stoics' contention that good people ought to extirpate all of the emotions. For if, as Proust repeatedly suggests, erotic love lies at the root of all the other emotions – if one cannot get rid of it except by a radical curtailment of object-love that would alter or remove compassion with it[1] – then we have not yet justified even the place of compassion in the ethical life. To do that, we will need to show that erotic love, too, can be part of a morally acceptable life. If the cost of keeping compassion in life is to keep, as well, this dangerous type of love, and

1 As we shall see in Chapter 10, that is not the novel's final word on the matter.

if this type of love can never be rendered morally acceptable, or even morally cooperative, then it might after all be better to do without the emotions altogether, relying on duty to motivate concern for others.

Proust's contention has great force. The argument of Part I has suggested that an intense form of object-love, which may as well be called erotic, underlies all of the adult emotions and colors them. The account of childhood ambivalence in Part I focused on need and incompleteness, rather than on sexuality narrowly construed (as desire for genital pleasure, for example). But the result was not a denial of Proust's contention; it was, instead, a rethinking of what sexuality is about, what forms of infantile eroticism lie behind it. Chapter 4 argued that the central drama in the infant's life is one of need and incompleteness, of an opening toward a radiant object accompanied by an almost intolerable need of the solace that object can give. Here we found the roots of later object-love and of erotic longing. Adult human sexuality does not aim merely at bodily pleasure and release: if it did, then the Cynic philosopher's advice to substitute masturbation for intercourse[2] would meet with universal acceptance, and everyone's life would be a lot calmer. It is because sexuality expresses deep needs that derive from infancy that it is both ethically valuable (a central form of aliveness to value) and ethically disturbing. In that sense sexual love, as Proust plausibly indicates, is a species of a more general category of erotic love and desire that has its origin in the child's longing to control the comings and goings of its mother, seen as the most important and marvelous creature in the world. But then, there really is reason to doubt whether the removal of erotic love would leave compassion and other emotions intact. Proust goes too far when he suggests that all friendly love is really concealed erotic love; and yet he is probably right to see the two emotions as intertwined, in such a way that we cannot count on retaining the energy of a beneficent compassion if we eliminate erotic love as a danger to morality.

We can make, as well, a related point. Erotic love involves an opening of the self toward an object, a conception of the self that pictures the self as incomplete and reaching out for something valued. The object is seen as valuable and radiant, the self as extending itself toward

---

2 Diogenes the Cynic, masturbating in the marketplace, said: "Would that it were as easy to fill the stomach by rubbing it."

that radiance. But that type of opening up of the self to value is risky, and, as we have already seen in Chapter 4, such a risky existence, depending so greatly on another, brings ethical problems with it. There may be no way of surmounting those ethical problems without living a life that bounds the self off against objects, denying its deep need for them and involvement with them. But if that is so, then compassion (and grief) will also need to be eliminated, as the Stoics held: for they too are proofs of a self that is too world-dependent, too "wonderstruck by external things."[3]

Thus even the limited ethical defense of emotions offered in Part II requires us to ask why erotic love has typically been seen by ethical thinkers as a danger, a disease that good thought ought to cure. And we need to examine the cures that have been proposed, to see whether they really do the trick of giving us love's energy and wonder without its danger – or, if they do not succeed in this, whether we can discover some other route by which the ethical life might accept and welcome love.

In Marcel's story we see many of the features of erotic love that philosophy has traditionally found disturbing, and has wished to cure. First and most obvious is love's partiality, which seems to threaten any ethical approach involving the extension of concern. Intense attachments to particular individuals, especially when they are of an erotic or romantic sort, call attention away from the world of general concern, asking it to rivet itself to a single life that provides in itself no sufficient reason for this special treatment, as it imperiously claims all thoughts, all desires. Erotic love is based on unequal concern, an unequal concern not explained by reasons: Marcel knows that there really is no rational basis for his choice of Albertine over the other cyclists. His choice is explained, if at all, by shadowy images reaching back into some distant past; perhaps it is explained only by the quirk of chance that lets him see her eyes before the eyes of the others. And such love exacts an intensity of focus that makes equal concern impossible. Marcel's book, the story of his love, contains no general social concern, no altruism (except, as we shall see, the altruism of art), no compassion. Shreds of gossip about the Dreyfus case appear and disappear – reminding us, by their rapid shifts as years pass, that there is a world of events and

3 Epictetus, defining tragedy.

people outside of Marcel's love, a world of justice and great injustice, and that he is lost to that world through love. We might say that because he continues to live a life of erotic love he never really moves beyond his own infancy. For his obsession with Mama is merely substituted another obsession, as tyrannical, as all-encompassing.

And if compassion raises questions about the excessive neediness of emotion, if compassion already seems to come hand in hand with the inclination to revenge, how much stronger must this excessiveness and this ambivalence seem in the case of erotic love, with its wish to abdicate control by putting one's happiness at the mercy of an unknown and ungoverned object, with its paralysis of prudence and choice, with its wish to surrender the inner precincts of the self to an incubus who is determined to create misery and upheaval. If, as Marcel suggests, love involves an *open sesame* that sends the external person down into the depths of the heart, then passivity and uncontrol are constitutive features of love. Marcel lives in a world of unbearably deep need. Even the beating of his heart seems to be not his own but hers, to give or to withhold.

A need this deep is rarely free of retributive wishes. The only way Marcel can prevent unbearable pain to himself is to inflict pain on Albertine. He sees his jealous demand that she sever all of her other friendships as the only way of "exorcising my hallucinations," "cur[ing] . . . the phobia that haunted me" (III.14). In his demand to know everything about her actions, he sees the only hope to "kill the intolerable love" he feels (III.93): "we feel that if she were to tell us everything, we might perhaps easily be cured of our love" (III.55). But the needs of such a love are so deep that, like and continuous with an infant's need for totality and comfort, they can never be fully or stably satisfied:

Jealousy, which is blindfold, is not merely powerless to discover anything in the darkness that enshrouds it; it is also one of those tortures where the task must be endlessly repeated, like that of the Danaides, or of Ixion. (III.147–8)

The life of the lover thus becomes the life of a jailer, who needs the perpetual threat of escape to goad him to new stirrings of love – and of cruelty.

What lies behind the hostility? In particular, we need to ask about

462

two emotions that have been closely linked to anger and aggression from the start of the inquiry: shame and disgust. Love seems in one way to be the emotion most opposed to shame: for the wish of love is to reveal the self and to be seen, whereas the reflex of shame is to hide. Love might also be opposed to disgust: for love breaks down boundaries between people and opens the personality to the activity of the other; disgust seals the self off from contamination by another. But this apparent opposition may mask an underlying dialectical structure. It may be precisely because love's openness is so extreme that it brings with it the reaction of shame and hiding; it may be precisely in order to avoid the extreme invasion of oneself by another that one calls disgust to one's aid, sealing the self from harm. All these connections remain to be further investigated; but they suggest that the relationship of love not just to one but to several negative emotions may be ethically problematic.

III. THE PHILOSOPHERS' DILEMMA

For such reasons, philosophers have not often been friends of erotic love.[4] Some would remove it altogether – if not from the entirety of life, at least from the ethical life. Kant, for example, holds that all sexual desire leads inexorably to the instrumental use of persons, and thus to the degradation of their humanity.

Sexual love makes of the loved person an Object of appetite; as soon as that appetite has been stilled, the person is cast aside as one casts away a lemon which has been sucked dry. Sexual love can, of course, be combined with human love and so carry with it the characteristics of the latter, but taken by itself and for itself, it is nothing more than appetite. Taken by itself it is a degradation of human nature; for as soon as a person becomes an Object of appetite for another, all motives or moral relationship cease to function, because as an Object of appetite for another a person becomes a thing and can be treated and used as such by every one . . . Sexual desire is at the root of it; and that is why we are ashamed of it, and why all strict moralists . . . sought to suppress and extirpate it.[5]

4 For an excellent anthology of philosophical treatments of the topic, with illuminating commentary, see Solomon and Higgins (1991).
5 Kant, *Lectures on Ethics*, Akad. pp. 163–4. By "human love," Kant means active concern, not strong emotion, as he shows by his distinction between "practical love" and "pathological" (i.e., passive) love in *The Doctrine of Virtue*.

Unlike the "strict moralists," Kant did not wish to eliminate sexual desire completely, given his interest in the family; but by restricting it to marriage he believed that he had surrounded it with external guarantees of concern and mutual aid, thus limiting its baneful tendencies.[6] He did not believe that it could ever be reformed from within. Although he uses the term "sexual love" for what he retains, it seems more accurate to say that he retains both sexual desire (accompanied by shame) and human love, eliminating sexual *love* completely from the well-lived ethical life.

But even philosophers who defend the ethical contribution of some other emotions tend to dislike the impure intensity of the erotic, which seems as subversive of the beneficent social passions as it is of nonpassionate calculation. Schopenhauer, who finds in compassion the root of all morality, notoriously detests women and the desires they inspire. The aim of our lives, properly understood, is fredom from bondage to the will, that is, to erotic striving. Adam Smith, who defends the ethical role not only of compassion but also of certain types of anger and fear and grief, argues that passionate erotic love forms no part at all of the moral equipment of the judicious spectator.[7] For the spectator will feel only those passions that one can feel *as* a spectator, a concerned onlooker who listens to all of the reasoning of those involved in the matter, but does not participate in their struggles. And Smith argues that from that point of view the specific reasons for lovers' passionate intensity, and their obsessive focusing on their objects, simply cannot be seen.

The trouble begins with the bodily experience of sexual desire, which is, Smith says, "perhaps, the foundation of love."[8] For a spectator looking at people who are in the grip of that passion usually fails to find in his external view of the object the source of the lovers' arousal. Thus he finds the entire scene one into which he "cannot enter," and feels it ridiculous or even disgusting. The real cause, Smith insists, for our experience of alienation and even disgust when we witness the sexual arousal of others is not that these are feelings shared with animals, and thus beneath our dignity. It is, instead, the moral fact that

6 See Herman (1993).

7 For a more extensive analysis of this part of Smith's argument, see "Steerforth's Arm: Love and the Moral Point of View," in Nussbaum (1990).

8 Smith (1976), p. 32.

we cannot see the grounds of their passions, we cannot enter into them with spectatorial empathy:

To the person himself who feels them, as soon as they are gratified, the object that excited them ceases to be agreeable: even its presence often becomes offensive to him; he looks round to no purpose for the charm which transported him the moment before, and he can now as little enter into his own passion as another person. When we have dined, we order the covers to be removed; and we should treat in the same manner the objects of the most ardent and passionate desires, if they were the objects of no other passions but those which take their origin from the body.[9]

Things are made worse, not better, when we add love to the picture. For if sexual desire without love is sometimes quirky, its operations difficult to understand, it is also fairly diffuse and unselective, and thus in many cases relatively easy to "see into." Smith does not talk about pornography, and uses his characteristic analogies to literary experience in such a way as to cast doubt upon its possibility – claiming that those who read narratives about the bodily appetites (hunger being his example) cannot find themselves sharing the appetite about which they read. But Smith is wrong. The actuality and efficacy of pornography shows that it is relatively easy to take on in one's own body the sexual feelings about which one reads, using the highly generalized image presented in the text as a receptacle for one's own fantasy.

The difficult thing is to take on love. For, as Smith argues, love is an intense response to perceptions of the particularity, and the particular high value, of another person's body and mind. This particular specialness is impenetrably obscure to the observer; it looks like an inexplicable quirk of fortune. Discussing love in a section entitled "Of those passions which take their origin from a particular turn or habit of the Imagination," Smith argues that if a friend has been wronged or benefited, the spectator can listen to the reasons for his anger or gratitude, and will be expected, as a friend, to share the emotion itself, insofar as it is based on those reasons. But love does not work this way. However much I try to describe the wonderful features of my lover to my friend, he argues, if it is not a friendship of esteem but a true erotic passion this explanation must always prove insufficient. "We never think ourselves bound to conceive a passion of the same kind, and for the same

9 Ibid., p. 28.

person for whom he has conceived it."[10] We may, he grants, sympathize with some general features of the lovers' situation: their fears for the future, their expectation of happiness. But the particularity of the attachment seems groundless, and thus ridiculous (though not "naturally odious").

As Smith is well aware, this is fortunate for the lover: for love is not only inexplicable, it is also exclusive. The lover does not *wish* his love to be shared or seen by any spectator, he wants to be the only one to see and feel just that for that person, and to receive those emotions in return. Love, in fact, is not simply a set of feelings and thoughts about an object, or even a mutuality of feeling and thought. It is, and Smith's account makes it clear that he knows it is, a mysterious and intimate way of life,[11] characterized by all sorts of hidden exchanges whose nature demands privacy and secrecy, and whose meaning is impenetrable to the observer, should there by bad fortune happen to be one.[12]

Smith focuses on love's exclusive character, which makes him think it inimical to general social concern, and on its apparent groundlessness, which makes it seem inappropriate in social life, which should be based on the giving and receiving of reasons. He says relatively little about our other two problems, love's painful dependency and its ambivalence – although his observations about exclusivity are not difficult to connect with his subsequent analysis of the "unsocial passion" of retributive anger. (He focuses, instead, on other ethical dangers: the danger of "the last ruin and infamy" for the woman, the danger of "an incapacity for labor" and "a neglect of duty" in the man [I.ii.2.5].) But we may without distortion add these two further problems to his account, since they undermine even further love's place in the life of the judicious spectator. Smith's argument makes it clear that one may be a strong ally of the emotions, and even of some intensely passionate emotions – for Smith's spectator will sometimes be extremely angry or extremely frightened, when the nature of the case warrants it – without having any approval at all of Marcel's passion, while finding it, in fact, a subversive enemy of the other good passions. In this passion above

10 Ibid., p. 31.

11 I am speaking here of mutual love; and of course quite a few accounts of love make it independent of reciprocation, as we shall see.

12 Smith (1976), pp. 32–3, analyzed in "Steerforth's Arm," in Nussbaum (1990), pp. 341–6.

all others one is blind to the good of others outside the relationship; in this one beyond others one is dependent on forces outside oneself that one does not control; in this one beyond others one is prone to anger and revenge.

Smith does strongly connect disgust to sexual love, when he argues that the object of desire is "offensive" to the lover after desire is satisfied, rather like food to the satieted eater. Thus sexual love in its very nature gives rise to a strong desire for the removal of the object – which we would carry out, he says, but for other, more tender sentiments that we may have toward her. Thus he regards as inevitable a certain misanthropic and, we should say, misogynistic tendency in sexual love, expressive of an ambivalence toward the body of the being to whom we are drawn with deep need. Although he says no more about the ethical dangers of such an emotion, and, indeed, seems to think it simply a natural part of (male) sexuality, we ourselves can see such dangers.

To hold that the judicious spectator does not feel love is not precisely to hold that a good human life should not contain love. But it is to say that love is always the occasion for a certain shame in the reasonable social life, for anxiety in the person who is striving to do good for others, and for mirth on the part of the onlooker. The primary reason Smith gives for putting up with it at all is Kant's: that it serves the purposes of reproduction (Smith calls its sexual component "the passion by which Nature unites the two sexes"). And it is pretty clear that, like Kant, he prefers a marital relation without love's dangers: for he connects love to female adultery and to male dissipation. It appears that we are most tolerant of love as a stage in premarital courtship.

Thus, ultimately, we endure love's ridiculous and even ugly propensities, insofar as we do, for the sake of other goods that it offers. But we don't want to talk about it too much, or shouldn't. For it can never "interest our companions in the same degree in which [it] interest[s] us." To the obvious point that we *are* fascinated by love stories, Smith has a ready reply: we are interested not in the love per se, but in the difficulties that beset the lovers, their hopes and fears, their guilt and anger. The exchange of loving confidences itself, should that be represented in narrative or dramatic form, would elicit only ridicule.[13]

13 Smith (1976), pp. 32–3, discussed in "Steerforth's Arm," in Nussbaum (1990).

But Smith is wrong. However difficult it is to represent erotic love successfully in narrative form, the love itself is an object of our most intense spectatorial interest. (Proust goes so far as to claim that *all* compelling narrative is at bottom about love, and involves the reader's reading of her own erotic desire.) Precisely *because* love is more mysterious than the other passions, precisely because we cannot easily catalogue the reasons for our loves, we look to narratives for the understanding we lack, or at least for a confirmation of our sense that there is a great mystery here. When we turn to stories we do not, to be sure, feel bound to form a passion of exactly the same sort for the same person on the basis of the same reasons. Reading about Marcel and Albertine does not make me more likely to go out and sleep with a cyclist (even though the substitution of genders that would be involved in that fantasy is in many ways invited by the text). But when we understand what is deep and compelling in their love we understand something about ourselves and our own depths. Such a story is, as Proust says, an optical instrument through which we inspect our own longing and its pain.[14]

And when we do inspect our love through stories and through poetry and music, we cannot easily draw Adam Smith's conclusion, that this is a merely ridiculous and undignified passion. We are likely to find in the erotic what Marcel finds there: a sense of mystery and depth, a tremendous power, that can make us wonder, at least, whether a life that forgoes this passion for the sake of acceptable social rationality would be impoverished, a life without radiance. One might even ask, although Marcel does not, whether such a life would not lack the strongest sources of social beneficence itself. Smith may be too hasty in attempting to sever benevolence from its impure foundations.

Accordingly, very few thinkers in the Western tradition have proposed the complete "extirpation" – as Kant and the Stoics put it – of erotic love. Although it is evidently one of the most dangerous of the emotions, it has also seemed one of the most necessary, even to philosophers who hate the emotions extremely. The Greek Stoics, who pro-

14 Proust, III.1089: "For it seemed to me that they would not be as 'my' readers but the readers of their own selves, my book being merely a sort of magnifying glass like those which the optician at Combray used to offer his customers – it would be my book, but with its help I would furnish them with the means of reading what lay inside themselves."

pose the complete "extirpation" of anger, and grief, and fear, and hope, and even pity, still wish to preserve for the wise man a certain species of *erôs*, and not a desexualized species either. They define it as "an attempt to form a friendship on account of the perceived beauty of young men in their prime" – a definition much mocked by Cicero, both for its inconsistency with their general antipassion program and for its homoerotic preferences.[15] They held that this reformed passion would provide the basis for a just and reasonable city.[16] In all this, as we shall see, they followed Plato's lead.

What we find emerging, therefore, in consequence of this perceived tension between love's energy for good and its subversive power, is a recurrent attempt to reform or educate erotic love, so as to keep its creative force while purifying it of ambivalence and excess, and making it more friendly to general social aims. This tradition centrally uses the metaphor of an "ascent," in which the aspiring lover climbs a ladder from the quotidian love from which she began, with all its difficulties, to an allegedly higher and more truly fulfilling love. In each case, moving the lover up the ladder involves both addition and subtraction; and we must ask whether what is left at the end still contains what was originally valuable and wonderful in love, whether it is still erotic at all, still love at all.

Part III examines four portions of this "ascent" tradition. It is such a pervasive feature of the history of Western philosophy and literature that one could write an illuminating history of moral thought from Plato to Nietzsche using that motif alone. I shall not attempt a continuous history here. Instead, I shall focus on three distinct types of ascent story that form their own continuous traditions within that larger tradition: an account of the ascent that focuses on contemplation of the good and beautiful; a Christian account of the ascent that investigates the role of humility, longing, and grace; and a Romantic account that rejects a static telos for ascent, holding that striving itself is love's transcendence. Finally, I shall consider an account of a reverse ascent or "descent" of love in which human desire sets itself the task of embracing the imperfect human world with love.

Each tradition claims to improve on the one that (in the order of

15 See Nussbaum (1995b) for an examination of the texts and their cultural background.
16 See Schofield (1999).

469

these chapters)[17] precedes it, by supplying something important that the previous one had lacked. To some extent I agree with those claims; thus the sequence of chapters is itself an ascending sequence. But in the end my own judgments are more complex: I find elements of ongoing ethical value in several distinct conceptions, and try to indicate, in Chapter 16, how I would make a whole (or nonwhole) out of those best elements.

The texts we shall examine do not all share the same account of erotic love, its nature, and its relationship to other types of love. In each case, therefore, I shall have to ask concrete questions about the initial characterization of erotic love, and about background cultural factors that may be involved in the differences among them. But I believe that there is sufficient overlap and common ground, both among the texts and between the texts and a modern reader's experiences, to yield a coherent debate. Indeed, it is partly because there is a coherent debate – because these texts refer to and criticize one another – that there is significant overlap among them, more than might have been the case had we simply set out to look at popular thought about love in each of the cultures in question.

In all cases, erotic love is characterized as involving an intense attachment to and longing for a particular person; this attachment may transform itself to take on other more general objects, but its beginning lies in personal attachment. Erotic love also involves characteristic ways of viewing the beloved person, who is seen as radiant and wonderful, and also as necessary for the lover's happiness. Finally, the beloved person is also seen as independent – as uncontrolled and unpossessed, not simply a part of the lover, or submissive to his will. Whether this separateness is pleasant or terrible (or both) will be a matter for debate; but it is a feature that fundamentally shapes love's projects. These beliefs about love are, we might say, the common ground of the ascent tradition.

---

17 To that extent, there is a chronological order: the Platonic tradition is known to, and the target of, the Christian ascent tradition; the Romantics know and criticize both Platonists and Christians; Whitman and Joyce reflect on all three tendencies. But of course there are Platonists who repudiate Romanticism (Proust), Christians who repudiate both Platonism and Romanticism (the modern Thomists discussed in Chapter 12), and so forth. In that sense, the sequence is not chronological.

IV. PUPILS OF THE ASCENT

Each of these traditions is not simply a tradition of thought but a way of life. Each of these views about ascent also proposes ways in which real people should ascend, converting their flawed human loves into better loves. To take the measure of such a view, we need, then, to be able to imagine what the change would be like, and what elements of people's lives survive it. I shall therefore hold the debate together further by returning periodically to Marcel and, especially, Albertine as aspiring, potentially "ascending" pupils, asking what they would have to think, desire, be, in order to accomplish the task each of these thinkers has set out for them.[18] Marcel and Albertine, of course, are fictional characters. (So too, in a sense, are all of us as we love and are loved in real life.)[19] The view of love expressed in Proust's narrative, using Marcel and Albertine as its material, is one of the views we shall be investigating. Although there are some elements of Proust's view that I have provisionally accepted in setting up the problem to be treated in Part III, I shall ultimately be quite critical of several features of Proust's idea of love. Since we want a hypothetical pupil who follows Plato's advice, and Augustine's, and Spinoza's – not only that of Marcel, the internal author, or of Proust, the author behind the author – we can best avoid confusion between our imagined pupil and Proust's own controversial view by focusing not on Marcel but on Albertine – concerning whose inner world Proust's reader actually learns nothing at all.

Albertine, or A, as I shall call her henceforth, is a convenient blank space within which we can construct the narrative of each ascent story. In addition, since the child we have imagined all along is female, A can

18 Readers will recognize a device that I used in Nussbaum (1994), when I investigated the education of the imaginary pupil Nikidion in the various schools of Hellenistic philosophy. I see no reason not to repeat this strategem.
19 When Proust says this, the claim is one of an austere solipsism. Because he cannot imagine knowledge of the other person as other than possession, he believes that we are doomed to loving a creation of our own fantasy: see Chapter 10, and "Love's Knowledge" in Nussbaum (1990). I do not accept his contention, as will become evident; indeed, I diagnose his conception of the goal as issuing from a pathological form of narcissism. So when I say this, I mean only that creative activities of imagination and interpretation are central to our ability to make contact with another person, and to imagine ourselves as well.

function as the continuation of that child's story. And finally, because the tradition we shall describe is for the most part, strikingly, a tradition of men writing about men,[20] it seems reasonable enough to imagine a female pupil, whose perceptions and reactions may, like those of Molly Bloom, complicate the philosophical landscape, even while they illuminate it.[21]

V. THE NEO-STOIC THEORY AND THE NEED FOR NARRATIVE

To begin talking about love I have turned to Proust. And the plan of Part III, as just described, involves a nonlinear investigation of love through literary texts of many kinds, one of them also a musical text, and several also philosophical. Why have I diverged here from the analytical method used in Parts I and II, where philosophical and literary works were cited, but where they did not provide entire chapters with their principle of organization?

Love is not a topic easily investigated in analytical philosophical prose; nor does it lend itself easily to conventional forms of linear argument. Smith was on the right track when he insisted on the disproportionate role, in love, of mystery and particularity; and conventional philosophical texts are usually bad at conveying these qualities. Short

---

20 And indeed, if we accept the received view according to which Albertine is a surrogate for various male love objects that Proust was really thinking about, even the fictional Albertine herself is a male.

21 Why is there only one example of women's writing in Part III? In *Love's Knowledge*, discussing Proust's view, I used as my foil a short story by Ann Beattie. In the early drafts of the lectures that became this book, I used at this point a novel by Joyce Carol Oates, *You Must Remember This*, whose female protagonist, Enid, became the imaginary pupil. But the unfortunate difficulty with using contemporary fiction is that it is rarely well-known enough to serve, without extensive further commentary, as a jumping-off point for a reflective transformation. This is particularly true if one wants to address a heterogeneous multinational audience, who may simply not know Beattie, or even Oates, at all. If one does use such a text, furthermore, one has to gloss it elaborately, whereas what is most desirable is, as I have said, a blank space. For all of these reasons, although gender differences are a major subtheme of this book, and although there are numerous female writers in literature who might have illuminated these themes, I have chosen to use an abstract Proustian pupil here, and to approach the theme of gender as it occurs within each text, whether written by a male or a female. We shall see that the rejection of a certain type of masculinity, and a corresponding strong identification with the female, is a central theme in Mahler, Whitman, and Joyce.

of attempting the Proustian task of writing the story of one's own love – a task that requires, as Marcel notes, both literary talent and a lifetime of selfless dedication to literature – the best route into the topic seems to me to be to examine texts written well by others. Part III is therefore a series of readings of texts, with philosophical commentaries on those readings. The selection of texts is not haphazard; its principles are described more fully in the next section. And the movement of the whole account (together with the reflections on the readings) ought to give a sufficiently clear picture of the story that I would attempt to tell if I were to undertake, *per impossibile,* Proust's enterprise. At the same time, the texts stress the sheer variety and multiplicity of love, and thus provide more and more varied "optical instruments" for readers who are eager to use such a commentary to study their own experience.

There is a further reason for turning to love stories in order to investigate love. I have characterized all emotions as complex object relations; and I have argued that most of the emotions of adult human beings cannot be well understood without looking at the history of object relations that informs them, as the past shadows the present. But what is true of all emotions to some degree is true most especially of love. It cannot be well understood unless we examine it as part of the complex fabric of a story that extends over time.

We now come upon a complexity in the relationship of love to the neo-Stoic theory of emotions that I have been developing. For love, while an emotion, is also a *relationship*. I may feel love for someone, or be in love with someone, and that love is itself an emotion in the sense described here; but there is another sense in which love is present only if there is a mutual relationship. Different writers emphasize different aspects of this family of experiences, some focusing on the object-directed emotion, some on a relationship of interaction, mutual emotion, and mutual awareness of emotion. This will concern us as we examine the accounts in turn. But if it is already the case that an object-directed emotion needs to be illuminated by thinking of the story of which it is a part, it is more abundantly clear that the relational and interactive aspects of love require narrative for their complete investigation.

To the extent that a thinker holds that love is not present without a mutual relationship – as, for example, Aristotle does in his account of *philia,* or friendly love – this thinker seems to be either defining love as not simply an emotion or else rejecting the account of emotions that I have defended here. Aristotle in a general way accepts an account of emotion not unlike my own. He does, however, hold that love – or at least *philia*[22] – is not merely an emotion. Although it involves emotion, it also has requirements that go beyond the emotional. I believe that Aristotle's account is persuasive: there are types of love that do have requirements beyond the emotional, and these are among the most important types of love for the purposes of normative ethics. But this observation does not call our account of emotions into question: for, as I have phrased the objection, it is simply that the emotion of love is insufficient for the full experience of human love as that is relevant for ethics. In other words, the term "love" is used equivocally, to name both an emotion and a more complex form of life. Our object-relations account may be adequate to describe the emotions, without giving a complete account of the fuller form of life of which emotions of love are often a central part.

Such a reply, however, is slightly too hasty: for it imagines that the emotions involved in love are unaffected by the presence or absence of a reciprocal relationship of the sort Aristotle depicts. This is plainly not the case. In a reciprocal relationship of Aristotle's sort, the emotions involved a conception of the object as a person who wants and actively seeks my good, and for whom I both want and actively seek the good. Moreover, lovers will have emotions toward their relationship itself, and the activities it involves. Thus we cannot even understand the emotional aspect of love fully without seeing how it is frequently related to interactions and exchanges of the sort Aristotle is thinking about. This complexity does not mean that we cannot investigate love with the perspective of a theory of emotion such as I have mapped out; but it does mean that any such investigation has to concern itself with the whole fabric of love, not just with isolated instances of strong emotion. This gives us reason, even from the perspective of the neo-Stoic account, to take a particularly keen interest in narrative accounts of love, which can illuminate the emotional aspects not only by investigating the relationship between past and present emotions, but also

---

22 For attempts to understand Aristotle's views about *erôs*, on the basis of the scanty evidence that survives, see Price (1989) and Sihvola (forthcoming).

by setting emotions in their relationship to actions and interactions, those other elements of Aristotelian love.

Two further questions now arise about the relationship between erotic love and the neo-Stoic view. Both, as we shall see, give us still more reason to be interested in narratives. One is the question of sexual desire. Erotic love, unlike many other emotions, does appear to be bound up with a desire that has at least some necessary bodily elements. Does this mean that its definition will be different in structure from the definitions of other emotions, mentioning those bodily elements of arousal and excitement as necessary for the emotion?

This is a very tricky question, and one whose answer will vary with different accounts of erotic love. There is, first, the problem of getting a good account of the sexual aspect of erotic love, and of the role of bodily elements in that. As I have observed in Chapter 2, commenting on reductive definitions in the social science literature, even sexual arousal is difficult to define in purely physiological terms, and it is unclear whether one wants to include any particular physiological condition (for example, as in Chapter 2, genital arousal as measured by penile or vaginal blood volume) in the definition of arousal. We noted in Chapter 2 that this measure certainly did not give us a sufficient condition for sexual arousal (because such physical conditions sometimes occur in contexts that would not plausibly be described as erotic, such as hanging); and it was not fully clear that it gave us a necessary condition, given the possibility of experiences that it seems reasonable to describe as sexual arousal (involving sensation and fantasy) in people with various handicaps that prevent erectile functioning. Certainly, however, sexual *desire* has no physiological sufficient condition, and no physiological necessary condition, for closely related reasons. (If one could not have sexual desire without genital arousal, impotence would not be the problem that it is.) As for erotic love – in Chapter 2 I said that we would need to wait until Part III to apply the penile plethysmograph to Heathcliff. Here I can say that if we did so, the result would be quite uncertain. *Wuthering Heights* confronts us with a type of extremely intense erotic love, coupled with strong desires that are in some sense erotic, and in that large sense sexual, that seems, nonetheless, to have little to do with genital sexuality. Heathcliff connects genital arousal with aggression and cruelty, as we know from Isabella's narrative. Whether he connects his love for Cathy with any such genital state is extremely uncertain. Cathy's relationship to the physical is extremely unclear: the more intensely she loves, the more she appears to become a flame or a wind, rather than a body of flesh.

This complex dissociation of erotic love from genital sexuality is a common theme in texts about love. The dissociation is especially strong in the Christian tradition, which attempts to appropriate love's emotional striving without the sins of the flesh; but we see it as well in the Platonic ascent, which quickly moves beyond beautiful bodies, and even in Proust. Marcel's erotic love for Albertine, though complexly linked to physical sexual acts, is not defined in terms of those acts or their physical conditions. As he states, sexual intercourse is one of the strategems he chooses to relieve his agony for a time, and possibly also as a way of expressing (vainly) a kind of fleeting possession.[23] But the intercourse and its physical manifestations are not themselves the love.

It seems plausible to say that erotic love is inseparable from some type of sexual desire, meaning by that some kind of desire for intercourse and other related bodily acts. This desire need not be conscious, and it need not take the form of an actual plan or project. (If one extends erotic love to nonhuman objects, as does Plato, then it cannot be linked to such projects, though there may be analogous fantasies of union or "being-with.")[24] As we shall see, this idea that erotic love cannot be the love it is without sexual desire is contested by some Christian authors, and yet I think we should accept it, at least tentatively, as a guide to what is distinctive about this type of love, as contrasted with other instances of love. On the other hand, since we have already insisted that sexual desire itself is a matter of thought and fantasy more than of any particular bodily manifestation, this does not make erotic love dependent on any particular bodily manifestation. So I see no reason to think that erotic love has a relation to the physical that requires us to modify in any fundamental way our neo-Stoic view.

In short: "upheavals of thought" are often linked to other upheavals – but the love itself is in the upheaval of mind. We need, however, to keep pursuing this issue as we investigate the emotion, because it is

---

23 Here he seems to be agreeing with Aristophanes, in Plato's *Symposium*: see Chapter 10.

24 Thus in the *Symposium* he speaks of a kind of intercourse with the object of knowledge: see Chapter 10.

very complicated and many-sided. This we can do well if we focus on narratives that do show us some of the links between love and sexual desire. Indeed, it is difficult to know how else we would pursue the links – given that scientific accounts of sexual desire usually deliberately leave love to one side, as do many psychoanalytic accounts. (Among the latter, the ones that are complex and nonreductive enough to incorporate an adequate idea of love are also more like narrative or poetry, and thus are not exceptions to my general suggestion.) We must keep returning to this question, however, as we examine each account in turn.

A final question about the relationship between love and the neo-Stoic theory brings us to yet one more reason for seeking understanding through narratives. This is the question of whether love has a relationship to desires for action, and to projects and plans of various sorts, that is unlike that of other emotions. I said in Chapter 2 that emotions frequently have a very close and intimate connection to motives and desires, and also to projects and plans; nonetheless, we said that they should not be defined in terms of those motives and projects. This was so, I argued, because quite a few emotions are not linked with any particular course of action: grief, for example, or calm joy. And I suggested that even when an emotion type has strong links with a course of action – as does fear, say, with flight – this link is contingent, not an essential part of the definition. Although someone who fears the enemy will, other things being equal, flee, the courageous soldier (as Aristotle describes him) will not flee, because, although afraid, he judges that to flee would be shameful. I think that something like this is true of love. Although love is often linked with projects of possession and control, or with more beneficent projects of helping the loved one – and although some prominent accounts of love do make such projects a part of the definition of love – probably what ought to be said instead is that love is a particular kind of awareness of an object, as tremendously wonderful and salient, and as deeply needed by the self. The project of possession (or of helping) is then a response to that awareness. At any rate, one should carefully distinguish the awareness from the project of possession (or of helping), which in no way follows automatically from it. If Proust describes a form of love that has the desire for possession at its very heart or as its essence, perhaps he is erring – taking as essential something that is a nonessential concomitant of a special form of awareness of an object – or perhaps he is describing a narrow subclass of experiences, in which that desire really is essential, and colors the very nature of the awareness.

VI. NORMATIVE CRITERIA

In order to assess the various accounts of love's reform, we need some benchmarks of comparison. According to my account of emotions, the assessment of emotions is part and parcel of the overall assessment of a person's value judgments and cognitive attitudes: how well do they fit the world, and how far do they embody appropriate perceptions of value? Nonetheless, I said in Part I that we could describe a mutually supporting relationship between an account of emotional health and a normative ethical account (or a family of such accounts) that stressed flexibility, reciprocity, and mercy.

In speaking about compassion, similarly, I stressed the need to supply compassion with an independently defended ethical theory that would give definite accounts of the three judgments; but I also suggested that the psychological mechanisms underlying compassion support an extension of concern and beneficence. Giving a very general account of how a reasonable ethical theory might answer the three judgments, I illustrated some of the contributions compassion might make to the public life of a pluralistic liberal democracy.

When we talk normatively about love we are talking, clearly, about matters both personal and social. We are not confining ourselves, as we did in Chapter 8, to the sphere of justice and the basic scheme of cooperation in a society, but venturing into the area of comprehensive ethical theory, concerning which we should not expect all citizens to be in agreement. On the other hand, at least part of what we are searching for is an extension of the "reasonable political psychology" mapped out in Part II: we want to know whether we can find an account of love that really does make it reasonable to expect that the emotional life of citizens will support pluralistic liberal-democratic institutions. Although the arguments that follow do not strenuously observe this distinction between political values and comprehensive values, and although it thus remains an open question how many of this part's conclusions could be made part of a political "overlapping consensus," my tentative judgment is that the normative criteria set out here are reasonable ones for all citizens to share. Loves that do not have these features should certainly be tolerated, but we can see that they are less likely to be supportive of the goals of a liberal-democratic society. Thus, for example, a comprehensive view of human life based on Proust's idea of love, with its emphasis on jealousy and the desire for possession, is likely to be in a deep tension with some reasonable goals of citizenship, in a way that a different normative conception of love, focused on reprocity, would not be.

In asking normative questions about conceptions of love, we would do well to begin with the problems the philosophical tradition has identified, namely, with love's links to excessive neediness and a related vengefulness, and to a narrow partiality of concern. And, in fact, the therapeutic accounts we shall study all explicitly address these three problems, claiming to have produced a love that is free of them. We need to assess these claims. My account of early childhood love suggests that in asking questions about excessive neediness we would do well to focus on pathological shame, seeing a persisting shame at the very fact of one's own needy humanity as a danger sign, a warning that narcissistic projects of manipulation and control may be in the offing. Chapter 4 also suggests that in thinking about love's connection to aggression we would do well to focus on the management or containment of disgust. An ascent of love that encourages disgust, with its bounding off of the self from contamination, is unlikely to have surmounted harmful aggression in a stable way.

But an adequate assessment of these ascent therapies also requires some positive normative criteria. Although we cannot evaluate these accounts completely without defending a complete ethical theory, we can focus, at least, on the following desiderata, which many otherwise different ethical theories emphasize:

1. *Compassion.* The view of love (or, rather, the love that is left in someone who lives according to the view) should make room for and support general social compassion. The compassion supported by love should be built upon reasonable accounts of all three of the judgments Part II identified as constituents of compassion: reasonable accounts, that is, of the seriousness of various human predicaments, of our responsibility for these predicaments, and of the proper extent of concern.

2. *Reciprocity.* The view of love (or, rather, the love that is left in

someone who lives according to the view) should make room for and support reciprocal relationships of concern in which people treat one another not just as things, but as agents and as ends, and in which they respond to one another with the "subtle interplay" described by Winnicott. Any account of love that purports to show how love can become a force for good in society ought to be able to show that it can handle this challenge – making room for reciprocity both inside the relationship of erotic love itself and also in other social relationships to which the love is closely linked. Thus, there are actually two questions here: does the love itself contain reciprocity, and does it support other reciprocal relationships? These points are in principle independent, in the sense that a reciprocal love might be so exclusive that it would discourage all other relationships, reciprocal or otherwise, and a love focused on possession rather than reciprocity might prove compatible with reciprocal relationships in other areas of life. On the other hand, we can see that there is a plausible link between them: for example, if men are encouraged by a normative picture of love to think of women as objects for their use and control, this is not likely to encourage reciprocal relationships between men and women in social and political life. Love gives us understandings of value that we then translate into other spheres.

3. *Individuality.* Any view of love that is going to be ethically good in itself, or conduce to further social goods, should recognize and make central the fact that human beings are individuals. This is an elusive notion. One aspect of individuality is *separateness*. By this I mean that people have distinct bodies and lives, and lives that are their own to live. Each pursues a separate course of life from birth to death, a separate course of joy and grief, elation and sorrow, that never fuses organically with the life of anyone else (except before a child is born, entering this world of objects). The food given to A does not miraculously arrive in the stomach of B (unless B is that prebirth child); the satisfaction of D does not remove or balance out the misery of C. Nor is this separateness merely spatio-temporal: each person has just one chance at life in this world, a chance to live a life that is that person's life and nobody else's.

A second aspect of individuality is *qualitative distinctness*. All people (even identical twins, and even the clones of the future) have distinct properties, over and above the sheer spatio-temporal differences involved in separateness. They have their own distinct talents and tastes, projects and plans, flaws and virtues, and these are wrapped up together in a way that makes it natural to name each by a proper name.

Of these two aspects of individuality, what I have called separateness seems the more significant, if by this we mean separateness not in the mere spatio-temporal sense, but in the richer sense suggested here. However similar people are in their qualitative properties, the fact that each has just one life to live, that person's own life, is a very salient ethical fact. However much influenced by another, or wrapped up in another, only I can live my own life. Consider snowflakes. Each one is qualitatively distinct, or so we are told. So each has that sort of individuality, and each is even spatio-temporally distinct. And yet we would not think of snowflakes as having "individuality" in the sense that we think relevant to our humanity, or to ethics.[25]

These three features seem important for any ethical view that we are likely to find attractive, and they can be shared by ethical views of several different kinds. They are also good features for a view that is likely to support the mutual respect of citizens in a liberal-democratic society – so any view of love that shores them up is likely, ceteris paribus, to be socially appealing, and any view of love that subverts them is likely to be socially suspect. Indeed, it seems to me that in insisting on these three features we need not leave the sphere of political consensus at all: they can be endorsed by a wide plurality of reasonable ethical conceptions. We shall see, in fact, that several of our ascent conceptions prove supportive of all three features – even though they belong to quite different comprehensive ethical/religious traditions.

How, then, can love reform itself, so as not to be excessively needy, vengeful, or partial, and so as to be supportive of general social compassion, reciprocity, and respect for individuality?

---

25 For the formulations in these paragraphs, I am much indebted to Charles Larmore.

CONTEMPLATIVE CREATIVITY: PLATO, SPINOZA, PROUST

I. CONTEMPLATIVE ASCENT

The pattern of reform that I shall call the "contemplative ascent" lies at the heart of the Western philosophical tradition. Articulated first by Plato, the pattern is influentially developed by Plotinus and finds adherents throughout history, from the later Neoplatonists to Augustine and other Christian thinkers, to Spinoza and, in recent times, imaginative writers such as Virginia Woolf[1] and Marcel Proust. I shall focus here on Plato, Spinoza, and Proust. Plato gives the pattern its defining features; Spinoza deepens the account of love's necessary ambivalence and of the social benefits of ascent; Proust, alluding directly to the Platonic ladder, places it within a narrative framework, motivating it more explicitly, developing Spinoza's account of ambivalence, envy, and jealousy, and making clear what it comes to in a life.

The general idea behind this ascent pattern is that the cure for the vulnerability of passion is the passion for understanding.[2] By focusing on that intellectual goal, and on the goal of creativity that the tradition links with it, one finds oneself able to deal with the very same worldly objects – or so it is claimed – without agonizing dependency, without ambivalence and the desire for revenge, without the self-centered partiality that makes love a threat in the social life. I turn now to Plato's *Symposium*, the source for this entire tradition – and also for Christian and Romantic views of the ladder of love as well, since they react to and critize Plato's account.

---

1 For the influence of Plato's *Symposium* on Woolf's *To the Lighthouse*, see Wyatt (1978).
2 Compare Epicurus: "By the *erôs* for true philosophy every bad passion is undone."

II. ARISTOPHANES: LOVE AND ORIGINAL WHOLENESS

Before the ascent of love is even in question, Plato's *Symposium* offers several accounts of unreformed love.[3] As it does so, it reflects a powerful cultural paradigm according to which *erôs* is understood not as an emotion essentially bound up with a relationship of mutuality, but rather as a longing for the possession of something seen as valuable and urgently needed.[4] Lovers long for sexual intercourse, and they see intercourse as involving the active control or possession of an object. But what they are trying to achieve through this intercourse is something more complex, more urgent, and more problematic.

In the view of the comic poet Aristophanes, whose diagnosis seems the most pertinent to the eventual cure,[5] A's desire to make love with M is nothing less than a desire for her own wholeness or completion – for a "healing" of the needy, incomplete condition shared by all human beings. His myth recalls a fictive time when humans were not needy and incomplete. Instead, he says, they were whole and round (189D ff.) – telling a version of the archaic Golden Age story that has a particularly deep connection with our account of infantile omnipotence and its magical transformations. Thus the myth taps a memory of infantile wholeness that is likely to lie deep in many, if not most, lives. Even our shape, he continues, was not the awkward pointy shape, with its soft undefended front parts, that now reminds us of our vulnerability every time we move. Instead, we were round and symmetrical, and could roll in any direction. The spherical shape was typically understood, in Greek antiquity, as the shape of completeness or perfection; it is also similar to the shape of the fetus, curled up inside its mother's

---

3 I have examined this account at length in Nussbaum (1986), Chapter 6; here I am far briefer, and I focus on the material about creation, which I did not treat in the earlier project, and on some important divergences from my earlier interpretation. I do not include here an account of the *Phaedrus*, which I still believe to be significantly different from the *Symposium* in its emphasis on mutuality of both action and passion: see Nussbaum (1995b).

4 The best account I know of the popular evidence is in Winkler (1990); see also Halperin (1989), for a claim that Plato's metaphysical picture is continuous with the material of popular culture.

5 See the analysis in Nussbaum (1986), Chapter 6, which I still support.

body, or of the newborn infant, cradled in its mother's arms. (Aristotle notes that limbs have the function of moving creatures from place to place, and therefore are suited only to creatures with needs: the heavenly spheres have no need of any such organs – see *De Caelo* I.12, discussed in Chapter 15.) We were "awe-inspiring in force and strength," and "had great ambitions" (190B).

Humans, in consequence, assailed the gods, with the aim of establishing their control over the universe as a whole (190B). Thus the pursuit of omnipotence leads to an act of disastrous aggression. Instead of wiping us out completely, Zeus simply, by making us "weaker," made us humans – creating for us the condition of need, insecurity, and incompleteness that sets an unbridgeable gulf between us and the gods. He accomplished the change by cutting the spherical beings in two, so that they walked on two legs – and then he turned their faces around so that they would always have to look at the cut part of themselves, and thus be "more orderly" (190E). Incompleteness is revealed to us, then, in the very form of our bodies, with their pointy jutting limbs, their oddly naked front parts. The navel represents the gods' sewing together of what they have cut, and is thus a "memorial of our former suffering (*mnêmeion tou palaiou pathous*)" (191A). Even this small detail suggests that the myth is intended to capture the traumatic character of birth into a world of objects: for of course what the navel really reminds us of is the *pathos* of separation from the mother, and the beginning of a needy life.

Each person has some dim idea of a former whole state, and goes about, forlorn, looking for his or her "other half." According to Aristophanes, this search is the origin of sexual desire, and the goal of desire is to be fused, once again, with that half, in a state of primal unity. The idea of uniting with one's "other half" at first leads people to forget about food and the rest of life: because they can't stop hugging one another, A and M (let us imagine) will soon die (191AB). For this reason, he goes on, Zeus, by switching people's genitals around, made a kind of penetration possible through sexual intercourse, so that "they could have satiety from intercourse and stop it and turn to their work and take care of the rest of life" (191C). In other words, the necessarily intermittent structure of sexual intercourse, with its cycles of need and repletion, is the only thing that prevents sex from killing us off; its strong pleasure is at odds with our concern for anything outside. By that insertion of one person's body into another's we attain something like the roundness and wholeness of "our earlier nature." The special importance the lover attaches to the object derives from the sense that this and only this one is the cure for her incompleteness, and that sexual love will be her healing. Describing two lovers lying together, Aristophanes conjectures that their deepest wish would certainly be to be fused with the other, so that all longing and incompleteness would come to an end:

If Hephaistos, standing over them with his tools as they lay together, were to ask them: "What is it, o human beings, that you want to get for yourselves from one another?" – and, if, when they couldn't come up with anything to say, he were to ask them again, "Isn't it this that you desire, to be in the same place as one another as much as possible, and not to leave one another's side either by day or by night? For if indeed it is this that you want, I am prepared to weld and melt you together into the same being, so that instead of two you would become one, and live a common life as one, both of you, as long as you live, and when you die, you would die together and even in Hades you would be one instead of two. See if it is this that you want, and whether it would satisfy you to achieve this." Hearing this, we know that not one person would refuse . . . (192DE)

This complicated passage gets to the heart of the ambivalence involved in the wish for restored totality. For of course in a way the idea of fusion does capture a cherished goal of restored wholeness. And yet, at the same time, it promises immobility, the loss of limbs, of movement, of erotic striving and sexual activity themselves. The wish of human beings is to be godlike; it is also (perhaps) to enjoy human life. These wishes, Aristophanes suggests, are tragically woven together. Thus the sexual act itself, though viewed by its participants as a healing, is actually the acting out of a complex, contradictory, and in part impossible fantasy. Sex would be human – and an occasion of joy rather than frustration – only if that wish were to be given up; but Aristophanes suggests that it never can be or will be given up: no lover would refuse Hephaistos' offer.

This profound portrait of the roots of erotic love says in effect that love of this sort is the acting out of a primitive fantasy of restored omnipotence. It seeks the magical result of complete control over the "transformational object," and derives its deep power from its connection with these early projects. But these projects must fail, since we are finite and mortal. And moreover, in addition to its power of distraction, love of this infantile sort, focused on possession and control, seems to prevent people from attaining the sort of relationship with one another within which real support and mutual aid are possible. It is no wonder that the dialogue is filled with images of favoritism and partiality, and also with the signs of love's "mad" excess and ambivalence – most vividly depicted in the self-destructive passions of Alcibiades, but present as well in the dialogue's frequent joking references to jealousy and madness and revenge (e.g., 219C–E, 217E–218A, 213D5–6, 213D7–8). If this is what *erôs* is, it urgently demands reform.

III. DIOTIMA: LOVE AS CREATION IN THE FINE AND GOOD

Before A can begin the ascent of love described by Socrates' teacher Diotima, she must understand the definition of love that Socrates learned from her, which goes beneath and in a subtle way revises the Aristophanic description. For love, it now develops, is indeed a desire for possession of an object – but the object must have a special character and description. For the object must be fine[6] and good.[7] "Love is not love of the half or of the whole, if that does not in some way happen to be good" (205E). Indeed, she claims, the various types of striving that are commonly found – love of money, love of sport, love of philosophical study, love of sex – are all species of the same passion, though in general we reserve the name *erôs* for the sexual kind (205D). A is asked to see what all her pursuits have in common – her gymnastics with her piano playing, her studies in school with her adoration of M. All are species of a common enterprise, in which all human beings are engaged: the effort to make the good one's own. And what is the person who does possess the good? This person is a flourishing and complete person (*eudaimôn*). The lovers described by Aristophanes are, then, really not seeking an "other half," except incidentally. A deeper

---

6 In what follows, I use "fine" rather than "beautiful" to translate *kalon*, in order to bring out the fact that it is a highly general moral-aesthetic term, treated here as interchangeable with "good."

7 For the apparent interchangeability of *kalon* and *agathon* in Diotima's argument, see especially 204E, 201C.

and more powerful explanation of their project is that they are seeking a good for themselves, and, through that good, their own flourishing.

A, then, is already asked to see a certain unity in these varied pursuits, and thus a certain highly general homogeneity in their objects. What one person gets by money-making, another gets through sexual love. This does not directly entail that there is some one thing, the good, varying only in quantity, in terms of which the different objects are all commensurable. But to subsume them all under the rubric "good" is to make a powerful move in that direction. And if A knows anything about Socratic arguments, she will understand the push toward homogeneity as a pervasive feature of that way of thinking: if two things share a common predicate P, then, however much they differ in other ways, *qua* P they must be just the same. Whether he is talking to Meno about bees, or to Euthyphro about piety, Socrates will not allow a common term not to be univocal in the many instances of its application: it must designate one common form or structure that, *qua* falling under that predicate, all bearers of that predicate share.[8] If A is a cagey analyst of arguments, she will notice that an earlier argument between Socrates and Agathon is valid only on the assumption that the beauty or goodness that is love's object is homogeneous wherever it occurs, in such a way that lacking one instance of it is sufficient for lacking it altogether.[9]

What she wants from M is, then, the possession of a good for herself. The object of her passionate desire is that good, the good for her that resides in M, and not the entirety of M at all, insofar as he has features that are not part of that good. This will seem intuitively plausible to her. For how often she has wished that M were not jealous and possessive, were not determined to look into her every action, were willing to marry her, were not determined to deny his love for her. How often, too, she has wished that the love they share were not a source of constant instability and quarreling. She wants the good of it clearly, and how much she would like to be able to separate this powerful good – his wit, his intellect, his sweet childlike need for her – from the fights over a casual remark on the train, or the boredom that

8 See *Euthyphro* 5D, 6DE and *Meno* 72AB.
9 See Nussbaum (1986), pp. 178–9.

ensues once M has reassured himself that she is faithful. In this way we all tend to want the good parts of the person we love and to wish away the bad parts, the parts that do not strike us as offering a good for us.

Once she begins thinking in this way, taking apart the woven strands of M and their passion and separating them into the good and the bad, it also seems plausible to her to believe that the good part has some pretty close connection with the good for herself that she pursues in other activities – in riding her bicycle, in laughing with her friends. For isn't she in all cases trying to be complete and to flourish? And aren't these all ways that she has of pursuing that single aim?

But before ascent can begin, Diotima has one more important addition to make to the Aristophanic picture. The Aristophanic lover thought of the object of love (the "beloved") as the other half, and the goal of love as becoming united with the other half. We have now reinterpreted that, understanding the object to be the good of the person, and the goal to be one's own flourishing. But Diotima insists that this is not the entire story. For our entire pursuit of flourishing is constrained at all times by awareness of our own mortality (207C ff.). We don't just want to possess the good, we want to possess the good forever (206A, 207A). But we know that we cannot achieve this. We therefore seek to create something of ourselves, engendering it out of ourselves in the good or fine thing we encounter[10] – something that will itself outlive us and bear our identity.[11] We do this, each of us, in ways that bear the mark of our own sense of who we are. Thus some seek, like the other animals, a continuity of physical procreation (207CD, 208DE). These are the ones who conceive of themselves as fundamentally bodies, and the project of engendering oneself as fundamentally bodily, requiring another body as its vehicle (209A). Others, however, identify themselves more fundamentally with their moral character, their speeches, their human achievements of various sorts. This sort of reproductive desire requires a receptive character and soul as its vehicle – although Diotima adds that the body must also be attractive, for the procreative activity is still at its base erotic, and bodily desire still plays a part in it (209B). In intimacy with a suitably receptive whole of body and character, this person will engender creative productions –

10 On the mixed gender metaphors in the language of this passage, see Evans (1993).
11 Here and in what follows I am in agreement with the interpretation of the passage in Kosman (1976).

speeches and works – in which her identity may live on. And it is this, not sexual intimacy itself, that is the true goal of love.

A is asked, then, to look back at her lovemaking with M, and to see herself as trying to achieve not the impossible Aristophanic goal of possessing the whole of the person, a goal linked so closely with jealousy and revenge, but instead a goal both more benign and more attainable: the goal of creation. The claim is that all along A's fundamental wish has been to use her intimacy with M as a vehicle by which she can create representations of herself, of her commitments and character and aspirations, that will outlive her and give her possession of the good not only during her lifetime but even after her death.

At this point A is likely to rebel. For she does not see herself in this picture of creative aspiration. She certainly is not drawn to M as a vehicle for physical reproduction: if she did become pregnant, their affair would probably end. Nor, it seems to her, does she see him as a vehicle for any other sort of reproduction of herself in speech or action. What draws her to him is a powerful need for his entire body and being, a need that she links with a threat to the security of her identity, not with its perpetuation. She can be convinced that she is aiming at something good for herself, and that this aim has something in common with other ways in which people aim for the good. And yet it is much more difficult to make her believe that it has anything to do with surviving her own death by creative action.

Well, what is it that she sees in this man? Isn't it, after all, the fact that he is an artist, that he has erudition and talent that she admires, that cultivate in her a taste for the creation of refined opinions and poetic phrases?[12] That he beckons to her from a world of refinement and wit, in which she can create speeches very different from the coarse schoolgirl argot that captivated him when he met her? The idea that she will become better, and create something that is itself fine and good, is a powerful ingredient in her love. Even in the maternal comfort she gives him there is an element of creation: for then, when

---

12 See, for example, III.10: "Albertine, even in the discussion of the most trivial matters, expressed herself very differently from the little girl that she had been only a few years earlier at Balbec." She has political opinions; she criticizes works of art; she quotes from Racine. "As soon as she entered my room, she would spring on to my bed and sometimes would expatiate upon my type of intellect, would vow in a transport of sincerity that she would sooner die than leave me" (III.11).

he creates as artist, she creates with him, she partakes in his works as their necessary precondition and background. And of course it is the novel's point that she succeeds, in this way, in creating and immortalizing herself: her speeches, her looks, her comforting gestures, all take on immortal life in his work of literary art.

If A can be convinced that this is her goal, she is ready for Diotima's ladder. For even to take the first step she must grant all of these points: that the object of her love is not M but the good in him; that this good is closely akin to, if not thoroughly homogeneous with, all the other goods that people pursue in their many projects and actions; and that her ultimate goal in this love is to reproduce and perpetuate herself.

Now she hears from Diotima that the first step in love's ascent, the step suited to a young person such as herself, is "to go to fine bodies, and first, if the teacher gives correct guidance, to become the passionate lover of one body, and there to engender fine speeches" (210A). This she has done; and her speeches, if not "fine speeches" of the sort Socrates has in mind, are more expressive of herself than any that would satisfy him. Notice that A even fits neatly into the Greek pederastic model, with its emphasis on asymmetrical age, initiation, and education, and its devaluing of physical reproduction.

"Then [s]he must notice that the fineness of a given body is akin to that in another body, and if it is necessary to pursue bodily fineness, it is very foolish not to consider the fineness of all bodies to be one and the same" (210B). In other words, noticing that the difference between M and other attractive bodies is relatively small, where the attractiveness itself is concerned, she decides to neglect those small differences (if indeed there remain any) and to think of her project as one of pursuing this fineness wherever it turns up. This seems to mean that A should seek sexual relationships with other people as well, rather than remaining obsessively fixed on M: for in these relationships too she can express and thereby reproduce herself. A is relieved to hear this. Perhaps (though we never know for sure) she has been doing this all along; perhaps she has not. But this advice certainly gives her an independence and a stability that she would not have if she were faithful to M, with his jealous obsessiveness. She is now in a more stable situation, vastly less dependent on the vicissitudes of a particular person; she can to a far greater degree choose the circumstances in which she will gratify her desire for love. She has begun to disentangle the good in M from the bad. "Noticing this she sets herself up as the passionate lover of all fine bodies, and relaxes her excessively intense passion for the one, looking down on it and thinking it trivial" (209B).[13]

If A is really deeply in love with M and faithful to him, she will be very reluctant to undertake any such move. For (let us suppose) she responds to M in a mysterious way, and she does not feel that he is simply one among many attractive bodies. The whole idea does not make sense of what she feels. On the other hand, she has already granted to Diotima that what she seeks in M's body is something good and fine for herself, something connected with her own flourishing. She has agreed that not all aspects of the real M conduce to her flourishing. So once she has begun to think in this way, it will seem more natural for her to take the next step, granting to Diotima that there may be quite a few people who have similarly fine properties of body, that might have a similar relationship to her wishes for herself.

But A's creative desire includes, we have said, much more than mere bodily sensations; it focuses on the reproduction of something in herself that she feels as spiritually or intellectually deep. Therefore it will be natural for her to feel a dissatisfaction with this stage, and to move toward a deeper concern for the character and psychology of her partners, a concern that had already played a prominent role in her original passion for M. She will "consider the fineness of the soul more worthy of esteem than that of the body, so that if a good person has even a little charm[14] that will be enough, and she will passionately love him and care for him and create and seek out speeches of that sort, speeches that will improve the character of the young" (210BC).

A now has a small question: how, precisely, did we move from the good for A to the morally good? A has never been particularly keen on morality. (Indeed, it was her defiant attitude that drew M to her.) She thought that what Diotima was talking about was fulfilling one's own deepest needs for self-expression. And now Diotima is talking about esteem, and speeches that improve people's character. But perhaps what most deeply expresses A is not so worthy of esteem, and maybe the speeches of her passion will not improve anyone's character. They might be about leaping over an old man on the beach, a gesture that

---

13 Compare the recipe for curing obsessive love in Lucretius IV.
14 Notice that physical attraction is still required, since the love in question is still fundamentally sexual.

fascinates by its amoral boldness. Her love is of the soul, but it does not follow from that that this love has morally improving properties. Diotima now reminds her that what we are talking about is realizing one's own conception of flourishing. Sexual love is one of many ways in which people attempt to put their idea of what is most important on the map of the world. But then, insofar as she is making such an effort to draw these characteristics out of herself and to reproduce them in the world through her love, she must after all think that there is something good and fine about them, whether in a narrowly moral sense or not. Insofar as she lets certain characteristics stand for her to all eternity, she is endorsing them as worthy of attention and even honor. (And we can see that A does strive, as the novel goes on, to abandon her coarse boldness and to cultivate refinement of taste.) Whether she is right or wrong, there is an evaluative component to her love, it bears the impress of her view of *eudaimonia*.

All of this A should concede. And yet, she will suggest, it is one thing to say that there is something wonderful and fine about her passion, something expressive of her view of *eudaimonia*; it is quite another to say that she will give it out in speeches to improve the moral character of the young. Well, what does A think the young should read? Romantics believe in Romantic representations, Dionysians in Dionysian representations; A, though a little of both, seems most drawn to M's sui generis mixture of classical erudition and deep emotion, in short, to the novel-in-the-making in M's life. She creates herself as a part of that novel. Would she then not hesitate to give the young the scenes of Proust's novel in which her passion, and her daring, and her maternal sweetness, are described and set down forever? Or if she does hesitate, as she does – for, after all, she eventually leaves M – isn't it because she has reservations about the passion itself, about its adequacy as a complete expression of herself and what she wants from life? Because she also loves her friends, and her bicycle, and her polo cap – in short, her freedom. She has a sense that all of this is really part of a complete human life for her and for others like herself (perhaps she will think of women in particular), and that not all of her being is conveyed by what she does while being guarded as M's prisoner. Thinking about how what she creates out of herself might work as reading for others forces her to concede that her conception of *eudaimonia* is incomplete without a sense of what kind of life, in society, makes a woman such as herself free and not a prisoner. And this already leads her to a social vision, a vision that she really could convey to others as a text that would stand for her and the entirety of her thought – "so that she is forced once again to reflect about the fineness of customs and laws and to see that there is a relatedness in all of this, so that she will think the fineness of bodies something trivial" (210C).[15] It is only at this point, and not before, that bodily love and bodily fineness get diminished: it is the thought of the educative properties of discourse pertaining to the soul, not the thought of the soul itself, that forces their depreciation.

Now A has granted that her interest is in *everything* that she considers fine – not in M alone but, insofar as she is creative, in the entirety of what she cares about, so that she can create something adequate to stand for herself in her fullness. This means thinking not just about public morality, but also about learning and understanding: for as a student and a musician she knows that this has its own peculiar fineness, and no image of herself would be truly complete without that (cf. 210C). By now she has moved far away from M, simply by surveying reflectively the whole of her conception of the good:

... and looking at the vast reach of the fine [s]he will no longer, like some servant, loving the fineness of one boy or man, or of one way of life, remain enslaved to that and be contemptible and of little account; but turned toward the vast sea of the fine and reflecting, [s]he will give birth to many fine and splendid speeches and thoughts in the abundance of her searching for understanding ... (210D)

At this point things even out. At this distance, the difference between one fine thing and another does not bulk large in A's vision. For as a reflective student of Socrates she recalls that things that are fine or good are, qua fine and good, thus far alike; and this means that she can think of her many pursuits of the good as having a unity, her many good objects as part of a single "sea," insofar as they answer to her aspiration for the good. A now creates abundantly, riding all over the

---

15 Usually the steps up the ladder are taken to be (1) one fine body, (2) all fine bodies, (3) fine souls, (4) the fine in laws and customs, (5) the fine in the sciences, (6) the wide sea of the fine, (7) the fine itself. But notice that in the text the third and fourth steps are actually presented as one: the consideration of the soul itself *forces* the consideration of customs and laws. I have tried here to convey the mechanism through which I believe this takes place.

countryside, loving her friends and fellow citizens, and loving, above all, the process of thought that brings her into a serene and controlling relation with so much goodness.[16]

M has not disappeared from A's life. For at each stage the objects left below are included in that which is loved, though assigned the lower status of the relatively "small" or "trivial."[17] But *how* is M included? Presumably A now sees him as one of the many fine bodies and souls, all of whom she in turn loves as parts of the "vast sea of the fine," and all of whom provide her with abundant occasions for her own creation. She will hardly know his name – for in the very first step she has already committed herself to the pursuit of his fineness rather than to *him*; in the second stage she has decided that it was foolish not to treat all fine bodies as alike for her creative purposes. Already at that point, she could say of herself what M so often says of her: that he is just one of a series, that his particular properties hardly matter. But by now, looking at the whole array of the good, she hardly sees individual persons at all; insofar as she sees them, their bodies will seem to her a set of peculiar shapes without urgent reference to her own erotic need. Indeed, her own body will seem increasingly impersonal to her, increasingly distant from her most urgent purposes; for it is with her mind that she controls the world.

But the final vision is yet to come – and it takes A away from even this calm, contemplative interest in distinct persons and objects. "All at once," she sees the tremendous radiance of the good and fine in all its

16 I have not attempted to replicate the entire argument of Nussbaum (1986), Chapter 6, insofar as I still agree with it. I focus on the role of creativity, which I did not sufficiently stress in that account, and I weaken the claim that all fine things are seen as absolutely the same insofar as they are fine – although I still believe that to be the conclusion to which Plato's general metaphysics of value forces him. I try to motivate the steps of the ascent to a greater extent from within A's own antecedent search for flourishing, thus to some extent diminishing its remoteness. But I still insist that there are ample indications in the text that the ascent strategy is not a neutral description of the way desire currently is; it is a therapeutic program undertaken for reasons of health, because the strains of ordinary *erôs* are too costly. And I still insist (see the following discussion) that, like those of the other members of the contemplative ascent tradition, the Platonic programme requires the lover to give up beliefs about the particularity and irreplaceability of the loved one that are an intuitive part of most experiences of passionate love.

17 For an account of the ascent as "inclusive," and an interesting set of observations on the role of need and dissatisfaction in motivating the passage from one level to another, see Moravcsik (1972).

unity; and she sees that this good of the world is permanent, eternal, beyond the particularities and mutabilities of bodies:

It is always, and neither comes to be nor passes away, neither grows nor decays . . . [S]he will see it as itself by itself with itself, eternal and unitary, and see all the other instances of the fine as partaking of it in such a manner that, when the others come to be and are destroyed, it never comes to be any more or less, nor passively suffers anything . . . In this place . . . if anywhere, life is livable for a human being, the place where [s]he contemplates the fine itself. If ever you see that, it will not seem to you to be valuable by comparison with gold and clothing and fine boys and youths, the sight of whom at present so inflames you that you, and many others, provided that you could see your beloved boys and be continually with them, are prepared to give up eating and drinking, and to spend your whole time contemplating them and being with them. What do we think it would be like . . . if someone should see the beautiful itself – unalloyed, pure, unmixed, not stuffed full of human flesh and colors and lots of other mortal rubbish, but if he could see the divine fineness itself in its unity? Do you think life would be miserable for a person who looked out there, and contemplated it in an appropriate way and was with it? Or don't you understand that there alone, where [s]he sees the fine with that faculty to which it is visible, it will be possible for [her] to give birth not to simulacra of excellence, since it is no simulacrum [s]he is grasping, but to true excellence, since [s]he is grasping truth? And as [s]he brings forth true excellence and nourishes it, [s]he will become god-loved, and, if ever a human being can, immortal? (210E6–212A7)

M is nowhere to be seen. For he cannot be seen at all by the intellectual faculty that is now preferred to all of the senses. And that intellectual faculty sees the absolute eternal unity of the fine in the universe as a whole, which does not change when individual fine things go in and out of existence. This unity is not even comparable to M. And the "being-with" or intercourse it offers, the pure light of intellectual understanding, itself so far surpasses the good of her physical erotic love that she now cannot even contemplate the two together. They do not belong to the same faculty of sight, and "the sight of intellect begins to see clearly as the sight of the eyes begins to grow dim" (219A). She sees now that all along it was this unity that she loved, and that all her love for M was an attempt to get beyond M to this divine good.

There are no barriers to creativity for A now. For the object of her love will not refuse her, or surprise her, or leave her, or drive her to suicide, or extinguish her thought in the sweat of passion. Her love is free of instability and painful need: for its object is always available, and always steady, as is the activity in which she grasps the object. For these reasons it is free from ambivalence as well: for offering no barrier to her control of her world, it gives her no incentive to revenge. And since her object is the whole of the world's goodness, and the unity in that goodness, her love does not play favorites. She does not obsessively devote herself to the one, but attends with impartial and neutral fairness to the claims of all. And yet, we may fairly say that it is the same *erôs* that has driven her all along, with much of its splendor and its ferocious energy. For it was her longing for goodness that propelled her to and up the ladder, goading her on until all obstacles to its full satisfaction were removed. If M is still in the world, she can only wish him this deep fulfillment.

We now have an account of love that preserves love's energy and beauty, without crippling passivity, without anger and vengefulness, without narrow partiality – a love that supports social and political helpfulness, rather than turning away from the social, a love that embraces the entire world with even-handed joy.

Should a person attached to the reasonable norms we have identified be satisfied with this reform? We can take final stock of the contemplative proposal only when we have seen its further refinements in Spinoza and Proust. But three worries are already on the scene, closely connected to what the ascent has subtracted from the flawed love with which it began: a worry about compassion, a worry about reciprocity, and a worry about the individual.

1. *Compassion.* In order to ascend beyond her bondage to earthly love, the Platonic lover is asked to treat earthly need and longing as so much "mortal rubbish." Attaching herself to an immortal object, she renounces dependence on earthly goods and becomes as close to immortal herself as any mortal can. In the process, she would appear to call disgust to her aid, bounding herself off from the detritus of mere worldly existence. But this transition means that she may not be so good at seeing what ordinary people need and want, how they suffer, and why that matters. Recall Marcus Aurelius' injunction (Chapter 7)

that we should consider losses befalling others as similar to a child's losing a toy: reasons for a lofty parental comforting, but not for the real pain of compassion. People who suffer look like children – or, to use Epictetus' term, fools. They suffer only because they have a diseased sense of what has importance. Plato adds that, seen from this lofty vantage point, their concerns are actually disgusting.[18] The aspiring lover bounds herself off from all that rubbish – "mud, hair, and dirt," as Parmenides would say.[19]

In this sense, Socrates' and Plato's harsh repudiation of pity and their attack on the tragic poets are of a piece with Plato's ascent story; they are entailed by its reorientation of value. To the lover who has ascended, the hungry, the bereaved, the sick, those who are persecuted and suffer from their persecution – all look like, indeed are, fools, who have been "wonderstruck by things external" when they should have been pursuing their own enlightenment. Socrates on his deathbed reproves pity; both Xanthippe and Apollodorus must leave the room. Not tears, but calm arguments, are his response to earthly suffering. Aristotle said that a person who believes himself to be above all calamities will not experience compassion; he called this a *hubristikê diathesis*, an overweening disposition.

Thus, insofar as the ascending lover does become or remain involved in politics (and we wonder, as does Plato's *Republic*, whether the flawed social world will hold her interest that strongly), she will not be inclined to relieve hunger, to heal the sick, to oppose persecution, or in general to do any of the things we usually think of under the rubric of fighting for justice. Or if she does them, she will do them, at best, in

18 This strategy is similar to that of Marcus in VI.13: "How important it is to represent to oneself, when it comes to fancy dishes and other such foods, 'This is the corpse of a fish, this other thing the corpse of a bird or a pig.' Similarly, 'This Falernian wine is just some grape juice,' and 'This purple vestment is some sheep's hair moistened in the blood of some shellfish.' When it comes to sexual intercourse, we must say, 'This is the rubbing together of membranes, accompanied by the spasmodic ejaculation of a sticky liquid.' How important are these representations, which reach the thing itself and penetrate right through it, so that one can see what it is in reality."

19 *Parmenides* 130CD: Parmenides asks Socrates if his theory does not commit him to recognizing Forms corresponding to "hair and mud and dirt, or anything else that is especially dishonorable and base." Socrates answers, "In no way . . . To think that there is a Form of these things would be too strange." This passage is actually a clearer indicator of disgust than *Symposium* 211E, where *phluaria*, which I translate as "rubbish," clearly indicates disdain for the pettiness of mortal pursuits, but less clearly the thought that they are actually repellent.

Marcus' spirit, with a little bit of contempt, and even disgust, for those who are distressed at their lot. Social morality begins from "circumstances of justice":[20] from the perception, that is, that we are in a situation of competition for scarce resources that we badly need. The Platonic ascent makes those circumstances disappear: for contemplation is always available, no matter how reduced one's life circumstances. There is no competition for it, and all can equally enjoy it. From such a vantage point, justice cannot be seen.

2. *Reciprocity.* A good normative account of love, I have argued, should emphasize the element of reciprocity and respect for agency that is present in some types of love. Important in itself, this factor is all the more important when we think of love's relation to general social concerns. Aristotle's account of *philia* is a good example of an account that combines strong emotion with interactions of a respectful and reciprocal kind. The lovers' emotions themselves contain these concerns: they wish one another well for their own sakes, and each lover's love sees the other as an agent and a separate life. That is why Aristotle's view of personal attachments, attractive in itself, also offers a promising basis for general social concern.

The Platonic lover, by contrast, viewing the object of her love as a seat of valuable properties, and therefore as a suitable vehicle for creation, neglects in the process the other person's own agency and choice – a point long ago made with great force by Gregory Vlastos, who saw this as a central defect in Platonic theory and a central area in which the Christians had made progress.[21] From the moment she gets onto the Platonic ladder, A does not concern herself with what M does or chooses. He is an object of her admiring contemplation, not a will whose independence she desires and fosters. From her contemplative viewpoint, there is ultimately no difference between loving a person and loving a scientific system, or the beauty of the entire world.[22] This is not exactly selfishness, since Platonic creativity gives unstintingly to

20 Hume's phrase, picked up by Rawls.
21 Vlastos (1981).
22 Price (1989) argues that a close relationship with a single beloved remains a part of the Platonic ascent. But he grants that the beloved is there as a vehicle of a creative activity that is addressed to the world in general. See also Vlastos (1981), who calls the conception "spiritualized egocentrism," and denies that the creative acts of the lover are chosen to "enrich the lives of persons who are themselves worthy of love for their own sake."

the entire world. But it is an unpromising attitude toward another person, and therefore an unpromising basis for attitudes toward other citizens in the political realm. Citizens don't so much want other citizens' contemplation as their cooperation in their efforts to act and be.

3. *Individuality.* I have said that an account of love should acknowledge as salient the fact that people are individuals – qualitatively distinct and, especially, separate, having their own lives to live. Any stance either in the personal life or in the wider social life that does not respect both of these aspects of individuality is bound to be deeply flawed. On the other hand, if we should find an account of personal love that does show a due recognition and embrace of these features of the person – so difficult, often, to recognize and to embrace – this might well be an account of love that, attractive in itself, could also inform the political life. (So I shall claim about Dante, Mahler, and Joyce.)

Plato's account, however, respects and embraces neither separateness nor qualitative difference. As Vlastos, once again, saw: to love people as seats of the good and the fine is precisely not a way to embrace the individuals that they are. It does not see their separateness – for after a while all particular seats of the fine simply look like bare containers, hardly salient at all, and all instances of the fine simply look like drops in "the wide sea of the fine." The idea that each person has her own distinct life to live simply plays no role in the analysis. As for qualitative distinctness, Plato's ascent leaves out of account, and therefore out of love, everything about the person that is not good and fine – the flaws and the faults, the neutral idiosyncrasies, the bodily history. In a very fundamental way it refuses to embrace the very fact of difference. It loves only what is of a piece with the ideal good. The other parts, we might say the all-too-human parts, it refuses to embrace. It is no surprise that this refusal goes hand in hand with an illiberal perfectionist politics, a politics that respects the choices of citizens only insofar as they come up to an externally imposed moral mark. Nor does the ascent seem promising as a way of loving real human beings in the personal life. "I'll love you only to the extent that you exemplify properties that I otherwise cherish." This attitude has no room for mercy, for an embracing unconditionality in love that seems well suited to a life of imperfection and vulnerability.

These points about separateness and qualitative distinctness are not simple. For the Platonic ascent has also given up much that would create impediments to individual love in both of these senses. The jealous insecure lover hates the freedom of the other – and one of the central motivations in both Spinoza and Proust is to produce a love free of that kind of possessive grasping. Nor can a lover preoccupied with her own neediness and insecurity do very well in seeing truly the real particularity of the other: for personal need often forms a fog that obscures a clear perception.

Nonetheless, despite the great achievements of the Platonic ladder, we suspect that A has climbed too high – out of reach of human need and imperfection, and therefore out of reach of an altruism, whether personal or political, that can constructively address real human beings.

IV. SPINOZA: THE BONDAGE OF THE PASSIONS

Spinoza's account of the therapy and ascent of love owes a large debt to the Platonist tradition.[23] But he goes well beyond Plato in the depth of his diagnosis of love's ills and, therefore, in his account of why and how understanding brings the cure.[24]

Unlike Plato's, Spinoza's account of the ascent of love begins from an explicit theory of emotion that provides a strong theoretical basis for what follows. The account of emotion itself derives from the Greek and Roman Stoics; but Spinoza articulates it in a novel way and puts it

23 Some of this influence is mediated by the Stoic tradition of therapy, which itself is in many ways indebted to Platonism, but which adds other features that are of particular interest to Spinoza, in particular the interest in distinguishing active control from passive dependence. On this see Nussbaum (1994), Chapters 9–10.

24 In what follows I shall in general use the translation of Samuel Shirley (1982); but I follow A. Rorty (1991) in rendering *laetitia* by "elation" rather than "pleasure," *tristitia* by "dejection" rather than "pain." Shirley's choices are just wrong for these Latin words, even in their nonphilosophical uses and although there are generic uses of *hêdonê* and *lupê* in Greek Stoics texts that are quite distinct from their ordinary uses to denote bodily pain and pleasure (*hêdonê* is the fresh judgment that good things are at hand, *lupê* the fresh judgment that bad things are at hand), the Latin words used to translate these special generic usages register the fact that Cicero found the bare terms "pleasure" and "pain" to be too misleading, and used *voluptas gestiens* (Seneca uses *gaudium*) and *aegritudo*. Neither the Stoics nor anyone else would suppose that one could entirely remove (bodily) pleasure and pain. Curley (1985) is better than Shirley, using "joy" and "sadness"; but these are too indeterminate – for there is a well-established distinction between *gaudium*, which is in Stoic terms a permissible thing, or a thing of which there is a permissible species, and *laetitia*, which is the inappropriate passion; this distinction is developed by Augustine in *The City of God* and is clearly in the background for Spinoza.

to work in the service of his Platonic aims. It is in many ways similar to the theory defended in Part I, and focuses in a similar way both on the emotions' link with need and, consequently, on their necessary ambivalence.

For Spinoza, emotions such as fear, grief, anger, joy, and love always involve the appraisal of a situation for its bearing on the person's own well-being. Emotions are not simply impulses or drives, but highly selective patterns of vision and interpretation. In experiencing fear, for example, I am not simply shivering or shaking; I am assessing a situation in the world with reference to myself and my well-being, and judging that my well-being is threatened by the situation. Spinoza thus incorporates what we found valuable in the Stoic view, emphasizing the emotions' cognitive content and their intentionality. Like Keith Oatley, whose views are discussed in Chapter 2, Spinoza holds not only that emotions involve an appraisal of a situation, but also that they generally involve awareness of a transition in the person's own condition, from greater to lesser well-being, or the reverse. In other words, events and persons outside the self are marked in the emotions only insofar as they spell change, or likely change, in the self. (As we shall see, there is one salient exception to this claim, one emotion that does not require alteration for its genesis.) I have argued in Chapter 2 that Oatley was wrong to insist on change or transition in the case of every single emotion – for surely we don't want to say in advance that joy, or anger, or love cannot remain in a person unless the situation outside her is changing. Spinoza, as we shall see, deals with this objection up to a point, by allowing a certain type of love and joy to be independent of transitions. I think he still insists too much on transitions, but, nonetheless, the account in most respects promises a rich explanation of emotional experience, going beyond Plato but remaining faithful to the essence of his program. Let us now see what Spinoza will say to our aspiring pupil.

Spinoza's account begins from a fundamental Platonic assumption: that all beings endeavor to preserve their being (*Ethics*, Pr. 6, III). Indeed, what a thing *is* is none other than this self-maintaining tendency (Pr. 7). The situation of beings like ourselves is in consequence complex. On the one hand, as parts of the world of nature we are passive before its events, and highly limited in the power we have to persist and maintain our being (Prs. 2 and 3, IV). Our ability to effect our own flourishing is "infinitely surpassed by the power of external causes" (Pr. 3, IV). It is impossible for a human being not to be a part of nature and therefore not to endure passively the effects of external causes (Pr. 4, IV). Indeed, every individual thing in nature is such that it can be destroyed by the power of some superior thing (Axiom, IV). On the other hand, our distinctive form of self-maintaining activity is mental. And the mind has, as we shall see, powers of transcendence that can potentially remove the person from this passive state.

Given our nature, we need many things. In particular, we need one another – "nothing is more advantageous to man than man" (Schol. Pr. 18, IV). We also need food, shelter, and many other types of sustenance. These facts lead us to focus on our own *transitions* – that is, on external parts of the world as having a significance for the status of our project of flourishing in our being. Some objects enhance our projects and our power, some diminish them. Emotions, Spinoza holds, are our recognitions of these significant relations to external things, and thus in effect acknowledgments of our own neediness and passivity, for good or for ill, before these external things. To have emotions is therefore, he argues, to be in a state of "bondage": "For a man at the mercy of his emotions is not his own master but is subject to fortune" (Preface, IV). Most people live in this way, "being driven hither and thither by external causes, never possessing true contentment of spirit" (Schol. Pr. 42, V).

It is important to notice that for Spinoza, as for my own theory, "bondage" to emotions is, in effect, bondage to the needed external objects whose salience the emotions register. Spinoza's complaint is not that love, hate, fear, and the rest are so strong that they debilitate us; it is not that their sheer force keeps us in bondage. The problem lies with the relation they express between us and the world. In emotions we are acknowledging the salience or importance of parts of the world, and consequently a bondage to the world. So the problem of bondage can be solved only by coming to be less needy, by not seeing things outside ourselves as essential for our well-being. Spinoza derives this idea from Stoicism, and his program of extirpation of emotion is directly modeled on Stoic ideas.

All this A will find relatively familiar territory, given her study of Plato. What is new is the emphasis on the necessary passivity of the human being in the world of nature, and on the way in which this passive dependence checks and inhibits our very being, which is a project of seeking our own flourishing. For Spinoza, in effect, the very humanness of life is a problem to be solved.

Where in all of this is love? Love, Spinoza argues, is an awareness of a significant transition in the direction of greater flourishing (i.e., "elation"), combined with the idea of an external cause of that transition (Definitions of the Emotions 6, III). In other words, it is both necessary and sufficient for love that we find a person (or thing) extremely helpful to us, in preserving our being. Indeed, love is nothing other than the recognition of that significance. This does not mean that Spinoza is denying the intensity of the emotion that lovers experience; but he is saying that what that intensity is all about is the attempt to protect and enhance our selves. Love certainly involves seeing another person as salient and essential; but he says that the content of our thought is that the other person is essential *to us*, someone without whom our well-being will suffer. In all of this, he is in great agreement with Plato.

But Spinoza also claims to go beyond Plato: for he insists that earlier philosophical definitions of love, in terms of possession of an object, do not go as deep as his does: his expresses the "essence" of the phenomenon, the others merely one of its properties. What he seems to be saying is that mere possession of an object is not intelligible as a goal without reference to the needs of the self: the reason why we want to control the one we love is that we recognize the urgent importance of that one to our very being, and therefore want to secure to ourselves the source of the desired transitions in our being (Explication, Definitions of the Emotions, df. 6, III). Goodness all by itself is not enough: we must bring the object into relation with our own urgent strivings in order for its goodness to be something for us, to excite our emotions. His argument is very close to an argument about early childhood attachment that we will find in Proust: the source of miraculous transitions is cherished *as* the source of those transitions, and it is this that explains the anxious desire to control its life.

Spinoza adds that the strength of any emotion will be proportional to our appraisal of the power of the object relative to our own power (Schol. Pr. 20, V). Thus love is predicated on our awareness of relative weakness and insufficiency vis-à-vis external objects, and is stronger the greater our feeling of relative weakness toward the object.

A is given little explanation of why it is M that she loves. M clearly has the power to affect her being, but Spinoza's theory does not tell her why that is the case. We cannot appeal to the fact that she loves him, for it is the love that we are trying to explain. Spinoza has little to say, however, about why we are in thrall to some objects and not to others. If he were to say that it is because we notice that they help us in other ways, independent of the love, he would make an implausible claim: for we love people with whom we have had no prior relation of inter-dependence; and we do not love some (the grocer, the mailman) on whom we depend for daily support. It must be the case that the need we feel for the person is internal to the love – but then, we really do not have any account of why some people inspire it and others do not. (Here Proust will claim to have taken a decisive step forward.) Spinoza seems content to leave things mysterious, and perhaps that is not such a bad decision.

Nor does Spinoza explain the specifically erotic need that A feels for this particular man, the fact that she has needs for him that are very different from those she has for her father, or her mother, or her sister, all of whom do much to preserve her being. Indeed, it is never made fully clear what role the erotic as such plays in Spinoza's account. That erotic love is central to the analysis is clear: for example, in the discussion of jealousy in Proposition 35, III (Scholium), where he exemplifies his general thesis by speaking of the jealousy a lover feels when thinking of the woman he loves in the arms of a rival. The theory is compatible with Proust's idea that all love is fundamentally erotic and has its roots in a child's eroticized perception of infantile weakness and maternal omnipotence. But the origins of erotic jealousy and its connections with earlier loves and jealousies are never elaborated.

Spinoza's theory does, however, explain the connection A feels between the depth of her love and her feeling of powerlessness. The intensity of her love, he points out, is proportional to the deep need she acknowledges, the need that makes it impossible for her to flourish without M. Such love tends to be obsessive, Spinoza argues, riveting the mind to a single object and blotting out any thought of any other parts of the world (Schol. Prop. 44, IV). "Emotions are as a general rule excessive, and keep the mind obsessed with one single object to such an extent that it cannot think of anything else."

Since all objects of love are independent of the lover, Spinoza continues, all love of external objects must be ambivalent in this way. For the very same object that can cause a beneficial transition in my being may also, in virtue of its very separateness, fail to cause that transition, or cause one of an opposite sort. Its very externality and independence make it undependable, and anyone who loves will inevitably become aware of this undependability. The awareness of a thing's power to cause a diminution of my well-being is nothing other than the emotion of hate (Schol. Prop. 13, III). The very externality of the thing A loves makes her hate it: for she can never completely possess it, and thus must always feel the pain of anxiety and frustration (Props. 13 and 14, III; Appendix 19–20, IV):

Emotional distress and unhappiness have their origin especially in excessive love towards a thing subject to considerable instability, a thing which we can never completely possess. For nobody is disturbed or anxious about any thing unless he loves it, nor do wrongs, suspicions, enmities, etc. arise except from love towards things which nobody can truly possess. (Schol. Prop. 20, V)

And when once we experience both love and hate toward the same object, the two emotions will ever thereafter be joined in our thought of that object (Prop. 14, III).

Insofar as the object of love is independent of the lover, furthermore, the beloved may love and attend to someone else: thus nonpossession dooms the lover not only to hatred, but also to jealousy and envy. Indeed, jealousy may be defined as "vacillation arising from simultaneous love and hatred accompanied by the idea of a rival that is envied" (Schol Prop. 35, III). These two emotions bring yet another: for the jealous lover, imagining his beloved in the rival's sexual embrace, cannot think of her without disgust:

[F]or he who thinks of a woman whom he loves as giving herself to another will not only feel pain by reason of his own appetite being checked but also, being compelled to associate the image of the object of his love with the sexual parts of his rival, he feels disgust for her. (Schol. Prop. 35, III,)

Thus the very love that turned the lover outward toward the object now leads to a contraction of the world, as he bounds himself off against the dangers that this openness has occasioned. Love of women, for Spinoza, is inherently linked to misogyny.

In short: A's love for M is a kind of bondage, born of her passivity. Since it is her nature to flourish, she hates her bondage, and both hates and loves its cause. The person who loves, Spinoza tells her, endeavors to keep present and to preserve that which she loves; the person who hates endeavors to remove and destroy that which she hates (Schol. Prop. 13, III). But to live one's life at the mercy of hate and retributive desire cannot be good (Prop. 44, IV). "He who wishes to avenge injuries by returning hate for hate lives a miserable life indeed" (Schol. Prop. 46, IV).

This account of love's necessary ambivalence once again deepens the Platonic diagnosis, in ways closely linked to our account of infantile emotion in Chapter 4. Plato thinks of jealousy and rivalry; but he does not go back to the depths of a child's helpless need for the figures who both comfort and desert him, the agonizing alternation between feeding and emptiness, between security and cold loneliness, that characterizes the earliest days of a human life. Spinoza summons that life history into view, through his emphasis on passivity and helplessness – in ways that link his view closely to the contemporary views of Bowlby, Fairbairn, and Klein. If we think of the infant's alternating experience of being held and being left alone, as the parent now approaches, and now recedes to go about his or her own separate life, we will have a good way of understanding Spinoza's insistence on the original ambivalence of love. Like Bowlby and Fairbairn, Spinoza posits no innate aggression to explain the origin of human wickedness, but instead traces aggression to this experience of the separateness and uncontrollability of needed objects – to our reaction to a world that makes us suffer. Thus the Spinozistic account invites A to search in her past for the shadowy memories of parental comfort and abandonment that presage and shadow and become intertwined in her love for M.

It is a terrible thing to realize that she hates the person she loves. Spinoza agrees with contemporary psychologists that the realization that both hatred and love are directed toward one and the same object occasions a fearful crisis in the mental life. "All emotions of hatred are bad," he concludes. "He who wishes to avenge injuries by returning hate for hate lives a miserable life indeed." Like the Greek and Roman Stoics, Spinoza is inspired to dissect the emotions in large part because of his views about the damage caused by anger and hatred in public life; his defense of religious toleration and his insistence that we must free ourselves from bondage to ambivalent emotions are, for him, parts of a single project, and any criticism of his radical anti-emotion program must show its ability to grapple well with those questions.

But how, for Spinoza, can the bondage to hatred be overcome? Spinoza announces that hatred can be overcome and "extinguished" by love, and that "he who strives to overcome hatred with love is surely fighting a happy and carefree battle" (Prop. 46, IV, with Schol.). But it is so far mysterious to A how any such victory could be accomplished. Surely it is not through her erotic love for M that she will conquer the ambivalence attendant on that love. For Spinoza's arguments have shown her that the more she focuses on that love, the more unbalanced will be her hate, and the more distorted and partial her vision of the world. She is right. It is not through that love at all that the victory will be accomplished. The passage in question speaks of "living under the guidance of reason." And we shall now see that it is intellectual guidance, and intellectual love, that will set A free.

V. SPINOZA: FREEDOM THROUGH UNDERSTANDING

Spinoza teaches A that understanding brings freedom. But what is this understanding, and how does it free? In the Platonic ascent, A gradually "relaxes" the grip of her "excessively intense passion" through reflection on the many good things that she cares about, and on their underlying unity. All of her reflection is directed toward the good; and it will propel her upward only if she is willing to see the good as essentially unified and harmonious, her initial love as forming simply one piece of a larger whole. At crucial points she is asked to consider fine things as intersubstitutable, one with another. Spinoza, however, promises her that she need not circumscribe her vision in this way, nor need she lose sight of the particularity of each thing's essential nature. To be released from her bondage, she need not turn her thoughts away from the messy impure elements of her life: she need only take up a new attitude toward the same life, making it an object of intellectual understanding.[25]

The crucial fact that she must realize is that mind as such is free; its

---

25 This aspect of Spinoza's therapy is particularly well treated by A. Rorty (1991), and I am largely in agreement with her more detailed account in what follows.

power cannot be checked by nature's influences. Insofar as her mind is lodged in a body, and insofar as the body needs a certain support from the world of nature, thus far mind is itself not free from external causal influences (Prop. II, III). But thought is by its own nature something free from passivity, something active and under our control. It is essentially by focusing on the active power of her mind, and by deploying that power in understanding herself and her predicament, that A will overcome the ambivalence of her love. Her love is a confused cognition, Spinoza repeatedly insists – meaning by this that in its obsessive character it presents what is significant and salient in the world in a distorted way, and presents our own powerlessness to ourselves in a way that is both unclear and false. (This is Spinoza's way of making the Stoic claim that emotions are all forms of false belief.) Simply turn the light of reflection on that emotion, however, and its character will begin to be transformed: "A passive emotion ceases to be a passive emotion as soon as we form a clear and distinct idea of it" (Prop. 3, V); "the more an emotion is known to us, the more it is within our control, and the mind is less passive in respect of it" (Corollary, Prop. 3, V).

So far A has been living in her love, and allowing her mind to be buffeted by the vicissitudes of M's erratic behavior. But suppose that she begins to wake up, and to ask herself about the orgins of her love, its merits, its overall role in her life – then the emotion itself will appear to her with a new clarity, and it will no longer simply inundate her. Seeing its causes and its effects, she will begin to have the idea that she can manage and control it. And the very activity of understanding, with its exhilaration born of the sense of secure control, itself assists control: for it diminishes the urgent sense of need for a completion that only another person's body can supply. As Spinoza says: "insofar as we understand the causes of pain, it ceases to be a passive emotion; that is, to that extent it ceases to be pain" (Schol. Prop. 18, V).

A turns, then, to the perspicuous description of her love for M, its causes and its effects. But in order to describe it well she must grasp the ideas it instantiates, and its place in the causal nexus of nature as a whole. She must, that is, turn her thoughts both to philosophy and to natural science. She might do this by writing a book dealing with the emotions. Such a book, to achieve the effect desired by Spinoza, would probably need to have a content rather different from that of this book, which supports and endorses all too many "confused cognitions" to win his approval. And yet it is also true that any philosophical book on the topic, insofar as it embodies thought about emotions and their causes, does have at least some of the Spinozistic effect. By focusing on the project of understanding, one renders oneself, for a time, less immersed in the emotions that are being described. I shall follow that suggestion later, in talking about Proust. But we can already see that if A were to articulate in writing a clear idea of childhood longing and hatred and ecstasy, to that extent – harrowing though the process of remembering and writing would be – she should be less passive toward that history. She would have given it a form, made it a part of an explanatory project that she has mapped out and executed with a great deal of joy. Spinoza seems correct to say that the understanding of one's own pain can be one of the most exhilarating activities in the world.

But the therapy undertaken by A under Spinoza's guidance will probably not really produce anything so novelistic. Her literary production will differ from that of the novelist in both form and content. Its content will be designed to sever her thoughts from her obsessive concern with a single object (Prop. 2, V); it will do this, above all, by asking her to focus on general causal patterns, and on her love as merely one instance of a larger design (Props. 9 and II, V; Schol. Prop. 20, V). And her text will ask her to see the larger pattern as necessitated through and through, the entire natural world as an orderly deterministic system in which no particular exists in isolation (Prop. 6, V).

These general metaphysical and scientific thoughts soon take her well beyond the world of particular human interactions, and well beyond the topic of love. That topic would eventually become tiresome to her, and she would regard the choice to write on that topic alone as a sign of continued bondage, no doubt indicative of other sorts of bondage in her life. Nor will just any kind of theoretical and philosophical prose suit her. Were she asked to give the Gifford Lectures, for example, she would hardly choose this topic, so riveted to human pain, nor this style, so laden with particular perceptions. A's Gifford Lectures would be about the entire order of the universe, in its interlocking harmony. That is to say, they would be (as Gifford Lectures should be) about God. "He who clearly and distinctly understands himself and his emotions loves God, and the more so the more he understand himself and his emotions" (Prop. 15, V). But it is a sign of this clear and distinct understanding that she would focus on the larger framework in which she, and her emotions, play a minor role.

This commitment to universal understanding entails that A's Gifford Lectures not relate philosophy to literature, or choose narrative approaches and structures. For Spinoza repeatedly insists that his own highly abstract geometrical way of writing is the correct way to show relations and objects as they exist from the point of view of a cured and God-oriented understanding. Narration, by contrast, focuses the mind too insistently on particulars, seeing them as important not just as parts of the causal nexus of the universe, but in their own right. Literature is an accomplice of a diseased understanding. Even as Augustine will turn, cured, from confessional autobiography to biblical commentary, so A, following Spinoza, will turn from storytelling and story reading to geometry.

The understanding of God is not for Spinoza, as the understanding of the forms is for Plato, opposed to or contrasted with an understanding of particular things. "The more we understand particular things, the more we understand God" (Prop. 24, V). But particulars are understood in a special way – that is to say, under the form of eternity, playing the part that they play in the eternal causal sequence of the universe. When her mind is able to apprehend things – and its own essence – in this way, grasping the whole, it has knowledge of God. And this knowledge brings a special kind of contentment, and a special kind of love – an elation that is accompanied by the idea of oneself, and also of God, as its cause.

This love is not contingent on any particular state of the body, or on any external event. Therefore it need not come to a halt at any time (Prop. 34, V, Corollary; Prop. 37, V). Nor is it tarnished by ambivalence (Prop. 18, V, Corollary). And since it is the common property of all human beings, she will not envy anyone else this understanding, but will realize that the understanding is made the more complete the more other people enjoy it (Prop. 20, V; Prop. 35, IV; contrast Props. 32–34, IV). This means that, far from keeping her insight to herself, she will communicate it to others, expressing her love of God through actions that benefit all human beings. By explaining her lectures on natural theology to M, A will overcome her ambivalent love for him with true love. And in her own being she will overcome her hatred of a universe that makes her suffer with love of the entire order of things.

VI. PROUST: USING INDIVIDUALS AS STEPS

As a boy he longs for his mother's goodnight kiss. There is an aching absence in his soul that he calls love. He wants to be filled up, consoled, comforted; he wants the nullification of the acute pain of feeling and thought. And even though his mother's kiss brings comfort, its effect is so transient that its happy imminence is already tainted with the pain of its departure, "so much so that I reached the point of hoping that this good night which I loved so much would come as late as possible, so as to prolong the time of respite during which Mamma would not yet have appeared."[26] But the price of the absence of pain, that is to say of love, is the extinction of awareness, the absence, one might say, of a life. Habit, that "clever arranger who makes all things habitable," prevents him from truly dwelling in himself. He wishes to possess the entirety of his life, which is to say the story of his longing, without the terrible intermittence of love itself, with a constancy and solidity of consciousness that love itself does not permit.

Many years later, he tells us in this very passage, waking up in the night, he feels a primitive longing for comfort that is the legacy of these childhood experiences. As we mentioned in Chapter 4, he tries to mother himself by pressing his cheeks against his pillow, and he thinks that soon "someone will come to his aid. The hope of being comforted gives him the courage to suffer."[27] He now dreams of a woman, and feels sexual arousal, as he senses the warmth of his body mingling with hers. He feels his body pressed down by her weight – as if she were, indeed, a calming and consoling maternal presence, as well as a sexual partner.[28]

We know from this point on that what Marcel will later call the "general form" of his loves points backward toward the past, toward the solitary anxieties of the child who longs passionately for his mother's goodnight kiss and for her reassuring embrace, which blots out alarming stimuli from the world. In his longing for a return to a womblike state of oneness – even in the dream, he wants to "become

26 Proust, I.13–14.
27 I. 10.
28 Strictly speaking, the entire narrative is in the *imparfait*, and the experience of waking in the night is said to be followed sometimes by sound sleep, sometimes by nightmares of "childish terrors," and sometimes by this dream of erotic tenderness.

one with" the woman he sees – he comes to view even his mother's arrival with pain, because he has learned that he is not in the womb, but in a world in which external objects, having arrived, soon depart again.[29]

Proust's novel contains traces of many philosophical accounts of love and its therapy. But the Platonist ascent tradition informs the structure of the narrative at a deeper level, I think, than any other. Plato gives the narrator his definition of love: "Love, in the pain of anxiety as in the bliss of desire, is a demand for the whole . . . We love only that which we do not wholly possess" (III.102). And Plato's ladder of love gives the narrator a pivotal image for the trajectory of his thought and desire. In a composite allusion to both the *Symposium* and the *Phaedrus*, placed at the heart of his theoretical account of his own literary project and its material in his life, he writes:

Every individual who makes us suffer can be attached by us to a divinity of which he or she is a mere fragmentary reflection, the lowest step in the ascent that leads to it, a divinity or an Idea which, if we turn to contemplate it, immediately gives us joy instead of the pain which we were feeling before – indeed the whole art of living is to make use of the individuals through whom we suffer as a series of steps enabling us to draw nearer to the divine form which they reflect and thus joyously to people our life with divinities. (III.935)[30]

Here we see not only the Platonic idea of using individuals as steps on the way to a general form that they imperfectly instantiate, but also the idea, common to both Plato and Spinoza, that an intellectual project addressed to the material of one's life converts life's pain to solid joy. We now need to examine the way in which this idea is worked out in the narrative itself: asking, first, why it is that the love of real people in life yields only agony and instability, and, second, why the ascent of love should take, as it did not for either Plato or Spinoza, the form of narrative art.

Love is a form of painful awareness of a gap or lack in the self,

---

29 I.21.

30 Where Kilmartin renders "*degré*" literally as "step," I have written "series of steps," which conveys more accurately, I think, the distributive meaning of the original. The passage is a fragment in Proust's journals, without a clear placement in the text. It has been inserted by editors into the middle of a discussion of truths derived from reality by the intellect as opposed to impressions of memory. This does not seem quite right, since the passage alludes to the whole work of the artist in basing his narrative on past loves.

accompanied by a demand for a restoration of wholeness. It has its roots in the child's unhappy anxious longing for his mother; and this desire to possess an elusive source of comfort colors every subsequent love. When Albertine appears before him on the beach, in the company of the little band of cyclists, it is the sheer separateness of her will that inspires his desire. His love of her follows the pattern set by its beginning: excruciating longing, issuing in projects of possession and wholeness that can never be fulfilled, punctuated by moments of comfort that are tainted before they arrive by either the pain of jealousy or the deadness of indifference. "We love only that which we do not wholly possess." Agonizing neediness, obsessive partiality of vision, and the evils of jealousy and hate – all three of the Platonic–Spinozistic flaws in love are emphasized here, and traced, through narrative, to the experience of childhood helplessness at which Spinoza only abstractly gestured.

As we have recorded, such a lover cannot but be cruel to the loved one, in his attempt to control her every movement and thought. Albertine can escape from his jealousy only when she is unconscious and has ceased, for the time, to be a separate human being:

When I returned she would be asleep and I saw before me the other woman that she became whenever one saw her full face . . . I could take her head, lift it up, press her face to my lips, put her arms round my neck, and she would continue to sleep, like a watch that never stops, like a climbing plant, a convolvulus which continues to thrust out its tendrils whatever support you give it. Only her breathing was altered by each touch of my fingers, as though she were an instrument on which I was playing and from which I extracted modulations by drawing different notes from one after another of its strings. My jealousy subsided, for I felt that Albertine had become a creature that breathes (*un être qui respire*) and is nothing else besides . . . (III.109)

In this way, her sleep realised to a certain extent the possibility of love . . . By shutting her eyes, by losing consciousness, Albertine had stripped off, one after another, the different human personalities with which she had deceived me ever since the day when I had first made her acquaintance. She was animated now only by the unconscious life of plants, of trees, a life more different from my own, more alien, and yet one that belonged more to me. Her personality was not constantly escaping, as when we talked, by the outlets of her unacknowledged thoughts and of her eyes. (III.64)

Thus is it only when a human being becomes a plant that she can be loved without hatred.

Proust's novel addresses itself to a reader who is eager for understanding of her own loves and their form, who would like to use the novel as an "optical instrument," so as to see herself more clearly (III.949). So let us imagine our pupil A – who is distinct from the fictional Albertine, just as (for Proust) any real person is necessarily distinct from any fictional character, a character being always the amalgamation of several different life experiences – reading the novel and applying it to her own life. She will see that the love of ordinary life brings no joy. Even the pleasure she longs for with M is "in fact only experienced inversely," through the anguish of its incompleteness and instability (III.909).

Nor can she, from her position of immersion within her own life, even understand the structures of that life: for the routines of life, together with our vanity, our incessant jealousy, our mechanisms of self-comfort and self-concealment, operate always to conceal from the self the structure of its own love, with its oscillation between anguish and deadness, its repetitious and obsessive pursuit of the impossible. Her ordinary existence exemplifies a process of self-concealment, a process

which, in those everyday lives which we live with our gaze averted from ourself, is at every moment being accomplished by vanity and passion and the intellect, and habit too, when they smother our true impressions, so as entirely to conceal them from us, beneath a whole heap of verbal concepts and practical goals which we falsely call life. (III.932)

Moreover, within life itself she can never achieve toward M himself either accurate vision or true altruism: for all her dealings with him are marred by the self-comforting structure of her aims.

The ascent of love is made possible by art – to some extent by the self-scrutinizing work of the reader of fiction, to a far greater extent by the task of writing one's own life story.[31] Unlike Spinoza, who thinks

31 It is unclear, as it is also in Plato and Spinoza, whether the ascent is thought to be available to all human beings, or only to those who are specially talented. Proust, like Spinoza, tends to portray the artist's success as depending on a special effort of will and on a renunciation of which few would be capable. It is this mode of life above all that sets the artist apart from the crowd. On III.931, he writes that all people have the materials of art within them, but most do not seek to shed light on them; therefore

of narration as too mired in emotion to be a vehicle of freedom, Proust plausibly argues that narration is the only true source of freedom, since only through narration do we master the general form of our love, with all its causal connections – at the same time making this mastery a gift to the reader. The task of the ascent, then, is to turn one's own life into a work of literature, using other people as steps on the ladder. The task is a labor more of decipherment than of creation, as one probes one's past for the text "which has been dictated to us by reality, the only one of which the 'impression' has been printed in us by reality itself" (III.914). Its goal is the disocvery "of what, though it ought to be more precious to us than anything in the world, yet remains ordinarily for ever unknown to us, the discovery of our true life, of reality as we have felt it to be" (915). The raw materials of this work are impressions that have been stored up in us by life itself (914); these must be recaptured and then assembled by the work of memory and intellect, until in the end we have recovered our own lost selves (935), and have immobilized by contemplation all that had previously eluded us (909). But this task is, then, in effect, the inverse of the usual operations of daily life, in which we live "with our gaze averted from ourselves" (932). For daily life buries the significant beneath habits and jealousies and vanities that mask its significance; art dispels the false covering and reveals the real material of life. It is for this reason that it is only the work of art, and not daily life, that can be called life fully[32] lived (932, 931). "Experience had taught me only too well the impossibility of attaining in the real world to what lay deep within myself" (910).

Before A can attempt this task with any hope of success, she must sever her connection with M, and, indeed, with all of the people she intimately loves or has loved, and seek an undisturbed condition within which the internal book of passion may be discovered. "It is our passions which draw the outline of our books, the ensuing intervals of repose which write them" (945). She should not attempt this, if possi-

---

their past is "like a photographic dark-room encumbered with innumerable negatives which remain useless because the intellect has not developed them."

32 On III.931, Kilmartin translates, "Real life, life at last laid bare and illuminated – the only life in consequence which can be said to be really lived – is literature." But it has recently been recognized that Proust's almost illegible handwriting actually has "*pleinement,*" "fully," and not "*réellement,*" "really," at this point.

ble, until she has loved a number of different people – for the reality that is characteristic of literary art requires the grasping of general forms, and this, in turn, requires many experiences (945):

[T]he writer, in order to achieve volume and substance, in order to attain to generality and, so far as literature can, to reality, needs to have seen many churches in order to paint one church and for the portrayal of a single sentiment requires many individuals. (III.945)

Indeed, "infidelity toward the individual" is a prerequisite for the appropriate creative posture (945). The artist in her is delighted not by this or that particular love, but by a general form of love and desire that emerges from all of the concrete experiences, in the unity of one portion of her past with another: for she "is nourished only by the essences of things," in these alone she finds her "sustenance and delight" (III.905).

The material of literary creation will not be just the good and fine in things, as Plato argued. A will find in the painful, the hateful, the despicable, the grotesque rich material for her contemplation. (Here Proust sides with Spinoza and not with Plato.) Calm and happy times, indeed, Proust holds, are the least valuable to her, since they are times of spiritual dullness, in which keen perceptions are not stored up.

Where love is concerned, she will see the unity of one past love with another, and of what she has called love with other pains (for example, the pain of travel) that she has not previously connected with love (911). All such pains and disappointments are simply "the varied aspects which are assumed, according to the particular circumstances which bring it into play, by our inherent powerlessness to realise ourselves in material enjoyment or in effective action" (911). Thus at bottom, for Proust as for Spinoza, love is all about powerlessness and neediness.

The pain of A's love for M must now "detach itself from individuals so that [sh]e can comprehend and restore to it its generality" (933–4). M will become for her an instantiation of a general form of love and desire whose vicissitudes she endeavors, in general, to comprehend. The remembered pain of their love will now be surpassed "by [her] curiosity to learn the causes of this calamity" (433): as in Spinoza, causal understanding quiets pain. Reaching back to their love in memory, she will now view him as a model who has "quite simply been posing for the artist at the very moment when, much against [her] will, [he] made [her] suffer most" (939). And in this way, in the very process of causing her pain, M has brought his stone "for the building of the monument" that is her narrative artwork (941). In fact, she will come to think that he really never was much more for her than a projective construct of her own imagining and desire, a fictional character already; and the austere truth of this recognition will itself console her for the fact that he did not love her enough (932–3).[33] She will come to understand the truth that art reveals: that we are always alone, however much we love. "Man is the creature who cannot escape from himself, who knows other people only in himself, and when he asserts the contrary, he is lying" (459).

Remembering the pain of love will itself be painful: and A will relive her suffering with the courage of a doctor who experiments on himself (942). But the suffering is mitigated by the narrative project in which it is embedded: "At the same time we have to conceptualise it in a general form which will in some measure enable us to escape from its embrace, which will turn all mankind into sharers in our pain, and which is even able to yield us a certain joy" (942–3).

For the life of art is a life of joy, a joy closely related to Spinoza's intellectual joy, and connected by Proust with a kind of immortality and life beyond the world. The raw material of self-knowledge and artistic expression is pain. But to use this pain *as* raw material for a work of universal communicative power and formal beauty is a profound delight (935) and a consolation. It not only supplies the artist with an endlessly fascinating active task, subject to no circumstantial vicissitudes and managed by her alone; it also enables her to escape her own bondage to the present moment and to possess the form of her life as a whole, thus defeating time and moving as close to immortality as any human being can (905–6).

One might suppose that the good of other human beings would not figure in this life at all. This is in a way true, since M has ceased to

---

33 See Nussbaum (1990), "Love's Knowledge," for a discussion of the relationship between skepticism and consolation. I argue that Marcel's adoption of criteria for knowledge of the other that are impossible to satisfy is a strategem connected with fear of openness toward the other, and that it prepares the way for a skeptical conclusion that is more welcome than painful.

exist for A as a real person with real needs. On the other hand, the work of the artist gives readers a powerful tool for self-understanding that they may use to uncover the reality of their own selves, and thus progress toward their own immortality. Indeed, Proust instructs A at this point that, earthly relationships being marred as they are by jealousy and personal longing, it is only in the act of creating a work of art, in the artist's sense of obligation to her theme and to her audience, that true giving to others may take place.

In an important passage in which Marcel describes his thoughts on the death of Bergotte, the novelist, he turns to Plato's theory of recollection, announcing that the novelist bears into this world trace memories of moral obligations contracted in another world – and, realizing that he cannot fulfill these obligations in ordinary human relations, he realizes them through his art.

All that we can say is that everything is arranged in this life as though we entered it carrying a burden of obligations contracted in a former life; there is no reason inherent in the conditions of life on this earth that can make us consider ourselves obliged to do good, to be kind and thoughtful, even to be polite . . . All these obligations, which have no sanction in our present life, seem to belong to a different world, a world based on kindness, scrupulousness, self-sacrifice, a world entirely different from this one and which we leave in order to be born on this earth, before perhaps returning there to live once again beneath the sway of those unknown laws which we obeyed because we bore their precepts in our hearts . . . (III.186)

Proust is making more than one claim here. One claim is that the artist's pure dedication to art is the only example of pure dedication that we have in this world. But he also says that this dedication is an example of "kindness" and "self-sacrifice" – because he thinks of the novel as a gift to its readers. Only in this act do we see selfless giving to others – every – face-to-face human relationship being marred by jealousy and possessive desire. The relationship between author and reader is free from excessive, crippling dependency, free from ambivalence, even free, in a necessary way, from partiality – for the work addresses itself to all alike. It does not know where it is placed in the lives it addresses.

Nor is this the end of the artist's gift: for the gift also creates for the reader a possibility of unselfish and undemanding love, therefore of knowledge of another's mind.[34] All of our attempts to know the mind of another real person are doomed by our jealous projects: we are always seeing some aspect of our own needs and wishes. Before the work of art, by contrast, these obstacles fall away, and true knowledge can take place.[35] An artist's style

is the revelation, which by direct and conscious methods would be impossible, of the qualitative difference, the uniqueness of the fashion in which the world appears to each one of us, a difference which, if there were no art, would remain for ever the secret of every individual. Through art alone are we able to emerge from ourselves, to know what another person sees of a universe which is not the same as our own and of which, without art, the landscapes would remain as unknown to us as those that may exist on the moon. (931–2)

And this means that art offers us the only possibility of genuine human contact, and therefore the only possibility of a love that is reciprocal rather than solipsistic.

VII. THE PURSUIT OF WHOLENESS

We now have two more accounts of a love that has love's energy, beauty, and wonder without its crippling passivity, without distraction, without ambivalence – a love that supports reflection rather than seeking its extinction, a love that embraces the entire world with even-handed joy. If in Plato the lover confined her attentions to the fine and good, Spinoza and Proust show that this need not be the case: contemplation can also find joy in the ugly and the grotesque, and even, and above all, in the lover's own history of pain. Thus love is purified of

---

34 This claim would appear to be in some tension with the claim that the artist offers the reader a set of optical instruments through which to view herself and her own love (III.1089, quoted in Chapter 9). I think it need not be. As Proust says, so it is: when we read his novel, we are made more keenly aware of the structure of our own love and its particularity, and, at the same time, we encounter another mind, the mind of a distinctive being who animates the text as a whole. In part we discover ourselves through our likeness to this being, but in part, too, through our unlikeness.

35 A significant corollary of this is that the artist, being the only type of human who can be known by another, is also the only sort who can be immortal. Thus "the idea that Bergotte was not permanently dead is by no means improbable." His books "kept vigil like angels with outspread wings and seemed, for him who was no more, the symbol of his resurrection" (III.186).

the obstacles that stand between it and a beneficent concern for all humanity.

Once again: what should a person attached to benevolence and justice say about this achievement? Have we in fact discovered a reform of love that keeps love's creativity without its problems? Let us revisit and deepen our three worries: about compassion, about reciprocity, about the individual.

1. *Compassion.* According to the Stoic therapy of emotions from which Spinoza borrows, no emotion involving a high appraisal of the importance of earthly goods and persons should remain in the cured person's life. As we saw in Chapter 7, compassion must depart as surely as anger, grief, and fear, since in pity we acknowledge that the misfortune befalling another has deep importance for the self. In the process we set ourselves up for fear at our own uncertain prospects, and even for anger at the cause of our suffering. Spinoza does not hesitate to draw the Stoic conclusion. He repudiates pity as a painful acknowledgment of human weakness (Prop. 50, IV) and an inappropriate response to the necessary and determined suffering we see.[36] Like the Stoics, he argues, further, that pity is inextricably bound up with the bad passions of envy and hate: our pity at the misfortune of others has as its opposite number our envy at their good fortune and our hatred of them for having power over us. The only way to get disentangled from hate is, then, to be less passive toward the world altogether – and then we will not pity, any more than we will envy or fear.

Just as Plato repudiates the suffering of tragic heroes, then, holding that a really strong person will be self-sufficient, and seeing pity as part of an undignified worldview, so too Spinoza. He does of course endorse benevolence and beneficence insofar as reason dictates these attitudes and actions – but, like Plato, his perfected lover is too high above the world to see why hunger, and mourning, and persecution,

---

36 Nor does his critique rest on a contrast between pity and compassion: he denies the difference between pity (*commiseratio*) and compassion (*misericordia*), "unless perhaps pity has reference to a particular occurrence of emotion, while compassion has regard to a set disposition to that emotion" (Definitions of Emotions, III, 18). Note, as well, that the translator seems to make no distinction: for *commiseratio* would surely, in terms of both the tradition and its etymology, be more plausibly translated as "compassion," and *misericordia* is the standard Latin equivalent to the Greek *eleos*, standardly rendered as "pity."

and loss have great weight for people and why their relief, in consequence, is a matter of political urgency. Like Marcus Aurelius, he will regard people as childish, perhaps even a little disgusting, insofar as they mind these things. He refuses to allow himself to be contaminated by them.

Proust is more complex: for he insists that his novel itself is a work of compassion, in which the artist has sacrificed his ease for needy humanity. He portrays his work as the emissary of a world of true altruism and sympathy beyond the ravages of jealousy and human love. There is much that seems compassionate in the work – with its searching portrayal of grief and mourning, its tenderness toward the vicissitudes of human suffering. At one point the narrator even states that the compassion for suffering is stronger, even, than the pleasures of love (III.435).

And yet there is reason to feel that the initial compassion is negated by the austerity of the novel's ending, in which we understand all human relationship to be fictitious, all loss therefore as loss merely in fiction. The corollary of loneliness is self-sufficiency. The artist's primary aim has become her own immortality, something that has only a tangential connection with the happiness of the reader. Nor does he seem to be alive to general social concerns. The political events of Proust's time appear through the narrative at a great distance, as so many signs of human folly and inconstancy; and we see why this must be so. No person who follows Proust's advice about love would take a risk for Dreyfus – even an intellectual risk – or get enmeshed in class struggle. Those things are mere distractions from the all-consuming project of self-contemplation. In the end, then, just as the novel adopts a view about the object of sexual love that implies that all sexual acts are essentially masturbatory, so too it adopts a view of sympathy and altruism – even, I think in the end, of the artist's altruism – that implies that all such altruism is at bottom egoistic self-gratification. This happens, as in Plato, out of the search for self-sufficiency.

Is there compassion at least for the beloved? M remains important to A in two ways: as a vehicle for creation, and as a part of the reality that contemplation studies with joy. In Plato, he turns out to be a relatively insignificant vehicle for creative thought and speech, since, like any real person, he evidently contains so much less goodness than other objects that A could contemplate, and his goodness is so mixed up with bad and neutral properties. In Spinoza's view, he fares somewhat better, since she may study the whole of him and not simply his goodness, and since the understanding of her own history is permitted to play a particular role in transcending her pain. And in Proust he fares best of all, since he will be a major source for the work of art she will create. Nonetheless, we have to say that M himself, and the happiness of M, vanish from view. He is, to use Proust's image, just an artist's model, just an occasion for a creation that transcends and leaves behind his reality. If she acts beneficently for his sake, it is only insofar as he is a part of the whole world to which her creative activity is addressed. If he really needed her, she could not see it.

In short, the boundaries of the lover's world, while appearing to expand, through love's embrace of the universe, have actually contracted, through the lover's repudiation of the human meanings of events and people in that world. To love human beings *more geometrico*, or even as fictional personae, is to push them away, not to embrace them.

2. *Reciprocity.* Plato's love, though unselfish and creative, appears to lack respect for the lover's separate agency and for reciprocal elements in the love, treating the beloved object simply as a seat of desirable properties. What do we find in Spinoza and Proust? As the lover progresses there is certainly less and less desire to possess or control individual people, less jealousy, less selfishness in the usual sense. But is there any sense of respect for the other person's choices? If A follows Spinoza, she will view every part of nature as a part of an interlocking whole, and the distinction between agents and other parts becomes relatively insignificant; only her own agency is an object of concern to her. In Proust, the agency of the beloved object is central – but as a primary cause of the artist's past suffering. In her cured artistic condition, A will regard M only as a model, the origin of a literary character; and the freedom to manipulate that character will belong entirely to her.[37]

---

37 See Vlastos (1981), p. 32: "Since persons in their concreteness are thinking, feeling, wishing, hoping, fearing beings, to think of love for them as love for objectifications of excellence is to fail to make the thought of them as *subjects* central to what is felt for them in love." Vlastos does not clearly distinguish this criticism from the point about altruism, but the two issues are logically independent, clearly. One might be very

3. *Individuality*. Both Spinoza and Proust consider separateness in the object to be a source of pain, something to be *defeated* rather than respected and loved. The fact that they have their own lives to live is precisely the problem. In Spinoza separateness is even disgusting, since jealousy over nonpossession is inextricably linked to a disgusting set of thoughts about sexual infidelity. As for qualitative particularity, this also plays an ever-diminishing role in the increasingly abstract contemplative concern of these two followers of Plato. Unlike Plato, Spinoza and Proust do not restrict A's view to what is fine and good in the object – so their views might seem to promise a richer grasp of particularity. But how far do they take us? Spinoza does permit A to see M as a particular – for, after all, that is what everything is. But increasingly it is not the specificities of his particularity that interest her – the bodily idiosyncrasies, the concrete history, even his flaws and faults – for she will increasingly see him as just one of many particulars locked together in nature's whole. And for therapeutic purposes she will be actively discouraged from focusing on those concrete aspects of him – his body, in particular – that used to inspire her with need and longing (as well as with violent disgust). Proust's narrator does continue to see the particular loves of his past – but only as so many signs of general essences, and of the general form of his love. It is for this reason that when A writes her Proustian artwork, the man she will portray there will not be M in all of his concreteness. It will be a rather abstract composite of several parts of her history.[38] It will not be surprising if the resulting literary character is as lacking in particularity as is Albertine herself – whose individuating traits fluctuate inconstantly through the novel, consisting in great measure of her tendency to recall to the narrator childhood feelings of pain.

Again, as with Plato, these points about separateness and particular-

___

concerned with fostering the other person's interests without respecting his or her autonomy: this happens (innocuously) in the love of a parent for a very young child, and (in a more troubling way) in the mutual love of the citizens in Plato's ideal city. On the other hand, it might be possible to respect other people's freedom while not seeking to benefit them for their own sake. This happens in one way in Stoicism, to the extent that the wise person construes respect as requiring the refusal of pity; it happens, as well, in certain types of enmity.

38 See III.876: "In this book in which there is not a single incident which is not fictitious, not a single character who is a real person in disguise, in which everything has been invented by me in accordance with the requirements of my theme . . ."

ity are not simple. For by removing jealousy and insecurity, Spinoza and Proust have also gotten rid of some of the most powerful impediments to individual love – as Proust records by emphasizing that ethical relations from the "other world" of kindness are possible *only* in the relationship between artist and reader. Both in Spinoza and in Proust, lovers ascend beyond the obstacles imposed by the insecure ego – but only by leaving behind the sight of the real-life individual in all his or her erotic complexity. This seems tolerable to Proust because on his account the individual as such never has been the object of love. The people we love, he concludes, are the ones we see least clearly of all: they are merely "a vast, vague arena in which to exteriorise our thoughts . . . And it was perhaps my fault that I did not make a greater effort to know Albertine in herself."

Thus the ascent succeeds only by getting so high above real people that the specificity of their human existence cannot be seen. All three of our thinkers seem to believe that only in this way can the terrible excessiveness and ambivalence of love be cured. What should we say to A about this? If we agree with their diagnosis but remain discontent with their conclusion, we face, it seems, a difficult choice, especially where social life is concerned: either no hope of overcoming hate, or an overcoming that also wipes out compassion, reciprocity, and particularity, except in the contemplative relationship between philosopher and God, or between reader and text.

The diagnosis of our therapists can now, however, be questioned. For they all begin with an understanding of love that derives from a picture of infantile helplessness and the infantile wish for omnipotence – that sees the wish of love in terms of the restoration of totality and a "Golden Age" needless state. We might say that they express what we have called pathological narcissism: for they long for complete control over the world, and they refuse to abandon that wish in favor of more realistic human wishes for interchange and interdependence. Their characterizations of what human life is like are distorted by their wish, for they see only agony and misery wherever there is incompleteness and a lack of dictatorial control, only the disgusting wherever there is a body going its own way. Rather than learning to live in a world in which every lover must be finite and mortal, the contemplative lover finds marvelously ingenious devices to satisfy the desires of infancy –

deploying, to remarkable effect, the wonder and curiosity that are so prominent in a human infant's initial makeup. Rather than renouncing the wish for totality in favor of a more appropriate human wish, this lover has continued to be motivated by infantile omnipotence and has for this very reason had to depart from a world in which the infant's wishes can never be satisfied.

None of my three normative criteria *can* be satisfied, so long as the ascending lover continues to hold onto omnipotence, or complete control of the good, as a goal. Reciprocity requires a willingness to live alongside others who are equals, and this means a willingness to admit limits to one's own control of good things. One cannot hate the very fact of another person's uncontrolled existence and still live with others on terms of reciprocity and justice. Compassion typically involves seeing oneself as one among others, similarly vulnerable, with similar possibilities for worldly misfortune. One cannot have compassion for others if one is unwilling to acknowledge the reality and the salience of another human life alongside one's own. And, as Proust admits, seeing the particularity of another truly and clearly requires a stance that does not try to incorporate or swallow that other particular, the stance of one who is willing to live in a world where there are agencies external to the self that go on being the way they are. In that sense he is absolutely correct: it *was* his fault that he did not get to know Albertine as she was in herself. But it was his fault not (as he thinks) because he fell in love with her, but on account of the specific goal he set for himself in love, and the account of love he adopts, so well suited to that underlying goal.

In short, any version of the ascent of love that is going to deliver a promising mode of either personal or social relations should not be built on the aim for godlike omnipotence, and the combination of anguish and arrogance that go with that infantile aim.

Why do they choose this aim? Why, to put it differently, is the Platonic ascent so attractive to A, and to many of us? Why has it had such appeal throughout the history of thought? Proust's diagnosis can stand for all three: it is because of shame. Proust depicts our condition as one of unendurable weakness and need, and he depicts us as riven not only by pain but also by shame about this condition of need. (Similarly, Aristophanes' formerly proud humans, who assailed the gods, are embarrassed and ashamed to have merely human bodies.)[39] Because our anguish at being a part of the whole is so unendurable, there will be no cure for love unless we become masters of the whole. Because our helplessness is so shameful, we must become like gods. This sense that one cannot hold up one's head unless one closes off all possible sources of pain and uncontrol, a condition that Part I identified as pathological narcissism, dooms the Platonic lover. One day, recognizing that in kissing Albertine he is really embracing and trying to possess the image of his mother, the narrator acknowledges this limitation. People like him, he says,

know that their emotions and actions are not in a close and necessary relation to the loved woman, but pass by her side, brush up against her, surround her like the tide that crashes along the rocks – and this awareness of their own instability increases still further their conviction that this woman, whose love they so much desire, does not love them . . . [T]his fear, this shame, bring about the counter-rhythm, the ebb-tide, the need . . . to take back the offensive and to regain esteem and control.[40]

It is this starting point that dooms his project to ethical inadequacy. Each of these three visions of a complete love is marred by the particular narcissistic stance of its author[41] toward the world of value.

So too A, cycling along the beach, is self-sufficient. She has had a philosophical education that lifts her beyond shame, beyond revenge, beyond instability – but also, beyond politics, friendship, and human love.

39 Spinoza defines shame in a broader way, simply as "pain accompaied by the idea of some action of ours that we think that others censure." But it is clear that the lover's felt powerlessness is the sort of thing he censures in himself, and thus he will think that others censure it. It is, after all, "bondage," a condition in which one is "not one's own master but is subject to fortune."

40 My translation of the French rendered by Moncrieff and Kilmartin at II.857–8 (see the more extensive quotation in Chapter 4). Shame is a theme of long standing in the novel. Consider, among others, the scene at Balbec where the young Marcel, annoyed that Charlus speaks in a vulgar way about his grandmother, frankly says, "What, Monsieur! I adore her!" – and is promptly told by Charlus that it is shameful to acknowledge one's sentiments openly, just as ridiculous as to have anchors embroidered on one's bathing-dress (I.823). In the Raoul Ruiz film *Time Regained*, this moment is especially well rendered.

41 In Proust there is most room to doubt: for after all, Marcel is not Proust. But the text creates no space in which Marcel's distinctive vision of the world may be criticized from within.

11

THE CHRISTIAN
ASCENT: AUGUSTINE

1. OMNIPOTENCE AND THE SIN OF PRIDE

The contemplative ascent set itself a goal: to retain the energy and beauty of erotic love while ridding it of three grave defects: its partiality or uneven focus, its excessive neediness and dependency, and its connection with anger and revenge. All three versions of the ascent appeared to achieve this goal, purifying love through the joy of understanding. And yet the claim to have rendered the lover godlike and self-sufficient, no longer needy, introduced grave problems, both for the love itself and for related social concerns. A lover who repudiates bondage to human need is ill-placed to assess properly the needs of other humans, or to see the importance of coming to their aid; thus it is no surprise that all three Platonic thinkers repudiate compassion as something contaminated by bondage to worldly objects. Nor will a lover whose original aim involves the possession or incorporation of the good be likely, so long as he or she retains and even fulfills that aim, to appreciate the worth of political reciprocity, or of respect for the dignity and separateness of others. And a lover who focuses on objects as sources of good and well-being will be unlikely to love them in all their full particularity. I have suggested that these three defects in Platonic love all derive from what I have called a pathological narcissism, but what, from our present perspective, we might call the vice of pride, the idea that one can and should achieve godlike omnipotence, removing all passivity and need. This project, which animates both Plato and Spinoza, is plausibly said by Proust to be based on infantile projects of possessing and incorporating the loved parental object, projects that, if not renounced in favor of other aims, render the lover solipsistic and incomplete as a lover of real human beings.

We turn now to the Christian rewriting of the ascent of love, which focuses its criticism of Plato on just this point. The Greek philosophical tradition is seen to be in the grip of the sin of pride, the false belief that human beings can by their own efforts make themselves godlike. Our ascending lover should certainly get rid of many impurities and flaws, including the primary ones that the Platonists attempt to cure. But in the process she must attempt to retain and deepen her sense of inadequacy and incompleteness, thinking of this very state, and its recognition, as conditions of her salvation.

II. HUNGER AND THIRST

We hear sighs of longing and groans of profound desolation. We hear love songs composed in anguish, as the singer's heart strains upward in desire. We hear of a hunger that cannot be satisfied, of a thirst that torments, of the taste of a lover's body that kindles inexpressible longing. We hear of an opening that longs for penetration, of a burning fire that ignites the body and the heart. All of these are images of profound erotic passion. And all of these are images of Christian love. Christian love both ascends and descends, both purifying the will and recovering a receptivity and vulnerability that the Platonist ascent had surmounted. In the process, the emotions, seen as acknowledgments of neediness and a lack of self-sufficiency, are restored to a place of value in the good human life. For while it is good to ascend, removing sin from the heart, it is also good to acknowledge one's deep need for sources of good outside oneself, and therefore not to ascend beyond the condition of imperfect humanity. In these chapters I shall investigate this double movement of ascent and descent, focusing on two thinkers who use, and transform, the traditional image of love's ascent: Augustine and Dante.

Throughout his career, Augustine repeatedly contrasts two types of love: human or earthly love, and Christian love, whose core is the love of God.[1] He repudiates the one and urges us, disdaining it, to cultivate

---

1 Not all Christian love is love of God: there may be human loves that are distinctively Christian. But these other loves are suffused by the love of God, and, as we shall see, their real object always is, in a way, God. So understanding Augustine's view of the love

the other. Repeatedly he speaks of the progress of the soul as an ascent of love and desire from the earthly to the heavenly, an ascent that strips away and leaves behind the merely human in love. This rejection of ordinary human passion is nowhere more vividly expressed than in the *Confessions*, where Augustine movingly recalls his own intense delight in earthly love, portraying this delight, with contrition, as a deviation from the true love and the true passion. Thus he repudiates the example of Dido and her consuming love for Aeneas:

I was forced to memorize the wanderings of some person called Aeneas, while I was unaware of my own wanderings, and to weep for the death of Dido, who killed herself for love, when meanwhile, in my most wretched condition, I endured with dry eyes the fact that I myself, in these matters, was dying from you, God, my life. For what is more wretched than a wretch who does not pity his own self, and weeps for the death of Dido, which was caused by love of Aeneas, but does not weep for his own death, which was caused by not loving you, God?[2]

Augustine's identification with pagan *erôs* was no mere schoolboy exercise; it was a paradigm that shaped his sense of his identity as a desiring subject. That paradigm is here dismissed with scorn, as a form of both sin and self-avoidance.

And yet, as even this passage of denial suggests, the *Confessions* is itself a deeply erotic work, a work filled with expressions of erotic tension and erotic longing. God is addressed throughout in language that Dido might well have used to Aeneas: "my beauty," "most beautiful one," "my life," "my light," "my sweetness." The central metaphors of the work express passionate longing and receptivity: images of hunger, of thirst, of an emptiness that desires to be filled. We encounter passages like this one:

of God is our central task. On Augustine's doctrine of love, see Brown (1967), Arendt (1929, 1996), Di Giovanni (1964); on the spiritual journey of Christian life in general, see Gilson (1949); for a fine general account of Augustine's philosophy of mind, see O'Daly (1987); on his relationship to pagan culture, see Marrou (1938). For an interesting account of the role of desire in the *Confessions*, see Miles (1992), and for a fascinating account of the relationship of this work to Augustine's biography, see Wills (1999).

2 *Confessions* I.13. All translations from Augustine are my own. Wills suggests, plausibly enough, that *The Testimony* is a better translation of the title, *Confessiones*, than *Confessions*: *confiteor* means to acknowledge or testify, not simply to confess in the narrow sense. I retain the traditional title for clarity's sake.

You blew fragrantly upon me, and I drew in the breath; and I pant for you. I tasted you and I hunger and thirst for you. You touched me, and I burned for your peace. (X.27)

And this one:

Let me leave them outside, breathing into the dust and filling their eyes with earth, and let me enter into my chamber and sing love songs to you, groaning inexpressible groans in my long wandering, and remembering Jerusalem with my heart stretching upward in longing. (XII.16)

This is not language that the Stoic or Spinozistic wise man would use, extirpating the passions. Nor is it the language of any form of the contemplative ascent. For while the ascending lover in that tradition is still a desiring subject, she lacks this lover's deep vulnerability to external influence, a vulnerability that paints the world in non-Platonic colors, locating the most urgent good things outside the self rather than within. In short, we are brought back, it seems, to the world of the emotions, seen, as Spinoza has urged us to see them, as recognitions of our necessary passivity and neediness in a world that we do not control. In some manner Christian love has reopened the space within which fear, and anxiety, and grief, and intense delight, and even anger, all have their full force. And correct love promises no departure from these other emotions – if anything, it requires their intensification. In short, correct love is very much like the old erotic love. Dante – quoting Virgil's Dido – will say of his own passionate response when Beatrice appears before him in her chariot, "I recognize the signs of the old passion" ("Conosco i segni dell'antica fiamma" [*Purg.* XXX.48 – see Chapter 12]). Something is the same here, however much is different. Something is preserved, however much is repudiated.

I shall now try to trace the "signs of the old passion" in Augustine and, in the next chapter, in Dante, both of whom explicitly set themselves the task of rewriting and correcting the pagan ascent of love. For each there are deep psychological links between earthly and heavenly love; for each it is important to argue that the good Christian life is more volatile and erotic than the Platonic tradition has wished love to be. They represent different points of view within the Christian tradition, and I shall be investigating their differences, as well as their shared ideas. I cannot hope to do justice to the whole thought of either about love, since both have careers of great internal complexity. In the case of Dante, I shall focus on the *Commedia*. In the case of Augustine, I shall focus on several works written just after his conversion, and then on a transitional period leading up to the *Confessions*. I shall allude more briefly to some later arguments in *The City of God*.

III. THE PLATONIC LADDER AND RATIONAL SELF-SUFFICIENCY

Augustine is a disciple as well as a critic of the Platonist ascent. Profoundly influenced by Neoplatonic versions of the *Symposium*'s ladder of love,[3] he uses these ideas, early in his career, as positive paradigms for the Christian life that can easily be recast in Christian terms. I shall argue that in early works such as *De quantitate animae* and *De Genesi contra Manicheos*, Augustine endorses a Platonist characterization of the contrast between earthly love and perfected love, holding up the contemplative self-sufficiency of the philosopher as a goal both available to and good for the faithful Christian in this life. The good Christian life becomes, as it goes on, a life progressively emptied of erotic longing and tension. Later, however, Augustine comes to think this view of ascent unacceptable: the goal it promises is both unavailable and inappropriate. In the *Confessions* he advances a picture of ascent (or ascent combined with descent) that gives a more substantial and more positive role to certain ingredients of ordinary human love.[4]

In the Platonist tradition, Augustine found an account of love's ascent that emphasized the self-sufficiency of the intellect, as it moves from stage to stage, and the complete self-sufficiency of the lover, when he or she reaches the final stage. At the top of the ladder, the philosopher, contemplating the fine and good, is free from all neediness and dependency, both internal and external. The object of his contemplation is eternal and unchanging; it never varies in quality or relation.

3 I do not take any stand on the vexed question of whether Augustine actually read Plotinus, or only heard of the views at second hand. This is irrelevant to my argument, since he clearly is familiar in a general way with the structure of the Platonist contemplative ascent.

4 My account of Augustine's development is close to that advanced in Brown (1967), a work for which I have much admiration. In many respects I am simply giving more elaboration and philosophical structure to the picture he has laid out. But I believe that he has not presented a complete picture of the arguments that lead Augustine to reject the Platonic ascent: see note 9 to this chapter.

The person who contemplates it is therefore entirely secure – nothing that happens in the world can alter or diminish his happy activity. At the same time, the philosophical lover is internally stable, minimally dependent on internal passions that might distract him from contemplation. His intellect, which contemplates the eternal forms, becomes increasingly like what it contemplates, pure and unvarying, impassive and hard. Its activities, completely transparent to the lover, yield accounts embodying truth and true excellence. He is the one lover who has gotten beyond the tension of erotic longing, since he has found an object that satisfies his longing to "be with" the beloved always.

In Plotinus' version of the *Symposium* ascent, the one that most influenced Augustine,[5] it becomes clear that even the lover's mortality is no impediment to the full perfection of his bliss. For the acts of the perfected intellect do not take place in time at all (*Enn.* I.5); thus the lover's bliss does not depend on time for increase or completion. Longer is not better; or rather, there really is no 'longer' when one is dealing with contemplation. Plotinus states unambiguously that the person who pursues a philosophical ascent correctly can achieve in this life a complete and self-sufficient state, beyond all seeking:

What then is the good for him? He is what he has, his own good . . . The person in this state does not seek for anything else; for what could he seek? Certainly not anything worse, and he has the best with him. The person who has a life like this has all he needs in life. (I.4.4, cf. I.6.9)

Such a person, ceasing to need, ceases to be erotic.

In many ways, Augustine sets himself in the Platonist ascent tradition. Repeatedly, he uses the metaphor of ascent to speak of the Christian development of love and desire. He sometimes enumerates the stages of this ascent in a manner that shows the influence of the Platonist texts that moved him. Repeatedly, too, he speaks of the disdain for earthly love that is so much stressed by Plato as a product of ascent. And he seems to endorse the central structural principle used by Plato to explain how love can move upward: the fundamental kinship of all

---

5 Because we cannot be sure in what version Augustine encountered Plotinus (see note 3), it is all the less clear how, precisely, he interpreted various disputed points in Plotinus' complex and contested text. I reconstruct his Neoplatonism, simply, from his own doctrines in the works under discussion.

fine things. In two early works, however,[6] Augustine goes beyond these general Platonist commitments – which persist in some form throughout his career. Here he embraces a more thoroughgoing Platonism, defending the life of contemplative self-sufficiency as a valuable and available Christian ideal.

The complex philosophical dialogue *De Quantitate Animae* ends with an account of the ascent of the soul from vegetative and sensory life to contemplative perfection. The ascent has seven stages (70ff.). The soul progresses to each new stage by freeing itself from impediments to contemplation. Intellect and will are the propelling forces in its movement. The first three stages bring the human being to ordinary adulthood. On top of the nutritive and vegetative life with which he is born, he quickly develops the use of his perceptual faculties and, later, the arts and abilities of reason. Only at stage four does he begin to reject any of the influences and activities of earlier stages. Here, Augustine says, is where true goodness begins (73). In stages four, five, and six, the soul gradually detaches itself from the influences of the body and the senses. From the painful struggle against worldly distraction that characterizes stage four,[7] it moves, by intellectual effort and strength of will, to the purity of stage five, as the soul "holds itself most joyfully in itself" (74). At this point the soul has a conception of its own power; at this point, then, it can turn itself outward, in stage six, to contemplation of truth (75). It now may advance, in stage seven, to the perfection of contemplation.

As the soul advances, its confidence grows, soon excluding all anxiety and uncertainty. At stage four the soul still feels some fear of death, though a fear tempered by the thought of divine Providence. By stage five, however, the soul advances toward contemplation "with a huge and unbelievable confidence."[8] In stage six, the soul's desire for truth is described as "most perfect," "best," "most correct" (75). Nowhere

---

6 Both works are dated to 388 C.E.: they are thus among his earliest postconversion writings.

7 ". . . labor, et contra huius mundi molestias atque blanditias magnus acerrimusque conflictus" (73).

8 "Ingenti quadam et incredibili fiducia pergit in Deum, id est, in ipsam contemplationem veritatis." One can see here how superficial the Christian modification to the Platonist conception has been: the name of God is explicated by a reference to the contemplation of truth.

after the conflict of stage four is there any serious opposition to the movement of the rational will, which has now been "freed," "purified," "cured." Indeed, by stage six we are told that intellect itself has "purified itself and freed itself from all desire and corruption of mortal things" (75).[9] At the last stage the ascent is completed in the perfection of philosophical self-sufficiency, a state which, Augustine assures us, has been attained by outstanding people in this life:

We have now arrived at the vision and contemplation of truth, which is the seventh and final step. Nor is it a step any longer, but a kind of stopping place to which these steps lead up. What its joys are, what the full enjoyment of the highest and true good is like, what serenity and eternity is in the air – how can I describe all this? It has been described by certain great and incomparable souls, insofar as they thought it ought to be described, souls whom we believe to have seen these things, and to be seeing them still. (76)

In *De Genesi contra Manichaeos*, Augustine depicts a similar process of ascent. The soul travels, again, through seven stages. The stages are now mapped onto the seven days of the Creation, a procedure that produces some changes in their order and content. The nature of the final stage, however, emerges with particular clarity. After six "days" of action and motion, there is a stopping place, a "day" of rest. Purified from all sin and bodily distraction, "having spiritual fruits, that is, good reflections (*cogitationes*) by virtue of the stability of his mind," the human being can now have a rest and a peace that are truly comparable to God's peace: the peace of perfection, null disturbance, and clear sight: "After the very good works of these (so to speak) six days, let the human being hope for perpetual rest, and let him understand what it means to say, 'On the seventh day God rested from all his works' " (I.25).

In these two passages, Augustine takes over all of the essentials of the Platonist ascent tradition, with minor modifications, as a description of an available and good Christian life. As soon as the person weans himself from the influence of the temporal and the sensible, he achieves a remarkable independence. Intellect propels itself continuously upward, interested only in its own self-sufficient activity. It generates its own motion, waiting for nothing, receptive to nothing. (Even

---

9 "Ipsa cogitatio ab omni cupiditate ac faece rerum mortalium sese cohibuerit et eliquaverit." Compare the reflexive verbs of Brunetto Latini in Dante's Hell – see Chapter 12.

the receptivity of faith, not mentioned at all in *De quantitate*, figures in *De Genesi* only as the early precondition for the beginning of intellectual activity, in stage one. Once intellect takes over, it no longer plays a role.) Because of this extraordinary freedom from circumstance, the soul's aim is completely fulfilled. Ascent and motion cease in consequence. The seventh step is no step at all, but the quiet dwelling place (*mansio*) at the top of the steps. The seventh "day" is no "day" of action at all, but a "day of rest," in which the soul exists outside of change. Breathing the air of eternity, the previously aspiring human being knows what it means to say that God rested from his labors. And, as the Platonic ascent would have it, he is godlike in his rest, he takes the place of God in God's own story.

IV. INCOMPLETENESS AND THE UNCERTAINTY OF GRACE

As we can see already, this "air" of serenity and eternity is not the air that Augustine is breathing in the *Confessions*. Nor is the Platonist goal endorsed in that work as one appropriate for a Christian life. From the *Confessions* itself, and from a roughly contemporary work, the *Ad Simplicianum de diversis quaestionibus* (A.D. 396), we can elicit Augustine's reasons for turning from the Platonist picture. Augustine's criticisms of Platonism fall into two categories. He argues, first, that the Platonist goal is not attainable in this life; second, that it is not, in any case, a good or appropriate Christian aim.[10]

Augustine's Platonist works insisted that the perfected life has been lived by actual human beings. The ascent involves a difficult struggle, but the struggle can be won. By the time of the *Confessions*, however, Augustine is no longer sanguine about this possibility. The desires and activities of our fleshly existence, to which we are strongly bound by both habit and memory, are a heavier load than the Platonist tradition believes. The Platonist, who speaks of casting off the burdens of the body, underestimates the tightness of the link between soul and body, the extent of the pressures that drive even the most zealous soul back to its old habits. Augustine's deep grief at his mother's death, for

---

10 Brown stresses the first group of arguments. Even his chapter title, "The Lost Future," implies that some goal, still desirable, is simply being found to be unavailable. But I believe that the second group of arguments has even greater importance.

example – which he could not assuage even by the most earnest prayer – "impressed on my memory by this one piece of evidence the strength of the chains of habit, even against a mind that is no longer fed on deceiving words" (*Conf.* IX.12). One can never correct oneself fully enough, watch one's impulses carefully enough. The power of sexual desire, the distractions of worldly cares, so mar his efforts to contemplate that he now concludes that Platonist bliss is entirely unavailable to a human being in this life. He mourns the loss of this high hope:

At some moments you admit me into a feeling that is very unlike my usual state. If it were perfectly accomplished in me it would be I know not what – but it never shall be in this life. The painful weights drag me down again to things here. I am reabsorbed in my habits. I am held fast, and I weep a great deal, but still I am very much held fast. Such is the power of the burden of custom. Here I am able to stay, but unwilling; there I will to be, but I am not able. I am wretched on account of both places.

However much A may try to sever her connection to M and to their bodily pleasure, the habits of that love and the desire that power it will seize her unawares, impeding her progress.

There is another reason why the ascent cannot take place as the Platonist depicts it: Plato has omitted a crucial causal factor, which is not within the individual's own control. In *Confessions* VIII, Augustine tells us that the central defect of the Platonist books is their failure to mention grace and to depict the ascending soul as waiting, always, for grace. "No man says there, 'Shall not my soul wait upon God, seeing that from him cometh my salvation?' " (VIII.21). Augustine retrojects these criticisms to the time preceding his conversion; but, as his early postconversion works show, they did not dawn on him until somewhat later. The crucial turning point seems to have been in the account of grace he gives to Simplicianus.

Simplicianus has asked Augustine to explicate a verse from Paul's Epistle to the Romans: "It is not in the power of the one who wills, nor of the one who runs, but in the power of God, who has pity" (IX.16: "neque volentis neque currentis sed miserentis est Dei"). Interpreting the verse, Augustine argues that the human being cannot hope by his own will and effort to be adequate for his own salvation. His own activity – both external (running) and internal (willing) – always proves insufficient. Or to put it more precisely, his own effort is insufficient for the right sort of internal and external activity. Right willing itself, he now insists, depends upon desire for a good object; and desire itself is a response of delight and love that is summoned up in us by an external call and is not perfectly ours to control. Unless something "happens our way" ("*occurat*") which delights and moves the soul's faculty of desire in the appropriate manner, the will can in no way be moved. "But that this something should happen our way, is not in the power of the human being" (*Ad Simplic.* I.Qu 2.22). We can be moved to faith and appropriate effort only by being struck in such a way that our will is correctly set in motion. "But who embraces in his soul something that gives him no delight? And who has it in his power to determine that that which can delight him should happen his way, or to determine that it should delight him when it does happen his way?" (I.Qu 2.21). Different people are moved and touched in different ways, by different sorts of external calls (14); desire's responses are idiosyncratic, unpredictable, and not transparent to reason. God's call may come to us in such a way that it moves us, or it may not. He may choose to move us to delight and love (for He always *can* do this), or He may allow our hearts to remain cold (16). This may seem unfair; but these are the ways of God's secret justice, which we cannot hope to understand. As Paul has written, "He pities those he wishes, and He hardens those he wishes" ("*quem vult obdurat*"). And there is no reliable relationship between the character of our human efforts and the likelihood of being called in the requisite way. As Brown writes, "Augustine now moves in a world of 'love at first sight,' of chance encounters, and, just as important, of sudden, equally inexplicable patches of deadness."[11]

Thus A, as Augustine's Christian, ascending not through the pure and active intellect, but through the complex psychology of receptivity and love, is deeply at the mercy of contingency, in two ways. She must depend for ascent not on her own self-control but on aspects of her personality that she neither governs nor fully understands. And these responsive elements in her personality depend, in turn, for their happy activation, on the mysterious ways of God's call. She cannot count on a stable perfection. Such progress as she does make is not made primarily through her own effort. The future, as Brown's chapter title puts

11 Brown (1967), p. 155.

it, is "lost." Her story is one of unending longing, of bewilderment and unstable motion. God is indeed eternal, perfect, and just, whereas the objects of earthly love are inconstant, mutable, and liable to moral error. But the inscrutability of that justice and the seeming arbitrariness of that perfection make A's subjective experience as a Christian lover very much like her old love.

Does Augustine still think of the Platonist ascent as good for Christian humans, yet sadly unavailable? Or does his new moral psychology lead, at the same time, to the creation of a new Christian norm? I think that the second is clearly the right option: the Platonist ladder is an altogether inappropriate path for the good Christian soul. It is in this line of argument that we find the really deep contribution of Augustine to the ascent tradition we are following.

Let us return to the difficulties for Platonism that come from the power and significance of memory. It is clearly Augustine's view that we *cannot* free ourselves altogether from psychological continuity with our past through memory and habit. We are bound indissolubly to the parts of ourselves that cause moral trouble by their undependability, their independence of control by reason. Above all, in *Confessions*, our sexuality serves Augustine as an example of the ungovernable from which we can never sever ourselves, for it exerts its influence even in our dreams (X.30).

The Platonist project, then, is doomed. But I believe it is just as clearly Augustine's view that we *ought not* dissociate ourselves from our past in the way that the Platonist urges. Certainly we can and must combat the sinful urges that are fed by a certain sort of memory. But memory is also crucial to a person's sense of identity and continuity in time. A really successful dissociation of the self from memory would be a total loss of the self – and thus of all the activities to which a sense of one's own identity is important. "I cannot comprehend the power of my memory," Augustine writes, "since I cannot even call myself myself apart from it" (X.16).

But this means that without memory, which with its links to sin makes perfection impossible, the soul cannot progress at all. The search for goodness, self-knowledge, and knowledge of God that the *Confessions* movingly records presupposes, throughout, Augustine's own sense of himself as a continuous temporal being. This temporal history may be a non-necessary property of his soul; it is still crucial to his salvation. Self-knowledge, insofar as he achieves it, is said to be a "fruit" of confession, that is, of an activity that centrally involves the drawing forth of his past through memory. His search for God, he explicitly declares, must be carried out "in the fields and broad meadows of memory, where there are treasure chests of innumerable images brought in from things of all sorts experienced by the senses" (X.8). Memory is a capricious faculty. It does not always obey the will, nor is its material always available for deliberate inspection. But Augustine cannot have its fruits without its difficulties and darkness. To cut it away, as the Platonist ascent urges, would be to forfeit the sense of self, therefore to cease to aspire and to love:

I do these things within, in the vast court of my memory. For there I have at my disposal the sky, the earth, the sea, along with everything that I have been able to experience in them – and, in addition, all the things I have forgotten. There I myself happen upon myself (*mihi occurro*). And I recollect what, when, and where I did something, and how, when I did it, I was affected. (X.8)

The Platonist, in cutting away from A all susceptibility to contingent occurrences, cuts away the susceptibility to an occurrence that is central to growth and knowledge: the one in which a person "happens across" himself. The use of the vocabulary of the *Ad Simplicianum* is no accident. Human development is irreformably a matter of happening. An adequate view of moral growth must be built on this psychological reality.

The Platonist might attempt to counter this objection. Surely, he could say, we can allow ourselves to retain, in memory, enough connectedness with our past to ground the sense of self and of personal continuity, without retaining the sinful memories that vex our contemplative efforts. As for these, if we can rid ourselves of them, we certainly ought to do so; and we need not fear that in so doing we will be lost to ourselves. Augustine would probably deny this as a psychological claim. For, to judge from what he sees fit to remember and record in the *Confessions*, so much of his history is taken up with sin that very little basis for his sense of personal continuity would survive if the memory of all that were erased. Indeed, he believes that the normal course of every human life, from infancy onward, is thoroughly steeped in sin. But even were he to concede to the opponent this point about connectedness, he has a further argument that would suffice to take him to his anti-Platonist conclusion. This argument concerns the connection between memory and responsibility.

In Augustine's view, every deed one has ever committed is a deed for which one is going to be judged by God. The Christian, therefore, in order to be maximally prepared for this judgment and maximally able to make an adequate confession, must be not less mindful of his past than another, but more mindful, not less concerned with what his bodily self has done, but more concerned. He must cultivate a very keen sense of his own continuity and unity. He must dredge up the past, rather than severing himself from it. To use the words in which Nietzsche perceptively analyzes the operations of the Christian "bad conscience," he must, working on himself, "breed an animal with the right to make promises."[12] The work of self-recollection and self-scrutiny carried out in the *Confessions* would seem both unproductive and risky to a Platonist; to a Christian it is of the deepest importance. On the other side, the Platonist curriculum of progressive dissociation from the bodily self and progressive identification with the pure intellect would seem to the Christian the creation of a fiction about the self that impedes true self-knowledge and appropriate responsibility.[13] To live with these fruits of memory, however, is to live, as well, with all of its hazards. When you explore the meaning of your past, you cannot guarantee, nor does Augustine think you can, that the power of the past will not surprise you. The Christian can only, then, take the risks and confess continually.

Furthermore, and most important of all, this world of chance encounters is the only world in which a Christian can live in the correct relation to God. The Platonist goal of godlike self-sufficiency is now seen by Augustine as a form of deep impiety. To pursue such a goal is to commit the sin of pride, which is based on the belief that one can

---

12 See *Genealogy of Morals* II. The extent of Nietzsche's sympathy with Augustine's project should not be underestimated: for Nietzsche, this "bad conscience," though unfortunately linked in the Christian tradition with hatred of this world and of the body, is also the "pregnancy" out of which all great creative achievement and all philosophy must grow.

13 Here there would appear to be an especially sharp critique of Plotinus, *Ennead* I.6 (much indebted to Plato's *Symposium*), where self-knowledge is equated with knowledge of the *good* that you are. Once again, it may be disputed precisely how Plotinus understands the role of the bodily in the perception of beauty; but it is reasonable to suppose that Augustine understood Neoplatonic doctrine to urge a progressive separation of soul from bodily distraction.

live according to oneself and under one's own control. The *Ad Simpli-cianum* makes it clear that a recognition of the uncertainty of grace and of God's decisive power over our internal, as well as external, lives was an essential part of being a good Christian. Openness, waiting, longing, groaning become forms of worship and acknowledgment. If you are a human being, the sort of being who does not suffice for its own salvation, it is a deep sin to live and think as if you were sufficient. As Augustine later writes in *The City of God,* "What is pride but a craving for perverse elevation? For it is perverse elevation to forsake the ground in which the mind ought to be rooted and to become, and to be, grounded in oneself" (XIV.13). Love, we might say, should not ascend too high, or prop its ladder on the wrong sort of ground.

If we now look ahead to the more systematic theoretical development Augustine gives these issues in *The City of God,* we find that the entirety of the ancient ethical project, with human flourishing in this world as its central goal, is denounced as infected by pride:

But those who have supposed that the ultimate good and evil are to be found in the present life . . . all these persons have sought, with a surprising vanity, to be happy in this life and to get happiness by their own efforts . . . Those philosophers . . . strive to manufacture for themselves in this life an utterly counterfeit flourishing by drawing on a virtue whose fraudulence matches its arrogance. (XIX.4)

But this means that the emotions, defined in the Stoic–Spinozistic way as recognitions of our bondage to the external, reenter the best life as forms of human excellence and appropriate rationality. For it is appropriate to acknowledge the truth; and emotions are acknowledgments of the truth of our profound neediness. The Stoics who taught the extirpation of passion are now repudiated as "interested in words more than in truth" (XIV.9). The City of God has a different standard of public and private rationality:

Among us Christians, on the other hand, in accordance with the Holy Scriptures and their healthy doctrine, the citizens of the holy City of God, living in accordance with God in the pilgrimage of this present life, fear and passionately desire, grieve and rejoice, [14] and because their love is right, all these emotions of theirs are right. (XIV.9)

14 "metuunt cupiuntque, dolent gaudentque": here Augustine succinctly lists the four well-known generic categories of passion in Stoic taxonomies, all of which the Stoic would seek to extirpate. (The taxonomy is arranged along two axes: a temporal axis

The difference is made by the rightness of the object of the Christian's love and fear and joy. Augustine does not disagree with the Stoics that it is inappropriate to have emotions about earthly events and persons, seen as needed by the self. The other world is the object of this longing: "They fear eternal punishment, they passionately desire eternal life. They grieve because they are still groaning within themselves, waiting for the redemption of their bodies; they rejoice in hope because 'there shall come to pass the saying that is written: Death is swallowed up in victory.'" (XIV.9)

After enumerating other proper occasions for Christian emotion – both self-regarding and on behalf of others whose salvation the Christian desires – Augustine proves his point by going carefully through the careers, first of Paul, then of Jesus, and demonstrating with ample citations the range of emotions that were exemplified in their virtuous lives. He insists that Christ's emotions were not feigned, but genuine, since he was really human and really suffering in a human body. When, then, we read of his anger and grief, we must not doctor the reports – we must take them to heart, as paradigms for ourselves (XIV.9). And we must conclude from this example that even though emotions may at times mislead us, no good life would be possible without them. To those who argue that the good Christian may have *caritas* or *dilectio* (translating the Greek *agapê*) but not *amor*, Augustine replies with extensive textual argument, showing that the emotion of Peter toward Christ is described by both Peter and Christ as *amor*, and that both words can be used of appropriate, as well as inappropriate, emotions (XIV.7).[15]

As for those who exalt the *apatheia* of the Stoic wise man, they are doubly foolish. For "if *apatheia* is that condition in which no fear frightens and no grief pains, it must be avoided in this life if we wish to live rightly, that is, according to God." And, furthermore, "if *apath*-

---

[present/future] and a good/bad axis: see Nussbaum [1994], Chapter 10.) In XIV.8, Augustine has quoted Virgil's enumeration of the four categories: "Hine metuunt cupiuntque, dolent gaudentque" (*Aen.* 6.278–9). His general aim in that chapter is to show that these emotions can belong (as can will, *voluntas*) to both good and bad alike.

15 The Latin *amor* and *amare* of Augustine's version of John 21 translate Greek *philia* and *phileô*; not surprisingly, Jesus did not ask Peter, "Do you have *erôs* for me?" But since Augustine's version occludes the distinction between *philia* and *erôs*, so too, in many ways, does his discussion.

eia is defined as that condition in which no emotion at all can touch the soul, who would not consider this stupor worse than any of the vices?" (XIV.9)

The example of Christ indicates that it is not always wrong to have emotions about earthly people and events. The Christian, however, following Christ, will not view attachments to others as deep personal needs. The deep need of all is for salvation, and appropriate emotions ultimately have that focus. Thus Christ suffered and grieved because he was still in the body and in the world; he longed for the perfection of Heaven. Even his pity for humans (as we shall see at greater length in the following section) focuses on the impediments to their salvation. It is real pity, because Christ (and, following him, the good Christian) really loves human beings and views their moral blindness as a really painful diminution of his life (see also IX.5). On the other hand, the pity focuses at all times on the distance of humans from the perfected condition: it does not treat life's reversals and pains as bad in and of themselves.

In short, the difference between the City of God and the earthly city lies not in the presence of strong emotions, but in the emotions' choice of objects. And in a sense the diseased, swollen earthly city is closer to God, because more passionate, more willing to turn outward and to search for an adequate object, than the torpid city of the Stoic wise man, wrapped in its own fatal pride. Such people, "not roused or stirred, not swayed or inclined by any emotion at all, rather lose all humanity than attain true tranquillity. For the fact that something is tough does not make it right, and the fact that something is inert does not make it healthy."[16] (XIV.9) Ascent must take place within the context of our humanity, not by attempting, out of pride, to depart from it.

V. THE VIRTUE OF LONGING

We are now prepared to understand what we find in the *Confessions*: a love of God characterized not by a neat intellectual progression toward contemplative purity, but by a pervasive sense of longing, incompleteness, and passivity. This love has more in common with the

---

16 "Non enim quia durum aliquid, ideo rectum, aut quia stupidum est, ideo sanum."

Platonic picture of ordinary love than with its reformed version. The metaphor of ascent still appears, but rarely. In its place we tend to find the image of a journey that goes on and on – especially a journey deep into the inner spaces of the mind. We even find images of a *descent* of the soul into itself, with proper humility. Instead of exaltation, we find poverty and lowness, dust and ashes (e.g., X.28, I.6); instead of the fullness of the Platonist soul, emptiness and barrenness (e.g., X.28, II.10); instead of the ease with which that soul, once purified, turns to contemplation, we find toil and labor (e.g., X.39, X.16, X.40); instead of safety, danger (X.35, 39); instead of light, darkness and obscurity, fog and mist (II.2, X.5). Instead of purity and health, we find sickness, hunger, and thirst; God is invoked as "my intimate doctor" (X.3, II.10; X.27, 28, 43).

Augustine plainly views himself as continually in danger. He stresses his openness to external happenings, depicting himself as a container (I.2, 3) that stands open to receive what God will choose to pour in (I.2, 5). Nor does he feel confident that his own internal processes are fully under his own control. In his own aspiration he exemplifies the very difficulties about grace that he describes theoretically in the *Ad Simplicianum*. For he prays that God should present Himself to him, happen his way, in such a manner that his soul may be moved by love and delight:

Hear, Lord, my prayer. Let my soul not fall short under your discipline . . . so that you might become sweeter to me than all enticements that I used to follow, and so that I might love you most firmly and embrace your hand with all the strength of my heart. (I.15)[17]

Through prayer, Augustine can make a powerful effort to become responsive to the right, and only the right, stimuli. But this effort does not guarantee success.

The final aim of this earthly lover, like that of his Platonist counterpart, is a complete union with the beloved object, in which all desire and emotion will at last be stilled. But this goal is now seen to be both impossible and inappropriate to this life:

When I shall be united to you in every part of myself, there will be for me no more sorrow or toil, and my life will be alive, in every way full of you.

---

17 Cf. X.29: "O love, you who always burn and are never extinguished, divine love, my God, set me on fire."

But now . . . since I am not yet full of you, I am a burden to myself. My joys, which ought to be lamented, contend against my sorrows, concerning which I ought to rejoice. And which way the victory will go, I do not know. (X.28)

The first part of the passage points to the unattainability of the lover's aim while human life continues. The equally important second half insists that the sorrow arising from unattainability is precisely what the Christian ought to value for himself in this life, the pride of a human joy just what he should avoid. [18] What is appropriate to this life is not erotic union, but erotic longing, distance, incompleteness. The wanderings of Aeneas have been rejected in favor of wanderings even more painful and laborious; and Augustine resembles Dido more than he does the somewhat Stoic Aeneas, whose journey was prompted by *pietas* rather than by love. The subjectivity of the two states has great similarity; the moral difference, which is huge, is made by the difference in their objects.

A now wants to know where we are with our account of the continuity and discontinuity between human and divine love. If she takes the Christian path rather than the one the Platonists map out for her, where will she find herself? One way to let her know will be to tell her a love story, and to let her see whose story it seems to be.

Imagine, then, we tell her, that you have for many years been deeply involved in a passionate relationship that has brought you neither stable satisfaction nor a quiet conscience. You have felt yourself to be the slave of forces beyond your control, both external and internal. You feel that your entire life is out of order. (She will have no trouble telling herself this, for all this is in fact her story.) For the sake of living and living well, you feel that you ought to turn away from the person whom you have loved, blinding yourself to that person's beauty and power, closing yourself to the deep influence that your response to this beauty exercises over imagination and action. You see that to succeed in this you must not merely avoid the immediate stimulus of that person's physical presence; you must also close off his access to your feelings through habit and memory, and the memory of habit, and the habit of remembering.

While you are struggling with these things, with uneven success, you are suddenly struck – briefly and obscurely, in an uncertain, momen-

18 Cf. also *Epistles* XXVII.I: he finds delight in his very longing.

tary encounter – by another person. You feel strangely moved. You see your own responses only dimly: you cannot even begin to describe what has happened. You are exhilarated; you have a sense of motion toward something, a vague, undefinable hope. And yet you feel hopelessly far from whatever it is you want from this person, far even from being able to say what it is you want. After all, you know almost nothing about the object of this longing. You can barely give him a name. All you can do is to learn from others about who he is and what he has done. And this increases both your interest and your sense of distance. You feel convinced that this hope is the hope of a better and more fruitful life, if you could only allow yourself to be touched by it deeply enough to change. You want to respond. You also want to want to respond. But at the same time, of necessity, you continue on with the old life, since that is where your life is lived. You easily become reabsorbed in your old relationship; and when you are reabsorbed you find that you do not even want to care about anything or anyone else. The power of habit and the memory of your own previous actions and feelings, stand between you and any change. You know that what must happen now is that the new person must approach you and call to you. And you must respond. But you know that you cannot guarantee your own response. He must call to you in just the right way, so that you will respond. You hope that you will be such, and that the call will be such, that your life will change; but you do not control this. You want it to happen, but you do not control happenings. What is more, you do not even see or become aware of all that is happening. You know that much of the drama is being played out in depths of memory that are not fully accessible to consciousness. You do not, however, want to sever yourself from memory and its power. For your history, as the person who has those memories and has loved that powerful love, is constitutive of whatever you are and bring to anything new in life. If the new lover does not call to and move that, it is not you that he calls and moves.

So you go about, feeling sick a great deal of the time, and powerless, and ugly;[19] feeling thirsty, and dark, and endangered. Whether you will be united with the person and life that you long to want, or whether the power of habit and the obtuseness of desire will hold you where

---

19 Cf. *Conf.* X.27: "in ista formosa deformis inruebam."

you are – this is, to you, the most mysterious matter in the world. You feel like a child lost in a dark wood.[20] And yet it is not that you long for a life without these pains and risks, a life lived in your own power. For you obscurely judge that this contest full of bewilderment and exposure, motion and tension, is the only way to deal, humanly, with these human questions.

The drama of Christian love in Augustine is something like this human love story. It is similar both in structure and in subjective experience. But we can now take one further step, following the lead of the anti-Stoic arguments of *The City of God*. Human love and Christian love, human emotion and Christian emotion, are not merely two similar stories. They are two parts of the same story. There is only one faculty of love and desire in the human being; the only way a human being changes in her love is to redirect that same love toward a new object. It is the same love that loves Dido and loves God. The change from earthly love to heavenly love is not, then, for Augustine, simply *like* my story of the person who changes lovers. It is one *example* of that story. And whether your life story plays out that example of change or some other – this, we already know, is not up to you. So much depends on how you are called, and how you like it when and if you are. So, we might finally say, whether your life is the human story of a change from M to N, or whether the N who happens your way and calls and moves you is in fact God – all this is a part of the drama of human love and a matter of inscrutable mystery. But to live in that mystery and that openness of expectation is (if, in God's judgment, it turns out to be so) the good life for a human being.

VI. THE MERELY PROVISIONAL WORLD

It should be clear by now why I regard Augustine's account of the Christian ascent as a major philosophical achievement and a decisive progress beyond the Platonic accounts: because it situates ascent within humanity and renounces the wish to depart from our human condition. I have suggested that any attempt to reform human love so as to make it more compatible with general social aims must criticize the wish of the infantile lover for possession and control, fashioning, within the

20 Cf. *Conf.* X.4, 35.

ascent, a new wish and a new aim. This Augustine does, in the process recapturing much of our humanity that the Platonists have cast aside.

Does Augustine's ascent solve the three problems the Platonists claimed to solve? It would appear that it does solve the problem of unevenness or partiality. In loving God, A also loves the entire world of God's creation. In loving God in humanity, she really does see all human beings as equal; and the Christian idea that all human beings are equal in the sight of God has certainly been among the foundational ideas in moving society toward equal concern for the deprived, the poor, and the different. As Augustine writes in the *Homilies on the First Epistle of John*, "You ought to wish all men to be your equals . . . He is your brother, alike you are bought; one is the price paid for you and you are both redeemed by the blood of Christ." Excessive neediness, as well, is cast aside, since A relies on an object that can never fail her, however inscrutable its operations may be.

About revenge and anger there is surely, however, room for doubt. In relying on God's justice and God's mercy, and in fashioning her emotions after that norm, A will not extirpate all anger, and indeed she will retain a desire to take revenge upon God's enemies. It was not without reason that Nietzsche stressed the vengeful elements in Christianity. Although it was surely hasty of him to conclude that these elements reveal the essential goal of Christian ethics to be revenge by the weak against the strong, and thus revenge on the very conditions of human life itself, nonetheless there is a disturbing emphasis on anger in Augustine, which might make us reconsider his attack on Stoic *apatheia*. Spinoza, following the Stoics, believes a central goal of the ascent of love to be the transcendence of anger and hatred, which poison human relations. His ideas of religious toleration seem a distinct advance over many of the Christian views they criticize.

We can agree with Augustine in thinking that at least some occasions for anger will remain in the best life – anger, for example, against various types of harm and injustice – without being convinced that he has circumscribed this passion sufficiently, where social relations are concerned. So much of Augustine's literary output expresses anger – against heretics, pagans, unbelievers, Jews. Anger and hatred based on the mere fact that someone follows a different religious conception, or even none at all – these are elements of Augustinian Christianity with which modern Christians have to wrestle, in fashioning a Christianity that can join with other religions in a pluralistic society. And certainly Augustine is no friend to such a pluralist politics: he pursues, instead, a politics of anger and retribution based on the dominance of the one true doctrine – in a dogmatic way that frequently seems in deep tension with his own admissions of the uncertainty and the mystery at the heart of human life.

But instead of pursuing this line further – and we will certainly return to it in subsequent chapters – let us now examine the three areas of social life in which the Platonist ascent seemed to have its greatest difficulties, asking whether Augustine's reformulation avoids those difficulties.

At this point, it is inevitable that what I say will take a stand on religious matters on which readers will differ. Even to assess the Augustinian project from the point of view of an ideal of social relations that contains no explicit religious commitment is a project that the committed Christian may view as not quite the right way to go about things. And of course there will be found in any group of readers many varieties of Christian belief, and of other forms of religious and secular moral commitment, that will influence their response to what is said. To put my cards on the table, then, what I shall say henceforth is said from the point of view of someone who has converted from Christianity to Judaism, and whose undertanding of Judaism gives the moral sphere considerable autonomy and centrality, seeing the concern of God for man as essentially moral and political, focused on this-worldly concerns and actions, and intelligible from the point of view of a this-worldly use of intelligence.[21] It is in order to investigate the relationship between Judaism and the Christian ascent that I have chosen to focus upon Mahler in Chapter 14, and I shall have more to say about these matters at that time. I shall now address my three questions, though in a different order.

1. *Individuality.* In loving God, Augustine emphasizes, one loves each and every human being – not only the good parts but also the flaws and faults, and not only as stepping stones to one's own artwork but in themselves. At the same time, it is a little unclear what role is left in *The Confessions* for loving real-life individual people. For what one loves above all in them is the presence of God and the hope of

---

21 See my "Judaism and the Love of Reason" (1999d).

salvation. As Hannah Arendt puts it well in *Love and Saint Augustine*, "[T]he lover reaches beyond the beloved to God in whom alone both his existence and his love have meaning . . . The Christian can thus love all people because each one is only an occasion, and that occasion can be everyone." (96) There is therefore a question about the extent to which the individual is really loved as such, as either a separate life or a qualitatively particular life. I postpone that question here, however, since it will be a major theme of my discussion of Dante in Chapter 12.

2. *Reciprocity.* Does this love acknowledge the importance of reciprocity, and a respect for human agency, both in the love relationship and in other social relationships that may be affected by it? It would be impossible to answer this fully without an extensive account of other works of Augustine's; but, confining ourselves to the texts we have discussed, there are certainly questions in this area, because there are questions about precisely what the lover's attitude toward fellow humans is to be. Augustine portrays the ascending Christian as radically isolated in her confessional zeal, retreating from the world to be alone with God. There is some question as to how this confessing lover can be said to have a neighbor at all.

I have said that there is a recognition of human equality, and this seems clear. But the equality that the solitary lover perceives in her acts of confession is an equality of abjectness, sinfulness, and need. In our common descent from Adam, that is to say, in our original sinfulness, is the foundation of our fellowship: in the *Confessions*, fellow citizens are companions in fate, participants in a situation of mortality (X.4.6). "The whole world was guilty from Adam," Augustine writes in a later text, *Against Julian the Pelagian*. And in *The City of God* (1.9), again, our fellowship is to be found in our wickedness as members of the world of sin. It is this thought of peril that, according to Augustine, impels us toward our neighbor (*Comm. on Paul's Epistle to the Galatians* 56).

The doctrine of original sin will be assessed in different ways by different readers, in keeping with their religious and experiential views. To me, as expressed here, it is a doctrine that diminishes the force of this-worldly moral distinctions based on this-worldly conduct and acts. It seems wrong to equate all humans in their sinfulness, and wrong to base social relations on a recognition of equal sinfulness. There is, I think, too much abjectness in this, too much unwillingness to grant that a human being may in fact become, and be, good, and that there is all the world of difference between the evil and the good. This entails a related failure to acknowledge individuality: each is treated as sinful, even before each has had a chance to live a life. The idea that in Adam we all sin is surely intended to compromise the idea that our engagements and choices in this world are at the core of who we are.

One can appreciate the problem by thinking about Hannah Arendt's fascinating study of Augustine, *Love in St. Augustine,* written in Germany in 1929. In this work, Arendt writes sympathetically about precisely this element in Augustine – the sense of equal wickedness and evil – seeing it as an appealing foundation for a community of equals. But in hindsight this seems an especially perverse and unfortunate view to be taking, especially when one considers that she is taking up this view as a substitute for Jewish views about virtue and human reciprocity. In the Jewish conception – as I think also to a great extent in later Thomistic Christian conceptions[22] – the human being is perfectly capable of being good, and the dignity of moral agency is the appropriate foundation for community. All persons respect one another's agency, and one of the ways that they do this is to blame the bad and praise the good, making a very sharp distinction, for example, between Arendt and those who persecute her. Augustine's own view of grace, not the only possible view surely, and one that attaches far less value to our earthly performances than most others, allows too little room for this dignity of agency. It therefore yields an inadequate foundation for political reciprocity. Augustine makes us a community of abject and rather helpless beings, victims of our inheritance, a community in which Arendt is not crucially different from those who will try to destroy her. Dante will attempt to show that it is possible to retain the Augustinian emphasis on receptivity and emotion while still building in far more respect for this-worldly moral choices.

3. *Compassion.* It is of course plain that Augustine's account restores compassion, along with other emotions, to a place of centrality in the earthly life. Human beings are to relate to one another as needy and incomplete, and recognizing the need of another should give rise to Christian love. However, we sense that the reasons for Augustinian

---

22 This is complicated by the role of grace in the Thomistic conception, which is both disputed and various: see further in Chapter 12.

compassion are not exactly the same as the reasons that recommended compassion in Part II, as a foundation for some valuable types of political action. In Part II, I argued that the good social agent should care when people are hungry, when they mourn, when they are persecuted – and should, in her compassion, see the remediation of those bad states of affairs as an urgent task of earthly politics. This is of course exactly how compassion functions in many parts of the Christian tradition, not least in the social doctrine of the contemporary Roman Catholic Church, with its scathing attacks on inequality and its admirable concern for the eradication of hunger, persecution, and other ills of earthly life.

Is this, however, the focus of compassion in Augustine? I believe not. Our sense of incompleteness is focused insistently on our sinfulness, and on our remoteness from God. What we see with compassion in our neighbors is this same sinfulness, this same need for God's grace. This means that Augustinian love is committed to denying the importance of the worldly losses and injustices to which my neighbor may attach importance, in order to assert the primacy of the need for God and the potential for grace. As Hannah Arendt put the situation very concisely:

Just as I do not love the self I made in belonging to the world, I also do not love my neighbor in the concrete and worldly encounter with him. Rather, I love . . . something in him, that is, the very thing which, of himself, he is not. "For you love in him not what he is, but what you wish that he may be." This not only preserves the isolation of the lover who is concerned about even those nearest to him only insofar as he loves God in them. It also means that for the neighbor as well love is merely a call to isolation, a summons into God's presence . . . Death is irrelevant to this love, because every beloved is only an occasion to love God. The same source is loved in each individual human being. No individual means anything in comparison with this identical source.

If this is a correct account of Augustine – and with some tentativeness I shall endorse it – it shows why we have reason to be alarmed at the insistent otherworldly direction of this longing. Death is irrelevant, real suffering in this world is irrelevant, all that is relevant is coming into God's presence.

To see how problematic this doctrine of love is, we have only, again, to consider Arendt, writing this from her 1929 situation. She takes from Augustine a lesson that may well have calmed her, but one that could not have been useful in directing her actions and speeches in the world in which she found herself. In the view she would have absorbed from her own Jewish tradition, both God and man are to care intensely about each earthly instance of injustice and wrongful death, directing compassion altogether toward the theater of history and not at all toward the shadowy and uncertain realm that may or may not lie outside it. As a follower of Augustine, Arendt learns that the griefs and pains of anti-Semitism, wrongful death, and hatred are not in the scheme of things really relevant – because those who hunger and thirst shall be filled by God, those who mourn shall see God. Whereas Judaism would have taught her that God's sphere of concern is this life, that all of our moral achievements take place in this life, if at all, and that those achievements thus have enormous weight, her reading of Augustine tells her that all of these acts and relations pale before something of far greater significance. As she herself concludes, "This indirectness breaks up social relations by turning them into provisional ones."

Nietzsche claimed that this attitude toward this-worldly virtue would inspire lassitude. Longing for the other world puts people to sleep in this world. The virtues of a merely provisional social world are "soporific virtues," because the focus on the beyond discourages risk taking and enterprise here and now. The aim of slipping off into beatitude distracts moral attention from the goal of making this world a good world, and encourages a focus on one's own moral safety that does not bode well for earthly justice. "Blessed are the sleepy ones," concludes Zarathustra – "because they shall soon drop off."[23] He is hasty, once again, when he indicts the entirety of the Christian tradition for this failing. But he is not wrong about something that is real in Augustine – and unpleasantly linked, perhaps, with Augustine's deep interest in the political control of the church, which sometimes requires docile, obedient – we might even say sleepy – subjects.

Why does Augustine believe that there is a radical and original equality of all human beings in sin? For this is not a universal Christian belief. Many Christian views – including Dante's, as we shall see – give this-worldly striving a central place in salvation. Why does Augustine direct longing away from this-worldly virtue, invoking our boundless

---

23 Nietzsche, *Thus Spake Zarathustra*, Part I, "On the Virtuous."

and equal sinfulness? Once again, this is a complicated question, to which we can give only a partial and incomplete answer. The primary ingredient in human sinfulness, for Augustine, is our disobedience to divine authority; another closely, and complexly, related ingredient is the nature of our this-worldly sexual longing. In his account of the Fall in *The City of God* XIV, Augustine makes it plain that disobedience is the central issue: sexuality was present in the Garden before the Fall, and was part of our original good human nature. Sexuality was good because it was obedient: we were able to use our organs the way we now use gardening tools, at the direction of the will (XIV.10). The unpredictable and ungovernable character of human sexuality as we now experience it is the fitting punishment for our original sin of disobedience: "the return for disobedience was nothing other than disobedience" (XIV.15). Our bodies now elude our control, just as we eluded God's:

At times, without intention, the body stirs on its own, insistent. At other times, it leaves a straining lover in the lurch, and while desire sizzles in the imagination, it is frozen in the flesh; so that, strange to say, even when procreation is not at issue, just self-indulgence, desire cannot even rally to desire's help – the force that normally wrestles against reason's control is pitted against itself, and an aroused imagination gets no reciprocal arousal from the flesh. (XIV.17, trans. Wills)

This lack of control over ourselves makes us, fittingly, ashamed. The original inhabitants of the Garden were not ashamed of their genital activities, because they used their parts obediently, and at the discretion of the will. It is when sexuality is bound up with disobedience, uncontrol, and ungovernability that a shame falls upon human beings that renders them all equally low. They are "confounded by the disobedience of their flesh . . . Thus modesty, prompted by shame, covered that which was disobediently aroused by desire against a will condemned for disobedience."[24]

Thus our separate and disobedient flesh is the consequence of our separate and disobedient will – and both become objects of a profound

---

24 *City of God* XIV.17, "confusi inoboedientia carnis suae . . . Quod itaque adversus damnatam culpa inoboedientiae voluntatem libido inoboedienter movebat, verecundia pudenter tegebat." See the excellent discussion of this passage in Wills (1999), pp. 130–36.

and equalizing shame. Augustine reads the myth of shame at our nakedness as a myth, ultimately, about the recalcitrance of the will, and
about sexuality only inasmuch as it remains a central example and sign
of the recalcitrance of the human will to divine authority. What he
does not like about human life, in the end, is that we cannot stop
thinking for ourselves, that we want to know good and evil for ourselves, and thus disobey a commandment that it would have been easy
to obey. Our bodies reveal our uncontrolled character, in the way that
they rebel against even our own commands. In consequence, we must
cover ourselves in shame, and wait for a time when we will again be
submissive to the authority of God.

Augustine had apparently restored the emotions to a place of honor
in the good life – and with them, the needy and imperfect aspects of
our humanity. He had condemned the pride with which the Platonist
tradition denounces as shameful any imperfection, any humanness.
And yet his own conception of Eden, and the sin that banished us from
Eden, is based, in its own way, on primitive shame, as is his idea of
love's ascent. For Augustine the disobedience of the will – and the
sexuality that is its sign – make us the human beings we know, so
unlike those automata that procreated in the Garden, using their genitals like gardening tools. These creatures were sexual, but in a deep
way nonerotic: they had no passionate attachment to pieces of the
world; so long as they were good, they were not curious or striving.
We might say that in our sense they were without emotion. It is thus a
very basic fact about humanity – our need for objects, our keen hunger
to know and to control the sources of good – that is original sin. And
thus a basic aspect of our humanity becomes a fitting object of boundless shame; it is this very condition that renders us hopelessly alike so
far as merit is concerned. The politics of Eden is this: be ashamed of
your longing for objects, your curiosity to know them, and your very
wish to originate independent actions. Be so ashamed that you see this
as radical evil, and yield your will before the authority of the church.
But also: be consoled, for this is a merely provisional world, and the
actions you would like to undertake here do not matter greatly; all of
your suffering will ultimately be made up by the transcendent beauty
of coming into the presence of God.

Let us now return one last time to Arendt. The idea that the independent will itself – and sexuality itself, seen as a metaphor for the ungov-

ernable will – are fundamentally evil in their separateness and their lack of docility is perhaps a consoling idea, in a world where real political engagement is enormously costly and uncertain of success. Thinking Augustinian thoughts of radical evil mitigates the suffering of having to obey evil powers in the world. It supplies the powerless with a project – coming into God's presence – that does not rely on their ability to will good action here and now. But again: the price that is paid is too high. The price is a profound shame – if not at all uncontrol, as with the Platonists, still, at a very fundamental element of our humanity – our independence, our willfulness, our sexual and moral unpredictability. Instead of taking action as best we can, we had better cover ourselves, mourn, and wait.

In the end, then, Augustine assails as the origin of evil the very root of a liberal politics. Fascist authority is not wrong just because it is the *wrong* authority, but because *any* such illiberal authority has the wrong relation to the human will. We find here the politics of shame again, in a new guise, now animated by a hatred not of weakness but of independent strength. Instead of Chapter 4's person of steel, the person who is dust and ashes. These two are less different than they at first appear: both normative pictures involve shame about human reality. Don't we have to like human action, even in its imperfection, if we are to figure out how to live decently in this world?

Here again, then, in a very different way, ascent has carried the lover too far beyond the realm of worldly need, suffering, and injustice for her to be quick to fight for the neighbor's right, or to assuage the neighbor's pain. Injustice is real and not just provisional, hunger is real and not just provisional. A must recognize these facts as she ascends, or else her ascent will take her away from morality itself.

556

12

THE CHRISTIAN
ASCENT: DANTE

I. SIGNS OF THE OLD LOVE

The Heavenly Pageant halts before Dante. Turning to the triumphal
chariot, the prophets sing the passionate words of the Song of Solomon, "Come with me from Lebanon, my bride."[1] Angels above
shout the joyful cry of the Gospel, "Benedictus qui venis," "Blessed
are you who come in the name of the Lord"[2] – and also, scattering
flowers, Anchises' tender words of mourning for the fate of Marcellus,
"Manibus o date lilia plenis," "O give lilies with full hands."[3] Read-

---

1 *Song of Solomon* 4:8. (The words "with me" are not explicit in Dante's Latin version,
   "Veni, sponsa, de Libano.") The context is among the most intensely erotic and lyrical
   in the *Song*: "Your lips are like a scarlet thread, and your mouth is lovely . . . Your two
   breasts are like two fawns, twins of a gazelle, that feed among the lilies . . . Come with
   me from Lebanon, my bride; come with me from Lebanon . . . You have ravished my
   heart, my sister, my bride, you have ravished my heart with a glance of your eyes . . .
   How sweet is your love, my sister, my bride! how much better is your love than wine,
   and the fragrance of your oils than any spice! Your lips distil nectar, my bride; honey
   and milk are under your tongue; the scent of your garments is like the scent of Lebanon
   . . . (4:3, 5, 8, 9–11, King James translation, Revised Standard Version).
      A valuable account of the role of Beatrice in the poem is in Von Wright (1994), who
   argues that she is a counterpart to Penelope, and thus an antitype to the egocentric
   voyager Ulysses; thus the poet expresses the idea that an adequate conception of love
   involves renouncing the desire to control the universe, and accepting one's own human
   vulnerability, a goal he symbolically connects with the feminine. On this account, there
   would also be a close connection between Beatrice and Molly Bloom.
2 *Matthew* 21:9, the shout of the crowd greeting Jesus as he enters Jerusalem. Note that
   though the Latin uses a masculine adjective, the phrase serves as a welcome to Beatrice.
3 *Aeneid* VI.882 ff.:
   heu, miserande puer, si qua fata aspera rumpas
   tu Marcellus eris. manibus date lilia plenis,
   purpureos spargam flores animamque nepotis
   his saltem accumulem donis, et fungar inani
   munere. . . .

ers who, with Dante, have followed Virgil's guidance up to this point, seeking an understanding of love through the eyes of his pre-Christian sensibility, are likely to experience a jolt. These words of grief seem inappropriate to a context of joyful welcome. There will be more such jolts, as Virgil, and the pagan sensibility, depart from the poem.

I have often seen at daybreak (Dante now observes) the eastern horizon glow rose, the sky above hang limpid and serene – and the sun's face come forth veiled in mist, so that the eye can look at it without pain. Even so, from that chariot, from within a cloud of flowers, a lady appeared before me, her white veil crowned with olive, her cloak green (symbol of hope), and, beneath it, in her gown, the color of living flame (symbol of Christian love).[4] This lady is not unknown to Dante, nor he to her:

My soul – such years had passed since last it saw
    that lady and stood trembling in her presence,
    stupefied, and overcome by awe –

now, by some power that shone from her above
    the reach and witness of my mortal eyes,
    felt the great power of the old love.

The instant I was smitten by the force
    which had already once transfixed my soul
    before my boyhood years had run their course,

I turned left with the same assured belief
    that makes a child run to its mother's arms
    when it is frightened or has come to grief,

to say to Virgil: "There is not within me
    one drop of blood unstirred. I recognize
    the tokens of the ancient flame." But he,

he had taken his light from us. He had gone,
    Virgil had gone. Virgil, the gentle Father
    to whom I gave my soul for its salvation!

4 "Di fiamma viva," *Purg.* XXX.33. The colors signify faith (white), hope (green), and Christian love (red): thus the "flame" of Christian love is introduced prior to, and prompts, Dante's acknowledgment of his own "flame."

Not all that sight of Eden lost to view
    by our First Mother could hold back the tears
    that stained my cheeks so lately washed with dew.

"Dante, do not weep yet, though Virgil goes.
    Do not weep yet, for soon another wound
    shall make you weep far hotter tears than those!"

*   *   *

"Look at me well. I really am, I really am Beatrice.
    How dared you make your way to this high mountain?
    Did you not know that here man lives in bliss?"[5]

Now, at the moment when Virgil and pagan virtue have taken their departure from the poem, at the time when Dante, having completed the ascent through Purgatory, is purified of sin, he acknowledges his passionate love for Beatrice – using Virgil's own words, the words used by Dido to acknowledge her passion for Aeneas, which she recognized as "the old love," the love she had once felt for her husband Sychaeus. "Agnosco veteris vestigia flammae. Conosco i segni dell'antica fiamma."

And now, even as he weeps for the loss of Virgil's gentle guidance, he is addressed by his own name. This is the first and only time that the word 'Dante' appears in the *Commedia*. The poet indicates that he records it "of necessity" (63). Its emphatic placement in the line, its isolation in the text, and the explicit reference to the anomaly of its mention all combine to give it enormous emphasis. It is as if Dante is being addressed in all his individuality for the first time. And the object

5 *Purg.* XXX.34–57, 73–75. I cite John Ciardi's translation (1977), though I have rewritten line 36, where Ciardi writes "stupefied by the power of holy awe": no word corresponding to "holy" is in the original. Some comments: in line 39, "d'antico amor senti la gran potenza" points more vividly than does the translation to the fact that it is the *same* love, the *old* love – and prepares for line 48, "conosco i segni dell'antica fiamma," which links the image of flame with acknowledgment of the continuing presence of the love. Line 48 is a translation of Virgil, *Aeneid* IV.23, "agnosco veteris vestigia flammae," in which Dido, acknowledging her love for Aeneas, recognizes it as "the old" love that she had once felt for her dead husband Sychaeus. (On flame as erotic image in Virgil, see Knox [1950].) At line 49, no image of "light" actually appears in the Italian, a literal rendering of which is, "But Virgil had left us bereft of him." In line 73, the emphatic and repetitious "Guardaci ben! ben son, ben son Beatrice," "Really look – I really am, I really am Beatrice" – has not been fully captured in the translation; and the significant fact that "Beatrice" is answered by the rhyming "*felice*" is captured only imperfectly.

of his passion, she who sees him with loving particularity of vision, she too draws attention to her own individuality. "I really am, I really am Beatrice," "Ben son, ben son Beatrice." The name is placed in close relation to its rhyme "*felice*," "blessed," – indicating, once again, that it is in the context of Christian salvation, and of worldly love seen in the context of salvation, that individuality is most truly realized, and loved.

This passage makes, then, several claims on behalf of the Christian love that survives the ascent through Purgatory. First, it claims that this Christian love is a love of the *individual*: both of the person's separate agency and of his qualitative particularity. Beatrice sees and loves not some aspect or part of Dante, and not some generic notion of fallen humanity, but *Dante*, the very man to whom she was passionately linked in earthly life. And it is as her very self – "look closely," she challenges him, "Guardaci ben," – that he sees and loves her. Second, with its unique stress on the poet's name, the scene suggests a claim that is developed in many ways throughout the *Commedia*: that it is in the context of Christian salvation that we find the *truest* and *most adequate* love of the individual, a love that most completely sees and loves the individual in all of his or her distinctness and uniqueness. Individuality is not just preserved in beatitude, it is heightened.

Finally, the passage seems to claim that Christian love is really *love* of the individual: it is not some distant contemplative appreciation, but "the ancient flame," the very passion that Dante felt for Beatrice on Earth, a passion linked with wonder, awe, and profound upheaval. The scene is both physically sensuous and deeply emotional. Dante's very heart melts (97–99). In the next canto, feeling "a thousand desires hotter than flame," he satisfies his ten years' thirst (XXXI.118, 128–30; cf. XXXII.2).

In order to begin to understand Dante's idea of love's ascent, we can set over against this central paradigm two other loves with which the poem has acquainted us. For, as readers, we are invited at this point to recall the erotic passion of Paolo and Frencesca, blown like birds by the winds of Hell, together for all eternity, their gentle hearts once and forever seized by love, "which absolves no beloved one from loving."[6]

6 Amor, ch'al cor gentil ratto s'apprende,
        prese costui della bella persona
        che mi fu tolta; e 'l modo ancor m'offende.

At that stage in his journey, Dante was moved to faint from pity at their fate[7] – seeing "how many sweet thoughts, how much desire, brought them to this mournful condition" (V.112–14). And now, in the narration of his encounter with Beatrice, we discover allusions to certain aspects of their doomed love – to its intensity of desire, to the uniquely strong bond its passion creates between two individuals, a bond that survives death itself. But even as Francesca used the language of Christian absolution to praise a sinful bodily desire, so Dante now uses the language of pagan desire to signify his spiritual love, which has been purified of lust.[8] Paolo and Francesca are in Dido's company in Hell.[9] Dante uses Dido's words of passion to acknowledge a love that has found salvation.

And since Beatrice's words immediately follow the departure of Virgil and the light of pagan reason from the poem, we are led, too, to consider the cases of pagan rational love with which the poem has acquainted us: above all, perhaps, the love between Dante and his teacher of Aristotelian philosophy, Brunetto Latini, a love based on mutual respect for merit and dignity, mutual well-wishing, and mutual hope of high achievement and renown.[10]Although this love is Aristote-

> Amor, ch'a nullo amato amar perdona,
> mi prese del costui piacer sì forte,
> che, come vedi, ancor non m'abbandona.
>
> Amor condusse noi ad una morte. (*Inf.* V.100–107)

7 V.140–1: ". . . sì che di pietade/io venni men così com' io morisse." On the refusal of pity to the damned, see section V of this chapter.

8 In Canto XXVII, Dante, gathering courage from Beatrice's name, follows the instruction of the Angel of Chastity and passes through the wall of fire that burns away lust. It is here, apparently, that the last "P" is stricken from his brow. Thus here the reference to the pagan erotic image of flame takes on a Christian and, in a sense, profoundly unerotic significance. See section V.

9 *Inferno* V.85: "uscir della schiera ov' è Dido." It is noteworthy that Dido is in the company of the adulterers for having been unfaithful not to a living husband, but to his memory: "ruper fede al cener di Sicheo" (IV.62). Although to be sure the emphasis is on a broken promise, the promise is to the person's ashes, not to the person. That this counts as infidelity seems to me quite problematic, although commentators have little to say about it, simply citing the parallel to *Aeneid* IV.552: "non servata fides cineri promissa Sichaeo." It is worth noting that this circle contains no remarried widowers.

10 *Inferno* XV. Dante addresses Brunetto – whose features are so scorched by the fire that he can hardly be recognized – by the reverential "*Ser*"; he calls Dante his "son," and Dante speaks of his paternal kindness. Brunetto urges Dante to "follow his star," and Dante recalls that Brunetto's teaching concerned "how the human being makes himself

lian rather than Platonic in its emphasis on mutuality in respect,[11] it is also strongly linked with our Platonic contemplative paradigm, in its emphasis on goodness as the basis of love and on the self-sufficiency of personal creative achievement for a kind of immortality – also, clearly, in its connection with the homoerotic love for which Brunetto is damned.[12] The tradition of pagan contemplative love disappears from

immortal." In the famous closing lines of the canto, Dante compares Brunetto to a runner in the foot race at Verona, and, he says, "to the winner, not the loser." Compare the account of the virtuous pagans in *Inf*. IV, where respect for merit and virtue is the central theme, and yet this respect is shown as existing in a dome shut off from the light of the sun. This, of course, is where Socrates, Plato, and Aristotle – as well as Empedocles, Democritus, Heraclitus, Diogenes, Seneca, and Cicero – are all placed, and the life of pagan philosophy with them.

11 On the relationship between Platonic *erôs* and Aristotelian *philia*, see Nussbaum (1986), Chapter 12, and especially Vlastos (1981), pp. 3–4 and note 4. Vlastos argues that "friendship" is inadequate as a rendering of *philia*: " 'Love' is the only English word that is robust and versatile enough to cover *philein* and *philia*." The inadequacy is the more patent in Dante, where Platonic and Aristotelian paradigms are interwoven in the depiction of pagan love, and where explicit theory traces all desire and motivation to *amore*: see especially *Purg*. XVI, XVIII; also XXIV, where Dante states that the whole poem signifies the internal dictation of love (52–4).

12 See *Inferno* XV. It is a peculiarity in the structure of the *Commedia* that while in *Inferno* heterosexual and homosexual lust receive extremely different treatments – the former being treated as a species of *akrasia* appetite, the highest up and therefore lightest among the sins, the latter as a form of violence against nature, much lower down – in Purgatory the two sins are treated as exactly similar, and similarly light in comparison to pride, envy, etc. This follows, it seems, from the fact that Hell is organized around Aristotelian categories classifying the acts for which the damned are damned, while Purgatory is organized around the Christian classification of standing dispositions of the personality. But it may also reflect the fact that homosexuality in Hell is associated with the overweening and self-sufficiency of the Platonic tradition (see further in the following text). In Purgatory, by contrast, the most prominent homosexual lovers are courtly love poets, who do not stand up for pagan self-sufficiency; presumably their ethical stance is more open to repentance than is Brunetto's. Finally, we may possibly see in the wavering treatment of homosexuality some ambivalence on the poet's part toward the Thomistic treatment of the issue, which marked a new phase of aggressive hostility in the history of the church. See Boswell (1980), not reliable in all respects but correct in its observation that this period marked a rise in hostility. In the *Purgatorio*, Dante draws attention to the symmetrical treatment of heterosexual and homosexual offenders in the rather comical description of the souls of the lustful, who form two bands that pass one another, moving in opposite directions, and kiss one another as they pass – like two processions of ants, he says, rubbing noses as they meet – the one group calling out "Sodom and Gomorrah," the other (heterosexual) group denouncing the lustfulness of Pasiphae (XXVI). It is very striking that heterosexual lust is here represented by a case of bestiality, and is thus apparently rendered more monstrous and "unnatural" than the homosexual love for which Dante's friends and fellow poets are suffering.

the poem with Virgil – to be replaced by something more volatile, more mobile, more vulnerable and humble. Wonder and awe, success and victory, even respect for merit and creativity – all take on a new meaning, as Brunetto's Platonic view of the world, according to which "the human being makes himself immortal" by intellectual deeds (*Inf.* XV.85), is replaced by an acknowledgment of human neediness and insufficiency before God's grace.

As A thinks of the ascent of her own desire, she would keep before her both of these earlier paradigms. For Dante's portrait of the love of Paolo and Francesca, while owing to the tradition of courtly love certain features that make it unlike her love for M – its emphasis on the "gentle heart," its depiction of the lovers as doves rather than as fiercer animals – still captures some central features of her own experience of passion, especially when it depicts lovers as passive before inexorable currents of desire, as lacking wholeness and even identity, and as determined in some mysterious way to be bound to a particular person for all eternity. Being a well-brought-up French Catholic (let us suppose), she knows that if she had indeed died in the midst of that love she would herself have become one of that flock, floating on the winds. On the other hand, she has now studied with the Platonists. They have promised her flourishing and even a kind of immortality. So she would have to be intensely interested in the fact that this "salvation" is now located deep in Hell. Having studied with Augustine, she would connect this location with his condemnation of the sin of pride involved in the Platonic tradition.

As she thinks about the ascent, she will be asking questions about agency and reciprocity: for this seemed a signal problem for the Platonist tradition, and perhaps for Augustine as well.[13] She will inquire about individuality, asking whether Dante's account includes her very concrete love for M as a separate and distinct person, who is also qualitatively unique. She will also be asking questions about love's focus on this world, wondering to what extent Dantean love will re-

---

13 See Vlastos (1981), who points out, correctly, that Aristotelian *philia* contains real altruism, in its insistence that the loved one should be benefited for his or her own sake, not just for the sake of one's own ends. I have argued that some of these elements are already present in Plato's *Phaedrus*: Nussbaum (1986), Chapter 7.

quire her to view this world of human life as merely provisional, to what extent it will permit her to continue to have intense concern for its people and events. As she asks all of these questions, she will look for differences between Dante's Thomistic account of love and its Augustinian predecessor.

Dante is intensely attentive to these questions. Even more steeped in classical paradigms of love than was Augustine, he sets himself to rewrite them, drawing on Augustinian insights and reconfiguring those insights with the help of the paradigm of courtly love poetry within which he first found his voice as a poet and lover. But there is a difference. Dante will not dismiss the entirety of the pagan tradition. As a devotee of Aristotle and Aquinas, he will remain faithful to Aristotelian insights about the dignity of agency and the perception of particularity, attempting a fusion of what is best in the pagan and the Christian traditions. In the process, striving in this world assumes a new dignity, and even Paradise is cognizant of virtue.

II. AGENCY AND THE ROMANCE OF GRACE

What, then, makes the love of Beatrice for Dante, and of Dante for Beatrice, a love of the individual – that is, a love that attends both to the separate agency and to the qualitative particularity of an individual person? And why is it alleged to be more truly a love of the individual than are other types of love? The two components of individuality are clearly distinguished in the poem, and both are given enormous emphasis, both in its overall narrative of Dante's progress and Beatrice's compassion and in its account of the love between them.

Dante emphatically focuses on the capacity of Christian love to show respect for each person's separate agency and thus to create relationships based on reciprocity. He singles out this feature as central to Christian love, and as a feature that distinguishes it from the erotic courtly love of Paolo and Francesca (of A in her former life). Beatrice seeks Dante's salvation; but this salvation, as she knows, must be achieved by his own will, though aided by divine grace. Indeed, Dante is not ready to meet Beatrice until he has purified his will of external influences that would deform it and mar its autonomy. Excessive attachments to earthly goods are such influences; Dante must be purified of his love of material objects, of fame, and of sexual pleasure, before he is ready to be declared fully autonomous. It is only when he has passed through the fire that disciplines the lustful that he is ready to be a free agent. Virgil can now leave him to his own guidance:[14]

> I have led you here by grace of mind and art;
>> now let your own good pleasure be your guide.

> * * *

> Expect no more of me in word or deed:
>> here your will is upright, free, and whole,
>> and you would be in error not to heed

> whatever your own impulse prompts you to:
>> lord of yourself I crown and mitre you. (*Purg.* XXVII.130–1, 139–43)

Only in the context of Christian salvation, then, does the will have its full integrity. But this means that it is only in the context of salvation that two people can love one another with full respect for subjecthood and agency.[15]

Why should we think this? We can understand Dante's claim more fully if we return to his portrait of Paolo and Francesca. For they are depicted as being passive with respect to their love. In Hell they are swept along by conflicting gusts of wind – "di qua, di là, di giù, di su li mena" (*Inf.* V.43) – because this is how desire tossed them around in life, as they subjected the freedom of their wills to the force of bodily desire. Even in the appealing and tender aspects of their love they are depicted as passive: "like doves summoned by desire,"[16] they come at Dante's call. Using the language of courtly love poetry, powerfully appealing to Dante as a leading participant in that poetic movement, Francesca depicts the very ideal of love as that of a gentle passivity, a being-seized. She and Paolo are the objects of its verbs, never the subjects:

---

14 Virgil must, of course, leave the poem at this point in any case, being a pagan.
15 This does not mean that only two completely purified people can love in this way; for one may show respect for agency by devoting oneself to the search for salvation. "In the context of salvation" means, then, in the course of a devout Christian life.
16 *Inf.* V.82–4. The passage makes a subtle point: they do direct themselves toward Dante "carried by their will" ("dal voler portate"), but only after desire has roused them ("dal disio chiamate").

Love, so quickly kindled in the gentle heart,
>seized my lover with passion for that sweet body
>from which I was torn unshriven to my doom.

Love, who absolves no beloved one from loving
>seized me with such a strong desire for him
>that, as you see, it has not left me yet.

Love led us to one death.[17]

Seized rather than seizing, led rather than leading, they surrender their agency – not so much to one another as to a power that guides them.

The sense we have is of people who cannot see the individuality and agency in one another, because they have insufficient respect for their own. They do not regard life as something involving agency or deliberation at all, because they are captivated by the idea of surrender to the forces of passion. But this means that they do not really treat one another as fully human: just as they allow themselves to be used as objects by the buffeting winds of desire, so they buffet one another. Dante is suggesting that this attitude is highly conducive to adultery, the sin for which they are damned: once one submits rational agency to desire, essential moral judgments are absent.

And yet Dante is not Kant. Although, like Kant, he criticizes the way in which erotic lovers lack a full sense both of their own humanity and of that of their partner, he does not represent their passion as ugly; indeed, he clearly finds their tender susceptibility deeply appealing. The attraction of this image of gentle passivity for Dante is one of the major temptations with which he must contend during his journey, as a human being and as a poet – as a courtly love poet who is also a Christian Aristotelian.

It therefore becomes a major task of the poem to show Dante that he can have the susceptibility of the gentle heart without its sinful passivity. Transformations in the image of the dove track his progress. In the second canto of the *Purgatorio*, Dante encounters Casella, friend and fellow love poet. Dante begs him for some of the love poetry that "used to quiet all my longing" ("quetar tutte mie voglie" [II.108]). Casella then begins to recite Dante's own early love poem, "Amor, che

---

17 *Inf.* V.100–107, quoted earlier in note 5. I have translated the lines myself, following the version I gave in "Love and the Individual" in Nussbaum (1990). I rely on Ciardi in lines 101–2, but for the rest give a more literal version.

ne la mente mi ragiona," "Love that discourses to me in my mind" –
profoundly ambiguous words at this point in the poem, since love may
"seize" the mind, removing its agency, or, on the other hand, it may
become the agency of a righteous will. Dante, Virgil, and the others all
listen, forgetting their higher purpose, "content as if nothing touched
the mind of any, . . . rapt and attentive to his notes" ("fissi e attenti"
[II. 117–18]).

Cato's rebuke now rouses them from their passivity: what negligence
is this! "Run to the mountain, to strip off the sloth that prevents God
from being manifest to you." The dove image now returns, transformed:

As when doves collected at their feeding, picking up wheat or tares, . . . if
something appears that frightens them suddenly leave their food lying, because they are assailed with a greater care (perch' assaliti son da maggior
cura); so I saw that new troop leave the song and go towards the slope, like
those who go they know not where . . . (II.124–32)[18]

These doves have a goal, albeit one they imperfectly comprehend. They
are not simply tossed about, they are agents. They are not, however,
self-sufficient or, in Platonist style, self-propelling. They are still susceptible doves. They are agents not in spite of, but in virtue of, their
willingness to be susceptible to the influence of the "greater care."
Quasi-erotic passivity and agency now are allies. The next time that
Dante is "rapt and attentive," his object is the smile of Beatrice (*Purg.*
XXXII.I), a smile that quenches his thirst, and draws his eyes to her
"with the old net" (XXXII.6).

As the poem shows in numerous ways, this love exemplifies the new
combination of agency and susceptibility, wholeness of will and receptivity. For Beatrice does not simply seize Dante in a loving embrace.
Her first act, indeed, is to charge him with his faults, with the worldly
ambition and material concern, the "false images of good" (XXX.131)
that have separated him from her. Before they can be together in love,
he must examine himself, confess, and repent. This confession is at
once a supreme effort of will and an act of loving passivity:

---

18 I give the literal prose version of Dante (1958), since Ciardi, to preserve rhyme, is
    forced to distort some parts of the sense that are important for my argument ("assaliti
    . . . da maggior cura" becomes "taken by a sudden scare," which is both weaker and
    lacking in the comparative dimension of the original).

Confusion joined to terror forced a broken
   "yes" from my throat, so weak that only one
   who read my lips would know that I had spoken.

As an arbalest will snap when string and bow
   are drawn too tight by the bowman, and the bolt
   will strike the target a diminished blow –

so did I shatter, strengthless and unstrung,
   under her charge, pouring out floods of tears,
   while my voice died in me on the way to my tongue.[19]

This highly complex image reformulates the relationship between agency and passivity. As a follower of pagan philosophy, Dante is an archer, his bow aiming at the target of the good human life.[20] His effort is an effort of his own agency and will, and his will has dignity. But he can be a Christian agent only by being, at the same time, the bowstring that breaks, confessing its own inadequacy.[21] To put it another way, he can have his poetic voice as a Christian love poet only by losing his voice, in tears of humility and awe. We are on our way to the mysterious harmony of *disio* and *velle*, longing and willing, with which the poem famously ends.[22] He can have that harmony only by allowing the "wheel" of his soul – desire and will both – to be "revolved" by heavenly love.

Now we can begin to understand how the poem's conception of agency criticizes the pagan ascent of love, as well as the unreformed love from which ascent begins. For in Brunetto's way of seeing the world the human being is self-sufficient for the achievement of the highest good – opposed by Fortuna, to be sure (*Inf.* XV.93–6), but still for the most part capable of attaining *eudaimonia* by his own efforts. He teaches Dante "come l'uom s'etterna" – and in that reflexive verb is his damnation. Ethical agency in Plato and Aristotle has moved beyond the directionless passivity of Francesca (of Plato's Alcibiades, a "slave" to

---

19 *Purg.* XXXI.13–21, Ciardi translation.
20 Aristotle, *EN* 1094a22–4, an image also used commonly in Hellenistic ethics. It would no doubt be well known to Dante.
21 See also the use of the same image in *Par.* I.120–5 – where the bow is drawn by divine Providence, and guides receptive mortals to their goal.
22 *Par.* XXXIII.143–5: "ma già volgeva il mio disio e 'l velle, / sì come rota ch'igualmente è mossa, / l'amor che move il sole e l'altre stelle."

passion). But in giving up their susceptibility to the external force of passion, the pagan philosophers abandon something crucial, Dante holds, for the attainment of the highest good. In that sense Brunetto is indeed further from salvation than are the drifting lovers: for they at least acknowledge the necessity of another's love for their good. This loving dependency can be educated so that it will eventually take an adequate object, an object that could not be attained by will alone.

Brunetto's damnation is, of course, not directly caused by this pagan attitude, and I have argued (note 12, this chapter) that Dante's attitude to same-sex relations is complex, shifting, or so it would appear, from *Inferno* to *Purgatorio*. But we can now perhaps gain a better understanding of that asymmetry. Brunetto's confidence that human beings are sufficient for their own salvation is closely related to his violence against the rules of the church (more rigid by far than those of pagan culture). His sin is treated as a sin of violence, not of lust, because it embodies a willing defiance of natural law, as understood in Thomistic doctrine. By contrast, souls who have same-sex relations but then repent have, in that act of repentance, given up their defiance, submitting their souls to the laws of a higher power. What remains in them is simply lust. Thus it is appropriate that, in Purgatory, the same-sex lustful should be given the same punishment as the heterosexual lustful. What differentiates Brunetto from Guido Guinicelli is, simply, Brunetto's conviction that he is superior to natural law.

So far Dante's critique of the pagan ascent is related to Augustine's, in its emphasis on the need for longing and mourning, rather than a prideful self-sufficiency. But he preserves much more than Augustine does of the pagan emphasis on reflective life planning and choice, the dignity of the human will. He does not hold that we are all alike in our disobedience, that original evil has reduced us to equal lowness. Our virtues and our striving have great weight, and grace is not radically independent of those strivings, as it is for Augustine.

What Christian love requires, in effect, is a new combination of susceptibility and the active use of reason, Aristotle's "clear distinctions" (*Par.* XI.27) with the lover's gentle heart. When Aquinas appears before Dante in Paradise, he supports, to some extent against the Augustinian tradition, the Aristotelian emphasis on taking charge of one's own search for the good through one's very own reflection:

He ranks very low among the fools, who affirms or denies without making clear distinctions ... since often a belief, rushing ahead, inclines us to the wrong conclusion, and then pride binds our intellect. It is worse than vain for a person to cast off from the shore, if he fishes for truth without the art – for he does not return the same as he set out.[23]

All this is in the tradition of the pagan ascent. And the entire structure of Paradise is shaped by a sense of the dignity of striving: souls are classified by their characteristic achievements, and Aquinas' dignity derives directly from his intellectual and moral merit.

But Dante's Aquinas is not Aristotle – or even Plato, with his more erotic account of the self-propelling movement of the intellect. His very first words to Dante are words of love that seem at home in courtly love poetry:

> Since the ray of grace from which true love is kindled –
> and then by loving, in the loving heart
> grows and multiplies ...[24]

And immediately after his praise of the philosophical art, Aquinas warns against the false pride of the intellect, and describes the unpredictable operations of grace:

> Men should not be too smug in their own reason;
>   only a foolish man will walk his field
>   and count his ears too early in the season;
>
> for I have seen a briar through winter's snows
>   rattle its tough and menacing bare stems,
>   and then, in season, open its pale rose;
>
> and I have seen a ship cross all the[25] main
>   true to its course and swift, and then go down
>   just as it entered port again.

Here Aquinas acknowledges a truth in Augustine's reading of "neque volentis neque currentis sed miserentis est dei": will falls so far short of sufficiency for its goal that grace can rescue a most unpropitious effort and damn one that was almost complete. And yet efforts of the will are

---

23 *Par.* XIII.115–23, my translation.
24 *Par.* X.83–5, Ciardi translation.
25 *Par.* XIII.130–8, Ciardi translation.

given a dignity that they are not in Augustine, as central constituents of a person's flourishing.

The world of Christian love, in short, is a world of sudden reversals, a world of philosophical self-government, but ruled by surprising incursions of strange influence.[26] Platonism is too focused on the self-government of reason to admit a love so needy, so open to the action of the other; Augustinian love does not retain sufficient respect for the lover's freedom and choice. The self-propelling motion of philosophical intellect must be infused with the "intelligence of love."[27]

III. PERCEIVING THE INDIVIDUAL

The love of Dante and Beatrice is, then, a love that respects subjecthood and freedom – in the singular manner in which it is mingled here with passivity, with what we might call the romance of grace. To that extent, it recognizes the fact that each person is a distinct individual, having only a single life to live. Is it also a love of the qualitatively particular? It is among the poem's most central concerns to establish that it is. In taking this stand, Dante's Thomistic view argues against the Augustinian tradition, according to which much of the qualitative particularity of persons – their flaws and faults, their idiosyncrasies, their very bodies and their histories – are all incidental accretions from the world of sin, to be disregarded in the context of redemption.[28] Augustine still wishes to maintain that each soul is a distinct individual, a new beginning, having its own life to live.[29] And yet, he omits so much of the lives individuals have actually led that we wonder, in the end, whether the integrity of their distinctive individual engagements has been preserved. Here we see a link between the two components of individuality: insofar as our qualitative particularity expresses what we have made of ourselves, the distinctive lives we have

---

26 Notice that the souls in Paradise are still susceptible lovers: they move toward Dante as fish in a fish pond move toward any external incursion, taking that to be their food; and they call out, "Behold – one who will increase our loves" (V.100–105).

27 *Purg.* XXIV.51: here Bonagiunta cites the opening line of one of Dante's own lyrics, "Donne ch'avete intelletto d'amore." It is clearly Dante's view that all forms of love involve cognitive representation; and he depicts his poetic task as that of taking down dictation from the internal speech of love (XXIV.52–4).

28 On this see especially Freccero (1986), pp. 16–29.

29 *City of God* XII.21, arguing against the view that newborns are simply recycled souls.

led, to treat those particular traits as inessential is to fail to respect the integrity of our personal distinctness. Reacting against Augustine's treatment of persons, Dante emphasizes these components of particularity throughout the poem, as he does most strikingly in the scene with which I began.

It is hardly necessary to argue that Beatrice's love for Dante embraces his faults, as well as his virtues. From the very beginning of her intervention in his fate, this is abundantly clear. As she appears before Virgil (*Inf.* II), pleading for "l'amico mio" (61), she stresses the fact that, inspired to leave Heaven by compassion for Dante's fallen condition, she does not cease to be fully herself, or her love to be a fully personal love: "I' son Beatrice che ti faccio andare," she insists (70). The essence of this love is "*pietà*," compassion, but a compassion thoroughly mixed with personal love. As soon as Lucia, "enemy of all cruelty," summons her, she hastens to "succor" her beloved, hearing the sound of his weeping. In the confrontation I have already discussed, her stern yet loving concern for his sinful state prompts his tearful confession.

Nor is their love without attention to idiosyncrasies that express the lives they have set themselves to lead, and that make each of them distinct from all the other souls that stand in need of salvation. Beatrice loves Dante's poetic career, his aspirations.[30] We feel that she knows well, and lovingly embraces, his entire history, even while, in her speech of denunciation, she narrates its faults. This recognition seems essential to a recognition of him as a person with a distinct life to live: could one be said to recognize *Dante*, without recognizing these engagements? Moreover, his very body is, for her, a part of his identity: she calls him by name, recognizes him, looks at him with love.

On his side, the emphasis on particularity is all the more marked – as, in a sense, it needs to be, since the reader's doubt will surface most strongly here. How can this "donna beata e bella" (*Inf.* II.53) really be, really be, Beatrice herself, as she so emphatically insists? (After all, she was a girl when she died, and he had only met her once.) Mysteri-

---

30 For example, in *Inf.* II he is identified to her by Lucia as "he who loved you so much that for your sake he left the vulgar herd" (104–5). It is of course also important that many properties that to an Augustinian would be morally irrelevant become relevant to Dante's scheme of salvation: for in Paradise souls are classified by their characteristic pursuits and ideals.

ously, it is so. Dante recognizes her, even before he sees her face, by the power of passion that she arouses in him, the "occulta virtû che da lei mosse" (*Purg.* XXX.38). He feels, we know, "the old love" in her presence; her whole history, and theirs, is present in her eyes, which satisfy his ten years' thirst for her. Even though, strictly speaking, the resurrection of the body has not taken place,[31] Dante is, without any doubt, in the presence of the bodily form of the woman whom he loves. And that body, Aquinas argues, is an essential part of the person, even in his or her redeemed condition.[32] This fact is nowhere more stressed than at the very end of the *Paradiso*, when Beatrice has ascended to her heavenly throne:

I lifted up my eyes and saw her where she made herself a crown, reflecting from her the eternal beams. From the highest region where the thunder sounds no mortal eye is so far, were it lost in the depths of the sea, as was my sight there from Beatrice. But to me it made no difference, for her image came down to me undimmed by anything between.[33]

Her particularity transcends all barriers. In that full particularity he loves her.

The poem stresses, furthermore, that with particularity as with agency, Christian love surpasses the forms of earthly love that are its alternatives. This is so because "the world is blind" ("lo mondo è cieco," *Purg.* XVI.66). The lure of material goods, of fame and honor – all this creates a "fog" around the sight of the individual[34] that blocks him or her from truly perceiving the particularity of other individuals, and to some extent from being truly perceived. The sins that are purged in Purgatory are all different forms of false love (see *Purg.* X, XVI, XVIII), love in which the soul has taken excessive interest in objects that are not worthy or true objects for its love, or defective interest in those that are. And this deforms the love of persons, who are worthy

---

31 See *Par.* XIV, where the souls are depicted as filled with desire for their dead bodies ("disio de' corpi morti," 63) – not only for their own, but for those of their loved ones (61–6).

32 For discussion of this aspect of Aquinas' Aristotelianism, see Nussbaum and Putnam (1992). Separated souls cannot perceive the particular things of this world without their bodily organs, Aquinas argues, and thus have only a confused and indistinct perception, until the resurrection of the body restores their faculties.

33 *Par.* XXXI.73–78, trans. Sinclair, with my changes.

34 Cf. "purgando la caligine del mondo," *Purg.* XI.30.

objects of love, in manifold ways. In pride, one attends only to one's own standing. This leads to a failure to see the needs of those one loves, and to a desire to lord it over them. In envy, one fixes on the possessions of others, and becomes competitive rather than truly loving. In anger one is filled with resentment at slights to oneself, and so cannot fully attend to the particular history and the needs of another. In sloth and in gluttony, one is slow to respond to another's need. Lust, finally, is also seen as a deformation of individual love. The suggestion is that the lustful, focusing as they do on their own pleasure and excitement, are imperfectly able to notice and respond to the needs of the person whom they love, or even to take in their full particularity. A person who is seen as a vessel of pleasure is not (as Aristotle already had argued) seen truly for what he or she *is*. How do Paolo and Francesca see and respond to one another? He sees her as a "bella persona" (and she notes that this bodily form is hers no longer); she sees him as a source of "*piacer*," and calls him "*costui*," "that one." Never does she mention his name.[35]

Nor are lovers immersed in worldly concerns easily perceived by the eyes of love. For they identify themselves with superficial attachments – to money, to status, to food, to physical pleasure – and wallow in these pursuits in a way that masks their deeper selves from view. It is in this sense that the purification of sin is not a self-destruction but a self-cleansing and a self-revelation.

We might suppose that Platonic love would fare better by these tests: for in his account of creation in the beautiful, Plato also criticizes loves that focus on superficial characteristics. This critique is developed further by Aristotle, who contrasts love based on the essentials of a person's character with more superficial forms of attention to status, reputation, pleasure, and wealth. But Dante's poem ultimately denies that a love that focuses on the merits of the loved one's character can yield a satisfactory notion of particularity in love. For any love that stays fixed on merit cannot take in the whole history of the individual, the whole particularity of that history, with its defects, its body, its flaws and faults. It cannot have the tender compassion of this love, its mer-

---

35 Dante's conception of the worldly obstacles to particular perception and love is close to the contemporary conception developed by Iris Murdoch in philosophical writings such as Murdoch (1970, 1977), but also in novels such as *The Bell, The Black Prince*, and *The Sacred and Profane Love Machine*.

ciful understanding of the struggles of the individual will within a tangled history.

IV. CHRISTIAN LOVE IS LOVE

Like Augustine, Dante stresses, moreover, that this redeemed love is really love. Throughout the poem he insists on the multifaceted character of love, the basic form, he argues, of all human desire and motivation (*Purg.* XVII.91–140). His entire poem, he tells us, is the writing of love within him: when Bonagiunta asks him whether he is the poet who wrote the lyric that begins, "Ladies who have the intelligence of Love," Dante replies, "I am one who, when love breathes in me, takes note, and in whatever way he dictates, I go on to signify" (*Purg.* XXIV.49–54). In that sense, any human relationship involving desire and action is bound by definition to be a relationship of love. As Virgil says to Dante, "Neither Creator nor his creatures move, / ... but in the action / of animal or of mind-directed love" (XIV.91–3). So we might suppose that Dante has not so much answered the question as avoided it.

But Dante does not stop there. He is at great pains to satisfy his reader that the love between himself and Beatrice is indeed the same erotic passion that had linked them in life. And in describing those "signs," Dante carefully associates their love with paradigms of romantic/erotic love that have already been present in the poem. We find awe, trembling, being overcome ("di stupor tremando affranto," *Purg.* XXX.36). We hear of a "hidden power" emanating from the loved one and binding the lover.[36] We witness tears and upheaval. We discover, in short, all the susceptibility of the "*cor gentil,*" as Dante has both enacted and poetically represented it. We even find the image of melting (XXX.97–9), well known at least since Plato's *Phaedrus* as an image for erotic susceptibility and "madness."[37]

On the side of Beatrice, we find, from the beginning of the poem, deep disturbance and concern for Dante's well-being, combined with a

---

36 For this motif in ancient Greek beliefs about *erôs*, see Winkler (1990).

37 On the *Phaedrus*, see Nussbaum (1986), Chapter 7; Nussbaum (1995b); and Halperin (1986). Charles Singleton, in his classic Dante commentary (1973), also compares Augustine, *Confessions* VIII.12, the account of Augustine's misery and tears before his conversion.

passionate emotionality that is never more apparent than in her first appearance before him. Commentators have frequently remarked on the fact that the solemn speech in which she denounces Dante for his sins is also a deeply personal and angry statement of betrayal.[38] She is recognizable as the Beatrice of the *Vita Nuova*, the real passionate woman who has loved Dante and loves him still.

Let me now return to A, who has accompanied Dante on his journey through Hell, and up the mountain of Purgatory. The same love moves her now that moved her at the start, when she had gone wrong by excessive attention to bodily passion. She will recognize now that her love for M was an impediment to her will's freedom. In its nature it made her into a passive object, rather than an agent. This made true flourishing impossible, and it also made it impossible for her to love M in an adequate way. She saw him, too, as an object rather than as a subject, and she had inadequate regard for his practical engagements as a separate and distinct individual with his own life to live. She will recognize, as well, that her many sins made her less fully her own particular self, and prevented her from seeing his particularity truly. In pride she believed that she could take any risk and never come to harm; this pride very likely prevented her from seeing his vulnerability and his need for her. Her tendency to anger at M's jealousy, similarly, created a "fog" that focused attention on wrongs to herself, rather than on the causes of jealousy in his own insecurity and need for love. Her envy of M's family, so much more cultivated than her own, made her incapable of kindness and decency. And at many times she was simply too lazy to do anything good, sluggish in her pursuit of all of her goals. Finally, her absorption in physical passion turned him, for her, into a body far more than an entire person. She has none of the novel-reader's knowledge of his fears and hopes, of his terror in the night and his pain at all new surroundings.

As she ascends the mountain, and each of the letters P (representing sin, *peccatum*) is removed from her brow, she will become less like the willful A inside the novel, the defiant A who jumped over the old man

38 XXX.104–45: Singleton, *ad loc.*, speaks of her "cutting sarcasm," and writes, "The Beatrice who is known to readers of the *Vita Nuova* now comes prominently to the fore" – a Beatrice who in that early work is *not* an allegorical figure.

on the beach, the A who could see truly neither M nor herself, and more like the implied author of the *Commedia*, the keen and merciful perception of human particularity that animates the text as a whole. But she will not lose her separateness or her qualitative distinctness: she will still remain A, with her own talents and achievements, her own tastes and her own bodily form; and she will still have a special love for M. She will work hard to save him from the sin of pride involved in the Platonist ascent, forgoing for a time beatitude itself. She will focus on his particular story, rather than on a general form of love that he exemplifies. And when, after ten years' absence, she appears before him, she will call him lovingly by his name.

V. THE TRANSFORMATIONS OF BEATITUDE

All this is so. And yet each of the elements of earthly love, while present, has also undergone a subtle transformation, in the context of salvation. Dante's love is passion; and yet it is also religious fear and longing. Beatrice is a real loving woman; and yet she is also an allegorical figure of Mother Church. Dido's recognition of her "ancient flame" led on to the intensity of earthly *erôs*; Dante's recognition of his leads upward toward confession and toward paradise. How does this affect the claim of this love to have solved the problems of the Platonist ascent without incurring its difficulties?

Once again, as with Augustine, we may fairly claim that at least two of the three problems that Platonic love wished to solve are really solved. Dante's excessive neediness is cured with his sins; his Christian love is stable and gives him stability. Even more clearly in Dante than in Augustine, this is a love that is not narrowly partial, but all-embracing in its concern, moved by compassion for all of fallen humanity. All people are really equal in its sight, and all are really people. There is no text in all of literature that has more sheer love and curiosity about a wider range of human lives. It really does embrace the world with love.

It is especially interesting that for Dante – as not, I think, for Augustine – love can move outward to embrace humanity while retaining intense attachments to particular individuals. In the sight of Heaven, Beatrice is still Dante's lady and he her lover – whereas Augustine feels the need to repudiate his tie to his mother in order to perfect his love.

In this sense, Dante's love promises an attractive approach to this-worldly political life, where we most urgently need to learn how to balance concern for the equality of all humans with our special ties to our own families and fellow citizens.

Once again, however, with anger and revenge we have problems. I have stressed that we should not wish for a complete extirpation of anger; and there is much worthy anger in Dante's poem, at corruption, fraud, treachery, and injustice. Especially beautiful is the light of anger that shines out of the starry souls who loved earthly justice, and who are "moved to anger once again / against the buyers and sellers in the temple" (*Par.* XVIII.121–2). These are the just rulers, who love this world, the "soldiery of Heaven" (124). Even in Heaven, they care passionately about the sufferings of Hungary, the corruption of Norway, the troubles of Navarre (XIX.136–49).

But we also find a less appealing anger, directed at those who erred simply by following their own convictions, often with moral rectitude. Although the poem certainly stresses the extent of divine mercy, its treatment of the virtuous pagans and especially of the heretics – whose flaming torment Dante is encouraged to find delightful – leaves a modern reader wishing for a more Spinozistic approach to this particular problem.

But this is a problem with which Dante wrestles profoundly, setting the tone for a debate on heresy and toleration that continues to the present. By choosing Virgil as the poet's guide through Hell and most of Purgatory, and by giving the virtuous pagans enormous reverence, Dante brings forward the problem of moral pluralism. The poem is, in the end, orthodox for its own time. It represents the virtuous pagans as doomed to inhabit Limbo, even though they could not have become Christians, and it represents those who know and refuse the true doctrine as more profoundly damned. But by depicting pagans as virtuous and good guides to the moral and political life, Dante raises in any reader's mind the question of the good political regime and its proper attitude toward the presence within itself of irresolvable disagreements about the ultimate good, associated with different ethical and religious conceptions. Even in Dante's treatment of the heretics there is great complexity. Although Dante is encouraged to applaud their torments, he also gives us the noble figure of Farinata, whose dignity rises above his punishment:

Erect,
> he rose above the flame, great chest, great brow;
> he seemed to hold all Hell in disrespect. (*Inf.* X.34–36)

In one way, Farinata's dignity, like Brunetto's, is an aspect of his sin, his contempt for Hell of a piece with the heretical rejection of the afterlife for which he is damned. But as in the case of Brunetto, the appealing aspect of his dignity is left standing, challenging the Christian conception to reflect and to learn. Virgil urges Dante to speak respectfully to him, and Dante does so. Thus Dante in no way conceals the fact that noble men, men of great significance, have been heretics – and he opens in the reader's mind, again, the question of how a reasonable state should treat these differences, a question to which the reader may find a different answer.

The Thomistic tradition has, of course, given rise to quite a few different positions on toleration over the centuries, and it is one of the most attractive features of contemporary liberal Thomism – and by now, through Vatican II, of contemporary Catholic social doctrine – that this form of unseemly anger against one's fellow citizens is removed far more effectively than Dante here removes it. Dante's vision is in this sense the source for an ongoing tradition of reflection about the ascent of love that has by now in some respects progressed beyond him. But it is the stress in Dante's Thomism on the dignity of the will, and the importance of respect for the will's autonomy, that led to this progress. Thus we find in Dante the seeds of a more satisfactory position on the social limits of anger than he himself gives us.

Let us turn, next, to our three desiderata for a view of love that will provide a suitable basis for social morality, the three that posed acute problems for the Platonic ascent. Dante's basic conception is one of the viable ones that we will still have standing, so to speak, at the end of the day. Its signal achievement is the way it has managed to make a fruitful marriage between the Augustinian rehabilitation of the passions and classical respect for the dignity of agency. This enables it to give attractive answers to all three of our questions. What I shall do here, then, is to raise some questions about each of the three items, questions with which the Thomistic tradition has continued to wrestle.

1. *Reciprocity*. Concerning reciprocity and respect for fellow citizens as agents, we do see a decisive advance over both the Platonic and the Augustinian traditions. The general ethical stance of Dante's Christian Aristotelianism involves a very strong respect for the other person's agency and freedom, which is a central ingredient of good human loves, and also, by implication, of social and political institutions.

At the same time, the Aristotelian idea of reciprocity is deepened by Dante's complex understanding of love's strange combination of agency with passivity. We are to see persons as centers of choice and freedom, but also as needy and demanding of care, as both independent and dependent. This is a very good starting point. Politics has all too often seen the citizen either as just a dependent receiver (with no respect given to agency and freedom) or else as just an agent (with no recognition of neediness and dependency). Social contract doctrines, for example, tend to imagine citizens only as agents, as "fully cooperating members of society over a complete life," to use John Rawls's significant phrase. But no human being is like this: we all have periods of profound neediness and dependency – most obviously in infancy and in old age, but neediness and the demand for care are woven through the fabric of our lives. These needs for care must be met, and societies must arrange for them to be met well, without neglect of the needy, without exploitation of the givers of care.

Arrangements that stress only need, neglecting agency, are even more profoundly flawed, since they seem to show no respect for persons at all. Thus a state that provides for people's material well-being without allowing them liberty of choice in some central areas of life is failing to recognize them as centers of choice and agency. They are just live bodies, not persons with their own lives to live.

To strike the right balance here, we need an adequate political conception of the person. Dante gives us a very promising such conception, which promises a basis both for liberal institutions and for an attentiveness to care that is frequently absent from liberal institutions. Aristotle's conception of the human being already emphasizes this combination of need and agency, but Dante's insistence on a need for compassionate care from others surely goes beyond any explicit doctrine of Aristotelian politics.[39]

39 On this interpretation, Dante's ideas find their appropriate modern fulfillment in Thomist social-democratic ideas, for example those of Jacques Maritain: see Maritain (1943, 1951). See particularly Maritain's insistence that the political liberties support

Dante's position on church authority and the limits of toleration leaves us, here again, with questions about how far his particular doctrine can support a political stance based on respect for choice and on reciprocity. The difficulty lies deep: Dante's anxiety about difference informs his very picture of the relationship of one Christian soul to another, preventing him from characterizing these relationships as truly reciprocal. It is of the essence of Dantean love to be given in freedom. And yet, despite the many beautiful images of the soul's free movement that inhabit Dante's text, there is also a powerful message of control and scrutiny. Individuals are free – to be "correct" or "incorrect," as we know as early as the famous third line, "che la diritta via era smarrita." Finding one's own way means – finding the *right* way: and the rightness or wrongness of a way is to be defined not simply by the insights of faith, but by the authority of the worldly institution that Beatrice represents.

It is not just that this work holds that there is a best conception of the good human life. Plato and Aristotle hold that too. But Aristotle holds that it is up to us to argue about that, and that what he says might possibly be shown to be wrong by some perfectly good human argument. And argument should always continue so long as there are considerations to be addressed. In that sense he and his readers are equals and fellow searchers. For Dante, by contrast, the arbitration of divergent views about the good is the task of church authority. In this sense, the reason of human individuals is not in the least free. Examined about love by St. John near the summit of Paradise, asked how his bow was directed at love's target, Dante answers:

> ". . . By the arguments of philosophy
>   and by authority that descends from here
>   such Love has clearly stamped its seal upon me."[40]

This comes out clearly in the relationship between Beatrice and Dante. For love, in the context of dogma, infantilizes him:

and are supported by economic and social rights (for example, Maritain [1951], pp. 103–7), and his recommendation that people from different religious and secular traditions can endorse for political purposes a list of human rights (Maritain [1951], Chapter 4).

40 *Par.* XXVI.25–7, trans. Ciardi. See also XXVI.16–18: "The Good that is this cloister's happiness / is the Alpha and Omega of the scripture / love reads to me with light and heavy stress."

As a scolded child, tongue tied for shame, will stand
    and recognize his fault, and weep for it,
      bowing his head to a just reprimand,

so did I stand.[41]

As he acknowledges the justice of her rebuke, Beatrice becomes – not his beloved mistress, not his friend, not his equal, but a scolding mother. There is, finally, no real reciprocity in the relationship, to the extent that Beatrice is not just herself but also a figure of the church. Instead, there is a quite Augustinian abjectness, a shame at one's naked incompleteness.

Consider in this light, as well, the role of disgust in the poem. Now, in a sense, Hell is all about disgust. The tradition in which Dante is working represents the punishment of sinners in Hell, and the sinners themselves as objects of a violent and visceral disgust that serves to cordon off good Christians from sin, reinforcing their determination not to be contaminated by the foulness of the sin they inspect. Such, presumably, is the motivation for portraying Hell as stinking, sulfurous, sticky, a stagnant swamp, and so forth. One could not have a clearer demonstration of the mechanism described in Chapters 4 and 6, by which people project these properties onto objects in order to bound them off from the self. Dante inherits this material, and presumably he could only with difficulty have depicted Hell without it. But his poetic creativity denies him such a refuge. Whatever the traditional nature of his material, he has elaborated it with relish and brilliance, creating the most unforgettable portrayals of the disgusting in all of world literature. No poetry I know uses smell and bodily effluvia to greater effect.

In ethical terms, Dante uses disgust in a classic way – to bound of his surrogate, and his readers, from the material they witness. Even where sin and crime themselves are concerned, as I have argued in Part II, this is a dangerous strategem: for it says, in effect, that these creatures are not like us, not vulnerable as we are vulnerable. Where heresy and deviation from church authority are concerned, to bound off one's fellow humans as disgusting is particularly problematic, of a piece with the use of disgust in long traditions of anti-Semitism, misogyny, and

---

41 *Purg.* XXXI.64 – 67, trans. Ciardi.

other forms of hatred. Here a consequence of the minimal ethical view I have defended emerges clearly, and controversially: disgust at one's fellow human beings is always questionable, whatever its foundation. It is always a threat to genuine reciprocity, whether in love or in the social life.

In short, Dante's Aristotelianism points in two directions. On the one hand, it points toward a view that was unknown in his day, but which has become familiar as a type of Catholic liberalism (instantiated in the views of thinkers such as Jacques Maritain, John Courtney Murray, and, more recently, David Tracy). On this view, respect for agency takes a central position, preventing church authority from using coercive means to its goals, and enjoining public respect for divergent religions, even when one is convinced that they are in error. I have said that Dante's conception of the person as both free and needy promises a particularly attractive version of such a position. On the other hand, his view points toward Augustinian abjectness and shame, seeing in church authority the only remedy for disobedience. In this view, citizens are children, and the church is the only parent. On such a view, reciprocity should never be the basis for politics in this world.

2. *Individuality.* Dante's achievement centers around individuality, both separateness and particularity. He stresses that the cured Christian lover can embrace many elements of the particular person that Platonic love could not, or could not fully, embrace: the idiosyncrasies, the flaws and faults, the history, the particular talents and affinities that chart our course in life. But what about the body and its sexual desires? We have been speaking of the ascent of erotic love. When I make the claim that the love of the purified Dante for the blessed Beatrice is the "same love" that bound them in life, I am, then, implicitly claiming that this love is still erotic passion, and this, in turn, would appear to suggest that it still has bodily desire as one of its integral components. I have said that no particular bodily manifestation or reaction is essential for erotic love; but the desire for bodily connection is harder to sever from erotic passion, if it is really to be the same passion. What has become of the sexual element in Dante's love?

In Augustine's love of God, we can be certain that bodily desire plays no role. The love is still erotic in the sense that it is an intense longing for an object of attachment who is seen both as wonderful and as necessary for the person's well-being. But for Augustine sexual desire is a sign of our uncontrol, and thus cannot be a part of any adequate love. It plays no positive role at all for him in the life of a Christian. It is a major obstacle to the self-perfecting of the Christian agent, and among the primary reasons why Augustine concludes that perfection cannot be achieved in this world. When we regain our perfected bodies at the Last Judgment, sexual desire will be no part of them. Because of his rather Platonic severing of the identity of the soul from that of the body, he has difficulty explaining why the resurrection of the body is important at all.

Dante's love claims to embrace the body. He is also heir to a Thomistic Aristotelian psychology according to which the embodied nature of the soul is an essential part of its very identity. It is clear that he does endorse the resurrection of the body as an essential part of personal resurrection. If he really followed Aristotle, he would hold, as well, that sexual desire is a necessary and appropriate part of our human equipment. Used properly – in relation to the right person, at the right time, in the right relation to other pursuits, sexual activity, and the desire that prompts it, are parts of virtue. And Aristotle makes it clear that deficiency in sexual desire and activity is just as serious a deviation from virtue as the corresponding excess; indeed, "such lack of feeling is not human . . . and if there is someone to whom none of these [bodily pleasures] is delightful, and one does not differ from another, that person is far from being a human being."[42] Nor does Aristotle limit the standard of appropriateness to reproductive use within marriage. His only comment pertinent to the marital use of sexuality is a condemnation of *moicheia*, which is the violation of another man's wife or sometimes daughter, seen as a grave offense against the man. This leaves a lot of room for other uses of sexuality, in accordance with the norms of his time, both within and outside of marriage.[43] Because Aristotle shows no sign of thinking that sexual desire is per se sinful, he does not have great concern to regulate its expression.

42 *EN.* 1119a6 – 10; strictly speaking, Aristotle is discussing all bodily pleasures here, not singling out sexual pleasure. See also *De Anima* II.4, where he calls the desire for reproduction "the first and most natural capability of all that has life."

43 For good discussions of Aristotle's views on sex and love, see Price (1989), Price (forthcoming), and Sihvola (forthcoming).

But on this point Dante's Aristotelianism is heavily qualified by the Augustinian tradition. He argues carefully that the body was created separately from the soul, which is the source of our worth, and made by a special act of God.[44] Though very difficult to square with his Aristotelian hylomorphism, this view is important to his Christian ethical stance. As for the body's sexual desires, he can accept them only in the context of a view according to which nonprocreative sexual indulgence is sinful, and mutual pleasure, communication, and emotional expression are never sufficient to legitimate a sexual act. One may pursue these purposes insofar as they, in turn, protect and reinforce the reproductive bond; but they do not justify a sexual relationship that has no reproductive purpose.

The idea that sex is delightful in itself (and in combination with other nonreproductive human aims) is certainly present in the poem – for example, in its relatively sympathetic treatment of the lustful in Purgatory, who occupy the highest, thus the least grave, region of sin.[45] In the company of the lustful are poets with whom Dante was closely affiliated. And yet, the final position of the poem is that any love is better the closer it is to chastity (procreation in marriage always excepted). But this means that if there is any depth of passion that demands sex for its full expression, or any knowledge of particularity and agency that seems to be completed only by sexual intimacy, or, indeed, any poetry that seems to be "dictated" by the body's love and expressive of its joy – these would have to be omitted from the ascent.

To be sure, Dante has made a powerful argument to the effect that sexual aims and ends frequently distract us from both the agency and the particularity of those we love. For, as he says, sexual emotions may cause lovers to surrender their agency so completely that they prove unable to seek the good of the other, or even to seek to understand it. And insofar as the intense pleasures of sex sometimes cause lovers to focus on their own sensations, and to see one another only as causes of sensations, sex can clearly have a deleterious effect on the effort to see

---

44 *Purg.* XXIV, the very canto in which Dante introduces the purgation of lust. It is significant that the learned discourse on this point is spoken by Statius, a Christian, rather than by Virgil.

45 See note 12 to this chapter on the relationship between heterosexual and homosexual lust in the *Purgatorîo* and the *Inferno.*

another person as a person. All this is compounded by the role, in sexual arousal, of fantasies that may not correspond well to the other person's reality, and may not survive the discovery of it.

But to say that such defects sometimes obtain is, first of all, not to show that sexual love does not contain other goods that offset them. Furthermore, nothing Dante says shows us that sexual love *must* go hand in glove with egoism and illusion. Nor does he argue against the proposition that Joyce and Whitman will very vigorously maintain, namely the idea that even the element of fantasy in sexual life can be a vehicle through which we reach across the gulf that separates one person from another, developing our imaginations in ways that prove highly pertinent to seeing one another as fully human, whether in relationships of intimacy or in wider social relationships.

Dante loads the dice, A would feel: for he gives her, as examples of erotic fantasy, a Paolo and Francesca who behave like two starry-eyed teenagers. They seem far too immature to comprehend one another as individuals, or to express that comprehension, or even the aspiration toward it, through sex. This is all the more peculiar when we note that the real-life Francesca has been married for ten years at the time of the events narrated and has a daughter nine years old. Dante's choice to infantalize her expresses his view, perhaps not the right view, of the passion she represents. In his own case, he gives us true passion and true perception of the particular. But the way to Beatrice is through the purifying flames of chastity, in which alone, he argues, human beings find true delight.[46]

One may accept everything else in the ascent, while remaining uncertain about this particular feature, and also puzzled by it. Dante's attitude toward sexual desire is more puzzling than is Augustine's, because disobedience and ungovernability do not seem to be the essence of earthly sexuality, as he depicts it, nor is his attack on sexuality focused on the way it expresses a sinful condition of the will. On the other hand, his attack is not simply an attack on deception and infidelity, such as we might find in Aristotle, or in the Jewish tradition: it is too insistently focused on the very nature of bodily desire for that. So we

---

46 The Angel of Chastity is called "l'angel di Dio lieto," "the joyful angel of God" (*Purg.* XXVII.6); his song is "Happy are the pure in heart," "Beati mundo corde" (8).

remain puzzled as to what, precisely, the problem is, and why the body as such is seen as the seat of a problem.

I can conclude this line of questioning by talking, in fact, about flame. In the Roman poetry on which Dante was raised, and particularly in Virgil, flame is a persistent symbol of erotic passion – of its suddenness, its intensity, its power of both destruction and creation. It is frequently linked with the image of the serpent, a creature both potentially lethal and symbolic of fertility and flourishing.[47] This imagery is used to suggest that sexuality brings great beauty and richness to human life, a beauty that may be inseparable from some degree of danger to the self and to morality. In Dante, all of these values have been quite deliberately reversed. The serpent is now thoroughly evil, with no redeeming features: as in Augustine, he is the sinuous seductive tempter who brings sin to the previously rational and will-governed inhabitants of the Garden, whose fertility was thoroughly separable from desire. And flame is now no longer that which ignites desire in the body. In its symbolic connection with Christian love, it becomes, in Purgatory, the purifying instrument of chastity, which burns desire away, leaving the will whole and clean. The "signs of the ancient flame" are not really the signs of the *ancient*, the pagan, flame, with all its ambiguity and its double splendor. What claims to be the same love is to that extent profoundly different. A must ask herself whether she wants the old flame, with all its moral peril, or the new flame that will destroy a fundamental part of her love; whether she wants rescue from the new serpent, evil in his very nature, or the forked tongue of the old serpent, which brought both death and life.

3. *Compassion.* Dante again makes a decisive advance by making compassion for human suffering a fundamental part of the ascent. Beatrice, like all of the souls in Paradise, is motivated by *pietà*. The image of Christ's compassion for humanity, and his chosen agony, stands before the Christian lover as a paradigm, and this paradigm directs even those who are blessed to turn their attention back to the Earth. As in Augustine, we know that a great part of this compassion is addressed to the condition of sin, and the possibility of redemption. But Dante's portrait of compassion is more insistently worldly and

---

47 See Knox (1950) on Virgil; and Nussbaum (1994), Chapter 12, on Seneca.

social. He makes it perfectly plain that the earthly search for justice and human well-being is a matter of tremendous importance. To that extent, compassion, including heavenly compassion, must continue to turn itself back to the world, concerning itself with the feeding of the hungry, the protection of the persecuted, the consolation of those who mourn. St. Francis's voluntary poverty and his compassion for all suffering people make him one of the central "heroes" of the *Paradiso* (XI).

Furthermore, higher even than Aquinas and the philosophers of church doctrine are the Just Rulers, whose intense love shines like light, as they cluster, birds of passion (XVII.73 ff.), spelling out the name of what they love:

> In five times seven vowels and consonants
>> they showed themselves, and I grasped every part
>> as if those lights had given it utterance.
>
> The first words of that message as it passed
>> before me were DILIGITE IUSTITIAM.
>> QUI IUDICATIS TERRAM were the last.
>
> Then, in the fifth word, at the final M
>> they stayed aligned, and silvery Jupiter
>> seemed to be washed in a golden glow around them.

"Love justice, you who are judges of the Earth." And as if to indicate their abiding love of the Earth, they linger on the M, and ornament it with lilies. Although all the fiery souls speak with a single voice, they have not ceased to care about political affairs in the nations of the world: instead, they all care for all of the nations: Norway, Hungary, Portugal, Venice, Navarre, the entire world is illuminated by their radiance. Anger at corruption and compassion for the world are complexly linked in their glory.

There are, again, tensions. As a modern reader, one is jolted by the insistent refusal of compassion to the damned souls in Hell, especially when one realizes that damnation and salvation are frequently a matter of chance. (Francesca, for example, would no doubt have sought absolution had her husband not killed her by stealth. Although his punishment is worse than hers, we still might feel, unlike Dante, that Dante's pity at her plight is appropriate.) As Dante learns his lesson more and more thoroughly, he becomes more and more disdainful and hard toward the pain that he encounters. In *Inferno*, Canto V, he faints from pity. By Canto XIX, he can say, "Stay there, for you are rightly punished." In Canto XXXIII, he refuses the plea of a soul to open its frozen eyes, saying, "It was a courtesy to be rude to him," "E cortesia fu lui esser villano." This moment is all the more striking because this is a soul whose body still lives on Earth, and who still has, therefore, a chance of redemption.

Finally, in Dante's portrait of Paradise the attention of the redeemed souls to this world, and their laudable compassion, is in an ongoing tension with Dante's evident desire to represent them as complete and lacking in nothing. As I mentioned at the outset, Dante takes the tender words of grief used by Virgil at or the premature death of the child Marcellus and recasts them, in the Earthly Paradise, as words of welcome and celebration: "O give lilies with full hands." Here is surely an Augustinian moment in Dante – a moment when Arendt's Augustine, who judges all earthly loves and ties to be merely provisional, rises to the surface. The death of a child, the poem suggests, is nothing in the context of eternity, where all losses will be made up. There is simply no room for loss or grief in salvation. Joy is assured for all eternity, and the only use for Virgil's lines – the only use for the lily, flower of death – is to celebrate. Similarly, the lovers of justice adorn with lilies the final letter M in the word "Earth" – apparently because they are celebrating the justice they praise, even though they are aware that it does not yet exist on Earth. The joy of their outcry seems incompatible with any thought that their use of the lily is an expression of grief for its absence there.

In salvation there is indeed no loss. The worst thing that can happen to a saved person, as the result of an earthly misfortune, is to reside a bit further away from God than other saved souls. But, as Dante sees it – encountering Piccarda Donati, who is kept low down for having been raped[48] – "Everywhere in heaven is paradise, even if the grace of the highest good does not rain there in the same measure." One cannot help feeling that this doctrine is in some tension with the desire to represent the world as a place whose events matter greatly, even from the point of view of salvation.

---

48 *Par.* III; see Canto IV for an attempt to justify this result.

The image of Heaven as a place of self-sufficiency, and a place of beatitude in the sense of an end to mourning, cannot ultimately be reconciled with the idea of ongoing compassion for human life. Compassion is incomprehensible without mourning; if these things are important, they are important. A must ultimately choose between regarding this world as merely provisional and regarding it as a scene of signficant struggles, between the harmony of Heaven and the blazing letter M in the word "Earth," as the souls speak with light the phrase, "Love justice, you who judge the Earth."

13

THE ROMANTIC ASCENT: EMILY BRONTË

I. THE LEAP OF DESIRE

" 'If I were in heaven, Nelly,' " she said, " 'I should be extremely miserable.' " [1]

I dreamt, once, that I was there . . . [H]eaven did not seem to be my home; and I broke my heart with weeping to come back to earth; and the angels were so angry that they flung me out, into the middle of the heath on the top of Wuthering Heights, where I woke sobbing for joy.

Cathy's soul cannot live in the Christian Heaven. For her soul, she explains, is the same as Heathcliff's soul, and the heavenly soul of Linton is as different from theirs " 'as a moonbeam from lightning, or frost from fire' " (95). Much later, as she lies on her deathbed, now the wife of Edgar Linton, thinking the Linton thought that what she wants is an escape into " 'that glorious world' " of paradise and peace, Heathcliff watches her with burning eyes. At last she calls to him:

In her eagerness she rose and supported herself on the arm of the chair. At that earnest appeal he turned to her, looking absolutely desperate. His eyes, wide and wet, at last flashed fiercely on her; his breast heaved convulsively. An instant they held asunder, and then how they met I hardly saw, but Catherine made a spring, and he caught her, and they were locked in an embrace from which I thought my mistress would never be released alive: in fact, to my eyes, she seemed directly insensible. He flung himself into the nearest seat, and on my approaching hurriedly to ascertain if she had fainted, he gnashed at me, and foamed like a mad dog, and gathered her to him with greedy jealousy. I did not feel as if I were in the company of a creature of

---

1 Emily Brontë, *Wuthering Heights* (New York: Modern Library, 1943), p. 94. Hereinafter page references to this edition will be given in the text.

my own species: it appeared that he would not understand, though I spoke to him; so I stood off, and held my tongue, in great perplexity. (188–9)

Once again, as in Augustine and Dante, love is a flame that animates the eyes, a lightning bolt that pierces the fog of our obtuse daily condition; once again love's energy causes the lover to leap away from the petty egoism of the daily into an ecstatic and mutually loving embrace. But we know we are far from the world of the Christian ascent, even in its most erotic form. Cathy's spring is not an upward, but a horizontal movement – not toward Heaven, but toward her beloved moors and winds, severed from which she would find Heaven miserable; not toward God but toward Heathcliff, the lover of her soul. Nor is there redemption into Heaven in this work; there is, if anything, a redemption *from* a world dominated by the imagination of Heaven, into a world that the pious Ellen Dean can recognize only as an animal world, a world inhabited by creatures of a different species, who probably do not understand language, so thoroughly are they identified with the energy of the body. A few hours after Cathy's death, Heathcliff, as Ellen Dean tells us, in a sudden "paroxysm of ungovernable passion," dashes his head against the knotted trunk of a tree, splashing the bark with blood, "and, lifting up his eyes, howled, not like a man, but like a savage beast being goaded to death with knives and spears" (197). It is in his world alone, it would seem, that flame is truly found. As Cathy says to Edgar Linton, " 'Your cold blood cannot be worked into a fever: your veins are full of ice-water; but mine are boiling, and the sight of such chillness makes them dance' " (139).

In both the Platonic and the Christian pictures, love's ascent leads ultimately – whether in this life or the next – to a resting place in which there is no more longing and striving. Desire, propelling itself upward, seeks, and finds, its own extinction. The vulnerability that gave birth to desire is for all time removed – and, with it, the body seen as a seat of vulnerability and uncontrol, and therefore as an object of shame.[2] In Romantic conceptions of love's ascent, striving itself, and the peculiarly human movements of embodied erotic effort, become an ascent and an end in themselves, in no need of redemption by a static and extratemporal telos. Indeed, redemption is found in the very depth of exposure

---

2 The body that will join the soul at the Last Judgment is a purified and perfected body, no longer vulnerable to disease or unchaste desire.

in erotic effort – redemption from the clutter of everyday life and its superficial cares, which obscure from the self its own true being. In the very extent of the lovers' exposure to pain and risk in love, a risk so profound that it courts death, there is the most authentic expression of pure and purified life; and there is an expression of both agency and particularity in love that is, so it would seem, unavailable to any less reckless passion.

The Platonic lover and the Christian lover had to be redeemed from the ordinary world to a purer world; so too here. But the direction of redemption is not from striving and temporality and embodiment toward peace and stasis; it is, rather, from a hollow simulacrum of peace to the vibrant energy of the committed soul; striving is now given full value as an end. Romantic lovers will still, like the Christian lover, cast aspersions on false attachments to worldly status and worldly goods, which are still seen as impediments to authentic personal love. But their Heaven is not Edgar Linton's static paradise, it is the vibrant realm of earthly passion, in which nature and the body become the very essence of the loving soul. They will still have the Christian lover's concern for free agency and for particular perception in love. But this concern can no longer be housed, it would seem, within a conventional system of religious authority; agency must find its own direction from within itself, and its way looks to the conventional Christian like the way to Hell.

In the next two chapters I shall consider two very different versions of the Romantic ascent, asking whether it is an ascent at all, and whether its critique of the Christian ascent is valid as a critique of Augustine and Dante, or only as a commentary on degenerate instances of Christian piety that Augustine would also find prideful and dead. Finally, we must ask whether this love can stand in any fruitful relationship to community and to general compassion. Romantic love will claim that it uncovers deep sources of spiritual richness and personal authenticity without which any morality of human concern is dead. But the question must be what happens next – whether love can find a way back to compassion, or whether its absorption in the particular is so deep that it must simply depart from the world.

The two works that I shall examine give very different answers to these questions. Brontë issues a defiant challenge to all systems of conventional social virtue, suggesting that the Christian ascent is doomed in its very nature to produce chilly and inauthentic human relations. This is so, she will suggest, because of its relationship to the deep reasons why human beings shroud themselves in egoism and refuse true love. Up to a point, as we shall see, Brontë expresses a radical Augustinian Christian sensibility, convicting the conventional Christian world of self-protectiveness and pride. But her challenge ultimately reaches beyond the conventional, to challenge the roots of Augustinian Christianity itself. The novel is therefore structured around an opposition between Christian pity and authentic love, in which Heathcliff cannot "see out" of his love to a general concern for others, and in which the conventionally compassionate gaze of Ellen Dean cannot "see into" his passion, though its intensity lures and fascinates her. (Seeing Heathcliff staining the tree trunk with his own blood, she remarks, "It hardly moved my compassion – it appalled me: still, I felt reluctant to quit him so" [197].)

For Mahler, by contrast, the Christian ascent – in a reconfigured and distinctively Jewish form – can accommodate the erotic striving of the Romantic soul, producing a wonderful triumph of universal compassion over egoism and envy, of reciprocity and equality over hierarchy. Romantic ideas of authenticity give Christianity new sources of richness, a new promise of a fruitful relationship to the earthly struggle for justice. Mahler will acknowledge the obstacles to love on which Brontë also focuses; but in the view of the Second Symphony, those obstacles can be surmounted by Romantic striving itself.

In short: the Romantic lover claims to bring to the Christian world an energy and a depth of commitment that it has lost. Can it do so without forfeiting Christian pity and turning us into animals?

II. DARK OUTSIDERS

A preliminary observation. In each of the four works we shall henceforth consider, we discover the figure of an outsider or alien – closely linked, in all four cases, with the point of view of the implied author of the work. These aliens are of dark complexion, suspiciously soft and sensuous, of ambiguous gender or sexuality. They are mocked and hated by the Christian world around them, which shrinks from their too-intimate, too-penetrating gaze. The dark-skinned gypsy Heathcliff is both male and, as a double of Cathy, female; in the self-exposure of his passion he defies conventional norms of manly control. Mahler alludes musically to images of the Jew as dark alien, as woman, as bearer of a receptive and sensuous type of creativity that is anathema to conventional German music culture. Whitman's poet–speaker depicts himself as identical with the black slave's body sold at auction, with the woman who hides her desire behind the shutters of a fine house, with the male who gazes with erotic longing at other male bodies. Bloom the Jew is the antitype to Blazes Boylan, that emblem of conventional "piston"-like masculine energy; soft and sensuous, unaggressive, he sleeps with his head at the wrong end of the bed.

All four of these outsiders claim, however, that they are in their strangeness the true brothers of Christ, and that their strangeness offers in some way the authentic model of Christian love. Heathcliff, at first a Satanic figure, ultimately claims the true descent from Christ's selfless sacrifice. Mahler's work claims to exemplify, as against his rivals, an authentic Christian music culture. Whitman's speaker portrays Christ as his loving comrade, like him a wanderer and an alien. Bloom reminds the Irish anti-Semites that "Christ was a Jew like me."

For all four texts, a primary obstacle to the social success of love's ascent is a ubiquitous hatred and fear of the alien. According to these texts the dominant Christian cultures of the nineteenth and early twentieth centuries are far from being free from resentment and anger. Indeed, they are poisoned by loathing and fear of outsiders – by racial prejudice, sex inequality, anti-Semitism, hatred of the homosexual. These hatreds, related to one another in complex ways, have been aided and abetted by at least some instances of institutionalized Christianity, much though they appear to be incompatible with Christianity in its authentic form. Such societies, the texts argue, are unable to embody true reciprocity and equality, true compassion. Our four texts connect this fear of the alien, in different ways, with shame about one's own body and sexuality – suggesting that the Christian ascent has failed to rid society of anti-Semitism and racial prejudice precisely because it has insufficiently addressed the roots of this shame.

All four works were themselves aliens and outsiders in their own societies. Their too-intimate gaze at the nakedness of the human being was greeted with fear and, especially, with disgust. *Wuthering Heights* was called "coarse and loathsome"; "there is such a general roughness and savageness . . . as never should be found in a work of art."[3] Mahler's symphony alludes, as we shall see, to the anti-Semitic response that commonly attended his early works: they were found decadent, parasitical, morally rotten. The first edition of Whitman's *Leaves of Grass* was hailed as "a mass of stupid filth" whose author "should be kicked from all decent society as below the level of a brute."[4] Joyce's *Ulysses* was the object of censorship and litigation for decades; one American reviewer called it "the most infamously obscene book in ancient or modern literature . . . All the secret sewers of vice are canalized in its flow of unimaginable thoughts, images and pornographic words."[5] The works set out to cross-examine their Christian audience,[6] eliciting the very responses of shame and anger that they wish to problematize and, perhaps, to treat. We must ourselves confront the shocking in these works, or we will have no chance of understanding what they set out to do.

With these ideas in mind, let us turn to *Wuthering Heights*.

III. LOCKWOOD'S SHAME

We must begin with two features of the novel that are likely to be forgotten by readers who have read the novel years ago, or whose memory is colored by the Hollywood film version. These are: the character of the work's narrator, Mr. Lockwood, and the ubiquity in the text of hatred and revenge. The novel begins as follows:

I have just returned from a visit to my landlord – the solitary neighbor that I shall be troubled with. This is certainly a beautiful country! In all England, I do not believe that I could have fixed on a situation so completely removed from the stir of society. A perfect misanthropist's heaven; and Mr. Heathcliff and I are such a suitable pair to divide the desolation between us. A capital

---

3 Reviews quoted in Barker (1994), p. 91.
4 Quoted in Reynolds (1995), pp. 346–7.
5 James Douglas in the *Sunday Express*, quoted in de Grazia (1992), p. 26. See my further discussion in Nussbaum (1999b).
6 The Douglas review of Joyce continues with an attack on its allegedly blasphemous character: ". . . its unclean lunacies are larded with appalling and revolting blasphemies directed against the Christian religion and against the holy name of Christ – blasphemies hitherto associated with the most degraded orgies of Satanism and the Black Mass" (de Grazia [1992], p. 26).

fellow! He little imagined how my heart warmed towards him when I beheld his black eyes withdraw so suspiciously under their brows, as I rode up, and when his fingers sheltered themselves, with a jealous resolution, still further in his waistcoat, as I announced my name. (3)

The work opens, then, with the refusal of community. The city man has come to the country to avoid, it seems, the "stir" and bustle of superficial social forms. But what attracts Mr. Lockwood to Thrushcross Grange is not simply is wildness, its promise of intensity. It is, at the same time, its desolation, its emptiness of love. It is, at the same time, retentiveness and self-sufficiency.

The man through whose eyes this strange world is described for us is a city man, a refined society man, a man of means. His usual occupation in the country is hunting – which he calls "devastat[ing] the moors" (360). His usual milieu is "the stirring atmosphere of the town" (359). His usual vacation choice is "a month of fine weather at the seacoast" (7). His choice of the desolate isolation of Thrushcross Grange is, however, not accidental: it grows from the "peculiar constitution" that led his mother to predict that he "should never have a comfortable home" (7). This constitution is shortly revealed as an inability to accept the reciprocation of love:

While enjoying a month of fine weather at the seacoast, I was thrown into the company of a most fascinating creature: a real goddess in my eyes, as long as she took no notice of me. I "never told my love" vocally; still, if looks have language, the merest idiot might have guessed I was over head and ears: she understood me at last, and looked a return – the sweetest of all imaginable looks. And what did I do? I confess it with shame – shrunk icily into myself, like a snail; at every glance returned colder and farther; till finally the poor innocent was led to doubt her own senses, and, overwhelmed with confusion at her supposed mistake, persuaded her mamma to decamp. By this curious turn of disposition I have gained the reputation of deliberate heartlessness; how undeserved, I alone can appreciate. (7)

The entire story, then, is made possible because Lockwood is afraid and ashamed of love. In a gesture that parallels Cathy's refusal of Heathcliff, he pretends that he does not have the feelings that he evidently does – why? Because to him the reciprocation of love is more terrifying than its nonreciprocation, because the gaze of desire, seeing into his own desire, makes him passive and ashamed of his own softness, the snail without its shell. Because a life of watching and romantic narration is manageable, and a life of passion is not. His name is significantly chosen: he locks his vulnerability away behind the wooden exterior of conventional social forms.

Nor is this locking without its clear psychic cost. The first night he spends under the roof of Wuthering Heights, stranded by a snowstorm, Lockwood is tormented by a dream. He falls asleep reading Cathy Linton's journal, in which she has been describing her brother Hindley's cruelty to Heathcliff. He now dreams that he is in a chapel, where the Reverend Jabes Branderham is delivering a sermon divided into four hundred and ninety parts, each discussing a separate sin. "They were," he notes, "of the most curious character: odd transgressions that I never imagined previously." As he reaches "the First of the Seventy-First," which is the "sin that no Christian need pardon," Lockwood protests: he is tired of listening, tired of forgiving. " 'Fellow-martyrs, have at him!' " he calls to the crowd. " 'Drag him down and crush him to atoms, that the place which knows him may know him no more.' " Jabes now turns to him with a fearful intensity. " *'Thou art the man!'* " he cries. " 'The First of the Seventy-First is come. Brethren, execute upon him the judgment written. Such honour have all His saints!' " The assembly rushes around Lockwood, determined to crush him to death. He wakes, seeing that the noise of the crowd's blows is identical with the tapping of a fir tree branch outside his window.

Lockwood now falls asleep once more – this time to dream of the arm of Cathy Linton, reaching through the casement, calling " 'Let me in – let me in . . . I'm come home. I'd lost my way on the moor.' " He is terrified, and "terror made me cruel." He puts the woman's wrist against the broken window pane "and rubbed it to and fro till the blood ran down and soaked the bedclothes." Next he plugs the hole in the windowpane with books, stopping his ears to "exclude the lamentable prayer." "I'll never let you in," he shouts, "not if you beg for twenty years."

Lockwood's dream reveals a depth of guilt and anxiety that can only be discharged, it seems, in ferocious aggression against anyone who sees into his situation. What is the four hundred and ninety-first sin, the sin that no Christian need pardon? Is it the erotic love he has felt, or is it his snail-like shame, his inability to express and reciprocate love? We do not know: we know only that Lockwood wants to murder the eye that sees him, to wipe out the reminder of his nakedness. We know only that he is haunted by the piteous voice of an unknown woman, trying to force her frozen arm through a crack in the casement. He longs so intensely to open the casement that he is forced to adopt three stratagems to prevent himself from yielding. He stops his ears; he piles up books, the armory of the intellect; he bloodies the arm that has reached too far inside. As he says: terror made me cruel.

By framing the narrative in this way, Brontë makes us consider from the start that the obstacles to deep love are not only obstacles created by superficial social deadness and hypocrisy – though, as we shall see, they do include these. The obstacle to Lockwood's love is in his own shame and fear, which make him flee the nakedness of reciprocated passion. He is both kin to Heathcliff and his opposite pole – fascinated by his darkness, drawn to his gloomy integrity and depth, to the depth of life in the countryside, where people live "more in earnest, more in themselves, and less in surface, change, and frivolous external things" (72). But at the same time he is ice to Heathcliff's fire, the self-protective snail to Heathcliff's total exposure, shame to his almost bestial shamelessness, observation and narration to his total immersion. Self-protection has exacted a price in his inner world: for the effort required to repel the objects that ask to be let in is so great that it produces a poisonous cruelty and envy directed at all in the world who are not locked up: at the dark alien above all, whose gaze reveals to him his own fear of penetration. Later, having lost the chance to court the younger Cathy out of fear of danger, thus repeating the refusal of love that has led him to the moors, Lockwood can only watch Cathy and Hareton with "a mingled sense of curiosity and envy," and, "feeling very mean and malignant," "skul[k] round to seek refuge in the kitchen" (363–4).

The famous Lawrence Olivier film of the novel had one great virtue: the nobility and clarity of Olivier's Heathcliff, who has an evident greatness of soul, a towering generosity of passion and thought, that the other inhabitants of this dark world all lack. In another way, however, the film is a disastrous distortion. For it makes the world of the novel, if dark, still "romantic" in an acceptable and even pretty way. It more or less completely omits one of the novel's most striking characteristics: the obsession of its narrators and of almost all the other characters with anger, revenge, even cruelty. The story, as recollected by the internal narrator, Ellen Dean, begins with an act of Christian charity. Mr. Earnshaw comes home from Liverpool with a gypsy child, "a dirty, ragged, black-haired child" (42). "You must e'en take it as a gift of God," says Mr. Earnshaw to his wife, "though it's as dark almost as if it came from the devil" (42). The child was homeless and starving in the streets. He had inquired for his guardian, and, getting no reply, refused to leave him as he had found him. Earnshaw now takes the alien into his home, determined to treat him as the equal of his own children.

From this auspicious beginning, however, we soon move on to a world dominated by envy, prejudice, and violence. The children refuse to allow Heathcliff into their room. Ellen Dean exiles him to the stair landing. Hindley and Ellen come increasingly to hate him, and they torment him without cease, both physically and psychologically. Heathcliff, all the while, endures Hindley's blows without retaliation; he "said precious little, and generally the truth" (44). Because Mr. Earnshaw favors Heathcliff, "all hated, and longed to do him an ill turn" (47).[7] The torture accelerates at Mr. Earnshaw's death. Heathcliff is relegated to servant status, mocked and humiliated. When at last he turns against his oppressors, throwing a dish of applesauce at Edgar Linton, the pattern of the violent plot is set. Envy and retribution dominate the novel, in scene after scene of brutal and uncontrolled physical violence in which every character partakes. Cathy pinches her devoted servant Ellen "with a prolonged wrench, very spitefully on the arm" (83). She slaps her on the cheek, shakes little Hareton until he is white, and hits her suitor Edgar on the ear (83). Hindley takes a knife to his own son and threatens to cut off the little boy's ears (86). Heathcliff and Cathy talk with pleasure of how Isabella Linton's face might be turned black and blue "every day or two" (125). Edgar Linton, overcome by "mingled anger and humiliation," strikes Heathcliff "full on the throat a blow that would have levelled a slighter man" (136). Cathy dashes her own head against the sofa until she lies as if dead, with "blood on her lips" (139). The marriage of Heathcliff and Isabella contains, it appears, both physical violence and sexual sado-

7 This is a judgment made by Mr. Earnshaw, as reported by Ellen, who does not believe it. But the reader has ample reason to believe it.

masochism.[8] Heathcliff holds the dying Cathy's arm so fiercely that Ellen sees "four distinct impressions left blue in the colorless skin." Heathcliff dashes his head against the knotted tree trunk, splashing it with his blood (197), and throws a knife at Ellen, who mocks his grief (213). Little Hareton is observed "hanging a litter of puppies from a chair-back in the doorway" (214) – as Heathcliff had once hanged Isabella Linton's little dog (170).

As Lockwood says: terror and shame produce cruelty. From the petty quarrels and the petty revenge of Edgar and Isabella (56) to the grand obsessive sweep of Heathcliff's entire life, the desire to retaliate for a slight or humiliation produces most of the action of the book, until every love is mingled with disdain or hatred. Hindley hates Heathcliff and avenges on him his own father's deficient love. Later, reduced to a drunken shadow of his former self, his eyes gleaming with "burning hate," he contemplates a final act of violence against the man who has robbed him of his property (206). Isabella hates the Heathcliff who abuses her. Edgar "abhors" Heathcliff "with an intensity which the mildness of his nature would scarecely seem to allow" (215). Heathcliff, from the beginning mocked and humiliated for his dark skin, his poverty, and his unknown origins, devotes his entire life to revenge against Hindley and the Lintons, making himself master of Hindley's fortune, leading Isabella into a life of misery. Just as he can play the gentleman better than the gentlemen, just as he can play the moneymaker better than the moneymakers, so too can he play at envy and violence – although his heart is altogether elsewhere, although he could do no harm to his beloved Cathy, although he would and does give her his entire life. The others torment out of fear; only Heathcliff torments out of love.

8 This aspect is veiled in obscurity. Isabella breaks off – "But I'll not repeat his language, nor describe his habitual conduct: he is ingenious and unresting in seeking to gain my abhorrence! I sometimes wonder at him with an intensity that deadens my fear: yet, I assure you, a tiger or a venomous serpent could not rouse terror in me equal to that which he wakens." (170). It is compatible with these lines that Heathcliff's sadism consists in mockery and humiliation, rather than in physical sexual cruelty. But the intent to cause suffering and humiliation of some painful sort is central to Heathcliff's plan: "he told me . . . that I should be Edgar's proxy in suffering, till he could get hold of him" (170). Isabella's narration of the marriage does not acknowledge any pleasure in Heathcliff's cruelty; but Heathcliff sees it: "But no brutality disgusted her: I suppose she has an innate admiration of it . . ." (177).

IV. PITY AND CHARITY

The novel creates two antagonistic worlds: the world of the Lintons, a world of (allegedly) Christian "pity," "charity," and "humanity," and the world of Heathcliff, a world of love from the point of view of which the Linton sentiments appear watery and self-serving. Isabella Linton, writing home to Ellen after her marriage to Heathcliff: "How did you contrive to preserve the common sympathies of human nature when you resided here? I cannot recognize any sentiment which those around share with me." (160) Ellen is moved to compassion for Heathcliff's loss, but she cannot really feel compassion for him – so far has he, in her view, put himself outside the common behavior of human beings. "Do you understand what the word pity means?" she has asked him long before. "Did you ever feel a touch of it in your life?" (179) It would appear that the Linton world is the world of compassion and the moral virtues, whereas Heathcliff's world is amoral and impervious to sympathy.

But things are not so simple. We have seen already that the world of the Christian characters is portrayed as the source of poisonous cruelty against the alien. Heathcliff can give back what he gets – but he is not the initiator of violence, nor is it clear that his refusal of the Lintons moral sentiments is to be simply condemned. For the world of the Lintons, the heavenly world, is depicted as also a shallow world: an indoor world, by contrast to the wild and passionate world of the moors, a world of stasis by contrast to Heathcliff's and Cathy's restless motion, a world of ungenerous and spiteful social judgments, by contrast to the sweep and size of all of Heathcliff's passions. When Cathy announces her plan to marry Edgar, Ellen Dean asks her where the obstacle is:

"Here! and here!" replied Catherine, striking one hand on her forehead, and the other on her breast: "in whichever place the soul lives. In my soul and in my heart, I'm convinced I'm wrong." (93)

At this point ensues the passage with which this chapter opens, which we can now understand more fully. Ellen is wrong, Cathy continues, because Heaven is not a place in which her soul could ever be happy. She dreamed that she was in Heaven, and wept for the Earth; and "the angels were so angry that they flung me out into the middle of the heath on the top of Wuthering Heights; where I woke sobbing for joy" (95). Heathcliff's soul, she continues, is made of the same stuff that hers is, he is "more myself than I am," while Linton's soul "is as different as a moonbeam from lightning, or frost from fire" (95). And after Heathcliff's angry rejection of pity, he insists that these heavenly sentiments, in the Linton world, produce a kind of Hell, the absence of real passion:

Oh, I've no doubt she's in hell among you! . . . You say she is often restless, and anxious-looking; is that a proof of tranquillity? . . . And that insipid, paltry creature attending her from *duty* and *humanity*! From *pity* and *charity*! He might as well plant an oak in a flowerpot, and expect it to thrive, as imagine he can restore her to vigour in the soil of his shallow cares! (180)

Where is, then, the real Heaven of emotion, and where its Hell?

There is an ambiguity, then, in the novel's treatment of Christian charity. On the one hand, charity presents Heathcliff as demonic and scarcely human; on the other hand, charity stands accused, itself, of shallowness, fearfulness, and self-protection. There is a corresponding ambiguity in the imagery used of Heathcliff, who is depicted as bestial and demonic – but also as a figure of authentic Christian love. He is "savage" (32, 54), a "cannibal" (207), a mad dog (188), an "evil beast . . . waiting his time to spring and destroy" (126), a "bull," a "tiger or a venomous serpent" (170), a "brute beast" (207), a "savage beast being goaded to death with knives and spears" (197). "A half-civilized ferocity lurked . . . in the depressed brows and eyes full of black fire" (112).

But he is no *mere* beast: for at the same time Heathcliff is depicted repeatedly as an inhabitant of Hell, as, ultimately, the Devil himself. From the first, his looks evoke the comparison: "You must e'en take it as a gift of God," says old Mr. Earnshaw, "though it's as dark almost as if it came from the devil!" (42). His dark peering eyes are like "devil's spies," not "confident innocent angels" (66). Mrs. Dean judges him "diabolical," the house an "infernal house" (77) – by contrast to the Linton house, which is like Heaven (56). Again and again he is called a devil and a fiend (101, 160, 203, 204, 206, 212, 214; cf. 'hell' at 165, 186, 133). Clearly, it is not a minor devil that he is seen to resemble, it is Lucifer himself, whose pride leads him to rebel against all religion, all moral authority. When he refuses Ellen Dean's compassion after Cathy's death, she cries, "Your pride cannot blind God! You tempt Him to wring them [sc., his nerves], till He forces a cry of humiliation." (196)

On the other hand, however, it is only Heathcliff, in this novel, who gives his life for another. All of the other characters hold something back, insist on control and calculation, insist on seeing all round about them, their mind and eyes not fixed on any one. And this means, Brontë suggests, that in a very real sense they are already half-dead. What the Devil's spies of Heathcliff's countenance see in their faces is avoidance, eyes deflected away from the world and from those whom they are alleged to love. When Edgar Linton dies, his "rapt, radiant gaze" on the heavenly world, "none could have noticed the exact minute of his death, it was so entirely without a struggle" (334). The love of Heathcliff for Cathy contains the total exposure of self to other from which Lockwood shrinks in fear and in shame. Only Heathcliff permits his very soul to be at risk. The other is in him and is him. In her death he dies, in a surrender, incomprehensible to the narrators, of reason and of boundaries. At Cathy's death, the blood of Heathcliff's head is spattered on the bark of a tree, "a repetition of other [scenes] acted during the night" (197).

The dead sentiments of Linton are linked with social morality, and both of these with self-protective control and calculation. Heathcliff's entirely unguarded love is linked, by contrast, with a deeper sort of generosity and the roots of a truer altruism. There is no character but Heathcliff in this novel who really sacrifices his life for the life of another, none who acts against his own interests with sincere and uncompromised altruism. For he refrains from doing any harm to Edgar for fear that Cathy would suffer by his loss, and sacrifices his own interests at every turn to hers, both before and after her death. The capacity to throw away all self-centered calculation is at the heart of real altruism and authentic (Christian) morality. And in this sense Heathcliff – despite the vindictiveness forced into his character by abuse and humiliation – is not only the only living person among the dead, the only civilized man among savages, he is, in a genuine if peculiar sense, the only Christian among the Pharisees, and – with respect to the one person he loves – a sacrificial figure of Christ himself, the only one who sheds his own blood for another. The novel suggests that only in this deep exposure is there true sacrifice and true redemption. At the novel's end, only Heathcliff's tombstone is not covered by moss; and a child tells Lockwood that he has seen Heathcliff and Cathy walking on the moors. "They are afraid of nothing," Lockwood grumbles – referring ambiguously to the ghostly couple and to the younger living couple who have just returned from a loving walk. "Together they would brave Satan and all his legions."

V. OUR OWN HEARTS, AND LIBERTY

What, then, is the novel's critique of the Christian ascent? It works at two distinct levels. The first level is a critique of the Christianity depicted in the novel; up to a point we may suppose that this is a critique of a degenerate, imperfect Christianity. At this level, four grave charges are made. First, the Christian sentiments of the pious characters are shown to be in large part hypocritical. The Lintons, Joseph, Ellen Dean, all pay lip service to pity and charity, but – as Ellen Dean at least has the grace to admit (108) – all behave selfishly and vindictively most of the time. Joseph's rigid piety is a way of tyrannizing over the house; Edgar and Isabella are vain and "petted" children whose love is contaminated by vanity. All engage in vindictive actions, all seek to humiliate their enemies. And whereas Heathcliff's revenge is grand and caused by love, theirs is petty and self-serving. These degenerate sentiments, however, do derive nourishment from the institutionalized Christianity the characters know: for they have all learned to justify their acts using images of divine anger and retribution. Heathcliff's pride, says Ellen, tempts God to wring his nerves "till He forces a cry of humiliation." So the first charge is that institutionalized Christianity does too little to discourage vindictiveness and hatred.

Second, institutionalized Christianity is charged with supporting a world of social hierarchy that excludes the poor and the strange, the dark-skinned and the nameless. For the Linton world, Heathcliff's dark looks and lower-class manners must keep him apart from a Cathy who is taught that to marry him would "degrade" her (95). The good Christians are too prompt, we feel, to baptize Heathcliff as fiend and devil; it is an all-too-convenient way of repudiating a look that they do not like, a sexuality that frightens them. From the perspective of Christian piety, Cathy sees Heathcliff as terribly unlike herself, his love as unworthy. From the perspective of her love, these distinctions of rank vanish, and he is "more myself than I am." To him as well, she is his life, his soul; and nothing but her refusal can divide them. The second charge, then, is that Christianity will only realize its true potential if it embraces these differences and teaches a truly universal love.

Third, conventional Christianity, it is charged, teaches people to look to a static paradise in which all movement and striving cease. It thus teaches them to denigrate their own movement and striving, to cultivate the small Linton virtues rather than the large risk-taking virtues. This is a point made much later by Nietzsche; it emerges here in the contrast between Edgar, who dies before his death, and Heathcliff, who has no interest in any static telos. Cathy, torn between the two conceptions of the end, at last prefers the this-worldly striving of Heathcliff, the "ramble at liberty" (55) that was always her own and Heathcliff's delight. The love of Earth is an end in itself. An obsessive theme in Emily Brontë's poems and essays, it is often, as here, associated with the theme of personal liberty. The heavenly world is depicted as one in which agency has been surrendered, at last, to authority, a world in which one's place is fixed for all eternity. The world of nature and the earth, by contrast, is a world in which the heart can roam freely, and its agency is whole: "Give we the hills our equal prayer," Emily wrote in a poem of 1841, "Earth's breezy hills and heaven's blue sea ; / We ask for nothing further here / But our own hearts and liberty." As Charlotte Brontë wrote, describing Emily's physical breakdown when she was sent to a boarding school where she could not roam around on the moors: "Liberty was the breath of Emily's nostrils; without it, she perished."[9]

We may add that the strength and agency of the female is a topic of special importance to Emily, from the juvenilia onward. Whereas Charlotte Brontë spent her childhood depicting heroines who were passive and languid, Emily from the start depicted them as equal agents, who are degraded by an enforced passivity. In their historical essays about the Siege of Oudenarde, written while in Belgium, Charlotte makes the women passive supporters of the men; Emily writes: "Even the women – that class condemned by the laws of society to be a heavy burden in every instance of action or danger, on this occasion put aside their

9 Quoted in Barker (1994), p. 236.

degrading privileges and played a distinguished role in the defense."[10] Here, she again sees the female as degraded by a static privileged role, and dignified only by risk-taking action.

In this third critique, Emily, known to many acquaintances as the most philosophical and rigorous of the Brontë children, goes straight to the heart of the question of agency and freedom in the Christian ascent. The directedness of longing toward a static telos, she suggests, diminishes the significance of human agency and its liberty. The provisional character of all earthly relations squeezes them into small Linton sentiments. As Heathcliff says, it is like planting an oak in a flowerpot. This world, the suggestion is, will always remain a Hell if we are allowed to aim at redemption from it, rather than at the amelioration of life within it, and led to anticipate the end of striving, rather than to respect the dignity of the striving itself.

Finally, the Christian world of the novel is charged with a neglect of one of the greatest of the human faculties, the imagination. None of the Christian characters imagines the life of another with vivid sympathy. Lockwood and Ellen Dean skulk around the edges of the world of the novel watching and waiting; their damaged inner lives call out to the characters with a mysterious longing; but this longing is distorted by malice. Only Heathcliff, from the beginning, knows how to imagine the hearts of his fellows. Only he consoles Cathy on her father's death; only he can inhabit her soul, and move so close to her that their two souls are as one. Heathcliff's heart, by contrast, is treated obtusely from the start by all of the Christian characters around him, who can penetrate no deeper than the color of his skin, so little have their faculties of wonder been cultivated. What is called Christian pity is but a shell, until it is infused and given life by the visitation of that "sterner power" – as Emily writes in another early poem.

How far do these four charges touch the Christian ascent itself, and how far are they merely indictments of a lifeless and degenerate Christianity? Would a keenly alive, surgingly erotic Augustinian Christianity contain all that Brontë calls for here? (In asking these questions I do not step outside the world of the text itself; for Emily was an extremely learned classical scholar whose education included much essay writing

10 Quoted in ibid., pp. 387–8.

on just such Christian themes. Indeed, her teacher in Brussels, M. Heger, expressed the view that Emily ought to become a philosopher: she had "a head for logic, and a capability of argument, unusual in a man, and rare indeed in a woman.")[11] So: what is this philosophical mind expressing, and how far does it cut into the views we have studied?

We have already had questions for both Dante and Augustine about anger and intolerance, and about the hierarchies created by them. Christianity will need to become more inclusive of the alien and the stranger than either of these two ascents has yet been, in order to satisfy her demand. A still deeper challenge lies in the Romantic defense of liberty and imagination, values that are difficult to accommodate fully within a universe in which desire points insistently toward Heaven. Dante, I have said, took up this challenge to at least some extent, restoring dignity to the this-worldly will and denying that earthly relations and acts are merely provisional. But there remained questions about the freedom of the mind within a context of authority, and about the significance of this-worldly striving within a universe that points toward eternity. One can imagine a Romantic reformulation of the Thomistic Christian universe – and Mahler, in effect, will propose one. But it does require a serious reformulation of the ideal, not just a criticism of people who fail to live up to the norm.

VI. "DON'T LET ME SEE YOUR EYES"

We must now move, however, to the deeper level of the novel's critique. For the novel's critique of Christian charity does not address itself only to these elements, revisable in principle. Indeed, it traces all of these defects – especially cruelty to and hatred of the alien – to deeper human motives that not only are not cured but are very much nourished by Christian teaching.

The love of Heathcliff and Cathy requires, we said, a total exposure of self to another's touch and gaze. In this way it courts a risk so total that it verges toward death. To one who loves totally, no defense can exist. The other is in oneself and is oneself. For to allow one's boundaries to be porous in this way is not to be the self that one was, and in

---

11 Quoted in ibid., p. 392.

society is. It is, indeed, to be an alien and a gypsy, to give up on the hard shell of self-sufficiency with which all of these characters protect themselves.

The real question of the novel, we must now see, is not why Heathcliff cannot have Cathy. That is a material and social and political question, and in the end a superficial one. The deeper question is why Cathy cannot accept Heathcliff, why she must be false to him, and to her own soul. Why is she driven to choose someone who cannot truly love her over someone who sees and loves and *is* her, a civilized but superficial sexual flirtation (the "poor fancy you felt for Linton" [189]) over a profound passion of the body and the spirit, the conventions of stable public married life over a life that contains and acknowledges her real self? "The sea could be as readily contained in that horse-trough, as her whole affection be monopolised by him!" (175) And yet she chooses that "love" over the love that is the identity of her own soul.

It is not enough to say that the situation Heathcliff can offer her involves pain and adversity and social exclusion. This is true, but it is no explanation. As Heathcliff says:

Because misery and degradation, and death, and nothing that God or Satan could inflict would have parted us, *you*, of your own will, did it. I have not broken your heart – *you* have broken it; and in breaking it, you have broken mine . . . *Why* did you betray your own heart, Cathy? (189)

Why indeed. Cathy's story, I think, is another version of the story of Mr. Lockwood. The extreme exposure of true passion, and its links with pain and death, are as intolerable, ultimately, to her as they were to our narrator. A part of her is Heathcliff. But she cannot bear the nakedness of that part, she is driven to cover it over with the clothing of the Linton life, with marriage and children, with social forms and hierarchy, with a life that is a revenge against both her and him, against the naked self that he calls forth in her. In seeking to protect herself from the risk of death, however, she kills not only him but also her own soul, and forces him to hate as well as love her. He says, holding her, "Kiss me again; and don't let me see your eyes! I forgive what you have done to me. I love *my* murderer – but *yours*! How can I?" They draw close only then, in the grief of impending death, "their faces hid against each other, and washed by each other's tears" (189–90). Heathcliff, who lives in and fully acknowledges the depth of his passion, is by this very act of acknowledgment placed outside the human species. For it is most human to avoid being seen with the eyes of love.

What are these people ashamed of? What do they fear, in fearing love? They fear and are ashamed of being given to and for others, which means that they fear following the image of Christ. But at the same time, the fear and shame take the body and its erotic passions as their object. Lockwood thinks of himself as a snail, curling up inside his shell to avoid encountering the gaze of passion. The snail without the shell is what he is ashamed to be. This is a deep image of the nakedness of the body, seen as an emblem of our helplessness, our penetrability, our givenness to the world's influences and to death. The object of shame and fear is not sexuality in and of itself, but sexuality experienced as a sign of our helpless insufficiency. Love, Brontë suggests – including and especially true Christian love – requires us to be in our insufficiency, given to the world and to others. Christianity, however, reacts to our shame by telling us to cover ourselves – with a fig leaf, with a snail's shell, with the hope of Heaven, the submission to authority, the flame of chastity. It tells us that yes, we should be ashamed of our nakedness, we should shrink from the powerful gaze of love. So there is ultimately, she suggests, a deep inconsistency between radical Augustinian openness to grace and the Augustinian attitude toward the body and the worldly person. We cannot give our bodies to the world as Christ did if we cannot manage, first, to inhabit them and make them ourselves.

The Christian response to primal shame – no easily eliminable aspect of Christian teaching – is thus seen to be in league with the refusal of love. But the refusal of love is, we have said, at the root of the hatred of the gaze of the woman, of the alien, the alien's all-too-fleshy dark presence, the woman's all-too-palpable embodiment. It is then Brontë's somewhat obscure suggestion that Christian morality is more than accidentally linked with racial hatred and misogyny.

But it is not as if she offers a viable alternative. The life of Heathcliff is unlivable in the world. It will not be tolerated by human beings, who have a deep need to be or to become snails and to inflict pain upon those who are not. Nor is it, perhaps, even livable in itself, for already it wears its death upon its face. She offers us, then, a powerful dream of a love that is permitted to enter in at the casement, a love that wears the nobility of true humanity – only to show us that we all will scrape the arm against the pane of broken glass, and pile our books against the opening, and shout, "I'll never let you in, not if you beg for twenty years."

VII. PHANTOMS OF THOUGHT

Is there a Heaven buried within this novel's Hell? Does the love of young Cathy and Hareton, whose development occupies the entire second half of the novel, show possibilities for the harmonious reconciliation of Edgar Linton's pity and Heathcliff's passion? Cathy is introduced as a hopeful fusion of the best elements of the two lines:

Her spirit was high, though not rough, and qualified by a heart sensitive and lively to excess in its affections. That capacity for intense attachments reminded me of her mother: still she did not resemble her; for she could be soft and mild as a dove, and she had a gentle voice and pensive expression: her anger was never furious; her love never fierce: it was deep and tender. (221)

And there are hopeful signs in her relationship with Hareton – as she eventually shows him gentle compassion, teaching him to read, and as his sexual strength evokes in her an intensity that Linton Heathcliff could not even perceive.

And yet there is something unconvincing in the union. The most hopeful point is the manly vulnerability of Hareton, whose willingness to risk humiliation and shame for the sake of passion show the potential for real love. But there is an obstacle in the character of his lover. For young Cathy, her father's daughter, spoiled and petulant, has none of the first Cathy's demonic intensity of spirit. Just as she plays at loving a Linton who cannot possibly offer her any real emotion, so later she plays at being the civilizing force who will bring Hareton into line. She seeks him out more because she is bored than because she loves or needs him, and the very notion of deep erotic and spiritual vulnerability seems foreign to her. As she bends over her reading lover, teasing him for his mispronunciation with a "voice as sweet as a silver bell," saying "Recollect, or I'll pull your hair!" (363), we know that we have here but a pale shadow of the woman who clings to Heathcliff with an embrace that was her death. Hareton, following her flirtatious petty lead, will soon, we feel, be as dead as she.

Is there ascent and reconciliation, then, in the act of narration itself, in the perspectives of Ellen Dean and Lockwood, the riveted onlookers, who see and are moved by the depth of love without being drawn away altogether from general social concerns? We have no reason to think so. The self-protective, snail-like character of Lockwood that keeps him in the world also prevents his heart from admitting anything closer to love than envy and spite, its twisted shadows. He sees enough of Heathcliff that we may see him too. But in the end he does not acknowledge the part of Heathcliff that is in himself. Nor does Ellen Dean show herself capable of real love, in her self-protective avoidance of risk – from the time when she is punished by old Mr. Earnshaw for callously making Heathcliff sleep on the stairs (44), to her passive collaboration with cruelty years later, as she pities young Cathy but shuts her door for fear of being moved to risk danger. "I didn't wish to lose my place, you know" (345). What she says of the whole world is surely true of her, at least: "we *must* be for ourselves in the long run; the mild and generous are only more justly selfish than the domineering" (108).

There is no final summation to be given here, because there is no positive proposal. The sensibility of this work tragically refuses all solutions, finding the roots of social degeneration deep in the human being's very way of being in the world. It imagines a Christianity reformed so as to remove hierarchy and revenge, so as to validate the claims of this-worldly striving and of the imagination. Then it takes the vision away, leaving us only with an image that haunts the reader's dreams, a hand groping at the casement. We think that we are people of sympathy and charity; we think that we love and permit ourselves to be loved. Chances are that we really don't. Chances are that we, like so many, are cleverly hedging our bets. And there's no social justice, just as there's no love, that can come from that.

Three headstones rest side by side on a slope next to the moor near Wuthering Heights. Edgar Linton's is "harmonised by the turf and moss creeping up its foot." Cathy's is "grey, and half buried in heath."

Only Heathcliff's is bare. Lockwood the observer "lingered around them, under the benign sky," watching "the moths fluttering among the heath and the harebells," listening to "the soft wind breathing through the grass." He wonders "how any one could ever imagine unquiet slumbers for the sleepers in that quiet earth." A small boy tells Lockwood that he has seen Heathcliff and a woman walking on the moors together. "He probably raised the phantoms from thinking, as he traversed the moors alone" (399). These phantoms of thought persist, to haunt any lover who has made compromises with life.

14

THE ROMANTIC
ASCENT: MAHLER

I. THE HOT STRIVING OF LOVE

The violins and violas joyfully leap up, bursting into a realm of brightness, where the harp celebrates their arrival.[1] The contralto voice now follows – the dark voice that has sung of the terrible neediness of human life – celebrating, in her free springing movement, release from "all-penetrating pain." With a sensuous soaring movement the two female voices spiral around one another, like serpents made of light, coiling through the sky with the strings and harp, winged by their own passionate energy:

> Mit Flügeln, die ich mir errungen,
> In heissem Liebesstreben
> Werd' ich entschweben
> Zum Licht, zu dem kein Aug' gedrungen!

> With wings that I have won for myself
> In the hot striving of love
> I will soar away
> To the light to which no eye has penetrated.

The choice of two female voices is significant: for, as we have seen, Mahler frequently drew attention to the connection of his creativity with a female or receptive element in the personality, which is, as he puts it, "played on by the spirit of the world."[2] And as the voices rise

---

1 Mahler, Second Symphony, fifth movement, section "Mit Aufschwung, aber nicht eilen" (no. 44 in the score).
2 On the whole (though of course this is a simplification), Mahler tends to assign expressions of vulnerability and need to female voices – as in "Das irdische Leben" and the "Abschied" of *Das Lied von der Erde*. Male voices face death in a different way – with

to the hidden world of light, wrestling upward in separate striving movements, each uttering separately the passionate words of love, they arrive together at the summit, at the words "zum Licht" – the soprano a third above the contralto, suddenly hushed in triumph. In their ecstatic serenity they have exchanged positions, so that in their descent the contralto is now a third above. As Mahler wrote in one of his several programs for the work, there is in this realm no judgment and no hierarchy, "no great and no small," just the illumination of an overwhelming compassionate love. "We know and are."[3]

II. THE REDEEMING WORD

Mahler's symphony has a text, written in large part by its composer. In an 1897 letter to Arthur Seidl, he writes, "Whenever I plan a large musical structure, I always come to a point where I have to resort to 'the word' as a vehicle for my musical idea."[4] As I have argued in Chapter 5, this does not really mean that the music relies upon the word or simply illustrates the word in a programmatic manner: usually we have to rely on the music to make precise the emotional trajectory of the words. Nonetheless, Mahler, strongly influenced by his career in opera and by the Wagnerian idea of the *Gesamtkunstwerk*, also attached importance to the creation of a totality of emotional expression melding verbal and musical ideas. He describes the way in which, for the Second, he searched "through the whole of world literature, including the Bible, in search of the redeeming Word – and in the end I had no choice but to find my *own* words for my thoughts and feelings." This suggests that the words are not merely incidental to the musical idea, but part and parcel of the idea of redemption that the music is working out. It suggests, as well, that the work's relation to conventional religion will be complex: for it is striking that the Bible did not provide Mahler with his "redeeming Word."

a military toughness and stoicism ("Der Tamboursg'sell") that sometimes degenerates into madness ("Revelge"). On Mahler's metaphors for his own creativity, which link it to a feminine passivity and receptivity, see Chapter 5.
3 Mahler, program for the 1901 performance in Dresden; quoted in Lagrange (1973), pp. 785–6.
4 Trans. E. Wilkins, quoted in Mitchell (1975), pp. 172–3. Mahler here compares himself to Beethoven in the Ninth Symphony, and comments that the Schiller text is inadequate to embody Beethoven's musical idea.

But the full story of the genesis of the fifth movement text draws our attention even more markedly to the relation between words and music. The first movement of the symphony was completed in September of 1888 – as the first movement of a symphony in C minor, but without any overall conception of the work.[5] The movement was entitled "*Todtenfeier*" ("Funeral Rite"), and Mahler described it as issuing out of some agonized thoughts about death and the meaning of life – including, as Natalie Bauer-Lechner reports, a vision of himself dead on a bier, surrounded by flowers.[6] At the same time, the movement was clearly not written as simple "program music," toward which Mahler had been developing an increasing antipathy. More classical in structure than the First, it has frequently been seen as Mahler's first major attempt to win a place in the classical symphonic tradition.[7] The attempt, however, did not immediately win favor. In 1891, Mahler played the movement for the influential conductor Hans von Bülow, who had been reasonably supportive of Mahler's career as conductor.[8] Bülow reacted by covering his ears and exclaiming that if this was music he knew nothing about music.[9]

The second, third, and fourth movements of the symphony were probably completed during the summer of 1893 – although Mahler seems to have been uncertain about their order, and still unclear about the overall trajectory of the work.[10] But then composition came to a halt. Mahler planned to use a chorus in the final movement, and was unable to proceed because he could not find a suitable text.[11] Although

---

5 See Mitchell (1975), p. 162; at this date the First Symphony was not yet called a "symphony," so this movement was not described as belonging to a "second symphony." The earliest full score of the movement (which Mahler also called "*Todtenfeier*") bears the date September 10, 1888.

6 For discussion of this incident, see Mitchell (1975), p. 162.

7 See ibid., p. 163, and note 41, pp. 261–2, on the alleged sonata form of the movement.

8 See ibid., p. 278, note 56.

9 See the discussion of this incident in ibid., pp. 162ff.; La Grange (1973), pp. 294ff.; Blaukopf (1973), pp. 97ff.; and especially Reik (1953), who has a very interesting interpretation of the Mahler/Bülow relationship.

10 The full score of the Scherzo bears the date July 16, 1893. (The closely related St. Anthony song was completed on July 8 in vocal and piano score, on August 1 in full score.) The "*Urlicht*" was completed in full score on July 19, 1893. Bauer-Lechner's memoir contains many anecdotes pertaining to this period. Mahler seemed unhappy with what he felt to be an excessive contrast of mood between the second and first movements (see Mitchell [165]).

11 He also expressed the fear that a choral final movement could easily seem a superficial imitation of Beethoven's Ninth – see Blaukopf (1973), p. 97.

it has sometimes been suggested that he had the final movement fully sketched out and simply did not know what words he wanted to use for the final choral section, this supposition surely grossly underrates the extent to which words and music, for Mahler, form a unity, and the movement as a whole is crafted around the themes of resurrection and love that his text embodies. As Mitchell rightly says, the *"auferstehen"* theme runs right through the movement, and it is an apt setting for the first lines of the Klopstock/Mahler text; how absurd to suppose that he just happened to write the theme with a rhythmic and emotional structure that exactly suits and fittingly expresses those words – and then, a year later, happened on some words that just happened to fit in. Mitchell demonstrates convincingly that all of our evidence is compatible with, and best explained by, the idea that Mahler had only inchoate sketches of the final movement and knew that he wanted it to be a choral movement: but as to its more precise thematic and emotional trajectory, he was at a loss – until he could discover a text around which his ideas might crystallize.[12]

In February 1894, Bülow died in Cairo. A series of memorial events was organized. On March 29, 1894, Mahler attended a memorial service for Bülow in Hamburg, at which extracts from Bach's St. Matthew and St. John Passions were performed, and the boychoir of the *Michaeliskirche* performed the Resurrection Ode by Klopstock. As Mahler's friend Förster reports, the performance was deeply moving: "The effect was created not just by Klopstock's profound poem but by the innocence of the pure sounds issuing from the children's throats." He could not see Mahler's face during the performance. Shortly after this, Mahler conducted a memorial concert at the Hamburg Opera, beginning the program with the funeral music from Wagner's *Götterdämmerung*.

The experience of hearing the boychoir singing the resurrection text seems to have been a profound experience for Mahler. Förster sought him out to see how the service had affected him. He saw him sitting at his writing desk, with pen in hand. He turned to Förster and said, "Dear friend, I have it!" Förster says that he understood the meaning of his outburst: "As if illuminated by a mysterious power, I answered: 'Auferstehen, ja auferstehen wirst du nach kurzem Schlaf.' " Mahler looked at him "with an expression of extreme surprise. I had guessed

---

12 See Mitchell (1975), pp. 172–5.

the secret he had as yet entrusted to no human soul" – the Klopstock text was to be the basis for the final movement of the symphony.[13]

Even if we have some skepticism about Förster's evident self-dramatization, and his desire to establish that he understood Mahler better than anyone, nonetheless it is clear from other sources as well that the experience of the memorial service was a pivotal moment. In a letter to Arthur Seidl, written in 1897, Mahler reports that when the boychoir began to sing he felt as if he had been "struck by lightning": hearing the text, he knew that he had found the way of completing his symphony. "[E]verything became plain and clear in my mind! It was the flash that all creative artists wait for – 'conceiving by the holy Ghost'!" (Here again – see Chapter 5 – he uses feminine imagery of conception to describe his creative process.)

Composition of the vast fifth movement proceeded rapidly thereafter. Three months after the memorial, on June 29, Mahler writes to Fritz Lohr announcing its completion, using the imagery of pregnancy and labor: ". . . the arrival of a strong and healthy last movement of the Second. Father and child are faring appropriately in the circumstances . . . It received in holy baptism the name: 'Lux lucet in tenebris.' "[14]

Now the Klopstock ode is no great work. It is a rather banal invocation of conventional pieties. Mahler felt its inadequacy, since he both rewrote and supplemented it. Indeed, more than once he describes the text as his own.[15] And indeed, most of the words of the text, and all of its passion, are Mahler's own. And yet the memorial service clearly unlocked some deep reservoir of feeling in Mahler. The simple chorale, the theme of resurrection, and the pure voices of children all played, it seems, some role in this experience. Our attention is drawn to the fact that these words suggestive of the victory of creativity and love over deadness came to him during the funeral of a man who had both blocked and humiliated him – and, it would appear, on anti-Semitic grounds. We are invited to pursue the suggestion that the fifth movement has something to do with a creative artist's victory over obstacles

---

13 Förster's narrative is quoted in full in ibid., pp. 168–9.

14 'Light shines in darkness.' Quoted in ibid., p. 173.

15 See the passage quoted above, concerning the search through world literature for the "redeeming word"; and in a letter of July 10, 1894, to Arnold Berliner, he writes, "The 5th movement is magnificent and closes with a choral hymn whose text is my own" (quoted in ibid., p. 176).

to his creative striving – including, it seems likely, obstacles imposed by resentment and envy in his own inner world.[16]

Mahler was repeatedly drawn to the task of providing a narrative "program" for the Second, and yet repeatedly frustrated by the inadequacy of what could be conveyed in this way. He oscillates between refusal of the demand for narrative and an eager, indeed elaborate, fulfillment. In a letter to Max Marschalk in December 1895, he acknowledges that the symphony has a narrative structure having to do with a sequence of emotions, but refuses to provide a concrete program, saying, "The parallel between life and music is perhaps deeper and more extensive than can be drawn at present."[17] Later on, however, Mahler did, though with continuing ambivalence, produce three narrative programs of the work.[18] Although he writes to Alma that the program is merely "a crutch for a cripple" that "can give only a superficial indication, all that any programme can do for a musical work,"[19] nonetheless the fact that he was repeatedly drawn to tell the story of the work, and did so with great passion, is evidence that Mahler always felt the work to be about the real and urgent struggles and searchings of a human soul. His ambivalence concerns the likely effect on the average listener of putting the complexities of the music into a brief verbal digest: for, like a plot summary of a tragedy, it may draw the listener away from openness to her own deepest emotions, as evoked in the musical experience on the basis of attention to specifically musical forms. As Mahler remarked to Natalie Bauer-Lechner, "It isn't enough to judge a work of art by its content; we must consider its total image, in which content and form are indissolubly blended."[20]

16 On this account, the temptation to read Mahler in the terms of Kleinian psychoanalysis is understandable, and in a sense on the right track. On the other hand, the attempt at this in Holbrook (1975) seems heavy-handed and jargon-laden, too little concerned with the music.

17 Quoted in La Grange (1973), p. 784, and Cooke (1988), p. 53. Mahler remarks that he leaves the "interpretation of details to the imagination of each individual listener."

18 One was writted to Marschalk only a few months later; one was written to Natalie and Bruno Walter in January 1896; and the last was written for performances in 1900 in Munich and in 1901 in Dresden. He suppressed its publication at the last moment in Munich, but published it in Dresden.

19 December 20, 1901, quoted in Cooke (1988), p. 54.

20 Bauer-Lechner (1980), p. 37. Recall that Mahler, in the same conversation, said that "symphony" to him means "constructing a world with all the technical means at one's disposal."

All of Mahler's programs depict the symphony as "about" the life and death of a heroic and creative individual. The 1895 program calls him the hero of the First Symphony, and states that the symphony opens as he is being carried to his grave, "and whose life I imagine I can see reflected in a mirror from a high watchtower."[21] The 1896 (Walter) program gives a different account of the first movement: it "depicts the titanic struggle against life and destiny fought by a super-man who is still a prisoner of the world; his endless, constant defeats and finally his death." The 1901 program refers to the hero simply as "a well-loved man," and reverts to the funeral setting: "we" are standing near his grave, and "his whole life, his struggles, his sufferings and his accomplishments on earth pass before us."[22] All three accounts agree, too, that the contemplation of this hero's struggles raises for us the most urgent questions about the meaning of life: "Wherefore hast thou lived? Wherefore hast thou suffered? Is it all some great, fearful joke? We must answer these questions in some way if we are to continue living – yes, even if we must only continue dying."[23] We usually do not confront these questions, adds the 1901 version, because we are "blinded by the mirage of everyday life." But in the sharp experience of the funeral rites, "the confusion and distractions of everyday life are lifted like a hood from our eyes."[24] The point of view of the music is the point of view of such spectators, who, by imagining those struggles, dig into their own depths. The spectators' questions are answered, Mahler insists, only in the fifth movement. The three middle movements are described as "intermezzi," two pertaining to memories of the hero's life and the fourth showing the "questions and struggle of the human soul" coming to the fore.

One more piece of the background must now be mentioned. In his student days, Mahler was associated with a group of young socialists known as the Pernerstorfer Circle, whose interests included liberal politics, the idea of renewal from folk traditions, and a questioning of conventional religion in the name of a Nietzschean type of romanticism. His good friend Siegfried Lipiner, also a member of the circle, went on to write works indebted to Nietzsche's *Birth of Tragedy*, in

21 La Grange (1973), p. 784.
22 Ibid., p. 785.
23 1985 version, ibid., p. 784.
24 Ibid., p. 785.

which the artist's transcendance over pain and suffering is depicted as the central instance of human transcendence: we realize our own potential for godliness in the Promethean artist's defiance of pain and death, a victory that is apparently also a victory over egoism and petty selfishness.[25] This same Lipiner, in 1888, translated a Polish dramatic epic by Adam Mickiewicz, entitled *Dziady*, the German translation of which (in Lipiner's version) is *Todtenfeier*. Musicologist Stephen Hefling has attempted to locate very precise parallels between the Mickiewicz/Lipiner poem and the structure of the symphony's first movement – although in the end even he admits that Mahler made something altogether his own, that should be understood in its own right rather than through slavish reference to the Lipiner program. Most interpreters would probably go still further, seeing the detailed parallels to the Mickiewicz poem as less convincing than does Hefling. Mahler may indeed have begun with the rather absurd plot of the Polish poem in mind: but as he ponders the life of his dead hero, his questions and emotions surely took on a profoundly personal meaning that can be traced without reference to specific incidents.[26]

My own view is that we should certainly be aware of the Lipiner text as one more element lurking in the background; but surely it cannot have been a central ongoing inspiration, if Mahler insists that he has rejected all known literature as the source for his symphony's conclusion. Nor do I think that the text supplies anything terribly helpful toward the interpretation of the emotional trajectory of the first movement; Mahler's own programs are surely much more insightful. On the other hand, what is significant in Hefling's research, it seems to me, is his vivid portrayal of Mahler's Nietzscheanism and of his general intellectual milieu, skeptical of orthodox stories about redemption, but profoundly interested in Romantic/Dionysian ideas of striving and overcoming. I believe those general ideas are indeed pivotal in the symphony, shaping its approach to the theme of resurrection.

25 See the extract from Lipiner's writings cited in Hefling (1988): ". . . we suffer to the extreme, then, only bleeding, man wrests himself from his transitory self . . .", etc. The conclusion states that "the giant I" has been overcome.
26 I am grateful to Ed Cone for illuminating correspondence on this point. Cone points out that even the word "*Todtenfeier*" has different meanings in the Lipiner/Mickiewicz text and in Mahler's own usage: in the former, it means a folk festival for the dead; in the symphony it means the funeral celebration for a hero.

III. FOR THE SAKE OF STRIVING ITSELF

I. *Allegro Maestoso*. c minor.

The violins and violas enter abruptly, with a sound at once cutting and trembling, as if a knife were being moved very rapidly back and forth across a firm but fleshy object. They recede to a soft quivering, as the lower strings move deliberately forward with menacing attack, digging and scraping into the body. The passage suggests (and, perhaps, alludes to) the entrance of Hunding in Wagner's *Die Walküre*,[27] therefore suggesting the threat of loveless conventional authority against true creativity and authentic love.

As it unfolds, the movement seems to express an alternation between a hope of love and creation and a defeat by some crushing oppressive force; an alternation between achievement and its nullification, aspiration and its erasure. The implied listener is forced by the erratic progress of the music to confront the questions suggested in Mahler's program: What is all this striving for? What are we able to achieve? Isn't all this effort futile and meaningless? The world then becomes very still. ("*Beruhigend*" is marked in the score.) The otherworldly sound of the harp suggests the imminence of death.[28]

Hope is briefly found in nature and its sources of renewal, linked to the idea of love. But even as introduced, this thought is distant, as if in a memory or an unrealizable hope. And soon this hope, too, is undermined and out of reach, as the funereal progress of the first theme carries all before it, inexorably. We hear the *Dies Irae*, hymn of death, as the high strings tremble with anxious agitation. A theme associated with heroic achievement then appears and vanishes. The music arrives at a painfully dissonant fortissimo climax, a sound both crushing and shredding, striking again and again, as if the order and beauty of music itself had been defeated by the hideous randomness of the world. Then there is silence.

Out of the silence, the strings are reborn, with their jagged funereal theme. And they enter our awareness in a new way. For now, instead of being simply emblematic of struggle and opposition they also embody that which has survived the most hideous adversity. The life that

---

27 See La Grange (1973).
28 See comments in Chapter 5 on Mahler's use of the harp.

moves toward death (in Mahler's words, "continues dying") is still a human life, capable of striving. And however painful and fraught that striving, it has a strength that is capable of imposing order in disorder, music in chaos. It begins to dawn on the listener that one possible answer to the question, "What is this for?" is, "For the sake of the striving itself" – or even, since the striving has defeated dissonance and silence, "For the sake of music." The theme moves tentatively at first, like pieces that need to be put back together, then more firmly. A rapid chromatic descent from fortissimo to pianissimo brings the movement to an inconclusive and doubt-ridden end.

Mahler here orders a pause of "at least five minutes."

IV. THE SELF IN SOCIETY

II. *Andante*. A flat (and g-sharp minor)

The stately civilized sweetness of this movement is shocking, following the agonized introspective character of the first. Mahler expressed dissatisfaction with the contrast,[29] but he took no steps to revise or replace the movement.[30] The contrast, in fact, seems integral to the symphony's overall design. If it is exploring, as I believe it is, the contrast between the expression of the self in society and its purer and richer expression through solitary personal striving and a faith not determined by conventional forms, then it seems crucial for it to contain not only the sardonic and grotesque account of society that the third movement will provide, but also a reminder of society at its best – the pleasures of gratitude and good manners, the stately movement of gracious hospitality – organized society's best answers to the agonized questions of the first movement. Here Mahler's programs are at their most misleading – indicating, perhaps, that he did not have conscious or verbal access to the spring of his musical idea. For he speaks of this movement as "about" the hero's lost happiness, and even his love. And yet to one who listens to it after the first movement it seems staid and lacking in authentic passion. The traditional form of the *Ländler* does contain nostalgic suggestions of good times, but not of any passion that goes deep, involving the whole self. We find, in effect, organized society's

29 Reported in Bauer-Lechner (1980).
30 Contrast the eventual removal of the "*Blumine*" movement of the First Symphony.

answers to the agonized questions of the first movement: live a gracious, virtuous, pious life according to the social and religious forms
of the day, and do not ask too many questions. The hero remembers
how that world of good will and virtue once satisfied him. It can no
longer.

We can offer a musical proof of the incompleteness of the programs.
For they do not accurately describe the movement's musical form,
which has an ABABA structure. The A theme, the stately *Ländler*, is
what Mahler is describing. But he omits completely the agitated and
turbulent B theme, which contains reminders of the triplets and dotted
rhythms of the first movement. This theme puts the *Ländler* on the
defensive, so that its second entrance is stammering and hesitant. The
second theme then eclipses it; the mood of the movement turns omi-
nous, harsh dissonances erasing our memory of harmony. The first
theme returns at the end – but as a ghost of itself. Society does not
answer the deepest questions of the heart.[31]

V. A CRY OF DISGUST

III. *In ruhig fliessender Bewegung* (In calm, flowing movement).
c minor.

The third movement, closely related to the *Wunderhorn* song in which
St. Anthony of Padua preaches to the fishes, presents, by contrast, a
sardonic and despairing view of social forms, the meaningless bustle of
inauthentic activity in which the self loses itself in triviality and the
ambition for conformity eclipses true thought. In one program Mahler
writes that it is like watching a dance from a distance without hearing
the music – it all seems empty and pointless.[32]

The "*Fischpredigt*" song whose history and music are so closely
intertwined with the movement[33] takes as its theme the conformity and
hypocrisy of contemporary society in matters of religion. St. Anthony
goes to preach in the church, but the church is empty. So he goes out
to preach to the fish. They all swim up with their mouths gaping open

---

31 Compare Cooke (1988), p. 56: "The first movement's overpowering character has the
 effect of shrinking the vision of life's happiness here to a small space, and to a subdued
 and fragile thing."
32 1896 program.
33 It remains unclear which was completed first, and Mahler continued to link the two.

and eagerly swallow what they cannot possibly understand. Rich and poor fish, high and low fish, all "lift up their heads just as if they were rational creatures," listening to the sermon. Then they go away and do just as before, gorging themselves, stealing, making love. These themes of superficiality and mindless conformity can be felt in the Scherzo as well, but the subtly different orchestration gives them a darker and more sinister tone.[34] The restless movement, the weaving and diving and rising, suggest the directionless lives of people who have not delved into themselves to find their own words and sounds to answer the questions of life.

The movement is punctuated by several countermelodies, one of them of wonderful sweetness and beauty,[35] marked "*sehr getragen und gesangvoll*," "very drawn out and melodious." Mahler speaks of it as "the loveliest passage," and emphasizes the fact that it must occur only once, "like the aloe" which "can bear only a single flower." We glimpse genuine tenderness through the veil of the hypocritical charade, which returns to eclipse it.

Toward the end of the movement there is a high dissonant outcry that Mahler called a "cry of disgust" and "the fearful scream of a soul." The experience, Mahler wrote, is that of looking at "the bustle of existence," the shallowness and herdlike selfishness of society, until it "becomes horrible to you, like the swaying of dancing figures in a brightly-lit ballroom, into which you look from the dark night outside . . . Life strikes you as meaningless, a frightful ghost, from which you perhaps start away with a cry of disgust."[36] It dies away gradually, but its echo hangs quivering over the broken return of the first theme. The movement ends with a low shudder in the bass, contrabassoon, horns, harp, and tam-tam, a hollow sound emptied of human dignity.

Notice that in giving way to disgust the implied listener becomes, in effect, a Brontean Romantic, solitary and antisocial. She repudiates all social institutions as hypocritical and inauthentic. She says, in effect, "I vomit at those stultifying institutions. I refuse to allow them to become a part of my being." In the determination to retain her own absolute

---

34 For details, see La Grange (1973), p. 789. In particular, one should notice the supplementing of the B-flat clarinet by the E-flat clarinet (its first entrance marked "*mit Humor*") and the use of a switch of birch twigs on the large drum.

35 At 40 in the score.

36 Mahler, letter to Max Marschalk, cited in Cooke (1988).

purity, her refusal to live human life as it is, she turns her back on humanity.

VI. I WILL NOT BE WARNED OFF

IV. *"Urlicht"* ("Original Light"). D-flat major, middle section in b-flat minor.

Without any pause, with firm serene confidence, the unaccompanied contralto voice enters, soon joined by brass and strings. The human voice appears at this late point in the work without preparation, as if it were the cry of disgust itself that demanded a verbal response. The sound is that of a simple and dignified hymn tune or chorale. We have moved from the false surface of civilization to speech so simple, so childlike, that it is almost prior to civilization – and yet at the same time allied with a long tradition of choral religious music. The reference of the music is not so much to ordinary institutionalized church hymns as to the authentic religious emotion expressed in the music of Bach, a composer in whom Mahler had a passionate interest during this period.[37]

Mahler wrote to Marschalk, "The unexpected appearance of the alto solo casts a sudden illumination on the first movement."[38] The first movement already suggests (I have argued) that the committed uncompromising striving of the individual human being is itself the answer to the questions posed by death and suffering. Here this idea is confirmed and developed by the suggestion that it is in the work of the human artist – here, in particular, the musical artist – that we find an authentic spirituality that can answer the cry of disgust generated by the hypocrisy of institutionalized social forms. The expressive power of the musical tradition is linked with the simplicity of a child's faith, and both with a love of nature. The music answers the cry of disgust by turning to the perspective of a child, who simply lacks that emotion. In consequence, humanity no longer looks repulsive; instead, it looks, simply, needy:

O Röschen Rot!
Der Mensch liegt in grösster Not!

---

37 For Mahler's keen interest in Bach during this period, see Bauer-Lechner (1980) and La Grange (1973).
38 See La Grange (1973), p. 784.

Der Mensch liegt in grösster Pein!
Je lieber möcht'ich im Himmel sein!

Da kam ich auf einen breiten Weg:
Da kam ein Engelein und wollte mich abweisen.
Ach nein! Ich liess mich nicht abweisen.
Ich bin von Gott und will wieder zu Gott!
Der liebe Gott wird mir ein Lichtchen geben
wird leuchten mir bis an das ewig selig Leben!

O red rose!
Humanity lies in greatest need!
Humanity lies in greatest pain!
Much rather would I be in heaven!

Then I came upon a broad path.
Then an angel came and wanted to dismiss me.
Ah no! I did not allow myself to be dismissed.
I am from God and I would go again to God!
Dear God will give me a lamp,
will light my way to eternal blessed life!

In the simple words of the folk poem, we find a direct expression of intense personal feeling combined with universal compassion. The child thinks of its own destiny, and the salvation of its own life. (In the word "*Lichtchen*," used for the light that God will give, we probably can think of Mahler as making a connection to the first poem of Rückert's *Kindertotenlieder* (well known to him as poems long before he set them musically), in which the little child's life is described as a "*Lämplein*," a small lamp. Following this lead, we may imagine that what God in effect gives the child is its own small life, and that it is this life and nothing else that will light its way. At the same time, however, the concern of the child is for all humanity, and for all human suffering and pain. The suggestion is that in the child's intense and unadulterated faith – linked here with the spiritual life of music – we find a love that is at one and the same time intensely personal and universal, embracing the entire world in the way that music embraces the world, because it has avoided the calcification of the daily social round and its petty envy and competition. Going to a country town to find the three large bells he uses in this symphony, Mahler wrote of the disgust he felt at seeing the daily routine of town life, with its "dry-as-dust" people: "Every inch of their faces bore the mask of that self-tormenting egoism which makes everyone so unhappy! Always 'I, I,' – never 'thou, thou, my brother!'"[39] I am suggesting that this section of the symphony makes a similar point about the connection between authenticity and altruism: when one delves deep into the self, one finds sources of personal expression that are at the very same time unselfish and compassionate, in the way that the deepest music is also (one might argue) the most universal. This is expressed in the open simplicity of the vocal line, and in the quality of the contralto voice, at once personal and vibrant with pity.

An angel, somewhat surprisingly, attempts to dismiss the child from the path. And the child relies on herself and on God to win the struggle with this angelic opponent, who guards what appears to be a dark, though broad, road. The words are traditional – but Mahler, we may suppose, selects nothing without considering the fit of its imagery with his overall idea. So we are invited to notice the fact that the road is described in terms usually reserved, in conventional religious imagery, for the forbidden path of sin (virtue's path being "narrow"); and it is guarded by an angel who warns people away from it.

Here we have, I think, another development of the contrast between conventional religious morality and the authentic spirituality of Mahler's art. Mahler's life had been in many respects a turbulent and by conventional standards "sinful" one; his love affairs and his nervous instability were notorious, especially during this period of his life. As a Jew, furthermore, he was well aware of propaganda linking the Jew with softness and parasitism, un-German passivity, and spiritual rot. A particularly well-known example of these connections is the writing of Otto Weininger, a self-hating Jew and closeted homosexual, who wrote that the Jew was really a woman, and that both were wet, soft, passive creatures who could never create authentically.[40] Weininger makes one

39 Mahler (1985), p. 170.
40 Weininger's *Sex and Character* was published in 1902, and he committed suicide in 1903. His ideas, however, were, if extreme, still expressive of common currents in the Vienna of the era; Karl Kraus had published similar ideas earlier. See Otto Weininger, *Sex and Character* (trans. from the 6th German edition, London and New York: William Heinemann and G. P. Putnam's Sons, n.d.), pp. 306–22: ". . . some reflection will lead to the surprising result that Judaism is saturated with femininity, with precisely those qualities the essence of which I have shown to be in the strongest opposition to the male nature." Among the Jewish/feminine traits explored here is the failure to understand the national state as the aim of manly endeavor: thus Jews and women have an affinity for the ideas of Marxism. They also fail to comprehend class distinc-

further link between the Jew and the woman: both fail to see the importance of hierarchical class distinctions and the "preservation of the limits between individuals." Their egalitarianism is presumably not unconnected with their disgusting softness and ooziness: for disgust, as we recall, has the function of protecting and reinforcing hierarchical boundary lines. Mahler has introduced the idea of inclusive compassion for all of suffering humanity; in the following movement he will make the idea more emphatically egalitarian. So these social issues too are likely to be in the background.

Mahler's defiant identification with the female voice and his use of images of pregnancy must be seen in this context. His music had frequently been attacked, especially in these early years, as neurotic and unbalanced, as embarrassingly emotional and lacking in classical order. The small angel of conventional Christian piety (and conventional Christian music culture, and conventional hierarchical German society) says, don't be that sort of person, don't tread that rotten path. But the heart says no. I will be the person I am, and I will tread the path that I tread, and, what is more, God will help me, and it will turn out to be the path to personal redemption and the redemption of society through compassionate love. It is not difficult to see in the drama of angelic dismissal the history with Bülow, and other incidents of the kind, many of them colored by anti-Semitism. And the choice of this text expresses the response: the creative soul will follow its own path to God, and its little light, the light that is its life, will prove more powerful than all angelic dismissals.

Nor do we have to focus on the text by itself in coming to this understanding. For the music and the text are in an unusually fascinating unity, and the contribution of the music pins down this reading of the text. I have said that the simple dignity of the movement's chorale opening alludes to Bach. The middle section, the setting of "Da kam ich zu einen breiten Weg," is, by contrast, pure Mahler; its use of jumpy nervous movement and of bells anticipates sections of the Fourth Symphony, the child's journey to Heaven. The dismissing angel, however,

tions: they are "at the opposite pole from aristocrats, with whom the preservation of the limits between individuals is the leading idea" (311). Weininger also holds that woman (and, by extension, the Jew) is the bodily and sexual aspect of the human being: "Woman alone, then, is guilt; and is so through man's fault . . . She is only a part of man, his other, ineradicable, his lower part" (300).

has a melody that is like a conventional nursery tune, banal, saccharin, and sly; it reminds us of the sardonic perspective on conventional society in the third movement.

Up until now, we might say that the vocal line still expresses the spiritual nature of a child, and a child's simplicity: in a good performance one will generally hear a comparatively straight and nonoperatic tone. There is at this point a sharp transition of mood and of musical tone, as, in a passage that Mahler marks *"leidenschaftlich aber zart,"* "passionate but tender," the contralto bursts out, "Ach nein! Ich liess mich nicht abweisen! Ach nein! Ich liess mich nicht abweisen." "Ah no! I did not allow myself to be dismissed!" The passionate chromatic melody here is characteristic of Mahler at his most Mahlerian, that is to say, most unacceptable to conservative musical taste; and in performance this is generally signalled by the use of a tone with more vibrato, a more operatic sound. The voice is pointedly accompanied by two clarinets, instruments traditionally emblematic of the feminine and the erotic, and used by Mozart to that effect in defiance of religious opposition.[41] The child, in short, stands revealed as a woman, and (in the cultural symbolism of the day) as a Jew, and probably as a leftist; and both stand revealed as Mahler the composer, who will not be warned off, who repeatedly insists that the work of composition involves a feminine receptivity and a nonhierarchical compassion. Moreover, since this outburst of Mahlerian music is the culmination of a search that began with Bach, the suggestion is that it is Mahlerian music, with all of its "feminine" emotionality and nervous intensity, with its wings won in the hot striving of love, that is the true heir to the tradition of authentic spiritual searching that Bach's music inaugurates. Conventional respectability is, by contrast, inauthentic and dead.

We note that the outburst, while passionate, is indeed at the same time tender: the opposing figure of the angel is defeated not by malice or retribution or envious detraction, but simply by pursuing one's own light and continuing to be oneself.

For Schopenhauer, whose account of musical eroticism was the dominant one in Mahler's cultural context, music contains a representation of our embodiment and our sexuality. By listening to this repre-

---

41 The archbishop of Salzburg famously forbade Mozart the use of the clarinet in all works written for performance in that city. Their use in connection with female sexuality in *Così fan tutte* is especially fascinating.

sentation we are enabled to free ourself from bondage to these elements in ourselves, and increasingly to approach an undisturbed condition. For Mahler, by contrast, the movement of thought seems to go in just the opposite direction. By creating (or listening to) a representation of one's embodiment and its sexuality, we stand forth in it and allow it to stand for ourselves. We refuse to allow ourselves to be warned off by the angels, and we simply exist, tenderly and without resentment.

This is a pivotal moment in the entire ascent tradition that I have been mapping out. In the first place, it is a moment of defiant social inclusiveness, which says an emphatic no to intolerance and hate. The excluded alien says, I claim the right to ascend, and I shall do so, and nobody shall dismiss me. Second, it is a moment of joyous acknowledgement of the embodied self. Mahler does not shrink back into a snail's shell, like Mr. Lockwood, before the angel's command; nor does he discharge against the female and receptive elements in himself the anger of Lockwood's terror, which has to bloody the female hand that keeps so insistently forcing its way in at the window. He simply stands forth, speaking in a contralto voice, with a self-described passionate tenderness. He indicates that it is only when one can stand forth in one's own both masculine and feminine body, without either shame or malice, that one can defeat the forces of hatred and win the victory for love. I did not allow myself to be warned off, the child simply says. In that statement she finds a sign that society might come to be loving and just.[42]

The victory over primitive shame enables a victory over both aggression and disgust. No longer shrinking from the imperfections of the embodied self, the speaker ceases, as well, to cordon himself off against the disgusting imperfections of his fellow human beings. The victory over adversity can thus be won without rage or hierarchy.

VII. THE UNSEEN LIGHT

V. *Im Tempo des Scherzos; Wild herausfahrend, etc* ("In the tempo of a Scherzo; leading wildly forward, etc"). c minor / C major at the opening, with many modulations; ending in E-flat major.

---

42 See Adorno (1992), p. 8, who speaks of Mahler's struggle against "the curse of closedness."

The vast fifth movement opens with a quotation of the third movement's cry of disgust, a terrifying explosion. The opening material is dense with references to other portions of the work – the trembling strings and the later oboe triplets recall the opening movement, the use of the glockenspiel the *Urlicht*; there are many forecasts of the thematic material of the choral closing section. Only the Andante is out of the picture altogether – as if the adversity and suffering of a life, and the social obstacles that impede it, can all be taken up and transfigured into something noble, but comfort and good manners must simply be left behind. Soon we hear for the first time the theme associated with the winged ascent of love. The glockenspiel sounds, and there is a silence. Out of the emptiness, a distant horn calls in isolation. It is as if the sufferer is being summoned – to what? The *Dies Irae* is now heard, slow and hushed in the distance, against pizzicato strings. A mood of awe-filled suspense builds, as the triumphant *"auferstehen"* theme enters for the first time, quiet but definite, but ending with a downturn, as it does each time until the end.

An anxious passionate theme, later associated with the contralto's "O glaube," "O believe," is now introduced by the winds.[43] The *Dies Irae* returns, the Resurrection theme joins in, and the brass builds toward a triumphant climax, which includes the ascent theme. Suddenly, however, the expansive climax turns crushed and sour; a shrill cry from the piccolo. An uneasy silence ensues. It is, it seems, the hour of death and judgment.

A remarkable long percussion crescendo leads to a pounding cruel theme – as if something indifferent and hard is stepping on all that is human. The march that Mahler describes as the march of the dead to judgment now begins. It is worthwhile quoting two versions of his account:

To begin with, as faith and the church picture it: the day of judgment, a huge tremor shakes the earth. The climax of this terrifying event is accompanied by drum rolls. Then the last trump sounds. The graves burst open, all the creatures struggle out of the ground, moaning and trembling. Now they march in mighty processions: rich and poor, peasants and kings, the whole church with bishops and popes. All have the same fear, all cry and

---

43 La Grange points out that this theme has a close resemblance to Amfortas's theme in *Parsifal*.

tremble alike because, in the eyes of God, there are no just men. As though from another world, the last trump sounds again. Finally, after they have left their empty graves and the earth lies silent and deserted, there comes only the long-drawn note of the bird of death. (1896)

The voice of the Caller is heard. The end of every living thing has come, the last judgment is at hand and the horror of the day of days has come upon us. The earth trembles, the graves burst open, the dead arise and march forth in endless procession. The great and small of this earth, the kings and the beggars, the just and the godless, all press forward. The cry for mercy and forgiveness sounds fearful in our ears. The wailing becomes gradually more terrible. Our senses desert us, all consciousness dies as the Eternal Judge approaches. The last trump sounds; the trumpets of the Apocalypse ring out. In the eerie silence that follows, we can just barely make out a distant nightingale, a last tremulous echo of earthly life. (1901)

Of particular interest here is the insistence on the equal fear and vulnerability of all human beings – the rulers of the world are on the same plane as the poor, and the leaders of the church join their flock. This explains, I think, the strongly sardonic character of the march, which is filled with reminders of cheap brass band music.[44] Even the "O believe" and *"auferstehen"* themes appear in a cheap degenerate form, adulterated by the worldly life that proceeds to judgment. Everything is lurching, reckless and unstable; everything is contaminated and in need of purification. A brass band is heard offstage; it gets closer, eclipsing the passionate voice of the "believe" theme. A sweet melody briefly rises up in the strings – later set to the words, "you were not born in vain." Bells, and trumpets in the distance.

---

44 In the Nighttown episode of *Ulysses*, the following stage directions appear: "A fife and drum band is heard in the distance playing the Kol Nidre. The beaters approach with imperial eagles hoisted, trailing banners and waving oriental palms. The chryselephantine papal standard rises high, surrounded by pennons of the civic flag. The van of the procession appears headed by John Howard Parnell, city marshal, in a chessboard tabard, the Athlone Poursuivant and Ulster King of Arms. They are followed by the Right Honourable Joseph Hutchinson, lord mayor of Dublin, the lord mayor of Cork, their worships the mayors of Limerick, Galway, Sligo and Waterford, Twentyeight Irish representative peers, sirdars, grandees and maharajahs bearing the cloth of estate, the Dublin Metropolitan Fire Brigade, the chapter of the saints of finance in their plutocratic order of precedence, the bishop of Down and Connor, His Eminence Michael cardinal Logue archbishop of Armagh, Primate of All Ireland . . ." and so on for another half page. Mutatis mutandis, this passage is a cousin of Mahler's march.

We now hear, offstage, the single call of the horn – as at the movement's opening, sounding alone, then taken up by trumpets. Across the emptiness throbs the sensuous broken melody in the flute that Mahler called the "bird of death."

Until this point, Mahler stressed, the movement follows rather conventional Christian ideas of the Last Judgment – though with his characteristic humanitarian stress on equality before God, and his satirical depiction of the disordered and terrified procession of the formerly rich and powerful. The concluding section, however, contains, he repeatedly insists, something altogether unexpected and heterodox.[45] To understand what it is, we must begin by looking at the text. First, the complete and unaltered text of Klopstock's ode:

Auferstehn, ja auferstehn wirst du,
mein Staub, nach kurzer Ruh!
Unsterblichs Leben
wird, der dich schuf, dir geben. Halleluja!

Wieder aufzublühn werd' ich gesät!
Der Herr der Ernte geht
und sammelt Garben
uns ein, uns ein, die starben! Halleluja!

Tag des Danks! der Freudenthränen Tag!
Du meines Gottes Tag!
Wenn ich im Grabe
genug geschlummert habe,
erweckst du mich.

Wie den Träumenden wirds dann uns seyn!
Mit Jesu gehn wir ein
zu seinen Freuden!
Der müden Pilger Leiden
Sind dann nicht mehr!

Ach ins Allerheiligste führt mich
Mein Mittler dann; lebt'ich
Im Heiligthume,
Zu seines Nahmens Ruhme! Halleluja!

---

45 See, for example, the 1896 program: "What happens now is far from expected: no divine judgment, no blessed and no damned, no Good and no Evil, and no judge."

Rise again, yes rise again you will,
my dust, after a short rest!
Deathless life
will he who created you grant you. Halleluja!

To bloom again I am sown!
The Lord of the Harvest goes
and gathers us in like sheaves,
we who have died! Halleluja!

Day of thanks, day of joyful tears!
Your day, my God!
When I have slumbered long enough in the grave,
You wake me.

What an experience it will then be for us dreamers!
With Jesus we enter into his peace!
The sorrows of the tired pilgrims
Are then no more!

Ah, then my redeemer leads me
into the holiest place of all.
I shall live in the holy realm
to the glory of his name. Halleluja!

Mahler makes four changes in this text. First, he omits the third, fourth, and fifth stanzas. These stanzas express conventional Christian piety and a conventional image of heavenly peace, which puts an end to all striving and effort. In place of this static end-state, Mahler, as we shall see, focuses on the beauty of striving and love; nor does he mention Jesus or Heaven. Second, throughout Mahler omits the "Halleluja's, which add nothing to the content and suggest a static finality rather than a continuation of effort. Third, he alters "I am sown" to "you are sown." Although on the surface this simply makes the rhetorical address to "my dust" continue into the second stanza, it also has the effect of turning the poem outward to address all humanity. Finally, he substitutes for "*schuf*," "created," the word "*rief*," "called." God figures in the text, then, not as the creator of man, but as the one who calls the creative person to self-expressive action.

The rest of the text is Mahler's own. It must be quoted in full, before its musical embodiment can be examined.

O glaube, mein Herz, o glaube,
es geht dir nichts verloren!
Dein ist, was du gesehnt,
dein was du geliebt,
was du gestritten!

O glaube,
du warst nicht umsonst geboren!
Hast nicht umsonst gelebt,
gelitten!

Was entstanden ist,
das muss vergehen!
Was vergangen, auferstehn!
Hör' auf zu beben!
Bereite dich zu leben!

O Schmerz! Du Alldurchdringer!
Dir bin ich entrungen!
O Tod! Du Allbezwinger!
Nun bis du bezwungen!

Mit Flügeln, die ich mir errungen,
in heissem Liebesstreben,
werd' ich entschweben
zum Licht, zu dem kein Aug' gedrungen!
Sterben werd'ich, um zu leben!

Auferstehn wirst du
mein Herz, in einem Nu!
Was du geschlagen
zu Gott wird es dich tragen!

O believe, my heart, o believe,
nothing of you will be lost!
Yours is what you have longed for [or: yours is your longing]
Yours is what you have loved [or: yours is your love]
what you struggled for [or: your struggles].

O believe,
you were not born in vain.
Have not vainly lived,
suffered.

What has arisen
that must pass away!
What passed away, must rise!
Cease to tremble!
Prepare yourself to live!

O pain! you that pierce through all things,
From you I am wrested away!
O Death! You who compel all things,
Now you are compelled!

With wings that I have won for myself
in the hot striving of love,
I shall soar away
to the light to which no eye has penetrated.
I shall die, in order to live!

Rise again you will,
my heart, in an instant!
What you have fought for [or: your beating]
will carry you to God.

It is obvious that Mahler's own words have an intensely personal and passionate quality that Klopstock's do not. To begin with, they have considerable formal freedom. In the "O glaube" section Mahler departs altogether from Klopstock's tightly symmetrical stanzas, leaving even rhyme behind. When he returns to a rhyming stanza, it is in a far freer and more expressive form than that of Klopstock. There is a similar shift in content. With their references to love's striving and to the wings of Plato's *Phaedrus*, Mahler's stanzas convey a far more kinetic and erotic picture of ascent than do the placid words of the opening stanzas. But there is something more: the words really do fulfill Mahler's description, when he says that he has replaced the traditional Dantean hierarchies of reward and punishment by overwhelming love and simple being. For the ode subtly depicts the movements, the very being, of the striving heart as ends in themselves, in need of no punishment and no reward.

"Nothing of you will be lost," the contralto sings. And she develops this idea in the ensuing, ambiguous words. At first, one takes these words in the most obvious teleological sense: you now have everything you ever wanted, everything you ever loved and fought for. And they can certainly be taken in that way. But besides being unacceptable as a conventional account of heavenly reward (for everyone is a sinner and has loved and wanted inappropriate objects), the German clearly can and does have another sense, in which the accusatives are construed as internal or cognate accusatives (a construction common in ancient Greek as well as in German, and in English locutions like "fight the good fight"). An internal accusative introduces no object distinct from the activity mentioned in the verb: in effect it simply reinforces the verb, by mentioning again, as a substantive, the activity involved in the verb.[46]

Understood in this second way, the pronouns ("was") do not mention an additional object over and above the striving and longing; they simply mention, as substantives, the notions of striving and longing themselves. Thus, the very fact of your longing, the very fact of your love, your struggles (the love you have loved, the struggles you have struggled) – this is all yours. Both readings of the lines remain open, but the second (cognate accusative) reading ties them far more appropriately to the idea that "nothing of you" is lost. As we shall see, it is borne out by the music, which glorifies striving rather than promising the static possession of an object. No reward and no punishment, just being. When we get to the very last lines, which have an identical syntax, they are more easily taken in the second way. "What you fought for will carry you to God" is very unlikely to mean, "The (separate) object that you fought for will cause you to move toward God." (What would that object be, and why would it cause movement?) It is far more likely to mean, "The fact of your fighting for what you fought for (the fight you fought) will carry you to God." We may now note that the other simultaneous sense of the phrase, namely, "your beating" (the beating of the heart) has the internal accusative grammatical construction and can have no other. The heart beats a beat, it doesn't beat against some separate object. The same is true of a

---

46 See, for a list of typical examples, Goodwin and Gulick, *Greek Grammar* (1958), section 1049: *pasas hêdonas hêdesthai*, to enjoy all pleasures (Plato); *êutuchêsan touto to eutuchêma*, they were fortunate with this good fortune (Xenophon); *noson nosein*, to be ill with an illness (many sources); *hamartêma hamartanein*, to err an error, to commit an error; *plêgên tuptein*, to strike a blow; and so forth. English has fewer such constructions than inflected languages such as German and Greek.

third sense, "your beating the time," in which we find a reference not only to the life of music but also to Mahler's career as a conductor. Once again: the conductor beats a beat, he doesn't strike against some external object. I conclude that we are intended to hear the internal accusative constructions along with the other construction, until, in the last instance, we are pulled inexorably toward the internal accusative (although the other remains as a grammatical possibility), so that we focus on the nature of activity and striving themselves, as rewards in themselves.

What is being said, then – as is no surprise by this time – is that the reward of a life of striving and love is to have that life. That is you and yours and cannot be taken from you in any way, by any death or pain or opposition. The triple meaning of "*geschlagen*" reinforces the idea: not just some metaphysical struggle, but your very heartbeat, the passionate movements of your body – and, in music, your beating time – is what redeems you, is what redemption consists in.

We must now describe the music; I think we shall find that it bears out this meaning, as if the text is bursting out from the music, the overflowing expression of a musical idea.

Out of the silence of death – at a time when, in conventional terms, we expect to find the judge of the traditional *Dies Irae* stepping forward with his great book "in which everything is contained by which the world will be judged" – we hear, instead, the quiet simple voices of human beings singing in chorus, reassuring one another. "Soft and simple," Mahler writes, "the words gently swell up."[47] They sing unaccompanied, in simple chorale-like harmony. The resurrection theme that has been contaminated by the worldly clutter of the march now stands forth with naked dignity. On the words "brief Rest," the theme bends downward. The altered word "*rief*," "called," is now given tremendous emphasis, as the soprano solo soars upward above the chorus, singing, as Mahler marks the part, "very tenderly," and "inwardly." The second stanza continues the same pattern, with simple orchestration.

In a section marked "*etwas bewegter*," "somewhat more animated," we arrive at the beginning of Mahler's own text. The "O believe" theme has been heard before, in anxiety and anguish; it is now sung by

47 1896 program.

the contralto, with an intensity reminiscent of the "Ah! Ich liess mich nicht abweisen" of "*Urlicht.*" When we arrive at the ambiguous words, the music expresses a great intensity of longing and striving, with its syncopated rhythms and its chromaticism, its upward straining on "*geliebt.*" No static possession of an object is present in this music, and no static telos of any kind – instead, the beauty is all in the intensity of human effort itself, which now spreads over the orchestra, as the strings are instructed to play "*mit leidenschaftlichem Ausdruck,*" "with passionate expression."

The tenors and basses now enter alone, singing mysteriously of rebirth. "Cease to tremble!" they say, with a hush of expectation – then, bursting out with enormous joy, "Prepare yourself to live!" And whether this is the joy of life in another world or joy at the life one has had in this world, it is enormous joy in the act of living. The wings of love now ascend – we have reached the freely sensuous and joyful passage described at the opening of this chapter. The significance of assigning this erotic music to two female voices coiling around one another should be understood in the light of our reading of "*Urlicht*" – and of so many of Mahler's images of the feminine and the passive. The wings of ascent belong to the receptive, to those who feminize themselves in the sense of allowing themselves to be "played on by the spirit of the world" – those, we discover here, who permit themselves passionate erotic love. And the ideal of love here – as, indeed, in Plato's *Phaedrus*, from which the wings ultimately derive – is, as expressed in the vocal lines, an ideal of reciprocity and equality, of "no great and no small." The music unfolds with a generous ecstasy, its love unconstrained by any envy or anger, including all beings in its sweep.

What is the "light to which no eye has penetrated"? In an obvious sense, it is the light of Heaven. But the idea that *no eye* has seen the light of Heaven is, in Christian terms, an anomaly. Not only mystical experiences within this life – prominently recognized in both the Augustinian and the Thomistic traditions – but also the experiences of angels and perfected souls after death[48] involve the seeing of the heavenly light. Some translations reduce the difficulty by writing "no mortal eye" – but this is not, of course, what the text says. We can now note

48 Even though the resurrection of the body has not taken place, accounts of Heaven such as Dante's do depict visual experiences. And the ability of angels to see is stressed in many different parts of the Christian tradition.

that in Jewish eschatology the afterlife is not a bright, but a shadowy, place, rather like the Homeric underworld. And Judaism draws close to Romanticism in its insistence on finding the worth and meaning of a life within history, in its choices and striving in this life. It seems not too bold to see here, then, a distinctively Jewish picture of the afterlife as in itself shadowy and uncertain, to be given light only by the achievements of the person within this life. Mahler's Romanticism and his Jewishness are once again allied, in drawing attention to the light of the worldly life, rather than to any telos beyond this world.

In keeping with this emphasis, it is, I believe, worth at least entertaining a further idea. If my account of the work has been at all persuasive, musical creativity is among its central subjects. Mahler repeatedly associates music with darkness: it is the realm where "the dark feelings hold sway."[49] The idea that ideal experience must be a visual experience, that its illumination must be accounted for in terms of the eye, would be one that might well be resisted by a person whose deepest emotions unfold themselves in musical form. Mahler was rather dismissive of the visual arts, writing that they are hooked up with "external appearances" rather than with "get[ting] to the bottom of things."[50] Music, by contrast, cuts beneath habit. It can therefore shed a light that is, very precisely, unseeable to the socially corrupted eye. Mahler uses the idea of "illumination" in describing both the "Urlicht" and the final experience of heavenly love. But I believe that it is, precisely, an illumination unseeable because musical, a light emanating from the inner world where the "dark feelings hold sway." This is fully compatible with, and a further specification of, the work's Jewish eschatology.

The entire chorus now joins the ascent. It becomes the ascent of all mortal beings, rich and poor, female and male, winged by love. They now sing in triumphant unison, "I shall die, in order to live." And now the Resurrection theme returns, sung fortissimo by the entire chorus, accompanied by the full orchestra – with, now, the addition of the organ. The sounds of Bach chorale now perfectly fuse with the Mahlerian intensity of strings and brass, as the symphony celebrates the victory of authentic (musical) creation and the love it bears to all human

49 See Chapter 5.
50 Letter to Marschalk quoted in Mahler (1985), pp. 200–1.

beings. The strong and fully expressive self, addressed as "you, my heart," now finds no limits to its joy. Instead of curving downward, burdened beneath a weight, the last phrase of the theme soars confidently back up to b-flat: "Rise again, yes, rise again you will my heart, in an instant" – and the "instant," "(*in einem*) *Nu*," is held solidly, weightily, for almost a full bar, as if to direct our attention to the temporally extended and the bodily, through which and in which the victory has been achieved. The triple meaning of "*geschlagen*" – the heart's struggles, its physical beating, and its music's beat – is now expressed in the orchestra, as the percussion, brass, organ, and strings all strike together emphatically on the downbeat. The temporality and physicality of sound – for Schopenhauer, signs of the connection between music and nonredemption, bondage to the erotic will – become here the vehicle of redemption, and the redeemed existence.

Is there an otherworldly Christian salvation in this work? On the surface, there is.[51] On the other hand, it is emphasized that there is no "Last Judgment," no assignment of static positions. Being and love are the ends, and these ends are ends in this life and of this life. Mahler purposively omits portions of Klopstock's text referring to Jesus and to heavenly peace, substituting his own Romantic vision. Furthermore, in order to be a salvation for the self, the world of bliss must be a world of the heartbeat, of the body, of erotic striving, of continued receptivity and vulnerability – a world in which general compassion for human suffering yields a love as fully universal as music itself.

VIII. IMAGINATION AND JUSTICE

Mahler achieves, then, a triumphant fusion of the Christian ascent with the Romantic emphasis on striving and imagination. He does this in the context of a Jewish emphasis on this-worldly justice and the this-worldly body. In the process he provides extremely powerful answers to the questions we asked of Dante's Thomistic ascent: questions about authority and reciprocity, about the worth of earthly striving, about

---

51 It should be remembered that Mahler converted to Christianity in 1897, and was baptized in the very church where he had heard the Bülow memorial. Whatever the motives for conversion may have been – and surely they are likely to have been complex – Mahler no doubt sincerely embraced certain aspects of Christianity, which he associates here with a child's pure faith, and with compassion.

the body. This account of the ascent claims to have eliminated the narrowness in love, its excessive fearfulness, and its anger – while yielding a result that contains fully universal compassion, along with a robust commitment to human equality and reciprocity, to the equal dignity of Jew and gentile, woman and man. The strivings of the individual heart take precedence over conventional authority; worldly striving for justice and brotherhood is given its full weight in the context of eternity – indeed, permitted to define the context of eternity.

In some ways this ascent is to me the most completely satisfying of all that we shall consider. And yet two questions remain. One is simply a request for further information. We have a very general idea about the politics that this musical idea prefers – that it is inclusive, compassionate, dedicated to something like democratic reciprocity. But for obvious reasons there is not much specificity here, and we wonder exactly how the further development of the view would go. The musical realm, called by Mahler the realm "where the dark feelings hold sway," does not in the end suffice to tell us all that a social and philosophical view needs to tell us, although in some ways it gets at the depths of a political vision more powerfully than most verbal representations can.

The second question is about the everyday. This work, while claiming to solve the problem of our own all-too-human self-repudiation, is itself filled with disgust and repudiation: at everyday life, at its shortcomings and half-heartedness, at the very existence of fixed social forms. Acceptance of all humanity is achieved musically, but at a considerable distance from real human beings, who continue to be condemned from the viewpoint of authentic creativity. We wonder what this visionary perspective has to say about real people with their real and everyday shortcomings; we would need to know this, for example, in order to know what approach to the particular loves of real people is promised in the perspective of the work.

Nonetheless, despite these questions, we are left with a remarkable claim, the claim that love, while remaining human and embodied, can overcome hatred, exclusion, and resentment. Brontë expressed pessimism about the victory of love over hate, suggesting that our shame at our nakedness, encouraged by centuries of Christian teaching, would continue to produce misogyny and hatred, forcing those who can love and be loved to dwell outside the world. Mahler, at least here, is an optimist. He does not exactly propose a therapeutic solution to Brontë's problem. He just expresses the thought that one may simply overcome primitive shame and stand forth in one's own being, without disgust, without envy. And he indicates that the corporeality and sensuousness of music – rather than being, as in Schopenhauer, a device of escape from bondage to the body and to sexuality – will be, in fact, devices of acceptance and joy, that following the movements of this music is a way of accepting love.

15

DEMOCRATIC DESIRE:
WALT WHITMAN

I. A DEMOCRACY OF LOVE

Walt Whitman is a political poet, a poet who holds that poetry has an essential role to play in the life of the American democracy.[1] This is so because the poet knows what it is to see men and women as ends, and to see the boundless and equal worth of each and every one of them:

> He sees eternity in men and women, he does not see men and women as
> dreams or dots.

> For the great Idea, the idea of perfect and free individuals,
> For that, the bard walks in advance, leader of leaders,
> The attitude of him cheers up slaves and horrifies foreign despots. (BO
> 153–6)

The vision of democracy is in itself, for Whitman, a poetic vision, and citizens are those who "have left all feudal processes and poems behind them, and assumed the poems and processes of Democracy" (BO 185).

For Whitman, the democratic vision is, ultimately, a vision of love. In a poem entitled "Recorders Ages Hence," Whitman tells the future what to say about him: "Publish my name and hang up my picture as that of the tenderest lover / . . . Who was not proud of his songs, but of the measureless ocean of love within him . . ." But this idea of love is not cozy or bland. It will require a radical reform, he argues, in common religious and secular understandings of love. The poet–

---

[1] All citations to Whitman's poetry are to the Norton Critical Edition (Whitman 1973). I use the following abbreviations: SM for *Song of Myself*, BO for "By Blue Ontario's Shore," BE for "I Sing the Body Electric."

speaker considers American ideals of equality and freedom, and concludes:

> Underneath all is the Expression of love for men and women,
> (I swear I have seen enough of mean and impotent modes of expressing
>   love for men and women,
> After this day I take my own modes of expressing love for men and
>   women.) (BO 266–9)

Whitman's "own ways" of expressing love were not congenial to conventional American society. Although the 1855 first edition of *Leaves of Grass* was greeted with much praise, including a remarkable public letter from Emerson, denunciation began at that time and escalated gradually, Emerson himself eventually joining the chorus. The book was called "a mass of stupid filth," a "heterogeneous mass of bombast, egotism, vulgarity, and nonsense," whose author must be "some escaped lunatic, raving in pitiable delirium." Whitman "should be kicked from all decent society as below the level of a brute."[2] In large part, these reactions are addressed to the poems' treatment of sexual and bodily themes. Whitman insistently pursues these themes throughout his career, holding that the appropriate conception of democratic love cannot be articulated without forging a new attitude toward both the body and its sexuality. The poetry of equality must also be erotic, and erotic in a bold and defiant manner. And the erotic must be frankly sexual. What are these connections? What is the new conception of love that Whitman claims to bring to America? And why must this democratic love be erotic, and erotic in a sexual sense?

II. "I AM HE ATTESTING SYMPATHY"

Before we can approach these questions, we must understand the context and historical motivation of Whitman's project. The first edition of *Leaves of Grass* was published in 1855, just before the Civil War. Subsequent editions cover the period of the war, the second presidency of Abraham Lincoln, the death of Lincoln, and the Reconstruction.[3]

---

2 See Reynolds (1995), p. 346.
3 See the Norton Critical Edition, pp. xxvii–lv. The first edition of *Leaves of Grass* (LG) of 1855 contained "Song of Myself" and eleven other poems. The 1856 edition added twenty more poems and gave them all titles. The 1860 third edition brought the total

The great political theme of this poetry is the overthrow of slavery; the democracy Whitman addresses with love is the preserved Union; and racial hatred is the central problem to which Whitman's new conception of love is addressed. The 1871 epitaph for Lincoln, one of Whitman's simplest and most eloquent statements, leaves no doubt of Whitman's intense feeling on this matter:

> This dust was once the man,
> Gentle, plain, just and resolute, under whose cautious hand,
> Against the foulest crime in history known in any land or age,
> Was saved the Union of these States.

It is because the poet–speaker lacks confidence that conventional forms of religious morality can deal effectively with the question of racial hatred – and other related hatreds and exclusions – that he has concluded that his own mission requires a radically reformulated idea of love, one that cannot be straightforwardly derived from religion. In a remarkable poem of 1855,[4] "Now Lucifer Was Not Dead," the speaker, a black slave, imagines that he must be the dark angel Lucifer, excluded as he is from Heaven, and even from the Earth, by the pious Christians who surround him:

> Now Lucifer was not dead – or if he was, I am his sorrowful terrible heir;
> I have been wrong'd – I am oppress'd – I hate him that oppresses me,
> I will either destroy him, or he shall release me.

number of poems to 156. *Drum-Taps* was published separately in 1865, and a "Sequel" in 1865–66. The fourth edition of LG (1867), included 236 poems, incorporating the separately published items. An edition of 1871 contained only nine new poems, and an 1876 edition only a few. The edition of 1881 gave the work its final arrangement, and the "deathbed" edition of 1891–92, the final authorized text, added a few more poems, keeping the structure intact. A number of Whitman's published poems were excluded from LG, and some that found a place in earlier editions are not in the final edition. Other uncollected poems and manuscript fragments are also gathered in the Norton edition, with a detailed discussion of their history.

4 This poem appeared in the first edition of LG, and in subsequent editions until 1881, when it was excluded, along with the fascinating "O Hot-Cheek'd and Blushing," to be discussed later. Whitman's reasons for the exclusion are unclear; the Norton editor attributes it to a lack of fit with the context (in "The Sleepers," a visionary lyric). Whitman may have felt that the efforts of reconciliation after the war suggested deemphazing anger and revenge – see the following text. As for the shame poem, he may possibly have felt that it was superceded by the completion of "I Sing the Body Electric" – embryonic and incomplete in the first edition, not in its present form until 1851.

Damn him! how he does defile me!
How he informs against my brother and sister, and takes pay for their
blood!
How he laughs when I look down the bend, after the steamboat that
carries away my woman!

Now the vast dusk bulk that is the whale's bulk, it seems mine;
Warily, sportsman! though I lie so sleepy and sluggish, the tap of my
flukes is death.

Inverting traditional metaphors of blackness and whiteness, of God
and Devil, hunter and huntsman, Whitman shows the white Christian
as an informer, a callous sportsman making a game of human flesh, a
defiler of the true dignity of humanity, which in the poem is represented
by its darkness. Whiteness becomes a metaphor for brutality, the angelic a metaphor for disdain and contempt of humanity; humanity itself
is represented by the metaphors of the dark angel and of the animal,
the whale's bulky dusky body. Identifying himself with the hunted dark
body, Whitman writes a powerful prophecy of revenge – not as an
endorsement of hatred over love, but as a warning cry for justice, an
injunction to show real love before it is too late.

Whitman omitted this poem from the last two editions of *Leaves of
Grass*, perhaps simply for structural reasons, perhaps feeling that the
"charity" of which Lincoln spoke entailed, so many years later, a
deemphazing of anger and revenge.[5] But Lincoln's forgiveness was
never without teeth. In the Second Inaugural Address, the famous exhortation to show "malice toward none and charity toward all" (see
Chapter 8) is immediately followed by an exhortation to "firmness in
the right as God gives us to see the right" – and preceded by a damning
criticism of those who imagine that God could ever have sanctioned
the cause of slavery: "It may seem strange that any men should ask a
just God's assistance in wringing their bread from the sweat of other
men's faces."

Whitman, similarly, sets out to create a love that is just and firm in
the right, and yet capable of forgiveness and reconciliation. We will be
on the right track if we ask at every point in the poetic argument, how
does this phrase, this image, bear on the task of creating a new and
transfigured America – an America that truly practices equality and

5 See the previous note.

inclusion, that is free from the poisonous hatred of the outsider? And also, how does this poetic strategy bear on the more immediate task of binding together an America riven by the waste and horror of a war fought for the most basic and elementary starting point of justice, a war that has destroyed generations of citizens for the sake of establishing what should never have been in question?

> And I saw askant the armies,
> I saw as in noiseless dreams hundreds of battle-flags,
> Borne through the smoke of the battles and pierc'd with missiles I saw them,
> And carried hither and yon through the smoke, and torn and bloody,
> And at last but a few shreds left on the staff, (and all in silence,)
> And the staffs all splinter'd and broken.
>
> I saw battle-corpses, myriads of them
> And the white skeletons of young men, I saw them,
> I saw the debris and debris of all the slain soldiers of the war . . .
> The living remain'd and suffer'd, the mother suffer'd,
> And the wife and the child and the musing comrade suffer'd,
> And the armies that remain'd suffer'd. ("Lilacs," 171ff.)

It is in this tragic and yet still hopeful context that we should hear the poet's announcement, "I am he attesting sympathy" (SM 22.461). It is a cry for radical social change to move the nation beyond this time of cruelty, guilt, waste, and mourning. We are put on notice that this is not a facile sympathy, but, like Lincoln's, a sympathy with teeth, coupled with a prophetic call to this-worldly justice. Seeing eternity in men and women entails working for a society that treats every one of them as an end, and none as a mere tool for the ends of others.

I have mentioned men and women. And a second great historical development that Whitman witnesses and makes his own is the growing movement for women's equality. Whitman was a contemporary of the early suffragists. He was directly and deeply involved in the women's rights movement, both as journalist and as poet. In his journalism he spoke out against domestic violence and other forms of misogyny. Underlining the link between prurience and puritanism, he criticized the representation of women in pornography; he called for respect for prostitutes and a reform of their living conditions. Nor did he ignore inequalities internal to marriage: well before J. S. Mill's *The*

Subjection of Women (1869), Whitman made most of its central arguments, calling for the democratization of marriage and of opportunities and duties within marriage, for new ideas of sexual attractiveness that did not eroticize domination on the one side, submission on the other. And he went further than Mill, advocating equality and mutuality in sexual pleasure itself as a sine qua non of a healthy society. He even advocated premarital sex for women as an avenue toward women's full sexual equality.[6]

Given this journalistic background, it is not surprising that, from the first, women's issues were given a central place in *Leaves of Grass*. In an 1847 draft, he wrote, "I am the poet of women as well as men. / The woman is not less than the man." In the preface to the 1855 edition he continues in the same vein: "A great poem is . . . for a woman as much as a man and a man as much as a woman." In SM these words become the poetic lines, "I am the poet of the woman the same as the man, / And I say it is as great to be a woman as to be a man, / And I say there is nothing greater than the mother of men" (SM 21.425–7). And although Whitman continued to stress the importance of the woman's role as mother, it was in the context of a radical rethinking of the family structure in which the household would not divide functions by sex and in which there would be a true equality of respect: "The wife, and she is not one jot less than the husband, / The daughter, and she is just as good as the son, / The mother, and she is every bit as much as the father" ("A Song for Occupations," 33–5).

Whitman took issue with some strategies of the women's suffrage movement: for he felt that the narrow focus on voting rights would be unlikely to ameliorate problems of misogyny and unequal respect. He believed that women could gain full equality only through a radical change in relations between the sexes. In a prose article he writes:

To the movement for the eligibility and entrance of woman amid new spheres of business, politics, and the suffrage, the current prurient, conventional treatment of sex is the main formidable obstacle. The rising tide of "women's rights," swelling every year advancing farther and farther, recoils from it in dismay.[7]

---

6 See the good discussion in Reynolds (1995), Chapter 7. Mill's *Subjection* is greatly indebted to some American writers about women affiliated with the Abolitionist movement: see Hasday (2000). It is likely that Whitman had similar sources.

7 Cited in Reynolds (1995), p. 233, from Whitman (1963.4), vol. 2, p. 494.

And, in a related fragment,

[O]nly when sex is properly treated, talked, avowed, accepted, will the woman be equal with the man, and pass where the man passes, and meet his words with her words, and his rights with her rights.[8]

Among our central tasks will be to uncover his reasons for making these connections.

Finally, there is a political issue that emerges in Whitman's work in a more indirect and yet insistent manner: the issue of homosexual love. Whitman's highly erotic poems about love between males were found controversial in his own time, a time in which, as historians George Chauncey and Martin Duberman[9] have shown, there was in many respects less intrusive opposition to same-sex activity than we have frequently supposed. Nonetheless, there was opposition, and Whitman suffered greatly from it. It now appears likely, on the basis of new evidence marshalled by literary historian David Reynolds, that in his youth Whitman was dismissed from a teaching position in Southold, on the eastern end of Long Island, for a suspected sexual relationship with a student or students.[10] Twenty-one years old at the time, he was apparently, as a boarder in the schoolmaster's home, required to share a bed with other males, whether students or sons of the master we do not know. All details of the living arrangements, including the ages of Whitman's possible roommates, are pure conjecture.

At any rate, given Whitman's well-known lack of sexual interest in women and his keen interest in men, rumors began to circulate. They reached a notoriously aggressive local Presbyterian preacher, the Reverend Ralph Smith. (Smith was trained at Princeton University – a fact that would have been meaningful to Whitman, since Princeton, though in the North, made a specialty at this time of training the elite gentlemen of the South, allowing them to bring their slaves with them, as slaves, to its New Jersey campus.)[11] Smith alleged in a sermon that sexual acts had been committed and that Whitman should be punished.

---

8 Cited in Reynolds (1995), p. 213, from Whitman, *Notes and Fragments*, ed. Richard M. Bucke (Ontario: A. Talbot and Co., original edition 1899, repr. n.d.).
9 Chauncey (1994), Duberman (1991).
10 Reynolds (1995), pp. 70–80.
11 The slaves were typically freed on graduation; the black population of the town of Princeton still contains many descendants of these freed slaves.

Members of the congregation, whipped up into a frenzy of hostility, apparently formed a furious mob, hunted Whitman down where he hid, cowering under a neighbor's mattress ticking, seized him, plastered tar and feathers all over him, and rode him out of town on a rail. Severely injured by the attack, he took a full month to recover.

We have no way of knowing whether there was any truth in the accusations; Whitman's perceived prefererences would have sufficed to explain them, even without any other foundation; such assaults have been known to occur, not least in America. What is clear is that the incident was an exceedingly painful one, one that very likely shaped Whitman's attitudes, both toward established religions and toward America's dominant moral views.

In the aftermath of the event, which he carefully shrouded in secrecy, Whitman in later years frequently approached the topic of same-sex relations, writing very passionately and erotically about male-male love – but, at the same time, publicly denying that explicit sexuality was really what he had in mind. John Addington Symonds, finding in the poems of the Calamus sequence in *Leaves of Grass* a prophecy of homosexual liberation, wrote to Whitman asking pointedly about their sexual meaning. When Whitman denied any such meaning, calling Symonds's inferences "morbid" and "damnable," Symonds refused to give up and wrote again. At this point, Whitman replied with confusion: perhaps the Calamus sequence "means more or less what I thought myself – means different: perhaps I don't know what it all means – perhaps never did know . . . I maybe do not know all my meanings."[12] This same idea of hidden meanings can be found in a poem in a later edition of the Calamus sequence itself, entitled "Here the Frailest Leaves of Me" (1860):

> Here the frailest leaves of me and yet my strongest lasting,
> Here I shade and hide my thoughts, I myself do not expose them,
> And yet they expose me more than all my other poems.

In a related poem near the beginning of the Calamus sequence, he darkly hints at the danger his readers incur, in following him. Given the suggestive title, "Whoever You Are Holding Me Now in Hand" (1860), the poem begins as follows:

12 Quoted in Reynolds (1995), p. 396, from Horace Traubel, *With Walt Whitman in Camden*, 7 vols. (1905, rpt. New York: Rowman and Littlefield, 1961), p. 77.

Whoever you are holding me now in hand, . . .
I give you fair warning before you attempt me further,
I am not what you supposed, but far different.

Who is he that would become my follower?
Who would sign himself a candidate for my affections?

The way is suspicious, the result uncertain, perhaps destructive . . .

The whole past theory of your life and all conformity to the lives around
    you would have to be abandon'd. . . . (1–6, 9)

Although the ensuing account makes it plain that the "follower" is a
follower of Whitman's poetic vocation, in fact his devoted reader, the
erotic imagery continues:

Here to put your lips upon mine I permit you,
With the comrade's long-dwelling kiss or the new husband's kiss,
For I am the new husband and I am the comrade.

Or if you will, thrusting me beneath your clothing,
Where I may feel the throbs of your heart or rest upon your hip,
Carry me when you go forth over land or sea. . . . (19–24)

Thus the reader, who is for the most part imagined as male (voyag-
ing on the sea, walking in the woods, putting a book on his hip), but
who can by turns also become the bride awaiting her "new husband,"
becomes the recipient of Whitman's intense erotic attentions. I think
Whitman's warnings, these suggestions of danger and of hidden painful
matter, are far too deliberate for us to take at face value his claim to
Symonds that he does not know what he means.

Consider, finally, the remarkable poem about sexual shame that
Whitman published in editions of *Leaves of Grass* between 1855 and
1867, "O Hot-Cheek'd and Blushing":

O hot-cheek'd and blushing! O foolish hectic!
O for pity's sake, no one must see me now! my clothes were stolen while
    I was abed,
Now I am thrust forth, where shall I run?

Pier that I saw dimly last night, when I look'd from the windows!
Pier out from the main, let me catch myself with you and stay – I will
    not chafe you,
I feel ashamed to go naked about the world.

I am curious to know where my feet stand and what this is flooding me,
    childhood or manhood – and the hunger that crosses the bridge
    between.

The cloth laps a first sweet eating and drinking,
Laps life-swelling yolks – laps ear of rose-corn, milky and just ripen'd;
The white teeth stay, and the boss-tooth advances in darkness,
And liquor is spill'd on lips and bosoms by touching glasses, and the
    best liquor afterward.

The poem begins with a powerful evocation of primal sexual shame,
shame about the body and its naked exposure. The speaker imagines
fleeing for shelter to the shadows of a "pier" at nighttime: and the piers
of New York were even then, as they are now, associated with homosexual encounters. The speaker associates his flight to the pier with a
shame at being seen by the world. But then the poem shifts. Together
with the shame there is an insistent sexual curiosity and desire. Indeed,
sexual desire is seen as a hunger that bridges the gap between the
condition of childhood (the helpless powerlessness of the body) and
manhood (adult pleasure). It would appear that knowledge of this
hunger might possibly dissipate the childlike panic and the condition
of helpless shame. The speaker is standing on unknown ground,
flooded with arousal.

In the remarkable final stanza, the speaker now permits himself to
map the aspects of himself that the stolen clothes had covered. The
clothing itself now becomes erotic, a cloth that not only covers the lap,
but also "laps" the body as waves lap at the shore. First, the fabric
caresses the sweetness of arousal, "a first sweet eating and drinking."
Next, it touches "life-swelling yolks" and "ear of rose-corn, milky and
just ripen'd."[13] Although one should not overliteralize these striking
erotic images, it is hard not to see them as, inter alia at least, suggestive
of penis and testicles. The poet both has these (his clothes cover them)
and views them with erotic desire. And as so often in Whitman,[14] the
image of male genitalia is followed by an image of fellatio, as the teeth
of the poet, the white teeth, open around the "advancing" swelling of

13 The Norton editors write that the popcorn, popular at that time, had a rose-colored
    ear.
14 For other examples, see my discussion of SM.

a bodily organ.[15] In the poem's conclusion, shame is overcome, and liquid pleasure ensues.

The poem combines homoerotic imagery with an intensity of pleasure in a way that we may associate with the important lines in SM 5, where the poet's mystical vision of the unity of all creason in love is prefaced by a fantasy of erotic oral contact between the poet's body and his soul.[16] Whether it is a commentary on Whitman's unhappy experience must remain uncertain. It is certain, at any rate, that his own experiences of exclusion, shame, and the longing for fulfilled love and pleasure powerfully color Whitman's writing, not only here but also more generally, providing him with ways of understanding other social exclusions and hatreds, and giving him powerful incentives toward the rethinking of society's moral and sexual norms.[17]

III. A COUNTER-COSMOS: THE DEMOCRATIC BODY

From its beginning, Whitman's poetry announces its intention to subject traditional religion and morality to searching critical scrutiny, by the light of norms of equality, reciprocity, and human freedom. Whitman presents himself as, in a sense, a deeply religious poet, a follower of the life of Christ and a believer in a God who is the source of love. And yet he also arrogates to himself the right to interrogate all traditional systems of religious understanding to see how well they come up to his democratic ideal. What is important in both philosophical and religious teaching is not the authority of the teaching's source, but the quality of the love that is its content. In a poem entitled "The Base of All Metaphysics," Whitman, rather in the manner of Mahler – who, we recall, looked all through world literature including the Bible for

---

15 See the Norton edition, *ad loc*: " '[B]oss' originally designated a swelling or extension of an internal organ; later, any protuberance of 'embossed' book covers, metal ornaments, armor, etc."

16 "I mind how once we lay such a transparent summer morning, / How you settled your head athwart my hips and gently turn'd over upon me, / And parted the shirt from my bosom-bone, and plunged your tongue to my bare-stript heart, / And reach'd till you felt my beard, and reach'd till you held my feet."

17 Not, however, in every respect: Reynolds shows that taboos against masturbation are still endorsed by the poet, who had strong affiliations with antebellum purity reformers on this topic (see Reynolds [1995], pp. 199–200).

his "redeeming word," only to conclude that words of love had to emerge from his own imagination – announces that he has looked all through the major metaphysical texts of his tradition, only to conclude that what really counts is human love, and one's own ability to articulate that love and live it:

> Having studied the new and antique, the Greek and Germanic systems,
> Kant having studied and stated, Fichte and Schelling and Hegel,
> Stated the lore of Plato, and Socrates greater than Plato,
> And greater than Socrates sought and stated, Christ divine having studied long,
> I see reminiscent to-day those Greek and Germanic systems,
> See the philosophies all, Christian churches and tenets see,
> Yet underneath Socrates clearly see, and underneath Christ the divine I see,
> The love of man for his comrade, the attraction of friend to friend,
> Of the well-married husband and wife, of children and parents,
> Of city for city and land for land.

Accordingly, Whitman sets out to create his own counter-metaphysical system of love that will express what he sees as religious metaphysics' true basis. Setting himself in the tradition of the cosmological writing of both Greek and Christian philosophy, he attempts to create a democratic counter-cosmos, in which hierarchies of souls are replaced by the democratic body of the United States, which he calls the "greatest poem."[18]

> Walt Whitman, a kosmos, of Manhattan the son,
> ... No sentimentalist, no stander above men and women or apart from them,
> ... In me the caresser of life wherever moving, backward as well as forward sluing,
> To niches aside and junior bending, not a person or object missing,
> Absorbing all to myself and for this song. (SM 13.232–4)

Here is the new cosmology that Whitman offers us, to stand over against the cosmologies created by philosophical and religious systems: the finite mortal individual, democratic citizen, equal to and among others, who contains the world within himself by virtue of his resource-

---

18 Preface to *Leaves of Grass* (1855): "The United States themselves are essentially the greatest poem."

ful imagination and his sympathetic love. "I am he attesting sympathy" (SM 22.461), the poet announces. And "whoever walks a furlong without sympathy walks to his own funeral drest in his shroud" (SM 48.1272). The defects in earthly love are to be overcome not by any established system of belief – for the poet speaks holding "creeds and schools in abeyance" (SM l.10) – but by the capacity of the individual to extend the circles of sympathy outward to embrace everything in the world with equal love. The poetry itself is democratic, in its freedom of form and line, in its inclusion of slang words such as "sluing" that were usually taken to be inappropriate to the dignity of literature.

Religious sources of love are not scorned in this poetry – "I do not despise you priests" (SM 43.1096), the poet writes; the poet's faith, he continues, is "the greatest of faiths" as well as "the least of faiths" (1097). But on the way to Whitman's America, some remarkable changes have taken place in religion. First of all, as we have already seen in the poem about Plato and Christ, it is deprived of its claims to authority. "Now I re-examine philosophies and religions" (OR 6.83), announces the citizen. His reader is told, "You shall no longer take things at second or third hand, nor look through the eyes of the dead, nor feed on the spectres in books" (SM 2.35). And lest this appear to be the prelude to a new claim to quasi-religious authority, the speaker immediately adds, "You shall not look through my eyes either, nor take things from me, / You shall listen to all sides and filter them from your self" (2.36–7). The agency of democratic love is not, like Dante's will, "upright, pure, and whole" on account of its relation to a religious authority. Its integrity is itself and its own.[19]

Second, religion no longer promises transcendence of our needy mortal condition. God is imagined as immanent in the world and its energy – indeed, in one passage, as an erotic partner of the poet himself.[20] The speaker announces his mortality and hopes for no immortal-

19 In this sense, Whitman announces, animals are frequently better off than human beings – for they have escaped that subservience to institutionalized religion, that encasement in self-abasement, that has led to so much misery in the world: "They do not lie awake in the dark and weep for their sins, / . . . Not one kneels to another, nor to his kind that lived thousands of years ago." (SM 32.687–8, 690)

20 Whitman seduces the reader, inviting him to "stop this day and night with me" (SM 2.33). Even so, and in very similar terms, he issues an invitation to God. In one of the most audacious gestures in the *Song of Myself*, Whitman imagines God as a male companion who accepts the invitation to spend the night in his bed, only to leave his

ity. He is the poet of life and he is the poet of death. There "will never be any more perfection than there is now, / Nor any more heaven or hell than there is now" (SM 3.42–3). There is just life, renewing itself; and the only continuity for the human being is the continuity of nature and of human civilization. The transcendence it makes sense to strive for is the transcendence of partiality and faction in sympathy, of hierarchy in equal respect, of oppression in citizenship and voting, of hatred in love. Indeed, this is the reason why the poet, not the religious thinker, not the legal thinker, not the economist, is the "equable man,"[21] the model of rational judgment required by a democratic nation: for, as we shall later see, it is in the poetic imagination, far more than in the modes of thought proper to these other professions, that narrow sympathies are transcended.

Third, as we have begun to see from the very beginning, this poetry affirms the body and its sexuality as has no other account of love's ascent that we have examined. Right from the beginning of "Song of Myself," with its daringly erotic depiction of the relationship between the poet and his God, and between his body and his soul, it is plain that the rehabilitation of sex is a central feature of Whitman's counter-cosmology. And I think one of the central questions posed by this poetry, one of the insistent obstacles to its understanding and full reception, still must be: why is this theme so central? Why does Whitman believe that a new attitude toward sex and the body is involved in the solution to problems of hierarchy and racial hate?

IV. THE RECLAMATION OF THE BODY

Whitman takes on a double task, its two parts closely related: the restoration to human beings of interest in and love for the blood and guts and bones that they are; and the restoration of sexual desire to the center of the account of ethical value. The two tasks are in some obvious ways connected, since sex leads attention to the stuff of the

---

side in the morning: "As God comes a loving bedfellow and sleeps at my side all night and close on the peep of day" (SM 3.60). Later editions make the line less explicit: "As the hugging and loving bed-fellow sleeps at my side through the night, and withdraws at the peep of day with stealthy tread."

21 BO 10.137. On this section of the poem, see Nussbaum (1995a).

body, and sexual interest will become furtive and tinged with shame and disgust if that stuff is the object of disgust. By contrast, the idea that blood and guts are the scene of a great wonder and mystery, closely connected to the most valuable sort of sympathy and love, itself infuses sexuality with beauty.

Taking on this twofold task – above all in the poems that comprise the volume *Children of Adam* – Whitman represents himself as Adam before the Fall, and beckons to his reader, in language of noble simplicity, to join him in acceptance and delight:

> As Adam early in the morning
> Walking forth from the bower refresh'd with sleep,
> Behold me where I pass, hear my voice, approach,
> Touch me, touch the palm of your hand to my body as I pass,
> Be not afraid of my body.

Notice that it does not matter whether the reader is male or female, or, indeed, whether the reader's caress is or is not specifically sexual. What stands at the center of the stage is loving acceptance of the flesh, and the innocence of the flesh.[22] In Eden there is no shame at any part of the body, no fear of its touch. In that innocence no pleasure of the flesh is marked off as specially problematic, none is a sphere of moral guilt or suspicion more than any other. The poem connects this absence of shame, obscurely, with an open acceptance of Adam's personhood. There is something about Adam's attitude toward his body that will make it possible for the reader, if he or she shares it, to walk right up to him and look him in the eye. This looking in the eye, which Whitman connects with the absence of the bodily shame of "O Hot-Cheek'd and Blushing," is seen by him as a crucial element in democratic inclusiveness, which cannot, he suggests, be built on disgust and self-concealment. "Was it doubted," the poet asks, "that those who corrupt their bodies conceal themselves?" (BE 1.5) By "corrupt their bodies" he means, however, not what conventional morality means – by "corrupt" he means "refuse to honor and respect."[23]

22 Compare Nietzsche's phrase, "*das Unschuld des Werdens.*"
23 Here we discover another defect in Reynolds (1995): for he takes these remarks at face value and out of context, as evidence that Whitman condemns masturbation. In context they cannot possibly bear this meaning.

The central text of Whitman's counter-cosmology of the body is the remarkable poem, "I Sing the Body Electric," in which the poet affirms the Aristotelian view that the body is the soul, coupling it with the view that the body is itself a poem and the theme of poems. Since what is remarkable about this counter-poem can only be seen in its unlikely detail, its bulky comic incongruities, its thrusting into verse of the most apparently prosaic, we need to have before us a substantial portion of its final section:

O my body! I dare not desert the likes of you in other men and women,
    nor the likes of the parts of you,
I believe the likes of you are to stand or fall with the likes of the soul,
    (and that they are the soul,)
I believe the likes of you shall stand or fall with my poems, and that they
    are my poems,
Man's, woman's, child's, youth's, wife's, husband's, mother's, father's,
    young man's, young woman's poems,
Head, neck, hair, ears, drop and tympan of the ears,
Eyes, eye-fringes, iris of the eye, eyebrows, and the waking or sleeping of
    the lids,
Mouth, tongue, lips, teeth, roof of the mouth, jaws, and the jaw-
    hinges, . . .
Strong set of thighs, well carrying the trunk above,
Leg-fibres, knee, knee-pan, upper-leg, under-leg, . . .
The lung-sponges, the stomach-sac, the bowels sweet and clean,
The brain in its folds inside the skull-frame . . .
The voice, articulation, language, whispering, shouting aloud,
Food, drink, pulse, digestion, sweat, sleep, walking, swimming,
Poise on the hips, leaping, reclining, embracing, arm-curving and
    tightening,
The continual changes of the flex of the mouth, and around the eyes,
The skin, the sunburnt shade, freckles, hair,
The curious sympathy one feels when feeling with the hand the naked
    meat of the body, . . .
The thin red jellies within you or within me, the bones and the narrow
    in the bones,
The exquisite realization of health;
O I say these are not the parts and poems of the body only, but of the
    soul,
O I say now these are the soul! (BE 9.129–135, 144–45, 153–58, 161–
    64)

This unlikely and irregular cosmology, this cosmology of our finitude and imperfection,[24] is Whitman's replacement for Plato's world of transcendent forms, for the Christian cosmology of Hell, Purgatory, and Heaven. Traditional metaphysicians, he suggests, do not know "the curious sympathy one feels when feeling with the hand the naked meat of the body"; or, if they do, they have aggressively eliminated it from their accounts of human love. And they hasten, too, in their different ways, to disengage their art from the sense of bodily weight conveyed in this bulky line, with its awkward human grace. All have disengaged themselves from the comic clumsy joyful enumeration of the parts of which poets and other citizens are made. But, says Whitman, this means that they avoid the soul. For all our acts are bodily acts, and all our art is naked meat, and all our sympathy is blood.

Particularly striking is the poem's thoroughgoing opposition to both shame and disgust. This body, the poet – speaker's own, has no urge to cover itself. It stands forth confidently as what it is. And it gazes at the bodies of other men and women with interest and joy. Parts of the body that are typically found disgusting, and that certainly do not figure as objects of praise in lyric poetry, are now seen as beautiful. Bowels, lungs, stomach, brain, "thin red jellies," all are parts of human health, to be admired along with flowing hair and muscular thighs. In the soft and organic, the poem discovers an "electric" vitality and dynamism.[25]

The political significance of this recuperation of the body is, Whitman claims, vast. For the body is the evident basis of human equality: "Have you ever loved the body of a woman? / Have you ever loved the body of a man? / Do you not see that these are exactly the same to all in all nations and times all over the earth?" (BE 8.121–3) This question, placed immediately after the narrative of a slave auction, comments upon it: for what the poet sees is not the auction of a slave, it is "a woman's body at auction" (118). And that is the crime of it, since all bodies are equally worthy of respect. Focusing on the body, we reveal

---

24 Cf. Aristotle, *De Caelo* I.12, which argues that the most perfect bodily shape, the shape among bodily shapes most suited to express perfection, is the sphere, and the most perfect motion revolution in a spherical orbit; the lumpy and irregular shapes of human and other animal bodies, and their corresponding movements, are signs of their distance from this perfection.

25 Contrast Jünger's "man of steel," in Chapter 6: his dynamism is purchased at the price of becoming a machine, rather than a creature of flesh and blood.

ourselves to ourselves as equally needy and finite and mortal, and also equally noble and beautiful; we find a foundation for both equal support and equal respect and love. We then understand the ugliness and irrationality of treating some bodies as mere meat and others as spirits. We see that slave and free, laborer and manager, immigrant and native, rich and poor, "Each has his or her place in the procession" (BE 6.88).[26] Very much in the manner of Rousseau in *Émile* (see Chapter 6), Whitman connects a perception of common bodily humanity and vulnerability with the genesis of a highly critical and morally aggressive sympathy: thinking our humanity means realizing that hierarchies of power that subordinate some groups and treat them as mere things are artificial and indefensible.

And when we take as the focus of our love and sympathy not only the body but also its sexual organs, we will derive one further critical insight: we will see, Whitman argues, that the woman is of equal dignity and importance as the man. Misogyny, he repeatedly insists, derives from a disgust with our sexual organs and acts, the corollary to which is the evident desire to blame someone for inciting those acts. The female body has been seen as impure and unclean, the origin of our sinfulness. But when we think as Whitman urges, we no longer see the woman as flesh and the man as spirit, we come to see both as complementary agents in a democratic process, both spirit and body. "The male is not less the soul nor more, he too is in his place . . . The man's body is sacred and the woman's body is sacred." (BE 6.75, 83)

V. CARESSING DEATH

But what has this rehabilitation of the body to do with erotic love and desire? We might so far see Whitman's project as, in effect, one of returning us to Eden before the Fall, to a state in which (at least as Augustine imagines it) our bodies were indeed pure and holy, including their sexual organs and acts – but only because these acts were imagined to be free from desire, pleasure, and erotic longing; they were undertaken at the direction of the will for the purposes of reproduction. Whitman evidently does not seek to return us to Eden: he persistently

26 Notice Whitman's recognition of the importance of varying pronouns in this context, already in 1855: if what is being said is that there is no unmarked and no marked, then prounouns too must take their place in the procession.

represents his transfigured America as one that accepts, indeed is built on, passionate erotic desire as well as bodily health, one in which our deepest spiritual experiences are erotic, where sexual fulfillment is both among the deepest experiences and a model for others. We therefore now must ask: what does desire have to do with democracy, with racial equality, with the equality of men and women?

We may begin answering our question by returning to the initial reception of *Leaves of Grass*. Whitman's public was sorely divided about the merit of his more erotic poems. They were in agreement, however, about one thing: if Whitman was really speaking about sexual passion, his poems were vile. Thus the defenders against the charge of filth proceeded by denying the poems' erotic content: "I extract no poison from these leaves," wrote one Fanny Fern, contrasting Whitman's poems with popular romances in which "the asp of sensuality lies coiled amid rhetorical flowers." Edward Everett Hale, praising the book's "freshness and simplicity," insisted that "[t]here is not a word in it meant to attract readers by its grossness."[27] What is striking about these reviews is their total inability to talk about deep sexual longing other than in the language of corruption, poison, and filth. These Americans all seem to be in the grip of a profound disgust-misogyny and misanthropy, linked to an aggressive shame about the fact of desire. Apparently all will be well if sex is regarded as merely a set of clean body parts in motion. It is the desire in it that is deeply threatening, that is seen as tinged with the disgust of decay. It is the art in the complex poetry of it that would be a snake coiled in the Garden. The reviews reveal an America in which prurience and puritanism live side by side and take their nourishment from one another.

Both prurience and puritanism are nourished, it appears, by an urgent desire for total control. What seems intolerable is the deep exposure of self to other in real passion. What seems acceptable is a cleaned-up and superficial sex in which nobody looks very deeply into anyone else. Whitman's task, then, is not simply to get his audience to accept clean bodily parts. It is the far more difficult task of getting them to accept real longing. Let us now examine a pivotal sequence in *Song of Myself*, in which Whitman begins to make his case for the relationship between democracy and a more profound eroticism.

27 See Reynolds (1995), pp. 346ff.

Immediately after a section in which the poet's body, talking to his soul, concludes that the cement of the universe is love, we find the following sequence:[28]

A child said *What is the grass?* fetching it to me with full hands;
How could I answer the child? I do not know what it is any more than
    he.

I guess it must be the flag of my disposition, out of hopeful green stuff
    woven.

Or I guess it is the handkerchief of the Lord,
A scented gift and remembrancer designedly dropt,
Bearing the owner's name someway in the corners, that we may see and
    remark, and say *Whose?*
Or I guess the grass is itself a child, the produced babe of the vegetation.

Or I guess it is a uniform hieroglyphic,
And it means, Sprouting alike in broad zones and narrow zones,
Growing among black folks as among white,
Kanuck, Tuckahoe, Congressman, Cuff, I give them the same, I receive
    them the same.

And now it seems to me the beautiful uncut hair of graves.

Tenderly will I use you curling grass,
It may be you transpire from the breasts of young men,
It may be if I had known them I would have loved them,
It may be you are from old people, or from offspring taken soon out of
    their mothers' laps,
And here you are the mothers' laps.
This grass is very dark to be from the white heads of old mothers,
Darker than the colorless beards of old men,
Dark to come from under the faint red roofs of mouths.

O I perceive after all so many uttering tongues,
And I perceive they do not come from the roofs of mouths for nothing.
    (SM 6.99–120)

The poet looks at a simple natural object, which a literal-minded scientific physiologist would describe in literal terms: some blades of grass. His imagination, however, sees so many other and further shapes

---

28 See also Nussbaum (1995a), Chapter 2.

in the blades of grass before him: images of hope, of divinity, of human equality. We are reminded that the vision of human equality is just that, a vision, an imagining, a seeing of something in something. As we go around the world, we see what is before us – but also, insofar as we are at all human, so much that is not straightforwardly before us. Shapes in motion do not by themselves announce their meaning. It is only through the generous work of the imagination that we people the world around us with life, going beyond what is straightforwardly present in perception to suppose the presence of life and growth in the grass, of thought, feeling, and dignity in our fellow citizens. This exercise of imagination is already itself erotic – a reaching into the inside of a thing beneath its perceived surface, an insertion of oneself into the thing to explore its hidden recesses. Whitman shortly makes this eroticism explicit, caressing tenderly, in fancy, the bodies of the soldiers dead in the war, the lost children. If we refuse this probing, he suggests, we doom ourselves to the surfaces of things, to seeing nature, and one another, merely as a set of shapes in motion. This object-like vision of people he connects with slavery, mentioning the topic of race for the first time in the poem. To think the equality of black and white is to cast aside the idea that a human being can be a mere object, an "animate tool," as Aristotle defined the slave. It is to think, instead, that the black person has an inner world and a depth; it is to probe into this depth. But this thinking requires the poetic imagination; and this imagination, he now suggests, involves a form of erotic touching.

In the lines that follow the mention of democratic equality, the poet's imagination reaches deeper still, into the mystery of our mortality itself, the "beautiful uncut hair of graves." In the link between eroticism and the mystery of death he finds a very basic ingredient of democratic citizenship – for it is not so much in the shape and configuration of our bodies that we stand before one another as equal. Nor is it only in the dignity of our living acts. It is, as well, in our darkness, in the faint redness of our mouths, in the fact that we will be buried in the earth and give nourishment to the grass that comes after us.

Shortly after the section that answers the child's questions about the grass, we find the poem's first extended discussion of slavery. A runaway slave comes to the poet's house and stops outside. He hears "his motions crackling the twigs of the woodpile." The poet comes out and sits with him on a log; finding him weak and injured, he fills a tub "for his sweated body and bruis'd feet" – a clear reference to Christ's humility and service. He gives him a room "that enter'd from my own" – indicating thereby that he has no hesitation about bodily proximity in the night. He gives him clothes, puts plasters on the sores on his neck and ankles. The slave stays with the poet for a week before he goes farther north. "I had him sit next me at table," the poet concludes, "my fire-lock lean'd in the corner." We see equality, but feel, as well, the external menace and pressure of hate.

We might now expect a general philosophical rumination on racial equality and the hatred of the black man. We do find it, but in an extraordinary form. The next section of the poem is called by Whitman a "parable," drawing attention to its importance and its religious significance. But it is a parable that would not be found in the sermons of conventional religion.

Twenty-eight young men bathe by the shore,
Twenty-eight young men and all so friendly;
Twenty-eight years of womanly life and all so lonesome.

She owns the fine house by the rise of the bank,
She hides handsome and richly drest aft the blinds of the window.
Which of the young men does she like the best?
Ah the homeliest of them is beautiful to her.

Where are you off to, lady? for I see you,
You splash in the water there, yet stay stock still in your room.

Dancing and laughing along the beach came the twenty-ninth bather,
The rest did not see her, but she saw them and loved them.

The beards of the young men glisten'd with wet, it ran from their long
    hair,
Little streams pass'd all over their bodies.

An unseen hand also pass'd over their bodies,
It descended tremblingly from their temples and ribs.

The young men float on their backs, their white bellies bulge to the sun,
    they do not ask who seizes fast to them,
They do not know who puffs and declines with pendant and bending
    arch,
They do not think whom they souse with spray. (SM 11)

These lines depict female sexual longing, and the exclusion of the female, by morality and custom, from full sexual fulfillment, and from public recognition as a sexual being. They link this exclusion with the confinement of the female to the domestic, rather than the public, sphere. The placement of the section, and Whitman's announcement that it is a parable, invite us to link it to the story of the slave that has preceded it, seeing the woman as a figure for the excluded black man, who must also hide his desire from the white world, who also runs the risk of being seen as a metaphor for the feared intrusion of the sexual. But there is another excluded party who also hides behind the curtains. In the depiction of the woman's imagined sexual act, linked, as it is, to other oral-receptive imagery in other poems about the allure of the male body, Whitman also refers to the exclusion of the male homosexual, whose desire for the bodies of young men must be concealed even more than female desire must be. The easy joy of these young men depends on their not knowing who is watching them with sexual longing; and this is true of the situation of the homosexual male in society, at least as much as it is of the black man gazing erotically at the white woman, or the female gazing erotically at the male. As he says in Calamus: "Here I shade and hide my thoughts, I myself do not expose them, / And yet they expose me." The woman, then, is also the poet, caressing in fancy bodies that in real life shun his gaze.

The woman's gaze, like the gaze of the poet's imagination in the earlier section, is tenderly erotic, caressing the bodies in ways that expose their naked vulnerability, their soft bellies turned upward to the sun. And she caresses something more at the same time. The number twenty-eight signifies the days of the lunar month and also of the female menstrual cycle. The female body, in whose rhythms Whitman sees the rhythms of nature itself, is immersed in finitude and temporality in a manner from which the male body and mind at times recoils. (Havelock Ellis, writing eloquently about this passage, cites the elder Pliny's remark that "nothing in nature is more monstrous and disgusting than a woman's menstrual fluid.") In caressing the twenty-eight men, the woman caresses her own temporality and mortality, and at the same time sees it in them, approaches and makes love to it in them.

Why must the woman's gaze be hidden? And why, we still need to know, is the woman an appropriate figure for the black man, as well as for the male who desires men? We now must talk about gazing in America. In the South, in Whitman's time and later, there were certain offenses that could be committed with the eyes. Taking their cue, perhaps, from the biblical idea that to look at a woman with lust is already to commit a sin, white men in the Jim Crow South prosecuted black men for gazing with desire at a white woman. This crime was colloquially known as "reckless eyeballing,"[29] and it resulted in at least some prosecutions. In 1951, in Yanceyville, North Carolina, a black man named Mark Ingraham was prosecuted for assault with intent to rape for looking at a seventeen-year-old white girl in a "leering manner." The prosecution claimed that he "undressed this lovely little lady with his eyes." Thurgood Marshall sardonically characterized the so-called crime as "highway looking and attempting to want."[30] In 1953, in Atmore, Alabama, a black man named McQuirter was convicted of the same crime, apparently after simply walking too close to a white woman. The State Court of Appeals held that racial factors might be considered in assessing the defendant's state of mind.[31]

Beyond the impact of such convictions on individual lives, such uses of the criminal law set the tone for "a stigmatizing code of conduct"[32] for black men, which made mandatory downcast eyes, and a shame-filled concealment of desire.[33] Black men must wear their bodies with

---

29 See Ishmael Reed's grimly funny novel of this title (1986).

30 See the discussion in Greenberg (1994), p. 101. Though Ingraham was convicted and sentenced, the North Carolina Supreme Court eventually reversed the decision because it was evident that blacks had been excluded from the jury.

31 *McQuirter v. State*, 63 So. 2d 388, affirming the conviction on appeal. See the excellent discussion of this and related cases in Kennedy (1997), pp. 89–90. McQuirter was fined $500, a sentence that suggests a deterrent and symbolic purpose to the charge of attempted rape.

32 Kennedy (1997), p. 88: the code "demanded exhibitions of servility and the open disavowal of any desire for equality."

33 Consider this description, from Richard Wright's *Native Son* (1993a):
   He wanted to wave his hand and blot out the white man who was making him feel this. If not that, he wanted to blot himself out. He had not raised his eyes to the level of Mr. Dalton's face once since he had been in the house. He stood with his knees slightly bent, his lips partly open, his shoulders stooped; and his eyes held a look that went only to the surface of things. There was an organic conviction in him that this was the way white folks wanted him to be when in their presence; none had ever told him that in so many words, but their manner had made him feel that they did. (53–4)
   And see also Wright's "The Ethics of Living Jim Crow," in *Uncle Tom's Children* (1993b). Especially significant is the description of Wright's employment as a hall-boy

shame rather than with pride, in effect becoming a walking metaphor for the shamefulness of sexuality. For despite the lowered gaze, the black man by his very presence was, and frequently is, taken to be a threatening emblem of sexuality, emanating from a fictive Africa that has standardly been represented by white America as a wild place of unfettered eroticism.[34] Whitman understands that the black man is hated and feared in part because he is seen as an image of sexual longing and of the depth and power of the sexual; his gaze is itself, therefore, a contamination. And refusal of his sexuality is a central way of refusing him full equality.

Let us now consider the desiring gaze of a woman. Had the young men seen the twenty-ninth bather, we may conjecture that they would have scattered in shame and confusion. In Whitman's world, and surely not only there, the female was not supposed to look with desire, any more than was the black man; there was felt to be something monstrous, threatening, defiling, in the assertive and aggressive sexuality of a woman, something that threatened to sully the simple clear world of male control. (Recall Mr. Lockwood, in whom the gaze of desire prompted both fear and cruelty.) For Rousseau, human women (unlike the females of all animal species) have "unlimited desires" – and therefore must learn shame as a "brake," lest desire lead to disorder. "If woman is made to please and to be subjugated, she ought to make herself agreeable to man instead of arousing him."[35] Her modest concealment of desire was thus a crucial part of social order. Out of a related fear of disorder, Thomas Jefferson insisted that full citizenship for women was impossible, because they simply could not mingle freely with men: "Were our state a pure democracy, there would still be excluded from our deliberations women, who, to prevent depravation of morals and ambiguity of issue, should not mix promiscuously in gatherings of men."[36] Denial of erotic agency and relegation to a sphere

in a hotel frequented by white prostitutes and their johns, where he was often asked to bring refreshments to the rooms. " 'Nigger, what in hell you looking at?' the white man asked me, raising himself upon his elbows. 'Nothing,' I answered, looking miles deep into the blank wall of the room. 'Keep your eyes where they belong, if you want to be healthy!' he said. 'Yes, sir.' "

34 See the acute analysis in Young-Bruehl (1996), drawing on the treatment of this theme in such writers as James Baldwin, Calvin Hernton, and Eldridge Cleaver.

35 *Émile* V, 359, 358 (Bloom translation).

36 Quoted in Okin (1979), p. 249.

ruled by patriarchal power go hand in hand. Whitman, we sense, has identified an issue deeply lodged in America's founding conceptions of the citizen.

Let us consider, finally, the gaze of the homosexual. In the recent extremely fraught discussions of the admission of openly homosexual soldiers to the U.S. army, the central issue, which keeps on surfacing, is not that of forced sexual conduct or even of sexual harassment: for all agree that those are practices that should be forbidden no matter who engages in them. Nor, given recent scandals about the ubiquitous harassment of women in the armed services, do people argue that male-male harassment would be a greater problem. The central issue is, once again, the gaze. The scenario that is most feared is, once again, that of being seen naked in the shower by someone who desires or might possibly desire you – when you are aware of that possible desire and it does not hide behind the curtains. The desiring gaze of the open homosexual is at present the central reason advanced for denying these would-be soldiers jobs for which they are in other respects acknowledged to be qualified.

Whitman is on to something deep, then, when he focuses on the relationship between exclusion and erotic gazing, and when he links this issue of the gaze to all three of the forms of exclusion that preoccupy him. What is this something? Whitman suggests that the willingness to be seen by desire entails a willingness to agree to one's own mortality and temporality, to be part of the self-renewing and onward flowing currents of nature. It is because it touches us in our mortality that sex is deep and a source of great beauty. In the final poem of *Leaves*, he imagines embracing a male comrade, and says, "Decease called me forth." The deep flaw in Whitman's America, then, the flaw that for him lies at the heart of hatreds and exclusions, is a horror of one's own softness and mortality, of the belly exposed to the sun; the gaze of desire touches that, and is for that reason to be repelled. Over against this flawed America, Whitman sets the America of the poet's imagination, healed of self-avoidance, fear, and cruelty, and therefore able truly to pursue liberty and equality.

Whitman's rehabilitation of sex does not involve, as his critics frequently allege, an endorsement of "free love," a casual and promiscuous approach to sex. On the contrary, both in his prose writings and in his poems, he is a stern moralist, inveighing against promiscuity and the commercialization of sex, and especially against the treatment of persons as objects in pornography, which he views as highly subversive to democratic goals and processes. But, very much like D. H. Lawrence, he sees the prurient attitude toward sex expressed in pornography, and the commercialization of sex represented in the sex industry, not as inevitable features of erotic desire, but rather as features of the puritanical refusal of desire, of a piece with America's horror at the truly erotic gaze. Whitman persistently links these forms of false relation to persons with other American deformations, especially with an exploitative attitude toward nature, which cannot be seen in its awesome continuity of death and life by one who refuses his own mortality. Linking the poet's love of nature with the acknowledgment of the humanity of the sexual female, Whitman addresses these lines in 1860 to a common prostitute: "Not till the sun excludes you do I exclude you, / Not till the waters refuse to glisten for you and the leaves to rustle for you, do my words refuse to glisten and rustle for you."

Where, in all this, is the poet? In answering the child's questions, Whitman has depicted the poet as the one whose imagination does not shrink from caressing reality – including the reality of death and decay. In now depicting the poet as a being in hiding, whose fantasies must lurk behind the curtains, he connects American puritanism and prurience, in turn, with American philistinism, the refusal of the erotic imagination of the poet. The best way to defeat the power and depth of sex is to render it superficial, commercial, and unpoetic; the best way to defeat the gaze of the female is to pretend that she is just a thing to be bought and sold, like the slave at auction. But the poet threatens these structures of denial, and is for that reason a being to be feared and shunned. It is precisely for this reason that the poet is required as the public voice of democracy. "He judges not as the judge judges, but as the sun falling round a helpless thing" – seeing its every nook and crevice, seeing its helplessness sharply but with the illumination of love.

VI. MOURNING THE SUN

The ascent of love enacted in this work, like several others we have examined, links the overcoming of hatred with the attainment of an inclusive and impartial love, and both of these with an overcoming of an excessive fear of one's own softness and neediness. In the process of attaining these goals, Whitman, very much like Mahler, has insisted on the power of compassion to bind a community together, and insisted, too, on the importance of democratic equality and reciprocity to the successful reform of love. Like Mahler, he insists that the love that can accomplish these goals must be erotic and must view its own this-worldly striving as an end in itself. Both, though in their own way religious, reject conventional religion in favor of a more personal spirituality that lays great stress on the role of the artist's imagination. While Whitman's poetic execution of this project is in many respects more uneven than Mahler's musical execution, in Whitman there is at the same time, obviously, a greater concreteness of relation to the particular hatreds and vices of a real social world. Anger at the very conditions of human life – and at humans who symbolize those conditions – is replaced by anger against injustice and social hierarchy.

It seems plausible to think that Whitman's cosmos has solved the problems that motivated love's ascent while retaining an inclusive compassion, while creating a plausible picture of democratic reciprocity, and while embracing every distinct individual with delight.

There remain, however, several problems with this new cosmos. First, there are flaws of execution. Whitman's poetry is highly uneven, veering from the extraordinary to the embarrassing. Sometimes the all-encompassing presence of the poet figure seems to defeat the project: for he seems so omnipresent, so sure of himself, so all-inclusive, that the realities of need and pain about which he speaks vanish from view. We receive at many moments an impression of self-sufficient and rather complacent egoism, and this certainly subverts the poetic design. Especially problematic are many passages dealing with women and with heterosexual love. Not surprisingly, we find here a forced bravado, an aggressive phallic muscularity, that seems entirely at odds with the poetry's deeper purposes. It seems like what it is, a form of self-concealment; and self-concealment is precisely what this poetry regards as the core political sin. Take, for example, this passage, in "A Woman Waits for Me," perhaps the most embarrassingly bad of all of Whitman's poems, in which the poet imagines himself making love to all the women of America:

It is I, you women, I make my way,
I am stern, acrid, large, undissuadable, but I love you,

672

I do not hurt you any more than is necessary for you,
I pour the stuff to start sons and daughters fit for these States, I press
  with slow rude muscle,
I brace myself effectually, I listen to no entreaties,
I dare not withdraw till I deposit what has so long accumulated within
  me.[37]

These are words of someone who does not want to be seen into; and this is a person who, insofar as he takes that stance, cannot see well the equality of others.

This flaw of execution seems, then, a deep one, connected with avoidance of a vulnerability in the poet himself. Another problem lies even closer to the core of the project. This is the grand sweep of the poetry, its refusal of the messiness of everyday life, even while it is precisely everyday life that it claims to be loving. The emphasis on mystical erotic experiences of fusion and oneness are a large part of this problem. For bodies just don't fuse. Elbows and knees, and even the genital organs to which Whitman attaches so much importance, tend to get in the way. As Lawrence wrote of Whitman:[38]

Even if you reach the state of infinity, you can't sit down there. You just physically can't. You either have to strain still further into universality and become vaporish, or slimy: or you have to hold your toes and sit tight and practise Nirvana; or you have to come back to common dimensions, eat your pudding and blow your nose and be just yourself; or die and have done with it. . . . [E]ven at his maximum a man is not more than himself. When he is infinite he is still himself. He still has a nose to wipe. (846)

Lawrence is a little unfair, for Whitman speaks of caressing far more often than of fusing, of feeling the surface of the body far more than of merging with it. He is, in fact, frequently very preoccupied with the body's separateness and the obstacles it poses to unity; and in many passages he treats that separateness as a source of joy, rather than as a falling off from the sublime state. But there is something right in Lawrence's criticism. For Whitman does indeed often grandly shun the messiness of the everyday, in favor of a highly romantic account of American life that may in some respects serve to alienate us from our daily lives and bodies. One symptom of this is the utter lack of humor

---

37 "A Woman Waits For Me" (25–30), Norton edition pp. 102–3.
38 "Whitman," from *Nation and Athenaeum* 29 (1921), Norton edition pp. 842–50.

in the poetry; another is the sense we often have that aggressive athletic energy is being deployed to pick up things from where they are and put them on a map of the cosmos.

Finally, there is a complex problem at the very heart of Whitman's project. For his mission is, as I have suggested, to show the way to an acceptance of mortality, finitude, and loss, to enable us to mourn and therefore adequately to love. But that effort is to at least some extent compromised by his constant emphasis on the mysterious unity of all things in nature, the continuity and therefore immortality of all life. Frequently Whitman suggests that this continuity, somewhat mystically experienced, negates the finality of death: "I know I am deathless, / I know . . . I shall not pass like a child's carlacue[39] cut with a burnt stick at night." (SM 20.406–8)

But to teach that death is not really a loss, or not really death, is to undercut the entire attitude toward eroticism and loss that the poetry, at its finest, has been promoting. This problem goes deep, I think; for Whitman is increasingly enamored of mystical views of oneness derived from Indian philosophy; and he does not seem to grasp how much at odds these ideas are with his project of teaching America and Americans to accept death. We should not say that this causes his erotic project to fail; but it does create an air of confusion that periodically mars its expression. It means, among other things, that the individual does not have his or her full weight as an object of love in this poetry, or, what comes to the same thing, as an object of grief and mourning. All individuals are seen as curiously continuous with one another.

This confusion does not run straight through the work. Let us consider, by contrast, a moment when Whitman leaves his dalliance with the obscure metaphysics of unity and shows what the finitude of a human being really is, and what the mourning for the finite individual really is. Lincoln is the only truly individual object of love in Whitman's poetry, and his death inspired Whitman to express the tragedy of death and longing as nowhere else in the work. "When Lilacs Last in the Dooryard Bloom'd," the remarkable elegy on Lincoln's death, depicts the procession of Lincoln's coffin through the cities and towns of America. The poet imagines the grief of all who see it pass by, and mourn as for someone utterly irreplaceable. The whole of the nation is tinged

---

39 A variant of "curlicue": a flourish in writing, easily erased.

with death. He now asks himself what he can give his dead president, to adorn the walls of his burial chamber. He answers that it must be pictures of the land they both love, pictures made in his poetic words.

> Lo, body and soul – this land,
> My own Manhattan with spires, and the sparkling and hurrying tides, and the ships,
> The varied and ample land, the South and the North in the light, Ohio's shore and flashing Missouri,
> And ever the far-spreading prairies covered with grass and corn.

> Lo, the most excellent sun so calm and haughty,
> The violet and purple morn with just-felt breezes,
> The gentle soft-born measureless light,
> The miracle spreading bathing all, the fulfill'd noon,
> The coming eve delicious, the welcome night and the stars,
> Over my cities shining all, enveloping man and land.

We see the beauty of the land under the form of mortality, with the sharper sense of splendor, with the shiver down the spine, that signals the nearness of death. The poet gives his president the land they both loved – and, also, this very poem of the land, a poem of the way the nation is seen by someone who knows about his own end. Air, light, and words, hanging on the walls of a tomb.

In these lines, as in the poem's larger picture of the nation mourning its leader, we see the vision of a transfigured America, an America grown up to adulthood, no longer making infantile claims to self-sufficiency and immortality, this nation that so much likes to believe that it can have and do anything without cost. The poet gives his dead president a portrait of the nation from the point of view of a citizen of this transfigured democracy, a place of truly free and equal individuals, where all, capable of mourning, can let go of hate and disgust, and pursue a truly inclusive love.

Isn't there still, one might ask, a characteristic American optimism in these proceedings? Whitman, even in the process of acknowledging tragedy, has performed a characteristically American conjuring trick, turning tragedy into good news, mortality into a hope of justice. Death is not just the horror of death, it is also an opportunity for social progress. We don't defeat death, but in assuming a more honest relationship to it we enable ourselves to live better with one another. To this question or charge one can only reply, yes, it is so. (This very same sort of optimism is present, as well, in this book.) Does this determination to turn bad news into good show that Whitman in particular, and America in general, lack a full-fledged sense of tragedy?[40] If a full-fledged sense of tragedy entails giving up the hope that things can become better in this world, the answer to this question must be yes. But why should we accept this account of tragedy? For a confrontation with the reality of our condition should be just that, a confrontation with reality. And the reality was and is that there is both bad news and good news: things are in many ways bad, but they do get better sometimes, when people fight for justice. The situation of African-Americans and of women has changed greatly since 1855. The situation of homosexuals has changed, though somewhat less greatly. Whitman's poetry, with its sui generis combination of tragedy and optimism, has played its part in inspiring those who were working for all of these changes. One need not have the unrealistic fantasy that America could ever lack hate and disgust completely, in order to join Whitman in the project of pushing it back a little, day by day.

In one way, resignation without optimism would be far easier. To recognize that change is possible is, for Whitman, to assume the burden of working for change the whole of one's life. In that way, as he sees it, the recognition of mortality has as its natural corollary a redoubled attention to our duties in the world:

> I dare not shirk any part of myself,
> Not any part of America good or bad,
> Not to build for that which builds for mankind,
> Not to balance ranks, complexions, creeds, and the sexes . . .

> I will not be outfaced by irrational things,
> I will penetrate what it is in them that is sarcastic upon me, . . .
> I will make cities and civilizations defer to me,
> This is what I have learnt from America – it is the amount, and it I teach
>   again. (BO 17.282–5, 292–6)

40 See the related observations in my Preface to the updated edition (2001) of Nussbaum (1986).

In other words, realizing that we cannot make ourselves or our nation immortal, we can, and must, try for the available goal of making it equal and free.

Postscript. During the very hour on May 20, 1996, during which this chapter was being presented publicly for the first time,[41] as a Weidenfeld Lecture at Oxford University, the U.S. Supreme Court announced its decision in *Romer v. Evans*, declaring unconstitutional a Colorado law, Amendment 2, that denied local communities the right to pass nondiscrimination laws protecting the rights of gays, lesbians, and bisexuals. I quote from Justice Kennedy's majority opinion, in which one may possibly discern Whitman's spirit:

We find nothing special in the protections Amendment 2 withholds. These are protections taken for granted by most people either because they already have them or do not need them; these are protections against exclusion from an almost limitless number of transactions and endeavors that constitute ordinary civic life in a free society . . . It is not within our constitutional tradition to enact laws of this sort. Central both to the idea of the rule of law and to our own Constitution's guarantee of equal protection is the principle that government and each of its parts remain open on impartial terms to all who seek its assistance. " 'Equal protection of the laws is not achieved through indiscriminate imposition of inequalities.' " . . . A law declaring that in general it shall be more difficult for one group of citizens than for all others to seek aid from the government is itself a denial of equal protection of the laws in the most literal sense.

Or, as Whitman puts it – and we read these lines aloud later, to mark the occasion and honor the poet –

Whoever degrades another degrades me,
And whatever is done or said returns at last to me . . .
I speak the pass-word primeval, I give the sign of democracy,

41 Whitman was part of the plan for the Gifford Lectures from the beginning, and a first draft of this material was completed before I delivered those lectures; but since there were to be only ten lectures, only four devoted to the material that is now Part II, I decided to give one lecture on the contemplative ascent, one on the Christian ascent, one on the Romantic ascent, and the final one entirely on Joyce. Thus there had been no occasion to present the Whitman material before 1996.

By God! I will accept nothing which all cannot have their counterpart of
on the same terms. . . .

For the great Idea, the idea of perfect and free individuals,
For that, the bard walks in advance, leader of leaders,
The attitude of him cheers up slaves and horrifies foreign despots . . .

Without extinction is Liberty, without retrograde is Equality,
They live in the feelings of . . . men and . . . women. (SM 24.503–4, 506–
7; BO 10.154–8)

16

THE TRANSFIGURATION OF EVERYDAY LIFE: JOYCE

I. SCHOLASTIC QUESTIONS

Lying on her left side in the brass-quoited bed, "left hand under head, right leg extended in a straight line and resting on left leg" (737),[1] she watches her husband sleep, his feet near her face, his body curled up like a baby, his face near her bottom, "the indexfinger and thumb of the right hand resting on the bridge of the nose" (737). Watching, she considers his unusual request:

yes because he never did a thing like that before as ask to get his breakfast in bed with a couple of eggs since the *City Arms* hotel when he used to be pretending to be laid up with a sick voice doing his highness to make himself interesting to that old faggot Mrs Riordan . . . still I like that in him polite to old women like that and waiters and beggars too . . . if ever he got anything really serious the matter with him . . . wed have a hospital nurse next thing on the carpet have him staying there till they throw him out or a nun maybe like the smutty photo he has shes as much a nun as Im not . . . I wish some man or other would take me sometime when hes there and kiss me in his arms theres nothing like a kiss long and hot down to your soul almost paralyses you then I hate that confession when I used to go to Father Corrigan he touched me father and what harm if he did where and I said on the canal bank like a fool but whereabouts on your person my child on the leg behind high up was it yes rather high up was it where you sit down yes O Lord couldnt he say bottom right out and have done with it . . . Id like to be embraced by one in his vestments and the smell of incense off him like the pope (738, 740–41)

---

1 All citations from *Ulysses* are taken from the Modern Library edition (1961), and page numbers are given from that edition.

Do we find here the contemplation of the beautiful itself, as described to Socrates by the priestess Diotima?

We find a pair of feet about to brush a face, a face near a bottom. We find retrospective contemplation of a pornographic *mimesis,* a confessorial interrogation; prospective, of an appetitive osculation, a clerical seduction.

Do we find exemplification of the *amor intellectualis Dei* of which the great Spinoza tells us?

We find a jealous inquisitiveness, an unrepentant bodily vanity, a carnal concupiscence.

Is our scene washed by the tears of Augustinian contrition, the dew of redeeming grace?

By urine descending into "the domestic chamber pot" (770).

Do we encounter Dante purified, the last P stricken from his brow? Do we see before him the *donna beata e bella* in her triumphal car, figure of Mother Church?

We encounter Bloom,[2] "adorer of the adulterous rump." We encounter Mrs. Marion Bloom, a "bodily and mental female organism" (732), "fulfilled, recumbent, big with seed" (737).

Does the coloration of white and of red in the female's garments derive from the Dantean symbolism of Christian faith (white) and Christian love (red)?

From the seminal residue of Blazes Boylan (white). From menstrual omissions (red).[3]

And does Bloom the Jew soar upward on wings won in the hot striving of love, to a light to which no eye has penetrated?

"And O! then the Roman candle burst and it was like a sigh of O! and everyone cried O! O! in reptures and it gushed out of it a stream of rain gold hair threads and they shed and ah! they were all greeny

2 See p. 442, where Gerty MacDowell makes this accusation.
3 For Molly's verbal confusion, see p. 770 – "how much is that doctor one guinea please and asking me had I frequent omissions where do those old fellows get all the words they have omissions" – and also p. 781.

dewy stars falling with golden, O so lively! O so soft, sweet, soft! . . .
Mr. Bloom with careful hand recomposed his wet shirt. O Lord, that
little limping devil. Begins to feel cold and clammy. Aftereffect not
pleasant. Still you have to get rid of it someway." (366–7, 370)

And did Mrs. Marion Bloom spring into the arms of her fierce dark
lover Poldy, that alien to the bliss of heaven, the only double of her
soul?

"he says your soul you have no soul inside only grey matter because
he doesn't know what it is to have one . . . he had all he could do to
keep himself from falling asleep after the last time we took the port
and potted meat it had a fine salty taste yes because I felt lovely and
tired myself . . . if he was married Im sure hed have a fine strong child
but I dont know Poldy has more spunk in him . . ." (742, 741)

II. THE HOLY OFFICE

Our various versions of love's ascent have all attempted to preserve
love's energy and beauty while purifying it of deforming excesses. But
all of the accounts we have examined so far have something in common. All repudiate daily life. The very metaphor of ascent suggests to
us that there is something low about where we usually live and are. All
of our previous accounts – even Whitman's, in a way – wish to rise
above that ordinariness, departing not only from what we might call
the idolatrous aspects of the ordinary social world, its excessive preoccupation with money, fame, and revenge, but also from the everyday
functions of life and everyday objects, from mud hair and dirt, as the
Platonist would say. And this means that – despite a general agreement
in the Christian and post-Christian accounts that a truly adequate love
will embrace the flaws and imperfections of a human being as well as
the goodness – all of these ascents in a real sense repudiate us. Nobody
has a menstrual period in Plato. Nobody excretes in Spinoza. Nobody
masturbates in Proust (though in a certain sense also, nobody does
anything else). Augustine and Dante record such moments, but leave
them behind in Hell. Cathy and Heathcliff demonstrate their superiority to the Linton world by a demonic intensity that seems to lift them
straight out of the daily world. In Mahler, the daily social round is
dead and deadening; the ascending artist, bitten by his own cry of

disgust against this world, ascends to a creative realm in which love exists purified of the lapses of attention that make up much of our daily lives. In Whitman, the body and erotic desire are rehabilitated, but also transfigured, made part of the great march of justice in the world, rather than just being by themselves. As Lawrence said of the poetry, even if you reach eternity, you can't sit down there. In none of these texts, then, does love wear a real-life body with its hungers and thirsts and fantasies, its all-too-human combination of generosity with forgetfulness.

All of our texts show their repudiation of the daily in their form as well as in their content. The abstract prose of Diotima's speech, so different from the concreteness of the narrative that surrounds it; the geometrical demonstrations of Spinoza, in which he deliberately asks his reader to view human beings and actions as so many lines, points, and surfaces; Marcel's detached and condescending narration of the follies of ordinary humans and of his own former self – in all of these formal choices we see the commitments of the contemplative ascent. In Augustine, the narrative of daily life is part of the memory of sin; conversion shifts the text's attention upward, from autobiography to biblical commentary. Dante's poem, the internal dictation of his love, ascends in form as his own soul ascends, attending to individuals in a manner increasingly characterized by a focus on grace and salvation. In Brontë, the two narrators remain mired in daily life, but look out from this perspective toward a purer authenticity. Mahler's symphony attends to the pettiness of the everyday with a sardonic detachment that culminates in a cry of disgust; the recovery of joy begins with a child's innocent faith, untouched by the distractions of the ordinary. Whitman's cosmic poetry of the body calls all citizens to justice with its idealistic unifying sweep, leaving behind much of the messiness of the real-life body and mind.

All of these works create, then, a wide gap between the reader whom they construct and the real-life reader. This is a deliberate strategem to drive attention upward; but it runs the risk of compounding anger and disgust when we discover that we are still ourselves. In this chapter I turn to a work that closes the gap, without giving up on moral effort, and especially the struggle against hatred and revenge. As Joyce wrote in an early essay, "Life we must accept as we see it before our eyes, men and women as we meet them in the real world, not as we apprehend them in the world of faery." And if we imagine texts in Dante's way, as dictations of love, this is also a new expression of love.

Joyce put a name to the intellectual basis for his art. In his 1904 poem "The Holy Office," written just after a visit to Paris, during which Joyce spent a lot of time in brothels and much of the rest reading the *De Anima* in French translation, he wrote the following exuberant lines:

> Myself unto myself will give
> This name Katharsis-Purgative . . .
> Bringing to tavern and to brothel
> The mind of witty Aristotle . . .
> Ruling one's life by common sense
> How can one fail to be intense?

Joyce here makes some complicated connections: between Aristotelian philosophy and the acceptance of sexuality, between a life governed by Aristotelian everydayness and the intensities of the erotic. As the poem goes on, it becomes clear that its title describes both what Joyce opposes – the dogmas of church authority, which stand between humans and the acceptance of their humanity – and also what he proposes to carry out in his art – a holy sacrament of Aristotelian purgation,[4] in which the censorious metaphysics of the Irish Catholic Church will be carried away by the cleansing sewer-pipes of Joycean literary frankness:

> But all these men of whom I speak
> Make me the sewer of their clique.
> That they may dream their dreamy dreams
> I carry off their filthy streams . . .
> Thus I relieve their timid arses,
> Perform my office of Katharsis . . .
> And though they spurn me from their door
> My soul shall spurn them evermore.

The church will consider Joyce's frankly sexual art a kind of sewage. His defiant conceit turns the metaphor around, saying that it is the religious refusal of the body that is sewage, and that his art is an

---

4 Like most classically trained people of his time, Joyce was raised to think that "purgation" was what Aristotle meant by *katharsis*. I don't think so (see Nussbaum [1986], Interlude 2); but Joyce gets good mileage out of the idea.

Aristotelian pipe that will drain it off, leaving the body – and the soul – in peace and health henceforth. Diotima is turning her ladder upside down.

III. A DIVIDUAL CHAOS

"Mr. Leopold Bloom ate with relish the inner organs of beasts and fowls. He liked thick giblet soup, nutty gizzards, a stuffed roast heart, liver slices fried with crustcrumbs, fried hencod's roes. Most of all he liked grilled mutton kidneys which gave to his palate a fine tang of faintly scented urine" (55). So the Homeric protagonist of love's sublime descent, target of love's little ruses (367), begins his day. "Gelid light and air were in the kitchen but out of doors gentle summer morning everywhere" (55). He fixes Molly's breakfast tray, arranging the slices of buttered bread. The cat stalks around him. "Mr Bloom watched curiously, kindly, the lithe black form." He asks himself how a cat sees and understands. "Mrkrgnao! the cat said loudly."

Ulysses, like classical tragedy in the Renaissance Aristotelian mode, confines itself to the span of a single day. But tragic Aristotelian days have a plot whose events are held together by chains of probability and necessity. Bloom's day, June 16, 1904, like most human days, is a day full of accidents, a day that eludes all of the reader's most resourceful attempts to compose it into an orderly plot. Tragedy is philosophical because its plots manifest the essential nature of the human soul in its attempts to live well. Bloom's day is philosophical because it contains fried kidneys, a greedy cat with "avid shameclosing eyes," four slices of bread and butter; because Bloom, obeying in his own way the laws of probability and necessity, eats, defecates, masturbates, urinates, sleeps.

As Joyce later described the production of *Ulysses* in *Finnegans Wake,*[5] Bloom's morally sublime and truly heroic creator, "pious

---

5 The full text of the passage (Joyce [1959], pp. 185–6):

> Then, pious Eneas, conformant to the fulminant firman which enjoins on the tremylose terrain that, when the call comes, he shall produce nichthemerically from his unheavenly body a no uncertain quantity of obscene matter not protected by copiright in the United Stars of Ourania or bedeed and bedood and bedang and bedung to him, with this double dye, brought to blood heat, gallic acid on iron ore, through the bowels of his misery, flashly, faithly, nastily, appropriately, this Esuan

Eneas," followed a heavenly command that "when the call comes he shall produce nichthemerically from his unheavenly body a no uncertain quantity of obscene matter not protected by copriright in the United Stars of Ourania or bedeed and bedood and bedang and bedung to him" – until, "through the bowels of his own misery, flashly, faithly, nastily, appropriately," like a "squidself" writing "with this double dye," he "wrote over every square inch of the only foolscap available, his own body . . . (thereby, he said, reflecting from his own individual person life unlivable, transaccidentated through the slow fires of consciousness into a dividual chaos, perilous, potent, common to allflesh, human only, mortal) . . ." This is a text, then, in which life is written by the "double dye" of semen and excrement on the skin of the "unheavenly body"; in which life is imagined not Homerically but "nichthemerically" (in which we may also read the novel's anti-*them*atic, anti-moralizing structure, and its fascination with the events of night [*Nacht*] as well as, or even as opposed to [*nicht*], those of day [Gk. *hêmera*]); in which the reality of its characters' lives are not, like Christ's body and blood in the bread and wine of the Mass, transubstantiated, realized as substance, but "transaccidentated," realized as accident, as contingency in the slow fires of thought – and realized not as the stories of individuals but as the story of accidental fragmented "dividuals," oddly incoherently made up out of memory and fantasy, philosophical thought and genital arousal; a text that has always had, in consequence, a hard time in that exalted moral republic the United Stars of Ourania, which has never had a law of copriright, which is to say the right to write with or of one's own excrement (Gk. *kopros*). For that republic is, as Joyce came to know well, not alone but in its characteristic way unusually energetic in pursuing its allegiance to the chaste Ouranian Aphrodite described in Plato's *Symposium,* with her pure interest in the education of the young, and its disparagement of

Menschavik and the first till last alshemist wrote over every square inch of the only foolscap available, his own body, till by its corrosive sublimation one continuous present tense integument slowly unfolded all marryvoising moodmoulded cyclewheeling history (thereby, he said, reflecting from his own individual person life unlivable, transaccidentated through the slow fires of consciousness into a dividual chaos, perilous, potent, common to allflesh, human only, mortal) but with each word that would not pass away the squidself which he had squirtcreened from the crystalline world waned chagreenold and doriangrayer in its dudhud. This exists that isits after having been said we know.

her everyday cousin Aphrodite Pandemos, with her taste for bodily pleasure.[6] And by setting his muse in opposition to Ourania – in Greek myth, the muse of traditional cosmological writing[7] – Joyce tells us that his own muse is the creator not of a Whitmanian American cosmos, but of an anticosmos, and an anti-America, a world where the stars that guide people's lives are not united, as optimistic Americans so love to believe, and where dividuals in chaos do both un-Platonic and un-Christian not to mention un-American things.

The idea of a writing in which the commonplace and the accidental would be realized as fit objects of literary attention guided Joyce's literary production from a very early date. Already in 1900, at the age of eighteen, he had begun to write a series of prose passages that he called "epiphanies," referring (or counter-referring) to the manifestation of Christ's divinity to the Magi. But Joycean epiphanies were descriptions of ordinary things and people, in which "the soul of the commonest object . . . seems to us radiant." Such manifestations of life might be found even "in the vulgarity of speech or of gesture"; and the young Joyce shockingly continues (anticipating the imagery of the *Finnegans Wake* passage) that such confrontations with our own lives may justly be called "eucharistic."[8] To present an accident as an accident, to attend to the ordinary as ordinary – these seem small demands to impose on author and on reader, far indeed from the great spiritual transactions of the Mass. But maybe it's not so easy to see things as they are, and to recognize one's own disorderly self in them – especially in a society governed so long by the aspirations of philosophy and religion, and by the language of ascent, purification, and divinization of which those traditions are so enamored. Maybe there's a kind of grace in that, more difficult than purity.

6 See *Ulysses* (490), where (in Nighttown) the keeper of the Kildare Street Museum appears, "dragging a lorry on which are the shaking statues of several naked goddesses, Venus Callipyge, Venus Pandemos, Venus Metempsychosis . . ." Callipyge, "beautiful rump," alludes, clearly, to Bloom's fondness for Molly's; Metempsychosis to a thought that runs through the novel about Molly's request to her husband for a definition of that term.

7 See Plato's *Phaedrus* 259BC, where Socrates says that the philosophical life is dedicated to both Calliope, the muse of epic poetry, and Ourania.

8 This discussion is from *Stephen Hero* (Joyce [1955], pp. 30, 211–213), not from the early critical writings, but Ellman (1983), p. 83, treats it, plausibly, as explanatory of the fictions that Joyce shortly produced.

"This is my body," says Bloom, thinking that he would love to have a bath.[9]

What do these difficulties mean, though, for our lives, and the nature of our attention to those we love? Or: how does love's descent change love? Joyce steals back the sacramental vocabulary for the frying of a kidney, a cat's breakfast, a trip to the outhouse, a woman's sexual pleasure. But what is he doing to the ascent traditions when he does this?

And how does he engage the reader in his project – the reader who, whatever his or her nationality, is all too likely to be a citizen of the United Stars of Ourania, dedicated to order and ascent, all too likely to dislike this novel's accidental plotless nature and to see its inhabitants as alien dividual creatures far from himself? While we are on the subject of America, we can focus this question by noting that Judge John M. Woolsey, in the famous opinion declaring the novel not obscene, an opinion that shows much genuine appreciation of what Joyce is attempting, nonetheless finds its theme quite distant from himself and his own milieu: the "old Saxon words" used by Joyce's characters

are such words as would be naturally and habitually used, I believe, by the types of folk whose life, physical and mental, Joyce is seeking to describe. In respect of the recurrent emergence of the theme of sex in the minds of his characters, it must always be remembered that his locale was Celtic and his season Spring . . . [W]hen such a real artist in words, as Joyce undoubtedly is, seeks to draw a true picture of the lower middle class in a European city, ought it to be impossible for the American public legally to see that picture?[10]

9 "Enjoy a bath now: clean trough of water, cool enamel, the gentle tepid stream. This is my body.

He foresaw his pale body reclined in it at full, naked, in a womb of warmth, oiled by scented melting soap, softly laved. He saw his trunk and limbs rippippled over and sustained, buoyed lightly upward, lemonyellow: his navel, bud of flesh: and saw the dark tangled curls of his bush floating, floating hair of the stream around the limp father of thousands, a languid floating flower." (86)

10 Opinion of Judge John J. Woolsey in *U.S. v. One Book Called "Ulysses,"* (December 6, 1933), printed with the novel in the Modern Library edition, p. x. Another striking feature of the opinion is its methodology: for in constructing his test to see whether the "normal person" would find the novel obscene in accordance with the legal definition, Woolsey showed the work to two male acquaintances, "men whose opinion on literature and on life I value most highly." He feels free on this basis to "venture" a guess as to what a woman would say about its vocabulary, concluding that "almost all men" but only "many women" are familiar with the words in question. In an earlier struggle

From which one may infer that American judges don't think about sex, especially in the winter.

Ulysses deploys against such refusals of recognition three stylistic devices, which work together in complex interrelationship to baffle confuse entice enveigle and madden readers, until their readerly dignity is at least breached if not completely laid waste. These are: graphic inclusiveness, the heroic and mock-heroic, and humor. The text commands recognition, first of all, simply because it does set before the reader what, especially if caught off guard, he or she can hardly deny to be a part of life, in words he or even she can hardly deny recognizing. The astonishing concreteness of Bloom's day, of the fragmentary and complexly interwoven texture of his musings, in which the past jostles against the present and actions against memories, compels assent. "Is that Boylan well off? He has money . . . He tore away half the prize story sharply and wiped himself with it. Then he girded up his trousers, braced and buttoned himself. He pulled back the jerky shaky door of the jakes and came forth from the gloom into the air . . . Quarter to. There again: the overtone following through the air, the third. Poor Dignam!" (69–70) As Bloom says, "Life might be so" (69). Grief for a friend follows a trip to the outhouse, and both, as present moments, are wound round by snaking strands of memory and fantasy and expectation, which crawl through the mind's day, leaving no moment single, no love exclusive, no logical deduction uncolored by wish and regret. In these ways the text says, here, here in this confusion is the really whole cosmos (or noncosmos), here and not in those ordered

over the publication of the novel, the prosecution held that the primary danger was that "the mind of a young girl" would be corrupted by the book. Apparently Woolsey was not ready to make such an experiment.

For an extensively documented account of the various prosecutions of the novel, see Edward de Grazia, *Girls Lean Back Everywhere* (1992). De Grazia's title is taken from a 1920 defense of the book by its lesbian publisher, Jane Heap – who, de Grazia notes, was a cross-dresser and habitually spoke from a male-oriented perspective. Heap writes, of the Gerty MacDowell episode, "Mr. Joyce was not teaching early Egyptian perversions nor inventing new ones. Girls lean back everywhere, showing lace and silk stockings; wear low-cut sleeveless blouses, breathless bathing suits; men think thoughts and have emotions about these things everywhere – seldom as delicately and imaginatively as Mr. Bloom – and no one is corrupted." On this early trial in New York, see also Ellman (1983), pp. 502ff.

clarified probabilified well-plotted texts in which we are accustomed to look for our lives. Even the reader to whom a focus on consciousness is a familiar novelistic device – the reader, say, of Henry James, or of Proust[11] – would still be arrested by the surprising multiplicity and daily disorderliness of consciousness in this work.

But the novel is also an epic; and it deliberately, elaborately, sets itself up as a reworking of Homer's *Odyssey*, whose episodes provide its own with names. Joyce obsessively drew attention to this feature of the work, calling Bloom the modern epic hero. Moreover, it is not just the *Odyssey* to which the novel alludes. It is stuffed full of allusions, in style, structure, and content, to hundreds of texts both "high" and "low," including many of the great works of the Western philosophical and religious tradition. Plato, Augustine, Aquinas, Dante, Spinoza, all of these are here – alongside the daily newspaper, alongside *Matcham's Masterstroke* and *Ruby, Pride of the Ring*, alongside Mozart's *Don Giovanni* and the Gaelic Sports League, alongside a guidebook to Dublin and the medieval Irish sagas. In an obvious way, the allusions to the heroic tradition – especially in their ridiculous proliferation and their odd heterogeneity – serve to turn readers' attention downward, reminding them of the considerable distance between heroes of legend and the real people of their world. Instead of the impregnable wit of resourceful Odysseus, leader of his people, we have a Jew and a cuckold, an outsider who is mocked by many and cannot hold a job. Instead of Telemachus, heroic son of the hero, we have a tormented angry young writer who has not had a bath since the previous October (673). Instead of the faithful prudent Penelope, who waits for her husband for more than ten years, resisting all offers, we have the adulterous Molly, who has no intention of waiting around during the "10 years, 5 months, and 18 days during which carnal intercourse had been

11 For various accounts of Joyce's famous meeting with Proust, see Ellman (1983), pp. 508–9. According to William Carlos Williams, the two got on well so long as they could compare maladies; but when each denied knowledge of the other's work, the conversation ended. Joyce reported the event differently: "Proust would only talk about duchesses, while I was more concerned with their chambermaids." Another guest, a friend of Joyce's, recalls that as the party broke up Proust invited her and her husband back to his flat in a taxi; Joyce, uninvited, got in with them. "Unfortunately his first gesture was to open the window with a bang. Proust being sensitive to fresh air, Schiff immediately closed it." When they arrived, Proust still did not ask Joyce in, and Schiff had to persuade him to let the taxi take him home. Later, in a notebook, Joyce wrote, "Proust, analytic still life. Reader ends sentence before him."

incomplete, without ejaculation of semen within the natural female organ" (736). Instead of the measured dignity of the Homeric hexameter, we have a chaotic profusion of styles, high and low, parading through the mind and portraying the mind, offering us no stable place to stand and find purity.

The idea that we are engaged in a send-up of the heroic, a cutting of its pretensions down to the size of the real world, is one of the primary sources of humor in the text, and thus one of the primary ways in which the text hooks the reader into Joyce's "eucharistic" project. Among the simplest examples, we have the wonderful portrait of the drunken Irish nationalist in Barney Kiernan's bar, the Polyphemus of the *Cyclops* episode, as a hero out of the Irish sagas:

From his girdle hung a row of seastones which dangled at every movement of his portentous frame and on these were graven with rude yet striking art the tribal images of many Irish heroes and heroines of antiquity, Cuchulin, Conn of hundred battles, Niall of nine hostages, . . . Father John Murphy, . . . Francy Higgins, . . . Goliath, . . . the Village Blacksmith, Captain Moonlight, Captain Boycott, Dante Alighieri, Christopher Columbus, S. Fursa, S. Brendan, Marshal MacMahon, Charlemagne, Theobald Wolfe Tone, the Mother of the Maccabees, the Last of the Mohicans, the Rose of Castille, the Man for Galway, The Man that Broke the Bank at Monte Carlo, The Man in the Gap, The Woman Who Didn't, Benjamin Franklin, Napoleon Bonaparte, John L. Sullivan, Cleopatra, . . . Muhammad, the Bride of Lammermoor, Peter the Hermit, Peter the Packer, Dark Rosaleen, Patrick W. Shakespeare, Brian Confucius, Murtagh Gutenberg, Patricio Velasquez . . . (296–7)

The parody shows us the absurd contrast between the grandeur of legend and the facts of daily urban life: for the so-called hero is an ignorant brawler and anti-Semite who has no dignity and no stature. The pretenses of Ireland to heroic status are shown up, both in the content of the boastful catalogue and in its interminable stylistic flow. (I have cited a small fraction of the list of names.) Part of its antiheroic humor is its excessiveness.

But even here there is tenderness, not savagery. The text exemplifies the Irish habits of boasting and excessive talking even while it parodies them, and includes itself in its own critique. And since it so obviously finds delight in the exuberance of its deficiencies, since it is obviously having so much more fun being flawed than it would have had being perfect and classical, the reader is seduced into taking pleasure in the flawed and excessive, into thinking that perhaps it is in this world where things are not perfect and jokes go on a little too long that real heroism is to be found.

This double movement is characteristic of the novel throughout.[12] To those who are hooked on epic grandeur, the daily events of Bloom's life may seem mean. To those hooked on the drama of Dante's spiritual journey, Bloom's return to his "Beatrice" will seem vulgar. To those hooked on Platonic or Spinozistic contemplation, the preoccupation of these minds with "mud hair and dirt"[13] will seem perverse.[14] To those who react with disgust to bodily functions and their products, it will seem like one of the most disgusting books in the world.[15] But since the text draws the reader's attention and heart to these elements of daily life, and does so with tenderness, the first "take," which laughs at the absurd juxtapositions, soon leads on to a second set of thoughts, in which one wonders whether Bloom's simple kindness to Dignam's family, his small speech against racial intolerance, his silly poem to Molly, his kiss on her bottom, are not the material of whatever is real in heroism, and of whatever is generous and genuine in the spiritual life. Through humor the text seduces us to this thought.

12 For an excellent account of this, see Ellman (1983), p. 360. On page 416 he records a conversation between Joyce and his language pupil George Borach, in which Joyce says repeatedly that he chose the *Odyssey* because he found its subject "the most human in world literature," the most "all-embracing."

13 See Plato, *Parmenides* 130CD (quoted in Chapter 10, note 19), where Socrates expresses scorn at the idea that there would be forms of such unworthy objects.

14 The *New York Times* wrote on Feb. 23, 1921, that *Ulysses* was "a curious production, not wholly uninteresting, especially to psychopathologists." See de Grazia (1992), p. 14. A judge in the New York trial exclaimed, "[I]t sounds to me like the ravings of a disordered mind. I can't see why anyone would want to publish it!" (de Grazia [1992], p. 12)

15 An early reviewer wrote:

> I have read it, and I say that it is the most infamously obscene book in ancient or modern literature. The obscenity of Rabelais is innocent compared with its leprous and scabrous horrors. All the secret sewers of vice are canalized in its flow of unimaginable thoughts, images and pornographic words. And its unclean lunacies are larded with appalling and revolting blasphemies directed against the Christian religion and against the holy name of Christ – blasphemies hitherto associated with the most degraded orgies of Satanism and the Black Mass.

This reviewer, interestingly enough, uses just the image for Joyce's art that Joyce had used in reverse in *The Holy Office* – and, in a similar way, connects religious purity to disgust at the body.

What acrostic upon the abbreviation of his first name had he (kinetic poet) sent to Miss Marion Tweedy on the 14 February 1888?

Poets oft have sung in rhyme
Of music sweet their praise divine.
Let them hymn it nine times nine.
Dearer far than song or wine,
You are mine. The world is mine. (678)

Above all, *Ulysses* is a book about love. And whether or not Joyce intended to divulge the name of "the word known to all men" for which Stephen Dedalus searches throughout its pages,[16] its story of descent is the story of the descent of love, and its chaos is love's disorder – above all, that of erotic love, whose Pandemotic (or Pandemic?) muse is the dictator of the double-died squidink of the text. It contains serious theses about love that set it in connection with the philosophical tradition at many points. It appears to argue that it is only through love, and bodily love at that, that human beings can find an exit from solipsism and loneliness to the reality of another life.[17] It appears to argue that the creative imagination is itself erotic, a receptive form of forms, passive, masochistic, akin to the "surety of the sense of touch in" Bloom's "firm full masculine feminine passive active hand" (674).[18] It appears to argue that love is the great hope for public life as well, the great opposite to the "insult and hatred" that are themselves "the opposite of that that is really life."[19] But in all of the appearances of the erotic in the work we find the antiheroic doubleness I have

16 For the controversy surrounding the reconstruction of "love" as this word in Gabler's text, Ellman's initial approval and subsequent defection, and the Kidd correction, which leaves the word's identity implicit, see John Kidd, "The Scandal of Ulysses," *New York Review of Books*, June 30, 1988; Hugh Kenner, "The Scandal of Ulysses," October 27, 1988, and subsequent exchanges of letters; for Ellman's original discussion of "the word known to all men," see the Cubler edition of the novel (New York: Vintage, 1986), p. xii.

17 For a convincing argument that this is the theme of the Proteus episode, and that the episode plays off hylomorphic realist Aristotle against idealist Berkeley, only to cut the knot by the desire for a bodily caress, see the remarkable article by James Cappio (1981).

18 On this theme in Joyce generally, see Ellman (1983), pp. 51, 296, 368–70. Bloom is both androgynous and masochistic, as we see in the Circe episode, written at a time during which Joyce had been studying Sacher-Masoch's *Venus im Pelz*. Bloom is "a finished example of the new womanly man" (493). Compare, in the *Finnegans Wake* passage, "through the bowels of his misery."

19 Bloom to the Cyclops, (333).

already mentioned – when we discover in the Blooms' house a romantic novel "which must have fallen down sufficiently appropriately beside the domestic chamberpot" (653); when we notice that Bloom's haunting memory of Howth and the rhododendrons is followed by a less-than-romantic vision:

All quiet on Howth now. The distant hills seem. Where we. The rhododendrons. I am a fool perhaps. He gets the plums and I the plumstones. Where I come in. All that old hill has seen. Names change: that's all. Lovers: yum yum. (377)

As if to say: don't think you can have the grand stuff without this too. As if to say, maybe you can't have the grand stuff at all, because you have this too.

But to see what is actually happening to love, and what remains when Diotima's ladder is pulled away or turned upside down, I want now to look more closely at just three of the novel's episodes, in which we see its relation to the various ascent traditions with particular clarity. The three are: Nausicaa, Ithaca, and Penelope.

IV. "THE LOVE THAT MIGHT HAVE BEEN"

The summer evening had begun to fold the world in its mysterious embrace. Far away in the west the sun was setting and the last glow of all too fleeting day lingered lovingly on sea and strand, on the proud promontory of dear old Howth guarding as ever the waters of the bay, on the weedgrown rocks along Sandymount shore and, last but not least, on the quiet church whence there streamed forth at times upon the stillness the voice of prayer to her who is in her pure radiance a beacon ever to the storm-tossed heart of man, Mary, star of the sea. (346)

So begins the episode that culminates in Bloom's masturbation, as he looks at the legs and underwear of Gertie MacDowell – who, aroused by her own sexual fantasy of a dark mysterious stranger, raises her skirt for him as she leans back to watch the fireworks. Afterward, as he readjusts his clammy shirt, she limps off down the strand, and her lameness, concealed until then, dispels his fantasy. ("A defect is ten times worse in a woman . . . Glad I didn't know it when she was on show." [368]) The initial reverie of Gerty, the arrival of Bloom, his arousal and orgasm – all are narrated in the gushy woman's magazine prose that forms so largely the contents of Gertie's consciousness. As she limps away, the perspective shifts to that of Bloom's clipped and intermittently compassionate realism, as if the dispelling of the romantic fantasy had also dispelled the prose in which it is couched.

On the surface, then, we have a contrast of visions and styles, which appears to be a contrast between debased and debasing fantasy and the way things really are. On the one hand, we have the imagination and prose of Gertie about herself, with its combination of popularized romanticism and sentimentalized eroticized Christianity, and of both with a consumerism that feeds on the fantasies these traditions arouse:

Gerty MacDowell . . . was in very truth as fair a specimen of winsome Irish girlhood as one could wish to see . . . Her figure was slight and graceful, inclining even to fragility but those iron jelloids she had been taking of late had done her a world of good much better than the Widow Welch's female pills . . . Had kind fate but willed her to be born a gentlewoman of high degree . . . Gerty MacDowell might easily have held her own beside any lady in the land . . . Mayhap it was this, the love that might have been, that lent to her softlyfeatured face at whiles a look, tense with suppressed meaning, that imparted a strange yearning tendency to the beautiful eyes a charm few could resist.

On the other hand, we have Bloom's unvarnished perception:

Tight boots? No. She's lame. O!
   Mr Bloom watched her as she limped away. Poor girl! That's why she's left on the shelf and the others did a sprint. (368)

On the one hand, we have Gerty's perception of Bloom through the distorting lens of romantic fiction:

whitehot passion was in that face, passion silent as the grave, and it had made her his. At last they were left alone without the others to pry and pass remarks and she knew he could be trusted to the death, steadfast, a sterling man, a man of inflexible honour to his fingertips.

On the other hand we have Bloom as we have come to know him, with his real anxieties and sorrows – "Bold hand. Mrs Marion . . . Funny my watch stopped at half past four . . . Was that just when he, she?" (369) – and his realistic unsentimentalized perception of his body:

"This wet is very unpleasant. Stuck. Well the foreskin is not back. Better detach." (373)[20]

In this first reading of the contrast, according to which Gertie is deluded and Bloom realistic, we see the romantic tradition as a source of lies. The erotic scenario of *Wuthering Heights* is still recognizable in its degenerate woman's magazine form, and we see it as a scenario that has caused Gerty to fail to see herself clearly and to be unable to perceive Bloom as a person in his own right. The abrupt revelation of the gap between fantasy and reality arouses laughter, but, very rapidly, also compassion and even anger – for the way in which she has been made to view female perfection is a way that denies happiness to the real person she is, and forces her to turn her gaze away from herself. "Come what might she would be wild, untrammelled, free" (365). But she isn't, and the juxtaposition of her real condition and these Brontë-esque thoughts is both pathetic and enraging.

As we pursue these thoughts, however, we have to recognize that the simple contrast between fantasy and reality, Gerty's dream world and Bloom's real world, is so far much too simple. For Gerty's fantasies are not hers alone. They are broadly disseminated in her (and our) society, and they shape the possibilities of sexual arousal for both men and women. Therefore they are also reality. Because Gerty does not, cannot however hard she tries, fit the stereotype of the romantic woman, wild, untrammelled, free, she is destined to loneliness and mockery, and the closest she is likely to come to sexual intimacy is in this very encounter, and others like it. Bloom may be more reflective and self-critical than most of the Dubliners of the novel, but he is not sui generis. He simply assumes that sexual arousal required idealizing fantasy and could not have endured the confrontation with reality: "See her as she is spoil all. Must have the stage setting, the rouge, costume, position, music." (370)

This might lead us to a more radical condemnation of fantasy. For we could argue that the reason a woman like Gerty suffers loneliness

---

20 Is it a mistake that Joyce has not circumcised Bloom? Even given the religious anomalies of his upbringing, one might have expected the hold of cultural tradition to prevail. See also page 746, where Molly remembers her curiosity about whether Bloom is circumcised, and page 760, where she remembers a foreskin, although it is not clear whether the possessor is Bloom (whom she was thinking about before) or Mulvey (to whom her thoughts shortly turn).

and misery is to be found in cultural stereotypes that enforce a narrow idealized picture of erotic desirability; that the reason for Bloom's post-orgasmic disillusionment and repudiation is to be found in the idealization in which he too collaborates. Accepting the everyday would mean, then, throwing over the tyranny of fantasy.

Perhaps. And perhaps not. The proposal in a sense accepts everyday life, and yet in another sense does not do so at all. For it refuses to acknowledge the omnipresence of fantasy in sexual life. And it thus fails to accept a part of daily life that is central for both kindness and cruelty, love and hatred. It is not just that without fantasy we might have no erotic arousal at all, as Bloom plainly thinks. It is also that without the energy of fantasy we might not have the imagination of another's good and ill that the novel shows to be a central fact in the moral life. In that sense Gerty, who lavishes compassion on the imaginary dark lover, has not been ill served by the tradition, and is infinitely ahead, morally, of the Cyclops of the immediately preceding episode, who cannot conceive of the similar humanity of the Jews, but thinks of them as "nice things . . . coming over here to Ireland filling the country with bugs" (323). And there is, we suspect, more tenderness and more connection in the parallel fantasizing of Bloom and Gerty[21] than in the intercourse of Blazes Boylan, that foe of the imagination, with any object at all. Gerty's literary fantasy gives her a sense of Bloom's suffering that, though crude, is not altogether wide of the mark; and it gives her a sense of her own specialness and dignity that help her to get through life with a drunken abusive father, an ailing and miserable mother.[22] Bloom's fantasy, while it cannot fully include the real lame Gerty as a desirable sexual object, still permits him to focus on the beauty she does possess, and to look at her situation with compassion.

Furthermore, in demanding a perfect authentic sexuality, in which

---

21 It is not absolutely clear whether Gerty has an orgasm, though it is clear that she is extremely aroused; she alludes to masturbation on pages 358 (her confession to the priest) and 366 (there is absolution so long as you don't have intercourse before marriage), and the description of her perception of the fireworks strongly suggests an orgasm. Bloom believes that she is finding some sexual satisfaction in the proceedings.

22 "Nay, she had even witnessed in the home circle deeds of violence caused by intemperance and had seen her own father, a prey to the fumes of intoxication, forget himself completely for if there was one thing of all things that Gerty knew it was the man who lifts his hand to a woman save in the way of kindness deserves to be branded as the lowest of the low" (354).

two individuals confront the essence of one another's souls, enclosed by no constructed images, the antifantasy reading actually proves an accomplice of the very Romantic (and Christian) images it purports to repudiate. For who has said that it is so bad, so inauthentic, to be aroused by a fantasy that does not fully intersect with the other party's sense of his or her authentic self? What is it that makes us so upset with the idea that seems perfectly obvious to Bloom, namely, that Gerty is aroused by a fantasy that is not really him? As he says, "She must have been thinking of someone else all the time. What harm? Must since she came to the use of reason, he, he and he." (371) It is the deep grip of the Romantic tradition on our judgment that makes us so dissatisfied with this failure to merge in a moment of mystical rapture. And that tradition, as Bloom sees it, repudiates the way real people are. In Nausicaa we see those longings for completeness, but also their inevitable failure, seeing them as a part of "life unlivable, transaccidentated through the slow fires of consciousness into a dividual chaos." And in that chaos, and in the text's tenderness toward its protagonists, across the barriers of fantasy that divide and also join them, there passes a kind of love and sympathy, which one may notice as such (while not sentimentalizing it, while still taking note of its unsatisfactory and slightly ridiculous character) if one is not looking too hard for something else. As Bloom says: "Did me good all the same . . . For this relief much thanks. In *Hamlet*, that is. Lord! It was all things combined. Excitement. When she leaned back felt an ache at the butt of my tongue. Your head it simply swirls . . . Still it was a kind of language between us." (372)

V. BLOOM'S SPINOZISTIC ASCENT

In Ithaca, Bloom becomes, and fails to become, Spinoza.[23] The text has the form of a philosophico-scientific catechism, depicting the return home and midnight conversation of Bloom and Stephen, Stephen's departure, Bloom's preparations for bed, and his sleepy dialogue with

23 For explicit references to Spinoza, see pages 342 (in Bloom's list of famous Jews), 687 (another list of famous Jews), 708 (*Thoughts from Spinoza* is among the books on Bloom's shelf, next to *The Story of the Heavens* by Sir Robert Ball, which also provides Ithaca with some of its material), and 769 (where Molly remembers Bloom talking "about Spinoza and his soul that's dead I suppose millions of years ago").

Molly, as he settles into bed, his head near her feet. The episode has struck many readers as odd and tedious; Joyce called it "the ugly duckling of the book and therefore, I suppose, my favorite."[24] It is my favorite too, along with Penelope, since its humor derives from the incongruity of confronting philosophical detachment with the mundane facts of life. Ithaca looks down on life from the great height of Platonic or Spinozistic contemplation, seeing the objects there simply as items in the cosmos, unmarked by human emotion, not colored by personal need. Joyce described the episode's atmosphere as that of a "tranquilising spectrality," and the episode as "a mathematico-astronomico-physico-mechanico-geometrico-chemico sublimation of Bloom and Stephen," in which events are "resolved into their cosmic physical, psychical, &c equivalents ... so that not only will the reader know everything and know it in the baldest coldest way, but Bloom and Stephen thereby become heavenly bodies, wanderers like the stars at which they gaze."[25]

The world is so seen not only by the reader, but also by Bloom himself, who shows us the motivations he has to undertake this ascent, and its benefits. Throughout the novel, Bloom displays a scientific spirit. He wants to know how things work, and he is inclined – unlike Molly – to view ordinary daily objects as challenges to scientific explanation. Already in other cases, the passion for understanding serves to distance him from more troubling passions. Now, as he prepares to get into the bed recently vacated by Blazes Boylan, in which he will encounter "the presence of a human form, female, hers, the imprint of a human form, male, not his, some crumbs, some flakes of potted meat" (731), he has need of the "tranquilising spectrality" of the contemplative perspective – and he follows Spinoza's stylistic lead, regarding "human actions and desires exactly as if [he] were dealing with lines, planes, and bodies."

In what directions did listener and narrator lie?
Listener, S. E. by E.; Narrator, N. W. by W.: on the 53rd parallel of latitude, N. and 6th meridian of longitude, W.: at an angle of 45° to the terrestrial equator.

In what state of rest or motion?
At rest relatively to themselves and to each other. In motion being each

---

24 Joyce, letter to Harriet Weaver, quoted in Ellman (1983), p. 500.
25 Letters cited in Ellman (1983), p. 501.

and both carried westward, forward and rereward respectively, by the proper perpetual motion of the earth through everchanging tracks of never-changing space. (737)

In the world of Ithaca, all physical details are equal, and none is infused with emotional meaning. More space is devoted to the path of the water supply from Roundwood reservoir in County Wicklow to Bloom's faucet (671) than to the history of the "limitations of activity and inhibitions of conjugal rights . . . perceived by listener and narrator concerning themselves" (736), more space to the physics of boiling water (673–4) than to Bloom's ruminations about his own mortality (667). In this perspective, the emotionally charged events of Bloom's life do indeed appear in tranquilized form. Both his anger and anxiety over Boylan and the tender memory of his acrostic poem to Molly are examined from without, with the impersonality of the cosmic perspective. From this perspective, Bloom, thinking of his desire "to amend many social conditions, the product of inequality and avarice and international animosity" (696), thinks as well, and fatalistically, of the natural obstacles to the perfectability of human life:

There remained the generic conditions imposed by natural, as distinct from human law, as integral parts of the human whole: the necessity of destruction to procure alimentary sustenance: the painful character of the ultimate functions of separate existence, the agonies of birth and death: the monotonous menstruation of simian and (particularly) human females extending from the age of puberty to the menopause: inevitable accidents at sea, in mines and factories: . . . seismic upheavals the epicentres of which are located in densely populated regions: the fact of vital growth, through convulsions of metamorphosis from infancy through maturity to decay. (697)

If much of the humor in this solemn catalogue derives from the incongruous contrast it suggests between real human emotions and the philosophical perspective on them, we should remember, too, that the contemplative perspective is at this point Bloom's; the emotionless spectralized world is one to which his emotions drive him.

In the end, Bloom partly achieves Spinozistic calm and fatalism with respect to his own marriage, passing through a cycle of emotions that terminates, or so it would appear, in contemplative equanimity.

With what antagonistic sentiments were his subsequent reflections affected?
    Envy, jealousy, abnegation, equanimity.

Envy?

Of a bodily and mental male organism specially adapted for the superin-
cumbent posture of energetic human copulation and energetic piston and
cylinder movement necessary for the complete satisfaction of a constant but
not acute concupiscence resident in a bodily and mental female organism,
passive but not obtuse

*   *   *

Equanimity?

As natural as any and every natural act of a nature expressed or understood executed in natured nature by natural creatures in accordance with
his, her and their natured natures, of dissimilar similarity. As not as calami-
tous as a cataclysmic annihilation of the planet in consequence of collision
with a dark sun. As less reprehensible than theft, highway robbery, cruelty
to children and animals, obtaining money under false pretences, forgery,
embezzlement, . . . criminal assault, manslaughter, wilful and premeditated
murder. As not more abnormal than all other altered processes of adaptation
to altered conditions of existence, resulting in a reciprocal equilibrium between the bodily organism and its attendant circumstances . . . As more than
inevitable, irreparable. (732–3)

Does Bloom, then, become Spinoza? The comic extremity of his
effort to assume an external perspective toward Boylan and Molly
leaves room for doubt. So, too, does the catalogue of offenses he ranks
ahead of hers: to say that something is less reprehensible than murder
is hardly to commit oneself to equanimity about it, and the bewildering
heterogeneity of the list shows a frantic struggle to achieve detachment
more than it shows detachment itself. We see, in affect, the philosophical ascent in process, as a movement of thought inspired by need and
pain – and soon cancelled by love and desire:

In what final satisfaction did these antagonistic sentiments and reflections,
reduced to their simplest forms, converge?

Satisfaction at the ubiquity in eastern and western terrestrial hemispheres,
in all habitable lands and islands explored or unexplored (the land of the
midnight sun, the islands of the blessed, the isles of Greece, the land of
promise) of adipose posterior female hemispheres, redolent of milk and
honey and of excretory sanguine and seminal warmth, reminiscent of secular
families of curves of amplitude, insusceptible of moods of impression or of
contrarieties of expression, expressive of mute immutable mature animality.

The visible signs of antesatisfaction?

An approximate erection: a solicitous adversion: a gradual elevation: a tentative revelation; a silent contemplation.

Then?

He kissed the plump mellow yellow smellow melons of her rump, on each plump melonous hemisphere, in their mellow yellow furrow, with obscure prolonged provocative melon-smellonous osculation. (734–5)

Here love makes a fool of contemplation, forcing its sublime prose downward to a childish yet oddly tender babble. The impersonality of the narratorial voice becomes intimate cosmic love poetry, the reality of smell and taste get the better of the mind's detachment.

But we should not sentimentalize this ending, seeing it as the once-for-all victory of love over detachment. We should not think to ourselves, now Bloom has gotten in touch with his emotions, and there will now be a blissful happy ending in which all sexual and emotional barriers are removed.[26] This is a day in Bloom's life, fragmented as his life is fragmented, both Spinozistic and tender, both detached and yielding, both attentive and obtuse. It is not as if tender love and particular attention simply break through the walls of the universe once for all to seize the victory. Bloom's Spinozism is a deep ongoing feature in his mental life. It has its good points, pulling him away from vindictiveness and despair. But it also, as Molly makes clear, has its bad points. For in accepting her affair with Spinozistic fatalism as "more than inevitable" and as a natural and necessary adaptation to their "altered conditions of existence," he shows his usual, and to Molly very irritating, lack of practical resourcefulness with respect to her sexual needs. He gives up on giving her pleasure because he is preoccupied with his own impotence, and the tragic events that gave rise to it – whereas from her point of view it is stupid and irritating that he doesn't think what else might be done.[27] (She notes his ineptitude at oral sex in particular.)[28]

26 This, more or less, is the interpretation of Theoharis (1988).
27 Of his preference for her bottom, she comments, "simply ruination for any woman and no satisfaction in it pretending to like it till he comes and then finish it off myself anyway" (740).
28 "he does it all wrong too thinking only of his own pleasure his tongue is too flat or I don't know what he forgets that we then I dont" (773). For Molly's own fantasy of being licked by Poldy – frustrated by remembering her menstrual period – see page

If one were to announce the proposition, "Philosophical contemplation makes Bloom unable to satisfy his wife," this might sound absurd
– just as it may seem to some absurd to discuss such matters in the
exalted context of academic philosophy. But it is of such incongruous
juxtapositions, and such intimate perceptions and failures of perception, that real-life love, and philosophy if it is to tell the truth about
love, are made. This is why, from Joyce's viewpoint, academic philosophy, in its search for truth, must contain his novel and the material it
produces for attention.

And this is why, as Joyce insists, Ithaca must be followed by the
"human all too human" voice of Penelope.[29]

VI. THE FEMALE WORD

Molly's monologue begins and ends, famously, with the word "yes,"
which Joyce calls "the female word."[30] Its four "cardinal points," he
writes, are "the female breasts, arse, womb, and cunt expressed by the
words *because, bottom . . . woman, yes.*" He concludes his description
of the monologue with a parody of Goethe: "*Ich bin der* [sic] *Fleisch
der stets bejaht.*"[31] Molly stands, then, in opposition to Mephistopheles, the *spirit* who always says *no.*

Two responses to Molly have dominated critical writing about this,
the most controversial and perhaps most famous part of the novel: the
moralizing and the sentimental. Sometimes, as in Ellman's otherwise
wonderful biography, the two are combined. The moralizing critic is
usually preoccupied with the number of Molly's lovers – either to accuse her of rampant promiscuity (if the critic believes the long list given
by Bloom, which names twenty-five names with Bloom himself the
twenty-sixth, and ends "and so each and so on to nolast term"), or else

---

787, quoted later. (Bloom's revulsion at menstrual odors has been previously established, at page 375: "Like what? Potted herrings gone stale or. Boof! Please keep off
the grass.")

29 Letter cited in Ellman (1983), p. 501: "The last word (human, all too human) is left to
Penelope." Note the reference to Nietzsche, whom Joyce much admired.

30 Letter cited in ibid., p. 501. On the importance of the word in Joyce's conception, see
Ellman (1983), pp. 342, 373, 516, 521–2.

31 Ellman (1983), p. 501. See Goethe, *Faust*, Part I, 1337, where Mephistopheles, in
answer to Faust's question about who he is, says, "Ich bin der Geist, der stets verneint!"
Presumably Joyce's false gender is deliberate, in order to parody closely the German
original. Joyce's German was fluent.

to vindicate her honor – as when Ellman insists that it is only with Boylan that she has had complete intercourse after her marriage, and that we should forgive her this slip because she waited chastely first for over 10 sexless years (not to mention 5 months and 18 days). The sentimentalist is preoccupied with her role as a symbol of the affirmation of life, and wants to love everything she does, great earth mother that she is. This person gets some help from Joyce, who did tend to talk in rather grand terms about the "acknowledgment of the universe,"[32] who was interested in mapping Molly's body onto the universe, with its "four cardinal points," and who connects her with Dante in an apparently serious way, by calling the final page of his work "la dolce pagina dove il sì suona," a reference to Dante's description of Italy.[33]

To the moralist, one can only say that it is this attitude of rigid judgment of female sexuality that the entire episode (and indeed the entire novel) wishes to call into question. Joyce addresses himself to a long history of repudiation, in Western philosophy and literature.[34] Indeed, this history followed his footsteps: in the story of the prosecutions of the novel, the fear of unfettered female sexuality, and of the corruption of girls and women through reading about it, is in the forefront of the prosecutors', and some judges', minds.[35] Notably, the moralists are not concerned with the immorality of Boylan's conduct, or even of Bloom's.[36] (This asymmetry in male judgment is not lost on Molly.)[37] And, in a familiar fashion, they tend to treat sexual deviations

32 Ellman (1983), pp. 521–2, reporting a conversation between Joyce and the French translator of the episode.

33 Dante refers to Italy as "la dolce paese dove il sì suona."

34 For a perceptive discussion, see Andrea Dworkin's essay on Tolstoy's *The Kreutzer Sonata* in *Intercourse* (1987).

35 See de Grazia, (1992), pp. 1–39. The two episodes that were the targets of prosecution were Nausicaa and Penelope, both of which portray female sexual aggressiveness and pleasure. And Bennett Cerf of Random House insists that the final decision of the authorities to prosecute the book was based on the fact that Molly said too many dirty words. (This is presumably why de Grazia chose for his title a phrase alluding to female sexual aggressiveness.) As Jane Heap commented at the earlier trial, "If there is anything really to be feared it is the mind of a young girl."

36 See the catalogue of Bloom's sins on page 537. Even if the whole list is not veridical, he clearly visits prostitutes from time to time, as here, and his correspondence with Martha Clifford is a kind of adultery.

37 ". . . men again all over they can pick and choose what they please a married woman or a fast widow or a girl for their different tastes like those houses round behind Irish street no but were to be always chained up theyre not going to be chaining me up" (777, similarly 746).

as weightier than many other sins (for example, greed, selfishness, intolerance).[38] In Joyce's novel, by contrast, women's sex is not moralized in the way that greed and fanaticism are moralized; it is simply there, set forth in a thoroughly practical manner that shows, I would say, an extraordinary ability on the part of a male (especially at that time) to grasp female sexual experience and to narrate it without fear or sentimentality or moralizing.

As for the practical question raised by Molly's accusers and defenders, it is difficult for the reader of *Penelope* (and especially, perhaps, for the female reader) to believe in Ellman's chaste rehabilitation of Molly as a one-time adulteress. Ellman is surely correct that some of the men named in Bloom's list were not Molly's lovers; about several we know from elsewhere in the novel that they simply flirted with her, or paid her compliments. On the other hand, what entitles Ellman to conclude that in the course of approximately an hour a woman is obliged to think of every lover she has ever had? This is to invoke a principle of fictional closure that should surely be in doubt, given the experimental form of the novel as a whole. One could as safely infer that Zerlina is the only operatic role with which Molly the singer is familiar, since within the text she thinks only of Zerlina's music.[39] Molly is preoccupied with memory and anticipation of sex with Boylan. She has briefer memories of masturbation with Bartell d'Arcy, of kissing and masturbation with Gardner, of kissing with Mulvey, of various sexual acts with her husband. She looks forward to an affair with Stephen Dedalus. She makes general remarks about the importance of sexual variety.[40]

But Ellman claims that of her lovers "only Boylan has fully consummated the sexual act."[41] Now, first of all, this is a vague claim. Presum-

---

38 "O much about it if that's all the harm ever we did in this vale of tears" (780).

39 And also of a number of nonoperatic pieces: Gounod's "Ave Maria" (745), Rossini's "Stabat Mater" (748, cf. 82, 661), and "Love's Old Sweet Song" (754). On page 748 she alludes to a song called "the absentminded beggar," on page 774 to something called "O Maritana wildwood flower," and on 775 to some lines of a song, "two glancing eyes a lattice hid . . . two eyes as darkly bright as loves own star." As for *Don Giovanni*: she thinks of the duet "La ci darem la mano" at pages 780 and 781 (since it appears frequently in Bloom's thoughts as well, it is also mentioned on pages 63, 77, 93, 120, 441, 445, perhaps 622).

40 For example, "God knows hes change in a way not to be always and ever wearing the same old hat" (740).

41 Ellman (1983), p. 377.

ably Ellman means by "fully consummated" what Ithaca calls "complete carnal intercourse, with ejaculation of semen within the natural female organ" (736). This, however, may not be what Molly understands by the full consummation of the sexual act; indeed, as she makes perfectly plain, it is neither necessary nor sufficient for her own pleasure, to which she attaches some importance, and she expresses much irritation with men in general for their insistent focusing on this goal. But let us pass beyond this major quibble. We now find a certain amount of evidence that Molly has a range of experience that casts doubt on the Ellman claim. To take just one representative example, although she does not compare the penis of Boylan to that of any specific person, she makes claims about the feeling of its size inside her that are hard to square with the view that her sample consists of exactly two.[42] Furthermore, Ellman's central argument for moving the number of lovers downward – that otherwise Molly cannot count as an "everyday woman" (377) – raises questions about Ellman's own conception of what such everyday creatures are and do. One senses a puritanism behind the textual literalism.

As for the sentimentalists, who view Molly as a grand symbol of the affirmation of life, there is much in the text to support them. Above all, there is the poetry of the ending, in which Molly does in her fashion affirm her love for her husband, and does say a word that Joyce deliberately placed at the novel's end:

the sun shines for you he said the day we were lying among the rhododendrons on Howth head . . . the day I got him to propose to me yes first I gave him the bit of seedcake out of my mouth . . . my God after that long kiss I near lost my breath yes he said I was a flower of the mountain . . . yes that was why I liked him because I saw he understood or felt what a woman is and I knew I could always get round him and I gave him all the pleasure I could leading him on till he asked me to say yes and I wouldnt answer first only looked out over the sea and the sky I was thinking of so many things he didnt know of Mulvey and Mr Stanhope and Hester and Father and old captain Groves and the sailors playing all birds fly . . . and O that awful deepdown torrent O and the sea the sea crimson sometimes like fire . . . and how he kissed me under the Moorish wall and I thought well as well him as another and then I asked him with my eyes to ask again yes and then he

---

42 Consider page 740, where, focusing on men's sexual fetishes, she remarks, "theyre all so different."

asked me would I yes to say yes my mountain flower and first I put my arms around him yes and drew him down to me so he could feel my breasts all perfume yes and his heart was going like mad and yes I said yes I will Yes. (782–3)

Both love and acceptance are here, without a doubt – but in what form?

Let us begin with Joyce's allusion to Faust: "Ich bin der Fleisch, der stets bejaht." The body always says yes: this is on one level, no doubt, an expression of the affirmation of life in a world of finitude and imperfection. At the same time, however, it has a simpler meaning: Molly always, or at least very readily, says yes. The "yes" includes her adultery, her evasion, the mixed and multilayered and contradictory nature of her love. In the famous passage, Molly's thoughts run from one man to another; her pronouns are multiply ambiguous. First, inside her memory of her day with Poldy, she recalls her thoughts drifting to other men; then (both inside and outside of the recollection) she re-members Mulvey kissing her; then, in the words "I thought well as well him as another," she apparently returns to Poldy, but in a way that does not inspire confidence in the intensity of her focus. Her thoughts have a rhythm of ascending arousal and a tendency to stray from one scenario to another should it appear more arousing.[43] The word "yes," we recall, stands for Molly's genitals – which in effect say the "Yes" with which the novel ends – and which no doubt have powers of love and affirmation, but have also the power to wound the one loved through incompleteness of attention.

Now I think that the sentimentalists are inspired, here, by the same notions of romantic authenticity that make the Gerty episode hard to swallow. For what is really wanted here is a happy ending, in which Molly's attention, having strayed, comes back once for all to her true love Poldy, who really loves and understands her. This is not exactly false. Nor are such thoughts strangers to Poldy, with his "You are mine; the world is mine," or even to Molly, who longs for a real love letter like that anagram, with a characteristic combination of self-mockery and real longing: "in Old Madrid silly women believe love is sighing I am dying still if he wrote it I suppose thered be some truth in

---

43 Molly refers to her own habit of masturbation on 771, "he had me always at myself 4 or 5 times a day sometimes."

it true or no it fills up your whole day and life always something to think about every moment and see it all around you like a new world" (758).[44] The novel includes the romantic vision of life as a profound human wish. But it informs us as well that life is more fragmentary, less single-minded, and also in some surprising way more fun, in its sheer variety and incongruity, than the vision of the single-minded lets on. It suggests that if we had the real-life Heathcliff before us, and inspected the contents of his daily thought, we would probably find, there too, the shadowing of the present object by objects anticipated or remembered, the infidelity of the sexual imagination – in short, the surprising heterogeneity of life.

And so, in a far more significant sense than the romantic reader proposes, the final episode does indeed say yes – not without a moral stance and not without moral judgment, but with a mercy and tenderness that really do embrace the inconstancy and imperfection of the real-life reader and real-life love, whatever in that reader longs at heart for complete unblemished undying love and the inevitably imperfect and so often comic realizations of that longing.[45]

44 This reflection begins as a wish for a letter from Boylan, whose letter has disappointed her: "his wasn't much" – but of course Molly knows that he never could write a love letter. He's like most men, "the majority of them with not a particle of love in their natures." So her thoughts turn to a more general wish to get such a love letter – and of course it is only Bloom, among her lovers, who writes love letters. So he's in the background, at least.

45 And here another "Yes" may lurk in the background, although it is never the object of any direct allusion. At the end of *The Marriage of Figaro*, the count is rushing around calling for vengeance against his putatively unfaithful wife. When various characters plead for forgiveness, he refuses. The countess then steps out from her hiding place, revealing to him both the fact that she is not unfaithful and the fact that he has been caught in his plot to seduce Susanna. Kneeling before her, he humbly asks for forgiveness. In music of extraordinary tenderness, its line first gently sliding up and then bending down, she sings, "I am more merciful, and I say yes," "Più docile io sono, e dico di sì." Her love for her husband embraces him as he is, so likely to stray again – and the "yes," which is set to three notes, stepping down, suggests the movement of her love to her kneeling husband. Although, as I say, *Figaro* is nowhere quoted in the novel, and Zerlina in *Don Giovanni* is Molly's only mentioned Mozartean role, there is at least another connection to consider. If we do consider it, we have to note that Mozart's opera emphatically does not say yes to female inconstancy, it being a very important part of the plot that the women are always entirely faithful and only play at infidelity to snare the men.

VII. THE OPPOSITE OF HATRED

Is there a political vision in this novel? Or: how does this descent connect love with compassion? It would be too grandiose to say that there is a political theory here; but without a doubt there is a political stance – expressed both in the thoughts and statements of Bloom and in the narration as a whole. This stance combines scientific rationalism with a nonreductive concern for "the soul," for human emotion and aspiration; a concern for kindness with a passionate defense of sexual liberty (protection of the "law of copriright"); compassion for human suffering with an intense dislike of religious parochialism and obscurantism and of their relative, militant nationalism. "Are you talking about the new Jerusalem?" says the citizen.[46] "I'm talking about injustice," says Bloom.

"Force, hatred, history, all that," says Bloom. "That's not life for men and women, insult and hatred. And everybody knows that it's the very opposite of that that is really life." "What?" says Alf. "Love, says Bloom. I mean the opposite of hatred." In Bloom's view, ethnic, religious, and national chauvinisms are a prime source of the "insult and hatred" that oppose love and therefore life. After all, says Bloom, what *is* a nation anyway, but "the same people living in the same place" (331) – a deflationary definition that hardly satisfies the Irish nationalists. "I resent violence or intolerance in any shape or form," Bloom summarizes. "It's a patent absurdity on the face of it to hate people because they live round the corner and speak another vernacular, so to speak." (643)

Against this politics of division, violence, and hatred, Bloom sets up his own program of nonviolence, of scientific and technological progress, of education, and of compassion for material need, in accordance with a cosmopolitan conception of a common humanity.

The novel's vision is as democratic in its own way as Whitman's, opposing intolerance and exclusion, affirming the equal dignity (including the dignity that resides in the lack of dignity) of people of all backgrounds – and going beyond Whitman's nationalistic patriotism in its militant critique of nationalism itself: "Christ," Bloom reminds the

46 Later, in Nighttown, the "new Bloomusalem" is constructed by workmen from all the counties of Ireland. "It is a colossal edifice, with crystal roof, built in the shape of a huge pork kidney, containing forty thousand rooms" (484).

citizen, "was a Jew like me." (To which the "citizen" replies with the logic inherent in his position: "By Jesus, says he, I'll brain that bloody jewman for using the holy name. By Jesus, I'll crucify him so I will." [342])

The novel's sexual explicitness and its insistent sexual focus can now be seen to have political significance. For, first of all, they are a linchpin of the project of restoring the reader to acceptance and love of the body, with all of its surprises, with precisely that disobedient ungovernable character that leads Augustine to find there our original equality in evil. Such love, the novel suggests, with Whitman, is necessary if we are to take the body's needs as seriously as a compassionate politics requires. And a focus on the body's universal needs is an essential step on the way to the repudiation of localism, therefore of ethnic hatred. Second, by showing Molly Bloom as the one character in the novel who never entertains thoughts of revenge, by showing how Bloom's own impulse to revenge is cut short by his arousal as he kisses Molly's bottom, the novel suggests, again with Whitman, that the root of hatred is not erotic need, as much of the ascent tradition repeatedly argues. It is, rather, the refusal to accept erotic neediness and unpredictability as a fact of human life. Saying yes to sexuality is saying yes to all in life that defies control – to passivity and surprise, to being one part of a very chancy world.

Here Joyce partly agrees with Whitman, but goes beyond him in the mercy of his attention to the flawed particular. Whitman is prepared to accept desiring so long as the relevant minds are filled with the Great Idea of Democracy. Joyce is prepared to allow people to be their whole selves, both idealistic and flawed, both committed and straying. And this yes to humanity, Joyce suggests, is the essential basis for a sane political life, a life democratic, universalist, and also liberal, in which human freedom will be protected by the law of copriright. The ascent tradition, with its exorbitant demands, is seen with suspicion, as a possible accomplice of self-hatred and the hatred of others.

To discover liberal internationalism in Molly Bloom's slightly soiled sheets[47] might seem absurd. But perhaps no more absurd than the struggle of real imperfect people for justice and love. Bloom's fantasies

---

47 ". . . theres the mark of his spunk on the clean sheet I wouldn't bother to even iron it out" (780) – not to mention the crumbs of potted meat discovered by Bloom (731).

of just government are endorsed, even as they are gently mocked. Imagining what his life would be like if he were a high-ranking judge, Bloom charts "a course that lay between undue clemency and excessive rigour" aimed at "the repression of many abuses though not of all simultaneously," directed above all at upholding the rule of law against "all orotund instigators of international persecution, all perpetuators of international animosities, all menial molestors of domestic conviviality, all recalcitrant violators of domestic connubiality" (716).

The liberal democratic state too is governed by human beings. And it is not in spite of that, but because it acknowledges and enjoys that, that it can at least hope to get the better of hatred.

VIII. ASCENTS OF LOVE

We began Part III with a set of problems about erotic love: its excessive neediness, its uneven and narrow attention, and, above all, its likely links with anger and hatred (forged, in part, through its developmental connections with primitive shame and disgust). It seemed that in the absence of an account of love that shows how these problems could be solved, or at least minimized, it would be unwise to give emotions even the limited guiding role in normative ethical reasoning that Part II had assigned to compassion. Thus even the modest contention that emotions can play a valuable normative role was called into question by love's fundamental role in the entire emotional life, together with its evident difficulties. Not surprisingly, a long philosophical and literary tradition favorable to the emotions has seen it as essential to answer such objections to erotic love by showing that a form of love can be found that is free of these problems – and by mapping out a course of therapy to produce just such a love in the aspiring pupil. To demonstrate that such a therapy is both possible and attractive seemed to these thinkers necessary, if they were to avoid the Stoic conclusion that emotions always offer bad guidance and should be eliminated, as far as they can be, from the good ethical life.

The Platonist ascents, by turning attention upward toward the unchanging good, removed the three problems, but at the price of removing love so far from the world that it appeared to lose three good ingredients that seemed necessary, if love were ever to prove supportive of ethical good in the personal life and of general public concerns:

compassion, reciprocity (insofar as it rests on respect for the dignity of agency), and attention to the whole of the concrete individual. This failure, I argued, resulted from the infantile and narcissitic conception of love with which this ascent tradition begins.

The other traditions we investigated all attempted to move beyond the flaws that they found in the Platonist tradition. Augustine made a major contribution by restoring the flawed and imperfect individual to the scene of love – and yet his view left large questions about the extent to which earthly happenings, and earthly agency, still retained their dignity and significance. If we inhabit a merely provisional world, it is unclear what would motivate us to take risks in it for the sake of justice. Dante made a major step beyond Augustine when he joined to the Augustinian emotions an Aristotelian regard for agency, and in-sisted that human actions in this world have dignity and worth, even from the point of view of salvation. This view clearly remains of living significance, even from the perspective of Part II's concern with the foundations of a liberal-democratic society. Its contemporary defend-ers, however, have felt the need to criticize Dante (and Aquinas) in the areas of religious hatred, sexuality, and the scope of religious authority.

Brontë began from this point, posing a tragic dilemma: either, with Lockwood, we turn in shame from our bodily helplessness, thereby leaving ourselves open to the cruelty and misogyny that Lockwood derives from his fear; or else we exit from the social world altogether with Heathcliff, living a love that is in some respects the true descen-dant of Christ's sacrifice, but at the same time totally asocial and apolitical. Mahler's triumphant affirmation of the strivings of the crea-tive individual, body and soul, cut through this dilemma in a remarka-ble way. By seeing that our striving is itself an end, and by standing forth in the integrity of our worldly commitments, we defeat hatred by our very willingness to be. This view of the ascent is in many respects the one that I find most complete as an ideal, containing the best answers to the question about how love might triumph over hatred.

At this point we were left, I said, with two questions: with a request for information about how Mahler's wonderful but highly general idea might be connected to a political program and to relations with real individual people; and with a worry about the element of disgust with everyday people and things that figures so largely in Mahler's idealistic vision. Even though the artist's disgust is presented as a temptation to be overcome, it is unclear that it has been stably overcome, and indeed it remains a motif running throughout Mahler's work.

Whitman's vision of the political, closely linked to Mahler's vision in its insistence on an inclusive compassionate love that reclaims the body and its erotic striving as the object, and subject, of love, made the political aims and connections of the vision more concrete, giving us an idealistic but not for all that unrealistic picture of a grown-up America, in which recognition of incompleteness and mortality work to defeat hatreds based on fear of the outsider's gaze. And yet Whitman, like Mahler, is an idealist, giving us noble metaphors and stirring cadences that lift us beyond ourselves, urging us sternly to fight more perfectly, to love more inclusively. The particulars of daily life become lost at times in the cosmic sweep of his vision.

Such ideals are valuable, indeed necessary, in human life, especially in the part of life that is social and political. And yet they run a risk, which Joyce's text makes apparent: by lifting us above ourselves, they risk the cry of disgust when we discover our daily reality. But that cry of disgust, as Mahler's work shows, is itself a grave threat to any continued devotion to the ideal. What seems required, then, is an idealism that also shows mercy and love to the real, a dedication to justice that embraces the fact that the individuals we love do have a daily life, with potted meat and the chamber pot, and at the same time grand romantic yearnings and a serious faith in the soul. Only Poldy and Molly, of our sequence, in the very comic fragmentariness of their love, appear to embrace what is most human in love, including the soul – and only this text seems to embrace the love of the real-life reader – in a way that provides a necessary complement to the more idealistic versions of the ascent, lest they collapse in on themselves through their failure to tolerate what is real.

Thus our sequence of chapters began as, itself, a ladder, as each ascent tradition moved beyond the previous one, supplying something essential about love that the previous one had lacked. But that upward movement itself encountered difficulty, since we encountered more than one vital and attractive ideal (especially Dante, Mahler, Whitman), and since each attractive ideal that we encountered proved, itself, flawed and imperfect, unable to contain everything that the structure asked for in an account of love. The upside-down ladder of *Ulysses* reminded us that imperfection is just what we ought to expect of our human ideals, and people. It asked us to climb the ladder and yet, at times, to turn it over, looking at a real person in bed or on the chamber pot. Only in that way do we get the best from our ideals; only in that way do we overcome the temptation, inherent in all ideals, to despise what is merely human and everyday.

It seems logical that a series of discussions of the ascent of love would end with a total text, one that includes all the elements that I think a view of love should include. If I am correct, however, such a complete ending is false to the complexity of the problem, and perhaps itself an aspect of the problem. The longing for totality breeds intolerance of the dividual. We are left not with a total text, but with insights from several idealistic pictures that we may try to incorporate into the greater chaos of our lives: with Dante's lucid love of the individual, piercing the fog of envy, anger, and sloth; with Mahler's triumphant compassion, rising above envy, including the whole world of mortal striving in its embrace; with Whitman's political call to a democratic equality grounded in the recognition of mortality, with "the most excellent sun so calm and haughty, . . . the gentle soft-born measureless light."

But we are left, as well, with the more tentative and tender love of their comic counterpart, which expresses an attitude we badly need if we are to remain idealists without disgust. By ending with Poldy and Molly, who both endorse and tenderly mock the spirit of ascent, I have tried to indicate that even in their real-life imperfect form, indeed especially in that real form, in which the incompleteness and surprise of human life is accepted rather than hated, love and its allies among the emotions (compassion, grief) can provides powerful guidance toward social justice, the basis for a politics that addresses the needs of other groups and nations, rather than spawning the various forms of hatred that our texts have identified. In Poldy's sudden defection from Spinoza, in Molly's inconstant desire, in the way surprise and passivity are embraced in the movement of the text, we find a mercy and equity that we need to combine with our other, loftier visions – no doubt with our own mercy toward the uneven intermittence of attention and desire that inhabits our own imaginations.

It therefore seems fitting to end this Part, and thus this book, with one more description of love's triumphant ascent (345):

When, lo, there came about them all a great brightness and they beheld the chariot wherein he stood ascend to heaven. And they beheld Him in the chariot, clothed upon in the glory of the brightness, having raiment as of the sun . . . And there came a voice out of heaven, calling *Elijah! Elijah!* And he answered with a main cry: *Abba! Adonai!* And they beheld Him even Him, ben Bloom Elijah, amid clouds of angels ascend to the glory of the brightness at an angle of fortyfive degrees over Donohoe's in Little Green Street like a shot off a shovel.

BIBLIOGRAPHY

Abramson, L. Y., Garber, J., and Seligman, M. E. P. (1980). "Learned Help-lessness in Humans: An Attributional Analysis." In Garber and Selig-man (1980): 3–34.

Abramson, L. Y., Seligman, M. E. P., and Teasdale, J. D. (1978). "Learned Helplessness in Humans: Critique and Reformulations." *Journal of Abnormal Psychology* 87: 4974.

Adorno, T. (1992). *Mahler: A Musical Physiognomy.* Trans. E. Jephcott. Chicago: University of Chicago Press.

Adorno, T. W., Frenhel-Brunswik, E., Levinson, D. J., and Sanford, R. N., in collaboration with Aron, B., Levinson, M. H., and Morrow, W. (1950). *The Authoritarian Personality.* New York: Harper and Row.

Annas, J. (1984). "Personal Love and Kantian Ethics in *Effi Briest.*" *Philosophy and Literature* 8: 15–31.

Arendt, H. (1929). *Der Liebesbegriff bei Augustin: Versuch einer philosophischen Interpretation.* Berlin: Julius Springer.

Arendt, H. (1996). *Love and Saint Augustine.* Ed. and trans. J. V. Scott and J. C. Stark. Chicago: University of Chicago Press.

Austin, J. L. (1970). "*Agathon* and *Eudaimonia* in the Ethics of Aristotle." In *Philosophical Papers*, 2nd ed., 1–31. New York: Oxford University Press.

Averill, J. R. (1968). "Grief: Its Nature and Significance." *Psychological Bulletin* 70: 721–48.

Averill, J. R. (1979). "The Functions of Grief." In *Emotions in Personality and Psycho-pathology*, ed. C. Izard, 339–68. New York: Plenum Press.

Averill, J. R. (1980). "A Constructivist View of Emotions." In Plutchik and Kellerman (1980): 305–39.

Averill, J. R. (1982). *Anger and Aggression: An Essay on Emotion.* New York: Springer.

Baier, A. (1978). "Hume's Analysis of Pride." *Journal of Philosophy* 75: 27–40.

Baier, A. (1986). "The Ambiguous Limits of Desire." In Marks (1986): 39–61.

Bandes, S. (1997). "Empathy, Narrative, and Victim Impact Statements." *University of Chicago Law Review* 63: 361–412.

Barker, J. (1994). *The Brontës*. London: Orion.

Bartov, O. (1991). *Hitler's Army*. New York: Oxford University Press.

Bartov, O. (1996). *Murder in Our Midst: The Holocaust, Industrial Killing, and Representation*. New York: Oxford University Press.

Batson, C. D. (1991). *The Altruism Question: Toward a Social-Psychological Answer*. Hillsdale, NJ: Lawrence Erlbaum Associates.

Batson, C. D., Sager, K., Garst, E., Kang, M., Rubchinsky, K., and Dawson, K. (1997). "Is Empathy-Induced Helping Due to Self-Other Merging?" *Journal of Personality and Social Psychology* 73: 495–509.

Batson, C. D., and Shaw, L. L. (1991). "Evidence for Altruism: Toward a Pluralism of Prosocial Motives." *Psychological Inquiry* 2: 107–22.

Bauer-Lechner, N. (1980). *Recollections of Gustav Mahler*. Trans. D. Newlin. London: Faber and Faber.

Belgum, E. J. (1976). *Knowing Better: An Account of Akrasia*. Ph.D. dissertation, Harvard University.

Ben-Ze'ev, A. (2000). *The Subtlety of Emotions*. Cambridge, MA: MIT Press.

Bérubé, M. (1996). *Life as We Know It: A Father, a Family, and an Exceptional Child*. New York: Pantheon.

Blackburn, S. (1998). *Ruling Passions*. Oxford: Clarendon Press.

Blaukopf, K. (1973). *Gustav Mahler*. Trans. I. Goodwin. London: Futura.

Blum, L. (1980). "Compassion." In Rorty (1980): 507–17.

Bollas, C. (1987). *The Shadow of the Object: Psychoanalysis of the Unthought Known*. London: Free Association Books.

Bollas, C. (1992). *Being a Character: Psychoanalysis and Self-Experience*. New York: Hill and Wang.

Booth, W. C. (1983). *The Rhetoric of Fiction*, 2nd ed. Chicago: University of Chicago Press.

Booth, W. C. (1988). *The Company We Keep: An Ethics of Fiction*. Berkeley and Los Angeles: University of California Press.

Boswell, J. (1980). *Christianity, Social Tolerance, and Homosexuality*. Chicago: University of Chicago Press.

Bowlby, J. (1982). *Attachment and Loss*. Vol. 1: *Attachment*, 2nd ed. New York: Basic Books.

Bowlby, J. (1973). *Attachment and Loss*. Vol. 2: *Separation: Anxiety and Anger*. New York: Basic Books.

Bowlby, J. (1980). *Attachment and Loss.* Vol. 3: *Loss: Sadness and Depression.* New York: Basic Books.

Braithwaite, J. (1999). "Restorative Justice: Assessing Optimistic and Pessimistic Accounts." *Crime and Justice* 25: 1–127.

Briggs, J. L. (1970). *Never in Anger: Portrait of an Eskimo Family.* Cambridge, MA: Harvard University Press.

Briggs, J. L. (1978). "The Origins of Non-Violence: Inuit Management of Aggression." In *Learning Non-Aggression,* ed. A. Montagu, 54–93. New York: Oxford University Press.

Brontë, E. (1943). *Wuthering Heights.* New York: Modern Library.

Brown, P. (1967). *Augustine of Hippo: A Biography.* Berkeley and Los Angeles: University of California Press.

Browning, C. (1992). *Ordinary Men.* New York: HarperCollins.

Budd, M. (1985). *Music and the Emotions: The Philosophical Theories.* London: Routledge.

Cannon, W. B. (1929). *Bodily Changes in Pain, Hunger, Fear and Rage.* New York: Appleton.

Cappio, J. (1981). "Aristotle, Berkeley, and Proteus: Joyce's Use of Philosophy." *Philosophy and Literature* 5: 21–32.

Carstairs, G. M. (1967). *The Twice Born: A Study of a Community of High-Caste Hindus.* Bloomington: Indiana University Press.

Caston, V. (1992). *Aristotle on Intentionality.* Ph.D. dissertation, University of Texas at Austin.

Cavell, S. (1969). "Knowing and Acknowledging." In *Must We Mean What We Say?,* 238–66. New York: Charles Scribner's Sons.

Chauncey, G. (1994). *Gay New York.* New York: Basic Books.

Chisholm, R. (1956). "Sentences about Believing." *Proceedings of the Aristotelian Society* 56: 125–48.

Chisholm, R. (1957). *Perceiving: A Philosophical Study.* Ithaca: Cornell University Press.

Chen, M. (1983). *A Quiet Revolution: Women in Transition in Rural Bangladesh.* Cambridge, MA: Schenkman.

Chodorow, N. (1978). *The Reproduction of Mothering: Psychoanalysis and the Sociology of Gender.* Berkeley and Los Angeles: University of California Press.

Cialdini, R. B., Brown, S. L., Lewis, B. P., Luce, C., and Newberg, S. L. (1997). "Reinterpreting the Empathy-Altruism Relationship: When One into One Equals Oneness." *Journal of Personality and Social Psychology* 73: 481–94.

Coase, R. H. (1976). "Adam Smith's View of Man." *Journal of Law and Economics* 19: 529–46.

Coetzee, J. M. (1999). "The Philosophers and the Animals." In *The Lives of Animals*, ed. A. Gutmann, 15–45. Princeton: Princeton University Press.

Cook, N. (1990). *Music, Imagination, and Culture*. Oxford: Clarendon Press.

Cooke, D. (1959). *The Language of Music*. New York: Oxford University Press.

Cooke, D. (1988). *Gustav Mahler: An Introduction to his Music*, 2nd ed. Cambridge: Cambridge University Press.

Cooper, J. M. (1980). "Aristotle on Friendship." In *Essays on Aristotle's Ethics*, ed. A. Rorty, 301–40. Berkeley and Los Angeles: University of California Press.

Curley E., ed. and trans. (1985). *The Collected Works of Spinoza*. Princeton: Princeton University Press.

Damasio, A. R. (1994). *Descartes' Error: Emotion, Reason, and the Human Brain*. New York: Putnam.

Dante. (1958). *The Divine Comedy*. Trans. J. D. Sinclair. New York: Oxford University Press.

Dante. (1977). *The Divine Comedy*. Trans. J. Ciardi. New York: Norton.

Danto, A. (1984). "Philosophy And/As/Of Literature." *Proceedings and Addresses of the American Philosophical Association* 58: 5–20.

Davidson, D. (1976). "Hume's Cognitive Theory of Pride." *Journal of Philosophy* 73: 744–56.

Davidson, D. (1984). "On the Very Idea of a Conceptual Scheme." In his *Inquiries into Truth and Interpretation*, 5–20. Oxford: Clarendon Press.

De Grazia, E. (1992). *Girls Lean Back Everywhere: The Law of Obscenity and the Assault on Genius*. New York: Random House.

Deigh, J. (1994). "Cognitivism in the Theory of Emotions." *Ethics* 104: 824–54.

Deigh, J. (1996). *The Sources of Moral Agency: Essays on Moral Psychology*. Cambridge: Cambridge University Press.

Deigh, J. (1998). Review of Stocker (1996). *Philosophical Review* 107: 617–20.

Deigh, J. (2000). "Nussbaum's Defense of the Stoic Theory of Emotions." *Quinnipiac Law Review* 19: 293–307.

Descartes, R. (1989). *The Passions of the Soul*. Trans. S. H. Voss. Indianapolis: Hackett.

De Sousa, R. (1987). *The Rationality of Emotion*. Cambridge, MA: MIT Press.

Dickens, C. (1966). *David Copperfield*. Harmondsworth: Penguin.

Dickens, C. (1969). *Hard Times*. Harmondsworth: Penguin.

Di Giovanni, A. (1964). *L'inquietudine dell'anima: la dottrina dell'amore nelle "Confessioni" di Sant'Agostino*. Rome: Edizioni Abete.

Dover, K. J. (1989). *Greek Homosexuality*, 2nd ed. Cambridge, MA: Harvard University Press.

Drèze, J., and Sen, A. (1989). *Hunger and Public Action*, 2 vols. Oxford: Clarendon Press.

Duberman, M. B. (1991). *About Time: Exploring the Gay Past*. New York: Meridian.

Du Bois, W. E. B. (1996). *The Souls of Black Folk*. New York: Penguin.

Dworkin, A. (1987). *Intercourse*. New York: Free Press.

Eisenberg, N., and Strayer, J., eds. (1987). *Empathy and Its Development*. Cambridge: Cambridge University Press.

Ekman, P. (1975). *Unmasking the Face*. Englewood Cliffs, NJ: Prentice-Hall.

Ekman, P. (1993). "Facial Expression and Emotion." *American Psychologist* 48: 384–92.

Ekman, P., and Davidson, R. J., eds. (1994). *The Nature of Emotion: Fundamental Questions*. New York: Oxford University Press.

Ellman, R. (1983). *James Joyce*. New York: Oxford University Press.

Erikson, E. H. (1985). *Childhood and Society*. New York: Norton.

Evans, N. A. (1993). *Revealing Wisdom: Convention and Mysticism in Parmenides and Plato*. Ph.D. dissertation, Brown University.

Fairbairn, W. R. D. (1952). *Psychoanalytic Studies of the Personality*. London and New York: Tavistock/Routledge.

Foot, P. (1988). "Utilitarianism and the Virtues." In *Consequentialism and Its Critics*, ed. S. Scheffler, 224–42. New York: Oxford University Press.

Foucault, M. (1985). *The History of Sexuality*. Vol. 2: *The Use of Pleasure*. Trans. R. Hurley. New York: Pantheon Books.

Foucault, M. (1986). *The History of Sexuality*. Vol. 3: *The Care of the Self*. Trans. R. Hurley. New York: Pantheon Books.

Frank, R. H. (1988). *Passions within Reason: The Strategic Role of Emotions*. New York: Norton.

Freccero, J. (1986). *Dante: The Poetics of Conversion*. Ed. R. Jacoff. Cambridge, MA: Harvard University Press.

Frede, M. (1986). "The Stoic Doctrine of the Affections of the Soul." In *The Norms of Nature*, ed. M. Schofield and G. Striker, 93–110. Cambridge: Cambridge University Press.

Freeland, C. A. (2000). *The Naked and the Undead: Evil and the Appeal of Horror*. Boulder: Westview Press.

Freud, S. (1917). "Mourning and Melancholia." In *Standard Edition of the*

Complete Psychological Works of Sigmund Freud, 24 vols. Trans. James Strachey. Vol. 14. London: Hogarth, 1953–74.

Freud, S. (1920). *Beyond the Pleasure Principle*. In *Standard Edition of the Complete Psychological Works of Sigmund Freud*, 24 vols. Trans. James Strachey. Vol. 18. London: Hogarth, 1953–74.

Fridja, N. H. (1986). *The Emotions*. Cambridge: Cambridge University Press.

Friedan, B. (1981). *The Second Stage*. New York: Summit Books.

Garber, J., and Seligman, M. E. P., eds. (1980). *Human Helplessness: Theory and Applications*. New York: Academic Press.

Gewirtz, P. (1988). "Aeschylus' Law." *Harvard Law Review* 101: 1043–55.

Gibbard, A. (1990). *Wise Choices, Apt Feelings: A Theory of Normative Judgment*. Cambridge, MA: Harvard University Press.

Gilson, E. (1949). *Introduction à l'étude de Saint Augustin*, 3rd ed. Paris: J. Vrin.

Glover, J. (1999). *Humanity: A Moral History of the Twentieth Century*. London: Jonathan Cape.

Goldhagen, D. (1996). *Hitler's Willing Executioners: Ordinary Germans and the Holocaust* New York: Knopf.

Goodall, J. (1990). *Through a Window*. Boston: Houghton Mifflin.

Goodman, N. (1968). *Languages of Art*. Indianapolis: Bobbs-Merrill.

Gordon, R. M. (1987). *The Structure of Emotions: Investigations in Cognitive Philosophy*. Cambridge: Cambridge University Press.

Gosling, J. C. B. (1969). *Pleasure and Desire*. Oxford: Clarendon Press.

Gosling, J. C. B., and Taylor, C. C. W. (1982). *The Greeks on Pleasure*. Oxford: Clarendon Press.

Graham, G. (1990). "Melancholic Epistemology." *Synthese* 82: 399–422.

Green, O. H. (1992). *The Emotions: A Philosophical Theory*. Dordrecht: Kluwer Academic Publishers.

Greenberg, J. (1994). *Crusaders in the Courts*. New York: Basic Books.

Greenspan, P. (1988). *Emotions and Reasons: An Inquiry into Emotional Justification*. London: Routledge.

Griffiths, P. E. (1997). *What Emotions Really Are*. Chicago: University of Chicago Press.

Halberstadt, A. G. (1991). "Toward an Ecology of Expressiveness: Family Socialization in Particular and a Model in General." In *Fundamentals of Nonverbal Behavior*, ed. R. S. Feldman and B. Rimé, 106–60. Cambridge: Cambridge University Press.

Halliwell, S. (1984). "Plato and Aristotle on the Denial of Tragedy." *Proceedings of the Cambridge Philological Society* 30: 49–71.

Halliwell, S. (1986). *Aristotle's Poetics*. Chapel Hill: University of North Carolina Press.

Halliwell, S. (1989). *Plato: Republic X*, translation and commentary. Warminster: Aris and Phillips.

Halliwell, S. (1992). "Pleasure, Understanding, and Emotion in Aristotle's *Poetics*." In *Essays on Aristotle's Poetics*, ed. A. Rorty, 241–60. Princeton: Princeton University Press.

Halliwell, S. (1997). *Aristophanes: Birds, Lysistrata, Assembly-Women, Wealth*, translation and commentary. Oxford: Clarendon Press.

Halperin, D. (1986). "Plato and Erotic Reciprocity." *Classical Antiquity* 5: 60–80.

Halperin, D. (1989). "Plato and the Metaphysics of Desire." *Boston Area Colloquium for Ancient Philosophy* 5: 27–52.

Halperin, D. (1990). *One Hundred Years of Homosexuality and Other Essays on Greek Love*. New York: Routledge.

Hanslick, E. (1986). *On the Musically Beautiful*. Trans. G. Payzant. Indianapolis: Hackett (based on 8th ed.).

Harré, R., ed. (1986). *The Social Construction of Emotions*. Oxford: Basil Blackwell.

Hasday, J. E. (2000). "Contest and Consent: A Legal History of Marital Rape." *California Law Review* 88: 1373–1503.

Hefling, S. (1988). "Mahler's 'Todtenfeier' and the Problem of Program Music." *Nineteenth Century Music* 12: 27–53.

Heimann, P. (1989). *About Children and Children-No-Longer: Collected Papers 1942–80*. London: Routledge.

Henderson, L. N. (1987). "Legality and Empathy." *Michigan Law Review* 85: 1574–1653.

Herman, B. (1993). *The Practice of Moral Judgment*. Cambridge, MA: Harvard University Press.

Hilberg, R. (1985). *The Destruction of the European Jews*. New York: Holmes and Meier.

Hillman, J. (1960). *Emotion: A Comprehensive Phenomenology of Theories and Their Meanings for Therapy*. Evanston, IL: Northwestern University Press.

Hindemith, P. (1961). *A Composer's World: Horizons and Limitations*. Garden City, NY: Doubleday.

Hitler, A. (1962). *Mein Kampf*. Trans. R. Mannheim. Boston: Houghton Mifflin.

Holbrook, D. (1975). *Gustav Mahler and the Courage to Be*. London: Vision.

Hrdy, S. B. (1999). *Mother Nature: A History of Mothers, Infants, and Natural Selection.* New York: Pantheon.

James, H. (1909). *The Golden Bowl.* New York: Charles Scribner's Sons.

Joyce, J. (1955). *Stephen Hero.* New York: New Directions.

Joyce, J. (1959). *Finnegans Wake.* New York: Viking.

Joyce, J. (1961). *Ulysses.* New York: Modern Library.

Kahan, D. (1996). "What Do Alternative Sanctions Mean?" *University of Chicago Law Review* 63:591–653.

Kahan, D. (1998). "*The Anatomy of Disgust* in Criminal Law." *Michigan Law Review* 96: 1621–57.

Kahan, D., and Nussbaum, M. (1996). "Two Conceptions of Emotion in Criminal Law." *Columbia Law Review* 96: 269–374.

Kakar, S. (1978). *The Inner World: A Psychoanalytic Study of Childhood and Society in India.* Delhi: Oxford University Press.

Kant, I. (1980). *Lectures on Ethics.* Trans. L. Infield. Indianapolis: Hackett.

Kant, I. (1981). *Grounding for the Metaphysics of Morals.* Trans. J. W. Ellington. Indianapolis: Hackett.

Kant, I. (1983). *Ethical Philosophy.* Trans. J. W. Ellington. Indianapolis: Hackett.

Kennedy, R. (1997). *Race, Crime, and the Law.* New York: Pantheon.

Kenny, A. (1963). *Action, Emotion and Will.* London: Routledge.

Kernberg, O. (1985). *Borderline Conditions and Pathological Narcissism.* Northvale, NJ: Jason Aronson.

Kittay, E. F. (1999). *Love's Labor: Essays on Women, Equality, and Dependency.* New York and London: Routledge.

Kivy, P. (1980). *The Corded Shell: Reflections on Musical Expression.* Princeton: Princeton University Press.

Kivy, P. (1990). *Music Alone: Philosophical Reflections on the Purely Musical Experience.* Ithaca: Cornell University Press.

Klein, M. (1984). *Envy and Gratitude and Other Works 1946–1963.* London: The Hogarth Press.

Klein, M. (1985). *Love, Guilt, and Reparation and Other Works 1921–1945.* London: The Hogarth Press.

Knox, B. M. W. (1950). "The Serpent and the Flame." *American Journal of Philology* 71: 379–400.

Kohut, H. (1981a). "On Empathy." In *The Search for the Self: Selected Writings of Heinz Kohut: 1978–1981,* ed. P. H. Orstein, 525–35. Madison, CT: International Universities Press.

Kohut, H. (1981b). "Introspection, Empathy, and the Semicircle of Mental Health." In *The Search for the Self: Selected Writings of Heinz Kohut:*

1978–1981, ed. P. H. Orstein, 537–67. Madison, CT: International Universities Press.

Kosman, L. A. (1976). "Platonic Love." In *Phronesis*, Suppl. II: *Facets of Plato's Philosophy*, ed. W. H. Werkmeister, 53–69. Assen: Van Gorcum.

Kupperman, J. J. (1995). "The Emotions of Altruism, East and West." In Marks and Ames (1995): 123–38.

Kurtz, S. N. (1992). *All the Mothers Are One: Hindu India and the Cultural Reshaping of Psychoanalysis*. New York: Columbia University Press.

Labarrière, J.-L. (1993). "De la 'nature phantastique' des animaux chez les Stoïciens." In *Passions & Perceptions*, ed. J. Brunschwig and M. Nussbaum, 225–49. Cambridge: Cambridge University Press.

La Grange, H.-L. de (1973). *Mahler*. Vol. 1. Trans. W. Schumann and T. Sutcliffe. Garden City, NY: Doubleday.

La Grange, H.-L. de (1995). *Mahler*. Vol. 2. Oxford and New York: Oxford University Press.

Lange, C., and James, W. (1922). *The Emotions*. Ed. Knight Dunlap. Baltimore: Williams and Wilkins.

Langer, S. K. (1951). *Philosophy in a New Key*, 2nd ed. Cambridge, MA: Harvard University Press.

Langer, S. K. (1953). *Feeling and Form: A Theory of Art*. New York: Charles Scribner's Sons.

Lazarus, R. S. (1984). "On the Primacy of Cognition." *American Psychologist* 39: 124–9.

Lazarus, R. S. (1991). *Emotion and Adaptation*. New York: Oxford University Press.

Lazarus, R. S., and Lazarus, B. N. (1994). *Passion and Reason: Making Sense of Our Emotions*. New York: Oxford University Press.

Lazarus, R. S., Kanner, A. D., and Folkman, S. (1980). "Emotions: A Cognitive Phenomenological Analysis." In Plutchik and Kellerman (1980): 189–217.

Lear, J. (1990). *Love and Its Place in Nature: A Philosophical Interpretation of Freudian Psychoanalysis*. New York: Farrar, Straus and Giroux.

LeDoux, J. (1993). "Emotional Memory Systems in the Brain." *Behavioural Brain Research* 58: 69–79.

LeDoux, J. (1994). "Emotion, Memory and the Brain." *Scientific American* 270: 50–57.

LeDoux, J. (1996). *The Emotional Brain: The Mysterious Underpinnings of Emotional Life*. New York: Simon and Schuster.

Lesses, G. (1989). "Virtue and the Goods of Fortune in Stoic Moral Theory." *Oxford Studies in Ancient Philosophy* 7: 95–128.

Levinson, J. (1990). *Music, Art, and Metaphysics: Essays in Philosophical Aesthetics*. Ithaca: Cornell University Press.

Levitz, M. and Kingsley, J. (1994). *Count Us In: Growing Up With Down Syndrome*. New York: Harcourt and Brace.

Lewis, C. S. (1961). *A Grief Observed*. London: Faber & Faber.

Lifton, R. J. (1986). *The Nazi Doctors: Medical Killing and the Psychology of Genocide*. New York: Basic Books.

Lincoln, A. (1992). *The Portable Abraham Lincoln*. Ed. A. Delbanco. New York: Penguin.

Long, A. A., and Sedley, D. (1987). *The Hellenistic Philosophers*, 2 vols. Cambridge: Cambridge University Press.

Lopez, F. G., and Brennan, K. A. (2000). "Dynamic Processes Underlying Adult Attachment Organization: Toward an Attachment-Theoretical Perspective on the Healthy and Effective Self." *Journal of Counseling Psychology* 47: 283–300.

Lutz, C. (1988). *Unnatural Emotions: Everyday Sentiments on a Micronesian Atoll and Their Challenge to Western Theory*. Chicago: University of Chicago Press.

Lyons, W. (1980). *Emotion*. Cambridge: Cambridge University Press.

Mahler, A. (1985). *Gustav Mahler: Memories and Letters*, 3rd ed. Ed. K. Martner and D. Mitchell, trans. B. Creighton. Seattle: University of Washington Press.

Mahler, G. (1979). *Selected Letters of Gustav Mahler*. Ed. A. Mahler and K. Martner, trans. E. Wilkins and E. Kaiser. London and Boston: Faber and Faber.

Maier, S. F. (1970). "Failure to Escape Traumatic Shock: Incompatible Skeletal Motor Responses or Learned Helplessness?" *Learning and Motivation* 1: 157–70.

Mandler, G. (1975). *Mind and Emotion*. New York: Wiley.

Mandler, G. (1984). *Mind and Body: Psychology of Emotion and Stress*. New York: Norton.

Maritain, J. (1943). *The Rights of Man and Natural Law*. New York: Charles Scribner's Sons.

Maritain, J. (1951). *Man and the State*. Chicago: University of Chicago Press.

Marks, I. M. (1987). *Fears, Phobias, and Rituals*. New York: Oxford University Press.

Marks, J., ed. (1986). *The Ways of Desire: New Essays in Philosophical Psychology on the Concept of Wanting*. Chicago: Precedent Publishing Co.

Marks, J., and Ames, R. T., eds. (1995). *Emotions in Asian Thought: A*

Dialogue in Comparative Philosophy. Albany: State University of New York Press.

Markus, H. R., and Kitayama, S. (1991). "Culture and the Self: Implications for Cognition, Emotion, and Motivation." *Psychological Review* 98: 224–53.

Marrou, H.-I. (1938). *Saint Augustin et la fin de la culture antique*. Paris: Boccárd.

Massaro, T. M. (1989). "Empathy, Legal Storytelling, and the Rule of Law: New Words, Old Wounds." *Michigan Law Review* 87: 2099–2127.

Meyer, L. B. (1956). *Emotion and Meaning in Music*. Chicago: University of Chicago Press.

Meyer, M. F. (1933). "That Whale among the Fishes: The Theory of Emotions." *Psychological Review* 40: 292–300.

Miles, M. R. (1992). *Desire and Delight: A New Reading of Augustine's Confessions*. New York: Crossroad.

Mill, J. S. (1988). *The Subjection of Women*. Indianapolis: Hackett.

Miller, W. I. (1987). *The Anatomy of Disgust*. Cambridge, MA: Harvard University Press.

Minow, M., and Spelman, E. V. (1988). "Passion for Justice." *Colorado Law Review* 10: 37–76.

Mitchell, D. (1975). *Gustav Mahler: The Wonderhorn Years*. London: Faber and Faber.

Mitchell, D. (1985). *Gustav Mahler: Songs and Symphonies of Life and Death: Interpretations and Annotations*. London: Faber and Faber.

Moravcsik, J. (1972). "Reason and Eros in the Ascent Passage of the *Symposium*." In *Essays in Ancient Greek Philosophy*, ed. J. Anton and G. Kustas, 285–302. Albany: State University of New York Press.

Morris, H. (1971). *Guilt and Shame*. Belmont, CA: Wadsworth.

Morrison, A. (1989). *Shame: The Underside of Narcissism*. Hillsdale, NJ: The Analytic Press.

Murdoch, I. (1970). *The Sovereignty of Good*. London: Routledge.

Murdoch, I. (1977). *The Fire and the Sun: Why Plato Banished the Artists*. Oxford: Clarendon Press.

Murphy, J. G., and Hampton, J. (1988). *Forgiveness and Mercy*. Cambridge: Cambridge University Press.

Nagel, T. (1979). "What Is It Like to Be a Bat?" In his *Mortal Questions*, 165–180. Cambridge: Cambridge University Press.

Nattiez, J.-J. (1989). *Proust as Musician*. Trans. D. Puffett. Cambridge: Cambridge University Press.

Nietzsche, F. (1954). *The Viking Portable Nietzsche*. Ed. and trans. Walter Kaufmann. New York: Viking Press.

Nietzsche, F. (1966). *The Basic Writings of Nietzsche*. Ed. and trans. Walter Kaufmann. New York: Modern Library.

Nietzsche, F. (1968). *The Will to Power*. Trans. W. Kaufmann and R. J. Hollingdale. New York: Vintage Press.

Nietzsche, F. (1974). *The Gay Science*. Trans. W. Kaufmann. New York: Random House.

Nietzsche, F. (1976). *The Birth of Tragedy*. Trans. W. Kaufmann. New York: Vintage Press.

Nolen-Hoeksema, S. (1990). *Sex Difference in Depression*. Stanford: Stanford University Press.

Nussbaum, M. (1978). *Aristotle's De Motu Animalium*. Princeton: Princeton University Press.

Nussbaum, M. (1986). *The Fragility of Goodness: Luck and Ethics in Greek Tragedy and Philosophy*. Cambridge: Cambridge University Press. Updated edition with new preface, 2001.

Nussbaum, M. (1990). *Love's Knowledge: Essays on Philosophy and Literature*. New York: Oxford University Press.

Nussbaum, M. (1991). Review of Vlastos (1991). *New Republic*, September: 34–40.

Nussbaum, M. (1992). "Tragedy and Self-Sufficiency: Plato and Aristotle on Fear and Pity." In *Essays on Aristotle's Poetics*, ed. A. Rorty, 261–90. Princeton: Princeton University Press.

Nussbaum, M. (1993a). "Poetry and the Passions: Two Stoic Views." In *Passions & Perceptions*, ed. J. Brunschwig and M. Nussbaum, 97–149. Cambridge: Cambridge University Press.

Nussbaum, M. (1993b). "Pity and Mercy: Nietzsche's Stoicism." In *Nietzsche: Genealogy, Morality*, ed. R. Schacht, 139–67. Berkeley and Los Angeles: University of California Press.

Nussbaum, M. (1993c). "The *Oedipus Rex* and the Ancient Unconscious." In *Freud and Forbidden Knowledge*, ed. P. Rudnytsky and E. H. Spitz, 42–71. New York: New York University Press.

Nussbaum, M. (1994). *The Therapy of Desire: Theory and Practice in Hellenistic Ethics*. Princeton: Princeton University Press.

Nussbaum, M. (1995a). *Poetic Justice: The Literary Imagination and Public Life*. Boston: Beacon Press.

Nussbaum, M. (1995b). "Eros and the Wise: The Stoic Response to a Cultural Dilemma." *Oxford Studies in Ancient Philosophy* 13: 231–67.

Nussbaum, M. (1997a). *Cultivating Humanity: A Classical Defense of Reform in Liberal Education*. Cambridge, MA: Harvard University Press.

Nussbaum, M. (1997b). "Kant and Stoic Cosmopolitanism." *Journal of Political Philosophy* 5: 1–25.

Nussbaum, M. (1998). "Emotions as Judgments of Value: A Philosophical Dialogue." *Comparative Criticism* 20: 33–62.

Nussbaum, M. (1999a). *Sex and Social Justice*. New York: Oxford University Press.

Nussbaum, M. (1999b). " 'Secret Sewers of Vice': Disgust, Bodies, and the Law." In *The Passions of Law*, ed. S. A. Bandes, 19–62. New York: New York University Press.

Nussbaum, M. (1999c). "Invisibility and Recognition: Sophocles' *Philoctetes* and Ellison's *Invisible Man*." *Philosophy and Literature* 23: 257–83.

Nussbaum, M. (1999d). "Het Jodendom en de liefde voor de ratio." *Nexus* 23: 67–100. Dutch translation of "Judaism and the Love of Reason," forthcoming in *Among Sophia's Daughters*, ed. M. Bower and R. Groenhout. Bloomington: Indiana University Press.

Nussbaum, M. (2000a). *Women and Human Development: The Capabilities Approach*. Cambridge: Cambridge University Press.

Nussbaum, M. (2000b). "Reply [to Symposium]." *Quinnipiac Law Review* 19: 349–70.

Nussbaum, M. (2000c). "Duties of Justice, Duties of Material Aid: Cicero's Problematic Legacy." *Journal of Political Philosophy* 8: 176–206.

Nussbaum, M. (2000d). "The Future of Feminist Liberalism." *Proceedings and Addresses of the American Philosophical Association* 74: 49–79.

Nussbaum, M. (2000e). "Disabled Lives: Who Cares?" *The New York Review of Books*, January 11, 2000, pp. 34–37.

Nussbaum, M. (2001a). "Animal Rights: The Need for a Theoretical Basis" (review of Steven Wise, *Rattling the Cage*). *Harvard Law Review* 114: 1506–1549.

Nussbaum, M. (2001b). *The Fragility of Goodness*, 2nd ed., with new Preface. Cambridge: Cambridge University Press.

Nussbaum, M. (forthcoming). "Judaism and the Love of Reason." In *Among Sophia's Daughters: Philosophy, Feminism, and the Demands of Faith*, ed. M. Bower and R. Groenhout. Bloomington: Indiana University Press.

Nussbaum, M., and Putnam, H. (1992). "Changing Aristotle's Mind." In *Essays on Aristotle's De Anima*, ed. M. Nussbaum and A. Rorty, 27–56. Oxford: Clarendon Press.

Nussbaum, M., and Glover, J., eds. (1995). *Women, Culture, and Development*. Oxford: Clarendon Press.

Nussbaum, M., and Sen, A., eds. (1993). *The Quality of Life*. Oxford: Clarendon Press.

O'Daly, G. (1987). *Augustine's Philosophy of Mind*. Berkeley and Los Angeles: University of California Press.

Oates, J. C. (1996). *Zombie*. New York: Plume/Penguin.

Oatley, K. (1992). *Best Laid Schemes: The Psychology of Emotions*. Cambridge: Cambridge University Press.

Oatley, K. (1999a). "Meetings of Minds: Dialogue, Sympathy, and Identification, in Reading Fiction." *Poetics* 26: 439–54.

Oatley, K. (1999b). "Why Fiction May Be Twice as True as Fact: Fiction as Cognitive and Emotional Stimulation." *Review of General Psychology* 3: 101–17.

Oatley, K., and Bolton, W. (1985). "A Social Cognitive Theory of Depression in Reaction to Life Events." *Psychological Review* 92: 372–88.

Oatley, K., and Jenkins, J. M. (1992). "Human Emotions: Function and Dysfunction." *Annual Review of Psychology* 43: 55–85.

Oatley, K., and Johnson-Laird, P. N. (1987). "Towards a Cognitive Theory of Emotions." *Cognition and Emotion* 1: 29–50.

Okin, S. M. (1979). *Women in Western Political Thought*. Princeton: Princeton University Press.

Oliner, S. P., and Oliner, P. M. (1988). *The Altruistic Personality: Rescuers of Jews in Nazi Europe*. New York: Free Press.

Ortony, A., Clore, G. L., and Collins, A. (1988). *The Cognitive Structure of Emotions*. Cambridge: Cambridge University Press.

Parke, R. D., Cassidy, J., Burks, V. M., Carson, J. L., and Boyun, L. (1992). "Familial Contribution to Peer Competence among Young Children: The Role of Interactive and Affective Processes." In *The Family-Peer Relationships: Modes of Linkage*, ed. R. D. Parke and G. W. Ladd, 107–34. Hillsdale, NJ: Lawrence Erlbaum Associates.

Pennebaker, J. W., and Roberts, T.-A. (1992). "Toward a His and Hers Theory of Emotion: Gender Differences In Visceral Perception." *Journal of Social and Clinical Psychology* 11: 199–212.

Perry, J. (1979). "The Problem of the Essential Indexical." *Nous* 13: 3–21.

Piers, G., and Singer, M. B. (1953). *Shame and Guilt: A Psychoanalytic and a Cultural Study*. Springfield, IL: Charles C. Thomas.

Pinker, S. (1997). *How the Mind Works*. New York and London: Norton.

Piper, A. M. S. (1991). "Impartiality, Compassion, and Modal Imagination." *Ethics* 101: 726–57.

Pitcher, G. (1965). "Emotion." *Mind* 74: 326–46.

Pitcher, G. (1970). "The Awfulness of Pain." *Journal of Philosophy* 67: 481–92.

Pitcher, G. (1995). *The Dogs Who Came to Stay*. New York: Dutton.

Plutchik, R. (1962). *The Emotions: Facts, Theories, and a New Model*. New York: Random House.

Plutchik, R., and Kellerman, H., eds. (1980). *Emotion: Theory, Research, and Experience.* Vol. I: *Theories of Emotion.* New York: Academic Press.

Posner, E. A. (2000). *Law and Social Norms.* Cambridge, MA: Harvard University Press.

Posner, R. (1988). *Law and Literature: A Misunderstood Relation.* Cambridge, MA: Harvard University Press.

Posner, R. (1990). *Problems of Jurisprudence.* Cambridge, MA: Harvard University Press.

Posner, R. (1992). *Sex and Reason.* Cambridge, MA: Harvard University Press.

Price, A. W. (1989). *Love and Friendship in Plato and Aristotle.* New York: Oxford University Press.

Price, A. W. (forthcoming). "Plato, Zeno, and the Object of Love." In *The Sleep of Reason: Erotic Experience and Sexual Ethics in Ancient Greece and Rome*, ed. M. Nussbaum and J. Sihvola. Chicago: University of Chicago Press.

Prichard, H. A. (1935). "The Meaning of *agathon* in the Ethics of Aristotle." *Philosophy* 10: 27–39.

Proust, M. (1954). *Du côté de chez Swann.* Paris: Gallimard.

Proust, M. (1954). *Sodome et Gomorrhe.* Paris: Gallimard.

Proust, M. (1982). *Remembrance of Things Past*, 3 vols. Trans. C. K. Scott Moncrieff and Terence Kilmartin. New York: Vintage Press.

Quinn, W. (1993). "Putting Rationality in Its Place." In his *Morality and Action*, 228–55. Cambridge: Cambridge University Press.

Rachels, J. (1990). *Created from Animals: The Moral Implications of Darwinism.* New York: Oxford University Press.

Rawls, J. (1971). *A Theory of Justice.* Cambridge, MA: Harvard University Press.

Rawls, J. (1980). *Kantian Constructivism in Moral Theory: The Dewey Lectures. Journal of Philosophy* 77: 515–72.

Rawls, J. (1996). *Political Liberalism.* New York: Columbia University Press.

Reed, I. (1986). *Reckless Eyeballing.* New York: St. Martin's Press.

Reik, T. (1953). *The Haunting Melody: Psychoanalytic Experiences in Life and Music.* New York: Farrar, Straus and Young.

Reisenzein, R. (1983). "The Schachter Theory of Emotion: Two Decades Later." *Psychological Bulletin* 94: 239–64.

Reynolds, D. S. (1995). *Walt Whitman's America.* New York: Knopf.

Richardson, H. S. (1994). *Practical Reasoning about Final Ends.* Cambridge: Cambridge University Press.

Ridley, A. (1995). *Music, Value, and the Passions.* Ithaca: Cornell University Press.

Robinson, J. (1995). "Startle." *Journal of Philosophy* 92: 53–74.

Roiphe, K. (1993). *The Morning After: Sex, Fear, and Feminism*. Boston: Little, Brown.

Rorty, A. O. (1991). "Spinoza on the Pathos of Idolatrous Love and the Hilarity of True Love." In Solomon and Higgins (1991): 352–71.

Rorty, A. O., ed. (1980). *Explaining Emotions*. Berkeley and Los Angeles: University of California Press.

Rosaldo, M. Z. (1980). *Knowledge and Passion: Ilongot Notions of Self and Social Life*. Cambridge: Cambridge University Press.

Rousseau, J.-J. (1979). *Émile*. Trans. A. Bloom. New York: Basic Books.

Rozin, P., and Fallon, A. (1987). "A Perspective on Disgust." *Psychological Review* 94: 23–41.

Rozin, P., Fallon, A., and Mandell, R. (1984). "Family Resemblance in Attitudes to Foods." *Developmental Psychology* 20: 309–14.

Rudnytsky, P. L., ed. (1993). *Traditional Objects and Potential Spaces: Literary Uses of D. W. Winnicott*. New York: Columbia University Press.

Russell, P. H. (1991). *Light in Battle with Darkness: Mahler's Kindertotenlieder*. Bern: P. Lang.

Schachter, S., and Singer, J. E. (1962). "Cognitive, Social and Physiological Determinants of Emotional State." *Psychological Review* 69: 379–99.

Scheler, M. (1957). *Schriften aus dem Nachlass*. Band 1: *Zur Ethik und Erkenntnislehre*. Bern: Francke.

Schofield, M. (1992). "Aristotle on Imagination." In *Essays on Aristotle's De Anima*, ed. M. Nussbaum and A. Rorty, 249–77. Oxford: Clarendon Press.

Schofield, M. (1999). *The Stoic Idea of the City*, 2nd ed. Chicago: University of Chicago Press.

Schopenhauer, A. (1969). *The World as Will and Representation*, 2 vols. Trans. E. F. J. Payne. New York: Dover.

Schopenhauer, A. (1995). *On the Basis of Morality*. Trans. E. F. J. Payne. Providence and Oxford: Berghahn Books.

Schulhofer, S. J. (1998). *Unwanted Sex: The Culture of Intimidation and the Failure of Law*. Cambridge, MA: Harvard University Press.

Schweder, R., and Le Vine, R. A., eds. (1994). *Culture and Value*. Cambridge: Cambridge University Press.

Scruton, R. (1997). *The Aesthetics of Music*. Oxford: Clarendon Press.

Seligman, M. E. P. (1975). *Helplessness: On Depression, Development, and Death*. New York: W. H. Freeman.

Seligman, M. E. P. (1990). *Learned Optimism*. New York: Knopf.

Sen, A. (1982). *Choice, Welfare, and Measurement*. Cambridge, MA: MIT Press.

Sen, A. (1984). *Resources, Values, and Development*. Cambridge, MA: MIT Press.

Sen, A. (1985). *Commodities and Capabilities*. Amsterdam: North-Holland.

Sen, A. (1990). "Gender and Cooperative Conflicts." In *Persistent Inequalities: Women and World Development*, ed. I. Tinker, 123–49. New York: Oxford University Press.

Sen, A. (1995). "Gender Inequality and Theories of Justice." In Nussbaum and Glover (1995): 259–73.

Serafine, M. L. (1988). *Music as Cognition: The Development of Thought in Sound*. New York: Columbia University Press.

Sherman, N. (1989). *The Fabric of Character: Aristotle's Theory of Virtue*. New York: Oxford University Press.

Sherman, N. (1998). "Empathy and Imagination." *Midwest Studies in Philosophy* 22: 82–119.

Sihvola, J. (forthcoming). "Aristotle on Sex and Love." In *The Sleep of Reason: Erotic Experience and Sexual Ethics in Ancient Greece and Rome*, ed. M. Nussbaum and J. Sihvola. Chicago: University of Chicago Press.

Singleton, C. S. (1973). *Purgatorio*. Vol. 2: *Commentary*. Princeton: Princeton University Press.

Smith, A. (1976). *The Theory of Moral Sentiments*. Oxford: Clarendon Press.

Smuts, B. (1999). Untitled essay. In *The Lives of Animals*, ed. A. Gutmann, 107–20. Princeton: Princeton University Press.

Snow, N. (1991). "Compassion." *American Philosophical Quarterly* 28: 195–205.

Snow, N. (1992). "Compassion for Animals." Paper presented at the Central Division meeting of the Society for the Study of Ethics and Animals, Louisville, Kentucky, April.

Sober, E., and Wilson, D. S. (1998). *Unto Others: The Evolution and Psychology of Unselfish Behavior*. Cambridge, MA: Harvard University Press.

Solomon, R. C. (1976). *The Passions*. New York: Doubleday.

Solomon, R. C. (1993). *The Passions: Emotions and the Meaning of Life*, 2nd ed. Indianapolis: Hackett.

Solomon, R. C. (1999). Review of Griffiths (1997). *Philosophical Review* 108: 131–34.

Solomon, R. C., and Higgins, K. M., eds. (1991). *The Philosophy of (Erotic) Love*. Lawrence: University Press of Kansas.

Sorabji, R. (1993). *Animal Minds and Human Morals: The Origins of the Western Debate*. Ithaca: Cornell University Press.

Spinoza, B. (1982). *The Ethics and Selected Letters*. Trans. S. Shirley, ed. S. Feldman. Indianapolis: Hackett.

Spinoza, B. (1985). *The Collected Works*. Vol. I. Trans. and ed. by E. Curley. Princeton: Princeton University Press.

Stampe, D. W. (1986). "Defining Desire." In Marks (1986): 149–73.

Stern, D. (1977). *The First Relationship: Infant and Mother*. Cambridge, MA: Harvard University Press.

Stern, D. (1985). *The Interpersonal World of the Infant*. New York: Basic Books.

Stern, D. (1990). *Diary of a Baby*. New York: Basic Books.

Stinton, T. C. W. (1975). "*Hamartia* in Aristotle and Greek Tragedy." *Classical Quarterly* NS 25: 221–54.

Stocker, M., with Hegeman, E. (1996). *Valuing Emotions*. Cambridge: Cambridge University Press.

Subotnik, R. R. (1991). *Developing Variations: Style and Ideology in Western Music*. Minneapolis: University of Minnesota Press.

Taylor, C. C. W. (1986). "Emotions and Wants." In Marks (1986): 217–31.

Taylor, C. M. (1964). *The Explanation of Behaviour*. London: Routledge.

Taylor, G. (1985). *Pride, Shame and Guilt*. Oxford: Clarendon Press.

Thalberg, I. (1964). "Emotion and Thought." *American Philosophical Quarterly* 1: 45–55.

Theoharis, T. C. (1988). *Joyce's Ulysses*: An Anatomy of the Soul. Chapel Hill: University of North Carolina Press.

Theweleit, K. (1987, 1989). *Male Fantasies*, 2 vols. Trans. S. Conway. Minneapolis: University of Minnesota Press.

Tolstoy, L. (1962). *What Is Art?* Trans. A. Maude. New York: Oxford University Press.

Turner, T. (1998). "Desire, Emotion, and Value: Theoretical and Ethnographic Perspectives on the Role of Emotion in Social Action." Paper presented at the Fourth Congress of the International Society for Activity Theory and Cultural Research, Århus, Denmark, June.

Vetlesen, A. J. (1994). *Perception, Empathy, and Judgment: An Inquiry into the Preconditions of Moral Performance*. University Park: Pennsylvania State University Press.

Vetlesen, A. J. (1997). "Impartiality and Evil: A Reconsideration Provoked by Genocide in Bosnia." Department of Philosophy, University of Oslo, photocopy.

Vlastos, G. (1981). "The Individual as Object of Love in Plato." In his *Platonic Studies*, 2nd ed., 3–42. Princeton: Princeton University Press.

Vlastos, G. (1991). *Socrates, Ironist and Moral Philosopher*. Ithaca: Cornell University Press.

Von Wright, G. H. (1994). "Dante entre Ulises y Fausto." *Boletín Institución Libre de Enseñanza* 21: 7–14.

Waal, F. de (1989a). *Peacemaking among Primates*. Cambridge, MA: Harvard University Press.

Waal, F. de (1989b). *Chimpanzee Politics: Power and Sex among Apes*. Baltimore: Johns Hopkins University Press.

Waal, F. de (1996). *Good Natured: The Origins of Right and Wrong in Humans and Other Animals*. Cambridge, MA: Harvard University Press.

Waal, F. de, and Lanting, F. (1997). *Bonobo: The Forgotten Ape*. Berkeley and Los Angeles: University of California Press.

Walton, K. (1988). "What Is Abstract about the Art of Music?" *Journal of Aesthetics and Art Criticism* 46: 351–64.

Wechsler, H. (1959). "Toward Neutral Principles of Constitutional Law." *Harvard Law Review* 73 (1959): 1–35.

Weininger, O. (n.d.). *Sex and Character*. London and New York: William Heinemann and G. P. Putnam's Sons (based on 6th ed.).

Weinrich, J. (1980). "Toward a Sociobiological Theory of the Emotions." In Plutchik and Kellerman (1980): 13–35.

Weiss, J. M. (1968). "Effects of Coping Response on Stress." *Journal of Comparative and Physiological Psychology* 65: 597–703.

Weiss, J. M. (1970). "Somatic Effects of Predictable and Unpredictable Shock." *Psychosomatic Medicine* 32: 397–409.

Weiss, J. M. (1971). "Effects of Coping Behavior in Different Warning Signal Conditions on Stress Pathology in Rats." *Journal of Comparative and Physiological Psychology* 77: 1–13.

Weiss, J. M., Glazer, H., and Pohorecky, L. (1974). "Coping Behavior and Neurochemical Changes in Rats." Paper presented at the Kittay Scientific Foundation Conference, New York City, March 1974.

Weiss, J. M., Stone, E. A., and Harrell, N. (1970). "Coping Behavior and Brain Norepinephrine in Rats." *Journal of Comparative and Physiological Psychology* 72: 153–60.

Whitman, J. Q. (1998). "What Is Wrong with Inflicting Shame Sanctions?" *Yale Law Journal* 107: 1055ff.

Whitman, W. (1963–4). *Prose Works, 1892*, 2 vols. Ed. F. Stovall. New York: New York University Press.

Whitman, W. (1973). *Leaves of Grass*. A Norton Critical Edition. Ed. S. Bradley and H. W. Blodgett. New York: Norton.

Wikan, U. (1990). *Managing Turbulent Hearts: A Balinese Formula for Living*. Chicago: University of Chicago Press.

Williams, B. (1962). "Aristotle on the Good: A Formal Sketch." *Philosophical Quarterly* 12: 289–96.

Williams, B. (1973). "Egoism and Altruism." In his *Problems of the Self*, 250–65. Cambridge: Cambridge University Press.

Wills, G. (1999). *Saint Augustine*. New York: Viking.

Winkler, J. J. (1990). *The Constraints of Desire: The Anthropology of Sex and Gender in Ancient Greece*. New York: Routledge.

Winnicott, D. W. (1965). *The Maturational Process and the Facilitating Environment*. New York: International Universities Press.

Winnicott, D. W. (1986). *Holding and Interpretation: Fragment of an Analysis*. New York: Grove.

Winnington-Ingram, R. P. (1980). *Sophocles: An Interpretation*. Cambridge: Cambridge University Press.

Wise, S. M. (2000). *Rattling the Cage: Toward Legal Rights for Animals*. Cambridge, MA: Perseus Books.

Wispé, L. (1987). "History of the Concept of Empathy." In Eisenberg and Strayer (1987): 17–37.

Wittgenstein, L. (1967). *Zettel*. Trans. G. Anscombe. London: Blackwell.

Wolf, N. (1993). *Fire with Fire: The New Female Power and How to Use It*. New York: Fawcett.

Wollheim, R. (1980). *Art and Its Objects*, 2nd ed. Cambridge: Cambridge University Press.

Wollheim, R. (1984). *The Thread of Life*. Cambridge, MA: Harvard University Press.

Wollheim, R. (1987). *Painting as an Art*. Princeton: Princeton University Press.

Wollheim, R. (1999). *On the Emotions*. New Haven: Yale University Press.

Wright, R. (1993a). *Native Son*. New York: HarperCollins.

Wright, R. (1993b). *Uncle Tom's Children*. New York: HarperCollins.

Wurmser, L. (1981). *The Mask of Shame*. Baltimore: Johns Hopkins University Press.

Wyatt, J. (1978). "The Celebration of Eros: Greek Concepts of Love and Beauty in *To The Lighthouse*." *Philosophy and Literature* 2: 160–75.

Young-Bruehl, E. (1996). *The Anatomy of Prejudices*. Cambridge, MA: Harvard University Press.

Zajonc, R. B. (1980). "Feeling and Thinking: Preferences Need No Inferences." *American Psychologist* 35: 151–74.

Zajonc, R. B. (1984). "On the Primacy of Affect." *American Psychologist* 39: 117–23.

ACKNOWLEDGMENTS

This book derives from my 1993 Gifford Lectures, delivered at the University of Edinburgh. Portions were also presented as Messenger Lectures at Cornell University in 1993–94, as Hagerstrom lectures at the University of Uppsala, Sweden, in the spring of 1995, as Distinguished Visiting Lectures at the University of California at Riverside in the spring of 1996, as a series of lectures at the University of California at Irvine in the spring of 1996, and as the David Ross Boyd Lectures at the University of Oklahoma in 1997–98. Part III was recast and expanded for presentation as the Weidenfeld Lectures in European Comparative Literature at Oxford University in the spring of 1996. I am grateful for sabbatical support from Brown University, for visiting scholar appointments at Stanford University and the University of Chicago, for teaching relief and research support from the University of Chicago, and for an appointment at the Center for Ideas and Society at the University of California at Riverside, where criticism from the other fellows much improved my ideas.

In addition, portions of the manuscript have been presented in many places, including: Aarhus University (Denmark), Albion College, the American Philosophical Association (Eastern Division), Baylor University, Belmont University, Ben-Gurion University (Israel), the University of Bristol, Brown University, the University of California at Berkeley, the University of California at Riverside, Calvin College, The University of Chicago, the Chicago Psychoanalytic Institute, the City University of New York Graduate Center, Columbia University, Dartmouth College, the Dialog Seminars (Stockholm), Duke University, the Ethics Programme (Oslo, Norway), the University of Exeter (England), Franklin and Marshall College, Göteborg University (Sweden), the Institute for Classical Studies (London), the University of Helsinki, Illinois State University, the University of Indiana (Bloomington), the University of Iowa, the London School of Economics, the University of Maryland, Marquette University, the University of Michigan, Muhlenberg College, New York University, Northwestern University, the University of Notre Dame, Stanford University, the University of Swansea (Wales), the University of Texas at Arlington, Washington University (St. Louis), and the University of Warwick (England). I am extremely grateful to all the participants on these occasions for their helpful criticisms, from which I have learned greatly, and especially to: Paul Boghossian, Michael Bratman, Diemut Bubeck, Myles Burnyeat, Thomas D'Andrea, Ronald De Sousa, Ronald Dworkin, David Glidden, Anniken Greve, David Halperin, Angie Hobbs, Paul Hoffman, Terence Irwin, Frances Kamm, Pierre Keller, Jaegwon Kim, Richard Kraut, Jerrold Levinson, Alasdair MacIntyre, Richard Miller, Thomas Nagel, Catherine Osborne, Ross Parke, John Procope, Witold Rabinowicz, Andrews Reath, Jerome Schneewind, Bennett Simon, Maurya Simon, Michael Slote, Nancy Snow, Ernest Sosa, Michael Stocker, Gary Watson, Howard Wettstein, Unni Wikan, Bernard Williams, Nick Zangwill.

For comments on portions or all of the manuscript I am extremely grateful to: Kate Abramson, Ermanno Bencivenga, Edward Bond, Victor Caston, Edward Cone, John Deigh, Richard Eldridge, Richard Epstein, Lothar von Falkenhausen, Jonathan Glover, Stephen Halliwell, Patricia Herzog, Simo Knuuttila, William Landes, Stephen Leighton, Lawrence Lessig, William Miller, Herlinde Pauer-Studer, Richard Posner, Bernard Reginster, John Roemer, Jerome Schneewind, Nancy Sherman, Albert Silverstein, Walter Sinnott-Armstrong, Richard Sorabji, Cass Sunstein, Christopher Taylor, and two anonymous referees for the Cambridge University Press. Aaron Ben Ze'ev showed me the manuscript of his excellent book before it was completed, and gave me many very helpful suggestions. I am also grateful to Professor G. H. von Wright for valuable correspondence. I owe thanks to students in several seminars on these topics at Brown University and the University of Chicago: in particular, to Jeremy Caplan, Craig Duncan, Rick Furtak, Margaret Graver, Richard Hoffman, Craig Joseph, Jeremy Bendik Keymer, Joanna Norland, Douglas McDiarmid, and John Stone, all of whom wrote detailed comments on some of the material.

I am exceptionally grateful to several people who went through the whole manuscript during its final stages of revision, making extremely valuable comments: Jeremy Bendik-Keymer, John Deigh, Rick Furtak, Charles Larmore, and Keith Oatley. Rick Furtak brought both his astuteness and his meticulousness to the task of finishing the Bibliography and preparing the indexes. Terence Moore was a marvelously supportive and helpful editor from a very early stage of the project. Russell Hahn was an exemplary copyeditor, alert but not invasive.

To one person I owe a debt that is deep and inexpressible, and so I dedicate this book to Cass Sunstein.

ACKNOWLEDGMENTS

Portions of drafts of this manuscript have been previously published as follows:

A much earlier version of Chapter 1 appeared as "Emotions as Judgments of Value and Importance," in *Relativism, Suffering, and Beyond: Essays in Memory of Bimal K. Matilal*, ed. P. Bilimoria and J. N. Mohanty (New Delhi: Oxford University Press, 1997), 231–51, and, in Swedish translation, in *Tanke Känsla Identitet*, ed. Ulla Holm et al. (Gothenberg: Annama, 1997), 197–236.

A version of Chapter 3 has appeared as "Emotions and Social Norms," in *Culture, Thought, and Development*, ed. Larry Nucci, Geoffrey Saxe, and Elliot Turiel (Mahwah, N.J.: Lawrence Erlbaum, 2000), 41–63.

A version of parts of Chapter 4 has appeared in German translation as "Emotionen und die Ursprung der Moral," in *Moral im sozialen Kontext*, ed. G. Nunner-Winkler and W. Edelstein (Frankfurt: Suhrkamp, 2000), 82–115.

A version of some of the material in Part II (though with many substantive differences in position) appeared as "Compassion: The Basic Social Emotion," *Social Philosophy and Policy* 13 (1996), 27–58, also published with the same pagination under the title *The Communitarian Challenge to Liberalism* (Cambridge: Cambridge University Press, 1996).

A version of some of the material in Chapter 10 appeared as "The Ascent of Love: Plato, Spinoze, Proust," in *New Literary History* 25 (1994), 925–49.

A version of Chapter 11 and parts of Chapter 12 appeared as "Augustine and Dante on the Ascent of Love," in *The Augustinian Tradition*, ed. Gareth B. Mathews (Berkeley and Los Angeles: University of California Press, 1999), 61–90.

Some of the material in Chapter 12 appeared in "Beatrice's 'Dante': Loving the Individual?" in *Virtue, Love, and Form: Essays in Memory of Gregory Vlastos, Apeiron* special issue 1993–4, ed. T. H. Irwin and M. Nussbaum (published 1994), 161–78.

An earlier version of Chapter 13 appeared as "Wuthering Heights: The Romantic Ascent," *Philosophy and Literature* 20 (1996), 362–82.

An earlier version of Chapter 16 appeared as "The Transfiguration of Everyday Life," *Metaphilosophy* 25 (1994), 238–61.

SUBJECT INDEX

adaptation, 108, 129, 141, 301
aesthetics, 238–9, 248, 277–8
 see also art; music; narrative
African views of emotion, 24*n*, 26*n*,
 140, 153
alone, capacity to be, 149, 207–8
altruism, 335–42, 604
ambivalence, 13, 191–3, 209, 225, 297,
 394, 467, 485, 505–7
 see also anger; conflict; love
Americans, emotions of, 152, 153–8,
 159, 160, 161–5, 165–9, 172, 181,
 307–8, 313–4, 330, 343, 349, 392,
 406, 438, 663–76
 see also love, romantic
amygdala, as essential for emotion, 58,
 114
anger, 29, 43, 60, 63, 72, 73–4, 87, 98,
 119, 130*n*, 135, 141, 152, 159–61,
 162–3, 172, 207, 231, 234, 297,
 393–4, 527, 579
animals, 23, 64, 89–129, 136–8, 144–7,
 186–7, 202, 301, 427
 evidence of emotion in, 89–90, 119–25
 Stoic view of, 5, 39, 91
 unethical treatment of, 102–5, 317,
 333
 see also chimpanzees; cockroaches;
 dogs; elephants; snakes; spiders
anthropocentrism, 101*n*, 120, 258
anthropology, 143, 151–5, 159, 169
 see also social construction
anti-Semitism, 319–20, 334–5, 346–8,
 450–2, 595, 618, 628–9, 709
anxiety, 190, 229, 288
apathy, 122, 197, 301, 346*n*, 381, 389,
 400, 542, 603, 699

 see also Stoicism, normative
appetites, 24, 129–32, 191
appraisal, *see* evaluation
art, emotions in response to, 165–9,
 242, 250, 272, 351–2
 see also music; narrative; tragedy
ascent, 14, 457–81, 482–526, 697–702,
 710–14
 Christian, 469, 476, 527–56, 557–90
 Romantic, 469, 591–613, 614–44
Asian views of emotion, 24*n*, 26*n*,
 143*n*, 152–5, 158, 161, 211, 221*n*,
 291*n*, 301
assent to appearance, 37–8, 40, 45, 46,
 90
 see also judgment; perception
athletes, as objects of emotion, 55–6
attachment, 2, 6, 36, 76, 141, 180,
 198*n*
author, implied versus real-life, 252
awe, 54
 see also wonder
axiology, *see* value, nature of

behaviorism, 94–5, 263
belief, 48–9, 82, 136, 306, 386
 false, 35–6, 394
 metaphysical and cosmological, 152–
 3, 167
 unconscious, 71, 72
 see also propositions
blame, *see* punishment; responsibility
bodily sensations, 25, 57–8, 60, 76–8,
 98–9, 200–2, 658–63, 679–81, 688–
 90, 693–7, 700–2
 see also emotions, noncognitive views
 of

745